OXFORD CLASSICAL

*Published under the supervision
Faculty of Classics in the University of Oxford*

The aim of the Oxford Classical Monograph series (which replaces the Oxford Classical and Philosophical Monographs) is to publish books based on the best theses on Greek and Latin literature, ancient history, and ancient philosophy examined by the Faculty Board of Classics

The Homeric Hymn to Aphrodite

Introduction, Text, and Commentary

ANDREW FAULKNER

UNIVERSITY PRESS

OXFORD
UNIVERSITY PRESS

Great Clarendon Street, Oxford OX2 6DP

Oxford University Press is a department of the University of Oxford.
It furthers the University's objective of excellence in research, scholarship,
and education by publishing worldwide in

Oxford New York

Auckland Cape Town Dar es Salaam Hong Kong Karachi
Kuala Lumpur Madrid Melbourne Mexico City Nairobi
New Delhi Shanghai Taipei Toronto

With offices in

Argentina Austria Brazil Chile Czech Republic France Greece
Guatemala Hungary Italy Japan Poland Portugal Singapore
South Korea Switzerland Thailand Turkey Ukraine Vietnam

Oxford is a registered trade mark of Oxford University Press
in the UK and in certain other countries

Published in the United States
by Oxford University Press Inc., New York

© Andrew Faulkner 2008

The moral rights of the authors have been asserted
Database right Oxford University Press (maker)

First published 2008
First published in paperback 2011

All rights reserved. No part of this publication may be reproduced,
stored in a retrieval system, or transmitted, in any form or by any means,
without the prior permission in writing of Oxford University Press,
or as expressly permitted by law, or under terms agreed with the appropriate
reprographics rights organization. Enquiries concerning reproduction
outside the scope of the above should be sent to the Rights Department,
Oxford University Press, at the address above

You must not circulate this book in any other binding or cover
and you must impose this same condition on any acquirer

British Library Cataloguing in Publication Data

Data available

Library of Congress Cataloging in Publication Data

Data available

Typeset by RefineCatch Limited, Bungay, Suffolk

Printed and bound by CPI Group (UK) Ltd, Croydon, CR0 4YY

ISBN 978–0–19–923804–0 (Hbk)
ISBN 978–0–19–963949–6 (Pbk)

For my parents
πατρί τ' ἐμῷ χαίρω καὶ μητέρι κέδν' εἰδυίῃ

Preface

THE *Homeric Hymn to Aphrodite* has received a good deal of scholarly attention since it was first printed in Florence in 1488, but no extensive commentary has ever been produced on the poem. In the twentieth century, Allen, Halliday, and Sikes (AS 1904, AHS 1936), and Càssola (1975) treated the poem admirably in their editions of the entire corpus of the *Homeric Hymns*, but the attention that they were able to give to *Aphr.* was naturally limited by the broad scope of their work. J. van Eck (VE) gave individual attention to the hymn in his doctoral thesis presented to the University of Utrecht in 1978 (a commentary with a short introduction), but, despite many useful observations, he left much work to be done (N. van der Ben also offered much of value in his short response to van Eck in 1986).

The present commentary, a substantially revised and expanded version of my Oxford D.Phil. thesis, does not pretend to be exhaustive, but it does aim to be inclusive and draws upon linguistic, literary, historical, and archaeological evidence in order to throw light on the text of *Aphr.* and the questions that it raises. Ultimately, it is hoped that this book will provide the reader with the necessary tools to make informed decisions about the poem and related matters, and serve as a base for further scholarship. A good deal of attention has been paid to parallels (both linguistic and thematic) elsewhere in Greek literature. These are often an indispensable aid to understanding and are also given in order to help situate the *Hymn to Aphrodite* within the Greek poetic tradition. The purpose of including parallels in later Greek poetry may be less immediately evident. As has traditionally been the practice, these are at times provided where there is the possibility of *imitatio* (such cases are summarized in the Introduction). Later parallels are also, however, given when there is no question of *imitatio*: these are provided for those scholars working on later texts who will approach this commentary with an interest in this information, and in the belief that the practice of later Greek poets can shed light on earlier poetry. In certain respects my approach to the commentary might be described as traditional. I do, however, make use of work in the field of narratology, which I have become convinced is very profitably applied to ancient texts, and I have dedicated a good amount of time to considering parallels in Near Eastern literature, an avenue of research which has been fruitfully expanded by scholars in recent years. I have been cautious not to confine myself to *minutiae*. Textual problems and matters of interpretation of individual words or lines are dealt with as they arise, but an effort has always been made to indicate when and how they affect the wider interpretation of the passage, or the whole poem.

For a task of this kind, I have naturally benefited from the work of many scholars who have come before me; my debt to them is signalled throughout the book. I should also like to record here my thanks to several individuals: I am most grateful to Dr Nicholas Richardson, first my D.Phil. supervisor and then my adviser for the press; his constant willingness to read and discuss my work, his acute scholarship, and his many suggestions for improvement have greatly clarified and expanded my thinking. Dr Richardson, who is now preparing a commentary on three of the four long *Homeric Hymns* (excluding *Demeter*) for the Cambridge Greek and Latin Classics series, very kindly allowed me to see a draft of his own work on the *Hymn to Aphrodite* once my thesis was complete; it was a great help to compare our opinions on particular matters at this later stage. To Dr Malcolm Campbell I am indebted for the suggestion that I undertake work on *Aphr.*, and for much else as well. During my time as an undergraduate and research student at St Andrews University, I also profited from the learning of Professor Stephen Halliwell and the entire department there. I spent a very profitable six months in Amsterdam working with Professor Irene de Jong. Also while in Amsterdam, I benefited from the advice of Professor Jan Bremer and the late Professor C. J. Ruijgh. Back in Britain, my D.Phil. examiners Dr Richard Rutherford and Professor Alex Garvie both read my thesis with great care and offered many very valuable suggestions for improvement. I am grateful as well to Professor Gregory Hutchinson, Professor Jasper Griffin, Dr Ewen Bowie, and Dr Bruno Currie, for their helpful criticism and encouragement. Dr Martin West kindly read my thesis and made many suggestions for improvement. Dr

Stephanie Dalley patiently discussed Near Eastern parallels with me and read my work on this topic. Professor Makoto Anzai kindly hosted me in Japan. It is also a pleasure to thank Dr Christos Simelidis, with whom I have discussed various aspects of my work at every stage; his careful approach to textual criticism, and his firm command of Greek have often helped to clarify my arguments. Thanks are owed also to my colleagues at Mount Allison University, the University of Notre Dame, and now the University of Texas at Austin: in particular, Dr Bruce Robertson, Dr Leslie Shumka, Professor Keith Bradley, Dr Brian Krostenko, Dr Elizabeth Mazurek, Dr Catherine Schlegel, Dr Lawrence Kim, Professor Timothy Moore, Professor Paula Perlman, Professor Cynthia Shelmerdine, and Dr Andrew Riggsby. I am greatly indebted to Dr Leofranc Holford-Strevens, whose learned queries and observations have improved many parts of this book. One longstanding teacher deserves individual mention: Mrs N. Hare. For personal encouragement and support I am most grateful to my family: my parents, to whom I dedicate this book, and my brother Jonathan. Special thanks are due to my wife Kate Timmers, without whose understanding and support my work would be impossible, and whose own learning continues to inspire me. To the many others who have assisted me but must go unnamed here I am no less thankful.

I am also indebted to several institutions for support, without which I would not have been able to undertake this work. During my time as a D.Phil. student I was funded by: Universities UK, which awarded me an ORS scholarship; the University of St Andrews; the Sir Kenneth Dover Fund; Merton College, which provided support on every level; the Craven Committee, who kindly elected me to a Derby Scholarship from 2002–4; the Harold Wyam Wingate Foundation, which heroically granted me a scholarship in 2003–4; the École Normale Supérieure, which provided support for a nine-month stay in Paris; and the Japanese Society for the Promotion of Science, which generously awarded me a fellowship in order to visit Japan for one month. I would also like to thank the Bank of Cyprus Cultural Foundation, in particular Eleni Zapiti, for allowing me to see coins in their collection, and the many libraries around Europe who gave me access to their manuscript collections. Since completing my D.Phil.: the Crake foundation funded a one-year fellowship at Mount Allison

University in Canada; I spent a very profitable and stimulating year at the University of Notre Dame; and the University of Texas at Austin continues to support me generously in my research and teaching. Finally, I should like to thank the Press for undertaking to publish this work.

The section in my Introduction entitled 'The Aineiadai and Interpretation of the Hymn' is a slightly revised version of an article entitled 'Aphrodite's Legacy', published in *AJPh* 129. 1; it is used by permission of The Johns Hopkins University Press and the *American Journal of Philology*.

Halifax, Canada, 2007   A.F.

Contents

Abbreviations   xii

Introduction   1
    I. Summary of the Poem   1
    II. The Aineiadai and Interpretation of the *Hymn*   3
    III. Near Eastern Motifs   18
    IV. Overview of Language and Relationship to Early Poetry   23
    V. Date and Place of Composition   47
    VI. Impact on Later Literature   50
    VII. Manuscripts and Text   52

Text   57

Commentary   69

Works Cited   299
General Index   313
Index Locorum   319

Abbreviations

AB	*Posidippi Quae Supersunt Omnia*, ed. C. Austin and G. Bastianini (Milan, 2002).
AHS	T. W. Allen, W. R. Halliday, and E. E. Sikes, *The Homeric Hymns* (Oxford, 1936).
ANET	*Ancient Near Eastern Texts*, ed. J. B. Pritchard (3rd edn. with supplement; Princeton, 1969).
AS	T. W. Allen and E. E. Sikes, *The Homeric Hymns* (Oxford, 1904).
Bernabé	*Poetae Epici Graeci*, ed. A. Bernabé (2nd edn.; Leipzig, 1996–2007).
Black	*Apocalypsis Henochi graece*, ed. M. Black (Leiden, 1970).
BTM	B. R. Foster, *Before the Muses: An Anthology of Akkadian Literature* (3rd edn., Bethesda, MD, 2005).
CA	*Collectanea Alexandrina*, ed. J. U. Powell (Oxford, 1925).
CAD	*The Assyrian Dictionary*, ed. I. J. Gelb, B. Landsberger, et al. (Chicago, 1956–).
Càssola	F. Càssola, *Inni omerici* (Milan, 1975).
CEG	*Carmina Epigraphica Graeca*, ed. P. A. Hansen, 2 vols. (Berlin, 1983–9).
Cook	A. B. Cook, *Zeus*, 3 vols. (Cambridge, 1914–40).
Cooper	G. L. Cooper, *Greek Syntax*, 4 vols. (Ann Arbor, MI, 1998–2002).
Cougny	*Epigrammatum Anthologia Palatina: cum Planudeis et Appendice Nova*, ed. E. Cougny, iii (Paris, 1890).
Davies	*Epicorum Graecorum Fragmenta*, ed. M. Davies (Göttingen, 1988).
Dictionnaire	P. Chantraine, *Dictionnaire étymologique de la langue grecque* (Paris, 1968–80).
Diggle	*Tragicorum Graecorum Fragmenta Selecta*, ed. J. Diggle (Oxford, 1998).
DK	*Die Fragmente der Vorsokratiker*, ed. H. Diels and W. Kranz (6th edn.; Berlin, 1952).

Abbreviations

Enchiridium	J. van Leeuwen, *Enchiridium dictionis epicae* (2nd edn.; Leiden, 1918).
ETCSL	The Electronic Text Corpus of Sumerian Literature (http://etcsl.orinst.ox.ac.uk/), ed. J. A. Black, J. Baines, G. Cunningham, J. Ebeling, E. Flückiger-Hawker, E. Robson, J. Taylor, and G. Zólyomi (Oxford, 1998–2006).
Farnell	L. R. Farnell, *Cults of the Greek States*, 5 vols. (Oxford, 1896–1909).
FGrH	*Die Fragmente der griechischen Historiker*, ed. F. Jacoby (Berlin and Leiden, 1923–58).
Foster	B. R. Foster, *The Epic of Gilgamesh* (New York, 2001).
Fowler	R. Fowler, *Early Greek Mythography* (Oxford, 2000).
Frisk	H. Frisk, *Griechisches etymologisches Wörterbuch*, 3 vols. (Heidelberg, 1954–72).
Furley	W. D. Furley and J. M. Bremer, *Greek Hymns*, 2 vols. (Tübingen, 2001).
GDK	*Die griechischen Dichterfragmente der römischen Kaizerzeit*, ed. E. Heitsch, 2 vols. (Göttingen, 1963–4).
Gesch.	M. P. Nilsson, *Geschichte der griechischen Religion* (3rd edn.; Munich, 1967–74).
GG	E. Schwyzer, *Griechische Grammatik*, 2 vols. (Munich, 1939–50).
Gow	A. S. F. Gow, Theocritus: *Edited with a Translation and Commentary*, 2 vols. (Cambridge, 1950).
Grammaire	P. Chantraine, *Grammaire homérique*, 2 vols. (Paris, 1942–53).
GVI	*Griechische Vers-Inschriften*, ed. W. Peek (Berlin, 1955).
HT	J. La Roche, *Die Homerische Textkritik im Alterthum* (Leipzig, 1866).
IEG	*Iambi et Elegi Graeci* (ed. altera), ed. M. L. West, 2 vols. (Oxford, 1989–92).
Kern	*Orphicorum Fragmenta*, ed. O. Kern (Berlin, 1922).
Leaf	*The Iliad*, ed. W. Leaf, 2 vols. (London, 1900–2).
LfgrE	*Lexikon des frühgriechischen Epos*, ed. B. Snell et al. (Göttingen, 1955–).
LIMC	*Lexicon Iconographicum Mythologiae Classicae*, 8 vols. (Zurich and Munich, 1981–99).

Abbreviations

Lomiento — *Cercidas: Testimonia et Fragmenta*, ed. L. Lomiento (Rome, 1993).

LSJ — H. G. Liddell, R. Scott, H. Stuart Jones, R. McKenzie, and P. G. W. Glare, *Greek–English Lexicon, with a Revised Supplement* (9th edn.; Oxford, 1996).

Milet — T. Wiegand, *Milet: Ergebnisse der Ausgrabungen und Untersuchungen*, 4 vols. (Berlin, 1906–15).

M–W — *Fragmenta Hesiodea*, ed. R. Merkelbach and M. L. West (Oxford, 1967).

OC — A. Heubeck, S. West, A. Hoekstra, J. B. Hainsworth, J. Russo, and M. Fernández-Galiano, *A Commentary on Homer's Odyssey*, 3 vols. (Oxford, 1988–92).

OCD — *The Oxford Classical Dictionary*, ed. S. Hornblower and A. Spawforth (3rd edn., Oxford, 1996).

PCG — *Poetae Comici Graeci*, ed. R. Kassel and C. Austin (Berlin, 1983–).

Pf. — *Callimachus*, ed. R. Pfeiffer, 2 vols. (Oxford, 1949–53).

PG — *Patrologia Graeca*, ed. J. P. Migne, 161 vols. (Paris, 1857–66).

PLF — *Poetarum Lesbiorum Fragmenta*, ed. E. Lobel and D. L. Page (Oxford, 1955).

PMG — *Poetae Melici Graeci*, ed. D. L. Page (Oxford, 1962).

PMGF — *Poetarum Melicorum Graecorum Fragmenta*, ed. M. Davies (Oxford, 1991).

RE — *Paulys Real-Encyclopädie der classischen Altertumswissenschaft*, ed. G. Wissowa et al. (Stuttgart–Munich, 1893–1980).

SM — *Bacchylidis Carmina cum Fragmentis*, ed. B. Snell and H. Maehler (Leipzig, 1992).

SnM — *Pindari Carmina cum Fragmentis*, ed. B. Snell and H. Maehler (Leipzig, 1987–9).

TrGF — *Tragicorum Graecorum Fragmenta*, Göttingen, ed. B. Snell, R. Kanicht, and S. Radt, 5 vols. (Göttingen, 1971–2004).

TP — *Theognidis et Phocylidis fragmenta*, ed. M. L. West (Berlin, 1978).

VB — N. van der Ben, 'Hymn to Aphrodite 36–291—Notes on the *Pars Epica* of the *Homeric Hymn to Aphrodite*', *Mnemosyne*[4], 39 (1986), 1–41.

VE	J. van Eck, *The Homeric Hymn to Aphrodite* (Diss. Utrecht, 1978).
Voigt	*Sappho et Alcaeus*, ed. E. Voigt (Amsterdam, 1971).
Wack.	J. Wackernagel, *Kleine Schriften*, 3 vols. (Göttingen, 1953–79).

Abbreviations of ancient authors and their works are those of LSJ, with the exception of the *Homeric Hymns*. The latter are referred to as *Dion.*, *Dem.*, *Apoll.*, *Herm.*, *Aphr.*, and then *Hy(s)*. The *Iliad* and *Odyssey*, and Hesiod's *Theogony* and *Works and Days* are frequently referred to by their abbreviation alone (*Il.*, *Od.*, *Th.*, *Op.*) without reference to the author, except where this aids in clarification. I use the name 'Homer' to refer collectively to the *Iliad* and *Odyssey* in something like their present forms. Accordingly, although I refer conventionally to the *Homeric Hymns*, I otherwise use the adjective 'Homeric' to mean 'of, pertaining to, or characteristic of the *Iliad* and *Odyssey*'. The *Hymns* of Callimachus and Proclus are respectively referred to as Call. *Hy(s)*. and Procl. *Hy(s)*. Unless otherwise noted, fragments of ancient authors are cited from the following editions: those of [Hesiod] from M–W, of other early epic poets from Davies, of Sappho and Alcaeus from Voigt, of Pindar from SnM, of Bacchylides from SM, of iambic and elegiac poets from *IEG*, of other lyric poets from *PMG* and *PMGF*, of tragic poets from *TrGF*, of comic poets from *PCG*, and of Callimachus from Pf. Abbreviations of journal titles follow the conventions of *L'Année philologique*.

Introduction

I. SUMMARY OF THE POEM

1–52. *Prologue*
1–6. The proem celebrates Aphrodite's universal power.
7–33. Athena, Artemis, and Hestia, the three virgin goddesses who cannot be conquered by love, are hymned and contrasted with Aphrodite.
34–44. The poet celebrates Aphrodite's ability to conquer even Zeus in love.
45–52. The motivation for the narrative is introduced; Zeus turns the tables on Aphrodite and makes her fall in love with a mortal man, in order that she will no longer be able to boast about the affairs she kindles between gods and mortals.

53–199. *The core narrative: Aphrodite's seduction of Anchises*
53–63. Aphrodite spots Anchises on Ida, falls in love with him immediately, and retires to her temple in Paphos to perform her toilette. She bathes, is anointed with perfumed oils, and dresses.
64–91. Aphrodite leaves Paphos and crosses Mt. Ida to the hut of Anchises. On the way she is fawned upon by beasts, lions, and bears, which mate as she passes. When she arrives she finds Anchises alone at his hut and stands before him in all her finery; he falls in love with her immediately.
92–106. Anchises, suspecting that his visitor is a goddess, inquires which of the immortals she is, and promises to set up a temple to her in return for a prosperous and long life.

107–42. Aphrodite responds to Anchises. She tells an elaborate lie: she is a mortal Phrygian princess, the daughter of King Otreus, who was brought to Ida by Hermes in order that she should become Anchises' wife and bear him children.

143–67. Anchises is persuaded. Seized by love, he goes to bed with the goddess. He removes her clothing piece by piece and the affair is consummated.

168–91. Anchises falls asleep after he has lain with Aphrodite. The goddess retakes her true form and makes an epiphany to Anchises by waking him. He is terrified and, hiding behind his blanket, asks Aphrodite not to harm him.

192–290. *Aphrodite's Final Speech*

192–9. Aphrodite reassures Anchises that he will not be harmed and prophesies that she will bear him a son, Aeneas, who will rule amongst the Trojans.

200–38. Aphrodite expands upon the beauty and godlike nature of Anchises' lineage. She uses as *exempla* the divine affairs of Anchises' ancestors Ganymedes and Tithonus. Ganymedes was taken by Zeus, who recompensed his father Tros with a gift of divine horses. Tithonus was taken to live with Eos, but the goddess foolishly requested of Zeus only that Tithonus be made immortal, forgetting to ask that he also be made eternally young. Tithonus grew ever older until, eventually bedridden, he was unable even to move his limbs.

239–55. Aphrodite explains that she would not want a fate such as Tithonus' for Anchises; he is mortal and must die, while she, an immortal goddess, must for evermore endure the shame of the present affair. She will no longer be able to boast amongst the gods about the affairs she brings about between gods and mortals.

255–80. Aphrodite expands upon the future of Aeneas. He will be reared by mountain nymphs who live and die with the trees. But, once he has reached adolescence, the nymphs will bring him back to Anchises, who must take him straight away to Troy.

281–90. Aphrodite concludes her speech with a warning to Anchises not to tell anyone that he has slept with her. If someone asks who is the mother of his son, he is to say that Aeneas is the offspring of one of the nymphs.

291–3. Departure and final invocation
Immediately after finishing her speech, Aphrodite rushes back up to heaven. The poet then gives a traditional address of farewell.

II. THE AINEIADAI AND INTERPRETATION OF THE *HYMN*

The *Hymn to Aphrodite* is one of four long hymns surviving in the collection of *Homeric Hymns*,[1] thirty-three poems in hexameter verse of varying dates dedicated to gods or deified heroes.[2] The other long *Hymns*, to Demeter, Apollo, and Hermes, narrate the foundation of a god's cult and the establishment of his or her powers and spheres of influence; Demeter goes in search of her daughter Persephone and founds the Eleusinian Mysteries, Apollo is born and founds his cults on Delos and in Delphi, while the precocious young Hermes steals Apollo's cattle before the two are eventually reconciled and establish their own spheres of influence. In tone, *Aphr.* is most similar to *Herm.*; both lack the focus upon cult found in *Dem.* and *Apoll.* But even *Herm.* narrates the foundation of cult practice; the description of Hermes' sacrifice of two of Apollo's cattle next to the river Alpheios (vv. 105 ff.) can be connected to cult practice at Olympia, and it seems reasonable to suppose that the poem was composed for performance there.[3] In contrast, there is no specific connection to cult or ritual worship in *Aphr.*[4] The subject-matter of the narrative also sets *Aphr.* apart from the other *Hymns*, for on the surface it does not celebrate the goddess and the establishment of her powers, but

---

[1] The first *Hymn to Dionysus*, of which only fragments now survive, most probably had a length of over 400 lines; see West (2001c), 1. *Hy.* 7 to Dionysus contains 59 lines and *Hy.* 19 to Pan 49 lines, while the other *Hymns* vary in length from 3 to 22 lines.

[2] Cf. Clay (1997), 489–92. A quotation of the *Hymn to Apollo* by Thucydides (3. 104) indicates that this *Hymn* was circulating in the 5th c. Other *Hymns* must also have been circulating at that time, but they were most probably not collected together in any organized way until the Hellenistic period; see West (2003), 20.

[3] See Burkert (2001), 178–88, West (2003), 13–14.

[4] The description of her cult site in Paphos in vv. 58 ff. is stock epic material; see Comm. on 58–63.

rather places her in an embarrassing situation; Zeus turns the tables on Aphrodite and makes her fall in love with Anchises, an affair which results in the birth of Aeneas and a great deal of shame for Aphrodite.[5]

The *Hymn to Aphrodite* has often been understood as a poem intended to pay honour to a family of Aineiadai who once held power in the Troad.[6] This reading has been inferred from the prophecy about Aeneas' future as a ruler of the Trojans in vv. 196–7 (σοὶ δ' ἔσται φίλος υἱὸς ὃς ἐν Τρώεσσιν ἀνάξει | καὶ παῖδες παίδεσσι διαμπερὲς ἐκγεγάονται), which echoes a similar prophecy at *Il.* 20. 307–8 (νῦν δὲ δὴ Αἰνείαο βίη Τρώεσσιν ἀνάξει | καὶ παίδων παῖδες, τοί κεν μετόπισθε γένωνται). In more recent years, however, this position has been questioned. N. van der Ben first argued that the Aeneas-episode in *Il.* 20 is poetically justified within the narrative, and that there is therefore no reason to explain the passage as motivated by external factors.[7] In a subsequent article,[8] he applied this same principle to *Aphr.*, arguing that, instead of overtly praising Aeneas and his descendants, *Aphr.* is an aetiology of why the gods no longer have love-affairs with mortals that result in semi-divine offspring.[9] Concurrently, Smith quite successfully showed that the claims of later Greek historians for the existence of a family of

---

[5] See Comm. on 239–55.

[6] A very useful review of the literature on this topic up until 1980 is found in van der Ben (1980), 41–55. See also the summaries of previous literature by Lenz (1975), 159 ff., VE 69–72, Clay (1989), 153 n. 3. The most influential article arguing for this interpretation was written by Reinhardt (1956), who believed that *Il.* 20 and *Aphr.* were written by the same poet. More reasonable positions have since been taken by Hoekstra (1969), 39–40, Càssola 243–7, VE loc. cit., who recognize that the *Hymn* is almost certainly post-Homeric, but still accept that both it and *Il.* 20 were composed with the Aineiadai in mind.

[7] Van der Ben (1980). For him, Aeneas is a literary figure who functions as a contrast to Hektor, '(a) als de overlever tegenover hem die omkomt, en (b) als de afzijdige tegenover hem van wie het lot van de stad afhangt' (71–2); cf. Smith (1981*b*), 49–52). He also suggests that Aeneas is not presented in an over-favourable light in the *Iliad*, but the fact that Aeneas 'doodt niet veel tegenstanders en geen enkele "grote naam" ' does not to me seem significant in the face of the overt prophecy uttered by Poseidon, and the long account of his genealogy to Achilles.

[8] Van der Ben (1981).

[9] This interpretation has since been picked up and expanded by Clay (1989), 166–70, 192–3; it has also been recently adopted by Turkeltaub (2003*a*), 75–8.

Aineiadai in the Troad are not to be blindly trusted.[10] Support for the Aineiadai hypothesis had often been gained from the supposed veracity of these historical accounts and Smith's article pushed the Aineiadai firmly into the background. He himself went on to argue that the juxtaposition of mortal and immortal is the central unifying theme in *Aphr.* rather than any concern with the lineage of Aeneas,[11] and his work opened the way for alternative theories. Frangeskou has suggested that the poem is concerned essentially with the divine relationship between Zeus and Aphrodite rather than the juxtaposition of mortal and immortal; a story which illustrates that 'if for a while the gods oppose one another, in the end concord and mutuality prevail'.[12] This redirection of focus has in one respect been healthy; new literary approaches (in particular the work of Smith) have offered many valuable insights. On the other hand, the new theories have brushed aside all too easily the remarkable attention paid to the descendants of Aeneas and Anchises by the poem.

A few scholars have continued to support or admit the possibility of the Aineiadai hypothesis. Janko, West, and Edwards all maintain that, despite the lack of any reliable corroborative evidence from later historians, the existence of Aineiadai is a possible conclusion to draw from the prophecies of the two poems.[13] There is, it must be

---

[10] Smith (1981*b*). Particularly influential had been the claim of Demetrius of Scepsis (reported by Strabo 13. 1. 52 ff.) that a family of Aineiadai lived in the city of his name. Smith argues that this and other accounts by historians are not to be entirely trusted as evidence for the existence of the Aineiadai. On the other hand, there is no proof that they are entirely unreliable, even if they do embellish.

[11] Smith (1981*a*). Segal (1974) had already drawn attention to the juxtaposition of mortal and divine when examining *Aphr.* with a structuralist approach; see also Segal (1986) and King (1989).

[12] Frangeskou (1995), 13, who also denies that the poem could have been composed for Aineiadai. Cf. also the psychological interpretation offered by Bergren (1989), 41.

[13] See Janko (1982), 158: 'the *aition* proves knowledge of the Aeneadae, but not performance before them' and (1991), 13: '*Pace* Clay and others, not only must the Aeneadae have notoriously survived for the prophecy in *HyAphr* to have point, but Homer even links Hector with Scamandrius, co-founder with Ascanius of many cities in the Troad, by giving Astyanax that name (*Il.* 6. 402 ff.)'; West (2001*a*), 7; cf. (2003), 15: 'it is evident from a famous passage in the *Iliad* and a similar one in the *Hymn to Aphrodite* that there was an aristocratic family somewhere in the region that claimed descent from Aeneas and suzerainty over "Trojans", and that our poet [Homer] was one of a number in contact with this family'; more reserved is M. W. Edwards (1991),

admitted from the outset, no way to prove this position absolutely. On the other hand, there is good reason to admit it as a strong possibility. In *Iliad* 20, Poseidon's prophecy that Aeneas will be saved in order that the race of Dardanos will not be destroyed, and that his descendants will rule amongst the Trojans for generations to come (vv. 293–308), seems too explicit to be explained away merely as appropriate to the developing narrative. Extratextual motivation is made probable by the unique nature of the prophecy, for which there are no parallels in the Homeric epics. Aeneas' recounting of his genealogy to Achilles (vv. 200–58) earlier in the episode recalls the exchange between Diomedes and Glaucus in *Il.* 6. 119–236,[14] but the two episodes are in some important respects quite different. Not only is the Diomedes–Glaucus episode not followed by any prophecy about future glory, but it places less attention on a single individual than the Aeneas episode; between the account of his genealogy and the consideration of his fate by Hera and Poseidon, Aeneas is remarkably the focus of attention for almost three hundred lines, in what should properly be the beginning of Achilles' *aristeia*.[15] This is not to say that van der Ben's argument that this passage in *Iliad* 20 is internally coherent should be dismissed. The Aeneas episode is undoubtedly internally coherent, and Aeneas does act as a foil to Hector as he suggests.[16] But it is false logic to conclude that because something is an effective element in the development of the internal narrative it can have no further external significance.

In itself, the similar prophecy in the *Homeric Hymn to Aphrodite* could be explained merely as the result of imitation of the *Iliad*

301, commenting on *Il.* 20, 'It seems most likely that the monumental poet knew of a story that Aeneas continued to rule somewhere in the Troad; this does not prove that a royal line of Aineiadai, perhaps originating in Thrace, survived (or claimed to) in the mid-eighth century, but it is a reasonable hypothesis.' See also Griffin (1992), 200 n. 24.

[14] On the similarities between the two episodes see Kirk (1990), 171 ff.

[15] On the interruption of Achilles' *aristeia* proper see M. W. Edwards (1991), 286–7; also his comment (299): 'the expansive style of the narration, the relaxed tone of Akhilleus' speeches, and his willingness to listen to his opponent's lengthy discourse, are unexpected.'

[16] On his arguments see above, n. 7; cf. M. W. Edwards (1991), 298–9, who recognizes the literary functions of the Aeneas episode in book 20, while at the same time entertaining the Aeineadai-hypothesis.

passage.[17] However, the two prophecies are not the only evidence to support the position that the *Aphr.* was written with Aeneiadai in mind. Also significant is the concentrated interest in the birth of Aeneas and his lineage throughout the poem.[18]

The theme of future offspring

The birth of the semi-divine Aeneas is first foreshadowed in the prologue of the poem, significantly just before the narrative begins. The poet introduces the narrative by telling how Zeus has turned the tables on Aphrodite and made her fall in love with a mortal man in order that she should never again boast among the gods:

> ὥς ῥα θεοὺς συνέμειξε καταθνητῇσι γυναιξί
> καί τε καταθνητοὺς υἷας τέκον ἀθανάτοισιν
> ὥς τε θεὰς ἀνέμειξε καταθνητοῖς ἀνθρώποις. (*Aphr.* 50–2)
>
> that she mixed gods in love with mortal women
> who bore mortal sons to the immortals
> and that she mixed goddesses with mortal men.

These lines meditate upon divine–mortal unions and the offspring which result therefrom, with the last line referring specifically to unions of goddesses and mortal men. This attention to the issue of semi-divine birth signals what is to be one of the main themes in the narrative; the birth of Aeneas. To be more exact, v. 50 is followed by a line that specifies that sons result from the unions of gods and mortal women. Verse 52, which by nature of its similar structure is a counterpart to v. 50, is followed immediately by the narrative. The narrative cannot be said to be a direct counterpart to v. 51 because it describes the cessation of Aphrodite's boasting rather than being part of it; but, like v. 51, it does explain, albeit in a more specific

---

[17] Cf. AHS 351.
[18] VB 22 does not agree: he comments, 'Aeneas does not occupy an important position in the poem as a whole: the central event, the intercourse between Anchises and Aphrodite, is never motivated by his birth; neither in the proem, nor in the plan of Zeus, nor in the goddess' own account does it receive the slightest mention. Aeneas' birth merely belongs to the aftermath and is a painful reminder to Aphrodite of a love that was not to be.' In what follows, I shall show that the birth of Aeneas is in fact a central concern in the poem.

8   Introduction

manner, the offspring which result from the union of a goddess and a mortal man. If v. 51 and the narrative can be seen as counterparts in this latter respect, the distinction between boasting and the cessation of boasting becomes significant. These lines immediately preceding the narrative are introducing two interrelated themes: the birth of Aeneas and the cessation of Aphrodite's boasting.

Anchises himself hints rather openly at his future offspring in the prayer which he offers to Aphrodite when she first arrives on the mountain to seduce him. She comes in the disguise of a young Phrygian woman, but he is uncertain what to make of his unexpected (and radiant) visitor. To be on the safe side, he addresses her in prayer, asking for strong offspring and a long, glorious life (vv. 103–5).[19] Anchises' request that his offspring be strong is on one level a standard petition in prayer,[20] but for an audience who knew the story of his parentage, this request must have brought Aeneas to mind.

The issue of children arises again before the consummation of the seduction, during Aphrodite's long lie to Anchises about her mortal Phrygian origins and her method of arrival on the mountain (vv. 108–42). The disguised goddess claims that she was whisked away from dancing with her young companions by Hermes, who brought her to the mountain and prophesied that she would be his wedded wife and bear him children (v. 127 σοὶ δ' ἀγλαὰ τέκνα τεκεῖσθαι). Out of context, the phrase τέκνα τεκέσθαι is a standard description of wifely activity,[21] but in the mouth of the disguised Aphrodite it carries a certain irony: she conceives of the prophecy as part of her deception, but it will (to her great shame) in fact come true. Without being explicit (which, given the circumstances of Aphrodite's deception, the poet hardly could be), this mention

---

[19] Allen (1898), 25 and Bickerman (1976), 231 argue that Anchises' speech is nothing more than a flattering speech to a mortal woman, just like Odysseus' address to Nausicaa at *Od.* 6. 149 ff. Smith (1981*a*), 46–9 thinks that Anchises is uncertain about whether his visitor is a goddess or not, and there is good reason to follow his view. While Odysseus cautiously asks whether Nausicaa is a god or a mortal, Anchises makes no mention of mortality, but gives only a long list of possible goddesses; Odysseus likens Nausicaa to Artemis alone. See further Comm. on 92–106.

[20] Cf. Nestor's prayer to Athena at *Od.* 3. 380–1 ἀλλά, ἄνασσ', ἴληθι, δίδωθι δέ μοι κλέος ἐσθλόν, | αὐτῷ καὶ παίδεσσι καὶ αἰδοίῃ παρακοίτῃ.

[21] Cf. *Od.* 22. 324, *Dem.* 136, [Hes.] fr. 31. 4.

of children once again foreshadows the ultimate result of the encounter.[22]

After the union, a great deal of attention is openly paid to Aeneas' future. Apart from the explicit prophecy of his birth at vv. 196–7, Aphrodite mentions him as the result of her union with a mortal in vv. 252–5. That Aphrodite's love-affair with Anchises and the resulting birth of Aeneas are an embarrassment to the goddess, is no reason to doubt that the poet is honouring a family of Aineiadai, as Smith argues.[23] Thetis is not happy with her marriage to the mortal Peleus, but this does not affect the honour of Achilles. Similarly, Zeus is embarrassed about his affairs with mortals (a fact which this poem expands upon), but his offspring (Heracles, Sarpedon, etc.) are all still extraordinary mortals with great honour. The point is that Aeneas comes from divine stock, whether Aphrodite is shamed among the gods or not. Aphrodite expands upon Aeneas further in vv. 256–90, where she explains how her son will be reared by mountain nymphs, and how, when Anchises sees Aeneas for the first time, he is to take him immediately to Troy. This expansion is a continuation of her brief prophecy concerning Aeneas at vv. 196–7, and occupies a substantial part of the final section of the poem.

There is also a marked emphasis upon the godlike beauty and stature of Anchises and his lineage throughout the poem. Not only are Anchises and Aeneas on several occasions compared to the gods with honorific formulae (Anchises, v. 55 δέμας ἀθανάτοισιν ἐοικώς, v. 77 θεῶν ἄπο κάλλος ἔχοντα; Aeneas v. 279 μάλα γὰρ θεοείκελος ἔσται), but there is a long digression during Aphrodite's final speech about Anchises' glorious ancestors Ganymedes and Tithonus (vv. 200–38), who also had love-affairs with gods. The section is introduced with the general statement ἀγχίθεοι δὲ μάλιστα καταθνητῶν ἀνθρώπων | αἰεὶ ἀφ' ὑμετέρης γενεῆς [Ἀγχίσεω] εἶδός τε φυήν τε (vv. 200–1), and the whole family is again praised when introducing the specific case of Tithonus at vv. 218–19 Τιθωνὸν ... | ὑμετέρης γενεῆς ἐπιείκελον ἀθανάτοισι. In addition, the stress which this episode lays upon the family seems particularly remarkable, given

---

[22] The fact that her claims that she will be called the wife of Anchises and bear him children in vv. 126–7 are presented as a prophecy from the mouth of the god Hermes also serves to mark this information out from the rest of her lie.

[23] Smith (1981a), 70.

that the digression is somewhat unexpected following the epiphany of Aphrodite to Anchises. The goddess would naturally have made her departure after a relatively short speech.[24] The general subject-matter (divine–mortal love-affairs) is certainly not out of place in the poem,[25] but it is at least possible that the poet of *Aphr.* added the Ganymedes–Tithonus episode to an earlier account of the love-affair, in which Aphrodite revealed herself to Anchises, gave a short speech of prophecy and warning, and departed. Increased praise of Aeneas' lineage is one possible motivation for the addition of the episode.

All the above passages in *Aphr.* dealing with the birth of Aeneas and the glory of his race show that his lineage is a theme central to the narrative. While it is not possible, based upon this evidence, to conclude definitively that the poet of *Aphr.* was composing with a group of Aineiadai in mind, nor to gain any understanding of exactly what form such a relationship might have taken (the poem could, for example, have been composed for a specific situation such as a festival, or as a piece of court poetry),[26] the marked emphasis on the lineage of Aeneas in *Aphr.*, when combined with the explicit prophecies there and in *Il.* 20, gives considerable support to the hypothesis that the Aineiadai did exist and that the poet of *Aphr.* intended to praise them.

Shameful love: unions between gods and mortals

In laying aside the Aineiadai hypothesis, van der Ben and, following him, Clay instead explain the *Hymn to Aphrodite* as an aetiology of why gods no longer have love-affairs with mortals, and therefore why the age of semi-divine heroes has come to an end.[27] Accepting that the poem was written with Aineiadai in mind certainly does

---

[24] On epiphanies' most frequently coinciding with the arrival or departure of a god, see N. Richardson (1974), 208. Although it is on a much different scale, cf. the quick departure of Poseidon after his affair with Tyro at *Od.* 11. 248–52. See further Comm. on 191–290.

[25] See Comm. on 200–38.

[26] See Ballabriga (1996), who suggests that *Aphr.* is paying homage not to a ruling family in the Troad, but to the people of the city Aineia, in Thrace, who claimed descent from Aeneas.

[27] See above nn. 8, 9.

not preclude a concern with literary motifs. Indeed, one needs only to glance at the poetry of Pindar, or that of the later Theocritus and Callimachus, to see how specific contemporary reference and themes derived from literature can coexist happily. With respect to *Aphr.*, for example, Smith has successfully shown that there is a recurrent juxtaposition of mortality and immortality in the hymn. This is a common motif elsewhere in early epic,[28] and naturally so in this poem as well, in which the boundaries between god and man are quite literally crossed; Aphrodite's disguising herself as a young maiden when she approaches Anchises (see in particular vv. 82, 109–10) itself blurs the distinction between mortal and divine, and the affair closes with the explicit statement that a mortal has slept with a goddess (v. 168 ἀθανάτῃ παρέλεκτο θεᾷ βροτός). The incompatibility of men and gods in love (known also in the *Iliad* and *Odyssey*),[29] is then later developed in detail in the stories of Ganymedes and Tithonus (vv. 202–40), while the elaboration upon the semi-divine nymphs in vv. 257–72 explores the question of life and death.

In principle, then, one might adopt the theory that *Aphr.* narrates the end of Aphrodite's willingness to bring about sexual unions between gods and mortals, while at the same time accepting that the poem is principally intended to praise a family of Aineiadai.[30] The case, however, for reading *Aphr.* as an aetiology of why gods no longer have love-affairs with mortals has been exaggerated. In what follows, I shall revisit the arguments made in support of this reading of *Aphr.* and suggest that, while it is a possible implication of the narrative, the end of unions between gods and mortals is neither explicit nor necessarily implicit in the poem. I will also argue that, even if one accepts this as a literary motif in the poem, it is not as prominent a theme as has been claimed.

---

[28] On the motif in Homer see Griffin (1980), 162 *et passim*; cf. also Walcot (1991), 140–1 with examples from other *Hymns*.

[29] See Achilles' lament to his mother at *Il.* 18. 86–7 that she ever married Peleus. Also, Calypso complains to Hermes about the hardships of relationships between goddesses and mortal men at *Od.* 5. 118 ff.

[30] See e.g. West (2003), 15, 'Previously [Aphrodite] had enjoyed making other gods compromise their dignity by falling in love with a mortal; but by making her fall for Anchises, Zeus has put a stop to that for the future. However, the union that is an embarrassment for the goddess is a matter of glory for the heroic family that issues from it, and this is the real point of the poem.'

To begin, Clay suggests that such a reading of *Aphr.* is supported by something similar at [Hes.] fr. 204. 102–3 ἀλλ' οἱ μ[ὲ]ν μάκ[α]ρες κ[......]ν ὡς τὸ πάρος περ | χωρὶς ἀπ' ἀν[θ]ρώπων [βίοτον κα]ὶ ἤθε' ἔχωσιν.[31] She cites the interpretation of the fragment by Nagy, who thinks that it narrates the 'permanent separation of gods and men' by Zeus (translating μάκαρες as gods).[32] Given, however, the similarity with *Op.* 167 τοῖς δὲ δίχ' ἀνθρώπων βίοτον καὶ ἦθε' ὀπάσσας, it seems much more probable that West is correct that the fragment describes Zeus separating the sons of gods (i.e. μάκαρες = semi-divine heroes) from the rest of mankind to live on the island of the blessed.[33] Clay also compares *Cypria* fr. 1 for her assertion that *Aphr.* is narrating the permanent separation of men and gods,[34] but there Zeus' plan is simply to relieve the earth of too many men, with nothing said about their permanent separation from the gods. The frequent longing in the *Iliad* for an age when men were better certainly implies that the age of heroes is in decline at the time of the Trojan war,[35] and nostalgia for a time when men and gods interacted more closely is expressed in the Hesiodic *Catalogue*.[36] But a specific event which brings about the permanent separation of gods and men is not explicitly narrated anywhere in what survives of early literature. In fact, the poetic tradition elsewhere has mortal-divine relationships continue past this affair of Aphrodite and Anchises. The relative ages of heroes such as Achilles, Aeneas, and Sarpedon are not specified anywhere in Homer.[37] If one considers the order in which the two births are presented at Hes. *Th.* 1006–10 as indicative of age, Achilles would indeed be older; but in this case the birth of Aeneas is followed by Circe and Calypso bearing sons to Odysseus, a generation after the birth of Aeneas.[38]

I now turn to *Aphr.* itself. Van der Ben and Clay first seek support

---

[31] Clay (1989), 167–8.   [32] Nagy (1979), 220.

[33] West (1985), 119 ff. On the description of the island of the blessed in Hesiod, and the meaning of μάκαρες, see West (1978), 193–4.

[34] Clay (1989), 156–7, 167–8.

[35] See Clay (1989), 168–70 and West (1997), 116 ff.   [36] See [Hes.] fr. 1. 6–7.

[37] Noted by VB 32.

[38] The account of his sons by Circe and Calypso is probably later than the *Odyssey*, where sons are not mentioned at all—see West (1966a), 433—but there is no way to exclude that it was known by the poet of *Aphr.* (certainly post-Homeric; cf. Hoekstra 1969, 39 ff.).

for their reading in ll. 36–9 of the poem. After the prologue of the hymn, in which the three exceptions to Aphrodite's universal power, Athena, Artemis, and Hestia, receive mini-hymns, the poet returns to the theme of her universal dominance with the point that she conquers even Zeus in love:

καί τε πάρεκ Ζηνὸς νόον ἤγαγε τερπικεραύνου,
ὅς τε μέγιστός τ' ἐστί, μεγίστης τ' ἔμμορε τιμῆς·
καί τε τοῦ εὖτ' ἐθέλῃ[39] πυκινὰς φρένας ἐξαπαφοῦσα
ῥηϊδίως συνέμειξε καταθνητῇσι γυναιξί. (Aphr. 36–9)

She even leads astray the mind of Zeus who delights in the thunderbolt,
who is the greatest, and receives the greatest honour.
Deceiving his shrewd mind whenever she wants,
she easily mixes him in love with mortal women.

They take the aorists ἤγαγε and συνέμειξε as referring to a past situation;[40] according to this, Aphrodite coupled Zeus with mortal women once upon a time, but no longer. This is possible, but there is nonetheless good reason to take ἤγαγε and συνέμειξε as 'gnomic' aorists, understanding the text as a general condition. This is signalled by the repetition of the particle combination καί τε at the beginning of vv. 36 and 38. It is well established that the combination of τε with other particles most often indicates a general proposition or a habitual action.[41] Van der Ben tries to dismiss the significance of καί τε here by claiming that it indicates nothing more than climax, but it is far more natural to understand the passage as describing a habitual action of the goddess,[42] for an attributive statement is

---

[39] The subjunctive (ἐ)θέλῃ is read only by M (Leiden), while the other 21 MSS containing Aphr. all read the optative (ἐ)θέλοι. However, the reading is not crucial to whether the text is describing a habitual action or not. The subjunctive is more expected in a general condition such as this (cf. Od. 7. 201–2, 20. 85–6,), but the optative could also be used; see Comm. ad loc.

[40] Van der Ben (1981), 92–3, VB 4–5, Clay (1989), 163 n. 35.

[41] See Denniston (1954), 528, 'the great majority of cases in which τε is coupled with another particle contain general propositions, or describe habitual action.' Compare Od. 20. 85–6, where epic τε is combined with a 'gnomic' aorist in the description of a general attribute of Sleep.

[42] Ruijgh (1971), 913, in his comprehensive study of epic τε, agrees. He notes that ἤγαγε is ambiguous, expressing the nuance of climax (i.e. 'she conquers even Zeus'), but nonetheless considers συνέμειξε 'gnomic'. VB 5 thinks 'the idea of climax is present both at 36 and at 38'.

perhaps also preferable here on structural grounds. After the digression of vv. 7–33 (in which the poet expands upon the three exceptions to Aphrodite's power, Athena, Artemis, and Hestia), the poet returns with ring-composition (v. 33 τάων οὐ δύναται πεπιθεῖν φρένας οὐδ' ἀπατῆσαι ~ v. 7 τρισσὰς οὐ δύναται πεπιθεῖν φρένας οὐδ' ἀπατῆσαι) to the theme which he left at v. 6: the universal power of Aphrodite (vv. 34–5 τῶν δ' ἄλλων οὔ πέρ τι πεφυγμένον ἔστ' Ἀφροδίτην | οὔτε θεῶν μακάρων οὔτε θνητῶν ἀνθρώπων). The switch from the habitual to the strictly historic would be abrupt at this point and is made more naturally a few lines later after vv. 40–4. These lines move from a general description of Hera as an esteemed wife to the historic description of her birth in preparation for the introduction of the narrative at v. 45, just as the description of birth elsewhere in the *Hymns* acts as a transition between attributive and narrative sections.[43] Once again, one cannot rule out altogether that these lines are referring to Aphrodite's mixing of Zeus with mortal women as a thing of the past, but the presence of the particle combination καί τε and the structure of the prologue speak against it.

The overt focus of the narrative at least seems to lie elsewhere. The narrative is introduced at vv. 45 ff. by the statement that Zeus made Aphrodite sleep with a mortal man in order that she should not boast amongst the gods (v. 48 καί ποτ' ἐπευξαμένη εἴπῃ μετὰ πᾶσι θεοῖσιν); nothing is said about stopping her mischief for good. Moreover, as I have argued above, the themes of boasting and semi-divine birth immediately precede the beginning of the narrative in vv. 50–2, signalling their interrelated importance for the upcoming narrative.[44] It is the shame of having been led astray by Zeus, to sleep with a mortal man and give birth to a semi-mortal son, that will end Aphrodite's pleasurable boasting about such affairs amongst the gods; for Aphrodite will in future be reproached by the gods for

---

[43] See e.g. the mini-hymn to Hestia at *Aphr.* 21–32; a description of her birth by Kronos leads from an attributive section to a short narrative about the goddess. For the description of birth initiating a narrative see also the opening lines of *Herm.*, *Hys.* 15, 28. Conversely, at *Hy.* 7. 56–7 the description of Dionysus' birth acts as a transition from the narrative to the closing farewell.

[44] See pp. 7–8.

her own affair. The realization of Zeus' plan to stop her boasting is then confirmed later by Aphrodite's own words to Anchises: [45]

> αὐτὰρ ἐμοὶ μέγ' ὄνειδος ἐν ἀθανάτοισι θεοῖσιν
> ἔσσεται ἤματα πάντα διαμπερὲς εἵνεκα σεῖο,
> οἳ πρὶν ἐμοὺς ὀάρους καὶ μήτιας, αἷς ποτε πάντας
> ἀθανάτους συνέμειξα καταθνητῆσι γυναιξί,
> τάρβεσκον· πάντας γὰρ ἐμὸν δάμνασκε νόημα.
> νῦν δὲ δὴ οὐκέτι μοι στόμα τλήσεται ἐξονομῆναι
> τοῦτο μετ' ἀθανάτοισιν, ἐπεὶ μάλα πολλὸν ἀάσθην
> σχέτλιον, οὐκ ὀνομαστόν, ἀπεπλάγχθην δὲ νόοιο,
> παῖδα δ' ὑπὸ ζώνῃ ἐθέμην βροτῷ εὐνηθεῖσα. (Aphr. 247–55)

For me there will be a great reproach amongst the gods, for all time because of you; [the gods] who before feared my whisperings and clever plans, with which at some point I mixed all gods with mortal women; for my purpose tamed them all. But now my mouth will no longer open to mention this amongst the immortals, since I have been greatly led astray, terribly, unspeakably, and gone out of my mind, and have a child under my girdle having slept with a mortal man.

Van der Ben argues that Aphrodite has essentially lost the power to bring about love-affairs between gods and mortals, because she will no longer, for fear of reproach for her own actions, mention such unions to the gods.[46] This is a possible implication of vv. 249–51; the gods previously feared her plans, with which she mixed them all in love, for her will in the past tamed them all. But van der Ben goes too far in suggesting that 'the tenses and temporal adverbs she uses leave no doubt that such contacts belong definitively to the past.'[47] In fact, the only thing which clearly belongs exclusively to the past according to the goddess is the gods' fear of her whisperings and clever plans. The use of the past tense with the indefinite adverb ποτε in the parenthesis of vv. 249–50 (αἷς ποτε πάντας | ἀθανάτους συνέμειξα καταθνητῆσι γυναιξί) is not indicative of an activity which is exclusive to the past; Aphrodite did 'at some point' couple all gods

---

[45] Many scholars have understood Zeus' victory to be nothing more than the end of Aphrodite's boasting; see the useful summary of scholarship following this view given by Clay (1989), 166 n. 43, 193 n. 137.

[46] Van der Ben (1981), 90–1, VB 30–3; cf. Clay (1989), 192–3; the gods 'previously' (πρίν v. 249) feared her plans but no longer do.

[47] Van der Ben (1981), 90–1, VB 30–3.

with mortals, and she might well do so again.[48] On the other hand, the temporal adverb πρίν in v. 249 refers only to the fear of the gods; a point which is emphasized by the striking enjambment of τάρβεσκον in v. 251 after a parenthesis of more than a line. The implication that her activity is at an end in fact depends upon the qualifying phrase of the latter half of v. 251, 'for my purpose tamed them all' (πάντας γὰρ ἐμὸν δάμνασκε νόημα).[49] One possible interpretation of this phrase is, as van der Ben has suggested, that if the gods previously feared Aphrodite's plans 'because' (γάρ) she tamed them all, they are not afraid any more because she will no longer make them sleep with mortals. Even here, however, an outright halt to Aphrodite's mixing of gods and men is not necessarily implied. The first word of the phrase places stress upon the fact that her purpose tamed 'all' (πάντας) gods, an emphasis which builds upon her use of πάντας in v. 249. Aphrodite is not saying that the gods previously feared her simply because she made them sleep with mortals, but because she was successful in taming them 'all' in this respect. The reason for the change in their fear could, therefore, be the result not of an outright halt to her activity but of diminished freedom in such activity, brought about by her own personal embarrassment with Anchises; the gods were previously afraid because she tamed 'all' gods, whereas now her will is more constrained for fear of reproach. Again, this does not necessarily imply an end to such activity altogether.

In any case, however one understands the implication of vv. 249–51, Aphrodite's speech seems to focus more upon her shame and the cessation of her boasting. Aphrodite's words at vv. 252–3 (οὐκέτι μοι στόμα τλήσεται[50] ἐξονομῆναι | τοῦτο μετ' ἀθανάτοισιν) again do not make it explicit that her plans are at an end. What she says is that she will no longer 'mention "this" (τοῦτο) amongst the gods'. Even if

---

[48] See e.g. the prayer of Chryses at Il. 1. 39–41 εἴ ποτέ τοι χαρίεντ' ἐπὶ νηὸν ἔρεψα, | ἤ' εἰ δή ποτέ τοι κατὰ πίονα μηρί' ἔκηα | ταύρων ἠδ' αἰγῶν, τόδε μοι κρήηνον ἐέλδωρ; Chryses has 'at some point' made sacrifices to Apollo, but there is certainly no implication that he will not do so again in the future. See the translation of West (2003), 179 'at one time or another'.

[49] This clause also adds emphasis to the idea that 'all' the gods were subject to her will, following from πάντας | ἀθανάτους συνέμειξα in vv. 249–50.

[50] στόμα τλήσεται printed above is the conjecture of Matthiae (1800); see Comm. ad loc.

τοῦτο here could be referring to her νόημα ('purpose') in the previous line, intending that she will no longer exercise that will amongst the gods, it most naturally refers to the entire description of her mixing gods and mortals given in the previous three lines, intending nothing more than that she will no longer laugh and boast about such affairs. This is supported by the language of the passage; these words of Aphrodite contain an echo of the language used to describe Zeus' intention to end her boasting at v. 48 (εἴπῃ μετὰ πᾶσι θεοῖσιν ~ ἐξονομῆναι | τοῦτο μετ' ἀθανάτοισιν). Moreover, a fear of reproach for her folly is from the outset the central concern for Aphrodite in this passage. She begins her discussion of the consequences of her union with Anchises by mentioning the 'great reproach' (μέγ' ὄνειδος) which she will suffer amongst the gods for all time because of Anchises. Concentrated attention is then given to her shame at the end of the passage in vv. 252–5; emphasis is produced here by expanding across two lines on the theme of her folly (vv. 253–4 ἐπεὶ μάλα πολλὸν ἀάσθην | σχέτλιον, οὐκ ὀνομαστόν, ἀπεπλάγχθην δὲ νόοιο), which is 'unutterable' (οὐκ ὀνομαστόν).[51] Zeus has in the end been successful, and the laughing, boasting Aphrodite presented in the lines immediately preceding the narrative has been humbled and shamed. The poignant irony of Zeus' victory should not be overlooked here, for the outcome represents a very real aspect of sexual love; Aphrodite, the physical embodiment of love, must at times suffer painful shame and remorse, just as countless lovers have done and will continue to do. Importantly, this motif is known elsewhere in early epic. Aphrodite's shame amongst the gods is also a consequence of her affair with Ares recounted by Demodocus in *Od.* 8. When Hephaestus' chains trap Aphrodite in bed with Ares, all the gods stand around and laugh at her (*Od.* 8. 321 ff.). This is an episode that the poet of *Aphr.* probably knew; *Aphr.* 58–63, while formulaic, are largely identical with *Od.* 8. 362–5, while the description of Tithonus' inability to move his limbs at *Aphr.* 234 is very similar to the line which describes the inability of Ares and Aphrodite to move

---

[51] The manuscripts here read the meaningless ὀνοτατόν. Martin (1605/1755) conjectures οὐκ ὀνομαστόν 'unutterable', while Clarke (1740) suggests οὐκ ὀνοταστόν 'not to be made light of'; see Comm. ad loc. Both readings support Aphrodite's fear of her affair being talked about.

their limbs under Hephaestus' chains at *Od.* 8. 298. There too Hephaestus, like Zeus, is getting his revenge against Aphrodite, and the goddess of love suffers shame before the gods.

In summary, the position of van der Ben and Clay that the *Homeric Hymn to Aphrodite* provides an *aition* for why gods no longer sleep with mortals is possible but not certain. Opinions as to what is implied in the poem will undoubtedly continue to differ, but the case for the poem narrating the end of unions between gods and mortals has at least been overstated. It is not explicitly announced at any point before the beginning of the narrative, nor, as has been claimed, is it necessarily implicit in vv. 36–9, where there are good linguistic and structural reasons to believe that Aphrodite's power over Zeus is being described as an eternal characteristic. Even in vv. 247–55, it is neither explicitly stated nor necessarily implied that Aphrodite will no longer be willing to bring about unions between gods and mortals; the emphasis in Aphrodite's speech upon her previous power over 'all gods' ($\pi\acute{a}\nu\tau as$, vv. 249 and 251) makes it equally possible that what is implied is that her power has been diminished because of her own shame, but not entirely stopped. In any case, the central concern of the passage and the narrative as a whole seems to be Aphrodite's shame and the cessation of her boasting, the successful outcome of Zeus' intention announced in vv. 45 ff. The theme of Aphrodite's shame before the gods is one that is known elsewhere in early epic, and itself provides an important comment upon the nature of sexual love; sexual unions often end in shame for one or more individuals. Above all, these literary themes, however one chooses to rate their prominence, should be understood as working alongside the concentrated attention given to Aeneas and his descendants in the poem, rather than as competing interpretations.

III. NEAR EASTERN MOTIFS

The Greek love goddess Aphrodite developed as a composite figure, many components of which derive from the Near East.[52] Cyprus

---

[52] See Burkert (1985), 172 ff., West (1997), 56, and Budin (2003), *passim*.

was a focal point for her development and recent scholarship has demonstrated that Cyprus must have been a major centre for the transmission of Near Eastern culture to the Aegean; with Greek immigration into Cyprus in the twelfth and eleventh centuries BC, the island, geographically on the cusp between East and West, was a natural facilitator of cultural interaction, an environment ripe for the absorption of Near Eastern literary motifs into the Greek tradition.[53] It is therefore not surprising to find a good number of motifs in the *Hymn to Aphrodite* which can be paralleled in Near Eastern literature. This does not presuppose that the poet of *Aphr.* had any direct connection with the Near East,[54] but rather demonstrates the extent to which traditional epic material surrounding Aphrodite has been influenced by the transmission of cultural material from East to West. What follows is a summary discussion of material in *Aphr.* which finds parallels in Near Eastern literature. More detailed discussion can be found in the commentary.

Aphrodite's toilette in vv. 58–63, which draws upon material found in the description of her bathing in *Od.* 8 and in Hera's preparation scene before she sets off to seduce Zeus in *Il.* 14,[55] finds several parallels in Near Eastern literature. In a Sumerian sacred-marriage text,[56] the love-goddess Inanna bathes and anoints herself with oil as she sets out to seduce the mortal shepherd Dumuzi. Another Near Eastern preparation scene provides a parallel for Aphrodite's retreat to her Cyprian sanctuary; in the Sumerian *Song of Inanna and Dumuzi*, in which the goddess sings of her own power, Inanna tells of how she washes her head and adorns herself with precious stones in the island retreat of Dilmun.[57]

When Aphrodite then sets out from her sanctuary at Paphos to confront Anchises, she is first described crossing Ida. En route she encounters a pack of wild beasts, wolves, lions, bears, and leopards,

---

[53] See in particular Burkert (1992), 9 ff., West (1997), 611 ff. *et passim*; cf. N. Richardson (1991), 124.

[54] Although it seems probable that the poem has an origin in the Troad (see below, pp. 49–50).

[55] See Comm. ad loc.

[56] *ETCSL* 4. 08. 29 = *ANET* 639: 'Inanna bathed in water and anointed herself with sweet oil.'

[57] See Labat et al. (1970), 247–50, Penglase (1994), 166–7.

which she subdues and incites to copulation (vv. 68–74). The power which she displays over animals in this passage has prompted some to understand a conflation with the Asiatic Magna Mater/Cybele. This is not a necessary assumption,[58] but contamination with the Magna Mater is not the only possible source for the motif, for it occurs prominently in Near Eastern literature as well. In the *Descent of Ištar to the Nether World*, Ištar (who elsewhere has the title 'mistress of animals', *bēlet nammašti*)[59] leaves the earth, and bulls and asses are said to halt all sexual activity.[60] Ištar 's Ugaritic counterpart Astarte, who perhaps played some role in the development of the Paphian Aphrodite, is also portrayed as πότνια θηρῶν.[61]

Upon her arrival in front of Anchises, Aphrodite's clothing and jewellery are described in detail (vv. 85–90). This description is an elaboration of the brief mention of her dressing after her bath at vv. 64–5, and its postponement until this point in the narrative makes Anchises' amazement and fear at seeing the disguised goddess more vivid. She wears shining clothes (εἵματα σιγαλόεντα), a dress brighter than the sun (πέπλον ... φαεινότερον πυρὸς αὐγῆς), spiral bracelets and shining ear buds (ἐπιγναμπτὰς ἕλικας κάλυκάς τε φαεινάς), and elaborate golden necklaces (ὅρμοι); she shines like the moon (ὡς δὲ σελήνη). The strongest parallel for the description in Greek literature is again the preparation of Hera in *Il.* 14. 173–87, as she sets out to seduce Zeus: she is described wearing an ambrosial dress (ἀμβρόσιον ἑανόν), golden pins (χρυσείης ἐνετῆσι), a belt with a hundred tassels (ζώνην ἑκατὸν θυσάνοις), earrings with three projections resembling mulberries (ἕρματα ... | τρίγληνα μορόεντα), a fine linen kerchief which shines like the sun (κρηδέμνῳ ... | ... λευκὸν δ' ἦν ἠέλιος ὥς), and beautiful sandals (καλὰ πέδιλα).[62] However, the emphasis on clothing in both these passages seems to owe some debt to the Near East. A striking parallel for Aphrodite's seduction of Anchises is found in a Sumerian narrative, in which the goddess of love Inanna covers her entire body with jewellery before approaching the mortal herdsman Dumuzi.[63] The same motif is found in another

---

[58] See Comm. on 69–74.   [59] See West (1997), 56.
[60] *BTM* 501–2; cf. Penglase (1994), 173–4.   [61] See Budin (2003), 237 ff..
[62] See also the description of clothing at *Cypria* frr. 4–5, *Hy.* 6. 5–13. Cf. Janko (1992), 173; such scenes of adornment are almost always connected with seduction.
[63] *ETCSL* 4. 08. 20 = *ANET* 638.

sacred-marriage text already mentioned above, in which Inanna bathes, dresses, and appears to Dumuzi 'like the light of the moon', just as Aphrodite shines ὡς ... σελήνη;[64] Hera shines like the sun in the *Iliad*. Also, although not in the realm of seduction, a similar emphasis on clothing is found in the *Descent of Ištar to the Netherworld*. There the love-goddess puts on clothing and jewellery, which is then removed piece by piece as she descends into the world of the dead; when she returns to life she collects her clothing in reverse order.[65] In this Near Eastern text, the removal and donning of clothing is representative of the goddess's loss and reclaiming of her power as she moves in and out of the Netherworld. Aphrodite is not confronting the world of the dead, but her clothes are put on and taken off in a power struggle of seduction. Anchises is later described removing her clothing and jewellery piece by piece on their way to bed (vv. 162–6), and when they have finished making love she once again dresses (vv. 171–2) before appearing to Anchises in fully divine form; shamed by sleeping with a mortal (removal of clothing), she afterward regains her position of authority and control (re-dressing).[66]

Also remarkable here is the correspondence between the items which Aphrodite and Ištar wear: on her descent, Ištar loses a crown (~ ἐϋστέφανος, v. 6), earrings (~ κάλυκας, v. 87), beads around her neck (~ ὅρμοι, v. 88), pins (~ στήθεσσιν ἀμφ' and πόρπας, vv. 90, 163), a girdle of birth-stones (~ ζώνην, v. 164), and clasps around her hands and feet (~ ἕλικας, v. 87). Women and goddesses are frequently represented wearing elaborate jewellery in art of the Near East,[67] and Cyprus is again a probable route of transfer for this material. Jacqueline Karageorghis has compared the description of Aphrodite's clothing to figurines found at Paphos (possible representations of Aphrodite and her companions), which are portrayed with ear-caps in the shape of a flower, and other jewellery.[68]

---

[64] *ETCSL* 4.08.29 = *ANET* 639. See West (1997), 204–5, Penglase (1994), 174. For a goddess shining like the moon in Greek literature cf. *Dem.* 278–9, where φέγγος seems to imply moonlight (N. Richardson 1974, 253).

[65] *BTM* 500–1.

[66] See Comm. on 81–90.   [67] See J. Karageorghis (1977), 58–60.

[68] J. Karageorghis (1984), 363–5; cf. N. Richardson (1991), 127. Statues of Aphrodite from Cyprus frequently have conspicuously large necklaces (see *LIMC* ii, Aphrodite, nos. 98–110), and elaborate crowns inlaid with rosettes (see V. Karageorghis 1998, 203–9 and *LIMC* II Aphrodite, nos. 107–10).

Another motif in the poem may also derive ultimately from the Near East. After Aphrodite has slept with Anchises and revealed that she is a goddess, the hero, reduced to hiding behind his blankets, begs Aphrodite not to leave him a 'living invalid' amongst men (μή με ζῶντ' ἀμενηνόν ἐν ἀνθρώποισιν ἐάσῃς | ναίειν, ἀλλ' ἐλέαιρ· ἐπεὶ οὐ βιοθάλμιος ἀνήρ | γίνεται, ὅς τε θεαῖς εὐνάζεται ἀθανάτῃσιν, vv. 188–90). The terms ἀμενηνός and οὐ βιοθάλμιος have been taken to refer to 'impotency' by some, who once again suppose contamination with the Magna Mater/Cybele in the Troad. Others have denied that 'impotency' is implied here (taking the two terms to refer to physical strength more generally, rather than sexual potency), and pointed out that the danger of a man sleeping with a goddess is already known in Homer.[69] At *Od.* 10. 301 Hermes warns Odysseus about sleeping with Circe before making her swear an oath, lest she rob him of his manhood (μή σ' ἀπογυμνωθέντα κακὸν καὶ ἀνήνορα θήῃ). Also, at *Od.* 5. 118 ff. Calypso tells how the gods jealously harm men who have affairs with goddesses. This motif has long been recognized to have entered the Greek poetic tradition from the Near East; in the Gilgamesh epic, Gilgamesh angers Ištar by refusing to sleep with her and listing all of her lovers who have come to harm.[70] Regardless of whether 'impotency' is implied in the *Hymn to Aphrodite*,[71] we are dealing with the same motif here; Anchises fears physical punishment for having slept with the goddess of love, either from Aphrodite herself or the other gods.[72] The Homeric parallels make it unnecessary to suppose any direct indebtedness to the Near East, but the appearance of this motif is yet another example of how much influence the transmission of cultural material from East to West has had on the conception of Aphrodite in early Greek literature.

---

[69] See Comm. on 188–90.
[70] Foster 46 (Tablet VI 32 ff.). See West (1997), 403–12, cf. Germain (1954), 263–4.
[71] Which in fact seems likely, at least as a symptom of a more general physical decline; see Comm. on 188–90.
[72] This is made clear a few lines later in Aphrodite's response to Anchises' fear, οὐ γάρ τοί τι δέος παθέειν κακὸν ἐξ ἐμέθεν γε | οὐδ' ἄλλων μακάρων (vv. 194–5).

IV. OVERVIEW OF LANGUAGE AND RELATIONSHIP TO EARLY POETRY

Points of language are discussed in the commentary as they arise. This section will present a summary of the information collected and come to some general conclusions about the compositional technique of the poet and the relationship of the hymn to other early poetry. References to the commentary are given only where it is considered particularly relevant, and further help is to be found there far more often than is indicated.

Close attention has been paid in the commentary to the versification of *Aphr.* as it compares with other early hexameter poetry, in particular Homer, Hesiod, and the other *Hymns*;[73] parallels are given where present, while it is noted where language is unique to early hexameter or only found elsewhere in a particular author. Unless otherwise indicated, the parallels are adduced in order to elucidate the extent to which the poet of *Aphr.* is working within, and innovating upon, the tradition of hexameter composition. In some cases, however, it seems possible that the poet may have had a particular passage in mind; these are discussed below.[74]

Without entering into a lengthy discussion of the subject, it is necessary to say a few words in preface to this section about the question of oral vs. literary composition. Brevity is made possible by the fact that others have already examined the matter in depth.[75] I confine myself to a quick run-through of the evidence: a high number of Homeric formulae (even whole verses) has been claimed by several scholars to indicate oral composition.[76] This assumes, however, that an argument for oral composition can be based upon

---

[73] Early hexameter poetry is broadly understood here to include Homer, Hesiod, pseudo-Hesiod (including the *Catalogue of Women* and other fragments attributed to Hesiod in M–W), the *Hymns*, and the *Cycle* (*Cypria* etc.). The one exception to this is *Hy.* 8, which is unanimously considered to be very late (see AHS 384–5 and West 1970, who argues that it is the work of Proclus; it must be late given that it identifies Ares with the planet Mars).

[74] See below, §§3, 5.

[75] See Janko (1982), 18–41.

[76] See Notopoulos (1962), Preziosi (1966), Pavese (1972), and Postlethwaite (1979).

the density of formulae in a poem, a supposition which Kirk has successfully argued is flawed.[77] The argument must instead be advanced on grounds of formular *quality*, and even then any test for oral composition is a negative one; that is to say that criteria can be applied to test for signs of literary composition but not for orality itself.[78] One possible criterion is the breach of formular economy, of which Janko notes three cases in *Aphr.*: $Διὸς θυγάτηρ Ἀφροδίτη$ (3×) beside $φιλομμειδὴς Ἀφροδίτη$ (5×, once with $δ$' inserted),[79] $αἰδοίην ἄλοχον$ v. 44 beside $κουριδίην ἄλοχον$ v. 127, and $χαμαιγενέων ἀνθρώπων$ in v. 108 beside $καταθνητῶν ἀνθρώπων$ (5×, once in the otherwise identical v. 192);[80] another can be added if one accepts M's $ἰοστεφάνου Κυθερείης$ at v. 175 beside $ἐϋστεφάνου Κυθερείης$ (vv. 6, 287).[81] Even this, however, is not a sure sign of literary composition, as one cannot be certain that an oral poet was incapable of choosing different formulae as it suited him. There are similar breaches of formular economy in Homer (as the first example shows).[82] Similarly, levels of necessary enjambment in *Aphr.* accord with Homeric figures.[83] But then comparison with Homer too is uncertain, as we do not know whether the *Iliad* and *Odyssey* were themselves composed with the aid of writing.[84]

More noteworthy is the metrical evidence; *Aphr.* has very low frequencies of both hiatus (3.4%) and spondees before the bucolic

[77] Kirk (1966), Janko (1982), 19–20.

[78] Cf. Janko (1982), 40: 'The most important point to remember is that it is easier to disprove oral composition than to prove it.' Also, Kirk (1966), 157: 'Notopoulos has attacked a subtle and complex problem with an excessively blunt instrument—the idea that, because all oral poetry is formular, all formular poetry must be oral.' This principle must extend even to the *Iliad* and the *Odyssey*, whose formular nature in no way proves their purely oral origin. What the work of M. Parry has successfully shown is that the two great epics have developed from an established tradition of oral poetry, but not that the two poems as we know them are entirely the product of oral composition.

[79] The breach is also known in Homer (e.g. *Il.* 5. 312 besides 5. 375). On the possible difference of meaning in the two formulae as they are used in *Aphr.* see Comm. on 81 $Διὸς θυγάτηρ Ἀφροδίτη$.

[80] See Comm. on 108 $χαμαιγενέων ἀνθρώπων$.

[81] See Comm. on 175 $ἰοστεφάνου$.

[82] Cf. G. P. Edwards (1971), 55 ff., who makes the point that breaches of economy in Hesiod often have Homeric parallels.

[83] See Janko (1982), 32 for a table of figures.

[84] See above, n. 78.

diaeresis (23.9%).[85] The low frequency of hiatus is paralleled only by *Herm.* (5.2%; compare *Il.* 7.8% and *Dem.* 22.3%), a poem which is generally thought to be later and to show signs of literary composition,[86] while the percentage of spondees before the bucolic diaeresis is almost half of that of any other *Hymn* (*Herm.* has 44.8%; compare *Il.* 1 at 67.1%); the behaviour of *Aphr.* in these respects approaches Hellenistic figures (this is true also of the low levels of omission of the third-foot caesura in *Aphr.* (0.4%) and *Herm.* (0.2%), although the overall rarity of the irregularity makes it a less compelling piece of evidence).[87] Richardson remarks of *Dem.* that there is little to 'indicate whether the poem is the work of a "genuine" oral poet, or rather a good literary imitation of the traditional style'.[88] In the case of *Aphr.*, this metrical polish, combined with a certain elaborateness of structure,[89] may suggest that it is of the latter category; although Janko is right to point out that there are 'no means of deciding whether an oral poet could have created such a masterpiece or not'.[90] I am inclined to think that some use of writing is likely,[91] but it is admittedly impossible to know.[92] Nor is the issue of orality clarified by cases where the poet of *Aphr.* may have had certain passages of other early poetry in mind. An oral poet might well have composed with a particular episode in mind, and there is nothing in *Aphr.* to prove complex literary borrowing from or to written texts.

---

[85] The figures are taken from Janko (1982), 35–41. M. Parry ap. A. Parry (1971), 191–239 suggested that certain metrical irregularities in Homer may be due to the adaptation and juxtaposition of formulae in oral composition.

[86] See AHS 275–6, Janko (1982), 149–50.

[87] Janko (1982), 37; cf. Porter (1951), 51.

[88] N. Richardson (1974), 31.

[89] See vv. 58–63 and the discussion ad loc. Freed–Bentman (1954) argued partially on structural grounds that *Aphr.* was Hellenistic; on the date of the poem see below, pp. 47–9.

[90] Janko (1982), 180.

[91] Kamerbeek (1967), 389 and Hoekstra (1969), 46 agree.

[92] The dichotomy of 'literary' and 'oral' poet is, as N. Richardson (1974), 337–8 and Janko (1982), 41 are careful to point out, not a helpful one; various middle positions can be imagined.

1. Homeric language (Iliad and Odyssey)

Aphr. has often been called the most Homeric of the *Hymns*.[93] At first glance, twenty whole verses in the poem are identical, or almost identical with only small variations, to lines found in Homer:[94]

35 = *Od*. 9. 521	118 ~ *Il*. 16. 183
59 ~ *Od*. 8. 363	139 ~ *Od*. 13. 136/16. 231
60 = *Il*. 14. 169	143 = *Il*. 3. 149
61 = *Od*. 8. 364	163 = *Il*. 18. 401
62 = *Od*. 8. 365	184 = *Od*. 22. 311/343/366 (cf. v.l. *Il*. 21. 73)
63 = *Il*. 14. 172	193 ~ *Od*. 4. 825
68 = *Il*. 8. 47	215 ~ *Od*. 5. 150
97 ~ *Il*. 20. 8	234 ~ *Od*. 8. 298
99 = *Il*. 20. 9	235 = *Il*. 2. 5/10. 17/14. 161
109 ~ *Od*. 16. 187	238 = *Il*. 11. 669

Apart from whole verses, *Aphr*. also makes use of a large number of formulae found in the *Iliad* and the *Odyssey*. Extensive lists of these parallels are given by Preziosi,[95] and I shall not repeat them here.[96] Other criteria as well show the language of *Aphr*. to be archaic and very close to Homer.[97] The proportion of the neglect of

---

[93] See Clay (1989), 157 n. 15, who cites among others H. Groddeck: '*ὁμηρικώτατον iure appellari debeat.*'

[94] Cf. the list in Heitsch (1965), 23.

[95] Preziosi (1966); she lists both parallel and analogous formulae found in Homer.

[96] Parallels for particular lines can be found in the Comm.

[97] The following figures are taken from the study of Janko (1982), 42–94, who considers the chronological and regional implications of the results. This statistical method (as Janko is himself aware) must be treated with caution: not only are figures in some cases subjective, but one must allow for possible regional variation, coincidence, the personal style of an individual poet, the effect of the subject-matter upon the composition, and the general dearth of surviving material for comparison. West (1995), 204–5 rejects the method altogether as a measure of chronology in arguing that Hesiod is prior to Homer: 'The major determinant of the quantity of younger forms in a given poet is the extent to which his language diverges from the formulaic, and this depends on many other factors apart from his date.' Certainly, given that he is a mainland Boeotian poet, one might expect Hesiod's language to differ significantly from the *Iliad* and the *Odyssey*, both presumably products of Ionia (perhaps even the same poet), regardless of date. The criteria might be chronologically significant for poetry of the same region; for example, the figures for the *Odyssey* given by Janko are consistently more developed than those of the *Iliad* (see his comparative

digamma in *Aphr.* remains low (15.9%), closest to Homeric levels (*Il.* 17.2%, *Od.* 17.9%). Also, the percentages of more traditional morphs such as the a-stem genitive plural -άων (85.7%)[98] and the long o- and a-stem datives plural -οισι(ν), -ησι(ν) (80.3%),[99] as well as prevocalic o- and a-stem accusatives plural -ους, -ας (50% and 42.9%),[100] accord with Homeric figures.

2. Modification

On closer inspection, there is much that is not Homeric in the language of *Aphr.* In apparent contrast to the morphological criteria just discussed, Janko notes that *Aphr.* has a low level of the older

---

tables, pp. 72–4), but reliability breaks down as soon as one introduces geographical variation. Nonetheless, these criteria are a useful measure of traditional formulaic style (using the *Iliad* as a benchmark).

[98] If one accepts that v. 98 is a later interpolation (see Comm. on 97–9) the only case of an advanced a-stem genitive plural form νυμφῶν (for νυμφάων) in *Aphr.* is removed, making the percentage 100.

[99] N. Richardson (1974), 334–5 has reservations about using the criterion of long and short datives plural as a dating tool, given the low number of short forms in the otherwise apparently late *Herm.*, although this could be the result of false archaism as Janko suggests; the low percentage of certain contracted genitive singular forms -ου (for -οιο) in *Herm.* might also point in this direction.

[100] The value of this statistic is debatable. Indo-European *-ons, *-ans originally gave -ους, -αυς before vowels and -ος, -ᾰς before consonants, as in Cretan (reflected in the Gortyn Law-Code), but elsewhere (Thessalian, Arcadian, and several West Greek dialects) one set of the forms was used regardless of the subsequent word (see Buck, 1955, 68, G. P. Edwards, 1971, 41–2). Apart from a few disputed variants, the short forms are not found pre-vocalically in Homer (nor in *Aphr.* or the other *Hymns*, with the exception of one occurrence in *Herm.*), but there are a number of cases of -ᾰς in Hesiod (see West, 1966a, 85). Edwards suggests that these acc. endings were felt to be light by Hesiod, who accordingly placed them more often before consonants than vowels to keep them heavy as the tradition required (see G. P. Edwards 1971, 141–65; for the argument that this is a regional, mainland, variation see also Pavese, 1972, 190–2; 1974, 93–4), but it remains problematic that Boeotian, Hesiod's native dialect, does not have short acc. plurals (see Davies 1964). On the other hand, if examples of -ᾰς in Hesiod are the result of modification of traditional formulae (see Davies, 1964, G. P. Edwards, 1971, 151–4), one then wonders why there are not any examples in Homer. Janko (1982), 58–62, maintains that a switch towards preconsonantal position from the *Il.* to the *Od.* suggests that the accusatives plural also came to be regarded as short in the Ionic branch of the tradition and that prevocalic position would be expected to decline in later Ionic verse, but this remains uncertain.

and more traditional genitive singular form -οιο (39% ~ *Il.* 51.9%, *Od.* 46.6%), and a corresponding high level of irresolvable -ου (56% ~ *Il.* 37%, *Od.* 42.5%).[101] As was mentioned above, the frequency of hiatus and spondees before the bucolic diaeresis is far lower than in Homer, Hesiod, and the other *Hymns*. A good number of non-Homeric words, forms, meanings, and combinations will be listed below under the sections which examine the poem's relationship to Hesiod and other early hexameter poetry.[102] Also, despite the high number of Homeric formulae noted by Preziosi,[103] *Aphr.* can in fact be said to diverge from Homer in the practice of formulaic composition.

Hoekstra has shown that modification of traditional formulae in Homer, whether by declension, conjugation, substitution, separation, or mobility, is often accompanied by linguistic innovations such as quantitative metathesis, loss of digamma, and use of nu mobile to make position.[104] More importantly for our purposes, in extending his study to include *Apoll.*, *Dem.*, and *Aphr.*,[105] Hoekstra has demonstrated that the *Hymns* show several cases of modification with linguistic innovation which have no parallel in Homer; together these suggest that the language of the *Hymns* is at a more advanced stage of the tradition of hexameter composition than that of Homer.[106] Hoekstra's method has subsequently been adopted and

---

[101] See Janko (1982), 50–4. He also notes (64–9) that nu mobile is more frequently used in *Aphr.* than Homer (frequency of 47.8 per 1000 verses ~ *Il.* 35.6, *Od.* 37.2). The frequency of nu mobile is most probably dictated largely by region, as the mainlander Hesiod uses the device seldom (21.5‰) in contrast with the practice of the Ionian Homer.

[102] See also the lists below under §§9, 11.

[103] See n. 95.

[104] Hoekstra (1965). Hainsworth (1968), 58 ff. also demonstrated modification of formulae in Homer, but by defining the more traditional formula as the more frequent one. This approach has the advantage of being broader in its coverage, but the disadvantage of ignoring underrepresented formulae; see the evaluation of the two methods by Janko (1982), 10–12.

[105] Hoekstra (1969).

[106] Following the approach of Hainsworth (1968), Postlethwaite (1979) conducted a statistical study of the *Hymns* which comes to similar conclusions: he calculates that *Aphr.* has the highest frequency of mobility amongst the *Hymns* (once every 10.8 lines ~ *Il.* 33.4, *Od.* 25.5, *Dem.* 35.4, *Apoll.* 18.8, *Herm.* 20.7) and separation (once in every 4.8 lines ~ *Il.* 12.8, *Od.* 12.4, *Dem.* 6.1, *Apoll.* 7.3, *Herm.* 5.6); cf. the table of these results in Janko (1982), 153.

expanded by Janko, who includes the contracted genitive singular -ου (for the more traditional -οιο) and short dative plural endings as criteria for linguistic innovation.[107] Below is a list of the chief cases for innovative modification in *Aphr*. The evidence for modification is discussed in more detail in the commentary.

Line(s) in Aphr.	Innovation	Mode of modification	Homeric starting-point
6. πᾶσιν δ' ἔργα μέμηλεν ἐϋστεφάνου	nu mobile prevents hiatus in μέμηλεν	transposition	ἔργα μέμηλεν (5∪∪6×, *Il.* 5. 876 etc.)
9. οὐ γάρ οἱ εὔαδεν	neglect of digamma	transposition	ἐπεί νύ τοι εὔαδεν εὐνή (∪4∪∪5∪∪6×, *Il.* 14. 340 etc.)
29. κᾱλὸν γέρας ἀντὶ γάμοιο	Aeolic form κᾱλόν	P₂ and T₂ permutation[108]	κᾱλὸν γέρας (*Od.* 11. 184 etc.)
36. Ζηνὸς νόον ἤγαγε τερπικεραύνου	contracted genitive	declension and separation	Ζεὺς τερπικέραυνος (*Il.* 12. 252 etc.; cf. Διὸς ∪∪4∪∪ αἰγιόχοιο *Il.* 17. 176)
40. κασιγνήτης ἀλόχου τε	contracted genitive	declension	κασιγνήτην ἄλοχόν τε (*Il.* 16. 432/18. 356)
52. καταθνητοῖς ἀνθρώποις	short dative plural	declension	καταθνητῶν ἀνθρώπων (*Il.* 6. 123 etc.)
54. ἐν ἀκροπόλοις ὄρεσιν πολυπιδάκου	nu mobile makes position; also un-Homeric form ὄρεσιν	transposition	ἐπ'/ἐν ἀκροπόλοισιν ὄρεσσιν (∪4∪∪5∪∪6×, *Il.* 5. 523/*Od.* 19. 205)

---

[107] Janko (1982), 50–7, 152–5. Hoekstra (1969), 44 mentions one case of the contracted genitive -ου at 152, to which Janko adds three more (36, 40, 176). Against using the number of short datives plural before a consonant as a dating tool, see N. Richardson (1974), 334–5. These short forms are not a secondary development from -οισι, -αισι, and may derive from the original instrumental of o-stems (from which the fem. -αις was formed by analogy), or go back to Mycenaean through 'Achaean'; see Monro (1891), 86, Ruijgh (1958), 107–11. But they nonetheless appear to be introduced at times due to the modification of traditional formulae; see also *Grammaire*, i. 194–7.

[108] The notation P₂ and T₂ 'indicates formulae which were originally designed to serve after the penthemimeris and the trochaic caesura respectively'; Hoekstra (1965), 61 n. 2.

55. βουκολέεσκεν βοῦς	nu mobile makes position	transposition	βοῦς βουκολέεσκες (— 5⌣⌣6x, Il. 21. 448)
85. καὶ εἵματα σιγαλόεντα	neglect of digamma εἵματα	P₂ and T₂ permutation	ὅθι εἵματα σιγαλόεντα (Il. 22. 154) beside καὶ ῥήγεα σιγαλόεντα (Od. 6. 38, *καὶ Ϝείματα σιγαλόεντα)
118. ἐκ χοροῦ Ἀρτέμιδος	contracted genitive	declension	ἐν χορῷ Ἀρτέμιδος (Il. 16. 183)
126–7. παραὶ λέχεσιν καλέεσθαι	nu mobile makes position; also un-Homeric form λέχεσιν	transposition	παραὶ λεχέεσσι κλιθῆναι (⌣4⌣⌣5⌣⌣6x, Od. 1. 366/18. 213)
135. σοῖς τε κασιγνήτοις	short dative plural	transposition	κασιγνήτοισί τε σοῖσι (⌣4—5⌣⌣6x, Il. 5. 474)
147–8. ἀθανάτου δὲ ἕκητι διακτόρου . . . ǀ Ἑρμέω	quantitative metathesis Ἑρμέω and contracted genitive ἀθανάτου	separation	Ἑρμείαο ἕκητι διακτόρου (1— 2⌣⌣3⌣⌣4⌣⌣, Od. 15. 319)
152. τόξου ἀπ' ἀργυρέου	contracted genitive	transposition	ἀπ' ἀργυρέοιο βιοῖο (⌣4⌣⌣5⌣⌣6x, Il. 24. 605; although cf. line-beginning τόξου ἀπὸ κρατεροῦ Il. 8. 279)
169. βοῦς τε καὶ ἴφια μῆλα	neglect of digamma	transposition	βόας καὶ ἴφια μῆλα (⌣4—5⌣⌣6x, Il. 5. 556 etc.)
194. οὐ γάρ τοί τι δέος παθέειν	neglect of digamma in δέος < *δϜέος	inversion	οὐδέ τί τοι παθέειν δέος (2⌣⌣3⌣⌣4⌣⌣, Od. 5. 347)
212. εἶπεν δὲ ἕκαστα	nu mobile; in εἶπε(ν) it never makes position in Homer	conjugation	εἴπω τε ἕκαστα (Od. 3. 361)
232. καὶ εἵματα καλὰ διδοῦσα	neglect of digamma in εἵματα; cf. above on 85	transposition	εἵματα καλὰ (5⌣⌣6x, Od. 6. 111 etc.)

256. πρῶτον ἴδῃ φάος ἠελίοιο	neglect of digamma in ἴδῃ and use of aorist	meaning and conjugation: formula used of birth and with aorist only here and Apoll. 71, where digamma is also neglected.	'to live and see the light', ὁρᾶν/ὁρᾷ φάος ἠελίοιο (Il. 18. 61 etc.); see Comm. on 105.
261. [νύμφαι] κᾰλὸν χορὸν ἐρρώσαντο	Aeolic form κᾰλόν	P₂ and T₂ permutation	[νυμφέων] κᾱλοὶ χοροὶ ἠδὲ θόωκοι (Od. 12. 318; cf. Il. 24. 616).
267. τεμένη δέ ἑ κικλήσκουσιν	ἑ used for plural	substitution	Φᾶρον δέ ἑ κικλήσκ- ουσι (Od. 4. 355) [109]

The results are naturally to some degree subjective and the method suffers from a similar range of limitations for measuring relative chronology to the application of the linguistic criteria discussed above.[110] It is impossible to be certain that any of the individual cases is post-Homeric; the fact that a parallel is not found in surviving epic could be put down to mere chance. It is most improbable, however, that all the cases should be due to hazard, and the sheer quantity speaks in favour of post-Homeric, or at least non-Homeric, composition.

3. Homeric *imitatio*

There are several parallels with Homer where thematic and verbal similarities combine to raise the question of *imitatio*. Such instances are treated with an awareness that it is impossible to be certain of direct influence. One must always admit the possibility of a lost common model. That said, although one needs to advance with caution, the approach should not be abandoned altogether, and it does seem probable that the poet of *Aphr.* is drawing directly from

---

[109] More candidates for innovation could be added: see Comm. on 4 οἰωνούς τε διειπετέας, 49 γελοιήσασα, and 102 ὥρῃσιν πάσῃσι.
[110] See n. 97.

episodes in Homer.[111] There are two particularly strong cases for direct imitation, one from the *Iliad* and one from the *Odyssey*.

190. ὅς τε θεαῖς εὐνάζεται ~ *Od.* 5. 119 οἵ τε θεαῖς ἀγάασθε παρ' ἀνδράσιν εὐνάζεσθαι. Calypso speaks of the punishments which the jealous gods inflict when goddesses sleep with mortal men, and Anchises is afraid of such punishment after having slept with Aphrodite. The thematic link is strong, and specific enough not to give the impression of being formulaic. The case for borrowing is strengthened by the presence of the rare short form θεαῖς, which is found only in these two passages.

196–7 σοὶ δ' ἔσται φίλος υἱὸς ὃς ἐν Τρώεσσιν ἀνάξει | καὶ παῖδες παίδεσσι διαμπερὲς ἐκγεγάονται ~ *Il.* 20. 307–8 νῦν δὲ δὴ Αἰνείαο βίη Τρώεσσιν ἀνάξει | καὶ παίδων παῖδες, τοί κεν μετόπισθε γένωνται. Poseidon's prophecy about the future of Aeneas' race is echoed by Aphrodite. In this instance 'the specific nature of the circumstances referred to make a common formulaic source most unlikely'.[112]

Other cases are less certain, but still suggestive of direct imitation:

58–63. This scene, in which Aphrodite prepares herself before setting out to seduce Anchises, is with some small changes an amalgamation of lines from *Od.* 8. 362–5 (Aphrodite's toilette after sleeping with Ares) and *Il.* 14. 166 ff. (Hera's toilette before seducing Zeus). The thematic similarity between the passages is obvious. Was the poet combining elements from these two scenes in order to create his own version? Support for a direct link with *Il.* 14 is given by more parallels in the following passage 64–91. Not only do three lines (66–8) describing Aphrodite's departure from her sanctuary and approach to Ida correspond with consecutive lines in *Il.* 14. 281–3 that describe Hera's approach to Ida, but a similar structure (the unique doubling of the traditional arrival scene)[113] could be the result of imitation. On the other hand, it is extremely difficult to know whether the language and structure of preparation and approach represented in the two poems were elements of a traditional seduction scene of this type. Indeed, one might well expect such a seduction to belong more properly to the goddess of

---

[111] Cf. Janko (1982), 9 on the subtleties of establishing *exemplum* and *imitatio*.
[112] Hoekstra (1969), 39–40.
[113] See Comm. ad loc.

love than to Hera, and the fact that in *Il.* 14 Hera goes to receive the magical κεστὸς ἱμάς from Aphrodite before seducing Zeus may suggest that it is with her that the origins of the scene lie.[114] In the case of the similarity with *Od.* 8. 362–5, Aphrodite's preparation at her cult centre Paphos is very probably traditional material.[115]

40–4. The description of Hera as the daughter of Kronos and Rhea, and the wife of Zeus, is very similar to that at *Il.* 4. 59–61. In particular, v. 42 is almost identical to *Il.* 4. 59, with the difference of κυδίστην for πρεσβυτάτην.

109–10. οὔ τίς τοι θεός . . . | ἀλλὰ καταθνητή τε, γυνὴ δέ με γείνατο μήτηρ: Aphrodite's denial of her immortality is similar to Odysseus' response to Telemachus at *Od.* 16. 187–8 when he is asked whether he is a god. Other similarities between the content of Aphrodite's and Odysseus' lies and Anchises' and Penelope's responses to the falsehood might support the case for imitation here,[116] but this can equally be explained by stock material; again, the broad structure of these lines could have been a formulaic response to being likened to a god, upon which both these passages are based. The latter half of v. 110 γυνὴ δέ με γείνατο μήτηρ is paralleled by the opposite claim of divine parentage at *Il.* 21. 109 (= 1. 280), which appears to be formulaic.

118. ἐκ χοροῦ Ἀρτέμιδος χρυσηλακάτου κελαδεινῆς ~ *Il.* 16. 183 ἐν χορῷ etc. In the *Iliad*, the line describes Hermes spotting Polymele in the dance of Artemis before raping her. Here Hermes is said to snatch Aphrodite away from the chorus of Artemis. If there is borrowing here, the contracted genitive χοροῦ suggests that it is secondary.

203. ἥρπασεν ὃν διὰ κάλλος, ἵν' ἀθανάτοισιν μετείη ~ *Il.* 20. 235 κάλλεος εἵνεκα οἷο, ἵν' ἀθανάτοισι μετείη. Given the probability, discussed above, that the prophecy at *Aphr.* 197–8 has borrowed from the passage devoted to Aeneas in *Il.* 20, this line might also be the result of direct imitation.

---

[114] It is perhaps also significant that scenes in which the love-goddess adorns herself before seducing a lover are known in Near Eastern literature; see above, pp. 20–1. On the similarities between Hera's seduction and Aphrodite's persuasion of Paris see Janko (1992), 185 on *Il.* 14. 214–17.

[115] One may compare the preparation of Aphrodite in the *Cypria* (frr. 4–5); cf. Burkert (1992), 103–4, N. Richardson (1991), 124.

[116] See Comm. on 113–16, 143–54.

234. οὐδέ τι κινῆσαι μελέων δύνατ' οὐδ' ἀναεῖραι ~ *Od.* 8. 298, part of the episode of Aphrodite's affair with Ares. As discussed above, Aphrodite's toilette at v. 58–63 perhaps borrows from the end of the same episode.

4. Hesiodic language and theology

Aphr. has some words, forms, and other features of language in common with Hesiod, which are not in Homer:

Words

108. χαμαιγενέων ~ *Th.* 107.
263. ἐρόεις ~ *Th.* 245 etc.

Forms

24. πότνιαν (acc.) ~ *Th.* 926 etc.

Meanings and Uses

1. πολυχρύσου Ἀφροδίτης ~ *Th.* 980 etc.
65. κοσμηθεῖσα (with the meaning 'to array') ~ *Th.* 573.
74. ἐναύλους (with the meaning 'haunt') ~ *Th.* 129.
135. ὁμόθεν (with the meaning 'from the same blood') ~ *Op.* 108.
158. χλαίνῃσιν μαλακῇς (noun-epithet combination) ~ *Op.* 537.

Digamma and Prosody

9. οὐ γάρ οἱ ~ *Op.* 526.
22. Ἱστίη (–⏑⏑) ~ *Op.* 734 (Homer and *Th.* 454 – – –).
29. δῶκε καλὸν γέρας (cf. v. 261) ~ *Th.* 585, *Op.* 63.
245. νηλειές (lengthened form for νηλεές) ~ *Th.* 770.

There are also several elements of theology in *Aphr.* that are Hesiodic rather than Homeric. The most striking of these is certainly the presentation of Hestia as an anthropomorphic deity in vv. 21–32: she is not treated as such in Homer at all, while the myth of her combined position as eldest (in Homer it is Hera who is eldest) and youngest child of Kronos narrated in vv. 22-3 (due to his swallowing and regurgitating his children) is known at *Th.* 453-500. It has also been pointed out that the position of Zeus as the bestower of honours upon Hestia is chiefly Hesiodic.[117] Another less obvious example of Hesiodic theology might be found in the presentation of Artemis as the defender of cities of just men at v. 20; Artemis is rarely depicted in this role, which bears most resemblance either to Zeus' position as protector of just cities at *Op.* 225 ff., or (more fitting for Artemis) to the connection of her cousin Hecate with justice at *Th.* 404-52.

5. Hesiodic *imitatio*

The similarities between *Aphr.* and Hesiod are not as extensive as those between Hesiod and *Dem.*,[118] but they are nonetheless substantial. In certain cases, the parallels are significant enough to suggest direct imitation.

First of all, there are extensive parallels with the proem of the *Theogony*. Similar language describes the nymphs dancing upon Ida and the Muses dancing on Helicon: *Aphr.* 258-61 αἳ τόδε ναιετάουσιν ὄρος μέγα τε ζάθεόν τε | ... | ... | καί τε μετ' ἀθανάτοισι καλὸν χορὸν ἐρρώσαντο ~ *Th.* 2-8 αἵ θ' Ἑλικῶνος ἔχουσιν ὄρος μέγα τε ζάθεόν τε | ... | ... | ... | ... | ἀκροτάτῳ Ἑλικῶνι χοροὺς ἐνεποιήσαντο | καλοὺς ἱμερόεντας· ἐπερρώσαντο δὲ ποσσίν. Not only is the language similar (for ἐρρώσαντο cf. *Il.* 24. 616 [νύμφαι] αἵ τ' ἀμφ' Ἀχελώϊον ἐρρώσαντο), but the phrase ὄρος μέγα τε ζάθεόν τε is otherwise unique to Hesiod, and in *Aphr.* its use violates economy alongside the Homeric ὄρος καταειμένον ὕλῃ at v. 285.[119] In this case, the transitive use of ἐρρώσαντο[120] and the neglect of digamma in κᾰλόν suggest that *Aphr.* is secondary. Further evidence of influence from the proem may come from *Aphr.* 8 κούρην τ' αἰγιόχοιο Διὸς γλαυκῶπιν Ἀθήνην, which is identical to *Th.* 13. The verse could be formulaic, but given the other similarities just noted, imitation is worth considering;

---

[117] See Comm. on 22-3. [118] See N. Richardson (1974), 33-41.
[119] See Heitsch (1965), 22, Janko (1982), 25. [120] See Janko, loc. cit.

especially as in Hesiod the verse is part of a catalogue of gods, which would have been a fitting model for the less condensed list of goddesses here. If so, the awkward function of τε in the line in *Aphr.* suggests that it is secondary.[121]

There are also some striking parallels between *Aphr.* and the story of the creation of woman at *Th.* 561 ff. Chief of these is v. 29 τῇ δὲ πατὴρ Ζεὺς δῶκε καλὸν γέρας ἀντὶ γάμοιο ~ *Th.* 585 αὐτὰρ ἐπεὶ δὴ τεῦξε καλὸν κακὸν ἀντ' ἀγαθοῖο; the case for imitation is strengthened by the presence of short κᾰλόν in both lines (not found in Homer). Furthermore, there is another strong parallel just a few lines later at *Th.* 602–3 πόρεν κακὸν ἀντ' ἀγαθοῖο | ὅς κε γάμον φεύγων; note the thematic similarity of avoiding marriage.[122] If this were not enough, there is yet another parallel between *Aphr.* and this section of the *Th.*: v. 5 ἠμὲν ὅσ' ἤπειρος πολλὰ τρέφει ἠδ' ὅσα πόντος ~ *Th.* 582 κνώδαλ' ὅσ' ἤπειρος δεινὰ τρέφει ἠδὲ θάλασσα; in itself this could be formulaic, but given the other parallels in the vicinity, direct influence is probable.

Moving to *Works and Days*, several interesting parallels with Hesiod's description of winter at 504 ff. occur in the proem of *Aphr.* These are discussed by Janko,[123] who argues that *Op.* is borrowing from *Aphr.* Below is a summary of the evidence:

The main similarity is *Aphr.* 14 ἥ δέ τε παρθενικὰς ἁπαλόχροας ἐν μεγάροισιν ~ *Op.* 519–20 καὶ διὰ παρθενικῆς ἁπαλόχροος οὐ διάησιν [Βορέας] | ἥ τε δόμων ἔντοσθε ... μίμνει. The passages are thematically similar: Boreas blows through everything except sheep/ Aphrodite conquers everything except for three goddesses, and there are the shared motifs of the tender maiden and the works of Aphrodite. There are also the following linguistic similarities between the proem of *Aphr.* and the same section of *Op.*: (1) *Aphr.* 1/9 ἔργα πολυχρύσου Ἀφροδίτης ~ *Op.* 521 ἔργ' εἰδυῖα πολυχρύσου Ἀφροδίτης, (2) *Aphr.* 6 πᾶσιν δ' ἔργα μέμηλεν ~ *Op.* 531 πᾶσιν ἐνὶ φρεσὶ τοῦτο μέμηλεν (πᾶσιν follows a list of beasts in both cases), and (3) *Aphr.* 9 οὐ γάρ οἱ ~ *Op.* 526 οὐ γάρ οἱ (where there is the same rare neglect of digamma).

There certainly seems to be a direct link between the two poems (cf. also the similarity between *Aphr.* 264–5 τῇσι δ' ἅμ' ἢ ἐλάται ἠὲ

---

[121] See Comm. ad loc. [122] See Comm. ad loc. [123] Janko (1982), 165–9.

δρύες ὑψικάρηνοι | γεινομένῃσιν ἔφυσαν ἐπὶ χθονὶ βωτιανείρῃ and *Op.* 509–10 πολλὰς δὲ δρῦς ὑψικόμους ἐλάτας τε παχείας | οὔρεος ἐν βήσσῃς πιλνᾷ χθονὶ πουλυβοτείρῃ), but that *Op.* is the imitator is far from clear. As regards the parallel between *Aphr.* 14 and *Op.* 519–20, Janko argues that the mention of a tender maiden is more out of place as an object for Boreas not to blow through in *Op.*[124] However, the view that the young maiden is more out of place in Hesiod is ground altogether too subjective on which to base an argument of priority. Nor, as he proposes, is the idea that a poet might be more likely to draw from a proem than another part of a poem a convincing reason to favour *Aphr.* as prior.[125] There is also a notable similarity between *Aphr.* 14–15 παρθενικὰς ... | ἀγλαὰ ἔργ᾽ ἐδίδαξεν and *Op.* 63–4 παρθενικῆς καλὸν εἶδος ἐπήρατον· αὐτὰρ Ἀθήνην | ἔργα διδασκῆσαι πολυδαίδαλον ἱστὸν ὑφαίνειν (the creation of Pandora). The parallel phrasing once again suggests a connection, despite the fact that teaching skills to young women is a traditional activity of Athena (apart from *Od.* 20. 72 ἔργα δ᾽ Ἀθηναίη δέδαε κλυτά, cf. *Od.* 7. 109–11 and *Il.* 9. 390).[126] But there is nothing to indicate that *Op.* is the imitator. Janko suggests that the addition in *Op.* of the word παρθενική and Athena's role as the teacher of household tasks, absent in Hesiod's parallel description of the creation of woman at *Th.* 570–89, would be explained if the later version in *Op.* had been influenced by our poem. However, these additions in *Op.* do not necessarily have anything to do with *Aphr.*[127] In fact, another parallel from *Op.* could equally suggest that *Aphr.* has combined Hesiodic language: compare v. 14 ἡ δέ τε παρθενικὰς ἀπαλόχροας ἐν μεγάροισιν with *Op.* 256 ἡ δέ τε παρθένος ἐστι Δίκη and 519 καὶ διὰ παρθενικῆς ἁπαλόχροος. This is itself no certain proof, but the case for *Aphr.* being secondary may

---

[124] In this he follows the sentiment of West (1978), 288: '[Hesiod] attaches [the tender maiden] rather oddly to the list of creatures that Boreas does or does not blow through.' However, West also notes that Hesiod may have intended 'conscious humour in the paradox that [Boreas] does not penetrate her tender skin.'

[125] Janko (1982), 167, 227 notes a contrary case in the apparent influence of *Aphr.* 267 on *Dem.* 5 (see Comm. ad loc.).

[126] See West (1978) 159 on *Op.* 64.

[127] The word παρθενική, a lengthened form for the apparently more traditional παρθένος (7× Homer), appears only three times in Homer (*Il.* 18. 567, *Od.* 7. 20, 11. 39), but three times in *Op.* alone (63, 519, 699). The form is also well attested in Sappho and Alcaeus and cannot be considered as rare.

also be supported by the parallel of *Aphr.* 6 πᾶσιν δ' ἔργα μέμηλεν and *Op.* 531 πᾶσιν ἐνὶ φρεσὶ τοῦτο μέμηλεν; if there is imitation, the phrase is unusual at line-beginning in *Aphr.*, whereas μέμηλεν at line end in *Op.* has good precedent.

Finally, Janko suggests that the presence of Aeolic forms in Hesiod's description of winter (*Op.* 510 πίλνα, 526 δείκνυ, and 534 ἐπὶ νῶτα ἔαγε) are due to Hesiod's knowledge of a body of Aeolic poetry rather than to the influence of his father, who was from Cyme, speaking to him in the Aeolic dialect (one assumes that his father influenced the Aeolisms in the advice on seafaring given at *Op.* 618–94). This is a possibility,[128] but in that case the body of Aeolic poetry does not need to have included *Aphr.*[129]

On balance, the evidence of v. 6 ~ *Op.* 531, v. 14 ~ *Op.* 256, 519 seems to me to favour *Aphr.* as the borrower. At least, there is no strong evidence to suggest that *Op.* is secondary, and I therefore prefer to place *Aphr.* after both the *Th.* and *Op.* However, as Janko justly concludes his discussion of the matter, 'it would be wrong to claim that the proof of this is absolutely conclusive.'

6. *Aphr.* and *Dem.*

It has long been accepted that a large number of parallels between these two *Hymns* indicates some direct relationship rather than a common model, and scholars are for the most part in agreement that *Dem.* is more probably secondary.[130] This position is the more attractive one, but as usual when approaching the question of priority, it is necessary to proceed with caution. The similarities are the following:

---

[128] However, if this is the case, it is puzzling that the Aeolic influence has apparently been limited only to this passage. Janko comments that it is 'far from obvious' why influence from Hesiod's father should affect the description of winter; but surely descriptions of weather are just what one might have expected him to hear from his father in everyday speech.

[129] On Aeolisms in *Aphr.* see below, pp. 44–5.

[130] The fullest discussions of the issue are by Janko (1982), 163–5 and N. Richardson (1974), 42–3. See also Heitsch (1965), 38–40, Lenz (1975), 51 n. 1, VE 3, 24; only the last of these argues that *Aphr.* is secondary.

Overview of Language and Relationship to Early Poetry 39

31–2. πᾶσιν δ' ἐν νηοῖσι θεῶν τιμάοχός ἐστι | καὶ παρὰ πᾶσι βροτοῖσι θεῶν πρέσβειρα τέτυκται ~ Dem. 268–9 εἰμὶ δὲ Δημήτηρ τιμάοχος, ἥ τε μέγιστον | ἀθανάτοις θνητοῖσί τ' ὄνεαρ καὶ χάρμα τέτυκται (τιμάοχος is unique to these two passages).

58. θυώδεα νηόν ~ Dem. 355 θυώδεος ἔνδοθι νηοῦ (cf. 385 νηοῖο προπάροιθε θυώδεος).

82. παρθένῳ ἀδμήτῃ... εἶδος ὁμοίη ~ Dem. 145–6 παρθένος ἀδμής |... εἶδος ἀρίστη (note also μέγεθος καὶ εἶδος ὁμοίη in this order and metrical position elsewhere only at Dem. 275 μέγεθος καὶ εἶδος ἄμειψε).

136. οὔ σφιν ἀεικελίη νυὸς ἔσσομαι ~ Dem. 83–4 οὔ τοι ἀεικὴς | γαμβρός.

156. κατ' ὄμματα καλὰ βαλοῦσα = Dem. 194.

157. ἐς λέχος εὔστρωτον ~ Dem. 285 ἀπ' εὐστρώτων λεχέων (εὔστρωτος not in Homer or Hesiod).

173–5. ἔστη ἄρα κλισίῃ, εὐποιήτοιο μελάθρου | κῦρε κάρη, κάλλος δὲ παρειάων ἀπέλαμπεν | ἄμβροτον ~ Dem. 188–9 ἡ δ' ἄρ' ἐπ' οὐδὸν ἔβη ποσί, καί ῥα μελάθρου | κῦρε κάρη, πλῆσεν δὲ θύρας σέλαος θείοιο.

205. θαῦμα ἰδεῖν, πάντεσσι τετιμένος ἀθανάτοισι ~ Dem. 397 πάντεσσι τετιμ[ένη ἀθανάτοι]σιν (although cf. Th. 415, 449, 588).

257. νύμφαι βαθύκολποι ~ Dem. 5 κούρῃσι... βαθυκόλποις (adjective only of Trojan women in Homer).

279. μάλα γὰρ θεοείκελος ἔσται ~ Dem. 159 δὴ γὰρ θεοείκελός ἐσσι.

284. νύμφης καλυκώπιδος ~ Dem. 8 καλυκώπιδι κούρῃ and 420 Ὠκυρόη καλυκῶπις (καλυκῶπις not in Homer or Hesiod).

The evidence for individual cases is discussed in the commentary and is on the whole slight. As Richardson points out, the most significant instances for determining priority are Aphr. 31–2 ~ Dem. 268–9, and Aphr. 173–5 ~ Dem. 188–9 along with the other similarities in close proximity to this passage at Aphr. 156 and 157. In the former case, the fact that τιμάοχος is most probably an Aeolism gives it a more natural home in Aphr. (at 157 the rare term εὔστρωτος, known elsewhere first in the Lesbian Alcaeus, may favour priority on similar grounds) while synizesis in ὄνεαρ and necessary enjambment in Dem. also suggest that it is secondary.[131] As regards Aphr. 173–5,

---

[131] See Comm. ad loc., where more subjective arguments in favour of this position are also discussed.

the unique sense 'lintel' for μέλαθρον in *Dem.*, where in *Aphr.* it has its normal meaning 'roof-beam', perhaps favours the priority of *Aphr*. Also significant here is the fact that several parallels are collected in the same section of *Aphr*. (also 156–7) but are more spread out in *Dem*. Otherwise, in a case such as *Aphr.* 257 ~ *Dem.* 5, the short datives plural in the latter may be suggestive of secondary modification.

7. Other Hymns

Aphr. shares parallels and some unique points of language with other *Hymns*:

5. ἠμὲν ὅσ' ἤπειρος πολλὰ τρέφει ἠδ' ὅσα πόντος ~ *Apoll.* 21 ἠμὲν ἀν' ἤπειρον πορτιτρόφον ἠδ' ἀνὰ νήσους.

19. διαπρύσιοι (used as an adjective) ~ *Herm.* 336 (although with a very different sense).

44. ἄλοχον ποιήσατο κέδν' εἰδυῖαν ~ *Apoll.* 313 [Ζεὺς] ἐπεί μ' ἄλοχον ποιήσατο κέδν' εἰδυῖαν (Hera speaking).

156. ἕρπω (to a particular location) ~ *Hy.* 19. 22 ἐς μέσον ἕρπων.

168. αὖλις (of a cattle-fold) ~ *Herm.* 71 ἔνθα θεῶν μακάρων βόες ἄμβροτοι αὖλιν ἔχεσκον.

175. ἰοστεφάνου (?) ~ *Hy.* 6. 18.

177. τί νυ νήγρετον ὕπνον ἰαύεις ~ *Herm.* 289 ἀλλ' ἄγε, μὴ πυματόν τε καὶ ὕστατον ὕπνον ἰαύσῃς.

199. ἕνεκα (conjunction) ~ *Apoll.* 308?

256. ἴδῃ φάος ἠελίοιο (of birth) ~ *Apoll.* 71.

289. εἴρηταί τοι πάντα, σὺ δὲ φρεσὶ σῇσι νοήσας ~ *Apoll.* 544.

There is nothing in these to suggest a particular connection between the poems.

8. Relationship with other early hexameter poems

Aphr. also has some novel points of language and phrasing in common with other early hexameter poetry:

Pseudo-Hesiod

7. τρισσάς [θεάς] ~ fr. 233. 2 τρισσήν [γαῖαν].
24. ἐμνῶντο (form) ~ frr. 197. 7, 199. 4.[132]
52. καταθνητοῖς ἀνθρώποις (dat. plural) ~ fr. 1. 7.
141. γάμον ἱμερόεντα (noun-epithet combination) ~ frr. 37. 6, 211. 6.
199. ἕνεκα (conjunction) ~ fr. 180. 10? (cf. Apoll. 308 noted above).

Cycle

1. Μοῦσά μοι ἔννεπε ~ *Little Iliad*, Μοῦσά μοι ἔννεπε κεῖνα | ἔργα? (as transmitted by Plutarch *Sept. Sap. Conv.* 154 A).
5. ἠμὲν ὅσ' ἤπειρος πολλὰ τρέφει ἠδ' ὅσα πόντος ~ *Cypr.* fr. 7. 12 θηρί' ὅσ' ἤπειρος αἰνὰ (πολλὰ Peppmüller) τρέφει.
23. βουλῇ Διὸς αἰγιόχοιο = Hom. *Ep.* 4. 3.
46. μιχθήμεναι: the form is in the same metrical position and in an erotic context at *Cypr.* fr. 7.4 (in Homer only at *Il.* 11. 438 in a martial context).

There is nothing in these similarities to establish a particular link between the poems. Janko has also noted several linguistic similarities on the statistical level: like *Aphr.*, the *Cypria* has low levels of neglect of digamma (25%), advanced results for o-stem genitives singular (of 10 cases, 2 -οιο and 7 irresolvable -ου), and an apparent preference for Ionic Ζηνός (2 of 4 cases; in *Aphr.* 41.7%), as well as a similar level of nu mobile before consonants (40 cases per thousand verses; *Aphr.* 47.8).[133] He proposes that these similarities are due to the two poems' coming from a distinct Aeolic tradition known in Lesbos and the Troad, which was influenced by the Ionic tradition at a later date. There are indications that *Aphr.* was conceived in this region,[134] but whether the statistical results just mentioned link the *Cypria* to *Aphr.* remains questionable; it must be remembered that only about 50 lines of the *Cypria* survive in fragments, a base of

---

[132] See Comm. on 24–5 on possible influence from the catalogue on the unique pursuit of Hestia by Poseidon and Apollo.
[133] Janko (1982), 176.
[134] See below, pp. 49–50.

material which is insufficient for extracting reliable statistical results. The discrepancy between advanced o-stem genitive results and the otherwise Homeric levels of traditional morphs, which leads Janko to propose the theory of a separate tradition,[135] could be due simply to the individual style of our poet.[136]

9. Language in *Aphr.* not attested elsewhere in early hexameter poetry

There are a good number of words, forms, and combinations in *Aphr.* which are not found elsewhere in what survives of early hexameter poetry, or which are not found elsewhere in the whole of Greek poetry. In the following list, those entries marked with * are of the latter category:

Words

13. σατίνας (Sapph. fr. 44.13).
31. πρέσβειρα (E. *IT.* 963 etc.).
74. σύνδυο (Pi. *P.* 3. 81).
84. θάμβαινεν? (only once as a variant at Pi. *O.* 3. 32).
*87. ἐπιγναμπτάς.
*123. ἄκτιτον (known in Mycenaean: *a-ki-ti-to*).
159. βαρυφθόγγων (Pi. *I.* 6. 34 of a bowstring; of a lion B. *Epin.* 9. 9 etc.).
*189. βιοθάλμιος (cf. Pi. *O.* 7. 11 ζωθάλμιος).
246. καματηρός (Ar. *Lys.* 542 etc.).

---

[135] Janko (1982), 172–80: 'the results are just what we would expect of a tradition that possessed the principles of formular modification from an early stage, but, until a recent period of Ionic influence, lacked most of the innovations we have been discussing.'

[136] Janko doubts whether deliberate imitation of the Ionic style of Homer can explain this discrepancy on the ground that 'it is difficult to believe that a poet of the archaic period, with no lexica or concordances, could or would achieve such consistent archaism'; but is it really so difficult? The same poet has created a poem which has a more polished metre than other examples of early poetry. These two facts might be explained by the use of writing as an aid to composition (see above, pp. 23–5).

Form and Metre

49. γελοιήσασα (form only here with relative certainty).
*67. νέφεσιν.
*71. προκάδων (as from προκάς).
*94. ἠϋγενής (form of εὐγενής).
*112. εὐτειχήτοιο (elsewhere fem. acc. εὐτείχεον and εὐτείχεα Il. 1. 129 etc.).
114. Τρῳάς (feminine nominative singular; although cf. acc. -ᾱς Il. 5. 461 etc.).
*127. τεκεῖσθαι (future infinitive, beside τέξεσθαι Il. 19. 99 etc.).
179. τὸ πρῶτον (scanned short; although cf. Od. 3. 320 ὅν τινα πρῶτον).
*197. ἐκγεγάονται (future modelled on perfect).
*224. ὀλοιόν (lengthened masculine form from ὀλοός; cf. fem. ὀλοιή Il. 22. 5 etc.).
281. ἀρσίποδας (contracted form for ἀερσίποδες Il. 3. 327 etc.).

Combination and Meaning

*4. οἰωνούς τε διειπετέας (διιπετής in Homer paired with ποταμός).
*7. πείθω double accusative, the whole and the part (τρισσάς [θεάς] and φρένας).
*20. ἄλσεά τε σκιόεντα (although cf. Thgn. 1252 ἄλσεά τε σκιερά).
21. αἰδοίη κούρῃ (~ A.R. 4. 1491).
28. παντ' ἤματα (inversion of ἤματα πάντα ~ A.R. 4. 648 etc.).
39. συνέμειξε and ἀνέμειξε v. 52 (compounds of sexual intercourse Hdt. 4. 114).
*39. καταθνητῇσι γυναιξί (also at vv. 50 and 210).
*41. εἶδος ἀρίστη (used of Hera, a goddess, whereas elsewhere only of mortal women).
*47. ἀποεργμένη (meaning to stay away from sexual intercourse; cf. Paus. 2. 24. 1 ἀνδρὸς εὐνῆς εἰργομένη).
47. βροτέης εὐνῆς (~ Nonn. D. 48. 893; cf. Pi. I. 8. 36 βροτέων δὲ λεχέων).
71. θοαί (used of animals: ~ Pi. P. 4. 17 etc.).
*75, 161, and 173. εὐποίητος (used uniquely of three objects, a hut, a bed, and a roof-beam).

*78. νομούς . . . ποιήεντας (cf. E. *Cyc.* 61 ποιηρούς λιπούσα νομούς).
80. διαπρύσιον (used of the sound of a cithara).
82. παρθένῳ ἀδμήτῃ (~ Orph. *Hy.* 55. 25. In early epic only of animals; but παρθένος ἀδμής).
*88. ὅρμοι . . . περικαλλέες.
102. εὔφρονα (εὔφρων meaning 'gracious, kindly'; ~ Pi. *O.* 4. 12–13).
*104. θαλερὸν γόνον (cf. θαλερὸν γάμον *Od.* 6. 66 etc.).
*114. διάπρο (temporal = διαμπερές).
*123. ἄκληρον (meaning 'unallotted' land; cf. of a poor man *Od.* 11. 490).
133. ἀπειρήτην (of sexual experience; ~ Nonn. *D.* 15. 171–2 etc.).
*140. ἄποινα (meaning 'dowry'; elsewhere 'ransom' *Il.* 1. 23 etc.).
142. τίμιος γάμος (~ *Orac. Sib.* 8. 27).
162. κόσμον . . . φαεινόν (~ Nonn. *D.* 5. 83).
*168. ἀποκλίνουσι (meaning 'to turn back').
*169. νομῶν . . . ἀνθεμοέντων.
182. παρακλιδόν (of averting eyes; ~ Nonn. *D.* 29. 151–2).
199. ἕνεκα (as conjunction, otherwise attested with certainty in Hellenistic poetry A.R. 4. 1523 etc.; cf. *Apoll.* 308 and [Hes.] fr. 180. 10).
199. ἔσχεν ἄχος (grief does not have hold of someone with ἔχω in Homer, where cf. ἄχος εἷλε *Il.* 13. 581 etc.; ~ Alcm. fr. 116, etc.).
*229. εὐηγενής (of a beard; of noble people in Homer see *Il.* 11. 427, 23. 81, where v.l. εὐηφενής).
259. ἕπονται (meaning 'count amongst'; ~ Pl. *R.* 406 D).
267. ἠλίβατος (of a tree, where elsewhere of rocks and caves; although cf. v.l. πεύκη for πέτρα with the adjective at *Sc.* 421).
*267. ἑ (plural; cf. above under modification).
276. διέλθω (meaning 'to recount'; ~ Pi. *N.* 4. 72 etc.).
*291. οὐρανὸν ἠνεμόεντα (usually οὐρανὸς ἀστερόεις *Il.* 4. 44 etc.).

10. Dialects

Aeolisms

There are two legitimate claims for Aeolisms in *Aphr.*, the prosody κᾰλός (vv. 29 and 261) and the compound τιμάοχος (v. 31). The former is found also in Hesiod,[137] but the rarity of the latter (only here and *Dem.* 268) could betray an Aeolic origin. A single case is of course not decisive, but this would accord with other evidence.[138] The variant form πορδάλιες at v. 71 might also be Aeolic; however, not only should the majority reading παρδάλιες be followed, but the variant form is well-known in Homer.

Atticisms

Four graphic Atticisms are found in the poem, all contracted forms, v. 51 acc. plural υἱεῖς, v. 98 νυμφῶν, v. 125 ἐδόκουν and v. 267 τεμένη. All, however, are resolvable into Ionic forms (υἷας, νυμφέων, δόκεον, τεμένεα); also v. 98 is very probably a later interpolation. There is nothing therefore to suggest any Attic influence at the time of composition. On the contrary, the interpolation may suggest an Attic phase of transmission (although the other graphic changes could themselves easily be due to the negligence of Byzantine scribes). Other forms have been claimed as Attic (v. 31 τιμάοχος, v. 71 v.l. πορδάλιες, and v. 190 θεαῖς), but there is no evidence that they actually are.

Finally, as regards dialect, a marked preference for the East Ionic form Ζηνός (next to Διός) has been noted by Janko (41.7%; cf. *Il.* 8.1%, *Od.* 10.7% etc.).[139] He considers it is a case of 'hyperionism', but it could be the result of metrical convenience, or even chance. It is certainly no indication of origin.

11. *Aphr.* and Lesbian poetry

Moving away from early hexameter poetry, there are several striking parallels between *Aphr.* and the Lesbian poets Sappho and Alcaeus. The first of these comes in vv. 12–14 ἄνδρας ... | σατίνας καὶ ἄρματα ... | ἡ δέ τε παρθενικὰς ἁπαλόχροας ~ Sappho fr. 44. 13–17 σατίναι[ς] ... | ... | ... παρθενίκαν τ' [ἀπαλο]σφύρων | ... | ... ἄνδρες ὔπαγον ὐπ' ἀ[ρματ-. The rare word σατίνη occurs next in a fragment of Anacreon (*PMG* 388. 10). This and the other verbal similarities

---

[137] See above, p. 34. [138] See below, pp. 49–50. [139] Janko (1982), 62–4.

might suggest a direct relationship between the two poems, although this cannot be certain; not only does some of the similarity in this instance depend upon conjecture (ἀπαλοσφύρων?), but one cannot rule out a common model.

A common model seems most probable in the case of another strong link with Lesbian poetry at vv. 25–32: this short narrative about Hestia has a number of verbal similarities with a fragmentary hymn to Artemis (Sappho fr. 44a Voigt, although attributed by *PLF* to Alcaeus).[140] The unique nature of the Hestia episode makes it most unlikely that the Lesbian poet has borrowed from *Aphr.* for a hymn to Artemis, and while it is not impossible that a hexameter poet should borrow from a lyric poet, this seems less likely than a common model that has influenced both poets.

A third link is found between the Tithonus episode at vv. 218 ff. and Sappho fr. 58: v. 227 ναίε παρ' Ὠκεανοῖο ῥοῆς ἐπὶ πείρασι γαίης ~ fr. 58. 10 βάμεν' εἰς ἔσχατα γᾶς φέροισα[ν, v. 228 πρῶται πολιαὶ κατέχυντο ἔθειραι ~ fr. 58. 4 ἐγ]ένοντο τρίχες ἐκ μελαίναν, 12 πόλιον γῆρας, v. 233 κατὰ γῆρας ἔπειγεν ~ fr. 58. 3–4 ποτ' [ἔ]οντα χρόα γῆρας ἤδη and v. 234 οὐδέ τι κινῆσαι μελέων δύνατ' (~ *Od.* 8. 298) ~ fr. 58. 5 βάρυς δέ μ' ὁ [θ]ῦμος πεπόηται, γόνα δ' οὐ φέροισι. Here the similarities are more thematic than verbal; indeed, what is remarkable is that the legend of the eternal old age of Tithonus is not known in Homer or Hesiod, but in early poetry only here, in Sappho, and in a fragment of Mimnermus (fr. 4, *IEG* ii).[141] This connection is again perhaps best explained by a common model, or models.

Two other less substantial points of linguistic contact can be mentioned: v. 115 σμικρὴν παῖδ' ἀτίταλλε (a child is not qualified as small elsewhere in early epic, but cf. Sappho fr. 49. 2 σμίκρα μοι παῖς and Alcaeus fr. 75. 7–8 πάϊς | ... σμῖκρ[ο]ς, although cf. Thgn. 254) and v. 157 εὔστρωτον λέχος (other than *Dem.* 285 εὐστρώτων λεχέων, this is paralleled in early poetry only by Alcaeus fr. 283. 8 εὔστρωτον λέχος).[142]

---

[140] See Comm. on 25–32 for the parallels and a discussion of attribution.
[141] See AHS 366, VE 77–8. Homer does know of Tithonus as the husband of Eos.
[142] Cf. also Comm. on 40–4 on the attention paid to Hera in *Aphr.* and by the two Lesbian poets.

Whether the above-mentioned parallels arose through common models or direct borrowing (or a combination of both) is impossible to say with any certainty. Regardless, they are substantial enough to suggest that the poet of *Aphr.* was in contact with a body of poetry which was also available to Sappho and Alcaeus. This is one indication that the poem perhaps has its origins in the area of Lesbos and northern Asia Minor.[143]

V. DATE AND PLACE OF COMPOSITION

Opinion as to the date of *Aphr.* has varied widely; Reinhardt famously considered it to be by Homer, while Freed and Bentman took the extreme view that it was the work of a Hellenistic poet.[144] The majority, however, have taken a more moderate position, which has in recent years become the *opinio communis*: post-Homeric, but prior to the sixth century and the earliest of the *Hymns*.[145] With no external evidence to aid in the task, one must rely upon comparative chronology. The evidence has been discussed in the preceding sections and the results can be summarized here quite briefly.

It is almost certain that *Aphr.* is post-Homeric, but as to how far post-Homeric the linguistic evidence is not a reliable measure. It also seems most probable that the poem is later than both Hesiod's *Theogony* and *Works and Days*; Janko argues that *Aphr.* might be dated between the two Hesiodic poems, with the *Works and Days* having been influenced by *Aphr.*, but I do not see any evidence to support this view.[146] A *terminus ante quem* is provided by *Dem.* The

---

[143] See below. pp. 49–50.

[144] Freed–Bentman (1954), cf. Reinhardt (1956), both arguing on linguistic and stylistic grounds. Heitsch (1965) also thought it was the work of the same poet who composed *Il.* 20, but considered the latter to be a later interpolation in the main text of the *Iliad* (a view refuted by Lenz 1975).

[145] For a summary of early views see Janko (1982), 151, who himself prefers a 7th-c. date. VE 3–4 felt that it was composed near the end of the 7th c. in 'the hey-day of Greek lyric poetry'. Most recently, West (2003), 16 suggests that 'we shall not go far wrong if we place him [the poet] in the last third of the seventh century.'

[146] See above, pp. 35–8.

high number of parallels between the two poems makes a direct connection virtually undeniable, and although the case for *Aphr.*'s priority is not impermeable, the balance of the evidence suggests that *Dem.* is secondary.[147] The question, however, is *post* and *ante* what? The dates of these other poems are hardly certain.

The standard view has been that the *Iliad* is the product of the second half of the eighth century, and that Hesiod comes slightly later at the end of the eighth century. However, West has argued that the *Iliad* should be dated in the seventh century, some time between 670 and 640, a view which also involves dating Hesiod prior to Homer.[148] If one follows West's view, *Aphr.* can be placed securely in the latter half of the seventh century. If not (and it still remains an open question) *Aphr.* could be a product of the early seventh or even late eighth century; especially if there is truth in West's supposition that 'there cannot be a huge difference in time, probably a generation at most, between these two celebrations [*Aphr.* and *Il.* 20] of the Aeneadae'.[149] Janko (who dates Homer before Hesiod) dates the *Theogony* to the early seventh century making Hesiod a contemporary of Archilochus.[150] In this case as well *Aphr.* would be a product of the middle to late seventh century.

On the other end, *Dem.* does not provide a certain *terminus ante quem*. Both Richardson and Clinton favour a date in the late seventh century, but the poem could be as late as 550.[151] However, if one accepts that *Aphr.* was composed within roughly one generation of the *Iliad* it will not be later than the end of the seventh century, whichever view of Homer's date one takes.

The numerous similarities of language and themes between *Aphr.* and the Lesbian poets Sappho and Alcaeus might also be significant

---

[147] See above, pp. 38–40.
[148] West (1995), cf. (1966), 46; his argument that Homer borrows from Hesiod will remain controversial, but he has at least shown that there is no strong evidence that borrowing has taken place the other way.
[149] West (2003), 15; on the question of the Aineiadai see above, pp. 3–18.
[150] Janko (1982), 94–8, 228–31; this chronology is based upon the uncertain dating of the Lelantine War and Hesiod's performance at the funeral games of Amphidamas, which could have taken place at the end of the 8th c. West (1995), 219 is also open to dating the Hesiodic poems to 680 or 670.
[151] N. Richardson (1974), 5–11, Clinton (1986), 47.

for the purposes of dating.[152] The parallels do not necessarily indicate direct imitation in either direction, but they are substantial enough to suggest that the poet of *Aphr.* had access to a body of poetry similar to that which was available to Sappho and Alcaeus. This seems to me to favour a date in the latter half of the seventh century for *Aphr.*, closer to the time when Sappho and Alcaeus were active, but it is admittedly impossible to be certain.

To turn to the place of composition: until the end of the nineteenth century, *Aphr.* was considered by some scholars to have been composed in Cyprus, perhaps for a festival in honour of the goddess. This claim was based upon the use of the title Κύπρις at the beginning of the poem (v. 2), the closing phrase of the hymn which celebrates Aphrodite ruling over well-built Cyprus (v. 292), and the occurrence of the word σατίνη (v. 13), which was supposed to be Cypriot.[153] However, it is in fact most probably a loan-word in Aeolis and Ionia,[154] and this, combined with other evidence in the hymn, suggests an origin in the Troad rather than composition in Cyprus. At vv. 113–16, Aphrodite, disguised as a young Phrygian maiden in order to seduce Anchises, explains that she is able to speak both Phrygian and the language of Anchises because she was reared by a Trojan nurse; Phrygian inscriptions recently found at Daskyleion near the Hellespont suggest a long tradition of Greek and Phrygian interaction in the area, an environment which could well have inspired this unique reference to bilingualism.[155] Two possible Aeolisms (κᾰλός vv. 29, 261, τιμάοχος v. 31) and a number of parallels with Lesbian poetry also support an origin in northern Asia Minor.[156] In addition, if one accepts that the hymn was composed for a family of Aineiadai, this is evidence of an origin in Asia Minor. It is true that there is no reliable evidence to locate the dynasty with any

---

[152] See above, pp. 45–7. On the extensive points of contact and exchange between Lesbos and the Troad in the 7th c. see Spencer (1995).

[153] For a summary and refutation of this position see AHS 351.

[154] See Janko (1982), 169–70, who suggests it is possibly Thracian in origin. It is found rarely in Greek literature, elsewhere only at Sappho fr. 44. 13, Anacreon, *PMG* fr. 388. 10, E. *Hel.* 1311. See further Comm. ad loc.

[155] On the inscriptions see Brixhe (2002), 1–2. Foreign languages are alluded to in Homer (*Il.* 2. 803–4, 2. 867, 4. 437–8, *Od.* 19. 175), but this is the first explicit reference to bilingualism in Greek literature.

[156] See above on the dating.

precision whatsoever, but if Homer was also in contact with the family, they must have been found somewhere in northern Asia Minor. This would also speak against the possibility that the poem was composed somewhere on the mainland by a poet with a knowledge of northern Asia Minor and the poetic environment of that region.

VI. IMPACT ON LATER LITERATURE

To Allen, Halliday, and Sikes it seemed strange 'that such brilliant literature made little or no impression on subsequent readers'.[157] Van Eck disagreed with this comment based upon one parallel in Callimachus,[158] but offered little in the way of evidence to show that *Aphr.* was more influential than his predecessors supposed. His instinct, however, was correct; it in fact seems very probable that *Aphr.* was quite widely known in the Hellenistic period and beyond. What follows is a summary of the most remarkable cases.

1. Callimachus

As one might expect, there are a number of parallels in Callimachus' *Hymns*, a collection which would naturally have found a model in the Homeric Hymns:

19. διαπρύσιοί τ' ὀλολυγαί ~ Call. *Hy*. 4. 258.

20. δικαίων τε πτόλις ἀνδρῶν ~ Call. *Hy*. 3. 122 ἀλλά μιν εἰς ἀδίκων ἔβαλες πόλιν.

27. ἀψαμένη κεφαλῆς πατρὸς Διὸς αἰγιόχοιο ~ Call. *Hy*. 3. 26–7 ὡς ἡ παῖς εἰποῦσα γενειάδος ἤθελε πατρὸς | ἅψασθαι (~ Sapph. fr. 44a. 1–11).

173–4. μελάθρου | κῦρε κάρη: the almost identical phrasing in *Dem.* 188–9 seems to have influenced Call. *Hy*. 6. 57–8 Δαμάτηρ ... | ... κεφαλὰ δέ οἱ ἅψατ' Ὀλύμπῳ (cf. also ibid. 37 μέγα δένδρεον αἰθέρι

---

[157] AHS 349.
[158] VE 19 (on 20); AHS had in fact already noted this parallel when making their claim of overall dearth.

κῦρον; cf. later in Latin Claudian *Cons. Stil.* 2. 277). This of course does not imply any direct imitation of *Aphr.*, but given the other parallels above Callimachus may well have had this passage in mind as well.

2. Apollonius Rhodius

Some parallels in the *Argonautica* are also of interest, although they are less striking than those in Callimachus. All come from the proem of *Aphr.* Two are found in the Lemnos episode in the first book (an erotic encounter for the Argonauts):

2. Κύπριδος, ἥ τε θεοῖσιν ἐπὶ γλυκὺν ἵμερον ὦρσε ~ A.R. 1. 803 Κύπριδος, ἥ τέ σφιν θυμοφθόρον ἔμβαλεν ἄτην and 1. 850 Κύπρις γὰρ ἐπὶ γλυκὺν ἵμερον ὦρσε.

A third finds itself in the mouth of Aphrodite in book three:

7. πεπιθεῖν φρένας οὐδ᾽ ἀπατῆσαι ~ A.R. 3. 152 παρέξομαι οὐδ᾽ ἀπατήσω. Given that *Aphr.* is speaking it is worth considering an echo here, although note οὐδ᾽ ἀπατήσω at line end *Od.* 4. 348, 17. 139 and *Herm.* 545 (cf. another weak case in 199 ἔσχεν ἄχος ~ A.R. 3. 464).

3. Moschus

The most extensive parallels are found in Moschus' *Europa*, a fact which has been overlooked by previous commentators. It is very probable that he was drawing upon *Aphr.* for his erotic tale:

2. Κύπριδος, ἥ τε θεοῖσιν ἐπὶ γλυκὺν ἵμερον ὦρσε ~ Eur. 76 Κύπριδος, ἣ μούνη δύναται καὶ Ζῆνα δαμάσσαι and 1 Εὐρώπῃ ποτὲ Κύπρις ἐπὶ γλυκὺν ἧκεν ὄνειρον.

38. καί τε τοῦ εὖτ᾽ ἐθέλῃ πυκινὰς φρένας ἐξαπαφοῦσα ~ Eur. 78 παρθενικῆς τ᾽ ἐθέλων ἀταλὸν νόον ἐξαπατῆσαι.

81. στῆ δ᾽ αὐτοῦ προπάροιθε ~ Eur. 93 [Ζεύς] στῆ δὲ ποδῶν προπάροιθεν ἀμύμονος Εὐρωπείης (although cf. *Il.* 14. 297).

156. ἕρπε μεταστρεφθεῖσα [ἐς λέχος] ~ Eur. 111 ἡ δὲ μεταστρεφθεῖσα φίλας καλέεσκεν ἑταίρας.

4. Late Imperial/Byzantine

A certain echo of *Aphr.* is found in the hymnographer Proclus of the fifth century AD: *Hy.* 4. 13 πᾶσιν δ' ἔργα μέμηλεν ἐρωτοτόκου Κυθερείης ~ *Aphr.* 6 πᾶσιν δ' ἔργα μέμηλεν ἐϋστεφάνου Κυθερείης (cf. also *Hy.* 7. 8 καὶ χθονίων δαμάσασα θεημάχα φῦλα Γιγάντων ~ *Aphr.* 3 καί τ' ἐδαμάσσατο φῦλα καταθνητῶν ἀνθρώπων ~). Musaeus 79 αὐτίκα τεθναίην λεχέων ἐπιβήμενος Ἡροῦς may well have been thinking of Anchises' death-defying desire at *Aphr.* 149–54 (compare also Musae. 160 and *Aphr.* 156). Others: Q.S. 8. 466–7 δάμνατο δ' ὁππόσα φῦλα φερέσβιος ἔτρεφε γαῖα | ἠδ' ὅσα πόντος ἔφερβεν ἀπείριτος ἠδ' ὁπόσ' ὕδωρ (cf. 13. 402–3 Κύπρις ἥ περ ἁπάντων | ἀθανάτων δάμνησι νόον θνητῶν ἀνθρώπων) ~ *Aphr.* 3–5 ἐδαμάσσατο φῦλα . . . | . . . | ἠμὲν ὅσ' ἤπειρος πολλὰ τρέφει ἠδ' ὅσα πόντος, Nonn. *D.* 11. 296 ἐν οὔρεσι θῆρας ἐναίρειν ~ *Aphr.* 18 οὔρεσι θῆρας ἐναίρειν, Eudocia *de Martyrio Sancti Cypriani* 30 ἔννεπέ μοι τεὰ ἔργα ~ *Aphr.* 1 Μοῦσά μοι ἔννεπε ἔργα (cf. also *Homerocentones* 1. 1–3 μυρία φῦλα περικτιόνων ἀνθρώπων | . . . | ἠμὲν ὅσοι . . . | ἠδ' ὅσσοι beside *Aphr.* 3–5), Leontius Scholasticus, *AP* 16. 375. 1 ἔγρεο Κωνσταντῖνε, τί χάλκεον ὕπνον ἰαύεις ~ *Aphr.* 177 ὄρσεο Δαρδανίδη· τί νυ νήγρετον ὕπνον ἰαύεις, Theodoros Prodromos (12th c.) *Carmina Historica* 6. 42–3 ὡς δὲ σελήνη | χρυσείοισι πέπλοισι φαείνεται ~ *Aphr.* 89 [ὅρμοι] καλοὶ χρύσειοι παμποίκιλοι· ὡς δὲ σελήνη.

VII. MANUSCRIPTS AND TEXT

1. Manuscripts

Twenty-nine manuscripts, all of the fifteenth century,[159] are known to contain the *Homeric Hymns*. The poems are often transmitted

---

[159] Càssola writes that At perhaps belongs to the end of the 14th, following the opinion of several previous scholars. AHS, p. xxxvii, however, had placed it in the 15th c. on account of the quality of its paper. Wilson (1974) has closed the debate by identifying the scribe of the manuscript as Girard of Old Patras, active in the 15th c. M, which had been dated to the 13th or 14th c. by AHS, p. xviii, was proved to date from the beginning of the 15th c. by Irigoin (1970), on account of its watermarks; N. Richardson (1974), 65 n. 1 notes that Wilson agrees that the

together with the *Hymns* of Callimachus, Orpheus, and Proclus. Fuller descriptions can be found in Càssola 593–6 and AHS, pp. xi–xvii. Of these 29, the following 22 include the *Hymn to Aphrodite*. The sigla correspond to those of Càssola. All manuscripts contain *Hymns* 3–33 unless otherwise stated.

> D = Ambrosianus 120 (B 98 sup.). (*Aphr.* fos. 197^r–202^r).
> Q = Ambrosianus 734 (S 31 sup.). (*Aphr.* fos. 70^r–78^r).
> At = Athous, Vatopedi 671. (*Aphr.* fos. 207^v–211^v).
> Γ = Bruxellensis 74. (*Aphr.* fos. 53^r–59^r).
> Harv. = Harvardensis Coll Ms. Typ. 18. (*Aphr.* fos. 85^r–90^v).
> L = Laurentianus 32. 45. Contains *H. Hymns* 3–7 (*Aphr.* fos. 175^v–181^r).
> L$_2$ = Laurentianus 70. 35 (*Aphr.* fos. 90^r–95^v).
> L$_3$ = Laurentianus 32. 4 (*Aphr.* fos. 466^r–470^v).
> L$_4$ = Laurentianus Aedil. 220 (*Aphr.* fos. 71^v–77^r).
> M = Leidensis B.P.G. 33 H. Contains *H. Hymns* 1. 10–18. 4 (*Aphr.* fos. 46^v–48^v).
> N = Leidensis B.P.G. 74 C (*Aphr.* fos. 88^v–95^r).
> V = Venetus Marcianus 456 (*Aphr.* fos. 524^r–528^r).
> T = Matritensis 4562 (*Aphr.* fos. 73^r–77^v).
> E = Mutinensis Estensis 164 (α W 5. 16) (*Aphr.* fos. 70^v–76^v).
> A = Parisinus Graecus 2763 (*Aphr.* fos. 115^r–120^v).
> B = Parisinus Graecus 2765 (*Aphr.* fos. 45^r–50^v).
> C = Parisinus Graecus 2833 (*Aphr.* fos. 68^v–75^r).
> Π = Parisinus Graecus suppl. 1095 (*Aphr.* 152–293 [1–151 *foliis avulsis*] fos. 238^r–239^v).
> R$_1$ = Riccardianus 53 (*Aphr.* fos. 84^r–90^v).
> R$_2$ = Riccardianus 52 (*Aphr.* fos. 56^r–62^v).
> P = Vaticanus Palatinus 179 (*Aphr.* fos. 112^v–119^v).
> G = Vaticanus Reginensis 91 (*Aphr.* fos. 332^v–339^v).

This edition of *Aphr.* is based upon the most recent and complete study of the relationships between the manuscripts by Càssola.[160]

---

date 'is probably the first quarter of the 15th century'. Correspondingly, Gelzer (1994), 123–5, following D. Harlfinger, identifies the scribe of M as Ioannes Eugenikos, active in the 15th c. in Constantinople, where (or near where) he supposes M to have been written; his article provides a useful history of this remarkable MS.

[160] Càssola 596 ff.

```
                    Ω
         ┌──────────┴──────────┐
         │                     Ψ
         │          ┌──────────┴──────────┐
         │          Θ                     p
         │       ┌──┴──┐          ┌───┬───┼───┬────┐
         │       D     χ         ╱   ╱    │    ╲    ╲
         M       │    ╱ ╲       ╱   ╱     │     ╲    ╲
                At   a   b
                    ╱╲ ╱╲
                   E T L Π   A  Q B   Γ   V    C Harv. L₂ L₃ L₄ R₁ R₂
                                              P
                                              N
```

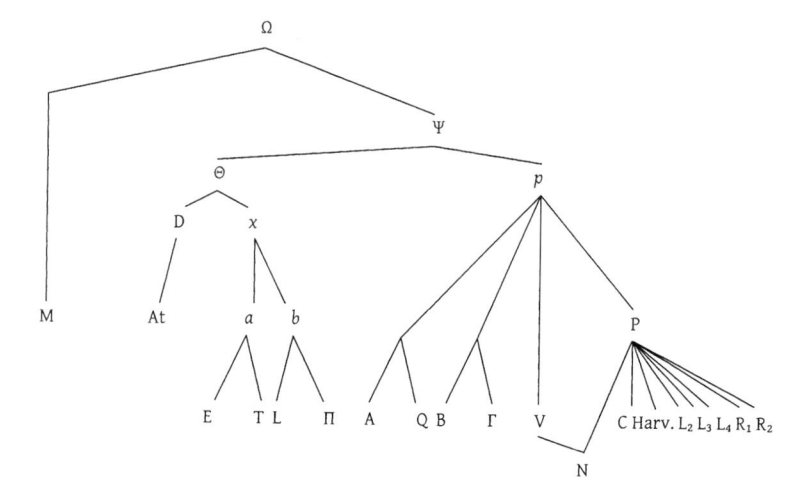

Much useful information is also found in the work of AHS.[161] The data from *Aphr.* are clearly insufficient to inform a reappraisal of the stemma codicum and no attempt has been made to undertake one. Càssola's stemma codicum is followed here, with the exception that only the manuscripts which contain *Aphr.* are included and the derivation of At from D, identified by Wilson (above n. 159), is reflected.

Manuscript G is unanimously considered to be a copy from the *editio princeps* and is therefore excluded from the stemma.[162]

Manuscript M, found in Moscow in the seventeenth century and moved to Leiden in the eighteenth,[163] stands apart from the other manuscripts with a number of unique readings: e.g. v. 8 γλαυκῶπιν M γλαυκώπιδ' Ψ, v. 10 ἄδον M ἄδεν Ψ, v. 18 πουλύχρυσα δέ M καὶ γὰρ τῇ (τοι AQ, τοῖ B) ἄδε, v. 38 εὖτ' ἐθέλῃ M εὖτε θέλοι (εὖτ' ἐθέλοι) Ψ, v. 66 Τροίης M Τροίην Ψ and κῆπον M κύπρον Ψ, v. 67 νέφεσι ῥίμφα M νεφέεσσι θοῶς Ψ, v. 114 Τρῳάς M Τρωός Ψ, v. 125 ψαύσειν M ψαύειν Ψ, v. 132 οὐ μὲν γάρ κε M οὐ γάρ τε Ψ, v. 135 δοιώ τε κασιγνήτω M σοῖς τε κασιγνήτοις Ψ, v. 139 οἱ δέ κέ χρυσόν τε M οἱ δέ τε χρυσόν κεν Ψ, v. 174 κῦρε M βύρε | ηὖρε | ἦρε Ψ, 175. ἰοστεφάνου M

---

[161] AHS, pp. xvii ff.; cf. also Humbert (1936), 12–18.
[162] See Càssola 613, AHS, p. xvii.
[163] See Càssola 597–8 and on its date and provenance above, n. 159.

ἐϋστεφάνου Ψ, v. 204 -οινοχοεύειν M -οινοχοεύοι Ψ, v. 205 τετιμένον M τετιμένος Ψ, v. 206 ἀφύσσειν M ἀφύσσων Ψ, v. 214 ἶσα θεοῖσιν M (et a marg.) ἤματα πάντα Ψ, v. 228 κατέχοιντο M κατέχυντο Ψ, v. 255 ζώνην M ζώνῃ Ψ.

In some instances I consider M's reading to be the better one (vv. 8, 10, 38, 66 Τροίης, 67, 114, 132, 174, 175, 214), but in a number of other cases M's reading is either inferior (vv. 66 κῆπον, 125, 204–6, 255) or clearly wrong (vv. 135, 228 etc.).[164] Van Eck mistrusts M on the grounds that it is 'inclined to "restore" Homeric forms, phrases or prosodic features', but van der Ben has successfully shown this claim to be unfounded; in the end, 'all cases must be decided on their individual merits'.[165]

2. The *editio princeps*

The *Hymns*, together with the *Odyssey*, were first printed in 1488, by Demetrius Chalcondyles in Florence. Scholars agree that Demetrius based his text for the most part on manuscript D, while also using a manuscript of the *x* family and one from the *p* family.[166] He is acknowledged as a talented editor, and made several corrections and improvements to the text. Those readings which appear to be Chalcondyles' own conjectures are indicated in the apparatus criticus.

3. Text and apparatus criticus

In preparing this text of *Aphr.*, all manuscripts which contain the poem have been collated or consulted by me. Of his own encounter with the manuscripts in 1975, Càssola 628 commented: 'Come era prevedibile, la collazione mi ha permesso di correggere qualche svista, generalmente non grave, e di colmare qualche lacuna, ma non ha portato grandi novità: gli studiosi più recenti (Goodwin, Allen,

---

[164] VB 2 lists 28 examples.
[165] VE 117–22, VB 2–4. N. Richardson (1974), 66 notes that M shows a tendency 'for "restoring" unmetrical "epicisms"' in four cases in *Dem.*, but M does not always favour Homeric forms; M alone has the un-Homeric ἰοστεφάνου at *Aphr.* 175.
[166] See Allen (1895), 154–60, Càssola 612–13.

Breuning, Humbert) conoscevano bene il materiale disponibile.' The same must be said for the present effort. Small errors in and inconsistencies between the apparatûs of previous editions have been corrected and verified. The apparatus does not aim to be exhaustive, but intends to offer a clear report of variants and errors without unnecessary clutter. Conjectures by editors of the *Hymns* after the *editio princeps* are indicated in the apparatus where they are deemed significant.

ΥΜΝΟΣ ΕΙΣ ΑΦΡΟΔΙΤΗΝ

τῶν εἰς Ὅμηρον ἀναφερομένων

Titulus ὕμνος εἰς ἀφροδίτην p: εἰς ἀφροδίτην Θ: τοῦ αὐτοῦ ὁμήρου ὕμνοι εἰς ἀφροδίτην M

Sigla

Omnes codices xv saeculi sunt

M   Leidensis B.P.G. 33 H
Ψ   consensus Θ et *p*
Θ   consensus D et *x*
At   Athous, Vatopedi 671
D   Ambrosianus 120 (B 98 sup.)
x   consensus *a* et *b*
a   consensus E et T
E   Mutinensis Estensis 164 (α W 5. 16)
T   Matritensis 4562
b   consensus LΠ
L   Laurentianus 32. 45
Π   Parisinus Graecus suppl. 1095

p   consensus AQBΓVP
A   Parisinus Graecus 2763
Q   Ambrosianus 734 (S 31 sup.)
B   Parisinus Graecus 2765
Γ   Bruxellensis 74
V   Venetus Marcianus 456
P   Vaticanus Palatinus 179

Singulis locis citantur
R_1 Riccardianus 53, ex P descriptus
R_2 Riccardianus 52, ex P descriptus
N   Leidensis B.P.G. 74 C, qui cum ex V tum ex P hausit

ΕΙΣ ΑΦΡΟΔΙΤΗΝ

Μοῦσά μοι ἔννεπε ἔργα πολυχρύσου Ἀφροδίτης
Κύπριδος, ἥ τε θεοῖσιν ἐπὶ γλυκὺν ἵμερον ὦρσε
καί τ' ἐδαμάσσατο φῦλα καταθνητῶν ἀνθρώπων,
οἰωνούς τε διειπετέας καὶ θηρία πάντα,
ἠμὲν ὅσ' ἤπειρος πολλὰ τρέφει ἠδ' ὅσα πόντος· 5
πᾶσιν δ' ἔργα μέμηλεν ἐϋστεφάνου Κυθερείης.
τρισσὰς δ' οὐ δύναται πεπιθεῖν φρένας οὐδ' ἀπατῆσαι·
κούρην τ' αἰγιόχοιο Διὸς γλαυκῶπιν Ἀθήνην·
οὐ γάρ οἱ εὔαδεν ἔργα πολυχρύσου Ἀφροδίτης,
ἀλλ' ἄρα οἱ πόλεμοί τε ἄδον καὶ ἔργον Ἄρηος, 10
ὑσμῖναί τε μάχαι τε καὶ ἀγλαὰ ἔργ' ἀλεγύνειν.
πρώτη τέκτονας ἄνδρας ἐπιχθονίους ἐδίδαξε
ποιῆσαι σατίνας τε καὶ ἅρματα ποικίλα χαλκῷ·
ἣ δέ τε παρθενικὰς ἁπαλόχροας ἐν μεγάροισιν
ἀγλαὰ ἔργ' ἐδίδαξεν ἐπὶ φρεσὶ θεῖσα ἑκάστῃ. 15
οὐδέ ποτ' Ἀρτέμιδα χρυσηλάκατον κελαδεινήν
δάμναται ἐν φιλότητι φιλομμειδὴς Ἀφροδίτη·
καὶ γὰρ τῇ ἅδε τόξα καὶ οὔρεσι θῆρας ἐναίρειν,
φόρμιγγές τε χοροί τε διαπρύσιοί τ' ὀλολυγαί
ἄλσεά τε σκιόεντα δικαίων τε πτόλις ἀνδρῶν. 20
οὐδὲ μὲν αἰδοίῃ κούρῃ ἅδεν ἔργ' Ἀφροδίτης
Ἱστίη, ἣν πρώτην τέκετο Κρόνος ἀγκυλομήτης,
αὖτις δ' ὁπλοτάτην, βουλῇ Διὸς αἰγιόχοιο,
πότνιαν, ἣν ἐμνῶντο Ποσειδάων καὶ Ἀπόλλων·
ἣ δὲ μάλ' οὐκ ἔθελεν ἀλλὰ στερεῶς ἀπέειπεν, 25
ὤμοσε δὲ μέγαν ὅρκον, ὃ δὴ τετελεσμένος ἐστίν,
ἁψαμένη κεφαλῆς πατρὸς Διὸς αἰγιόχοιο
παρθένος ἔσσεσθαι πάντ' ἤματα, δῖα θεάων.

1 ante 152 def. Π foliis avulsis   3 καταθνητῶν x: κατὰ θνητῶν MDp (simili discidio καταθνητ- vv. 39, 46, 50, 51, 52, 110, 122, 192, 200, 250)   4 διειπετέας Schulze (1892): διιπετέας Ψ: διιπετέα M   6 πᾶσιν δ' ἔργα AQPx: πᾶσι δ' ἔργα MBΓVD: πᾶσι δὲ ἔργα Hoffmann (1848)   8 γλαυκῶπιν M: γλαυκῶπιδ' Ψ   10–11 in unum conflaverunt ET   10 ἀλλ' ἄρα] ἀλλά ῥα MΓ   ἄδον M (ex ἄδον correctum): ἄδεν Ψ   13 σατίνας τε Barnes (1711): σάτινα Mpx: σκύτινα D   16 χρυσηλάκατον Mp: χρυσήλατον Θ   17 φιλομμειδής Atp: φιλομειδής MDx (similiter φιλομ(μ)ειδής vv. 56, 65, 155; cf. v. 49)   18 καὶ γὰρ τῇ ἅδε Aldus (1504): καὶ γὰρ τῇ (τοι AQ, τοί B) ἅδε Ψ: πουλύχρυσα δέ M   20 πτόλις Chalc. (marg. Γ): πόλις Θ: πόλεις M: πόνος p   22 ἱστίη px (ἱστιῆ L) Chalc.: ἑστίη MD   23 βουλῇ διὸς] διὸς βουλῇ ΓT

ΥΜΝΟΣ

τῇ δὲ πατὴρ Ζεὺς δῶκε καλὸν γέρας ἀντὶ γάμοιο,
καί τε μέσῳ οἴκῳ κατ' ἄρ' ἕζετο πῖαρ ἑλοῦσα. 30
πᾶσιν δ' ἐν νηοῖσι θεῶν τιμάοχός ἐστιν
καὶ παρὰ πᾶσι βροτοῖσι θεῶν πρέσβειρα τέτυκται.
τάων οὐ δύναται πεπιθεῖν φρένας οὐδ' ἀπατῆσαι·
τῶν δ' ἄλλων οὔ πέρ τι πεφυγμένον ἔστ' Ἀφροδίτην
οὔτε θεῶν μακάρων οὔτε θνητῶν ἀνθρώπων. 35
καί τε πάρεκ Ζηνὸς νόον ἤγαγε τερπικεραύνου,
ὅς τε μέγιστός τ' ἐστί, μεγίστης τ' ἔμμορε τιμῆς·
καί τε τοῦ εὖτ' ἐθέλῃ πυκινὰς φρένας ἐξαπαφοῦσα
ῥηϊδίως συνέμειξε καταθνητῇσι γυναιξίν
Ἥρης ἐκλελαθοῦσα κασιγνήτης ἀλόχου τε, 40
ἣ μέγα εἶδος ἀρίστη ἐν ἀθανάτῃσι θεῇσι,
κυδίστην δ' ἄρα μιν τέκετο Κρόνος ἀγκυλομήτης
μήτηρ τε Ῥείη· Ζεὺς δ' ἄφθιτα μήδεα εἰδώς
αἰδοίην ἄλοχον ποιήσατο κέδν' εἰδυῖαν.
τῇ δὲ καὶ αὐτῇ Ζεὺς γλυκὺν ἵμερον ἔμβαλε θυμῷ 45
ἀνδρὶ καταθνητῷ μιχθήμεναι, ὄφρα τάχιστα
μηδ' αὐτὴ βροτέης εὐνῆς ἀποεργμένη εἴη
καί ποτ' ἐπευξαμένη εἴπῃ μετὰ πᾶσι θεοῖσιν
ἡδὺ γελοιήσασα φιλομμειδὴς Ἀφροδίτη
ὥς ῥα θεοὺς συνέμειξε καταθνητῇσι γυναιξί 50
καί τε καταθνητοὺς υἷας τέκον ἀθανάτοισιν,
ὥς τε θεὰς ἀνέμειξε καταθνητοῖς ἀνθρώποις.
Ἀγχίσεω δ' ἄρα οἱ γλυκὺν ἵμερον ἔμβαλε θυμῷ,
ὃς τότ' ἐν ἀκροπόλοις ὄρεσιν πολυπιδάκου Ἴδης
βουκολέεσκεν βοῦς δέμας ἀθανάτοισιν ἐοικώς. 55
τὸν δήπειτα ἰδοῦσα φιλομμειδὴς Ἀφροδίτη
ἠράσατ', ἐκπάγλως δὲ κατὰ φρένας ἵμερος εἷλεν.
ἐς Κύπρον δ' ἐλθοῦσα θυώδεα νηὸν ἔδυνεν

30 πῖαρ Ψ: πεῖαρ M   31 ἐστιν MAQ: ἐστι cett.   36 τε Ψ: τι M
37 τ' (ἐστί) Ψ: om. M   38 εὖτ' ἐθέλῃ M: εὖτ' ἐθέλοι D : εὖτε θέλοι px
39 συνέμειξε West (2003): συνέμιξε codd.   καταθνητῇσι MΘ: καταθνητοῖσι p
42 τέκετο Ψ: τέκε M   46 μιχθήμεναι Mpx: μιγήμεναι D   49 γελοιήσασα
Ψ: γελάσασα M   φιλομμειδής Stephanus (1566): φιλομειδής codd.
50 συνέμειξε West (2003): συνέμιξε Ψ: σύμμιξε M   καταθνητῇσι MΘ: καταθνητοῖσι
p (cf. v. 39)   51 υἷας Faulkner: υἱεῖς codd.   τέκον M: τέκεν Ψ   52 τε
Ψ: δέ M   ἀνέμειξε West (2003): ἀνέμιξε codd.   53 δ' ἄρα οἱ D: δ' ἄρ' οἱ Mpx
57 ἐκπάγλως] ἐκπάγλης L: ἔκπαγλος Köchly (1881)

ΕΙΣ ΑΦΡΟΔΙΤΗΝ

ἐς Πάφον· ἔνθα δέ οἱ τέμενος βωμός τε θυώδης·
ἔνθ' ἥ γ' εἰσελθοῦσα θύρας ἐπέθηκε φαεινάς. 60
ἔνθα δέ μιν Χάριτες λοῦσαν καὶ χρῖσαν ἐλαίῳ
ἀμβρότῳ, οἷα θεοὺς ἐπενήνοθεν αἰὲν ἐόντας,
ἀμβροσίῳ ἑδανῷ, τό ῥά οἱ τεθυωμένον ἦεν.
ἑσσαμένη δ' εὖ πάντα περὶ χροΐ εἵματα καλά
χρυσῷ κοσμηθεῖσα φιλομμειδὴς Ἀφροδίτη 65
σεύατ' ἐπὶ Τροίης προλιποῦσ' εὐώδεα Κύπρον
ὕψι μετὰ νέφεσιν ῥίμφα πρήσσουσα κέλευθον.
Ἴδην δ' ἵκανεν πολυπίδακα, μητέρα θηρῶν,
βῆ δ' ἰθὺς σταθμοῖο δι' οὔρεος· οἱ δὲ μετ' αὐτήν
σαίνοντες πολιοί τε λύκοι χαροποί τε λέοντες 70
ἄρκτοι παρδάλιές τε θοαὶ προκάδων ἀκόρητοι
ᾔισαν· ἡ δ' ὁρόωσα μετὰ φρεσὶ τέρπετο θυμόν
καὶ τοῖς ἐν στήθεσσι βάλ' ἵμερον, οἱ δ' ἅμα πάντες
σύνδυο κοιμήσαντο κατὰ σκιόεντας ἐναύλους.
αὐτὴ δ' ἐς κλισίας εὐποιήτους ἀφίκανε· 75
τὸν δ' εὗρε σταθμοῖσι λελειμμένον οἷον ἀπ' ἄλλων
Ἀγχίσην ἥρωα θεῶν ἄπο κάλλος ἔχοντα.
οἱ δ' ἅμα βουσὶν ἕποντο νομοὺς κάτα ποιήεντας
πάντες, ὁ δὲ σταθμοῖσι λελειμμένος οἷος ἀπ' ἄλλων
πωλεῖτ' ἔνθα καὶ ἔνθα διαπρύσιον κιθαρίζων. 80
στῆ δ' αὐτοῦ προπάροιθε Διὸς θυγάτηρ Ἀφροδίτη
παρθένῳ ἀδμήτῃ μέγεθος καὶ εἶδος ὁμοίη,
μή μιν ταρβήσειεν ἐν ὀφθαλμοῖσι νοήσας.
Ἀγχίσης δ' ὁρόων ἐφράζετο θάμβαινέν τε
εἶδός τε μέγεθός τε καὶ εἵματα σιγαλόεντα. 85
πέπλον μὲν γὰρ ἕεστο φαεινότερον πυρὸς αὐγῆς,
εἶχε δ' ἐπιγναμπτὰς ἕλικας κάλυκάς τε φαεινάς,
ὅρμοι δ' ἀμφ' ἁπαλῇ δειρῇ περικαλλέες ἦσαν
καλοὶ χρύσειοι παμποίκιλοι· ὡς δὲ σελήνη

---

63 ἑδανῷ Clarke (1740): ἑανῷ Θ: ἐανῷ Μp   66 Τροίης Μ: Τροίην Ψ
Κύπρον Ψ: κῆπον Μ   67 νέφεσιν ῥίμφα Allen (1904): νέφεσι ῥίμφα Μ: νεφέεσσι
θοῶς Ψ   68–112 om. Μ   71 παρδάλιες ΘAQV: ποδάλιες ΒΓΡ
72 ᾔισαν Ilgen (1796): ᾖεσ(σ)αν Ψ   76 οἷον L: οἷον ΓD: οἷος ap   77 ἄπο
κάλλος Stephanus (1566): ἀπὸ κάλλος (vel ἀποκάλλος) codd.   79 οἷος L:
οἷος cet.   82 καί ΘPV: τε καί AQBΓ   84 θάμβαινεν p: θαύμαινεν Θ
87 ἐπιγναμπτάς ΒΓx: ἐπὶ γναμπτάς Dp rell.

ΥΜΝΟΣ

στήθεσιν ἀμφ' ἁπαλοῖσιν ἐλάμπετο, θαῦμα ἰδέσθαι. 90
Ἀγχίσην δ' ἔρος εἷλεν, ἔπος δέ μιν ἀντίον ηὔδα·
"χαῖρε ἄνασσ', ἥ τις μακάρων τάδε δώμαθ' ἱκάνεις,
Ἄρτεμις ἢ Λητὼ ἠὲ χρυσῆ Ἀφροδίτη
ἢ Θέμις ἠϋγενὴς ἠὲ γλαυκῶπις Ἀθήνη
ἦ πού τις Χαρίτων δεῦρ' ἤλυθες, αἵ τε θεοῖσι 95
πᾶσιν ἑταιρίζουσι καὶ ἀθάνατοι καλέονται,
ἤ τις νυμφάων αἵ τ' ἄλσεα καλὰ νέμονται,
{ἢ νυμφῶν αἳ καλὸν ὄρος τόδε ναιετάουσι}
καὶ πηγὰς ποταμῶν καὶ πίσεα ποιήεντα.
σοὶ δ' ἐγὼ ἐν σκοπιῇ, περιφαινομένῳ ἐνὶ χώρῳ, 100
βωμὸν ποιήσω, ῥέξω δέ τοι ἱερὰ καλά
ὥρῃσιν πάσῃσι· σὺ δ' εὔφρονα θυμὸν ἔχουσα
δός με μετὰ Τρώεσσιν ἀριπρεπέ' ἔμμεναι ἄνδρα,
ποίει δ' εἰσοπίσω θαλερὸν γόνον, αὐτὰρ ἔμ' αὐτόν
δηρὸν ἔϋ ζώειν καὶ ὁρᾶν φάος ἠελίοιο 105
ὄλβιον ἐν λαοῖς καὶ γήραος οὐδὸν ἱκέσθαι."
τὸν δ' ἠμείβετ' ἔπειτα Διὸς θυγάτηρ Ἀφροδίτη·
"Ἀγχίση, κύδιστε χαμαιγενέων ἀνθρώπων,
οὔ τίς τοι θεός εἰμι· τί μ' ἀθανάτῃσιν ἐΐσκεις;
ἀλλὰ καταθνητή τε, γυνὴ δέ με γείνατο μήτηρ. 110
Ὀτρεὺς δ' ἐστὶ πατὴρ ὀνομάκλυτος, εἴ που ἀκούεις,
ὃς πάσης Φρυγίης εὐτειχήτοιο ἀνάσσει.
γλῶσσαν δ' ὑμετέρην τε καὶ ἡμετέρην σάφα οἶδα·
Τρῳὰς γὰρ μεγάρῳ με τροφὸς τρέφεν, ἡ δὲ διάπρο
σμικρὴν παῖδ' ἀτίταλλε φίλης παρὰ μητρὸς ἑλοῦσα. 115
ὣς δή τοι γλῶσσάν γε καὶ ὑμετέρην εὖ οἶδα.
νῦν δέ μ' ἀνήρπαξε χρυσόρραπις Ἀργειφόντης
ἐκ χοροῦ Ἀρτέμιδος χρυσηλακάτου κελαδεινῆς.
πολλαὶ δὲ νύμφαι καὶ παρθένοι ἀλφεσίβοιαι
παίζομεν, ἀμφὶ δ' ὅμιλος ἀπείριτος ἐστεφάνωτο· 120

93 χρυσῇ codd.: χρυσέη Barnes (1711) 97 om. ET 98 del. Ruhnken (1749) 99 πίσεα Ruhnken (1749): πείσεα (ss. β) L: βήσεα cet. 105 ἔϋ ζώειν West (2003; ἐΰ ζώειν iam Barnes 1711): εὐζώειν codd. 110 τε codd.: γε Gemoll (1886) 111 ὀνομάκλυτος West (2003; ὀνομακλυτός iam Hermann 1806): ὄνομα κλυτός Ψ 113 τε Wolf (1807): om. Ψ 114 τρῳάς Μ: τρωός Ψ 116 γε Hermann (1806): τε codd. 118 χρυσηλακάτου MD: χρυσηλάτου px 120 ἐστεφάνωτο] ἐστεφάνωντο Ε

ΕΙΣ ΑΦΡΟΔΙΤΗΝ

ἔνθεν μ' ἥρπαξε χρυσόρραπις Ἀργειφόντης,
πολλὰ δ' ἐπ' ἤγαγεν ἔργα καταθνητῶν ἀνθρώπων,
πολλὴν δ' ἄκληρόν τε καὶ ἄκτιτον, ἣν διὰ θῆρες
ὠμοφάγοι φοιτῶσι κατὰ σκιόεντας ἐναύλους,
οὐδὲ ποσὶ ψαύειν δόκεον φυσιζόου αἴης· 125
Ἀγχίσεω δέ με φάσκε παραὶ λέχεσιν καλέεσθαι
κουριδίην ἄλοχον, σοὶ δ' ἀγλαὰ τέκνα τεκεῖσθαι.
αὐτὰρ ἐπεὶ δὴ δεῖξε καὶ ἔφρασεν, ἤτοι ὅ γ' αὖτις
ἀθανάτων μετὰ φῦλ' ἀπέβη κρατὺς Ἀργειφόντης·
αὐτὰρ ἐγώ σ' ἱκόμην, κρατερὴ δέ μοι ἔπλετ' ἀνάγκη. 130
ἀλλά σε πρὸς Ζηνὸς γουνάζομαι ἠδὲ τοκήων
ἐσθλῶν· οὐ μὲν γάρ κε κακοὶ τοιόνδε τέκοιεν·
ἀδμήτην μ' ἀγαγὼν καὶ ἀπειρήτην φιλότητος
πατρί τε σῷ δεῖξον καὶ μητέρι κέδν' εἰδυίῃ
σοῖς τε κασιγνήτοις οἵ τοι ὁμόθεν γεγάασιν· 135
οὔ σφιν ἀεικελίη νυὸς ἔσσομαι, ἀλλ' εἰκυῖα.
πέμψαι δ' ἄγγελον ὦκα μετὰ Φρύγας αἰολοπώλους
εἰπεῖν πατρί τ' ἐμῷ καὶ μητέρι κηδομένῃ περ·
οἱ δέ κέ τοι χρυσόν τε ἅλις ἐσθῆτά θ' ὑφαντήν
πέμψουσιν, σὺ δὲ πολλὰ καὶ ἀγλαὰ δέχθαι ἄποινα. 140
ταῦτα δὲ ποιήσας δαίνυ γάμον ἱμερόεντα
τίμιον ἀνθρώποισι καὶ ἀθανάτοισι θεοῖσιν."
ὣς εἰποῦσα θεὰ γλυκὺν ἵμερον ἔμβαλε θυμῷ.
Ἀγχίσην δ' ἔρος εἷλεν, ἔπος τ' ἔφατ' ἔκ τ' ὀνόμαζεν·
"εἰ μὲν θνητή τ' ἐσσί, γυνὴ δέ σε γείνατο μήτηρ, 145
Ὀτρεὺς δ' ἐστὶ πατὴρ ὀνομάκλυτος, ὡς ἀγορεύεις,
ἀθανάτου δὲ ἕκητι διακτόρου ἐνθάδ' ἱκάνεις

---

122 ἐπ' ἤγαγεν Barnes (1711): ἐπήγαγεν codd.   123 ἄκτιτον MDL: ἄκτιστον Ata   ἄτικτον p   125 ψαύειν Ψ: ψαύσειν M   δόκεον La Roche: ἐδόκουν codd.   φυσιζόου L: φυσιζώου cett.   130 post 131 D   132 οὐ μὲν γάρ κε M: οὐ γάρ τε Ψ nisi quod V οὐ γάρ τοι: οὐ γάρ τοι γε Stephanus (1566)   134 εἰδυ(ί)ῃ MDx: εἰδείῃ p   135 σοῖς τε κασιγνήτοις Ψ: δοιῶ τε κασιγνήτω M   136 νυός Θ: νηός M   post 136 add. εἴ τοι (τι) ἀεικελίη γυνὴ ἔσσομαι ἠὲ καὶ οὐκί MΘ: conflavit in unum οὔ σφιν ἀεικελίη γυνὴ ἔσσομαι ἠὲ καὶ οὐκί p   139 οἱ δέ κέ τοι χρυσόν τε Matthiae (1805): οἱ δέ κε χρυσόν τε M: οἱ δέ τε χρυσόν κεν Ψ nisi quod AQ οὐδέ τε χρυσόν κεν   141 δαίνυ Ga: δαίνυν LDp: δαῖνυ M   144 ἔρος Θ: ἔρως Mp   145 θνητή τ' codd.: θνητή γ' Wolf (1807)   δέ σε MDp: τέ σε x   146 ὀνομάκλυτος West (2003): ὀνομακλυτός M: ὄνομα κλυτός Ψ   ἀγορεύεις MΘN: ἀγοράζεις p rell.   147 ἀθανάτου M: ἀθανάτοιο cett.   δὲ ἕκητι Hermann (1806): δ' ἕκητι Ψ praeter N : δ' ἕκατι NM

ΥΜΝΟΣ

Ἑρμέω, ἐμὴ δ' ἄλοχος κεκλήσεαι ἤματα πάντα·
οὔ τις ἔπειτα θεῶν οὔτε θνητῶν ἀνθρώπων
ἐνθάδε με σχήσει πρὶν σῇ φιλότητι μιγῆναι 150
αὐτίκα νῦν, οὐδ' εἴ κεν ἑκηβόλος αὐτὸς Ἀπόλλων
τόξου ἄπ' ἀργυρέου προϊῇ βέλεα στονόεντα·
βουλοίμην κεν ἔπειτα, γύναι εἰκυῖα θεῇσι,
σῆς εὐνῆς ἐπιβὰς δῦναι δόμον Ἄϊδος εἴσω."
ὣς εἰπὼν λάβε χεῖρα· φιλομμειδὴς δ' Ἀφροδίτη 155
ἕρπε μεταστρεφθεῖσα κατ' ὄμματα καλὰ βαλοῦσα
ἐς λέχος εὔστρωτον, ὅθι περ πάρος ἔσκεν ἄνακτι
χλαίνῃσιν μαλακῇς ἐστρωμένον· αὐτὰρ ὕπερθεν
ἄρκτων δέρματ' ἔκειτο βαρυφθόγγων τε λεόντων,
τοὺς αὐτὸς κατέπεφνεν ἐν οὔρεσιν ὑψηλοῖσιν. 160
οἱ δ' ἐπεὶ οὖν λεχέων εὐποιήτων ἐπέβησαν,
κόσμον μέν οἱ πρῶτον ἀπὸ χροὸς εἷλε φαεινόν,
πόρπας τε γναμπτάς θ' ἕλικας κάλυκάς τε καὶ ὅρμους.
λῦσε δέ οἱ ζώνην ἰδὲ εἵματα σιγαλόεντα
ἔκδυε καὶ κατέθηκεν ἐπὶ θρόνου ἀργυροήλου 165
Ἀγχίσης· ὁ δ' ἔπειτα θεῶν ἰότητι καὶ αἴσῃ
ἀθανάτῃ παρέλεκτο θεᾷ βροτός, οὐ σάφα εἰδώς.
ἦμος δ' ἂψ εἰς αὖλιν ἀποκλίνουσι νομῆες
βοῦς τε καὶ ἴφια μῆλα νομῶν ἐξ ἀνθεμοέντων,
τῆμος ἄρ' Ἀγχίσῃ μὲν ἐπὶ γλυκὺν ὕπνον ἔχευεν 170
νήδυμον, αὐτὴ δὲ χροΐ ἕννυτο εἵματα καλά.
ἑσσαμένη δ' εὖ πάντα περὶ χροῒ δῖα θεάων
ἔστη ἄρα κλισίῃ, εὐποιήτοιο μελάθρου
κῦρε κάρη, κάλλος δὲ παρειάων ἀπέλαμπεν
ἄμβροτον, οἷόν τ' ἐστὶν ἰοστεφάνου Κυθερείης. 175
ἐξ ὕπνου τ' ἀνέγειρεν, ἔπος τ' ἔφατ' ἔκ τ' ὀνόμαζεν·
"ὄρσεο Δαρδανίδη· τί νυ νήγρετον ὕπνον ἰαύεις;
καὶ φράσαι εἴ τοι ὁμοίη ἐγὼν ἰνδάλλομαι εἶναι

148 Ἑρμέω Ψ: Ἑρμαίῳ M   152 ἄπ' Barnes 1711: ἀπ' codd.   προϊῇ Gemoll (1886): προίη ΜΘ: προίοι p   156 μεταστρεφθεῖσα] μεταστραφθεῖσα (ss.ε) ΕΤ
157 λέχος Ψ: λέχον M   ἄνακτι Ψ: αὐτή M   158 χλαίνῃσι(ν) Ψ: δίνησι M
159 ἄρκτων Ψ: ἐκ τῶν M   164 ἰδέ Ψ: ἠδ' M   169 ἀνθεμοέντων ΜΘ: ἀνθεμούντων p   170 ἔχευεν Mp: ἔχευε Θ   173 ἄρα codd.: πάρ Stephanus (1566)   εὐποιήτοιο Ψ: εὖ ποιητοῖο M: εὐποιήτου δὲ Ruhnken (1782)
174 κῦρε M: βύρε a: γῦρε bp: ἧρε D   175 ἰοστεφάνου M: ἐϋστεφάνου Ψ
178 εἴ τοι M: εἴ τι Ψ

ΕΙΣ ΑΦΡΟΔΙΤΗΝ

οἵην δή με τὸ πρῶτον ἐν ὀφθαλμοῖσι νόησας."
ὣς φάθ'· ὁ δ' ἐξ ὕπνοιο μάλ' ἐμμαπέως ὑπάκουσεν. 180
ὡς δὲ ἴδεν δειρήν τε καὶ ὄμματα κάλ' Ἀφροδίτης,
τάρβησέν τε καὶ ὄσσε παρακλιδὸν ἔτραπεν ἄλλῃ.
ἂψ δ' αὖτις χλαίνης ἐκαλύψατο καλὰ πρόσωπα,
καί μιν λισσόμενος ἔπεα πτερόεντα προσηύδα·
"αὐτίκα σ' ὡς τὰ πρῶτα θεὰ ἴδον ὀφθαλμοῖσιν 185
ἔγνων ὡς θεὸς ἦσθα· σὺ δ' οὐ νημερτὲς ἔειπες.
ἀλλά σε πρὸς Ζηνὸς γουνάζομαι αἰγιόχοιο,
μή με ζῶντ' ἀμενηνὸν ἐν ἀνθρώποισιν ἐάσῃς
ναίειν, ἀλλ' ἐλέαιρ'· ἐπεὶ οὐ βιοθάλμιος ἀνήρ
γίγνεται ὅς τε θεαῖς εὐνάζεται ἀθανάτῃσιν." 190
τὸν δ' ἠμείβετ' ἔπειτα Διὸς θυγάτηρ Ἀφροδίτη·
"Ἀγχίση, κύδιστε καταθνητῶν ἀνθρώπων,
θάρσει, μηδέ τι σῇσι μετὰ φρεσὶ δείδιθι λίην·
οὐ γάρ τοί τι δέος παθέειν κακὸν ἐξ ἐμέθεν γε
οὐδ' ἄλλων μακάρων, ἐπεὶ ἦ φίλος ἐσσὶ θεοῖσι. 195
σοὶ δ' ἔσται φίλος υἱὸς ὃς ἐν Τρώεσσιν ἀνάξει
καὶ παῖδες παίδεσσι διαμπερὲς ἐκγεγάονται·
τῷ δὲ καὶ Αἰνείας ὄνομ' ἔσσεται οὕνεκά μ' αἰνόν
ἔσχεν ἄχος ἕνεκα βροτοῦ ἀνέρος ἔμπεσον εὐνῇ·
ἀγχίθεοι δὲ μάλιστα καταθνητῶν ἀνθρώπων 200
αἰεὶ ἀφ' ὑμετέρης γενεῆς εἶδός τε φυήν τε.
"ἤτοι μὲν ξανθὸν Γανυμήδεα μητίετα Ζεύς
ἥρπασεν ὃν διὰ κάλλος ἵν' ἀθανάτοισι μετείη
καί τε Διὸς κατὰ δῶμα θεοῖς ἐπιοινοχοεύοι,
θαῦμα ἰδεῖν, πάντεσσι τετιμένος ἀθανάτοισι, 205
χρυσέου ἐκ κρητῆρος ἀφύσσων νέκταρ ἐρυθρόν.

179 οἵην Ψ: οἴκοι M   181 δὲ ἴδεν Ψ: δ' εἶδε M   183 χλαίνης ἐκαλύψατο VB 19: χλαίνη τ' ἐκαλύψατο Mp: χλαίνη τε καλύψατο Θ: χλαίνη ἐκαλύψατο West (2003)   186 ἔειπες Dbp: ἔειπας a (ss. ε): εἴειπες M   189 βιοθάλμιος Θ: βιοφθάλμιος Mp   190 γίγνεται Ψ: γίνεται M   ἀθανάτῃσι(ν)] ἀθανάτοισι(ν) ΠΓ   194 τοί τι Θ: τί τοι M: τι p   195 ἐπεὶ ἦ Allen (1904): ἐπειή codd.   197 ἐκγεγάονται codd.: ἐκγεγαῶτες Ilgen (1796): ἐκγεγάοντες Baumeister (1860)   200 ἀγχίθεοι Barnes (1711): ἄγχι θεοί codd.   202 ἤτοι codd.: ἦ τοι Allen (1904)   203 ἥρπασεν ὃν Hermann (1806): ἥρπασ' ἐόν Dp: ἥρπασ' ἑνὸν x: ἥρπασ' αἰνόν M: ἥρπασε ὃν Matthiae (1805)   204 ἐπιοινοχοεύοι D: ἐπιοινοχοεύειν M: ἐπὶ οἰνοχοεύοι La (E -εύει ss. οι): ἐπ' οἰνοχοεύοι ΠΓ: ἐποινοχοεύοι p   205 τετιμένος Dp: τετιμένον M: τετιμένονος x   206 κρητῆρος M: κρατῆρος Ψ   ἀφύσσων Ψ: ἀφύσσειν M

ΥΜΝΟΣ

Τρῶα δὲ πένθος ἄλαστον ἔχε φρένας, οὐδέ τι εἴδη
ὅππῃ οἱ φίλον υἱὸν ἀνήρπασε θέσπις ἄελλα·
τὸν δήπειτα γόασκε διαμπερὲς ἤματα πάντα.
καί μιν Ζεὺς ἐλέησε, δίδου δέ οἱ υἷος ἄποινα 210
ἵππους ἀρσίποδας, τοί τ' ἀθανάτους φορέουσι.
τούς οἱ δῶρον ἔδωκεν ἔχειν· εἶπέν τε ἕκαστα
Ζηνὸς ἐφημοσύνῃσι διάκτορος Ἀργειφόντης,
ὡς ἔοι ἀθάνατος καὶ ἀγήρως ἶσα θεοῖσιν.
αὐτὰρ ἐπεὶ δὴ Ζηνὸς ὅ γ' ἔκλυεν ἀγγελιάων 215
οὐκέτ' ἔπειτα γόασκε, γεγήθει δὲ φρένας ἔνδον,
γηθόσυνος δ' ἵπποισιν ἀελλοπόδεσσιν ὀχεῖτο.
"ὣς δ' αὖ Τιθωνὸν χρυσόθρονος ἥρπασεν Ἠώς
ὑμετέρης γενεῆς ἐπιείκελον ἀθανάτοισιν.
βῆ δ' ἴμεν αἰτήσουσα κελαινεφέα Κρονίωνα 220
ἀθάνατόν τ' εἶναι καὶ ζώειν ἤματα πάντα·
τῇ δὲ Ζεὺς ἐπένευσε καὶ ἐκρήηνεν ἐέλδωρ.
νηπίη, οὐδ' ἐνόησε μετὰ φρεσὶ πότνια Ἠώς
ἥβην αἰτῆσαι, ξῦσαί τ' ἄπο γῆρας ὀλοιόν.
τὸν δ' ἤτοι εἵως μὲν ἔχεν πολυήρατος ἥβη, 225
Ἠοῖ τερπόμενος χρυσοθρόνῳ ἠριγενείῃ
ναῖε παρ' Ὠκεανοῖο ῥοῇς ἐπὶ πείρασι γαίης·
αὐτὰρ ἐπεὶ πρῶται πολιαὶ κατέχυντο ἔθειραι
καλῆς ἐκ κεφαλῆς εὐηγενέος τε γενείου,
τοῦ δ' ἤτοι εὐνῆς μὲν ἀπείχετο πότνια Ἠώς, 230
αὐτὸν δ' αὖτ' ἀτίταλλεν ἐνὶ μεγάροισιν ἔχουσα
σίτῳ τ' ἀμβροσίῃ τε καὶ εἵματα καλὰ διδοῦσα.
ἀλλ' ὅτε δὴ πάμπαν στυγερὸν κατὰ γῆρας ἔπειγεν
οὐδέ τι κινῆσαι μελέων δύνατ' οὐδ' ἀναεῖραι,
ἥδε δέ οἱ κατὰ θυμὸν ἀρίστη φαίνετο βουλή· 235
ἐν θαλάμῳ κατέθηκε, θύρας δ' ἐπέθηκε φαεινάς.
τοῦ δ' ἤτοι φωνὴ ῥεῖ ἄσπετος, οὐδέ τι κίκυς

207 τρῶα MD*bp*: τρῶς *a* εἴδη Faulkner: ᾔδει codd. 212 τε codd.: δέ Wolf (1807) 214 ἀγήρως M*px*: ἀγήραος D ἶσα θεοῖσιν M (*a* marg.): ἤματα πάντα D*bp* 218 χρυσόθρονος MΘ: χρυσόθρονον *p* 224 ἄπο γῆρας Hermann (1806): ἀπὸ γήρας MD*p*: ἀπογήρας *x* 225 δ' ἤτοι MBΓΠ: δή τοι cet. 228 κατέχυντο Ψ: κατέχοιντο M 229 εὐηγενέος M: εὐγενέος Ψ: καὶ εὐγενέος Chalc. 230 δ' ἤτοι Hermann (1806): δή τοι codd.: ἦ τοι Allen (1904) 237 δ' ἤτοι Hermann (1806): δή τοι M*x*: δή τι D: δ' οὗτοι *p*: ἦ τοι Allen (1904) ῥεῖ MD*a*: ῥεῖ' *bp*

ΕΙΣ ΑΦΡΟΔΙΤΗΝ

ἔσθ᾽ οἵη πάρος ἔσκεν ἐνὶ γναμπτοῖσι μέλεσσιν.
"οὐκ ἂν ἐγώ γε σὲ τοῖον ἐν ἀθανάτοισιν ἑλοίμην
ἀθάνατόν τ᾽ εἶναι καὶ ζώειν ἤματα πάντα. 240
ἀλλ᾽ εἰ μὲν τοιοῦτος ἐὼν εἶδός τε δέμας τε
ζώοις, ἡμέτερός τε πόσις κεκλημένος εἴης,
οὐκ ἂν ἔπειτά μ᾽ ἄχος πυκινὰς φρένας ἀμφικαλύπτοι.
νῦν δέ σε μὲν τάχα γῆρας ὁμοίιον ἀμφικαλύψει
νηλειές, τό τ᾽ ἔπειτα παρίσταται ἀνθρώποισιν, 245
οὐλόμενον καματηρόν, ὅ τε στυγέουσι θεοί περ.
αὐτὰρ ἐμοὶ μέγ᾽ ὄνειδος ἐν ἀθανάτοισι θεοῖσιν
ἔσσεται ἤματα πάντα διαμπερὲς εἵνεκα σεῖο,
οἳ πρὶν ἐμοὺς ὀάρους καὶ μήτιας, αἷς ποτε πάντας
ἀθανάτους συνέμειξα καταθνητῇσι γυναιξί, 250
τάρβεσκον· πάντας γὰρ ἐμὸν δάμνασκε νόημα.
νῦν δὲ δὴ οὐκέτι μοι στόμα τλήσεται ἐξονομῆναι
τοῦτο μετ᾽ ἀθανάτοισιν, ἐπεὶ μάλα πολλὸν ἀάσθην
σχέτλιον οὐκ ὀνομαστόν, ἀπεπλάγχθην δὲ νόοιο,
παῖδα δ᾽ ὑπὸ ζώνῃ ἐθέμην βροτῷ εὐνηθεῖσα. 255
"τὸν μέν, ἐπὴν δὴ πρῶτον ἴδῃ φάος ἠελίοιο,
νύμφαι μιν θρέψουσιν ὀρεσκῷοι βαθύκολποι,
αἳ τόδε ναιετάουσιν ὄρος μέγα τε ζάθεόν τε·
αἵ ῥ᾽ οὔτε θνητοῖς οὔτ᾽ ἀθανάτοισιν ἕπονται·
δηρὸν μὲν ζώουσι καὶ ἄμβροτον εἶδαρ ἔδουσιν, 260
καί τε μετ᾽ ἀθανάτοισι καλὸν χορὸν ἐρρώσαντο.
τῇσι δὲ Σιληνοί τε καὶ εὔσκοπος Ἀργειφόντης
μίσγοντ᾽ ἐν φιλότητι μυχῷ σπείων ἐροέντων.
τῇσι δ᾽ ἅμ᾽ ἢ ἐλάται ἠὲ δρύες ὑψικάρηνοι
γεινομένῃσιν ἔφυσαν ἐπὶ χθονὶ βωτιανείρῃ· 265
καλαὶ τηλεθάουσαι ἐν οὔρεσιν ὑψηλοῖσιν
ἑστᾶσ᾽ ἠλίβατοι, τεμένεα δέ ἑ κικλήσκουσιν

241 τοιοῦτος Ψ: τοῖος M   244 τάχα γῆρας Map: κατὰ γῆρας Db (b ss. τάχα)   245 τό τ᾽ p: τό γ᾽ MΘ, nisi quod Π τό σ᾽   247 ἐν M: μετ᾽ Ψ   250 συνέμειξα West (2003): συνέμιξα codd. nisi quod a συνέμιξας καταθνητῆσι Ψ: καταθνητοῖσι M   252 στόμα τλήσεται Matthiae (1800): στοναχήσεται codd.: στόματ᾽ ἔσσεται Clarke (1740): στόμα χείσεται Martin (1605)   254 ὀνομαστόν Martin (1605): ὀνότατον codd.: ὀνοταστόν Clarke (1740)   255 ζώνῃ Ψ: ζώνην M   256 ἐπὴν Ψ: ἐπεί M   262 σιληνοί MDb: σειληνοί p: σεληνοί a   267 ἑστᾶσ᾽ Mp: ἕστασ᾽ Θ   τεμένεα Faulkner: τεμένη codd.

ΥΜΝΟΣ

ἀθανάτων· τὰς δ' οὔ τι βροτοὶ κείρουσι σιδήρῳ.
ἀλλ' ὅτε κεν δὴ μοῖρα παρεστήκῃ θανάτοιο
ἀζάνεται μὲν πρῶτον ἐπὶ χθονὶ δένδρεα καλά, 270
φλοιὸς δ' ἀμφιπεριφθινύθει, πίπτουσι δ' ἄπ' ὄζοι,
τῶν δέ θ' ὁμοῦ ψυχὴ λείπει φάος ἠελίοιο.
αἱ μὲν ἐμὸν θρέψουσι παρὰ σφίσιν υἱὸν ἔχουσαι.
"τὸν μὲν ἐπὴν δὴ πρῶτον ἕλῃ πολυήρατος ἥβη
ἄξουσίν τοι δεῦρο θεαί, δείξουσί τε παῖδα. 275
{σοὶ δ' ἐγώ, ὄφρα τοι αὖ τὰ μετὰ φρεσὶ πάντα διέλθω,
ἐς πέμπτον ἔτος αὖτις ἐλεύσομαι υἱὸν ἄγουσα.}
τὸν μὲν ἐπὴν δὴ πρῶτον ἴδῃς θάλος ὀφθαλμοῖσι,
γηθήσεις ὁρόων· μάλα γὰρ θεοείκελος ἔσται·
ἄξεις δ' αὐτίκα μιν ποτὶ Ἴλιον ἠνεμόεσσαν. 280
ἢν δέ τις εἴρηταί σε καταθνητῶν ἀνθρώπων
ἥ τις σοὶ φίλον υἱὸν ὑπὸ ζώνῃ θέτο μήτηρ,
τῷ δὲ σὺ μυθεῖσθαι μεμνημένος ὥς σε κελεύω·
φάσθαι τοι νύμφης καλυκώπιδος ἔκγονον εἶναι
αἳ τόδε ναιετάουσιν ὄρος καταειμένον ὕλῃ. 285
εἰ δέ κεν ἐξείπῃς καὶ ἐπεύξεαι ἄφρονι θυμῷ
ἐν φιλότητι μιγῆναι ἐϋστεφάνῳ Κυθερείῃ,
Ζεύς σε χολωσάμενος βαλέει ψολόεντι κεραυνῷ.
εἴρηταί τοι πάντα· σὺ δὲ φρεσὶ σῇσι νοήσας
ἴσχεο μηδ' ὀνόμαινε, θεῶν δ' ἐποπίζεο μῆνιν." 290
ὣς εἰποῦσ' ἤϊξε πρὸς οὐρανὸν ἠνεμόεντα.
χαῖρε θεὰ Κύπροιο ἐϋκτιμένης μεδέουσα·
σέο δ' ἐγὼ ἀρξάμενος μεταβήσομαι ἄλλον ἐς ὕμνον.

---

268 οὔ τι Μx: οὔτοι Dp   269 παρεστήκῃ Stephanus (1566): παρεστήκει ΜΘ: παρεστήκοι p   271 ἄπ' ὄζοι a (ex ἄπο ὄζοι correctum): ἄποζοι M: ἀπ' ὄζοι Ψ   272 δέ θ' Hermann (1806): δέ χ' codd.   λείπει codd.: λείποι Allen (1936)   275 τοι M: σοι Ψ   276–7 del. Hermann (1806)   276 ὄφρα τοι αὖ τά Kamerbeek (1967): ὄφρα ταῦτα codd.: ὄφρα κε ταῦτα Barnes (1711)   279 γηθήσεις ΜΘ: γηθήσαις p   280 ἄξεις ΜΘ: ἄξαις p   μιν Hermann (1806): νιν Ψ: νῦν M   281 εἴρηται] εἰρήσεται T   283 τῷ δὲ σύ QR₂: τῷδε σύ Ψ rell.: τῷδέ σοι M   284 φάσθαι Matthiae (1800): φασίν codd.   ἔκγονον Barnes (1711): ἔγγονον codd.   290 ὀνόμαινε Hermann (1806): ὀνόμηνε codd.   291 ἠνεμόεντα codd.: ἀστερόεντα Ruhnken   293 σέο West (2003): σεῦ codd.   ἄλλον ἐς ὕμνον] ἐς ἄλλον ὕμνον D

Commentary

Title. M has τοῦ αὐτοῦ ὁμήρου ὕμνοι εἰς ἀφροδίτην; for the plural ὕμνοι see N. Richardson (1974), 136 on the similar title in *Dem*. He places a full stop after ὕμνοι; *contra* Bücheler (1869), who suggested this might indicate that there was more than one *Hymn* to Demeter. Such titles also precede *Herm.*, *Apoll.*, and hymns of the later poets Callimachus, Orpheus, and Proclus. In the case of *Aphr.* the plural could plausibly refer to both this and the subsequent *Hy.* 6, which is also to Aphrodite. M, however, provides the separate heading τοῦ αὐτοῦ εἰς τὴν αὐτὴν ἀφροδίτην for *Hy.* 6 and, given the frequency of this formula as a title, N. Richardson's punctuation should also be followed here. The *p* MSS transmit the singular ὕμνος εἰς ἀφροδίτην (note that there is a stop after the singular ὕμνος in R₁).

1–44. The *pars epica* of the hymn, the story of the seduction of the mortal Anchises by the goddess Aphrodite and the engendering of Aeneas, is not introduced until v. 45. What precedes, a 'prologue' comprising attributive statements and events, can be divided into three main sections: (A) 1–6: invocation to the Muse and expansion upon Aphrodite's universal power, (B) 7–33: digression upon Athena, Artemis and Hestia, who alone escape Aphrodite's subjugation, and (C) 34–44: the point which the previous two sections have been building up to, that even Zeus, the greatest of gods, falls under Aphrodite's power; included is a short digression on Hera as Zeus' wife.

This lead-up to the main narrative is longer than that in any of the other major *Hymns* (the narrative begins in *Dem.* at v. 2, in *Herm.* at v. 3 and, more similarly delayed, in *Apoll.* at v. 30) and is certainly unique in structure. There is on a broad level an element of the *Priamel* in this first section, singling out 'one point of interest by contrast and comparison' (Race 1982, 7; see also generally on the *Priamel* Dodds 1960, 190 and West 1978, 269): (A) is a list of those affected by Aphrodite's power, (B) a contrasting list of exceptions to the rule, acting as a foil (cf. Porter 1949, 253), and (C) the rise to the climax or 'point of interest' (cf. Janko 1981*a*, 19). But such a schema is only partially applicable to this section and implies a straightforwardness which is not present. The revelation at v. 36 that Zeus himself is also a victim of Aphrodite is a climax somewhat undermined by the brief encomium to Hera that follows, just as the apparent climax of v. 6 πᾶσιν δ' ἔργα ... is swept away by τρισσὰς δ' οὐ δύναται of v. 7. The opening section is studded with false clues and the true point of climax comes only at v. 45 when the poet emphatically reveals what the thread of his narrative will be: τῇ δὲ καὶ αὐτῇ Ζεὺς γλυκὺν ἵμερον ἔμβαλε θυμῷ. There is a certain roughness of composition felt in these first 44 lines (cf. on *Aphr.* 10 ἀγλαὰ ἔργα *et passim*), and one can hardly call this elegant composition, but by using traditional material in a distinctive way the poet has effected with some skill the 'manipulation of the audience's expectations' (Janko 1981*a*, 19).

1–6 Proem. The hymn is remarkable from the outset, and the structure of the proem itself sets *Aphr.* apart from the rest of the Homeric corpus. On the surface it appears to follow hymnic and epic convention: an invocation to the Muse(s) is contained in nine of the thirty-one other surviving openings of the *Hymns* (cf. *Herm.*, *Hys.* 9, 14, 17, 19, 20, 31, 32, 33) as well as the openings of the non-hymnic *Il.*, *Od.*, *Thebais*, and *Epigoni* (see Lenz 1980, 21 ff., Race 1992, 20, Janko 1981*a*, 11). There are, however, substantial departures from the norm in this seemingly traditional embarkation.

It is unusual that in *Aphr.* the name of the goddess does not appear until the end of the first line, and not until after the initial verb (the latter is a trait shared only with *Apoll.* 1 μνήσομαι οὐδὲ λάθωμαι Ἀπόλλωνος; see Janko 1981*a*, 10 and cf. Furley i. 54). With the exception of *Hys.* 19 and 33 (which employ ἀμφί, followed by the name of the god's more prestigious father in the genitive), the name of the deity who is to be the subject of the poem is the first word in each of the *Hymns* which begins with an invocation to the Muse(s). On the first word of an epic poem acting as an announcement of its subject see West (1966*a*), 151 and N. Richardson (1974), 136, who

Lines 1-6—1

both list archaic parallels; a later example is Call. *Hy.* 3. In contrast, the name of the divinity being celebrated is always delayed in the later hymns of Proclus (cf. Devlin 1994, 35). Elsewhere in early poetry, there is a delay of Zeus' name until the second line after an invocation to the Muses in *Op.* 1–2; nor is such postponement foreign to lyric hymns (see the texts in Furley ii. 2. 6, 4. 5, 6. 2, 7. 1 etc.).

The suspended mention in *Aphr.* is partially explained on metrical grounds. In the overwhelming majority of its appearances, the name Ἀφροδίτη occupies the final place in the line; every instance in *Aphr.* is found there (cf. 1, 9, 17, 21, 34, 49, 56, 65, 81, 93, 107, 155, 181, 191) and of over 80 appearances of the name in Homer, Hesiod, and the *Hymns*, it is at a different position in the line only twice, *Il.* 9. 389 (Ἀφροδίτη ⌣⌣4—) and *Od.* 20. 73 (Ἀφροδίτη ⌣⌣2—). Nonetheless, the poet could have been more direct in introducing his divinity: *Hy.* 6 begins with an adjective referring to the goddess (αἰδοίην χρυσοστέφανον καλὴν Ἀφροδίτην) while *Hy.* 10 starts with an alternative epiclesis (Κυπρογενῆ Κυθέρειαν ἀείσομαι). Furthermore, in *Aphr.* it is not the goddess who is the object of song in the accusative, but rather her ἔργα (see on *Aphr.* 1 ἔργα).

The transition from introduction to expansion is made with a relative clause, a traditional device used in hymns to introduce a god's powers or general prestige; cf. *Apoll.* 2 ὅν τε θεοὶ κατὰ δῶμα (see Devlin 1994, 35, N. Richardson 1974, 135–6, Norden 1913, 168 ff.). The device is also found in Pindar, of Hora at *N.* 8. 1–2 Ὥρα πότνια, κάρυξ Ἀφροδίτας ἀμβροσιᾶν φιλοτάτων | ἅ τε παρθενηίοις παίδων τ' ἐφίζοισα γλεφάροις, or Hestia at *N.* 11. 1 Παῖ Ῥέας, ἅ τε πρυτανεῖα λέλογχας, Ἑστία etc.; or for expansion upon a victor, such as Psaumis at *O.* 5. 4. At *Dem.* 2 ἣν Ἀϊδωνεύς and *Herm.* 3 ὃν τέκε Μαῖα the relative leads directly into the main narrative of the hymn (for the relative introducing a narrative digression in epic see *Il.* 2. 547 and *Th.* 22; cf. West 1966*a*, 161 ad loc.).

1 Μοῦσά μοι ἔννεπε ἔργα: for the vocative Μοῦσα as the first word in the poem cf. *Op.* 1–2 Μοῦσαι . . . | . . . ἐννέπετε, Hippon. fr. 128. 1 Μοῦσά μοι Εὐρυμεδοντιάδεα . . . | . . . | ἔννεφ', Simon. *IEG* 92. 1 Μοῦσά μοι Ἀλκμήνης and *PMG* 938e. 1 Μοῖσά μοι. Cf. also the genitive Μουσάων at *Th.* 1 and the vocative at Ar. *Pax.* 775, *Ran.* 674. The striking resemblance of this opening line to *Od.* 1. 1 ἄνδρα μοι ἔννεπε

Μοῦσα πολύτροπον has focused the attention of previous commentators (cf. Gemoll 1886, 261, AH 352). A glance, however, at Hesiod reveals a similar formula, *Th.* 114 ταῦτά μοι ἔσπετε Μοῦσαι, and invocations of the Muse(s) to tell the poet (μοι) of events or facts are not uncommon in Homer; cf. ἔσπετε νῦν μοι Μοῦσαι at *Il.* 2. 484, 11. 218, 14. 508 and 16. 112, or σύ μοι ἔννεπε Μοῦσα at 2. 761. Cf. also *Hy.* 19. 1 ἀμφί μοι . . . ἔννεπε Μοῦσα.

For a comparable invocation of the Muse(s) in later literature cf. A.R. 4. 1–2 Αὐτὴ νῦν κάματόν γε, θεά, καὶ δήνεα κούρης | Κολχίδος ἔννεπε Μοῦσα. Callimachus probably began the fourth book of his *Aitia* Μοῦ]σαί μοι (fr. 86. 1). Plutarch transmits a possible opening line of the *Little Iliad*, Μοῦσά μοι ἔννεπε κεῖνα (*Sept. Sap. Conv.* 154 A), the original of which might have read ἔννεπε ἔργα after *Aphr.* (see West 1967, 439 and Bernabé, who follows his conjecture). In the fifth century AD, the Empress Eudocia may have had this line in mind at *de Martyrio Sancti Cypriani* 30 ἔννεπέ μοι τεὰ ἔργα. See also [Opp.] *C.* 3. 461, where ἔννεπέ μοι κἀκεῖνα πολύθροε Μοῦσα λιγεῖα follows from οἰωνούς τε δόλοισιν; cf. *Aphr.* 4.

ἔννεπε: Harder (*LfgrE* s.v) comments that this verb is used 'almost always of things which are of more than ordinary importance to the speaker and/or audience, and may imply a certain solemnity'. It is most common for the *Hymns* to begin with some form of ἀείδω, with a form of ἐννέπω found at the beginning of only *Aphr.* and *Hys.* 19, 32, 33; but there does not seem to be any particular pattern to its use, such as before a long poem/narrative, attributive section, etc. See Risch (1985), and cf. West (1966*a*), 190, S. West, *OC* i. 233, Campbell (1994), 7.

ἔργα . . . Ἀφροδίτης: the ἔργα of Aphrodite are the direct subject of the poet rather than the goddess herself (cf. Podbielski 1971, 18 ff., VE 9). The word occurs no less than seven times in the first 21 lines of the poem (1, 6, 9, 10, 11, 15, 21) and its prominence should not be dismissed as careless; by echoing v. 1 ἔργα πολυχρύσου Ἀφροδίτης/ ἐϋστεφάνου Κυθερείης the poet both emphasizes his central theme and demarcates the opening section (Porter 1949, 252). For more on the structural role of repeated ἔργον in *Aphr.* see below on 7–33; on repetition in early hexameter poetry see also Abramowicz (1972), 223 ff.

To suggest with van Groningen (1958), 105 that ἔργα πολυχρύσου

Ἀφροδίτης 'ne résume pas du tout le corps de l'ouvrage: la visite de la déesse chez Anchise ne fait certainement pas partie de ses ἔργα' is to attach too narrow a semantic field to the phrase. It should be understood to carry both a literal sense 'the works performed by Aphrodite' and a wider one 'sexual love'; cf *Op.* 521 οὔ πω ἔργ' εἰδυῖα πολυχρύσου Ἀφροδίτης: a young girl who has not been married does not yet know of the works of Aphrodite, i.e. sexual matters (see Podbielski 1971, 19). 'Similarly, just as by metonymy, the "works of Ares" mean "war"' (Clay 1989, 156); cf. *Aphr.* 10 ἔργον Ἄρηος.

Aphrodite's 'works' are connected with marriage at *Il.* 5. 429 ἀλλὰ σύ γ' ἱμερόεντα μετέρχεο ἔργα γάμοιο. See mention of her ἔργα also at [Hes.] fr. 124. 2 νοσφιδίων ἔργων πέρι Κύπριδος, A. A. 1207 τέκνων εἰς ἔργον, and Theoc. *Ep.* 4. 4 Κύπριδος ἔργα; similarly Musae. 141, *AP* 7. 221 (Anon.) and Philip of Thessalonica *AP* 9. 416. Cf. later Ant. Lib. *Met.* 21. 1. 5: Polyphonte is made to mate with a bear as punishment for initially spurning the ἔργα τῆς Ἀφροδίτης. Preston (1916), 33 discusses the erotic sense of *opus* in Latin poetry.

Sexual union, specifically that between gods and mortals, applies as a theme to the entire hymn. That ἔργα πολυχρύσου Ἀφροδίτης is generally understood to mean this, as well as the more literal 'works' performed by Aphrodite in her anthropomorphic form, allows for the delicate irony which will permeate the main narrative of the poem; Aphrodite will be conquered by her own devices!

πολυχρύσου: here and at *Aphr.* 9, 'very/brilliantly golden'. The epithet is never attached to Aphrodite in Homer but always used of cities or men: cf. πολυχρύσοιο Μυκήνης 'of much gold/wealthy' 3× (*Il.* 7. 180, 11. 46, *Od.* 3. 304; see Hainsworth 1993, 223, S. West, *OC* i. 180); it is used at *Il.* 18. 289 of Troy, and at *Il.* 10. 315 of Dolon to indicate his wealth (cf. Archil. fr. 19. 1 of King Gyges). For Aphrodite, Homer has only χρυσέη, *Il.* 3. 64 etc. (cf. West 1978, 288), despite the metrically equivalent formula Διὸς κούρης Ἀφροδίτης at 20. 105 (cf. Janko 1982, 26). Elsewhere in the *Hymns* there is the similar doublet φιλοστεφάνου Ἀφροδίτης at *Dem.* 102 (cf. N. Richardson 1974, 182). Only in Hesiod is the epithet used of Aphrodite; πολυχρύσου Ἀφροδίτης is found at *Op.* 521 (on the possible link between this and *Aphr.* 1/9 ἔργα πολυχρύσου Ἀφροδίτης see Introd., pp. 36–8), *Th.* 980, *Sc.* 8, 47, [Hes.] frr. 185. 17, 253. 3; remarkably, the goddess is called πολύχρυσος nowhere else in Greek poetry. Callimachus is the only other poet to apply the term to a god; he uses it of Apollo at *Hy.* 2. 34 πολύχρυσος γὰρ Ἀπόλλων, in a passage where the god is said to be clothed in gold (cf. Williams 1978, 39, 41), just as Aphrodite will be later in this hymn. It is used elsewhere of lovers at the anonymous *AP* 6. 283 πολυχρύσοις ἐπ' ἐρασταῖς, probably with the sense of 'dear'. See in Latin *Venus aurea* at Verg. *A.* 10. 16. In modern Greek one can still address a loved one as χρυσέ/χρυσή μου.

Aeschylus uses the epithet repeatedly in the parodos of the *Persae* (3, 5, 45, 53) to characterize the oriental lavishness of the Persians (cf. Hall 1996, 107 n. 3) and the word may carry an eastern flavour here as well; πολύχρυσος foreshadows Aphrodite's adornment with gold at *Aphr.* 65 χρυσῷ κοσμηθεῖσα etc., which has clear eastern parallels (see on *Aphr.* 81–90). Cf. also the description of her brightly shining jewellery at *Aphr.* 84 ff. (in particular vv. 88–9 ὅρμοι ...| καλοὶ χρύσειοι παμποίκιλοι) and her undressing at *Aphr.* 162–5.

2–6. Aphrodite is traditionally said to touch all with her power. Cf. the words of Hera at *Il.* 14. 198–9 δός νύν μοι φιλότητα καὶ ἵμερον ᾧ τε σὺ πάντας | δαμνᾷ ἀθανάτους ἠδὲ θνητοὺς ἀνθρώπους; also *Th.* 121–2 (cf. Janko 1992, 180), E. *Hipp.* 447–61, and later Q.S. 13. 402 (see below on *Aphr.* 3 ἐδαμάσσατο). Similarly, in Latin poetry cf. Lucr. 1. 19 *omnibus incutiens blandum per pectora amorem* (see Bailey 1947, ii. 589) and Ov. *Met.* 5. 366 *illa, quibus superas omnes, cape tela, Cupido* (see Barchiesi 1999, 115).

For the idea expressed in a list such as this one see E. *Hipp.* 1268–81, where the extent of Eros' power is detailed, and Barrett's note there (1964, 394): '"All nature" is often expressed by such lists.' See also S. fr. 941. 9–17. In Hellenistic literature, Eros views his domain of both land and sea at A.R. 3. 159–63 (see Campbell 1994, 142 ad loc., 123 on 3. 135–41). Elsewhere in early epic, however, Aphrodite's sphere of influence is limited to gods and humans (cf. West 1966a, 225 on *Th.* 204 ff.); here and in later literature (see above on E. *Hipp.* 1268–81, S. fr. 941, Lucr. 1. 1 ff.) it is extended also to include animals (see on *Aphr.* 69–74).

The passage is fluidly structured with the pairing of contrasting groups in vv. 2–5; Aphrodite has power over (i) gods and men, (ii) birds and beasts, and (iii) the creatures of both land and sea. Verse 6 then powerfully sums up the intended message with πᾶσιν at the beginning of the verse followed by 'explanatory' δέ (used here where one would expect γάρ; cf. Denniston 1954, 169, VE 11). Exceptions will soon be presented but for now the point has been established; the works of Aphrodite are a concern to all. For πᾶσιν in the first position of the line see *Il.* 2. 285, 5. 29, *Od.* 1. 71, 7. 180 etc.

Κύπριδος, ἥ τε θεοῖσιν: see the similar relative clause expansion upon a god at *Il.* 15. 144 Ἶρίν θ', ἥ τε θεοῖσι; also 2. 669 ἐκ Διὸς ὅς τε θεοῖσι and 7. 45 βουλήν, ἥ ῥα θεοῖσιν (cf. on *Aphr.* 1–6). On the 'gnomic' or 'omnitemporal' quality conveyed to the aorist ὦρσε by ἥ τε see Ruijgh (1971), 906 and Faulkner (2006).

There are two cases for later imitation of this line: most strikingly Mosch. *Eur.* 76 Κύπριδος, ἢ μούνη δύναται καὶ Ζῆνα δαμάσσαι (cf. Campbell 1991, 80), but also A.R. 1. 803 Κύπριδος, ἥ τέ σφιν θυμοφθόρον ἔμβαλεν ἄτην (see *Il.* 4. 444 ἥ σφιν . . . ἔμβαλε; cf. Campbell 1981, 15). Cf. also Call. *Hy.* 4. 308 Κύπριδος ἀρχαίης ἀριήκοον, ἥν ποτε Θησεύς.

Κύπριδος: the name is derived from Κύπρος (cf. *Dictionnaire* s.v.), the birthplace of Aphrodite; cf. *Th.* 199 Κυπρογενέα δ' ὅτι γέντο περικλύστῳ ἐνὶ Κύπρῳ (see West 1966a, 224). One would expect the name to be oxytone (Κυπρίς), like Λεσβίς from Λέσβος. It might be supposed that the barytone form goes back to Aeolic singers and is due to the recessive accent of the Lesbian dialect (see Wack. ii. 1166, Buck 1955, 85); the accusative form Κύπριν, proper to a barytone -ιδ-stem, is transmitted at *Il.* 5. 330 (although there emendable to Κύπριδ'), but otherwise not attested until the classical period ([A.] *PV* 650 etc.). Κύπρις appears five times in *Il.* 5 (330, 422, 458, 760, 883) but nowhere else in Homer (cf. Kirk 1990, 94 ff., Lorimer 1950, 442). The name is more common in later poetry; Apollonius goes so far as to use only Κύπρις, to the exclusion of the name Ἀφροδίτη (cf. Faerber 1932, 69, Campbell 1994, 11). For more on Aphrodite's Cyprian connections and her sanctuary and cult at Paphos, see on *Aphr.* 58–9.

The genitive Κύπριδος is not in Homer but cf. *Il.* 5. 458, 883 for Κύπριδα at line-beginning. For Κύπριδος at the first position in the line cf. Stesich. fr. 223. 3, B. *Dith.* 17. 10, *Epin.* 5. 175, *Enc.* 20B. 8 etc. Later, it is relatively common initially in A.R. (1. 615, 803, 2. 424, etc.); see also Call. fr. 110. 56, Posidipp. 119. 2, 126. 2, 141. 1 AB.

ἐπὶ γλυκὺν ἵμερον ὦρσε: the accusative γλυκὺν ἵμερον appears once in Homer at *Il.* 3. 139 within the formula γλυκὺν ἵμερον ἔμβαλε θυμῷ (cf. on *Aphr.* 45), and the nominative γλυκὺς ἵμερος three times, at *Il.* 3. 446, 14. 328, *Od.* 22. 500. See ἵμερον ὦρσε (5–6×) at *Il.* 23. 14 and *Od.* 23. 144 but never with γλυκύν. For tmesis of ἐπόρνυμι cf. *Il.* 9. 539 ὦρσεν ἔπι, *Od.* 5. 366, 385 ὦρσε δ' ἐπί, *Od.* 21. 100 ἐπὶ δ' ὤρνυε; Hesiod (*Th.* 523) has ἐπ' αἰετὸν ὦρσε. See also ὑφ' ἵμερον ὦρσε at *Il.* 23. 108 etc. The likeliest source of the tmesis ἐπί . . . ὦρσε seems to be the metrically equivalent formula ἐπὶ γλυκὺν ὕπνον ἔχευεν at *Od.* 2. 395 (appearing also at *Aphr.* 170), in which the poet has substituted ἵμερον ὦρσε; cf. also *Od.* 23. 144 ἐν δέ σφισιν ἵμερον ὦρσε. Ideas of love and sleep are elsewhere mixed; in *Th.* 121 λυσιμελής is an epithet of Eros; it is used of sleep in Homer (see West 1966a, 196–7).

Apollonius Rhodius is again a possible imitator at 1. 850 Κύπρις γὰρ ἐπὶ γλυκὺν ἵμερον ὦρσεν (cf. Campbell 1981, 16). As the single women of Lemnos entertain the Argonauts in their homes the sexual implications are clear: Aphrodite is stirring up desire of the most sexual kind (cf. the Lemnian episode in *Orph. A.* 477 and a description of Medea falling in love later in the same poem at v. 868). The first line of Moschus' *Eur.* is also reminiscent of this verse, Εὐρώπῃ ποτὲ Κύπρις ἐπὶ γλυκὺν ἧκεν ὄνειρον.

3 καί τ': here emphatically 'and also', as at 36 and 38, where Aphrodite conquers 'even Zeus' with her powers. The particle combination καί τε is common in *Aphr.*, appearing seven times at line-beginning (30, 36, 38, 51, 204, 261). Denniston (1954), 528 suggests that 'the great majority of passages in which τε is coupled with another particle contain general propositions, or describe habitual action' (cf. also Monro 1891, 301 ff.). The particle combination here signals the 'gnomic' or 'omnitemporal' aspect of the aorist ἐδαμάσσατο (see Ruijgh 1971, 23, 273, 763 ff., 913, Faulkner 2006). See also *Od.* 17. 485 for καί τε introducing a general truth which is described in present tense verbs (cf. Russo, *OC* iii. 42).

ἐδαμάσσατο: the 'gnomic' use of the verb here makes the augmented form preferable; 'gnomic' aorists rarely omit the augment in early epic (see West 1978, 243; there are only a few examples guaranteed by metre in Hesiod and later authors). It is often difficult to choose between the augmented or unaugmented form of aorists in Homer, where the MSS frequently differ (see *Grammaire*, i. 481–2); here all MSS elide τ' ἐδαμάσσατο. Cf. *Od.* 9. 516 of Polyphemus ἐπεί μ' ἐδαμάσσατο οἴνῳ (4⏑⏑5⏑⏑6×), where the scarcity of word-division after the fourth trochee (Hermann's Bridge) makes the elision of με more probable.

Used elsewhere of controlling horses (*Il.* 10. 403 etc.) and conquering in battle (*Il.* 1. 61 etc.), the verb also carries sexual undertones in Homer: see *Il.* 3. 301 ἄλοχοι δ' ἄλλοισι δαμεῖεν, the wives of the defeated are subdued by other men (see Kirk 1985, 308 'this might seem to imply rape rather than capture and concubinage, but probably both are envisaged'); less violently, see Thetis speaking of her marriage to Peleus at *Il.* 18. 432–3 ἐκ μέν μ' ἀλλάων ἁλιάων ἀνδρὶ δάμασσεν | ... καὶ ἔτλην ἀνέρος εὐνήν; or the erotic effect of Hera upon Zeus at 14. 315–16 οὐ γάρ πώ ποτέ μ' ὧδε θεᾶς ἔρος οὐδὲ γυναικὸς | θυμὸν ἐνὶ στήθεσσι περιπροχυθεὶς ἐδάμασσεν; also 14. 198–9 (quoted above on *Aphr.* 2–6). Love is connected with taming later in *Aphr.* at vv. 17 and 251 (see on *Aphr.* 17 for further examples).

Although intending no erotic context, Proclus produces a line with similarities to this one at *Hy.* 7. 8 καὶ χθονίων δαμάσασα θεημάχα φῦλα Γιγάντων. See also Q.S. 13. 402–3 Κύπρις ἥ περ ἁπάντων | ἀθανάτων δάμνησι νόον θνητῶν τ' ἀνθρώπων.

φῦλα καταθνητῶν ἀνθρώπων: the formula καταθνητῶν ἀνθρώπων occurs once in the *Iliad* (6. 123) and six times in the *Odyssey* (3. 114, 9. 502, 17. 587, 19. 285, 20. 76, 23. 126; see Kirk 1990, 172, Preziosi 1966, 173); also at [Hes.] frr. 70. 40, 204. 112, 343. 15, *Apoll.* 541. Its use here will be echoed four more times in *Aphr.* (122, 192, 200, 281; cf. also the dative plural at 52). The theme of human mortality in contrast with the immortality of the gods will be a significant motif in the hymn (see Introd., p. 11).

For φῦλα combined with this formula see the common φῦλ' ἀνθρώπων, *Il.* 14. 361, *Od.* 3. 282 etc. or φῦλα θνητῶν ἀνθρώπων at *Herm.* 578, [Hes.] frr. 43a. 6 and 240. 4; φῦλα is easily substituted in the metrically equivalent πολλὰ καταθνητῶν ἀνθρώπων at *Od.* 19. 285. Cf. also *Dem.* 352 φθεῖσαι φῦλ' ἀμενηνὰ χαμαιγενέων ἀνθρώπων (cf. N. Richardson 1974, 267). See later A.R. 4. 1165 φῦλα δυηπαθέων ἀνθρώπων, Q.S. 1. 135, 5. 45 φῦλα πολυτλήτων ἀνθρώπων, *Orph. A.* 1007 φῦλα πανημερίων ἀνθρώπων. Possibly modelling itself on the proem of *Aphr.*, cf. also Eudocia, *Homerocentones* 1. 1–3 Κέκλυτε, μυρία φῦλα περικτιόνων ἀνθρώπων | ... | ἠμὲν ὅσοι ... | ἠδ' ὅσσοι ... The term φῦλα is used in Homer to refer for the most part non-specifically to 'tribes' and is appropriate to the general statement of power desired here (see Kirk 1985, 256, 154).

4 οἰωνούς ... θηρία πάντα: in comparison with its masculine equivalent θήρ, the neuter θηρίον is rare in early Greek poetry. Any diminutive sense was lost at an early stage (cf. *Dictionnaire* s.v. θήρ); its two uses in Homer, at *Od.* 10. 171 and 180, are of an extraordinary stag: μέγα θηρίον ἦεν (see Heubeck, *OC* ii. 54 on its unusual size). See also Chantraine (1956), 66 on the use of the neuter form in Herodotus and Xenophon.

The next line in *Aphr.* (ὅσ' ἤπειρος ... ὅσα πόντος) gives θηρία to mean both 'land-animals' and 'sea-animals' (cf. *LfgrE* s.v.). *Cypr.* fr. 7. 12, however, singles out the neuter θηρία specifically as 'land-animals'. For θῆρες of sea animals see Pi. *N.* 3. 23 δάμασε δὲ θῆρας ἐν πελάγει, although the masculine also is more commonly separated from both fish and birds: see *Od.* 24. 291–2 ἐν πόντῳ φάγον ἰχθύες ... θηρσὶ καὶ οἰωνοῖσιν, *Op.* 277 ἰχθύσι ... θηρσὶ ... οἰωνοῖς (cf. West 1978, 226 ad loc.) and Alcm. *PMGF* 89. Cf. also Archil. 122. 7 μηδ' ἐὰν δελφῖσι θῆρες ἀνταμείψωνται νομόν and Emp. fr. 21. 15 DK θῆρές τ' οἰωνοί τε καὶ ὑδατοθρέμμονες ἰχθῦς. For the contrast between birds and beasts in later epic see Opp. *H.* 1. 704 οἰωνοῖσιν ἀμειλίκτοισί τε θηρσίν, Q.S. 3. 104 ἀθρόα φῦλα | θῆρές τ' οἰωνοί τε, and *Orac. Sib.* 3. 697 πάντα τε θηρία γῆς ἠδ' ἄσπετα φῦλα πετεινῶν.

οἰωνούς τε διειπετέας: a much-disputed word, διπετής appears four times in the *Iliad* (16. 174, 17. 263, 21. 268, 21. 326) and thrice in the *Odyssey* (4. 477, 4. 581, 7. 284), always of ποταμός (cf. [Hes.] fr. 320). Its use with οἰωνός in *Aphr.* is unparalleled elsewhere (for other epithets attached to οἰωνός cf. Alcm. 89. 6 οἰωνῶν φῦλα τανυπτερύγων, S. *Ant.* 1082 ἢ θῆρες, ἤ τις πτηνὸς οἰωνὸς φέρων). It has often been taken to mean 'fallen from the sky/Zeus', with the latter part of the word connected to πίπτω (cf. LSJ s.v., AHS 352, et al.). Objections that the first element διῑ- cannot mean 'from Zeus/the sky', requiring a genitive of source instead of a dative (cf. Hainsworth, *OC* i. 337 and Griffith 1997, 353–4), are partially muted by the later name Διιτρέφης in Aristophanes (Ar. *Av.* 798, 1442) alongside διοτρεφής in Homer (*Il.* 2. 445 etc.). Cf. the form διοπετές at E. *IT* 977 and διπετῆ at E. fr. 815. 2; διῑ- (original dative διϝει) and διο- seem interchangeable with little difference in sense while διῑ- provides the required long position in Homer.

Here, however, its use with οἰωνός implies that the second element is derived from πέτομαι 'to fly', rather than πίπτω; both etymologies are attested in ancient lexica (cf. *EM* 275. 21 ἀπὸ Διὸς πίπτων, ἢ πετόμενος) and oxytone accentuation, an Alexandrian issue in any case, does not exclude a derivation from πέτομαι (see similarly παλιμπετές *Il.* 16. 395, *Od.* 5. 27, cf. Griffith 1997, 354; Baumeister 1860 and VE amend to paroxytone). Thus Janko (1982), 155–6 is probably correct that 'the adjective means here "flying through the air" rather than "fallen from Zeus/the sky"'; for another adjective meaning 'through the air' cf. later at A.R. 2. 227 διηέριαι ποτέονται of the Harpies and οἰωνῶν τε διηερίων at [Opp.] *C.* 4. 391. Regardless of true etymology, this is the most obvious meaning of the word, and probably the one which was in the mind of our poet. (Treu's suggestion, 1958, 269, of understanding the preposition διa-, thus 'hindurchfliegend', is attractive as a popular etymology, especially given the form in Alcman ἀστήρ | ὠρανῶ διαιπετής, *PMGF* fr. 3. 66–7.) Humbach (1967), 279 unconvincingly derives the first element from διερός 'flüchtig, rasch'. Cf. on the word also Schmitt (1967), 44–6, 221–36, Heitsch (1965), 26–7, Renehan (1972), and Hooker (1979). Càssola 544–5 follows Schulze (1892), 237–8 in reading διειπετέας. The form is possible: Janko (1992), 341–2 claims that it rests solely on the weak authority of Zenodorus, but it is also the papyrus reading at E. *Hyps.* 133 διειπετῆ (Diggle) and Hsch. has both διειπετεος and διιπ-. It therefore seems reasonable to print this as the original form (cf. West 2003).

Hoekstra (1969), 44–5 points out that, if the poet modelled this on the prototype διιπετέος ποταμοῖο (in Homer always at ⌣4⌣⌣5⌣⌣6×), this would be a remarkable case of modification where a formula was 'declined, shifted, broken up and perhaps re-interpreted'; as always, however, it is impossible to know whether there was another prototype now lost (Hoekstra suggests *διιπετέες τ' οἰωνοί) and there is no linguistic innovation here to indicate modification.

5 ἠμὲν ὅσ' ἤπειρος πολλὰ τρέφει ἠδ' ὅσα πόντος: cf. *Th.* 582 κνώδαλ' ὅσ' ἤπειρος δεινὰ τρέφει ἠδὲ θάλασσα (on the relationship of these lines see Introd., pp. 35–6) and *Cypr.* fr. 7. 12 θηρί' ὅσ' ἤπειρος αἰνὰ (πολλὰ Bernabé) τρέφει (cf. West 1966a, 328). For ἠμέν . . . ἠδέ constructions in Homer see *Il.* 5. 751, 8. 395, 14. 234, etc.; in particular note the similar structure of *Apoll.* 21 ἠμὲν ἀν' ἤπειρον πορτιτρόφον ἠδ' ἀνὰ νήσους and Hy. 30. 3 ἠμὲν ὅσα χθόνα δῖαν ἐπέρχεται ἠδ' ὅσα πόντον. The sea nurtures also at Th. 107 οὕς θ' ἁλμυρὸς ἔτρεφε Πόντος, Pi. I. 1. 48 καὶ ὃν πόντος τράφει and E. Hec. 1181 γένος γὰρ οὔτε πόντος οὔτε γῆ τρέφει. Cf. the earth at Il. 11. 741 ᾗ τόσα φάρμακα εἴδη ὅσα τρέφει εὐρεῖα χθών, Herm. 570 ὅσα τρέφει εὐρεῖα χθών, A. Ch. 585 πολλὰ μὲν γᾶ τρέφει and E. Hipp. 1277 ὅσα τε γᾶ τρέφει. Three lines attributed to Alcman are similar; PMGF 89. 3–5 ὕλά (cod. φῦλα) θ' ἑρπέτ' ὅσα τρέφει μέλαινα γαῖα | θῆρές τ' ὀρεσκῷοι καὶ γένος μελισσᾶν | καὶ κνώδαλ' ἐν βένθεσσι πορφυρέας ἁλός.

Also later Orph. Hy. 85. 2 ὁπόσα τρέφει εὐρεῖα χθών and Chr. Pat. 336 (PG 163) ὅσα τε γῆ τρέφει κακά. A.R. 3. 530 has φάρμαχ' ὅσ' ἤπειρός τε φύει. Quintus perhaps has Aphr. in mind at 8. 466–7 δάμνατο δ' ὁππόσα φῦλα φερέσβιος ἔτρεφε γαῖα | ἠδ' ὅσα πόντος ἔφερβεν ἀπείριτος ἠδ' ὁπόσ' ὕδωρ.

ἤπειρος: as it is most commonly used in archaic epic, the term here simply signifies 'land' in contrast to the sea (Od. 5. 56 etc.). It can elsewhere be used to differentiate the 'mainland' from islands (Apoll. 21, n. prec., etc.). For a list of examples of the word with its different senses see LfgrE s.v.

6 πᾶσιν δ' ἔργα μέμηλεν: the phrase ἔργα μέμηλεν is found four times in Homer (Il. 5. 876, 9. 228, Od. 5. 67, 12. 116) always at line-end. The metrical position of the formula here is unique to early hexameter, although note the metrically equivalent οἷς δ' ὕβρις τε μέμηλε ... ἔργα Op. 238 and Herm. 267 ὕπνος ἐμοί γε μέμηλε. The fact that nu mobile in μέμηλεν prevents hiatus may suggest modification by transposition from line-end (cf. Hoekstra 1969, 41, Janko 1982, 166).

For phrasing similar to this line, Janko notes Op. 531 φεύγουσιν καὶ πᾶσιν ἐνὶ φρεσὶ τοῦτο μέμηλεν (for more on the relationship between Aphr. and Op. see Introd., pp. 36–8). Cf. also Il. 2. 614 ἔργα μεμήλει, 2. 338 μέλει πολεμήϊα ἔργα, and Op. 146 ἔργ' ἔμελε (see more examples at Campbell 1994, 267–8 on A.R. 3. 292 and Livrea 1968, 183, on Colluth. 229). The perfect μέμηλεν is a so-called 'intensive' perfect, used here as an equivalent to the present μέλει (type τεθνᾶσι); cf. GG i. 768. Monro 31 lists Homeric examples of this type, which he calls '*perfecta praesentia*'.

In the fifth century AD, Proclus clearly models his Hy. 4. 13 on this line: πᾶσιν δ' ἔργα μέμηλεν ἐρωτοτόκου Κυθερείης. For μέλει of love deeds in later poetry see A.R. 4. 794–5 of Zeus κείνῳ γὰρ ἀεὶ τάδε ἔργα μέμηλεν | ἠὲ σύν ἀθανάταις ἠὲ θνητῇσι ἰαύειν, and *Orac. Sib.* 1. 296 ἀνδράσιν οἷσι μέμηλε πόνος καὶ ἔργ' ἐρατεινά.

πᾶσιν δ'ἔργα: the neglect of digamma in ἔργα could be resolved by reading πᾶσι δὲ ἔργα (so Hoffmann 1848, 188; see Shackle 1915, 163, Càssola 624; MB*Γ*VD transmit πᾶσι δ' ἔργα), but there is no compelling motive to do so. Admittedly, no other instance of ἔργ-ον/α in *Aphr.* shows a definite neglect of digamma; it is preserved in vv. 1, 10, 11, 15 whereas in vv. 9, 21, 122 nu mobile obviates digamma-hiatus. However, digamma is certainly neglected in several occurrences of the word in Homer (see *Grammaire*, i. 135–6; cf. *Il.* 4. 470, 17. 279 etc.), and a Naxian dedication (*CEG* 403) suggests that Ionian poets were using nu mobile to avoid digamma-hiatus by the mid-seventh century (see West 2001*a*, 163). There is therefore no reason to assume its neglect a later addition to the text; *Aphr.* may be a product of the latter half of the seventh century (see Introd. pp. 47–9). Cf. below on *Aphr.* 203 ἥρπασεν ὄν.

ἐϋστεφάνου Κυθερείης: the formula appears at least once more in *Aphr.* at v. 287 (also perhaps 175). It is found in Homer only at *Od.* 8. 288, 18. 193 (cf. ἐϋστεφάνου τ' Ἀφροδίτης at *Od.* 8. 267), and in Hesiod at *Th.* 196, 1008; also at Thgn. 1339. Similarly, Aphrodite is 'well-garlanded' in the inscription on the famous 'Cup of Nestor' ἥμερος : hαιρέσει : καλλιστε[φά]νο : Ἀφροδίτες (see Buchner–Russo 1955 = *CEG* 454). She weaves garlands with the nymphs and Charites at *Cypr.* fr. 5. 1–2 ἡ δὲ σὺν ἀμφιπόλοισι φιλομμειδὴς Ἀφροδίτη | πλεξάμεναι στεφάνους εὐώδεας, ἄνθεα γαίης (cf. Boedeker 1974, 28). The epithet ἐϋστέφανος is used elsewhere in early epic of Artemis (*Il.* 21. 511 ἐϋστέφανος κελαδεινή), Demeter (*Op.* 300, *Dem.* 224 etc.; see N. Richardson 1974, 228), the heroine Mycene (*Od.* 2. 120), the city Thebes (*Il.* 19. 99), and Polymele ([Hes.] fr. 43(a). 1). It is used of Aphrodite in later epic at Q.S. 10. 318 ἐϋστέφανος Κυθέρεια and 1. 667 Κύπρις ἐϋστέφανος.

Aphrodite is garlanded in vase painting (*LIMC* ii, Aphrodite no. 1323 etc.), and often wears an elaborate crown in sculpture from Cyprus and the Near East (ibid., nos. 107–10, *Aphrodite in Peripheria Orientali* nos. 75 ff., and V. Karageorghis 1998, 203–9); she also appears on several coins from Cyprus with a rich crown or garland (see V. Karageorghis 2002, 319–22, James 1888, 187).

Κυθερείης: only twice in Homer, the name 'appears to be a later addition to the resources of the Kunstsprache' (Hainsworth, *OC* i. 365–6; cf. also Boedeker 1974, 20). Hesiod tells at *Th.* 198 that it is derived from Κύθηρα, the name of the island where Aphrodite arrived after her birth: ἀτὰρ Κυθέρειαν ὅτι προσέκυρσε Κυθήροις. An obvious popular etymology, this derivation has been questioned because of the unexplained short quantity of the second syllable in the name (see West 1966a, 223 and Page 1955, 127 n. 1 on the term in Sappho fr. 140. 1), but cf. Frisk s.v.: 'von der Insel (τὰ) Κύθηρα mit Kürzung des η wegen des Verses nach εὐπατέρεια u. a.' West (1997), 56–7 instead follows the work of Brown (1965; 1995, 245, 332) in deriving the name from Kuthar (*Kwtr*), a mythical ruler of Cyprus (known from a Syriac text ascribed to Bishop Melito of Sardes), who can in turn be identified with the Ugaritic god Kothar, the divine craftsman; as he points out, both Aphrodite's relationship with the craftsman Hephaestus in Homer and a close connection between Aphrodite's temple and smiths' workshops in Cyprus would make it fitting if Cythereia were in origin a female counterpart of Kothar (and Kothar was known to have female counterparts; see ibid. n. 238). Other explanations are at least no more certain: Morgan (1978), 115–20 proposes a connection with the IE root *$g^w hedh$-, giving a meaning 'goddess of desire'. Burkert (1992), 190 suggests that this name for Aphrodite, the goddess of incense (see below on *Aphr.* 58 θυώδεα), derives from the Semitic root *qtr*; 'cf., e.g., Hebrew *mequtteret*, "filled with fragrance".'

Whatever its actual provenance 'è certo comunque che i greci interpretavano Citerea come "dea di Citera"' (Càssola 545), and there is good reason to suppose that the poet of *Aphr.* is here drawing from the Hesiodic model. Aphrodite's two leading cult epithets Κύπρις and Κυθέρεια frame vv. 2–5, associating Cythera with Cyprus just as at *Th.* 192–3 πρῶτον δὲ Κυθήροισι ζαθέοισιν | ἔπλητ', ἔνθεν ἔπειτα περίρρυτον ἵκετο Κύπρον and 198–9 . . . Κυθήροις | Κυπρογενέα δ', ὅτι γέντο περικλύστῳ ἐνὶ Κύπρῳ. The pairing is found also at *Hy.* 6. 2 and 18 Κύπρου . . . Κυθερείης and together in the same line at both *Hy.* 10. 1 Κυπρογενῆ Κυθέρειαν and Thgn. 1386 Κυπρογενὲς Κυθέρεια. The Hesiodic passage has left its mark on the tradition and the combination of these two geographical adjectives does not seem 'distinctly strange' as Morgan suggests (1978, 117). Campbell (1994),

98 notes of the use of the name later at A.R. 3. 108 that it is '"high-sounding", "exotic-sounding even"'; it is not so exotic here, but it is certainly a term of 'colour'.

Pausanias (3. 23. 1) tells of a temple of Aphrodite Ourania on Cythera which was the oldest and holiest of all Greek shrines of the goddess, ἁγιώτατον καὶ ἱερῶν ὁπόσα Ἀφροδίτης παρ' Ἕλλησίν ἐστιν ἀρχαιότατον (cf. Hunter 1999, 126 on Theoc. *Id.* 3. 46). See also Herodotus 1. 105, who mentions the temple of the goddess on Cythera.

7–33. Three short digressions, mini-hymns to Athena (8–15), Artemis (16–20), and Hestia (21–32) now follow (on the hymnic nature of these passages cf. AS 350, Porter 1949, 252, VE 12 etc.). These examples of virginity, which contrast with the statement of Aphrodite's universal power in the previous lines, are contained within a traditional epic structure: τρισσάς at the beginning of v. 7 'underlines' the tripartite presentation of the goddesses (cf. Podbielski 1971, 22) while ring-composition, v. 33 repeating 7 almost verbatim, neatly encapsulates the three exemplars (cf. Janko 1981*a*, 19, Pellizer 1978, 119, Kamerbeek 1967, 394). Comparison with Aphrodite is effected through the use of vocabulary, which directs attention back to the first six lines: if slightly inelegant (so AHS 349), the repetition of ἔργα (-ον) at vv. 9, 10, 11, 15, and 21 purposefully echoes its use at vv. 1 and 6; different forms of ἁνδάνω (εὕαδεν 9, ἅδον 10, ἅδε 18, ἅδεν 21), as well as ἀλεγύνειν at v. 11, recall the sense of μέμηλεν at v. 6; δάμναται at v. 17 turns attention to ἐδαμάσσατο at v. 3 (cf. Podbielski 1971, 23). Although digressive, these short hymns are framed in the shadow of Aphrodite's actions.

7 τρισσὰς δ' οὐ δύναται πεπιθεῖν φρένας οὐδ' ἀπατῆσαι: τρισσός is not common in archaic poetry. For early examples, cf. [Hes.] fr. 233. 2 τρισσὴν γαῖαν and Pi. *P.* 8. 80 νίκαις τρισσαῖς. Euripides applies the word to a group of goddesses, Athena, Hera, and Aphrodite at *Hec.* 645–6 κρίνει τρισσὰς μακάρων | παῖδας, as does Sophocles when invoking Athena, Artemis, and Apollo at *OT* 164 τρισσοὶ ἀλεξίμοροι προφάνητέ μοι. Later the term is frequently applied to the Charites, a group of three from Hesiod onward (see below on *Aphr.* 61): Nonn. *D.* 42. 467 τρισσάων Χαρίτων, Meleager, *AP* 5. 139. 4, 5. 194. 1, etc.

The adjective τρισσάς is to be taken with θεάς understood: the immediate contrast with v. 6 is itself telling: 'all' <individuals> but not these <female individuals>. See also Bossi (1978), 23–4: 'il v. 33 τάων ... riprende infatti ... il nostro v. 7: e τάων (sc. θεάων) non potrà che corrispondere a un aggettivo (τρισσάς) che rimandi a θεάς'. The accusative κούρην ... Ἀθήνην corresponds to τρισσάς. For the phrasing here, cf. Il. 3. 236 δοιὼ δ' οὐ δύναμαι ἰδέειν and 8. 299 τοῦτον δ' οὐ δύναμαι βαλέειν.

The verb πείθω is not found elsewhere taking such a double accusative (whole and part construction; cf. Càssola 545), but cf. the compound from ἀπατάω taking this construction at Ar. Pax. 1099 μή πώς σε δόλῳ φρένας ἐξαπατήσας and, notably of sexual trickery, at Hes. Op. 373 μηδὲ γυνή σε νόον πυγοστόλος ἐξαπατάτω (cf. Bossi 1978). It is also worth noting that φρήν is often used in phrases with a double accusative (i.e. Il. 1. 362 τί δέ σε φρένας ἵκετο πένθος;) see LSJ s.v.

πεπιθεῖν ... οὐδ' ἀπατῆσαι: an innovative line. Il. 9. 184 ῥηϊδίως πεπιθεῖν μεγάλας φρένας Αἰακίδαο is the only other occurrence of the reduplicated aorist infinitive of πείθω in early poetry; it is found in the same metrical position (⏑⏑–4) elsewhere at A.R. 3. 536 πεπιθεῖν ἐπαρῆξαι ἀέθλῳ. See also Apoll. 275 Ἑκάτου πέπιθε φρένας. For οὐδ' ἀπατῆσαι at line-end compare οὐδ' ἀπατήσω, Od. 4. 348, 17. 139, Herm. 545. Later, see the speech of Aphrodite at A.R. 3. 152 παρέξομαι οὐδ' ἀπατήσω; the clausula in Aphr. would be a 'pertinent' model for these words of Cypris (Campbell 1994: 136), but this cannot be certain given the Homeric parallels.

8–20. Athena and Artemis are a duo of virgins later in the collection of *Hymns*, paired by succession in 27 and 28, where they are both identically called παρθένον αἰδοίην (27. 2, 28. 3). Gemoll (1886), 349 saw the style of the two hymns as so similar that he claimed they were composed by the same author (see also AHS 424). Even if this is not accepted, their pairing in the collection may reflect their relationship in *Aphr*. They are also paired as companions at the Rape of Persephone; cf. *Dem*. 424 and N. Richardson's note there (1974, 290–1). The two goddesses are later mentioned together as virgins at E. *Ion* 465–6 σὺ καὶ παῖς ἡ Λατογενής | δύο θεαὶ δύο παρθένοι. In Latin cf. Venus' words at Ov. *Met*. 5. 375–6 *Pallada nonne uides iaculatricemque Dianam* | *abscessisse mihi* for the similar contrast with these two goddesses. Note also at Call. *Hy*. 5. 15 ff. the inverse comparison of Aphrodite with Athena, this time in a hymn dedicated to Athena (Bulloch 1985, 127 gives further examples of Aphrodite and Athena contrasted). For more on Artemis' virginity see on *Aphr.* 16–20.

8 κούρην τ'αἰγιόχοιο Διὸς γλαυκῶπιν Ἀθήνην: the same line occurs at *Th.* 13, within the catalogue of gods in the proem. Given other similarities between *Aphr.* and the proem of the *Th.*, direct imitation is a distinct possibility; certainly the catalogue of gods would have been a fitting exemplar for the less condensed list of goddesses in *Aphr.* (Introd., pp. 35–6). The particle τε is more at home in the Hesiodic passage as a connective particle. What we expect here is τε followed by καί ... καί introducing the other two goddesses, but the exposition takes a longer and more complex path; instead, the other two goddesses are later introduced by οὐδέ (v. 16 apparently picking up v. 7 δ' οὐ δύναται, and v. 21 perhaps echoing v. 9 οὐ γάρ). Denniston (1954), 514 groups this under his 'irregular corresponsions' of τε ... δέ, and the particle must here be what Ruijgh (1971), 142 calls a 'preparative' coordinator. In *Il.* 10. 552–3 νεφεληγερέτα Ζεὺς | κούρη τ' αἰγιόχοιο Διὸς γλαυκῶπις Ἀθήνη the τε has clear connective force.

Athena is commonly referred to as the κούρη Διός in Homer (*Il.* 5. 733, 6. 304 etc.) and only twice are other individuals called such: Helen at *Il.* 3. 426 (see Kirk 1985, 327) and Aphrodite at *Il.* 20. 105. In the plural, the Muses and nymphs are often called the κοῦραι Διός (West 1966a, 161 lists some examples), and the Litai are once called such at *Il.* 9. 503.

γλαυκῶπιν Ἀθήνην: cf. *Aphr.* 94. Always at line-end, the noun–epithet combination is common in Homer, but only once in the accusative; *Od.* 1. 156. Cf. *Apoll.* 323, Hes. *Th.* 13, 888; see West's note (1966, 403) on the possible variant γλαυκώπιδ' Ἀθήνην: 'both forms of the accusative certainly existed'. M here has -ιν while the other MSS read -ιδ'. VE 15 follows Càssola in adopting the latter reading, on the weak grounds that M is 'inclined to "restore" Homerisms' (VB 3 successfully argues that this is unfounded; cf. on *Aphr.* 67). In this case, it is perhaps worth noting that M retains the form γλαυκώπιδ' Ἀθήνην at *Apoll.* 323. The case for M's veracity acquires considerable support if the poet of *Aphr.* did have *Th.* 13 in mind (see on v. 8 and Guttmann 1869, 53 n. 32). Cf. also AS 200, Breuning (1929), 107.

9 οὐ γάρ οἱ εὔαδεν: cf. *Il.* 14. 340, 17. 647 ἐπεί νύ τοι εὔαδεν οὕτως and *Od.* 16. 28 ὡς γάρ νύ τοι εὔαδε θυμῷ for this form of ἀνδάνω in Homer. The prosodic collocation οὐ γάρ οἱ here is rare; it is found elsewhere only at Hes. *Op.* 526 οὐ γάρ οἱ ἠέλιος δείκνυ with the same uncommon neglect of digamma in οἱ (see West 1978, 291 on the frequency of this neglect). There is no formulaic parallel in Homer and the neglect suggests post-Homeric modification (see Hoekstra 1969, 41–2). Matthiae (1805) unnecessarily conjectures οὐ γάρ οἱ ἅδεν to preserve the effect of the digamma in *Aphr.* Janko (1982), 166–7 points to the thematic similarity of the Hesiodic passage with 'the shared ideas of a force [Boreas in Hesiod] that subdues everything with certain exceptions, of the works of Aphrodite, and of the virgins at home', which combined with the rare neglect of digamma and similar phrasing makes borrowing a likely possibility; he argues, however, that Hesiod is the borrower here. While his suggestion that these themes are perhaps more at home in *Aphr.* has some truth, it goes little way to support a claim that Hesiod is the imitator (see Introd., pp. 36–8).

The aorist εὔαδεν here is 'gnomic' or 'omnitemporal' (see Faulkner 2006). Bornmann (1968), 87 comments on its 'valore presente' in Homer, within the formula νύ τοι . . . εὔαδε (*Il.* 14. 340, 17. 647, *Od.* 16. 28), and Callimachus (*Hy.* 3. 183, 187). It is used in this generic sense also at *Hy.* 14. 4. Only at *Dem.* 205 might it have a pure aorist meaning (see N. Richardson 1974, 205), although even there it could be understood as a historic fact with lasting present truth.

The verb is used later of virginity and chastity at A.R. 2. 501–2 εὔαδε γάρ οἱ | παρθενίη καὶ λέκτρον ἀκήρατον. It is used of ἔργα at Q.S. 1. 457 εὔαδεν ἐξ ἀρχῆς καὶ ὅσ' ἀνέρες ἔργα πένονται; cf. also Nonn. *D.* 3. 308 οὐ μὲν . . . εὔαδεν ἔργον.

10–11. The contrast intended in these two lines bears resemblance to that drawn by Zeus in his playful taunt of Aphrodite at *Il.* 5. 428–30 οὔ τοι, τέκνον ἐμόν, δέδοται πολεμήϊα ἔργα· | ἀλλὰ σύ γ' ἱμερόεντα μετέρχεο ἔργα γάμοιο, | ταῦτα δ' Ἄρηϊ θοῷ καὶ Ἀθήνῃ πάντα μελήσει. In *Aphr.* it is inversely Athena's concern with the deeds of war (ἔργον Ἄρηος, ἀγλαὰ ἔργ') that is juxtaposed with the ἔργα . . . Ἀφροδίτης, but the spirit of the two passages is similar (cf. Clay 1989, 160 n. 23). Cf. also Diomedes' taunt of Aphrodite at *Il.* 5. 347–51 and Idas' similar rebuke of the Argonauts at A.R. 3. 558–63

(Hunter 1989, 158 compares the latter to *Il.* 5, noted above). Apart from contrast, love and war share similarities, a *topos* which is frequently exploited in later literature (cf. Ov. *Am.* 1. 9. 1 *militat omnis amans*); in this poem Aphrodite 'tames' (δάμνημι) others in love, a verb also used of conquering in war (cf. on *Aphr.* 3 ἐδαμάσσατο and see Turkeltaub 2003b, 102–7). On the listing of attributes here see below on *Aphr.* 18–20.

Athena is coupled with Ares also at *Hy.* 11. 2–3 ᾗ σὺν Ἄρηϊ μέλει πολεμήϊα ἔργα | περθόμεναί τε πόληες ἀϋτή τε πτόλεμοί τε and Pi. *N.* 10. 84 σύν τ' Ἀθαναίᾳ κελαινεγχεῖ τ' Ἄρει; cf. also their pairing at Paus. 1. 8. 4, 5. 15. 6 and Lycurg. *Orat. AL.* 77 (see AHS 392). She is later worshipped with the cult title ἀρεία at Athens (Paus. 1. 28. 5) and Plataea (Paus. 9. 4. 1); cf. *RE* (1949).

ἀλλ' ἄρα: the particle combination ἀλλ' ἄρα underlines the positive affirmation of the preceding negative statement οὐ γάρ οἱ (see Podbielski 1971, 22 and cf. Denniston 1954, 42), as well as marking this line as a point of interest (on this see on *Aphr.* 42 δ' ἄρα). For other examples of ἀλλ' ἄρα cf. *Il.* 6. 418, 13. 716 (preceded by οὐ γάρ as in *Aphr.*), 24. 699, *Od.* 3. 259, and Hes. *Th.* 899.

πόλεμοί τε ἄδον ... | ὑσμῖναί τε μάχαι τε ... ἀλεγύνειν: cf. *Il.* 1. 177–80 αἰεὶ γάρ τοι ἔρις τε φίλη πόλεμοί τε μάχαι τε | ... | ... | ... ἀλεγίζω and Hes. *Th.* 926 ᾗ κέλαδοί τε ἄδον πόλεμοί τε μάχαι τε; also *Od.* 11. 612 ὑσμῖναί τε μάχαι τε and Hes. *Th.* 228 Ὑσμίνας τε Μάχας τε. The structure of v. 11, ... τε ... τε καὶ ἀγλαὰ ἔργ', is similar to *Od.* 13. 289, 15. 418, 16. 158 καλῇ τε μεγάλῃ τε καὶ ἀγλαὰ ἔργα ἰδυίῃ. The infinitive ἀλεγύνειν appears at line-end only at *Od.* 11. 186 and later A.R. 3. 1105.

Janko (1982), 160 suggests that the observance of digamma in ἄδον, unparalleled in Homer but found in Hesiod (Ϝάδον *Th.* 926; cf. ἄδον *Apoll.* 22), is a sign of archaism. However, digamma is only certainly neglected in the aorist of ἀνδάνω at *Il.* 3. 173 ἀδεῖν (for a full list of occurrences of the aorist in early epic see *LfrgE* s.v. ἀνδάνω), and its observance in this particular form ἄδον, which does not happen to be found in Homer, is not significant.

ἀγλαὰ ἔργ': used in the *Odyssey* only of the delicate crafts of women and entirely absent from the violence of the *Iliad* (cf. *Od.* 10. 223, 13. 289, 15. 418, 16. 158), the phrase is here uniquely entwined with war. It follows the Homeric use at v. 15, 'crafts of women', but cannot have that meaning here. Porter's 'deeds of prowess' (1949, 253), should not be entirely dismissed, following from ὑσμῖναί τε μάχαι τε (cf. *Il.* 8. 453 πολέμοιό τε μέρμερα ἔργα etc.), but the succeeding explicative asyndeton of πρώτη (nearly equivalent to πρώτη γάρ; cf. Denniston 1954, pp. xliii f., Humbert 1954, 87, 371) favours the idea that vv. 12–15 are an elaboration on what is intended; σατίνας καὶ ἅρματα, the skilled products of men. But this is not elegant composition, and the switch from wars to crafts is awkwardly abrupt.

The phrase introduces a sort of 'chiasmus' between vv. 11 and 15, which effects a contrast of the sexes: (*a*) ἀγλαὰ ἔργα, (*b*) a line relating to men, (*c*) a line which mentions the chariots of women and men respectively (see below on *Aphr.* 12–13 σατίνας), (*b*) a line relating to women, (*a*) ἀγλαὰ ἔργα. Similar to the separation of men and animals, birds and beasts, and land and sea creatures in the proem, the crafts of men and women are contrasted here in order to enhance the point that Athena has a hand in both. Cf. *Hy.* 20. 2 where ἀγλαὰ ἔργα is used of the crafts of Hephaestus (see AHS 411: = τέχνας generally).

12–13 πρώτη τέκτονας ἄνδρας ... ἐδίδαξε: Athena is the patron-goddess of carpenters at *Il.* 5. 61, 15. 412 and is said at *Od.* 8. 493 to have played a part in the construction of the famous wooden horse; her δμωός (i.e. the carpenter) is also the builder of the plough at Hes. *Op.* 430. Cf. later A.R. 1. 18–19 and 111 where she is behind the creation of the Argo; in Latin poetry see Catul. 64. 8–10 *Diva ... ipsa levi fecit volitantem flamine currum | pinea coniungens inflexae texta carinae*.

She, along with Hephaestus, is the first to teach such skills to humans; see *Od.* 6. 232–4 ὡς δ' ὅτε τις χρυσὸν περιχεύεται ἀργύρῳ ἀνήρ | ἴδρις, ὃν Ἥφαιστος δέδαεν καὶ Παλλὰς Ἀθήνη | τέχνην παντοίην (cf. AHS 410, Clay 1989, 160) and more parallels in the next note. A civilizing goddess (see Burkert 1985, 141), she is similarly the teacher of women's crafts below at v. 15 (ἐδίδαξεν) and elsewhere; see Hes. *Op.* 63–4 αὐτὰρ Ἀθήνην | ἔργα διδασκῆσαι, πολυδαίδαλον ἱστὸν ὑφαίνειν (on the possible relationship of these lines to *Aphr.* see Introd., pp. 36–8) and West's note there (1978, 159) for further parallels.

ἐπιχθονίους ἐδίδαξε: cf. *Hy.* 20. 2–3 ὃς μετ' Ἀθηναίης γλαυκώπιδος ἀγλαὰ ἔργα | ἀνθρώπους ἐδίδαξεν ἐπὶ χθονός. For phrasing similar to that in these two lines, see also later *Orph*. fr. 269. 2–3 Bernabé πρῶτοι τεκτονόχειρες, ἰδ' Ἥφαιστον καὶ Ἀθήνην | δαίδαλα πάντ' ἐδίδαξαν, Opp. *H*. 2. 21–3 δοῦρα … | … | Παλλὰς ἐπιχθονίους ἐδιδάξατο, and Syncellus' version of the *Apocalypsis Henochi Graece* 8. 1 (Black) Πρῶτος Ἀζαὴλ ὁ δέκατος τῶν ἀρχόντων ἐδίδαξε ποιεῖν μαχαίρας καὶ θώρακας καὶ πᾶν σκεῦος πολεμικόν.

σατίνας … ἅρματα ποικίλα χαλκῷ: a notoriously rare term, σατίνη is in opposition to ἅρματα also at Sappho fr. 44. 13–17, a similarity which Janko thinks might not be 'accidental' (1982, 169–70; see on *Aphr*. 14 ἀπαλόχροας and Introd., pp. 45–7); it is found elsewhere only in Anacr. *PMG* 388. 10 and E. *Hel*. 1311. The word supplies an eastern flavour, found elsewhere in the poem, which is perhaps more at home in Sappho's poem about Hector's marriage than in this mini-hymn to Athena.

The distinction in Sappho, made between σατίνας as carriages used by women and ἅρματα by men, while sustainable under the evidence of the other two appearances of the word, does not necessarily apply here (cf. Leumann 1959, 206–7, Page 1955, 71 n. 2); however, this distinction seems to be supported by the contrast of the sexes in vv. 11–15 (see on *Aphr*. 10–11 ἀγλαὰ ἔργα). Marzullo (1958), 157 prefers 'carri da trasporto e da guerra' (cf. Hsch. σατίναι· αἱ ἅμαξαι) but even this might be questioned if an etymology implying martial use is correct (see Janko 1982, 170 'war-waggon'). What seems certain is that, of Thracian or Phrygian origin, the word implies a carriage of particular 'eastern luxury' (see AHS 353). Cf. also Càssola (1975), 545, Somolinos (1998), 50, 69.

τε καί: the MSS read only καί; τε was inserted by Barnes (1711) in order to avoid hiatus. The low incidence of hiatus in the poem (see Introd., pp. 24–5) would seem to support this, and the τε could easily have dropped out along with the -ς of σατίνας (transmitted by no MS; it could have been lost because the word σατίνη was unfamiliar).

14 ἥ δέ τε παρθενικὰς ἀπαλόχροας: possible innovation through the combination of existing lines; cf. Hes. *Op*. 256 ἥ δέ τε παρθένος ἐστὶ Δίκη and 519 καὶ διὰ παρθενικῆς ἀπαλόχροος οὐ διάησιν | ἥ τε δόμων ἔντοσθε … μίμνει (for more on the possible connection between these two poems see Introd., pp. 36–8). Completing the verse, ἐν μεγάροισι(ν) is extremely common at line-end in Homer

(*Il.* 1. 418 etc.) and found in Hesiod at *Th.* 384 and *Op.* 377. If Pfeiffer's restoration is correct at Sappho fr. 44. 15 γυναίκων τ' ἄμα παρθενίκαν τ' [ἀπαλο]σφύρων, it is worth noting (see, however, the strong arguments of Page 1955, 64–5 against the restoration on grounds of space; more favourable is Janko 1982, 272 n. 131). Cf. later Theoc. *Id.* 8. 59–60 ἀνδρὶ δὲ παρθενικᾶς ἀπαλᾶς πόθος and Marc. Sid. 81 οἷά τε παρθενικῆς ἀπαλόχροος αἰνήσουσι.

ἡ δέ τε: the use of adverbial τε again suggests that the aorist form ἐδίδαξεν intends a permanent state of affairs, referring to Athena's role as patron of carpentry and women's crafts.

15 ἐπὶ φρεσὶ θεῖσα ἑκάστῃ: similar to *Od.* 4. 729 ἐνὶ φρεσὶ θέσθε ἑκάστῃ and *Il.* 13. 121 ἐν φρεσὶ θέσθε ἕκαστος, with ἐπί instead of ἐνί. The combination ἐπὶ φρεσί is more common in Homer than VE 17 suggests and is frequently preferred in tmesis with the verb τίθημι; cf. *Il.* 1. 55, 8. 218, *Od.* 5. 427, 11. 146 (v.l.), 15. 234, 18. 158, 21. 1 and also *Apoll.* 534. See West (1966*b*), 147–9, who proposes reading ἐπὶ φρεσὶ θῆσιν Ἀθήνη at *Od.* 16. 282 (codd. ἐνί).

16–20. Artemis is the most obvious choice for inclusion in a trio of virgin goddesses and her chastity is better known in Homer than that of Athena or Hestia (see on *Aphr.* 18–20). In Homer she carries the epithet ἁγνή (cf. *LfgrE* s.v.: 'casto, puro') on three occasions in the *Odyssey* (5. 123, 18. 202, 20. 71). The term, which is also used of Persephone in Homer (*Od.* 11. 386), is most commonly applied to Artemis and the implication of virginity is strongly present; at *Od.* 6. 109 when Nausicaa is compared to Artemis she is called παρθένος ἀδμής, for which there exists a variant παρθένος ἁγνή. For more on the use of the epithet see N. Richardson (1974), 222. In Christian literature ἁγνή is used of the Virgin Mary. A fragment assigned to either Sappho or Alcaeus (Sapph. fr. 44a Voigt) probably refers to Artemis swearing an oath of virginity as Hestia does later in *Aphr.* (see on *Aphr.* 25–32). In Callimachus she requests her virginity from Zeus at *Hy.* 3. 6: δός μοι παρθενίην αἰώνιον (see Bornmann 1968, 7–8).

Artemis is contrasted with Aphrodite later in E. *Hipp.*; cf. in particular 1301–2, where Artemis speaks of her as the most hated of the gods to those who prize virginity: τῆς γὰρ ἐχθίστης θεῶν | ἡμῖν ὅσαισι παρθένειος ἡδονή. The two goddesses are set in sharp contrast throughout the play (see Barrett 1964, 391–2).

16 οὐδέ ποτ': this combination at line-beginning emphasizes the introduction of the second of the three virgin goddesses; neither is Artemis 'ever' tamed by Aphrodite. Achilles employs it when speaking passionately to Agamemnon at *Il.* 1. 155 οὐδέ ποτ' ἐν Φθίῃ; see also 18. 283 οὐδέ ποτ' ἐκπέρσει. At *Dem.* 49 οὐδέ ποτ' ἀμβροσίης, it is used of Demeter abstaining from eating or drinking in mourning for her daughter. Cf. also Hes. *Th.* 796 οὐδέ ποτ' ἀμβροσίης, 802 οὐδέ ποτ' ἐς βουλὴν and *Op.* 230 οὐδέ ποτ' ἰθυδίκῃσι.

Ἀρτέμιδα χρυσηλάκατον κελαδεινήν: this formula does not appear elsewhere in the accusative. It may be an innovation here, based upon the genitive Ἀρτέμιδος χρυσηλακάτου κελαδεινῆς found at *Il.* 16. 183 and later in *Aphr.* at v. 118; if restored correctly, cf. also [Hes.] fr. 23(a). 18. The case for innovation is strengthened by the fact that the lengthened accusative form of the name Ἀρτέμιδα is found only in *Aphr.*, the usual form being Ἄρτεμιν; cf. *Hy.* 27. 1 Ἄρτεμιν ἀείδω χρυσηλάκατον κελαδεινήν.

χρυσηλάκατον κελαδεινήν: on these two epithets see Due (1965), Janko (1992), 343. χρυσηλάκατον is used only of Artemis in Homer and Hesiod. It is used of Amphitrite at Pi. *O.* 6. 104, Leto at *N.* 6. 36, one of the Nereids at *N.* 5. 36 and of the Charites at B. *Epin.* 9. 1. It must here mean 'with golden arrows' rather than 'with distaff of gold' (the latter given by LSJ s.v.). Artemis' connection with bows and arrows is made explicit only two lines later (ἅδε τόξα), and she is far from the domestic realm of spindles here. Cf. *Hy.* 27. 5 where the use of the epithet is followed five lines later by ἄγρῃ τερπομένη παγχρύσεα τόξα τιταίνει. That this epithet can elsewhere mean 'with distaff of gold', as apparently at *Od.* 4. 121 ff., is convincingly explained by an original meaning of 'reed' or 'cane' for ἠλακάτη, the common material for the construction of both distaffs and arrows (Due 4 ff.; see Hsch. χρυσηλάκατος· καλλίτοξος· ἠλακάτη γὰρ ὁ τοξικὸς κάλαμος).

κελαδεινός: used elsewhere of Ζέφυρον at *Il.* 23. 208 and of αὐλῶνας at *Herm.* 95, and later, adverbially, at A.R. 3. 532 of rivers and at Q.S. 14. 482 of wind. Due 2–3 prefers to understand the word as 'referring to the sounds of wild nature' rather than to the sound of the hunt, as explained by the scholiast to *Il.* 16. 183 (κυνηγετικῆς, παρὰ τὸν γιγνόμενον ἐν τοῖς κυνηγίοις κέλαδον, ὅ ἐστι θόρυβον). Cf., however, *Hy.* 27. 7–10 ἰαχεῖ δ' ἔπι δάσκιος ὕλη | δεινὸν ὑπὸ κλαγγῆς θηρῶν, where the resounding noise of Artemis in the hunt is stated in detail. Artemis is generally a noisy goddess; note the considerable racket of the phorminx, dances and shrill cries of women, which are her concerns at v. 19.

17 δάμναται ἐν φιλότητι: δάμναται recalls ἐδαμάσσατο at v. 3, underlining the contrast between Artemis' virginity and Aphrodite's erotic tyranny (cf. on *Aphr.* 10–11). For taming ἐν φιλότητι cf. Theia, the mother of Eos, at Hes. *Th.* 374 γείναθ' ὑποδμηθεῖσ' Ὑπερίονος ἐν φιλότητι. The beginning of the line is similar to *Th.* 122 δάμναται ἐν στήθεσσι νόον καὶ ἐπίφρονα βουλήν where Ἔρος is doing the taming (note δάμναται emphatically enjambed at *Od.* 14. 488).

For examples of love taming see above on *Aphr.* 3. Also note Sapph. frr. 1. 3, 102. 2, Archil. fr. 196 ἀλλά μ' ὁ λυσιμελὴς ὠταῖρε δάμναται πόθος, Pi. *P.* 11. 24 ἦ ἑτέρῳ λέχεϊ δαμαζομέναν; later, [Opp.] *C.* 2. 31 ἔρως ἐδαμάσσατο δριμύς, Nonn. *D.* 33. 316 Ἔρως με δάμασσε, Orph. *A.* 479 Ὑψιπύλην ἐρατοῖς ἐδάμασσεν Ἰήσων, Musae. 198 Ἔρως βελέεσσι δαμάζει.

φιλομμειδὴς Ἀφροδίτη: this formula is used four other times in *Aphr.* (see 49, 56, 65 and 155). At Hes. *Th.* 200 the epithet is explained by Aphrodite's birth from the genitals of Uranos (ἠδὲ φιλομμειδέα, ὅτι μηδέων ἐξεφαάνθη, see West 1966a, 88). However, Aphrodite's predilection for smiles and laughter is also well known in Hesiod and this may have been the earlier meaning of the epithet (see Kirk 1985, 326, *Dictionnaire* s.v. μειδιάω; *contra* Càssola); cf. Sapph. fr. 1. 14, and note *Hy.* 10. 3, where she is always smiling, αἰεὶ μειδιάει. At *Aphr.* 49 the formula is linked with laughter by immediately following ἡδὺ γελοιήσασα, which suggests that this is how it was understood in the poem (cf. Boedeker 1974, 31–4, who identifies this characteristic more generally with erotic contexts). Also, the frequency of this formula, if it is referring to her smiles and laughter, is particularly appropriate for the trickery which Aphrodite employs in the hymn. Hera's smiling is stressed at *Il.* 14. 222–3 (by repetition: μείδησεν, μειδήσασα) as she is about to deceive Zeus with Aphrodite's help; elsewhere, Aphrodite's laughter is matched explicitly with deception at Hes. *Th.* 205 παρθενίους τ' ὀάρους μειδήματά τ' ἐξαπάτας τε (see *LfgrE* s.v. μειδῆσαι 3a for more examples of deceptive smiles).

The formula is found elsewhere in archaic epic at *Il.* 3. 424, 4. 10, 5. 375, 14. 211, 20. 40, *Od.* 8. 362, *Th.* 989, [Hes.] fr. 176. 1 and *Cypr.* fr.

5. 1. In later hexameter poetry it appears at Nonn. *D.* 33. 36, 35. 148, 41. 205 with clear associations of laughing.

18–20. We now enter the wild realm of Artemis and, similar to the list of things which are a concern for Athena at vv. 10–11, there is a snappy list of Artemis' unamorous pursuits: she hunts beasts in the mountains with bow and arrow, takes pleasure in the phorminx, dance and piercing cries, revels in shadowy forests and is concerned with the city of just men. In the short *Hy.* 27 to Artemis there is a comparable presentation of her pursuits: v. 2 παρθένον αἰδοίην; vv. 4–5 ἣ κατ' ὄρη σκιόεντα καὶ ἄκριας ἠνεμοέσσας | ἄγρῃ τερπομένη παγχρύσεα τόξα τιταίνει; vv. 7–8 ὑψηλῶν ὀρέων, ἰαχεῖ δ' ἔπι δάσκιος ὕλη | δεινὸν ὑπὸ κλαγγῆς θηρῶν; v. 10 θηρῶν ὀλέκουσα γενέθλην; v. 15 Μουσῶν καὶ Χαρίτων καλὸν χορὸν ἀρτυνέουσα. Cf. also the list of pursuits at the beginning of Callimachus' *Hymn* to Artemis: vv. 2–3 ὑμνέομεν, τῇ τόξα λαγωβολίαι τε μέλονται | καὶ χορὸς ἀμφιλαφὴς καὶ ἐν οὔρεσιν ἐψιάασθαι. Listing of attributes and characteristic activities of a god is common hymnal practice and the title 'mini-hymn' is again strikingly appropriate for this section (see above on *Aphr.* 7–33).

18 καὶ γὰρ τῇ ἅδε: 'for in fact . . .' is preferable here to the alternative meaning of καὶ γάρ 'and also to her . . .' (cf. Denniston 1954, 108–9 on the particle combination); it has an explanatory function, adding emphasis to the positive affirmation of the preceding negative statement much as ἀλλ' ἄρα begins the list of Athena's concerns above in v. 10. Artemis cannot 'also', i.e. as well as Athena, be interested in hunting and bows, when these things have not previously been presented as concerning Athena. See a clear case of 'and also' in later hexameter poetry at Opp. *H.* 1. 687–8 καὶ γὰρ τῇ μαζοί τε καὶ ἐν μαζοῖσι γάλακτος | εἰσὶ ῥοαί; the seal is said 'also' to have breasts and milk for her young in relation to the dolphin, who was previously described as having these things.

Instead of καὶ γὰρ τῇ ἅδε, MS M alone reads πουλύχρυσα δὲ τόξα. AHS 353 suggest that a line may have been omitted here owing to *homoeomeson* between 18 and a now missing 18a, lightly offering καὶ γὰρ τῇ ἅδε <παρθενίη μέν τ' ἀγαμίη τε> | πουλύχρυσα δὲ τόξα καὶ οὔρεσι θήρας ἐναίρειν as an original reading (note the strange scansion of the first line and the impossible syntax in μέν τ'!). Shackle (1915), 163, had offered οὐ γὰρ τῇ ἅδε ἔργα πολυχρύσου Ἀφροδίτης | πουλύχρυσα etc. VE 18 rejects the proposed reading as implausible, but nonetheless accepts the explanation of a missing line as convincing. In fact there is little to lead to such a conclusion. There is no awkwardness in these lines that would imply that something has dropped out and all Artemis' chief attributes are amply presented in the existing verses; her virginity is indicated by negation in v. 16 (οὐδέ ποτ'), just as in the case of Athena (vv. 7 οὐ δύναται and 9 οὐ γάρ οἱ) and Hestia (v. 21 οὐδὲ μέν), and there is no reason to think the message was repeated here.

The insertion of πουλύχρυσα δὲ τόξα may be explained otherwise. The adjective πολύχρυσος is not elsewhere used of a τόξον, but Artemis' accoutrements are often golden; cf. her golden chariot at *Hy.* 9. 4 (παγχρύσεον ἅρμα) and her golden bow at *Hy.* 27. 5 (παγχρύσεα τόξα); see also Call. *Hy.* 3. 110–12 Ἄρτεμι Παρθενίη Τιτυοκτόνε, χρύσεα μέν τοι | ἔντεα καὶ ζώνη, χρύσεον δ' ἐζεύξαο δίφρον | ἐν δ' ἐβάλευ χρύσεια, θεή, κεμάδεσσι χαλινά. Artemis is in fact called χρυσηλάκατον two lines above and the scribe of M may have been influenced to insert πουλύχρυσα δέ where his exemplar was damaged or problematic, despite the lack of sense without a verb. Moreover, apart from this variant, the lengthened poetic form πουλύχρυσος is never found; this lengthened form, weakly used here *metri gratia*, may have been suggested by the use of the epithet πολύχρυσος twice of Aphrodite in this poem (see above on *Aphr.* 1).

τόξα ... ἐναίρειν: men are killed with bows at *Il.* 8. 296 ἐκ τοῦ δὴ τόξοισι δεδεγμένος ἄνδρας ἐναίρω; cf. the verb ἐναίρω used of human killing elsewhere at *Il.* 13. 483 φῶτας ἐναίρειν and at 20. 96 Τρῶας ἐναίρειν. For hunting mountain-beasts with bows see also S. *Ph.* 955–6 οὐδὲ θῆρ' ὀρειβάτην | τόξοις ἐναίρων.

οὔρεσι θῆρας ἐναίρειν: Artemis is described as a huntress of beasts in the mountains in very similar language at *Il.* 21. 485 ἤτοι βέλτερόν ἐστι κατ' οὔρεα θῆρας ἐναίρειν and she is the teacher of such tasks at 5. 51–2 δίδαξε γὰρ Ἄρτεμις αὐτή | βάλλειν ἄγρια πάντα, τά τε τρέφει οὔρεσιν ὕλη. Cf. also the description of Artemis' protégé at E. *Hipp.* 1129 κυνῶν ὠκυπόδων μέτα θῆρας ἔναιρεν. The goddess is called πότνια θηρῶν at *Il.* 21. 470 and in this role she is not only the huntress of animals but also their protectress (cf. Burkert 1985, 149, Kirk 1990, 59, N. Richardson 1993, 94, and on her protection of bears Anderson 1985, 15; see also on *Aphr.* 68–4 on μήτηρ θηρῶν). Her strong connection with mountains and beasts is elsewhere on full display in *Hy.* 27 (see above on *Aphr.* 18–20). Artemis' identification as *Jagdgöttin* is dominant in literature and art, and she is frequently depicted with her bow (*Gesch.* i. 483 ff.).

For similar language cf. also Pan bounding across the mountains at *Hy.* 19. 12–13 διέδραμεν οὔρεα μακρά, | πολλάκι δ' ἐν κνημοῖσι διήλασε θῆρας ἐναίρων. Nonnus, who mentions Ida just a few lines above, could have been thinking of *Aphr.* at *D.* 11. 296 εἰ ἐτεὸν μενέαινες ἐν οὔρεσι θῆρας ἐναίρειν.

19 φόρμιγγές τε χοροί τε: the lyre is associated with dance at *Il.* 18. 569–72 and *Od.* 8. 248–55, where the Phaeacians dance to the phorminx of Demodocus; note in particular the similarity of *Od.* 8. 248 αἰεὶ δ' ἡμῖν δαίς τε φίλη κίθαρίς τε χοροί τε to this line in *Aphr.* (noted by VE 18). Apollo, who plays the phorminx for the immortals at *Il.* 1. 603 and 24. 63, leads a grand dance of gods and goddesses with the instrument at *Apoll.* 182 ff., and Apollo and Hermes both dance in delight to the lyre at *Herm.* 505 ἄψορροι πρὸς Ὄλυμπον ἀγάννιφον ἐρρώσαντο | τερπόμενοι φόρμιγγι; cf. also *Sc.* 280 αἳ δ' ὑπὸ φορμίγγων ἄναγον χορὸν ἱμερόεντα and Pi. *N.* 5. 23–4 Μοισᾶν ὁ κάλλιστος χορός, ἐν δὲ μέσαις | φόρμιγγ' Ἀπόλλων ἑπτάγλωσσον χρυσέῳ πλάκτρῳ διώκων. A young accompanist is often depicted in art leading a chorus with a lyre, usually standing in the centre of the group of dancers (see Tölle 1964, 62, Heubeck, *OC* i. 362). More generally on the close connection between dance, rhythm, and music in Greek thought see Georgiades (1958), 37–8.

φόρμιγγές: Artemis is never actually in possession of a lyre in Homer, where the instrument is chiefly attached to her brother Apollo, and ownership is not implied here either. She is rarely depicted with the instrument in art (see *LIMC* ii, Artemis, 714–19 and comments there). The earliest of these examples of Artemis herself in possession of a lyre are dated to the end of the sixth century and the particular attribution of this instrument to the goddess may be a later development. She is more often found beside Apollo with his lyre. Her close relationship with her brother, with whom she shares several traits, may in fact explain her adoption of the instrument. It is also interesting that at Arist. *Rh.* 1413[a]1, the term 'stringless lyre' is pointed to as a metaphor for a bow, Artemis' most well-known possession (οἷον ἡ ἀσπὶς φαμέν ἐστι φιάλη Ἄρεως, καὶ τόξον φόρμιγξ ἄχορδος).

The nominative plural of φόρμιγξ is used only once in Homer and Hesiod at *Il.* 18. 495 αὐλοὶ φόρμιγγές τε βοὴν ἔχον, where it is also connected with shouts. Cf. also at line-beginning φόρμιγγα (*Il.* 23. 144) and φόρμιγγός (*Od.* 8. 99, 17. 262).

τε . . . τε . . . τ': for the connective structure of the line see *Il.* 9. 503, 16. 636 and *Od.* 11. 286. See also the use of τε above at v. 11.

χοροί: later in the hymn at v. 118 Aphrodite, in the disguise of a Phrygian girl, claims to have been snatched from a chorus of maidens and virgins in honour of Artemis (see ad loc.). In Homer her dance is mentioned at *Il.* 16. 183, where Hermes falls in love with the virgin Polymele while she is in a chorus of Artemis. Cf. her connection with dance elsewhere at *Hy.* 27. 15, Call. *Hy.* 3. 3, 13–15, 181, and 266. Artemis is also strongly linked to the chorus in cult, and young women often danced together in groups at cult festivals for the goddess (see in particular Calame 1977, i. 252–304; also Burkert 1985, 151, *Gesch.* i. 490 ff.). An armed female dancer (pyrrhic) is at least once depicted dancing around a temple of Artemis (*LIMC* ii, Artemis 113), as described at Call. *Hy.* 3. 240–3.

διαπρύσιοί τ' ὀλολυγαί: διαπρύσιος is not found in Homer or Hesiod as an adjective, but six times adverbially of shouting in the *Iliad* (8. 227 etc.; see Janko 1982, 156). It is also used of a wooded hill 'reaching right across' the plain at *Il.* 17. 748 (cf. M. W. Edwards 1991, 136). Connected with shouting it is probably best translated as 'piercing' or 'penetrating', referring to the high-pitched noise of the voice (see Kirk 1985, 317, Hainsworth 1993, 255, AHS 336). Later at *Aphr.* 80 Anchises is said to play his lyre διαπρύσιον, an instrument which is also mentioned at the beginning of this line (φόρμιγγες). For its use as an adjective, see *Herm.* 336 where Apollo derogatorily and uniquely refers to Hermes as τόνδε διαπρύσιον κεραϊστήν; cf. West (2003) 'thoroughgoing plunderer type.' The adjective is later used of the κέλαδον of cymbals at E. *Hel.* 1308. Cf. ὀξύς of the voice, 'shrill, sharp, high-pitched' (see *LfgrE* s.v. 3 for examples).

The only other time that the word is used of ὀλολυγαί is at Call. *Hy.* 4. 258 διαπρυσίην ὀλολυγήν, a case perhaps of direct influence. Cf. also the adverb connected with shouting later at A.R. 1. 1272 (τῆλε διαπρύσιον μεγάλῃ βοάασκεν αὐτῇ) where the distance of the shout is clearly emphasized. The etymology of the word is uncertain but it may originate from διάπρο (see *Dictionnaire* s.v.).

ὀλολυγαί: the word is found only once in Homer and Hesiod, of the ritual shouts of women praying to Athena at *Il.* 6. 301 (αἳ δ' ὀλολυγῇ πᾶσαι Ἀθήνῃ χεῖρας ἀνέσχον). The D scholia there comment φωνὴ δὲ αὕτη γυναικῶν εὐχομένων θεοῖς, and the restriction of this word to female ritual screams seems to be almost universal (see Deubner 1941; but cf. Dunbar 1995, 207, who points to the verb ὀλολύζω of male shouts at Ar. *Eq.* 616, 1327). At *Apoll.* 119 a group of goddesses shouts (ὀλόλυξαν) at the birth of Apollo, while the wives and the daughters of the Crisaeans are said to shout ritually (ὀλόλυξαν) to Apollo later in the same hymn at v. 445; it is the female Deliades who release a διαπρυσίην ὀλολυγήν at the birth of Apollo at Call. *Hy.* 4. 258; female celebrants are concerned with shouts (ὀλολυγαῖς) at Call. *Hy.* 5. 139; cf. also Alc. 130b. 19–20 ἄχω θεσπεσία γυναίκων ἴρα[ς ὀ]λολύγας ἐνιαυσίας.

The noun and its cognates are used more than once in connection with the birth of Apollo, but van der Mije, *LfgrE* s.v. nonetheless justifiably doubts the suggestion of VE 18 that these shouts in *Aphr.* may refer to Artemis' role as patron of childbirth. The epiphany of Apollo (albeit by birth) is reason enough to explain the ritual shouts at his delivery (cf. Bulloch 1985, 245), and with no particular mention of childbirth in *Aphr.* ὀλολυγαί was probably intended to refer simply to the shouts of female celebrants taking part in the aforementioned ritual dancing. At Ar. *Av.* 214–22 the lyre (φόρμιγγα) and dance (χορούς) are together associated with ὀλολυγή as they are here.

20 ἄλσεά τε σκιόεντα: the adjective σκιόεντα is used of clouds, halls and mountains in Homer, but never of forests. Applied to forests it probably implies 'shady/cool' as well as 'shadowy' and 'dark' (see S. West, *OC* i. 121 on *Od.* 1. 365–6). Artemis' connection with mountains, mentioned at v. 18, may have inspired an innovation from a formula such as οὔρεά τε σκιόεντα θάλασσά τε ἠχήεσσα, found at *Il.* 1. 157. Artemis' domain is said to include ὄρη σκιόεντα at *Hy.* 27. 4. There is a mention of the 'shady' mountains of Ida at *Apoll.* 34.

Forests are later occasionally called 'shady'. See Thgn. 1252 ἄλσεά τε σκιερά and Stesich. fr. 517. 8–9 ὁ δ' ἐς ἄλσος ἔβα δάφναισι κατάσκιον. The fifth-century tragic poet Diogenes mentions the worship of Artemis in a shady forest (*TrGF* 45. 1. 8 δαφνόσκιον κατ' ἄλσος Ἄρτεμιν σέβειν). See later also A.R. 4. 1715 and Theoc. *Id.* 7. 8.

98   *Commentary*

δικαίων τε πτόλις ἀνδρῶν: M transmits the plural πόλεις here, the Θ MSS have the singular πόλις, while the p group gives the improbable alternative πόνος; all are *contra metrum*. The conjecture of the metrically appropriate form πτόλις by the first editor Chalcondyles can be adopted with relative confidence, even though the reading of the singular presents certain difficulties. If the intention of the poet is to refer to Artemis' interest in cities of just men as a general attribute, the plural would be more natural; this may explain scribal correction to the plural πόλεις in M, and the problematic transmission in general.

Càssola 546 argues that the singular must be understood as a collective here (he cites comparable examples at *Od*. 5. 64, 6. 270; see *contra* VE 19), and this interpretation is probably the correct one. The attributes presented in the preceding lines are all clearly universal, and a switch to refer to a specific city would seem unnatural; especially when that city is not named. Callimachus uses the singular πόλιν collectively to refer to an attribute of Artemis at *Hy*. 3. 122 (ἀλλά μιν εἰς ἀδίκων ἔβαλες πόλιν), a passage which is very probably a deliberate and clever adaptation of this line in *Aphr*. There, by contrast, πόλιν more naturally follows on from a string of singulars (δρῦν, θῆρα), as the poet tells permanent truths by recalling Artemis' historic firsts; the fact that Callimachus seems to be deliberately echoing this line in *Aphr*. may indicate that there was originally a singular, which he took to be collective.

Elsewhere, Artemis is connected with a city in the singular in a fragment of Anacreon:

γουνοῦμαί σ' ἐλαφηβόλε
ξανθὴ παῖ Διὸς ἀγρίων
δέσποιν' Ἄρτεμι θηρῶν,
ἥ κου νῦν ἐπὶ Ληθαίου
δίνῃσι θρασυκαρδίων   5
ἀνδρῶν ἐσκατορᾷς πόλιν
χαίρουσ', οὐ γὰρ ἀνημέρους
ποιμαίνεις πολιήτας (*PMG* 348).

Anacreon uses the singular here to refer to a specific city; most probably Magnesia at the end of the river Lethaeus in Asia Minor, near to which there was the temple of Artemis Leucophryene; see

Page (1960), Bowra (1961), 273–4 (cf. Strabo 14. 1. 39 on rivers by this name). Her connection with a city of θρασυκαρδίων ἀνδρῶν (note how this echoes ἀγρίων δέσποινα θηρῶν three lines above), the citizens of which are οὐ ... ἀνημέρους, shows a concern with justice similar to that in *Aphr.*; but there is no reason to suppose that Anacreon had *Aphr.* particularly in mind.

Apart from *Aphr.*, Anacreon, and Callimachus, Artemis is not elsewhere identified as a goddess with connections to the city and justice. Callimachus' hymn to the goddess is somewhat of an exception in that it makes such a point of her connection with cities: she asks for a city at v. 18, is granted thirty cities by Zeus at vv. 33–5 (note the repetition of πτολίεθρα there), is concerned with cities and justice in vv. 122 ff., and is πολύπτολι at v. 225! Yet, if this all seems a bit much when compared with the sparse mention of this attribute elsewhere in literature, hyperbole may be the whole point; it is quite in line with Callimachus' literary programme to walk the 'path less trodden' (see Call. fr. 1. 25–8), and it also accords with the theme of jealousy and competitiveness with her brother Apollo, which is so prominent in the hymn (see Plantinga 2004, 258–64).

Her concern with just cities resembles more the role of Zeus as protector/punisher of the just/unjust cities described at *Op.* 225 ff. (cf. VE 19): there is no particular verbal similarity between Hesiod and *Aphr.* in this case, but it is interesting that Callimachus seems to be adapting the Hesiodic passage to suit Artemis as an avenger of justice in the lines following *Hy.* 3. 122 (see West 1978, 213), a verse which, as was suggested above, was probably inspired by this line in *Aphr.* (note also Libanius, *Or.* 5. 34, where Artemis is said to reward/ punish the just/unjust with the help of her father Zeus; cf. Bornmann 1968, 61). Also of note is her resemblance in this respect to the Hecate of the *Theogony*. In the section dedicated to Hecate by Hesiod (vv. 404–52; on the authenticity of the passage see West 1966a, 276 ff.), Hecate is said to sit beside kings in matters of justice (v. 434 ἔν τε δίκῃ βασιλεῦσι παρ' αἰδοίοισι καθίζει): again there is no verbal similarity with *Aphr.*, but the mention of justice is remarkable given Artemis' well-known connection with her cousin. The relationship between the two goddesses seems to have been early (see Wilamowitz 1931–2, i. 169 ff., Kraus 1960, 14). At A. *Supp.* 676 (cf. A. 140 Ἑκάτα; conjectured by Badham), Ἄρτεμις ἑκάτα is associated with the protection of women (cf. Johansen–Whittle 1980 iii. 41–2). In cult, Artemis-Hecate was later worshipped in Athens, with the epithet φωσφόρος (see Simon 1985, 152–3, Graf 1985, 228 ff., Kraus 1960, 85 ff.). Also in Asia Minor, where Hecate cult was most prominent, the two goddesses are found together: the earliest archaeological evidence for Hecate-worship, a round altar with an inscription on it *boustrophedon* (*Milet*, iii. 275–6; see Kraus 1960, 11 ff.), is found at Miletus, where Artemis was also worshipped; Pliny later reports a statue of Hecate in the famous temple of Artemis at Ephesus (*Nat.* 36. 32; cf. Kraus 1960, 39 ff.). However, similar to Artemis, the conspicuous connection with δίκη attributed to Hecate in the *Theogony* is not reflected in the evidence for her cult; she has an attachment to cities as the protectress of doors and gates (πρόπολις, προπύλαιος), but she does not seem to have been a goddess of justice.

Artemis' association with justice and cities in cult is rare, yet it seems to have been more prominent in Asia Minor. In his third *Hymn* (discussed above), Callimachus singles out the city of Miletus as a cult centre of the goddess, just after calling her πολύπτολι (vv. 225–6). She is called βουληφόρος in Miletus (*Gesch.* i. 498, Farnell ii. 468), and if Anacreon is referring to her connection with justice in the above fragment, it is noteworthy that his birthplace was Teos, not far from Miletus (cf. Simon 1985, 154 on her connection with these cities). Again in Asia Minor, the Ephesian Artemis wore a turret-crown on her head, 'the badge of the city-goddess' (see Farnell ii. 481, who points to her affinity in Ephesus with eastern goddesses such as Cybele). Elsewhere Artemis is identified with justice in Athens, where she was called βουλαία, and she is found in an urban setting at Olympia as ἀγοραία (according to Paus. 5. 15. 4). She is even invoked in the ratification of oaths in some treaties in Crete (see Willetts 1962, 272 ff.). However, given other signs that *Aphr.* is a product of Asia Minor (see Introd., pp. 49–50), it would not be unreasonable to attribute the mention of cities in *Aphr.* to some knowledge of Artemis cult in Asia Minor, where this side of the goddess seems to have been strongest.

Ultimately the poet may be emphasizing this rare attribute of the goddess for literary effect; just as Hestia is later in the poem said faithfully to swear oaths of virginity to Zeus, Artemis is a goddess connected to justice and social order in sharp contrast to the deceitful Aphrodite of vv. 7 and 33, who in cult had 'less to do than most of the other Greek divinities with the arts of civilization' (Farnell ii. 668, cf. Smith 1981a, 35 ff.).

21–32. The third virgin goddess to receive a mini-hymn is Hestia. The passage devoted to her is conspicuously the longest and the most extensive of the three presented to the chaste divinities (12 lines are set aside for her, as opposed to 8 for Athena and 5 for Artemis), and her mini-hymn moves beyond the simple attributive praise which Athena and Artemis receive. A short historical narrative, telling of her double birth, her refusal of the advances of Poseidon and Apollo, and her subsequent privileged placement in the centre of Zeus' house as a virgin, underlines her great honour. She is ὁπλοτάτη at v. 23, διὰ θεάων at v. 28, the recipient of πῖαρ at 30, and then emphatically she both is θεῶν τιμάοχος and πρέσβειρα τέτυκται at vv. 31–2, two lines which mirror each other in structure and intention (cf. Solmsen 1960, 8 n. 1). The place she occupies in the poem reflects this emphasis on her honour; as the oldest she has the final and most honoured position amongst the goddesses and she receives more extensive and detailed praise.

Hestia does not appear in Homer at all as a goddess, despite her great antiquity and the religious importance of the hearth throughout Greece (cf. *Gesch.* i. 78–9, AHS 417–18); she is first mentioned in literature as a personified goddess at Hes. *Th.* 452–3 (Ῥείη δὲ δμηθεῖσα Κρόνῳ τέκε φαίδιμα τέκνα, | Ἱστίην ...). Moreover, much of the story told in the short narrative in *Aphr.*—the pursuit of Poseidon and Apollo, and her swearing of oaths to Zeus—is not found elsewhere in literature. It may well be the innovation of this poet, based upon more than one literary model (see on *Aphr.* 22–3, 24–5, 25–32). Solmsen (1960) has argued convincingly that the poet of *Aphr.* is drawing at least partially upon Hesiod for this narrative (see on *Aphr.* 22–3), but his suggestion (followed by Podbielski, 26, VE 20) that the poet is aiming at a reconciliation between Hesiod and Homer, where Hera claims to be the eldest child of Kronos (*Il.* 4. 59), is not a convincing explanation for why Hestia has been introduced here. A programme of introducing such originality on grounds of literary reconciliation alone seems forced for an archaic poet; cf. Heitsch (1965), 20: 'Ob *h.Aphr.* hier nur eine ... Hesiodformulierung systematisch explizieren wollte, ist zweifelhaft.' Certainly, after having introduced the Hesiodic version of Hestia's birth and regurgitation as part of this unique elaboration upon the goddess, the poet might have felt it necessary to adapt the Homeric version of Hera's seniority (introduced in the hymn for other reasons; see below on *Aphr.* 40–4), but why has the poet expanded upon Hestia here in the first place?

Smith (1981*a*), 36 suggests that Hestia is attached to the other goddesses through her capacity as a destroyer of animals, in contrast with Aphrodite who represents reproduction; but this assumes a conscious preoccupation with life and death which again seems rather forced. A more convincing argument for her inclusion on literary grounds is that divinities often appear in threes in myth (cf. Podbielski 1971, 24). It may have been desirable for the poet to present a group of three goddesses in opposition to Aphrodite, and Hestia, carrying with her the associations of purity connected with the hearth, and the links with social order and society which Athena and Artemis display (see Smith 1981*a*, 35 ff.; cf. above on v. 20 on Artemis), would have been a possible candidate to complete the group. Heitsch (1965), 20 suggests that Dike, a personified virgin already at *Op.* 256, was perhaps the more obvious choice. But although she does have a seat next to Zeus, which is similar to the one which Hestia is granted at *Aphr.* 30 (πὰρ Διὶ πατρὶ καθεζομένη, *Op.* 259; see West 1978, ad loc. on Dike's privileged placement), she is not on the same level as Hestia in the pantheon.

As it stands, the section fits naturally into the development of the hymn and has an integral function. Her episode not only provides a further contrast to Aphrodite (cf. Porter 1949, 253), but also introduces the pivotal role which Zeus will play in the main narrative of the hymn; presented as he is in the Hestia episode, the father of the gods significantly becomes first the one that rewards Hestia for her chaste obedience, and then later the one who will punish Aphrodite for her promiscuity and deceit (cf. Clay 1989, 162, Smith 1981*a*, 37). Furthermore, his introduction here in a position of power and control heightens the ironic effect at v. 36, when Zeus himself is proclaimed to be a victim of Aphrodite. Note that Hestia's connection with Zeus is also explicit at *Hy.* 24. 5 (σὺν Διὶ μητιόεντι), and it was often the case in cult that she was associated with Zeus, the god of the state (see AHS 419–20).

Podbielski (1971), 26–7 suggests that 'les épithètes de la déesse, la description de ses fonctions cultuelles, sa position centrale dans tous les temples et tous les foyers, le caractère général de son culte souligné par la répétition du mot πᾶσι, l'explication de l'étiologie des rites . . .' all point to a cult hymn in honour of the goddess (cf. also Heitsch 1965, 20). The poet may well have been familiar with a cult of Hestia, but there is no indication of a particular cult connection in this passage. The repetition of πᾶσι and the stress upon her central position underline her pan-Hellenic glory amongst the pantheon of gods. Hestia was frequently worshipped as the hearth in the *prytaneion* or *bouleuterion* of cities (Farnell v. 348). The most famous hearth in Greece was certainly that at Delphi, in the temple of Apollo (cf. AHS 418, Süss, *RE* vii. 1288 ff.). She is connected with Delphi at *Hy*. 24. 1–2 (Ἑστίη, ἥ τε ἄνακτος Ἀπόλλωνος ἑκάτοιο | Πυθοῖ ἐν ἠγαθέῃ ἱερὸν δόμον ἀμφιπολεύεις), and elsewhere in a hymn dedicated to her by Aristonous of Corinth, where she is also said to occupy Olympus (*CA* 2. 2–3). She also had a famous hearth in Olympia (see Xen. *HG* 7. 4. 31; cf. Farnell v. 362 and for the archaeological evidence for the temple there see Drees 1968, 124 ff., Kirster–Kraiker 1967, 282). Pausanias reports that her sacred flame burnt there night and day, and ash from the hearth was brought each year to the altar of Olympian Zeus, contributing to its great height (5. 15. 9).

21 οὐδὲ μέν: 'nor indeed', as at A.R. 3. 388 (see Campbell 1994, 332 ad loc.), is preferable here to Denniston's 'nor again' (1954, 362). This line recalls both οὐ γάρ at v. 9 and οὐδέ ποτ' at v. 16 (on this awkward bit of structure see on *Aphr*. 8).

αἰδοίη κούρῃ: cf. of Hestia *Hy*. 29. 10 σὺν αἰδοίῃ τε φίλῃ. The adjective is not definitely joined with κούρῃ anywhere else in archaic poetry, but see the conjecture of West at [Hes.] fr. 180. 13 (κούρην τ' α]ἰδοίην ἑλικώπιδα). The pairing is in fact found only once more in Greek literature at A.R. 4. 1491 κούρης τ' αἰδοίης Ἀκακαλλίδος, ἥν ποτε Μίνως. The adjective αἰδοίη is elsewhere used of virgin divinities (παρθένον αἰδοίην is used of Artemis at *Hy*. 27. 2, Athena at *Hy*. 28. 3, and of the virgin Dike at *Op*. 256–7; cf. also the adjective with παρθένῳ at *Il*. 2. 514 and *Th*. 572), but it is also used of Aphrodite at *Hy*. 6. 1 and *Th*. 194 and is more generally indicative of the 'respect' or 'reverence' which a goddess inspires; see N. Richardson (1974), 227, Verdenius (1971), 5. On the original meaning of 'religious awe' of αἰδώς and its cognates see Hooker (1987). The term is elsewhere used of Demeter and Persephone at *Dem.* 374, 486, and of Maia at *Herm.* 5. Cf. below on *Aphr.* 44 of wives.

22–3. Kronos swallowed his children and then regurgitated them in inverse order; so the story is told in Hes. *Th.* 453–500. West (1966*a*), 293 suggests that 'the idea that the regurgitation was a second birth may have been developed so that Zeus, who grew up before any of these secondary births, could be counted as the eldest as well as the youngest'. In *Aphr.* Hestia is said to be both the firstborn of Kronos, but also the youngest on account of this regurgitation, and as Solmsen (1960) has argued, the poet of *Aphr.* seems to be drawing upon Hesiod for this part of the Hestia episode: at *Th.* 454 Hestia is mentioned first of all the children of Kronos and Rhea, and because Zeus is subsequently mentioned last at 457, 'tatsächlich der jüngste', it can be assumed that the children are presented in order of their birth (ibid. 2–3). This primary position of the goddess is made explicit in *Aphr.*, in contrast to Homer, where Hera claims to be the eldest (*Il.* 4. 59; see on *Aphr.* 40–44).

Solmsen has also suggested that further influence from Hesiod can be detected in the Hestia episode: Zeus is presented in *Aphr.* as the bestower of honours upon Hestia, which is a position in relation to the other gods that Bruno Snell points out is chiefly Hesiodic: 'erst für Hesiod hat Zeus "alles verteilt"' (Snell ap. Solmsen, 1960, 3). At *Aphr.* 28 Zeus gives Hestia a γέρας in compensation for remaining a virgin, and she is called τιμάοχος just two lines later; the two terms γέρας and τιμή are often found together in Hesiod, connected with the granting of functions by Zeus (cf. *Th.* 393, 395–6, 426–7; Solmsen 1960, 5, Podbielski 1971, 26); this same emphasis on γέρας and τιμή for Hestia is found at *Hy.* 29. 3–4 (ἕδρην ἀΐδιον ἔλαχες πρεσβηΐδα τιμὴν | καλὸν ἔχουσα γέρας καὶ τιμήν), but Zeus is not involved in the apportionment there. There is some danger in assuming that because Zeus' position in *Aphr.* corresponds with his function in Hesiod it is drawn directly from there; a fragment of Lesbian poetry provides striking parallels for the narrative following from v. 25 (see on *Aphr.* 25–32), where Zeus seems to be granting virginity to Artemis as he does to Hestia in *Aphr.*; Hesiod may at any rate not have been the only source with Hesiodic cosmic ordering. A similar caution could be issued about the myth of Kronos swallowing his children.

However, it seems very probable that the poet of *Aphr.* is drawing upon the *Th.*, given the combination of the above factors; a view which is supported by several striking linguistic similarities elsewhere between the two poems (see Introd., pp. 35–6).

The myth of Hestia's second birth and status as youngest and eldest may have been linked to a practice of making a libation to Hestia at the beginning and end of a sacrifice (see AHS 428 ff., *Gesch.* i. 338).

22 Ἱστίη: this Ionic form is found in all but three of the MSS (At, D, M), and should be printed here; ἑστίη is a common variant, cf. AHS 354, West (1966a), 293–4. For the prosody here (–⏑⏑ with epic correption), see *Op.* 734, *Hy.* 24. 1, 29. 1, 6, 11, and later Call. *Hy.* 4. 325 (cf. Mineur 1984, 251 ad loc.). ἱστίη appears at line-beginning with the prosody (– – –) at *Od.* 14. 159, 17. 156, 19. 304, 20. 231 and *Th.* 454. The enjambment of the name here (as at *Hy.* 29. 11) draws attention to it.

ἣν πρώτην τέκετο Κρόνος ἀγκυλομήτης: the formula τέκετο Κρόνος ἀγκυλομήτης is later used to refer to the birth of Hera at v. 42, as does its one occurrence in Homer at *Il.* 4. 59 (see on *Aphr.* 40–4). For a similar structure cf. *Th.* 137 τοὺς δὲ μέθ' ὁπλότατος γένετο Κρόνος ἀγκυλομήτης and *Il.* 20. 215 Δάρδανον αὖ πρῶτον τέκετο νεφεληγερέτα Ζεύς.

Κρόνος ἀγκυλομήτης: in the nominative elsewhere at *Th.* 137, 168, 473, 495 and once in Homer at *Il.* 4. 58; also in the accusative at *Th.* 18, while the genitive Κρόνου πάϊς ἀγκυλομήτεω appears five times in Homer (*Il.* 2. 205 etc.). The adjective is used only of Kronos in Homer, but twice of Prometheus in Hesiod, at *Th.* 546 and *Op.* 48.

The original meaning of the epithet may have been 'of the curved sickle'; see Cook ii. 549 n. 8 and *Dictionnaire* s.v. However, by the time of Hesiod the name clearly has the sense given in the *Suda* οἱ σκολιόβουλοι, 'crooked-planning' or 'cunning', evidenced partially by the fact that it is used also of Prometheus (see West 1966a, 158). It was probably understood in this way in *Aphr.* as well; at v. 42 the formula occurs just before Ζεὺς δ' ἄφθιτα μήδεα εἰδώς in the next line, and invites comparison between 'crafty' Kronos and his even more cunning son who defeated him.

23 ὁπλοτάτην: 'youngest'. This superlative form of the comparative ὁπλότερος is most often found in the *Odyssey* used of marriageable young women such as Polycaste at 3. 465 and Chloris, an ὁπλοτάτην κούρην at 11. 283 (cf. *LfgrE* s.v. ὁπλότερος and Burkert 2002, 32). Hestia fits into this same category, pursued by Poseidon and Apollo, although she will remain a virgin for eternity. The accepted derivation of this word in antiquity was from ὅπλον, the younger being those who were more able to fight and bear arms; see *EM* 628. 24 ff. Aristophanes plays upon this supposed original meaning at *Pax*. 1270 when he parodies the reported opening line of the *Epigoni*, νῦν αὖθ' ὁπλοτέρων ἀνδρῶν ἀρχώμεθα Μοῦσαι (see Olson 1998, 307), and Burkert (2002), goes so far as to suggest that this famous verse may have been the 'Weiche . . . die ein neues Gleis der Bedeutung erschloß' (see the discussion in Faulkner 2003). More attractive is an original derivation from the IE root *oplo*, 'strength' supported by Szemerényi (1977), 6, cf. S. West, *OC* i. 189–90, the younger being stronger and more generally able. Any sense of ὅπλον is certainly not felt here in *Aphr.* (cf. also Hainsworth 1993, 67).

βουλῇ Διὸς αἰγιόχοιο: this is not a Homeric phrase, and it recurs only once more at Hom. *Ep.* 4. 3 (*Vit. Hom.* 175) ἥν ποτ' ἐπύργωσαν βουλῇ Διὸς αἰγιόχοιο. Cf. also *Op.* 99 αἰγιόχου βουλῇ Διὸς and later Q.S. 6. 141 ὑποσχομένη βουλῇ Διός· οὐ γὰρ ἐῴκει.

The βουλή of Zeus is a central concern in *Aphr.*; his vindictive plans are what will set the narrative in motion at v. 45. His control of the second birth of Hestia here introduces his power over the gods. The βουλή of Zeus is often mentioned at the beginning of an epic poem, perhaps most famously at *Il.* 1. 5 (see N. Richardson 1974, 145 for a list of ancient examples).

Διὸς αἰγιόχοιο: the formula is quite common at line-end in Homer and Hesiod (*Il.* 2. 348, 2. 491, 15. 175, *Od.* 3. 42, 3. 394, *Th.* 25, 52, 735, 966, 1022). The epithet αἰγίοχος is only ever applied to Zeus. It is most often taken to mean 'aegis-bearing' by modern translators, but this is almost certainly not its original meaning. It was a hotly contested term even in antiquity: at *EM* 29. 6 ff., some are said to have claimed that it referred to Zeus' rearing in Crete by the goat Amalthea, others that it refers to the famous σκεπαστήριον he bears in the *Iliad* (made from a Cretan goat), others that it comes from his control of the roaring winds (καλεῖται γὰρ αἰγὶς ὁ ἄνεμος), and yet others that it recalls when Zeus took Aiga, the daughter of Pan, as his first wife. But none of these explains the second element of the word

-ϝοχος, which must mean something like 'carried by/riding upon', cf. ὀχέω/ὄχος (of vehicular or animal transport; see *Dictionnaire* s.v.). West (1978), 366 ff. offers the suggestion that the bleating of the snipe (αἴξ = goat, but was also the name of a bird) might have presaged a coming storm, and that the epithet originally referred to Zeus being borne along in a chariot pulled by such birds; comparable to Aphrodite's chariot being pulled by sparrows in Sappho. He also offers the example of Thor, the Germanic god of thunder whose chariot was drawn by goats; Zeus rides Amalthea in *Orph.* fr. 236 Bernabé (*testimonium: Recognitiones Clementinae*, tr. Rufinus 10. 19. 2 *ab ipsa caprae superpositus in caelum emissus est*; cf. West 1983, 133). The meteorological connection with roaring winds given in the *EM* may reflect this original sense; cf. *Il.* 17. 593 Κρονίδης ἕλετ' αἰγίδα θυσανόεσσαν.

Nonetheless, S. West (*OC* i. 163) is justified in claiming that for Homer the epithet had probably come to mean 'aegis-bearing'; the aegis is a frequent tool of Zeus in the *Iliad*, and it may have been the intended significance of the epithet in *Aphr.* as well. First and foremost, the epithet stresses Zeus' authority and power, the aegis being a symbol of his power (see Janko 1992, 261). Cf. also *Dictionnaire*, Frisk s.v. αἰγίς, *LfgrE* s.v.

24–5. The pursuit of Hestia by Poseidon and Apollo is not attested elsewhere in either literature or art, and the myth is very possibly an innovation of this poet. The lack of artistic representation and imitation of this story by later authors can perhaps be explained by the infrequent personification of Hestia in both cult and literature, even if the scene was known.

Jouan (1956) suggests that the author of *Aphr.* was drawing for this myth upon the Hesiodic *Catalogue* (frr. 210–11; cf. Dornseiff 1931), which tells of the pursuit of Thetis by Zeus. He argues that the model has been adapted in order to enhance the legend of Hestia, with Zeus having been replaced as a suitor by Apollo. The pursuit of Thetis by Zeus is also treated in the *Cypria* (fr. 2), and with Poseidon included at Pi. *I.* 8. 26 ff.; cf. as well [A.] *PV* 922–5. At the end of the *Theogony* (1006–10), which probably led on to the *Catalogue* (see West 1966a, 397 ff.), the stories of the mortal–divine unions of Thetis and Peleus and of Aphrodite and Anchises are mentioned one after the other (the unions are also compared at

Il. 20. 105–7, 203–9; cf. Lenz 1975, 36–7), and the model of the pursuit of another goddess who has a famous child with a mortal may have presented itself naturally to the poet of *Aphr.* (cf. Jouan 1956, 296). Yet, however desirable such an adaptation of this myth might be here, there is nothing to substantiate a direct link: 'Das Material des Hymnus zeigt wohl gewisse allgemeine Motivähnlichkeiten mit den von Jouan herangezogenen Parallelen, aber nicht eine wirkliche Übereinstimmung im einzelnen' (Lenz 1975, 143; cf. VE 21). The pursuit of Thetis would have been a natural model for this unique pursuit of Hestia, but for confirmation of whether the latter was inspired by a Hesiodic version of the former, the fragmentary remains are not forthcoming.

The appearance of Apollo and Poseidon as the pair of wooers here has been a further source of debate. If the episode was indeed adapted from a version of the pursuit of Thetis, the presence of Poseidon is more explicable, or at least less emphasized. Poseidon would merely be transposed, while Apollo would be a unique substitute for Zeus. On the other hand, Apollo is mentioned in the opening lines of a lyric hymn to Artemis, which offers clear parallels for the swearing of Hestia's oath here in *Aphr.* (see on *Aphr.* 25–32); this, or an earlier exemplar, could have suggested the god. On a formulaic level, the pairing of the two gods in a verse has Homeric precedent: Ποσειδάων καὶ Ἀπόλλων act together at *Il.* 12. 17 and 12. 34 to destroy the Achaean wall (cf. Jouan 1956, 297 and see below). However, their destruction of a wall in Homer is not an obvious model for them as amorous suitors. Their inclusion can be justified plausibly on literary grounds: Solmsen (1960), 7 n. 3 suggests that Hestia's refusal of the two most important gods after Zeus increases the praise of her virginity (cf. Podbielski 1971, 25–6). One might also suggest that by Hestia's refusal of the advances of Poseidon and Apollo, and her swearing an oath to Zeus, the supremacy of Zeus over the other gods is given that much more emphasis and honour; the balance of power between Poseidon and his brother Zeus is already known, and decided in favour of Zeus, at *Il.* 15. 184 ff.

Mommsen (1878), 2 suggests a solution based upon their inclusion in cult practice at Delphi, where Hestia famously sat at the central hearth, and both Poseidon and Apollo had an honoured place (see on *Aphr.* 21–32 on Hestia cult). But Delphi is not the only place that they are found together. Pausanias mentions statues of Poseidon, Apollo, and Aphrodite together in his description of Corinth (2. 2. 8). Poseidon had a famous and ancient cult at the Isthmus of Corinth (Farnell iv. 38–9), and Apollo also had a conspicuous temple in Corinth, just below Acrocorinth (see Salmon 1984, 59 ff.; a previous temple on the site of the present sanctuary of Apollo shares clay roof tiles with a temple of Poseidon at Isthmia, suggesting that there existed two early contemporary structures to the gods). Both these sites are in clear view of the cult-site of pan-Hellenic fame to Aphrodite at Acrocorinth. There was also worship of Poseidon and Apollo together at Potidaea in Chalkidike, an important colony of Corinth (see Alexander 1963, 23–5). AHS 325 point out a group of statues of Poseidon, Amphitrite, and Hestia described by Pausanias (5. 26. 2) at Olympia. The two gods are also linked by their connection with dolphins (see Schamp 1976, 100 ff.).

24 πότνιαν: 'lady' or 'queen'; the title is a common term of respect (σεβασμία, ἔντιμος, *EM* 685. 50), indicating authority and influence. The connection with prestige is well displayed at *Dem.* 492 πότνια ἀγλαόδωρ' ὡρηφόρε Δηοῖ ἄνασσα. The accusative is found elsewhere in early poetry only at *Th.* 11, 926, *Dem.* 203 and Alc. fr. 3. 1 (cf. West 1966a, 79, 156, N. Richardson 1974, 222, Janko 1982, 156). Of these occurrences, πότνιαν is at the beginning of the line only at *Th.* 926, a verse which also has similarities with *Aphr.* 10–11 (see ad loc); note also the nominative in this metrical position at *Dem.* 492, *Hy.* 30. 6 and Hom. *Ep.* 7. 1 (*Vit. Hom.* 249).

In Homer it is used for both mortals and goddesses, most often of mothers and Hera; also at *Il.* 21. 470 of Artemis, at 5. 592 of Enyo, at 6. 305 of Athena, of the nymph Calypso at *Od.* 1. 14 and 5. 149, and of Circe at *Od.* 8. 448 etc. It is often used of Demeter and Kore after Homer (cf. N. Richardson 1974, 161–2). Later, in a fragment of Euripides (*Phaethon* 228–31 Diggle) the term is applied to Aphrodite: τὴν Διὸς οὐρανίαν ἀείδομεν | τὰν ἐρώτων πότνιαν, τὰν παρθένοις | γαμήλιον Ἀφροδίταν | πότνια, σοὶ τάδ' ἐγὼ νυμφεῖ' ἀείδω; cf. of Peitho at *Op.* 73. On the etymology of the epithet (and the disyllabic πότνα *Od.* 5. 215, 13. 391, 20. 61) see *Dictionnaire* and Frisk s.v. It may have been applied to Athena in a tablet found at Knossos, *a-ta-na-po-ti-ni-ja*, and seems to have stood alone as a divine name on other tablets (see Chadwick 1957; Chadwick–Ventris 1973, 126–7; cf. Russo, *OC* iii. 112 for further discussion and bibliography).

ἐμνῶντο: the verb μνάομαι 'to woo/court' is 'am plausibelsten erklärt als Sonderentwicklung von μνάομαι „gedenken"' (Schmidt in *LfgrE* s.v., with bibliography). The verb is never used with this meaning in the *Iliad*, and is found first in the *Odyssey* of the suitors at 1. 39 etc. Callimachus plays wonderfully upon the two possible meanings at *Hy*. 2. 95 μνωόμενος προτέρης ἁρπακτύος (see Williams 1978, 81).

Apollo goes after Azantis with the verb at *Apoll*. 209 ὅππως μνωόμενος ἔκιες Ἀζαντίδα κούρην (assuming that Martin's conjecture is correct there; see AHS 230).

ἐμνῶντο Ποσειδάων καὶ Ἀπόλλων: this line is very similar to *Il*. 12. 17 δὴ τότε μητιόωντο Ποσειδάων καὶ Ἀπόλλων. The two names appear at line-end also at *Il*. 12. 34 and [Hes.] fr. 235. 5. Later, cf. the similar line at Colluth. 279 Ἴλιον, ἥν πύργωσε Ποσειδάων καὶ Ἀπόλλων, which tells of how Poseidon and Apollo built the walls of Troy for Laomedon; as Poseidon recounts at *Il*. 7. 446 ff. (cf. Livrea 1968, 208–9).

25–32. This passage is very similar in content and vocabulary to a fragment of a lyric hymn to Artemis:

```
     ] cανορες .. [
    ]μαι τὸν ἔτικτε Κόω . [
    Κρ]ονίδαι μεγαλωνύμω<ι>
    ]μέγαν ὅρκον ἀπώμοσε
    ]λαν· ἀΐ πάρθενος ἔσσομαι              5
    ]. ων ὀρέων κορύφαις ἔπι
    ]δε νεῦσον ἔμαν χάριν·
    ]. ε θέων μακάρων πάτηρ·
    ]ολον ἀγροτέραν θέοι
    ]. σιν ἐπωνύμιον μέγα·                  10
    ]ερος οὐδάμα πίλναται· (Sapph. fr. 44a. 1–11 Voigt)
```

The fragment was tentatively considered to be a work of Alcaeus by Lobel–Page (1952) on metrical grounds, but Treu (1968), 161–4 is probably right to attribute it to Sappho (adopted by Voigt; cf. also Liberman 1999, p. xciv). Refuting any metrical arguments, he suggests that the poet speaks personally through the poetry in the manner of Sappho, and also points to Philostratus' comment that

Sappho wrote hymns to Artemis (*VA* 1. 30). The evidence is not conclusive either way, but whether it is by Alcaeus or Sappho, this fragment supports the link between *Aphr.* and Lesbian poetry, which suggests itself elsewhere in the hymn (cf. on *Aphr.* 13 σατίνας and see Introd., pp. 45–7).

The uniqueness of the Hestia narrative in *Aphr.* makes direct borrowing from the latter improbable (cf. West 2002, 217). More likely would be the transposition of this episode from Artemis to Hestia by the poet of *Aphr.* This leaves two possibilities: *Aphr.* is either drawing directly on this fragment, or there was a common exemplar (or exemplars) for the two poets (cf. Treu 1968, 161–2). West's comment (loc. cit.) that 'Alcaeus will hardly have been the model for the hexameter poets' should be treated with caution; there is nothing *a priori* that denies the possibility of a hexameter poet borrowing from either Lesbian source. Nonetheless, borrowing from Sappho by the poet of *Aphr.* does seem less likely, and there is nothing to substantiate direct borrowing here in any case. A common exemplar sufficiently explains the similarities between the two passages.

This episode of virginity-granting by Zeus is also imitated later by Callimachus. In his third *Hymn* (6 ff.), Artemis asks for virginity from Zeus, δός μοι παρθενίην αἰώνιον, ἄππα, φυλάσσειν (v. 6), and is granted it with a nod of the head, πατὴρ δ' ἐπένευσε γελάσσας (v. 28), as is the case in the Lesbian fragment (see Page 1955, 264–5). Although the nodding of the head does not occur in *Aphr.*, it also seems to have influenced Callimachus directly (cf. above on *Aphr.* 20 δικαίων τε πτόλις ἀνδρῶν): Artemis playfully pulls upon Zeus' beard in order to precipitate his nodding in Callimachus, ὣς ἡ παῖς εἰποῦσα γενειάδος ἤθελε πατρὸς | ἅψασθαι ... (vv. 26–7), a detail which appears to be drawn from *Aphr.* 27 ἁψαμένη κεφαλῆς πατρὸς Διὸς αἰγιόχοιο. (The grasping of the head does not occur in the above fragment, but cf. v. 5, which may have read κεφα]λὰν· ἄϊ πάρθενος ἔσσομαι; if, however, a form of ἅπτομαι preceded, one would expect the genitive and not the accusative κεφαλάν.) Callimachus seems to have been aware of both poems, and, if one in fact existed, he may even have been in possession of a common exemplar.

Jouan (1956), 299 suggests that E. *Tr.* 979–81 ἢ γάμον Ἀθάνα θεῶν τινος θηρωμένη, | ἢ παρθένειαν πατρὸς ἐξῃτήσατο | φεύγουσα λέκτρα

... is taken from this passage, but while the petition is similar, the language is very different. Euripides may well have known *Aphr.* (see on *Aphr.* 16–20), but there is no evidence to suggest conscious borrowing from this passage (cf. VE 22). Much more similar is *Hy.* 29: the statement of Hestia's honour amongst gods and men in vv. 1–2 corresponds to *Aphr.* 31–2, vv. 3–4 ἕδρην ἀΐδιον ἔλαχες, πρεσβηΐδα τιμήν | καλὸν ἔχουσα γέρας καὶ τιμὴν correspond to *Aphr.* 29, also recalling the use of πρέσβειρα at *Aphr.* 32, and v. 5 ... ἵν' οὐ πρώτῃ πυμάτῃ τε suggests her status as eldest and youngest detailed at *Aphr.* 22–3 (cf. Janko 1982, 268 n. 25, Solmsen 1960, 8 n. 2, 9 n. 5).

25 ἡ δὲ μάλ' οὐκ ἔθελεν: the point of Hestia's refusal is made with force in this line; she 'certainly' (μάλ') did not want the attentions of Poseidon or Apollo, and refused 'firmly' (στερεῶς). The stage is being set for her great oath to Zeus. Cf. *Il.* 18. 434 πολλὰ μάλ' οὐκ ἐθέλουσα, where Thetis laments her unwilling union with Peleus at the hands of Zeus. The phrase ἡ δὲ μάλ' occurs at line-beginning seven times in Homer (*Il.* 12. 63 etc).

στερεῶς ἀπέειπεν: cf. the very similar *Il.* 9. 510 ὃς δέ κ' ἀνήνηται καί τε στερεῶς ἀποείπῃ, and also 9. 431 μάλα γὰρ κρατερῶς ἀπέειπεν (where Leaf i. 402 'may mean either *spoke out* as 309, or *refused their offers*'). Elsewhere, for firm refusal followed by the swearing of an oath see *Il.* 23. 42 αὐτὰρ ὅ γ' ἠρνεῖτο στερεῶς, ἐπὶ δ' ὅρκον ὄμοσσεν, where Achilles refuses to bathe until having performed funeral rites for Patroclus. Demeter 'firmly' refuses the pleas of Zeus and the other gods until she should see her daughter Persephone at *Dem.* 330 στερεῶς δ' ἠναίνετο μύθους.

26 ὤμοσε δὲ μέγαν ὅρκον: Agamemnon swears a great oath not quite of virginity, but that he never went to bed with Briseis at *Il.* 9. 132 ἐπὶ μέγαν ὅρκον ὀμοῦμαι (reported again at 9. 274). For the structure of this line see *Od.* 14. 331 ὤμοσε δὲ πρὸς ἔμ' αὐτόν. The combination μέγαν ὅρκον occurs in the same metrical position at *Il.* 19. 113. Hestia's serious oath here is accompanied by the touching of Zeus' head; similarly, although mischievously, Hermes threatens to swear an oath by his father's head at *Herm.* 274 εἰ δ' ἐθέλεις πατρὸς κεφαλὴν μέγαν ὅρκον ὀμοῦμαι.

ὃ δὴ τετελεσμένος ἐστίν: 'which has truly | indeed come to pass'; emphatic δή, see Denniston (1954), 203 ff. This latter half of the line recurs identically at *Il.* 1. 388, where Achilles speaks of the command of Agamemnon. The formula τετελεσμένος (-ον) ἐστί (ἔσται | εἴη) is common in Homer; see in particular Il. 18. 4 ἃ δὴ τετελεσμένα ἦεν, Od. 19. 547 ὅ τοι τετελεσμένον ἔσται.

27 ἁψαμένη: the language with which Hestia is said to swear an oath by touching or grasping Zeus' head (κεφαλῆς) has similarities with that of supplication: Eurycleia grasps the beard of Odysseus at Od. 19. 473 ἁψαμένη δὲ γενείου Ὀδυσσῆα προσέειπεν, and Dolon reaches for the beard of Diomedes at Il. 10. 454–5 γενείου χειρὶ παχείῃ | ἁψάμενος λίσσεσθαι; Hestia is well rewarded by Zeus for her actions. Thetis grasps under the chin of Zeus when supplicating him at Il. 1. 501 δεξιτερῇ δ' ἄρ' ὑπ' ἀνθερεῶνος ἑλοῦσα. On the customary gestures of supplication see Gould (1973), 76–7 = (2001), 25–6. Also, with language very similar to this line, Hecuba and Andromache grasp the head of the dead Hector in mourning at Il. 24. 712 ἁπτόμεναι κεφαλῆς. Cf. as well Thgn. 1010 κεφαλῆς δ' ἅπτεται ἀκροτάτης, of old age grasping hold of the head.

Callimachus is almost surely imitating this line at Hy. 3. 26–7 (see on Aphr. 25–32). For other parallels in later literature see Theoc. Id. 24. 6 ἁπτόμενα δὲ γυνὰ κεφαλᾶς μυθήσατο παίδων, where the action is a caress of tenderness (cf. Gow ii. 416). Cf. also Leonidas, AP 7. 648. 2 εἶπ' ὀλιγοχρονίης ἁψάμενος κεφαλῆς.

πατρὸς Διὸς αἰγιόχοιο: cf. Il. 7. 60, 11. 66, 22. 221 and Sc. 322.

28 παρθένος ἔσσεσθαι: the closest Homeric parallel is Od. 6. 33 ἐντύνεαι, ἐπεὶ οὔ τοι ἔτι δὴν παρθένος ἔσσεαι, where the phrase is a negation of virginity rather than an affirmation; Athena warns Nausicaa in a dream that she will not be a virgin for much longer. παρθένος (-ον) is at line-beginning at Il. 2. 514, 22. 128, Th. 514, etc. and ἔσσεσθαι is in the same metrical position at Il. 6. 339.

The original sense of the term παρθένος was perhaps just 'unmarried young woman' (see Chadwick 1996, 226–9), which normally implied virginity; cf. Od. 6. 109 παρθένος ἀδμής (of Nausicaa after an invocation of Artemis) etc. The contrast, however, between Hestia and Aphrodite in this passage makes the idea of virginity conveyed by the term more explicit than it often is (Chadwick does not mention this case).

πάντ' ἤματα: 'always/for ever'. This phrase is an inverted version of the more common ἤματα πάντα, which is found four times in Aphr. (148, 209, 221, 240), and frequently in early epic (cf. Bowra 1926,

174–5). This inverted version is not in Homer, Hesiod, or the other *Hymns*, and apart from *Aphr.* it seems to be mostly a Hellenistic construct. Aeschines uses the phrase in prose when reporting a Pythian oracle in indirect speech, *in Ctesiphontem* 108, καὶ αὐτοῖς ἀναιρεῖ ἡ Πυθία πολεμεῖν Κιρραίοις καὶ Κραγαλίδαις πάντ' ἤματα καὶ πάσας νύκτας, but this is possibly an inversion of the original hexameter (see Parke–Wormell 1956, 8, who restore ἐνδυκέως πάσας νύκτας τε καὶ ἤματα πάντα). Cf. Call. *Hec.* fr. 260. 51]ου γὰρ[. .] πάντ' ἤματα, ναὶ μὰ τὸ ῥικνόν, A.R. 4. 648 ἠέρα χεῦε θεὰ πάντ' ἤματα νισσομένοισιν, Arat. 20, 204. See also later [Opp.] *C.* 3. 48, *Orph. L.* 254.

δῖα θεάων: 'noble goddess' (West 2003, 161); this formula, a common one at line-end in Homer (*Il.* 5. 381 etc.), is probably a derivative of the equivalent δῖα γυναικῶν (see Hainsworth, *OC* i. 265). It is uncertain whether the epithet δῖος developed directly from the IE root **dei-* 'shine', a sense which seems preserved at *Il.* 14. 76 (see Janko 1992, 158), or from the Mycenean **Δίϝyος* 'of the god Zeus', as at *Il.* 9. 538 and *Dion.* 2 (cf. Hainsworth, *OC* i. 256). Properly δῖα is from δίϝ-yă; the thematic δίϝ-yo- would give fem. δίϝyā > δῖᾱ. Ruijgh (1967), 133, favouring a development from 'descendant of Zeus' to the generally applicable 'divine' or 'illustrious', suggests that the substantive feminine δῖα combined with θεάων or γυναικῶν had the original meaning 'the wife/partner of Zeus', which developed over time into an honorific title applicable to all goddesses and women in epic. Whatever the case, this phrase is simply honorific in *Aphr.* with no clear sense of either of the above etymologies. Cf. also *LfgrE* s.v. δῖος.

S. West (*OC* i. 73) suggests that 'the expression is used without regard to pre-eminence in the divine hierarchy', but although, as she suggests, the formula elsewhere seems appropriate to any goddess, its use of Hestia here is very much in the context of her pre-eminence; ὁπλοτάτην, τιμάοχος, πρέσβειρα etc.

29 τῇ δὲ πατὴρ Ζεὺς δῶκε . . . γέρας: γέρας/δῶρα + δοῦναι/πορεῖν are the usual expressions for the handing out of divine honours (see N. Richardson 1974, 263).

δῶκε καλὸν γέρας ἀντὶ γάμοιο: possibly modelled upon *Th.* 585 αὐτὰρ ἐπεὶ δὴ τεῦξε καλὸν κακὸν ἀντ' ἀγαθοῖο. The rare prosody κᾰλός (the Aeolic form; see below), found in both these lines, does not occur in Homer, but once more in both Hesiod and *Aphr*. (*Op*. 63 and v. 261); cf. Solmsen (1960), 9 n. 5, Heitsch (1965), 20–1. The use of this form could suggest post-Homeric modification of κᾱλὸν γέρας (*Od*. 11. 184 etc.) by alternation of P$_2$ and T$_2$ formulae (the notation P$_2$ and T$_2$ 'indicates formulae which were originally designed to serve after the penthemimeris and the trochaic caesura'; Hoekstra 1965, 61 n. 2); cf. the T$_2$ alternatives in Homer τὸ σὸν γέρας (*Il*. 1. 185), ἐμὸν γέρας (*Od*. 11. 175) etc. (see Hoekstra 1969, 42–3, Janko 1982, 153–4). Janko's point that there is another parallel (this time thematic as well, avoidance of marriage) for this line at *Th*. 602–4 ἕτερον δὲ πόρεν κακὸν ἀντ' ἀγαθοῖο | ὅς κε γάμον φεύγων καὶ μέρμερα ἔργα γυναικῶν | μὴ γῆμαι ἐθέλῃ, and another line in the vicinity (*Th*. 582) which is similar to *Aphr*. 5, strengthens the case for borrowing here (see Introd., pp. 35–6). See the later inscription *GVI* 1330. 6 παρθένος, ἐν δ' ἔλαχον σῆμα τόδ' ἀντὶ γάμο[υ], where a young virgin receives a grave instead of marriage; also an Attic inscription *c*.540 BC(?), *CEG* i. 24 σῆμα Φρασικλείας. κόρε κεκλέσομαι αἰεὶ | ἀντὶ γάμο παρὰ θεὸν τοῦτο λαχοῦσ' ὄνομα (see Càssola 1975, 546).

The prosody κᾰλός (cf. v. 261) is probably Aeolic (West 1966*a*, 82, Kamerbeek 1967, 386, VE 23; more sceptical is Janko 1982, 154, 170); see below on τιμάοχος.

καί τε: see on *Aphr*. 3. On the transition from narrative to attributive praise provided by the generic aorist ἕζετο see Faulkner (2006), 72.

μέσῳ οἴκῳ: Hestia is given a place in the centre of Zeus' house. She is said to have an honoured seat also at *Hy*. 29. 3 ἕδρην ἀΐδιον, but there her centrality is not emphasized as it is in *Aphr*. For such explicit identification with centrality note later Call. *Hy*. 4. 325, where Delos is called the hearth (ἱστίη), or centre of the Cyclades, and *Orph. Hy*. 84. 3 ἣ μέσον οἶκον ἔχεις πυρὸς ἀεναόιο, μεγίστου (see the discussion at AHS 355). Hestia's important place at Delphi, the ὀμφαλός of the earth, is indicative of her connection with centrality, but there is nothing to lead one to believe, like Mommsen (1878), 2, that this passage is making any particular allusion to the Pythian oracle (cf. on *Aphr*. 24–5).

κατ' ἄρ' ἕζετο: this formula occurs 13 times in Homer (*Il*. 1. 68 etc.), once in the *Hymns* (*Herm*. 365), but never in Hesiod. It is used only once in later literature at Q.S. 6. 160. On the meaning of ἄρα here see on *Aphr.* 42.

πῖαρ: 'the choicest fat'; from the IE root *peiH, 'swell' (see *LfgrE*). Before a meal a small sacrifice to Hestia was often made (cf. *Gesch.* i. 337–8, Heitsch 1965, 27), and as the personified hearth it was through her fire that the gods received sacrifices. πῖαρ is a noun here, as at *Il.* 11. 550 and 17. 659 οἵ τέ μιν οὐκ εἰῶσι βοῶν ἐκ πῖαρ ἑλέσθαι, used of the fat of bulls (see Hainsworth 1993, 283). At *Od.* 9. 135 and *Apoll.* 60 the word is used of soil, πῖαρ ὑπ' οὔδας; it could plausibly be taken as an adjective in this phrase, but is more probably also a noun, 'richness under the soil' (see AHS 211 citing Buttmann; *contra* Leaf i. 504. See also West 1997, 237 on the relationship between animal fat and soil in early literature). Cf. Sol. fr. 37. 8 πρὶν ἀνταράξας πῖαρ ἐξεῖλον γάλα. It is used of the fat (oil) of an olive later at A.R. 4. 1133 πῖαρ ἐλαίης.

For a γέρας including an abundance of food and drink, and an honoured seat, see the mortal equivalent at *Il.* 8. 162 and 12. 311 ἕδρῃ τε κρέασίν τε ἰδὲ πλείοις δεπάεσσιν.

31–2. Hestia is honoured amongst both gods and mortals. The same distinction between mortal and immortal honour is made less boldly at *Hy.* 29. 1 ff. Ἑστίη ἣ πάντων ἐν δώμασιν ὑψηλοῖσιν | ἀθανάτων τε θεῶν χαμαὶ ἐρχομένων τ' ἀνθρώπων | ἕδρην ἀίδιον ἔλαχες, and later at *Orph. Hy.* 84. 5–6 οἶκε θεῶν μακάρων, θνητῶν στήριγμα κραταιόν | ἀιδίη. These two verses in *Aphr.* are well balanced by the anaphora of θεῶν, placed immediately after the weak caesura and preceded by -οισι in both cases; and the repetition of πᾶσι(ν) also adds to their parallel structure. In v. 32, θεῶν must be taken as a partitive genitive with πρέσβειρα, although in the preceding line it could plausibly be taken with either νηοῖσι or τιμάοχος. The division after the weak caesura favours the latter reading 'most honoured of the gods in all temples', but 'most honoured in all the temples of the gods' gives roughly the same sense.

The most striking parallel for these lines is found in *Dem.*, the first of a number of similarities between these two hymns (see further Introd., pp. 38–40); *Dem.* 268–9 reads εἰμὶ δὲ Δημήτηρ τιμάοχος, ἥ τε μέγιστον | ἀθανάτοις θνητοῖσί τ' ὄνεαρ καὶ χάρμα τέτυκται. The fact that the same distinction between immortal and mortal honour is made, that τιμάοχος is unique to these two passages, and that τέτυκται ends the second line in both cases, seems to suggest a direct link between the two passages, rather than a common exemplar. The question of priority, although a matter of considerable delicacy, seems to favour *Aphr.*: (i) τιμάοχος is hardly awkward in *Dem.*, but given the honours which Zeus bestows upon Hestia, it is perhaps more at home in *Aphr.* (cf. Podbielski 1971, 91 n. 16). Less subjectively, other possible Aeolisms and a clear connection with Lesbian poetry seem to favour an Aeolic origin for *Aphr.* (see Introd., pp. 44–7), a fact which gives the probably Aeolic τιμάοχος a more natural origin in *Aphr.* (see Kamerbeek 1967, 387, Janko 1982, 163; cf. below on τιμάοχος); VE's conviction (24) that *Dem.* is prior because one would expect old religious language (Aeolic τιμάοχος) in *Dem.* rather than *Aphr.* has no basis. (ii) The distinction between gods and mortals in the two passages may also support *Aphr.* as prior. N. Richardson (1974), 249 has noted an awkwardness of this sentiment in *Dem.*, where it is somewhat unclear why Demeter is praised as a joy to immortals as well, and although any discomfort there is mild, the idea is perhaps more developed and comfortable in the environs of *Aphr.* (iii) Janko's observation (1982, 163) of prosodic irregularity (the form ὄνεαρ with synizesis only here; cf. Richardson 1974, 249) and necessary enjambment in *Dem.* also pushes *Aphr.* forward as the earlier version, although such stylistic evidence should be treated with caution.

31 πᾶσιν δ' ἐν νηοῖσι: cf. *Apoll.* 347 ἀλλ' ἥ γ' ἐν νηοῖσι.

τιμάοχος: only here and at *Dem.* 268. The forms τιμοῦχος and τιμῶχος are found in later Greek (cf. N. Richardson 1974, 249, Heitsch 1965, 38). The long -α, preserved instead of Ionic -η, may be an Aeolism as Kamberbeek (1967), 387 and Hoekstra (1969), 56 suggest (cf. Càssola 546, Janko 1982, 163); a later Aeolic inscription of the second century BC, from Methymna in Lesbos, records τῶν τιμώχων (Schwyzer 1923, 299). Zumbach (1955), 57, suggests it is an Atticism, but there is nothing to support this view (see N. Richardson 1974, 53, 249). For an overview of the possible Aeolisms found in *Aphr.* see Introd., pp. 44–5.

32 καὶ παρὰ πᾶσι βροτοῖσι θεῶν: for the structure of this line cf. *Il.* 9. 159 τοὔνεκα καί τε βροτοῖσι θεῶν ἔχθιστος ἁπάντων.

πρέσβειρα: not elsewhere in early hexameter. It may be an adaptation of πρέσβα θεά, used four times of Hera in the *Iliad* (5. 721, 8.

383, 14. 194 and 14. 243; cf. Janko 1982, 156, Zumbach 1955, 8, Hoekstra 1969, 13, Heitsch 1965, 25). The term means 'honoured': see Hsch. πρέσβειρα· προτιμητή and Suda πρέσβειρα· ἔντιμος. Elsewhere it first appears at E. IT 963 τὸ δ' ἄλλο πρέσβειρ' ἤπερ ἦν Ἐρινύων, but cf. Hy. 29. 3 πρεσβηΐδα. Aristophanes uses it twice, at Ach. 883 πρέσβειρα πεντήκοντα Κωπάδων κορᾶν (which the scholia report is a parody of a line of Aeschylus' Ὅπλων κρίσις, referring to Thetis, δέσποινα πεντήκοντα Νηρήδων κορῶν), and Lys. 86. It is used of Themis at A.R. 4. 800. See Orph. fr. 702. 4 Bernabé (315 Kern) πανδοχέα, πρέσβειραν, a hymn to Number which is claimed by some to be a work of Pythagoras (see Thesleff 1965, 173); cf. also Orph. Hy. 10. 2 οὐρανία, πρέσβειρα and 27. 13 οὐρανόπαι, πρέσβειρα, βιοθρέπτειρα. It is used later of the virgin Dike in Macedonius AP 11. 380. 1 παρθένος εὐπατέρεια Δίκη, πρέσβειρα πολήων, in the same metrical position. Cf. also its use at Opp. H. 2. 665.

33 τάων: this line, almost an exact replica of v. 7, brings the section devoted to the three virgin goddesses to a close with strikingly clear ring-composition; only τρισσάς is replaced by τάων. For τάων cf. Il. 5. 332, where it is used to introduce goddesses of war, Athena and Enyo, in contrast to Aphrodite: τάων αἵ τ' ἀνδρῶν πόλεμον κάτα κοιρανέουσιν.

34–9. In the face of these three exceptions, the poet now turns again to the point that all others, whether men or gods, are subject to Aphrodite's power. More important still, this general statement of vv. 34–5 acts as an introduction to the revelation that even Zeus is amongst the ranks of those subdued by the goddess. The elaboration of this point, spread over four whole lines (36–9), endows it with weighty importance, and signals its relevance for the upcoming narrative. There is particular irony in the presentation of Zeus' seduction directly after the episode in which he has rewarded Hestia for her chastity (Podbielski 1971, 28); the juxtaposition makes the motives for Zeus' announced revenge at v. 45 clear.

34 τῶν δ' ἄλλων οὔ πέρ τι πεφυγμένον: neuter τι appears to be used collectively here, as at Th. 7. 48 καὶ ἦν γάρ τι ('an element') καὶ ἐν ταῖς Συρακούσαις βουλόμενον τοῖς Ἀθηναίοις τὰ πράγματα ἐνδοῦναι (cf. LSJ s.v.). This may also reflect the intended point that nothing at all, beasts included (cf. Aphr. 2 ff.), escapes the power of Aphrodite. The particle περ adds emphasis to the negation here (see Bakker

1988, 89–90, Denniston 1954, 482); it is equivalent to οὐδαμῶς in later Greek. Cf. *Od.* 8. 212 τῶν δ' ἄλλων οὔ πέρ τιν' ἀναίνομαι οὐδ' ἀθερίζω. Also close to this line are *Il.* 6. 488 μοῖραν δ' οὔ τινά φημι πεφυγμένον ἔμμεναι ἀνδρῶν and 14. 427 τῶν τ' ἄλλων οὔ τίς εὖ ἀκήδεσεν. For more on the genesis of this line see Heitsch (1965), 27–8. On the perfect passive participle πεφυγμένος (-ον), used here and elsewhere with an active sense, see AHS 355–6.

The idea that neither gods nor mortals escape Aphrodite's subjugation is expressed in very similar language later at S. *Ant.* 787–90 καί σ' οὔτ' ἀθανάτων | φύξιμος οὐδεὶς οὔθ' | ἀμερίων ἐπ' ἀνθρώ|πων (cf. Furley ii. 271).

ἔστ' Ἀφροδίτην: of Aphrodite as the mother of Aeneas by Anchises, cf. *Il.* 5. 248/20. 209 εὔχεται (-ομαι) ἐκγεγάμεν, μήτηρ δέ οἵ ἐστ' Ἀφροδίτη; in *Aphr.*, however, ἔστ' goes with the participle πεφυγμένον, whereas it goes with the name Ἀφροδίτη in the *Iliad*. The accusative Ἀφροδίτην is found only twice in Homer at *Il.* 5. 427 and 14. 188; it is more common in Hesiod (*Th.* 16, 195, 822, 962 etc.). Cf. also *Hy.* 6. 1.

35 οὔτε θεῶν μακάρων οὔτε θνητῶν ἀνθρώπων: this line is an exact replica of *Od.* 9. 521, *Herm.* 144. See also similarly *Il.* 1. 339 πρός τε θεῶν μακάρων πρός τε θνητῶν ἀνθρώπων, *Od.* 5. 32 οὔτε θεῶν πομπῇ οὔτε θνητῶν ἀνθρώπων, [Hes.] fr. 25. 31 ἔκ τε θεῶν μακάρων ἔκ τε θνητῶν ἀνθρώπων etc. The antithesis of gods and mortals is intended to express universality, as it did in the proem (see on *Aphr.* 2–6 and VE 26); cf. later *Orph. Hy.* 41. 2 ἀθανάτων τε θεῶν ἠδὲ θνητῶν ἀνθρώπων.

36 καί τε: 'and even Zeus . . .'; the repeated use of this particle combination (here and at v. 38) once again suggests the generic quality of the aorists ἤγαγεν and συνέμειξε (see above on 3). The combination here also adds to the sense of climax (cf. Ruijgh 1971, 913). For καί τε emphatically in Homer cf. *Il.* 19. 86, where it also 'conveys a climax' (M. W. Edwards 1991, 247).

The sexual liaisons of Zeus with mortal women, and the children they bore, are well known from his own boastful (certainly insensitive) catalogue at *Il.* 14. 313 ff.: the wife of Ixion (Dia according to the scholiasts), Danae, Europa, Semele, and Alcmene (see Janko 1992,

203 ff. for more on these individual encounters). Reference to Zeus' experience with women became a stock element in later erotic epigram; cf. Theoc. *Id.* 8. 59–60 ὦ πάτερ, ὦ Ζεῦ | οὐ μόνος ἠράσθην· καὶ τὺ γυναικοφίλας (see Gow ii. 180 for further examples). For Aphrodite taming Zeus in love in later literature see explicitly Mosch. *Eur.* 76.

πάρεκ Ζηνὸς νόον ἤγαγε: Dolon blames his nocturnal spying on Hector with similar language at *Il.* 10. 391 πολλῆσίν μ' ἄτησι πάρεκ νόον ἤγαγεν Ἕκτωρ. There, πάρεκ may be taken with νόον to mean 'outside and beyond sense and reason' (Hainsworth 1993, 193), as at *Il.* 20. 133 and *Herm.* 547, with ἤγαγεν governing με; alternatively we may understand παρεξήγαγεν to take a double accusative (whole and part construction), as with the verb ἀπατάω of deceiving φρένας at *Aphr.* 7 (see ad loc.), which would relieve a certain awkwardness in the phrasing there. In *Aphr.* the use of the name in the genitive Ζηνός, denoting the owner of the νόον, is more similar to the construction found later at A.R. 4. 102 κῶας ἕλοντες ἄγοιντο πάρεκ νόον Αἰήταο, where πάρεκ is again taken with νόον, but this time to mean 'without the knowledge of' or 'behind the back of ', as at A.R. 1. 130, 1. 323 and Call. *Hec.* fr. 234 πάρεκ νόον εἰλήλουθας (cf. Livrea 1973, 39, Hollis 1990, 145); see the same sense without νόον at *Il.* 24. 434 πάρεξ Ἀχιλῆα. However, while Aphrodite may have contrived Zeus' amours behind his back, πάρεκ can hardly be taken with νόον here; the verb ἤγαγεν must govern νόον as an object, and πάρεκ is therefore to be understood adverbially with ἤγαγεν, i.e. παρεξήγαγεν, 'led (his mind) astray'; cf. similarly Archil. fr. 124b. 4 ἀλλά σεο γαστὴρ νόον τε καὶ φρένας παρήγαγεν. Aphrodite blames her affair with Anchises on a similar loss of mental faculties later in the hymn (ἐπεὶ μάλα πολλὸν ἀάσθην, v. 253).

Ζηνὸς: this East Ionic genitive form occurs often in *Aphr.*, five times (also vv. 131, 187, 213 and 215) alongside seven of Διός (the genitive form is found only 22 times in Homer), a fact which Janko (1982), 62–3 thinks is due to 'hyperionism'. Alternatively it could be due to metrical convenience, or mere chance; one of the cases is the result of the repetition of a line (vv. 131, 187).

τερπικεραύνου: more probably 'who takes delight in lightning' than 'hurler of the thunderbolt' as Leaf i. 518–19 prefers. He follows G. Meyer in deriving the first half of the epithet from τρέπω (suggested at Hsch. s.v., *EM* 753. 32–4), accepting metathesis of -ρε. Metathesis of -ρα is known for metrical variance in epic with such words as κάρτερος for κράτερος, but such a transposition of -ρε in τρέπω is not paralleled elsewhere, and is dubiously invoked here. Zeus' ability to throw thunderbolts is actually threatened later in *Aphr.* (288), but an attributive epithet indicating his pleasure in lightning is entirely appropriate for describing his general connection with the thunderbolt. The weather-god Zeus takes delight in lightning just as Athena and Artemis are delighted (ἁνδάνω) by their accoutrements in the proem of *Aphr.* (cf. VE 27). On τερπι-, see Bechtel (1914), 312, Chantraine (1967), 23, and now Meissner (2006), 19.

The epithet is applied to Zeus in the nominative, accusative, and dative in Homer, but never in the genitive. The contracted genitive form is suggestive of modification of line-end Ζεὺς τερπικέραυνος (*Il.* 12. 252 etc.), declined and split (the formula is split twice already in Homer at *Il.* 8. 2 and 16. 232) perhaps by analogy with Διὸς ⏑⏑4⏑⏑ αἰγιόχοιο *Il.* 17. 176 and Διὸς νόον (*Il.* 8. 143 etc.) | Ζηνὸς νόον (found only at *Op.* 483, 661, [Hes.] frr. 43a. 52, 303. 2); on the modification see Janko (1982), 52, 155.

37. There can be no doubt after this verse that Zeus is the greatest of all gods! The ABA structure of vv. 36–8 places emphasis upon this middle line; in vv. 36 and 38 καί τε is repeated at line-beginning, and ἐξαπαφοῦσα is a structural counterpart to τερπικεραύνου at line-end. Furthermore, v. 37 stands out on its own merit through assonance and alliteration. The two clauses are skilfully balanced by the repetition of μεγιστ- and the connective structure of the particle τε, while the whole line, with the exception of the -ρ in ἔμμορε, is made up of sounds from the word μέγιστος (for these points of structure see Porter 1949, 264; 1951, 39).

There is more than a touch of irony in this line, placed as it is between two verses which espouse Aphrodite's ability to conquer the 'greatest' of all gods in love. Although quite different in sense, this line has some structural and phraseological similarities with *Op.* 347 ἔμμορέ τοι τιμῆς, ὅς τ' ἔμμορε γείτονος ἐσθλοῦ. See also *Il.* 15. 189 τριχθὰ δὲ πάντα δέδασται, ἕκαστος δ' ἔμμορε τιμῆς, where the earth is split into three and honour is divided between Zeus and his brothers, Poseidon and Hades.

ὅς τε μέγιστός τ' ἐστι: Zeus is μέγιστος elsewhere in early hexameter poetry at *Th.* 49 ὅσσον φέρτατός ἐστι θεῶν κάρτει τε μέγιστος and *Hy.* 23. 1 Ζῆνα θεῶν τὸν ἄριστον ἀείσομαι ἠδὲ μέγιστον; in Homer he is addressed as Ζεῦ κύδιστε μέγιστε 6× in the *Il.* (2. 412 etc.) and his κράτος is also μέγιστον (*Il.* 2. 118 and *Od.* 5. 4). Cf. also *Il.* 15. 37–8, *Od.* 15. 185–6, and *Apoll.* 85, where the river Styx is described, ὅς τε μέγιστος | ὅρκος. Zeus receives the title later at B. *Epin.* 6. 1, E. *Ion* 1606, *Alc.* 1136, etc. See very similar language applied to Dionysus at Orph. *Hy.* 1. 8–9 ὅς τε μεγίστας | τιμὰς ἐν μακάρεσσιν ἔχεις.

The particle τε combined with ὅς expresses the permanence of the fact that Zeus is the greatest of gods, as at *Od.* 5. 4 οὗ τε κράτος ἐστὶ μέγιστον (cf. Hainsworth, *OC* i. 254, Ruijgh 1971, 906).

38 εὖτ' ἐθέλῃ: 'a common qualification in telling of a god's powers ... which explains why he does not always do what he is supposed to be able to' (West 1966a, 163); see εὖτ' ἐθέλωμεν of a common attribute of the Muses at *Th.* 28.

M is the only MS to read the subjunctive, accepted by Wolf (1807), Càssola, and Ruijgh (1971), 913. AS 203 argue that the optative should be preferred on the grounds that ἤγαγε and συνέμειξε are not 'gnomic' aorists and refer to past actions for which Aphrodite will now be punished. However, the particle combination καί τε at the beginning of the line suggests the generic quality of the aorist (see above on v. 3 and Faulkner 2006). It is more attractive to have an attributive statement here on structural grounds as well. After the ring-composition of vv. 7 and 33, the poem has picked up the statement of Aphrodite's universal power which was being made in the proem, and brought it to a certain climax (see on *Aphr.* 1–44 on the priamel structure of this prologue); it would be very awkward to switch from the characteristic to the strictly historic here in such an ambiguous fashion. This change takes place more naturally over vv. 40–4 (see ad loc.). On the implications of this reading for the interpretation of the narrative, see Introd., pp. 10–18.

It is possible to read the optative in a statement of general truth (see *Grammaire*, ii. 223, 259–60; e.g. *Il.* 4. 262–3 σὸν δὲ πλεῖον δέπας αἰεί | ἕστηχ', ὥς περ ἐμοί, πιέειν ὅτε θυμὸς ἀνώγοι), but the subjunctive is more expected. Achilles utters a general truth after Athena's intervention at *Il.* 1. 218 ὅς κε θεοῖς ἐπιπείθηται μάλα τ' ἔκλυον αὐτοῦ. More similar to the case in *Aphr.* is the declaration of an attribute of Sleep at *Od.* 20. 85–6 ὁ γάρ τ' ἐπέλησεν ἀπάντων | ἐσθλῶν ἠδὲ κακῶν, ἐπεὶ ἄρ βλέφαρ' ἀμφικαλύψῃ; as in *Aphr.*, adverbial τε signals the characteristic activity. Cf. Cooper iii. 2378 on *Il.* 5. 127–8 and Monro (1891), 270. To a strictly 'grammatical' mind the optative may have seemed preferable with so many aorists in the vicinity, and it might have been introduced as the *lectio facilior*. Note that the poet of *Aphr.* deviates from the strict rules of the sequence of tenses below at vv. 46–8 (see ad loc.).

ἐθέλῃ: θέλω is rarely a certain form in epic poetry (cf. AHS 209, VE 28), and, following the reading of M, ἐθέλ- should be printed.

πυκινὰς φρένας ἐξαπαφοῦσα: cf. *Il.* 14. 160 ὅππως ἐξαπάφοιτο Διὸς νόον αἰγιόχοιο, where Hera tricks Zeus into love-making. This formula is equivalent to πυκινὰς φρένας ἀμφικάλυψεν of love at *Il.* 14. 294, and πυκινὰς φρένας ἀμφικαλύπτοι found later at *Aphr.* 243. As Janko (1992), 198 notes, 'the expansion πυκινὰς φ. aptly stresses the intelligence that is overcome'.

For the genesis of the formula, see also at line-end *Th.* 537 Διὸς νόον ἐξαπαφίσκων, and 889 φρένας ἐξαπατήσας. The feminine participle occurs at line-end only here and *Apoll.* 379 ἐμὸν νόον ἐξαπαφοῦσα; otherwise it appears only once in a later fragment attributed to Alexander of Aetolia by Parthenius in his Ἐρωτικὰ Παθήματα (14, v. 19; see Lightfoot 1999, 465) μύθοις ἐξαπαφοῦσα. Moschus was possibly thinking of this line at *Eur.* 78 παρθενικῆς τ' ἐθέλων ἀταλὸν νόον ἐξαπατῆσαι (cf. Campbell 1991, 81).

πυκινὰς φρένας: apart from here and at v. 243, this phrase appears in early hexameter poetry only at *Il.* 14. 294. See. however, πυκινὰ φρεσὶ μήδε' ἔχοντες at 24. 282, 675, *Od.* 19. 353. Zeus has a πυκινὸν νόον at *Il.* 15. 461 (cf. Janko 1992, 279).

Theognis uses the combination while invoking Aphrodite's univeral power over all men in a similar manner at 1385–8 Κυπρογενὲς Κυθέρεια δολοπλόκε, σοί τι περισσὸν | Ζεὺς τόδε τιμήσας δῶρον ἔδωκεν ἔχειν, | δαμνᾶς δ' ἀνθρώπων πυκινὰς φρένας, οὐδέ τίς ἐστιν | οὕτως ἴφθιμος καὶ σοφὸς ὥστε φυγεῖν; there it is actually Zeus who grants her this power. See the phrase elsewhere at Stesich. *PMGF* S88. 19.

39 ῥηϊδίως: the ease with which Aphrodite brings about these unions between Zeus and mortal women is typical of divine action (see a list of Homeric examples at de Jong 2001, 81; in Hesiod at

Th. 254 etc.). 'ῥηϊδίως or ῥεῖα is an adverb frequently used in aretalogies, especially of gods' (West 1966a, 185).

συνέμειξε: the compounds συμμείγνυμι and ἀναμείγνυμι (v. 52) are not otherwise used of sexual intercourse in early hexameter. They are elsewhere attested of mixing or bringing two things together, such as food or materials for sandals (cf. *Il.* 24. 529, *Od.* 10. 235 for ἀνα-, *Herm.* 81 for συν-). Even outside epic the erotic sense is rare, and συμμείγνυμι appears elsewhere of sexual intercourse for the first time at Hdt. 4. 114 γυναῖκα ἔχων ἕκαστος ταύτην, τῇ τὸ πρῶτον συνεμίχθη (cf. AHS 356); in poetry see Ar. *Thesm.* 891 παιδὶ συμμεῖξαι λέχος. The simple form μείγνυμι is frequently used of sexual intercourse in epic and elsewhere (at *Aphr.* 46, 150, 287 etc.; see *LfgrE* s.v. μίσγω).

The compound verbs in *Aphr.* certainly carry the original sense of physically bringing two groups together, Zeus and mortal women, or more generally gods and mortals, but the sexual implications are also apparent. VE's argument (29–30) that it is the physical sense which is intended here, because it was the transgression of 'the boundaries between mortals and immortals ... and not love itself', which is regarded as shameful, is not convincing. Sexual intercourse, which produces offspring, is the physical interaction by which that boundary is crossed; it is not shameful for Athena physically to tug Achilles' hair in order to stop him from drawing his sword in *Il.* 1, but it would have been shameful if she had slept with him to calm his temper. The two senses go hand-in-hand, and it may even diminish the sexual meaning too much to say more temperately that 'der Geschlechtsverkehr, der natür. auch gemeint ist, wohl nicht primär [ist]' (B. Mader, *LfgrE* s.v. μίσγω). Aphrodite, the goddess of love, is after all the subject of these verbs and one should not imagine that she plans for Zeus to have a quiet cup of tea with mortal women.

καταθνητῇσι γυναιξί: twice more in *Aphr.* (vv. 50 and 250), this phrase is not found elsewhere in Greek poetry. For similar expressions of women as mortal cf. at line-end in Homer *Il.* 20. 305 γυναικῶν τε θνητάων and *Od.* 11. 244 θνητήν τε γυναῖκα.

40–4. The poet now moves to a short section in praise of Hera. She is the most beautiful of goddesses, the daughter of Kronos and Rhea, whom Zeus honoured by making his wife. Introduced by Zeus' deception of her in matters of love, the section is entered into with a natural air, and the simple mention of Hera, famous for her wrath against Zeus' lovers (Leto and others), does not seem out of place here. As the poem moves towards Zeus' act of revenge upon Aphrodite, the invocation of the strife she has caused between Zeus and his wife exemplifies the mischief caused by the love-goddess, for which some punishment is surely well deserved. Solmsen (1960), 11 argues that this section of praise is included in order to justify and make up for the poet's earlier attribution of the title 'oldest' to Hestia (see vv. 22–3 and πρέσβειρα v. 32). This seems improbable (cf. on *Aphr.* 21–32): are we to assume that the audience would have been insulted if the balance had not been redressed for Hera? Alternatively, the expansion upon the goddess here has an important transitional function. Until this point the poet has been speaking generically of Aphrodite's power over all living creatures. At v. 45 the narrative will be introduced and this section offers a gentle temporal gradient from one to the other. The presentation of Zeus' general deception of Hera in v. 40 progresses into praise of Hera's beauty in v. 41, her genealogy over vv. 42–3, and then the fact of her marriage to Zeus over vv. 43–4. While all these steps imply lasting honour for Hera, the last two, and especially the final one, present this as the result of specific events in the past: her birth and her marriage to Zeus. Moreover, in the final case it is Zeus himself who makes her his wife at v. 44 ἄλοχον ποιήσατο. Honour is being paid not only to Hera, but also to Zeus, who acts ἄφθιτα μήδεα εἰδώς; this helps to build up to his powerful act of revenge which will be revealed at v. 45.

The passage certainly has similarities with *Il.* 4. 59–61 καί με πρεσβυτάτην τέκετο Κρόνος ἀγκυλομήτης | ἀμφότερον γενεῇ τε καὶ οὕνεκα σὴ παράκοιτις | κέκλημαι, σὺ δὲ πᾶσι μετ' ἀθανάτοισιν ἀνάσσεις: not only does Hera speak of her honour in terms of her marriage to Zeus in both passages, but *Aphr.* 42 κυδίστην δ' ἄρα μιν τέκετο Κρόνος ἀγκυλομήτης recalls the language of her claim to seniority at *Il.* 4. 59. This is perhaps a case of direct imitation, in which case the poet has changed πρεσβυτάτην in order not to conflict with his previous tale of Hestia (the rare accusative κυδίστην may support innovation upon a previous model; see below on 42). Given that the poet seems elsewhere to be drawing directly upon the *Iliad* (see Introd., pp. 31–4), this is a distinct possibility here as well. On the other hand, it is worth noting the similarities, more in content than in language, between these lines and *Hy.* 12, a short hymn to Hera: Rhea is said to give birth to Hera in v. 1 Ἥρην ... ἣν τέκε Ῥεία, as at *Aphr*. 43; Hera is praised as an eminent immortal with regard to her beauty in v. 2 ἀθανάτην ... ὑπείροχον εἶδος ἔχουσαν, as at *Aphr*. 41; she is both the sister and the wife of Zeus in v. 3 Ζηνὸς ... κασιγνήτην ἄλοχόν τε, as at *Aphr*. 40; and she is called κυδρήν at the beginning of v. 4, a term similar to κυδίστην at *Aphr*. 42. This suggests that the content was stock material appropriate for a hymn to Hera, in which case one cannot easily rule out a common model for *Aphr*. and *Il*. 4. 59–61. As often, it is impossible to know for certain.

For other hymns addressed to the goddess see Sapph. fr. 17 and Alc. 129, although on the whole 'there is a remarkable dearth of hymns and prayers to Hera' (Furley i. 166; see n. 16 there for a list of prayers to Hera in the comic and tragic poets). The fact that, apart from *Aphr*. and *Hy*. 12, two major examples are offered by Sappho and Alcaeus, hints perhaps at the connection between *Aphr*. and Lesbian poetry displayed elsewhere in the poem (see Introd., pp. 45–7). As in the Lesbian examples, where Hera is hymned alongside Zeus (it appears to have been a Lesbian tradition to worship Hera, together with Zeus and Dionysus; cf. Furley i. 172, Page 1955, 168), her short hymn in *Aphr*. is intrinsically linked with the praise of her glorious husband. Note also a short hymn to Hera and Zeus in connection with marriage at Ar. *Av*. 1731–42, an occasion on which hymns celebrating the divine couple may have been sung (see Dunbar 1995, 757). On cult worship of Hera in Greece (particularly in Boeotia, Argos, and Samos), and her frequent connection with Zeus as his wife, see Farnell i. 179 ff., Nilsson i. 427 ff. Later, *Orph. Hy*. 17 is dedicated to Hera.

40 ἐκλελαθοῦσα: Aphrodite makes Zeus forget all about his beautiful wife Hera. Kamerbeek (1967), 390 should be followed in reading this reduplicated thematic aorist as causative: 'to cause to forget' + acc. Δία (understood) and genitive Ἥρης of the object forgotten. The compound ἐκλανθάνω is used in this sense with a genitive of the object forgotten at *Od*. 7. 221 (in tmesis), and with an accusative of the object forgotten at *Il*. 2. 600; it never has the meaning in epic 'to escape notice', as the simple form of the active verb does (cf. *LfgrE* s.v. λανθάνω). For the verb in the passive of forgetting about love see *Od*. 3. 224 ἐκλελάθοιτο γάμοιο and 22. 444 ἐκλελάθωντ' Ἀφροδίτης etc.

Ἥρης ... κασιγνήτης ἀλόχου τε: this formula does not appear elsewhere in the genitive, but see the accusative at *Il.* 16. 432 Ἥρην δὲ προσέειπε κασιγνήτην ἄλοχόν τε, 18. 356 Ζεὺς δ' Ἥρην προσέειπε κασιγνήτην ἄλοχόν τε and *Hy.* 12. 3 Ζηνὸς ἐριγδούποιο κασιγνήτην ἄλοχόν τε. As above at 36 τερπικεραύνου, the contracted genitive may suggest post-Homeric modification (cf. Janko 1982, 154). Kirk (1985), 381 compares the formula to the Homeric κασιγνήτη ἑτάρη τε (*Il.* 4. 441).

41 μέγα: adverbial, 'by far', as at *Il.* 2. 82 νῦν δ' ἴδεν ὃς μέγ' ἄριστος Ἀχαιῶν εὔχεται εἶναι (see *LfgrE* s.v. III 2 for plenty of examples). It should not, as VE 28 argues, be taken as an adjective with εἶδος. Hera has a physique no larger than any of the other gods, and nom. or acc. εἶδος is never described by μέγα in early epic; only the dative at *Th.* 153 μεγάλῳ ἐπὶ εἴδει (of the Hundredhanders). The earliest, and only, combination in epic poetry is at Theoc. *Id.* 25. 40 οἷόν τοι μέγα εἶδος ἐπιπρέπει (cf. Gow ii. 447).

εἶδος ἀρίστη: literally 'the best as regards form' = 'most beautiful'; εἶδος is an accusative of respect. This phrase is a fairly common way of indicating a mortal woman's beauty in Homer: in the *Il.* of Alcestis 2. 715, Laodice 3. 124, etc.; in the *Od.* of Periboia at 7. 57 and 8. 116; see also at *Dem.* 146 of Kallidike. Its application in *Aphr.* to Hera, a goddess, is unique. It appears rarely in later hexameter poetry; of Hypsipyle at *Orph. Arg.* 475 and once more at *App. Anth.* 3. 281. 18 (Cougny). Hera was connected with the beauty-contests of young women on Lesbos (see Page 1955, 168, and n. 4 there for a list of sources). The claim that Hera is the most beautiful of goddesses is surprising in a hymn to Aphrodite, who defeated Hera in the beauty contest judged by Paris.

ἐν ἀθανάτῃσι θεῇσι: the combination of noun and adjective appears twice elsewhere in early epic (*Il.* 3. 158 ἀθανάτῃσι θεῇς and Hes. *Op.* 62 ἀθανάτης δὲ θεῆς), but neither at line-end, nor with the long dative plural form of θεά. This may be an innovation based upon the formula ἐϊκυῖα θεῇσι (⏑⏑5 ⏑⏑6×), used to compare mortal females to goddesses at *Aphr.* 153, *Il.* 8. 305, 11. 638, 19. 286, *Od.* 7. 291, [Hes.] fr. 185. 23, and the masculine formula ἐν ἀθανάτοισι θεοῖσι(ν) (⏑4⏑⏑5⏑⏑6×) at *Il.* 1. 520, 7. 102, 15. 107, 21. 476, *Th.* 120, *Herm.* 458, *Hy.* 32. 16 (see also ἀθανάτοισι θεοῖσιν at *Aphr.* 142). Note in particular *Th.* 120 ἠδ' Ἔρος, ὃς κάλλιστος ἐν ἀθανάτοισι θεοῖσι and

Hy. 32. 16 ἐκπρεπὲς εἶδος ἔχουσαν ἐν ἀθανάτοισι θεοῖσι, where the extraordinary divine beauty of Eros and Semele is praised.

42 κυδίστην: on the relationship of this line with *Il.* 4. 59 see on *Aphr.* 40–4. The accusative κυδίστην is not otherwise found in early epic, and it appears only twice more at Thgn. 904 and A.R. 2. 719 (see on *Aphr.* 24 πότνιαν for another rare accusative). This perhaps strengthens the suggestion that the poet did have *Il.* 4. 59 (καί με πρεσβυτάτην τέκετο Κρόνος ἀγκυλομήτης) in his mind as a model, κυδίστην influenced by the accusative πρεσβυτάτην.

The adjective, literally translated 'most glorious', carries with it a sense of 'power' and 'strength'; it is most common in Homer in the vocative either of Agamemnon (*Il.* 1. 122 etc.) or Zeus (2. 412 etc.), kings in their respective spheres (note the vocative at *Aphr.* 108 of Anchises). The feminine form is used of the martial Athena at *Il.* 4. 515. Hera is not elsewhere κυδίστη but she is called Διὸς κυδρὴ παράκοιτις (*Il.* 18. 184, *Th.* 328 and *Hy.* 12. 4); cf. Leto, who is called Διὸς κυδρὴ παράκοιτις at *Od.* 11. 580 and is also κυδίστη at *Apoll.* 62.

δ' ἄρα: in general ἄρα underlines the interesting character of a fact being expressed, although this sense can be weakened when it is used in formulae such as κατ' ἄρ' ἕζετο above at *Aphr.* 30 (see Ruijgh 1971, 434 ff. for a concise but complete discussion of the particle, with bibliography). It here expresses the significance of Hera's birth, marking her out as a character of importance; cf. *Il.* 20. 236–9 where, in the long list of his genealogy, Aeneas marks the births of Tithonus, Priam, and Anchises with the particle-combination δ' ἄρα. Cf. on *Aphr.* 53 and see ἀλλ' ἄρα at v. 10.

43 μήτηρ τε Ῥείη: this is the most common form of the name Rhea in epic (see N. Richardson 1974, 171, West 1966a, 203, McLennan 1977, 39), but it is only once elsewhere found in this metrical position (*Il.* 14. 203 vulg., v.l. Ῥείας, cf. Janko 1992, 183); cf. *Th.* 135 Θείαν τε Ῥείαν, where note the structural similarity. Also, the name is not otherwise paired with μήτηρ until Nonn. *D.* 9. 175, 11. 241, etc. Rhea is explicitly mentioned as giving birth to Hera at *Th.* 453 and *Hy.* 12. 1. On the etymology of her name and the play upon it at Call. *Hy.* 1. 14 ff. see Hopkinson (1984b).

Ζεὺς δ' ἄφθιτα μήδεα εἰδώς: the formula Ζεὺς ἄφθιτα μήδεα εἰδώς occurs elsewhere five times in Hesiod (*Th.* 545, 550, 561, frr. 141. 26, 234. 2), once in Homer (*Il.* 24. 88), and once in *Dem.* (321; cf.

N. Richardson 1974, 262); the δέ is inserted into the formula only here and at Hes. *Th.* 550, both instances where there is necessary enjambment into the next line.

If there is a mild irony here after Zeus has been shown to be conquered by Aphrodite, it is more to the point that the tables are turning. This statement of Zeus' great cunning is building up to the announcement of his revenge in v. 45 (see on *Aphr.* 40–4).

44 αἰδοίην ἄλοχον: on the meaning of the adjective see above on v. 21, where it is used of Hestia. It is paired with the dative plural ἀλόχοισι(ν) at *Il.* 6. 250, 21. 460, *Od.* 10. 11, and *Apoll.* 148, but it is not elsewhere found with ἄλοχος. Janko (1982), 25 suggests that this combination arose through 'mobility' beside κουριδίην ἄλοχον (*Aphr.* 127; see on *Aphr.* 126–7).

ἄλοχον ποιήσατο κέδν' εἰδυῖαν: cf. the angry words of Hera at *Apoll.* 311–13 κέκλυτέ μευ ... | ὡς ἔμ᾽ ἀτιμάζειν ἄρχει νεφεληγερέτα Ζεὺς | πρῶτος, ἐπεί μ᾽ ἄλοχον ποιήσατο κέδν᾽ εἰδυῖαν. For ποιέω of marrying Hera see also *Th.* 921 Ἥρην θαλερὴν ποιήσατ᾽ ἄκοιτιν.

κέδν' εἰδυῖαν: the MSS unanimously transmit the e-grade form εἰδυῖαν, here and below at v. 134 εἰδυίη. The zero-grade Ϝιδ- was the earlier form, although the MSS of Homer and Hesiod often read the e-grade εἰδυῖαν in this and other similar formulae (ἔργ᾽ εἰδυῖα etc.); it is confirmed by the metre twice, at *Il.* 17. 5 and *Th.* 887. On this see West (1966a), 241, (1978), 62, S. West, *OC* i. 126, Hoekstra, *OC* ii. 190. There is no compelling reason to amend the transmitted readings in *Aphr.* for the sake of the older form.

Wives know κεδνά elsewhere in early epic at *Od.* 20. 57, 23. 182, 232 (mothers can too, *Od.* 1. 428, 19. 346, *Aphr.* 134; cf. Iambe at *Dem.* 195, 202), and are also themselves κεδναί at *Il.* 24. 730, *Od.* 1. 432, 22. 223.

45–52. The poet now abruptly turns the tables, introducing a narrative which will give the father of the gods his due revenge. The addressee has been prepared to some degree for this *conversio* by the preceding mini-hymn to Hera, which ends by praising Zeus for making Hera his wife with his capacity of eternal wisdom (see on *Aphr.* 40–4, 43). Nonetheless, there has been little warning that the revenge of Zeus, inciting Aphrodite to sleep with the mortal Anchises, will provide the main theme of the narrative to come. This is not even a well-known story; that Zeus was the instigator behind this famous sexual union is a variant of the myth confined to *Aphr.* (see on *Aphr.* 53–199).

The narrative proper does not begin until v. 53 with the introduction of Anchises on Ida (cf. Kamerbeek 1967, 394, Lenz 1975, 22, van der Ben 1981, 67 etc.), but v. 45 nonetheless marks the formal end of the prologue (cf. Podbielski 1971, 30); de Jong (1989), 13 n. 2 thus prefers to let the narrative commence at v. 45. One might say more precisely that the narrative is introduced here (Ζεὺς γλυκὺν ἵμερον ἔμβαλε θυμῷ | ἀνδρὶ καταθνητῷ μιχθήμεναι), but that things do not really get going until v. 53. Instead of launching straight into the narrative, the following lines elaborate upon the intention and the result of Zeus' counterattack: never again will Aphrodite be able to boast among the gods that she has mixed them with mortals because henceforth she will be a laughable victim herself! On the repetition of words signifying 'mortal' and 'immortal' in this section see on *Aphr.* 50–2.

45 τῇ δὲ καὶ αὐτῇ: this emphatic phrase at the beginning of the line lends force to the announcement of Zeus' revenge. Cf. in Homer οἳ δὲ καὶ αὐτοί (*Il.* 5. 520 etc.), although never at the beginning of the verse, and *Il.* 1. 437 ἐκ δὲ καὶ αὐτοὶ βαῖνον.

γλυκὺν ἵμερον ἔμβαλε θυμῷ: cf. *Il.* 3. 139 ὣς εἰποῦσα θεὰ γλυκὺν ἵμερον ἔμβαλε θυμῷ, where Iris fills Helen with longing for her former husband Menelaus and her homeland; this phrase is used twice more in *Aphr.* at vv. 53, 143. There is no sexual implication in the Homeric passage (see Kirk 1985, 281), although that sense is explicit here. The noun ἵμερος and its cognates are by no means confined to sexual longing (see Fernández-Galiano, *OC* iii. 309–10), but combined with γλυκύς it is on two of four occasions in Homer strongly erotic: the lusty words of Paris to Helen at *Il.* 3. 446 ὥς σεο νῦν ἔραμαι καί με γλυκὺς ἵμερος αἱρεῖ and, most strikingly, those same words uttered by Zeus during his seduction by Hera at 14. 328. The repetition of γλυκὺν ἵμερον here recalls v. 2, where Aphrodite is stirring up desire, underlining that things have been turned on their head; the seducer has become the seduced

45–6 ἵμερον ... ἔμβαλε θυμῷ | ... μιχθήμεναι: cf. the *Naupactia* (fr. 7a. 1–2) δὴ τότ' ἄρ' Αἰήτηι πόθον ἔμβαλε δῖ' Ἀφροδίτη | Εὐρυλύτης φιλότητι μιγήμεναι. D and At transmit the variant μιγήμεναι in *Aphr.*, which does not fit the metre. The form μιχθήμεναι is rare but it is found in the same metrical position in an erotic context at *Cypr.* fr. 7. 4, during the description of Zeus' passionate pursuit of Nemesis; also at *Il.* 11. 438 in a martial context. On μείγνυμι of sexual intercourse see on *Aphr.* 39 συνέμειξε.

46 ἀνδρὶ καταθνητῷ: ἄνδρες are καταθνητοί elsewhere only at *Il.* 10. 441–2 καταθνητοῖσιν ἔοικεν | ἄνδρεσσιν, *Op.* 484 ἄνδρεσσι καταθνητοῖσι and Thgn. 897 ἄνδρεσσι καταθνητοῖς, although they are not infrequently θνητοί. Cf. the metrically equivalent formula ἀνδράσι γε θνητοῖσι (*Il.* 10. 403, 17. 77, 20. 266 and *Od.* 10. 306) or ἀνδρός τε θνητοῦ (*Il.* 24. 259); *Hy.* 19. 33 has the similar ἀνδρὶ παρὰ θνητῷ.

46–8 ὄφρα τάχιστα | ... εἴη | ... εἴπῃ: the switch of moods here from optative to subjunctive has sufficient Homeric precedent; *Il.* 14. 163–5, 16. 650–1, 18. 308, etc. (see AHS 356, VE 29, Hahn 1953, 87 n. 199). Strictly, the optative should also follow in the second instance after the aorist ἔμβαλε in the main clause. The subjunctive after the historic tense here adds a vividness to Aphrodite's boasting amongst the gods, which is described in more detail in the following lines (cf. Janko 1992, 173 on the contrast of vividness at *Il.* 14. 163–5 noted above).

ὄφρα τάχιστα: a relatively common expression at this metrical position in Homer (12×: *Il.* 4. 465 etc.), it here underlines the eagerness of Zeus to take revenge on Aphrodite (cf. Kamerbeek 1967, 30, VE 46). Compare the eagerness of Elephenor to strip the armour of Echepolos at *Il.* 4. 465 λελιημένος, ὄφρα τάχιστα (see Kirk 1985, 387, 'eager to ...').

VB 6 suggests that, because 'the context contains nothing to indicate at what particular point in time, or for what immediate reason, Zeus decided to take action', τάχιστα should be understood 'in light of the means Zeus applies, *viz.* ἵμερος', desire which is to be quickly fulfilled (on the word see below on 91). We should not, however, expect divine time and motivation to be precisely stated here; it can be assumed that at some point Zeus decided enough was enough and enacted his revenge swiftly on Aphrodite.

47 μηδ' αὐτή: 'not even she ...'; complementing the emphatic τῇ δὲ καὶ αὐτῇ at the beginning of v. 45, this phrase underlines once again the remarkable reversal in Aphrodite's situation. The unit μηδ' αὐτ- does not occur elsewhere in Homer, Hesiod, or the *Hymns*.

Otherwise, in this metrical position, most similar is μηδ' αὔτως found in Hellenistic poetry at A.R. 3. 185, Arat. 869 and then later at Procl. *Hy.* 7. 6.

βροτέης εὐνῆς: the adjective βρότεος is uncommon and is not used of εὐνή elsewhere in archaic poetry. It is used only once in Homer, of the voice (φωνῇ δὲ βροτέῃ, *Od.* 19. 545), and in Hesiod of skin (βρότεος χρώς, *Op.* 416); of strength at [Hes.] fr. 204. 128 μένος βρότεον. Most similar is its use at Pi. *I.* 8. 36 βροτέων δὲ λεχέων, also of a bed. It is elsewhere combined with εὐνή only at Nonn. *D.* 48. 893 καὶ οὐ βροτέην ἴδον εὐνήν. The line may have been conceived from a familiarity with verses such as *Il.* 18. 85 ἤματι τῷ ὅτε σὲ βροτοῦ ἀνέρος ἔμβαλον εὐνῇ or 2. 820–1 Αἰνείας, τὸν ὑπ' Ἀγχίσῃ τέκε δῖ' Ἀφροδίτη | Ἴδης ἐν κνημοῖσι θεὰ βροτῷ εὐνηθεῖσα; these are also similar to *Aphr.* 199 and 255.

ἀποεργμένη: 'not even she should stay away from the mortal bed …'; this uncontracted form of the verb ἀπείργω appears four times in Homer (ἀποέργει at *Il.* 8. 325, *Od.* 3. 296 and ἀποέργασθε at *Il.* 21. 599, *Od.* 21. 221), but never in relation to sexual or marital contact. This use is unique to *Aphr.*, although cf. Paus. 2. 24. 1 γυνὴ μὲν προφητεύουσά ἐστιν, ἀνδρὸς εὐνῆς εἰργομένη.

48 καί ποτ': unsatisfied with the lack of a second negative particle here, Kamerbeek (1967), 390–1 proposes an emendation to either μηδ' ἔτ', or the even more divergent ἢ ποτ' ἐπευξαμένη εἶπεν. Certainly, in no other instance of καί ποτε in early epic is the force of a negative particle continued (*Il.* 1. 213, 6. 459, 6. 479, 7. 87, *Od.* 8. 461, 11. 623, *Apoll.* 325, *Herm.* 385). Yet no palaeographically plausible emendation of the unified MS tradition has been found and, although slightly awkward, 'logic demands that we understand the negation of μηδ' αὐτή to apply also to εἴπῃ' (VB 6); cf. VE's arguments (29) for the consecutive force of καί.

ἐπευξαμένη: the verb ἐπεύχομαι, which in Homer can mean either 'to pray' or 'to exult/boast', here clearly means the latter. Kirk (1985), 62 points out that while the verb normally implies a justified claim, it can 'also suggest a dubious boast' (see as well Adkins 1969, 26), such as at *Il.* 20. 102; Aphrodite's claims are not unjustified but they are about to become ironically and embarrassingly self-reflective.

Cf. the similarity of this line to *Il.* 6. 475 εἶπεν ἐπευξάμενος Διί τ' ἄλλοισίν τε θεοῖσι, and note there also the proximate occurrences of the τις-speech introduction καί ποτέ τις εἴπ- (vv. 459, 479). The participle ἐπευξάμενος occurs at ˇ2ˇˇ3 elsewhere only at *Il.* 10. 368 and *Od.* 14. 436.

μετὰ πᾶσι θεοῖσιν: cf. *Apoll.* 316 αὐτὰρ ὅ γ᾽ ἠπεδανὸς γέγονεν μετὰ πᾶσι θεοῖσι. See also ἐπεύξατο πᾶσι θεοῖσι at *Od.* 20. 238 and ἐπεύχετο πᾶσι θεοῖσι at *Od.* 14. 423 and 21. 203. The unit πᾶσι θεοῖσι(ν) is common at line-end in Homer: *Il.* 6. 140, 6. 200 etc.

49 ἡδὺ γελοιήσασα: the sweet laughter which accompanies Aphrodite's boasting resembles the vanity of the laughter of Paris as he boasts over the wounded Diomedes at *Il.* 11. 378–9 ὁ δὲ μάλα ἡδὺ γελάσσας | ἐκ λόχου ἀμπήδησε καὶ εὐχόμενος ἔπος ηὔδα. Cf. also the proud sweet laughter of the suitors at *Od.* 18. 111 ἡδὺ γελώωντες καὶ δεικανόωντ᾽ ἔπεσσι. Laughter is derisively sweet at *Il.* 2. 270, *Od.* 20. 358 and 21. 376 ἐπ᾽ αὐτῷ ἡδὺ γέλασσαν. On the feeling of superiority which laughter implies see D. B. Levine (1982). Cf. on *Aphr.* 17 φιλομμειδὴς Ἀφροδίτη.

γελοιήσασα: this participle, formed from the epic γελοιάω for γελάω, occurs with relative certainty only here (MS M alone has the unmetrical γελάσασα), although γελοίω- is a v.l. for γελώω- at *Od.* 18. 111, 20. 347, 390. This may be a modification by declension of ἡδὺ γελώωντες (*Od.* 18. 111; quoted in previous note), or by shifting of ἡδὺ γέλασσαν (*Il.* 2. 270 etc.; 5ˇˇ6×), but there is no linguistic innovation to support the case; see Hoekstra (1969), 45, Janko (1982), 156. Note *Batrach.* 172, which begins ἡδὺ γελῶν.

50–2. The alliteration in these lines creates a striking verbal effect and one can almost imagine the playful boasting of Aphrodite amongst the gods which this passage is intended to represent: ὥς ῥα θεούς ~ ὥς τε θεάς, συνέμειξε ~ ἀνέμειξε, καταθνητῇσι γυναιξί ~ καταθνητοῖς ἀνθρώποις. Moreover, the repetition in these lines signals the importance of the theme of mortal–divine relationships (on the motif see Introd., p. 11). The contrast between mortals and gods has already been made in vv. 46–8 (ἀνδρὶ καταθνητῷ and βροτέης εὐνῆς vs. [Ἀφροδίτη] and θεοῖσιν), and they are now explicitly juxtaposed in each line: v. 50 θεούς ~ καταθνητῇσι γυναιξί, v. 51 καταθνητοὺς υἷας ~ ἀθανάτοισιν, v. 52 θεάς ~ καταθνητοῖς ἀνθρώποις. There is even a sort of double chiasmus, which effects a balanced contrast of mortal and immortal gender: gods—mortal women—mortal sons/gods—goddesses—mortal men.

Despite their ornate internal composition, however, these lines might be thought to be somewhat awkward in the overall structure of the hymn. After apparently having entered the narrative in v. 45, the poet unexpectedly returns to attributive statements here, thereby prolonging the start of the narrative until v. 53. But if it temporarily impedes the forward progress of the hymn, this digression is far from superfluous. It is here for the first time that mention is made of the children which result from such unions. The poet is foreshadowing the birth of Aeneas (see Introd., pp. 7–8), and the point of καταθνητοὺς υἷας is made all the more poignant by its place in the imagined boasting of Aphrodite: 'ces mots résultent en quelque sorte de l'ironie, ainsi accrue de sa destinée' (Podbielski 1971, 30).

51 υἷας: all MSS transmit the contracted acc. plural υἱεῖς, which does not occur elsewhere in early epic; the contracted nominative υἱεῖς is found at *Il.* 24. 387, 24. 497, and *Od.* 15. 248, and the vocative υἱεῖς at *Il.* 5. 464. Buck (1955), 93 lists the contracted acc. form as Attic. Similar to δόκεον (MSS ἐδόκουν) at v. 125 (see ad loc.), this Atticism is resolvable and could quite easily have been a later alteration. It seems best to restore the common epic form υἷας (*Il.* 1. 240 etc.), given that there is no sure sign of Attic influence elsewhere in the poem; several resolvable forms and a possible interpolation at v. 98 instead suggest an Attic phase of transmission (see Introd., p. 45).

Also possible is υἱέας (*Il.* 2. 693 etc.). The first syllable of υἱός is often shortened in Homer (*Il.* 1. 489, 4. 473, etc.); although this does not occur in Homer in the acc. plural form, the shortening could here have been due to modification; the acc. plural occupies an unusual place in the line (⏑⏑4; elsewhere in early epic always at line-beginning, except for υἱέας ἐσθλούς 5⏑⏑6x, *Il.* 23. 175, 181 etc.).

τέκον: the Ψ MSS all offer the variant τέκεν, while M alone preserves the plural τέκον. VE 30, who has an unjustified mistrust of M (see Introd., pp. 54–5), prefers τέκεν, arguing that Aphrodite can be said to give birth to mortal sons through mortal women. He bases his argument upon the weak parallel that γαῖα is said to 'produce' sheep at *Od.* 19. 113. The sense there, however, is quite different and offers little support for the reading. In fact, there seems to be no parallel for Aphrodite giving birth (τίκτειν) through another agent and the plural, referring to καταθνητῇσι γυναιξί, should be preferred here.

The singular τέκεν has probably come in because of influence from the two singular verbs in vv. 50 and 52.

52 ἀνέμειξε: Porter (1949), 265 suggests that the alternation between συνέμειξε and ἀνέμειξε here adds to the assonance of the passage (see on *Aphr.* 50–2); the prefix complements the preceding syllable: συν- comes after θεούς, while ἀν- follows θεάς. This is dubious given that -ους [-ōs] does not contain a υ sound. Nonetheless, Schäfer's correction to συνέμειξε is unnecessary (cf. AHS 356); the alternation is probably for variety.

καταθνητοῖς ἀνθρώποις: this formula does not appear in Homer in the dative plural. The closest parallel is found at [Hes.] fr. 1. 7 ἀθανάτοις τε θεοῖσι καταθνητοῖς τ' ἀνθρώποις. See also *Dem.* 11 ἀθανάτοις τε θεοῖς ἠδὲ θνητοῖς ἀνθρώποις. The short dative plural perhaps suggests that the poet is innovating by modifying the genitive plural, found in Homer and five times in *Aphr.* (cf. Janko 1982, 155; on the genitive see on *Aphr.* 3).

53–199. The core narrative. The hymn is the main source for the story of Aphrodite's seduction of Anchises. The love-affair and the resulting birth of Aeneas are referred to cursorily elsewhere in extant early epic, but only here is the episode developed into a detailed narrative. The basic kernel of the story is known in the *Iliad*, at 2. 820–1 Αἰνείας, τὸν ὑπ' Ἀγχίσῃ τέκε δῖ' Ἀφροδίτη | Ἴδης ἐν κνημοῖσι θεὰ βροτῷ εὐνηθεῖσα (Aeneas' parentage is also alluded to at *Il.* 5. 312–13, 20. 208–9), and in Hesiod at *Th.* 1008–10 Αἰνείαν δ' ἄρ' ἔτικτεν ἐυστέφανος Κυθέρεια | Ἀγχίσῃ ἥρωι μιγεῖσ' ἐρατῇ φιλότητι | Ἴδης ἐν κορυφῇσι πολυπτύχου ἠνεμοέσσης. Otherwise, however, the early terrain is rather barren. V*E* 4 is almost certainly correct in supposing that these were not the only sources of the story for the poet of *Aphr.*, but what these sources might have consisted of can only be conjecture. The origins of the myth may owe something to the eastern tale of the union of the Sumerian love-goddess Inanna and the mortal herdsman Dumuzi (see *ETCSL* 4. 08. 1 ff. = *ANET* 637–44, cf. Penglase 1994, 170), although these were hardly direct sources of inspiration for this poet.

It is probable, nonetheless, that the poet has innovated to a considerable extent in creating his version of the story. The form and content of the prologue already suggest an innovative poet: a rather unorthodox build-up to the narrative (see on *Aphr.* 1–44), possible adaptation of a hymn to Artemis for the Hestia episode (see on *Aphr.* 25–32) etc. Yet, even if one has the impression of a good degree of innovation, it is still difficult to say with any certainty to what extent the poet has expanded scenes which were native to other accounts of the myth, and at which points he has added material which did not exist in other versions of the story. More traditional scenes such as Aphrodite's toilette (vv. 58–63), the description of her clothing and jewellery (vv. 85–90), or her epiphany (vv. 177–99) might be supposed more probably to have had a place in an existing tradition, even if in a more reduced form. These elements of Aphrodite's seduction of Anchises are paralleled in other extant seduction scenes; most notably Hera's seduction of Zeus in *Il.* 14. 153–351 and the affair between Aphrodite and Ares in *Od.* 8. 266–366, but also Helen's encounter with Paris in *Il.* 3. 374–447 (see Sowa 1984, 67 ff.); cf. as well Odysseus' meeting with Penelope in *Od.* 23. 153–372.

One element of the narrative has a particular claim to innovation by this poet; the instigation of the love-affair by Zeus (see van der Ben 1981, 93, Lenz 1975, 37, VE 5, Rose 1924, 12 etc.). That this element probably did not have a place in other versions of the myth is suggested by its lack of appearance in not only the brief references to the story in Homer and Hesiod, but also in all surviving accounts of the myth by later authors. In later Greek poetry the love-affair is referred to by Theocritus at *Id.* 1. 105–6 ff., 20. 34, in Nonnus at *D.* 15. 210 ff., and also several times in epigrams of the *AP* (Agathias Scholasticus 6. 76, anonymous 16. 168, Leontius Scholasticus 16. 357, Marcellus *App. Anth.* 1. 264 Cougny). In prose there is an account by Acusilaus surviving in the *Scholia* to Homer (fr. 39 Fowler), and a later one by Apollodorus 3. 141. Mention is made of the affair at Longus, *Daphnis and Chloe* 4. 17. 6. In Latin see Ov. *Ep.* 16. 203–4, and possibly Prop. 2. 32. 33–40 (where, however, the text is uncertain; it could refer to Paris and Oenone rather than to Venus and Anchises; see Camps 1967, 213). Punishment of Anchises by Zeus is also a frequent theme of later authors: Soph. *Laocoon* fr. 373. 2–3, Verg. *A.* 2. 649, Hyginus, *Fab.* 94 (see further references in Gow ii. 24 and cf. below on 286–8). Nowhere, however, is the role of Zeus as instigator mentioned.

53–7. Anchises is introduced for the first time in the poem. Zeus cast desire for him into the heart of Aphrodite. As a result of Zeus' action, Aphrodite fell in love with Anchises. Structurally, v. 53 echoes v. 45 through the repetition of γλυκὺν ἵμερον ἔμβαλε θυμῷ; this serves to recall the theme of Zeus' revenge after the digression of the preceding lines, and to set the narrative on its forward course once again. Alongside the echo, there is also clarification; what was stated vaguely above, ἀνδρὶ καταθνητῷ (v. 46), is now given precisely.

After the introduction of his name in v. 53, two lines of expansion then describe Anchises: an alpine cattle-herder endowed with immortal beauty. These lines also function to set the bucolic environment in which the love-affair will take place: Ida of the many springs. But this is only a short glimpse of the hero and his abode, and the poet quickly returns in vv. 56–7 to the world of the gods. Having described the scene, the poet tells how Aphrodite fell completely in love with Anchises upon seeing him (τὸν δἤπειτα ἰδοῦσα ... | ἠράσατ'; cf. on *Aphr.* 56). This is clever narration: although Anchises is actually described in vv. 54–5 by the primary narrator-focalizer (the poet; cf. de Jong 1989, 19), the small vignette of Anchises' life does not escape a certain focalization through the eyes of Aphrodite. The audience in effect sees what Aphrodite herself saw (Anchises from a distance and briefly, just as the narrator presents it to the audience) experiencing with increased vividness her 'love at first sight'.

53 Ἀγχίσεω: the prominent placement of Anchises' name at the beginning of the line marks the introduction of the new character and the start of the narrative proper. The name is frequently in the first position in the line in *Aphr.* (vv. 77, 84, 91, 108, 126, 144, 166, 192; v. 170 is the only exception), but never in Homer. Elsewhere in early poetry it is in this position only at *Th.* 1009 Ἀγχίσῃ ἥρωι.

The Homeric form of the genitive is Ἀγχίσαο. The form Ἀγχίσεω with synizesis, here and at *Aphr.* 126, occurs only once more in Greek poetry, in the much later Marcellus, *App. Anth.* 1. 264. 4 (Cougny) Ἀγχίσεω κλυτὸν αἷμα καὶ Ἰδαίης Ἀφροδίτης. On the synizesis, regular with -εω, -έων < -αο -άων, see *Enchiridium*, 47–50.

δ' ἄρα: on this particle combination, which helps to express the interest or importance of a fact being expressed, see on *Aphr.* 42. Also, 'a particle which marks realization or enlightenment is half-way to becoming a logical connective particle' (Denniston 1954, 40); here perhaps picking up on vv. 45–6 'and so . . .'.

54 ὃς τότ': note the relative expansion typical of hymnic openings (see on *Aphr.* 1–6). For similar phrasing in praise of extraordinary mortals cf. *Od.* 14. 205 ὃς τότ' ἐνὶ Κρήτεσσι θεὸς ὣς τίετο δήμῳ of Castor, *Dem.* 97 ὃς τότ' Ἐλευσῖνος θυοέσσης κοίρανος ἦεν of Celeus, etc.

ἐν ἀκροπόλοις ὄρεσιν: a possible case of modification by transposition from line-end ἐπ'/ἐν ἀκροπόλοισιν ὄρεσσιν, *Il.* 5. 523/*Od.* 19. 205; see Janko (1982), 155, Hoekstra (1969), 42. Modification is suggested by the form ὄρεσι(ν), which does not appear in Homer and has nu mobile make position. The similar form λέχεσι(ν) at *Aphr.* 126, again un-Homeric and with nu mobile making position, also suggests modification (see on *Aphr.* 126–7); cf. also νέφεσι(ν) at *Aphr.* 67 which shares these characteristics (see ad loc.). VE offers the enticing suggestion that the modification was modelled upon *Il.* 14. 157 Ζῆνα δ' ἐπ' ἀκροτάτης κορυφῆς πολυπίδακος Ἴδης. He bases his argument, however, on the weak grounds that the o-stem genitive πολυπιδάκου found in *Aphr.* is a *variant reading* at *Il.* 14. 157 (see n. seq.). More relevant is the corresponding context. The Διὸς ἀπάτη is initiated in *Il.* 14 by Hera seeing (εἰσεῖδε, v. 158) Zeus on Ida, just as Aphrodite sees (ἰδοῦσα, v. 56) Anchises before seducing him. Hera then retires to her θάλαμος to prepare herself, while Aphrodite returns to her sanctuary in Cyprus. Also, these two toilette-scenes share identical verses (see on *Aphr.* 58–63) and there is further linguistic similarity with *Il.* 14 at *Aphr.* 66 ff. (see ad loc.). The thematic similarities combined with the linguistic parallels make imitation an attractive possibility. See also *Il.* 14. 307 ἵπποι δ' ἐν πρυμνωρείῃ πολυπίδακος/-πιδάκου Ἴδης.

πολυπιδάκου: 'of many springs'. The epithet πολυπίδαξ is used only of Ida in Homer (*Il.* 8. 47, 14. 157, etc.), which is also called πιδήεσσα at *Il.* 11. 183. Strabo 13. 1. 43 comments that Ida is called πολυπίδακος because of the great number of rivers which flow from it (cf. Janko 1992, 173, Edwards 1991 245). Cook (1973), 306 reports of the present-day Kaz Dağ in the Troad, 'springs are numerous and very chill in the high part of the mountain'.

The radical o-stem genitive is the unanimous reading only here and at *Cypr.* fr. 5. 5; elsewhere the athematic πολυπίδακος is a variant, or vice versa. Aristarchus condemned the o-stem form at *Il.* 14. 157 as τελέως ἀγροικόν (on possible influence of this line upon *Aphr.* see the preceding note). Nonetheless, it predominates in the MSS in three of the five occurrences of the genitive in Homer, and it was probably in circulation quite early. Janko (1992), 172–3, 1978 provides several parallel examples of nouns and adjectives transferred to the *o*-stem declension in Homer, and, as he suggests, it may well have been the case that 'Homer himself wavered'. Thus, although the athematic acc. πολυπίδακα is used later at *Aphr.* 68, there seems to be no particular reason to normalize here by printing πολυπίδακος (so West 2003, following the conjecture of D'Orville). These parallels also preclude any indication of provenance in the form, which cannot be attached to a particular dialect (cf. Janko 1982, 170).

The adjective is first used of a location other than Ida at *Hy.* 19. 30, of Arcadia, and at Simonides fr. 15. 1 of Ephyre. In later poetry it is not common, and in contrast to its early usage it is never applied to Ida; see Ἀκρωρείης Theoc. *Id.* 25. 31, σκοπιάς A.R. 3. 883, λαιμῷ Nonn. *D.* 2. 276 etc.

55 βουκολέεσκεν βοῦς: Hoekstra (1969), 45 suggests possible modification by transposition of *Il.* 21. 448–9 Φοῖβε σὺ δ' εἰλίποδας ἕλικας βοῦς βουκολέεσκες | Ἴδης ἐν κνημοῖσι, both because of a strange rhythm and nu mobile making position. According to Fränkel's theory of verse division into four cola (Fränkel 1955, 111 ff.; 1962, 32–7), the division of cola in this line is irregular: both the A and C caesurae come later than is usual. This is the only such occurrence in *Aphr.*, although Fränkel (1955), 112–13 gives several examples of both A and C caesura displaced in the same line in *Il.* and *Od.* (e.g. *Il.* 1. 449). Hoekstra points out that the line has a 'highly unusual' rhythm, which combined with the presence of nu mobile making position, is a strong signal for modification here, where it would have been equally possible to have βουκολέεσκε βόας. Anchises is mentioned explicitly as a herder (βουκολέοντι) at *Il.* 5. 313.

δέμας ἀθανάτοισιν ἐοικώς: Aphrodite does not become infatuated with just any man, but one whose beauty is comparable to that of the gods. The godlike beauty of Anchises is a motif which recurs throughout the poem (see Introd., pp. 9–10). Conversely, Aphrodite lessens the gap between her and Anchises in the poem by taking the form of a young mortal virgin (v. 82).

This phrase does not occur elsewhere, but cf. *Od.* 3. 468/8. 14/23.

163 δέμας ἀθανάτοισιν ὁμοῖος, *Il.* 17. 323 Αἰνείαν ὤτρυνε, δέμας Περίφαντι ἐοικώς, *Apoll.* 400 δέμας δελφῖνι ἐοικώς. Later see Q.S. 6. 309 δέμας μακάρεσσιν ἐοικώς, of Paris.

56 τὸν δήπειτα ἰδοῦσα: 'as a result . . .'; ἔπειτα is causal here, explaining the effect of Zeus' action; δή, rather than having connective force as VE 31 claims, is emphatic (see VB 7; cf. Denniston 1954, 204). The participle ἰδοῦσα should be understood as narratologically 'coincident' with γλυκὺν ἵμερον ἔμβαλε θυμῷ (vv. 45, 53), in that it describes the same event from Aphrodite's point of view (see de Jong 1989, 19–20). τὸν δήπειτα is used in a causal sense also at *Aphr.* 209, of Tros' reaction to his son's mysterious disappearance.

The MSS have δ' ἤπειτα for δὴ ἔπειτα, as at *Th.* 405, 562 (see West 1966a, 100). Recent editors, Càssola, VE, and West (2003), print the Homeric form δήπειτα, while others have followed Hermann's correction to δὴ ἔπειτα. The Homeric form is hardly surprising here, and is preferable to Hermann's change of the transmitted reading (in support of the form see West ibid., N. Richardson 1974, 177, and *Enchiridium*, 70).

ἰδοῦσα ... | ἠράσατ': similar language describes Hermes' rapture at the sight of the mortal Polymele at *Il.* 16. 181–2 τῆς δὲ κρατὺς Ἀργειφόντης | ἠράσατ', ὀφθαλμοῖσιν ἰδών. 'Love at first sight' is a common motif in divine love-affairs with mortals. The summary to [Hes.] fr. 141, which tells the story of Zeus' affair with Europa, explains that he fell in love (ἠράσθη) with the mortal upon seeing her (θεασάμενος), a theme which recurs in the later version of the affair by Moschus *Eur.* 74 ff. (see Campbell 1991, 79). Other examples of erotic love following sight do not cross the divine–mortal boundary; Zeus is overcome by desire for Hera upon seeing her at *Il.* 14. 294 etc. (see Janko 1992, 198 and Gow ii. 51–3 for further examples). The theme of perception by sight is a frequently recurring one throughout *Aphr.*: at vv. 72, 84, 179, 185, 256, 278–9.

φιλομμειδὴς Ἀφροδίτης: see on *Aphr.* 17.

57 ἐκπάγλως: AS 204 rebut Köchly's correction (1881, 221) to ἔκπαγλος by citing ἔκπαγλα ἐφίλησ-α/ε (*Il.* 3. 415, 5. 423). Following this parallel, however, one would expect the adverb to go more naturally with ἠράσατο than εἷλεν (cf. the structure of *Od.* 5. 340 ὠδύσατ' ἐκπάγλως, ὅτι τοι κακὰ πολλὰ φυτεύει), but punctuation cannot come after ἐκπάγλως before δέ. One could read ἠράσατ' ἐκπάγλως, κατὰ δὲ φρένας ἵμερος εἷλεν (for κατὰ δέ after the main caesura cf. *Il.* 1. 436, 11. 811, 16. 325 etc.), although it is difficult to explain what would have caused the transposition of κατὰ δέ. Köchly's ἔκπαγλος is possible, but there are in the end no strong grounds to reject the almost united MS tradition (L₁ reads ἐκπάγλης, presumably after φιλομμειδής in the previous line); Aphrodite could just as well be seized 'exceedingly' by erotic desire as she could be seized by 'exceeding' erotic desire.

κατὰ φρένας ἵμερος εἷλεν: cf. περὶ φρένας ἵμερος αἱρεῖ at *Il.* 11. 89 and *Apoll.* 461. Sweet desire seizes both Paris and Zeus in the *Iliad* (3. 446, 14. 328, γλυκὺς ἵμερος αἱρεῖ), while in both episodes their φρένας are separately said to be enveloped by love (3. 442, and 14. 294 ἔρως φρένας ἀμφεκάλυψεν).

58–63. These lines are largely identical with *Od.* 8. 362–5, part of the so-called *Lay* of *Demodocus*, but with some significant variation (long noticed by scholars; see Matthiae 1800, 323–4, AHS 356–7 etc.). The differences are the following: (i) vv. 60 and 63 are not present in the *Odyssey* passage, and are instead identical with *Il.* 14. 169 and 172, lines from Hera's toilette before seducing Zeus; (ii) although v. 58 announces Aphrodite's arrival at Cyprus, as does *Od.* 8. 362, the phrasing of the two lines is in fact quite different (the structure of the verse in *Aphr.* resembles more the line that follows it); (iii) while it is identical with *Od.* 8. 363 in every other respect, *Aphr.* 59 uses the adjective θυώδης at the end of the line in place of the form θυήεις; (iv) thematically, the toilette in *Aphr.* has more in common with the preparation of Hera; both goddesses are setting out to conquer a lover, whereas in *Od.* 8 Aphrodite's short dressing scene comes after her embarrassing encounter with Ares.

As the sequence of verses in *Aphr.* stands, elaborate repetition and alliteration mark the passage: (i) three successive pairs of lines begin with parallel words and phrases, ἐς Κύπρον/ἐς Πάφον—ἔνθ'/ἔνθα—ἀμβρότῳ/ἀμβροσίῳ; (ii) at the centre of this triplet of paired lines there is the further threefold repetition of ἔνθα in vv. 59–61 (the Charites themselves mentioned in v. 61 of course also traditionally number three); (iii) there is assonance of -ους (following from ἰδοῦσα in v. 56) with ἐλθοῦσα (58), εἰσελθοῦσα (60), λοῦσαν (61), and θεούς (62); (iv) finally, the repetition of the adjective θυώδης at the beginning of the passage (58–9), and both ἑδανῷ and τεθυωμένον in the final verse, underline the fragrant quality of this toilette (see on *Aphr.* 58–9; note also εὐώδεα in v. 66).

Freed and Bentman (1954) suggest that the finely crafted structure of this passage seems more complicated than examples in Homer and Hesiod. The observation has been marred by their insistence upon the notion that such repetition could only be produced by a Hellenistic poet; but the reflection itself is not without value. Early poetry does contain examples of reasonably elaborate structure; cf. *Od.* 14. 395–400, 19. 329–34, *Th.* 721–5, *Op.* 1–8 (on which see West 1966*a*, 359; 1978, 136; also Fehling 1969, 313 ff.). *Od.* 8. 363–6 itself contains alliteration, assonance, and repetition: (i) paired ἐς/ἔνθα—ἀμβρότῳ/ἀμφί; (ii) repetition of ἔνθα in 363–4 (cf. also *Hy.* 19. 31–2); (iii) -ους repeated in λοῦσαν/θεούς of 364–5. However, there is no real parallel in early poetry for the intricate structure of these lines in *Aphr.* Podbielski (1971), 37 proposes that this points to 'l'époque terminale et décadente de l'épopée archaïque'. The criterion is hardly a precise dating tool, but one might reasonably say that it suggests a period after Homer and Hesiod (on the date of the poem see Introd., pp. 47–9).

AS 205 and Porter (1949), 268 n. 35 are rightly cautious about accepting any conscious adaptation of the two episodes in *Il.* 14 and *Od.* 8. In the former case, such a seduction scene should belong more properly to the goddess of love, and one might wonder whether there was a common Greek model for both *Aphr.* and *Il.* 14. On the other hand, given other cases of possible borrowing from Homer, it seems probable that the poet knew them in at least some form (see Introd., pp. 31–4).

58–9 θυώδεα νηὸν ... | ... βωμός τε θυώδης: the repetition of the adjective initiates a series of references to fragrance in this passage (cf. on *Aphr.* 58–63). The quality of sweet scent is appropriate to a preparation-scene where a divinity is involved (at *Od.* 5. 264 Calypso covers Odysseus in εἵματα θυώδεα after bathing him), to a divine dwelling-place (see θυώδεος Οὐλύμποιο, *Dem.* 331 and *Herm.* 322), and to the sanctuary of a beautiful woman (the θάλαμος of the sexually attractive Helen is θυώδης at *Od.* 4. 121); but the insistence on the point here is made especially for Aphrodite. She is well known for her fragrance in literature and cult; see Pirenne-Delforge (1994), 322–3, Lilja, (1972), 21–5, 44–5, and on the general erotic significance of fragrance 47 ff. There is a similar stress upon fragrance in consecutive lines in a later funerary epigram of Antipater Sidonius (*AP* 7. 218. 8–10): the grave, bones, and hair of the famous prostitute Lais, named τὴν θνητὴν Ἀφροδίτην in the poem, still produce sweet odours (on the use of perfume and bathing in the ἐρωτικὴ τέχνη of prostitutes, see Stumpp 1998, 105).

Given that fragrance is a known attribute of Aphrodite cult, and the emphasis on the point in this passage, the adjective θυώδης probably intends 'perfumed' in both cases here (cf. Casabona 1966, 118). This would be in contrast to θυήεις used of βωμός in Homer, which more plausibly refers to the smell of burnt offerings at the altar (see Kirk 1990, 302), but a certain play on words here would not be surprising. The form θυώδης used of βωμός is rare, and appears elsewhere in early poetry only at *Apoll.* 87–8 and then twice later in Nonn. *D.* 5. 270 and an epigram preserved at Paus. 7. 25. 1 βωμούς τε θυώδεις; only in Nonnus is the use of the adjective explicitly connected with sacrifice.

58 ἐς Κύπρον δ' ἐλθοῦσα: apart from *Od.* 8. 362 noted above, see the similar structure at 3. 159 ἐς Τένεδον δ' ἐλθόντες ἐρέξαμεν ἱρὰ θεοῖσι.

θυώδεα νηόν: cf. *Dem.* 355 θυώδεος ἔνδοθι νηοῦ and 385 νηοῖο προπάροιθε θυώδεος; the adjective is not used again of a temple until A.R. 1. 307 νηοῖο θυώδεος, Theoc. *Id.* 17. 123 θυώδεας ναούς etc. Janko (1982), 164 (also 226) comments rather too confidently though that '*Dem.*'s separated phrases . . . have a secondary look', although other similarities between the two poems seem to suggest that borrowing is in the direction of *Dem.* (see Introd., pp. 38–40). It should be kept in mind that the poet of *Dem.* is himself 'fond' of the adjective θυώδης (see N. Richardson 1974, 236).

59 ἔνθα δέ: so all MSS; δέ is also the vulgate at *Od.* 8. 363 (where τε is a v.l.), which may be significant if that passage was a model for *Aphr.* (see on *Aphr.* 58–63). Hermann (1806) nonetheless prefers to correct to τε (adopted by Càssola 1975). This is difficult to justify given the unanimity of the MSS here, and the presence of δέ as a vulgate or variant in similar phrasing elsewhere (cf. *Il.* 8. 48, 13. 21, *Hy.* 19. 31); δέ clearly had a place here for the ancients. Denniston (1954), 169 observes that δέ for γάρ is 'quite common' in Homer (cf. VE 32). Note also ἔνθα δέ just two lines below; the repetition is typical of the passage and provides a further chiasmus effect for the central triplet, ἔνθα δέ—ἔνθ' ἥ—ἔνθα δέ.

τέμενος βωμός τε θυώδης: cf. the formula τέμενος βωμός τε θυήεις (*Il.* 8. 48, 23. 148, *Od.* 8. 363). Note also *Apoll.* 87–8 ἦ μὴν Φοίβου τῇδε θυώδης ἔσσεται αἰεὶ | βωμὸς καὶ τέμενος; the 'violent enjambment' there seems to suggest modification of an existing formula (Janko 1982, 254 n. 13), although there is no particular reason to suspect direct imitation of *Aphr.*

60 θύρας ἐπέθηκε φαεινάς: Aphrodite 'puts to' or 'closes' the doors of her temple as Hera does at *Il.* 14. 169; at *Od.* 21. 45, *Th.* 732 the verb means to 'fit', in the process of building (cf. West 1966a, 362). The phrase recurs below at v. 256 of Eos shutting Tithonus in his bedroom.

φαεινάς: 'shining' or 'splendid'; used elsewhere of metal doors in Homer at *Il.* 14. 169, *Od.* 6. 19, 10. 230 etc., the adjective also qualifies the light of the moon (*Il.* 5. 555), fire (5. 215), Eos (*Od.* 4. 188) etc. When used of objects it takes on also a more concrete sense of 'splendid' or 'beautiful' (see Cianni 1974, 103). For a comprehensive list of uses in early poetry see Mugler (1964), 403–5 and cf. Handschur (1970), 89–92. Aphrodite's peplos is φαεινός at *Il.* 5. 313, and the adjective will describe her peplos and jewellery later in *Aphr.* at vv. 86–7, 162.

61–4. This bath-scene contains the three core elements of the typical scene noted by Arend (1933), 124–6: washing (λοῦσαν), anointing (χρῖσαν ἐλαίῳ), and dressing in new clothes (εἵματα καλά). The cleansing and dressing represent a renewal of beauty and strength for Aphrodite before she sets out to seduce Anchises (on her clothes and jewellery see below on 81–90). Bathing was a nuptial rite (see Pirenne-Delforge 1994, 142); as at *Op.* 522–3 and Semonides fr. 7. 63 ff., a woman washes and anoints herself with oil (cf. West 1978, 288). On the Greek view of bathing as 'healthy and refreshing', in Homer and later, see Yegül (1992), 6 ff. A similar bath of preparation for a love-goddess is known in Near Eastern texts: in a Sumerian sacred-marriage text, Inanna bathes and anoints herself with oil before confronting her mortal lover Dumuzi (*ETCSL* 4. 08. 29 = *ANET* 639); also in the Sumerian *Song of Inanna*, in which the goddess sings of her own power, Inanna tells of how she washes her head and adorns herself with precious stones in the mountain retreat of Dilmun, as in the case of Aphrodite's removal to her Cyprian sanctuary (see Labat et al. 1970, 247–50 and cf. Penglase 1994, 166–7).

61 Χάριτες: the Graces are traditional companions of Aphrodite in literature; cf. *Il.* 5. 338, *Od.* 8. 364–5, 18. 193–4, *Apoll.* 194–6, *Cypr.* fr. 5, Mosch. *Eur.* 71 etc. They are also paired with others close to Aphrodite, Himeros 'desire' at *Th.* 64 and Peitho 'persuasion' at *Op.* 73. In cult, however, they are not known to have been connected with Cyprus. Their most famous cult was at Orchomenos, where there was a sacred spring to Aphrodite, and they were also worshipped elsewhere in southern Greece and in Asia Minor (see West 1966a, 408, Hainsworth, *OC* i. 371, Campbell 1991, 76, AHS 357, *OCD* s.v. Charites). On these goddesses see also on 95–6.

62–3 ἀμβρότῳ ... | ἀμβροσίῳ: since Gemoll (1886) and AS, the trend has sensibly been to retain both these lines (earlier editors preferred to delete v. 63 as a variant; cf. Hermann 1806 etc.). Not only is repetition an integral part of the structure of this passage (see on *Aphr.* 58–63), but both lines introduce a fresh idea, and are not incompatible or redundant. Note the pairing of ἀμβροσίου/ἄμβροτον at *Il.* 5. 338–9; also ἀμβροσίῃ/ἄμβροτα in the same line at 16. 670 and 680.

62 οἷα θεοὺς ἐπενήνοθεν: the meaning of ἐπενήνοθεν and other similar forms (ἐνήνοθεν, ἀνήνοθεν, or κατενήνοθεν) is obscure. According to Frisk (s.v. ἐνθεῖν; cf. *Grammaire*, i. 423–4) they are reduplicated perfect and pluperfect forms derived from ἐνθεῖν (=ἐλθεῖν). Another theory finds an origin in ἄνθος, ἀνθεῖν, which probably had an original meaning 'growth', 'to grow' (see Aitchison 1963, 273–4). This latter suggestion seems the more plausible. An original meaning from 'to grow' can account sufficiently for the use of the compounds in Homer ('grow on the surface' is acceptable for ἐπενήνοθε at *Il.* 2. 219, 10. 134, while 'to spring up' suits ἀνήνοθεν at *Il.* 11. 266, *Od.* 17. 270); in the case of *Od.* 8. 365 and here in *Aphr.* ἐπενήνοθεν can be understood to have come to mean 'to be on the surface' or 'to cover', from an original sense 'to grow upon', also compatible with κατενήνοθεν 'to grow down over'/'cover' at *Dem.* 279 (see N. Richardson 1974, 253–4, *LfgrE* s.v. ἐνήνοθεν, and cf. LSJ s.v. ἐπανθέω). Compare as well the development of a meaning 'to be' or 'to become' in the perfect form πέφυκα from φύω 'to grow'; a similar sense arising from a verb 'to grow' is found also in other Indo-European languages (see *Dictionnaire* s.v. φύομαι, LSJ s.v. φύω for examples). Oil was offered to gods and used to anoint their statues across the Near East and in Egypt, a practice which may help to explain this image of 'oil-covered' divinities (on the uses of perfumed oil see Shelmerdine 1985, 123 ff., Adrados 1964). In English poetry, Milton, *Paradise Lost* 5. 55–7 evokes the image of an immortal radiating ambrosia (note also the enjambment) 'One shap'd and wing'd like one of those from Heav'n | By us oft seen; his dewie locks distill'd | Ambrosia...'.

Further difficulty has been caused here by the plural οἷα following the singular ἐλαίῳ. One possible solution is to treat οἷα adverbially, with ἔλαιον understood as the subject, 'as it covers gods' (Hainsworth, *OC* i. 371). The point, however, is not the manner in which the oil is applied, but its immortal nature, stressed by the enjambment of ἀμβρότῳ at the beginning of the line. Cf. vv. 174–5 κάλλος δὲ παρειάων ἀπέλαμπεν | ἄμβροτον, οἷόν τ' ἐστί... and *Od.* 18. 192–4 κάλλεϊ μέν οἱ πρῶτα προσώπατα καλὰ κάθηρεν | ἀμβροσίῳ, οἵῳ περ ἐϋστέφανος Κυθέρεια | χρίεται, εὖτ' ἂν ἴῃ Χαρίτων χορὸν ἱμερόεντα; here the singular οἷον could not fit the metre. AHS 357 suggest reading οἷα as a generalizing relative 'things which'; but this is also problematic and seems to imply an elaboration upon the processes of bathing and anointing, 'things' which cannot be understood to 'cover the gods' (their parallel of *Od.* 11. 536 describes 'two' processes summed up by οἷα, οὔτ' ἄρ βεβλημένος... οὔτ' αὐτοσχεδίην οὐτασμένος). A relative which expands specifically upon ἔλαιον ἄμβροτον still provides the most natural sense. Alternatively one might understand οἷα in relation to ἔλαιον as a collective noun; Aphrodite is covered in 'immortal oil', 'such [immortal oils] as cover the gods' (cf. πλήθει, οἵπερ δικάσουσιν at Pl. *Phdr.* 260 A; see Goodwin 1900, 218).

θεοὺς... αἰὲν ἐόντας: in the accusative, and divided by another word, this formula appears four times in the *Odyssey* (1. 263, 378, 2. 143, 8. 365; see separation in the genitive at *Herm.* 548). In the *Iliad*, however, it is only in the nominative and never divided (*Il.* 1. 290 etc.). This may suggest a later development (see Hoekstra 1969, 58 n. 5, Janni 1968, 157 ff.).

63 ἑδανῷ: Clarke's conjecture (1740, 730) of ἑδανῷ for MSS ἑανῷ and ἑανῷ has become the standard (West 2003 prints ἑ<δ>ανῷ). It is the vulgate at *Il*. 14. 172, where ἑανῷ and ἑανῷ also appear as variant readings. The substantive ἑᾱνός (ἑᾱνόν) 'dress' has been dismissed as incomprehensible, and both ἀμβροσίῳ and ἑανῷ have thus been taken as adjectives qualifying ἔλαιον. Because the adjective ἑανός has a long α, the correction to ἑδανῷ has been considered inevitable (so AHS 357 and VE 33).

Hurst (1976) has successfully argued that the substantive cannot be rejected on the grounds that dresses are not perfumed: the practice of treating garments with perfumed oil is known in Mycenean Linear B tablets at Pylos (PY fr. 1225, 1 *e-ra-wo, u-po-jo, po-ti-ni-ja*, 2 *we-a$_2$-no-i, a-ro-pa*; see Shelmerdine 1985, 124 ff.; 1998). Moreover, it is alluded to on several occasions in Greek poetry; at *Cypria* fr. 4. 7 Aphrodite wears τεθυωμένα εἵματα, which have been dipped in spring flowers; at *Apoll*. 184, Apollo goes to Pytho sporting ἄμβροτα εἵματα . . . τεθυωμένα; *Od*. 5. 264 has εἵματα . . . θυώδεα, *Dem*. 231 θυώδεϊ . . . κόλπῳ, and *Herm*. 237 σπάργανα . . . θυήεντα; one even finds ἀμβρόσι-ον/ος ἑαν-όν/ός at *Il*. 14. 178 and 21. 507, which instead of being the source of a false reading here (according to Lejeune 1963, 81), can just as well point to the appropriateness of the substantive.

Nonetheless, the substantive does not fit well into the sentence. Hurst translates '[oil] which was perfumed for her immortal dress', but as West (2001*b*, 122 n. 19) points out, τό ῥά οἱ . . . is awkwardly understood as referring to oil after an intervening noun ἑανῷ; the two other uses of the clause τό ῥά οἱ in early epic immediately follow either the noun it describes (*Od*. 21. 17), or a runover adjective describing a noun in the previous line (*Il*. 20. 146). Janko (1982), 161, (1992), 175 tries to relieve this problem by reading τό ῥά οἱ as referring to the dress, '[oil] for her dress, which [the dress] had been perfumed'. He does so by proposing a neuter ἑανόν, which he compares to the Sanskrit neuter *vásanam*; he further suggests that this better fits the context of *Il*. 14. 172. This too, however, is dubious. Even if one accepts the uncertain neuter ἑανόν, the translation 'oil for her dress' is problematic; the true dative expressing 'for' is rarely used of nouns denoting things in Greek (see Monro 1891, 136). Moreover, it does not better fit the context as he claims, either at *Il*. 14. 172 or here. In the former instance, Hera's dressing does not begin until

v. 178 and the mention of a dress at v. 172 is entirely out of place. Here, mention of a dress is more plausible given that Aphrodite's dressing begins in the next line (v. 64 ἐσσαμένη δ'. . .), but even so, a reference to the process of perfuming clothing would be rather clumsy at this point. It seems far preferable to understand ἑανῷ as a second runover adjective, and to adopt the conjecture ἑδανῷ (traditionally taken as 'fragrant' or 'sweet'; see a summary of literature on the meaning of the word by West, 2001b, 122–3, who himself proposes 'bridal' from the root in ἔεδνα/ἔδνα, a sense which would certainly fit the context here and in *Il.* 14); this must be favoured at *Il.* 14. 172 as *lectio difficilior* and could well have been an ancient variant at *Aphr.* too (again see West, 2001b, 122). It is also worth noting that ἀμβροσίῳ is naturally attached to ἐλαίῳ as a runover adjective based upon the parallel at *Il.* 23. 186–7 ῥοδόεντι δὲ χρῖεν ἐλαίῳ | ἀμβροσίῳ (of Aphrodite anointing Hector's body).

64–91. Aphrodite leaves her temple and sets out toward Ida. The scene is fantastic and full of colour, as she travels through the clouds and effortlessly tames exotic wild beasts. Such wonders follow naturally from her rejuvenating bath, itself fully exotic and divine, and continue to underline her divine nature and power (cf. Podbielski 1971, 39). Penglase (1994), 174 *et passim* compares the journeys of divinities in Mesopotamian mythology, where the increase and demonstration of power is a central feature (i.e. Ištar's ascent from the Nether World).

Her approach to Anchises follows the general pattern of the Homeric arrival-scene: (i) she departs; (ii) she arrives; (iii) she finds Anchises (playing his lyre); (iv) she appears close to him (see Arend 1933, 28 and cf. Sowa 1984, 81). Within this broadly traditional structure Lenz (1975), 123–4 (cf. also VB 8) has observed two particularities. First, the approach has been extended by doubling; Aphrodite initially leaves Cyprus (προλιποῦσα) and arrives at the general location of Ida (vv. 64–8: 'ungefährer Zielort'), before once again departing (βῆ) from her point of arrival on the mountain, and arriving at the more exact destination of Anchises' hut (vv. 69–75: 'genauer Zielort'). Second, more attention is given to the description of the journey itself than is normally the case; in particular her encounter with the animals on Ida. Neither of these characteristics lacks Homeric parallels (see Lenz 1975, 123 n. 3), but they are the exception rather than the norm. It is interesting therefore, that both are also part of Hera's approach to Zeus in *Il.* 14. 281–93: along with Sleep, she leaves her sanctuary (v. 281 βήτην) and arrives first on Ida (v. 283), then departs again (v. 285) and arrives finally to where Zeus is sitting (v. 293); Mt. Ida receives description, as the poet must explain how Sleep waits in a tall tree for Hera to finish her dirty work. These structural similarities are supported by linguistic parallels in consecutive lines between the two scenes; v. 66 προλιποῦσα ~ λιπόντε v. 281, v. 67 ῥίμφα πρήσσουσα κέλευθον ~ ῥίμφα πρήσσοντε κέλευθον v. 282, v. 68 Ἴδην δ' ἴκανεν πολυπίδακα, μητέρα θηρῶν ~ Ἴδην δ' ἱκέσθην πολυπίδακα, μητέρα θηρῶν v. 283. After the correspondences just a few lines above between Aphrodite's toilette and Hera's preparation in *Il.* 14 (see on *Aphr.* 58–63), this may be a further suggestion that the poet of *Aphr.* knew the Διὸς ἀπάτη episode (see Introd., pp. 31–4).

Structurally, the section is demarcated by ring-composition. It opens with the brief two-line mention of the beautiful clothes and jewellery which Aphrodite puts on when leaving Cyprus (vv. 64–5), and then closes with an elaborate description of what these actually consist of (vv. 81–90).

64. All the components of this line exist in Homer, but never together as here. See of Hera setting out to find Aphrodite at *Il.* 14. 187 πάντα περὶ χροῒ θήκατο κόσμον; note also 7. 207 πάντα περὶ χροῒ ἕσσατο τεύχεα. For dressing in εἵματα καλά see *Od.* 14. 154, 16. 79, etc., and cf. περὶ χροῒ εἵματα ἕστο *Il.* 23. 67, *Od.* 17. 203 etc. Aphrodite dresses herself in a similar manner at *Hy.* 6. 6 περὶ δ' ἄμβροτα εἵματα ἕσσαν and 14 πάντα περὶ χροῒ κόσμον ἔθηκαν. *Aphr.* 64 will be echoed later at vv. 171–2, when Aphrodite dresses after having slept with Anchises.

65 κοσμηθεῖσα: the verb κοσμέω means 'to array' here, but only ever 'to marshal' in Homer (*Il.* 2. 554 etc.; cf. Podbielski 1971, 86, Janko 1982, 156). It is found in this sense at *Th.* 573 (= *Op.* 72; of Athena dressing Pandora), twice in *Hy.* 6. 11–12 (of the Hours apropos of Aphrodite), and at *Phoronis* fr. 3. 3 (Davies). Also, if restored correctly, see the passive participle with this meaning (and in the same metrical position) at *Meropis* fr. 6. 5 [ὣς ἄρα κοσ]μηθεῖσα (Bernabé); elsewhere in epic poetry at Nonn. *D.* 34. 274, 43. 93.

This use may be another sign of post-Homeric composition. On the overlap of vocabulary for love and war see on *Aphr.* 10–11.

φιλομμειδὴς Ἀφροδίτη: see on *Aphr.* 17.

66 σεύατ᾽: the form occurs four times in Homer in this metrical position, normally used of movement immediately after dressing: Hermes rushes off at *Od.* 5. 51 after putting on his sandals and taking his sceptre, while at *Il.* 6. 505, 7. 208 it describes Paris and Ajax after putting on their armour. Only of Hera rushing to the snowy mountains of the Thracians to see Sleep (*Il.* 14. 227) does it not directly follow dressing, and even there her adornment takes place just a few lines above (vv. 169–86).

ἐπὶ Τροίης: only *M* has the genitive; the other MSS read the accusative. ἐπί + gen. for motion towards is reasonably well attested in early epic, although ἐπί + acc. is more common; for the gen. see *Il.* 3. 5, 5. 700, *Od.* 3. 171 (cf. *Grammaire*, ii. 107, GG ii. 470, AHS 358; at *Il.* 9. 588–9, 13. 665, 18. 531, *Od.* 10. 56, *Apoll.* 49 the sense is 'to go upon'). It is impossible to be certain, but M's reading seems preferable as *lectio difficilior*; accusatives in the vicinity (Κύπρον, κέλευθον, Ἴδην) and the fact that the accusative is the more common construction could have introduced the change.

προλιποῦσ᾽ εὐώδεα Κύπρον: *M* again has the lone variant κῆπον; the other MSS Κύπρον. Càssola 547 prefers κῆπον partially on the grounds that it is an improbable insertion for a scribe 'di sua iniziativa'; Κύπρον is naturally on everyone's mind after its mention at v. 58 (cf. VE 34). But such an insertion is not impossible (a later cult of Ἀφροδίτη ἐν κήποις was well known in Athens and elsewhere; see Pirenne-Delforge 48 ff., 63 ff.). Càssola further argues that the adjective εὐώδεα is more appropriate of a garden; as at Ar. *Av.* 1067 κήπους εὐώδεις. It is certainly more natural of flowers than of a large land mass (see *Dem.* 401, *Hy.* 19. 25–6, *Cypr.* fr. 5. 2, Pi. *N.* 11. 41 etc.; at Pi. *P.* 5. 24 Aphrodite is said to have a γλυκὺν κῆπον), but this may in itself provide an explanation for the insertion of κῆπον. Most importantly, κῆπον is somewhat out of place here; there has been no mention of flowers or vegetal growth up to this point to indicate that Aphrodite should leave a garden. If she were departing after the flower-filled episodes with the Charites in *Cypr.* frr. 4–5, this would be more expected. Also, given the insistence on scent in the preceding scene, it is not so surprising that εὐώδεα is used here of Cyprus (see above on 58–63, 58–9). Otherwise, the repetition of Κύπρον fulfills a pattern of ring-composition (arrival at Cyprus v. 58 ἐς Κύπρον ... departure from Cyprus v. 66 προλιποῦσ' εὐώδεα Κύπρον) that is also an element of Hera's toilette in *Il*. 14; Hera goes to her chamber at v. 168 (βῆ δ' ἴμεν ἐς θάλαμον), and leaves from her chamber after dressing at v. 188 (βῆ ῥ' ἴμεν ἐκ θαλάμοιο). In this respect it is also noteworthy that the poet of *Aphr*. makes use of ring-composition on more than one occasion elsewhere in the hymn (cf. on *Aphr*. 7–33, 69 οἱ δὲ μετ' αὐτήν etc.). As well, the place-name Κύπρος should be favoured after Τροίης at the end of the first hemiepes; the point of departure (place-name) is contrasted with the point of arrival (place-name). Cf. Eros leaving Cyprus at Thgn. 1277 τῆμος Ἔρως προλιπὼν Κύπρον, περικαλλέα νῆσον. See also Sappho fr. 86. 6]ας προλίποισα κ[, a possible prayer to Aphrodite; Fraenkel (1942), 56 suggests both Κ[ύπρον and κ[άποις as possible supplements (cf. Theander 1937, 468).

67 ὕψι μετὰ νέφεσιν ῥίμφα πρήσσουσα κέλευθον: this concludes a string of unique readings by M: νέφεσι ῥίμφα (preferred by most editors, Matthiae 1800, Breuning 1929, AHS, West 2003, etc.), while the other MSS have νεφέεσσι θοῶς (adopted by Humbert 1936, VE 35). VE suspects the reading in M as a correction to a better-known Homeric formula; cf. *Il*. 14. 282 ῥίμφα πρήσσοντε κέλευθον, 23. 501 ὑψόσ' ἀειρέσθην ῥίμφα πρήσσοντε κέλευθον and *Od*. 13. 83 ὑψόσ' ἀειρόμενοι ῥίμφα πρήσσουσι κέλευθον. Homeric formulae, however, abound in *Aphr*. (for a list see Preziosi 1966), and it is hardly surprising to find another one here (in any case this formula is usually of horses). Nor should his belief that M tends to restore Homeric forms be allowed to mislead on this occasion; M does show a mild tendency to restore unmetrical epic forms, but not to replace whole, graphically unsimilar words, as would be the case here (on M's tendencies see N. Richardson 1974, 66; cf. on *Aphr*. 8). The short form νέφεσι(ν), common in later prose, is not known elsewhere in epic and requires nu mobile here to make position. Quite fitting for this poet, such a form is paralleled twice in the hymn, by ὄρεσι(ν) v. 54 and λέχεσι(ν) v. 126 (see on *Aphr*. 54 and 126–7). It is necessary to insert nu mobile, but this is an easy scribal omission.

68 Ἴδην δ' ἵκανεν πολυπίδακα ...: cf. *Il*. 8. 47, 14. 283, 15. 151 (see on *Aphr*. 64–91). In Homer love-affairs between mortals and nymphs or goddesses 'cluster round the hills of Asia Minor, especially Mount Ida' (Griffin 1992, 201–2, with examples; cf. on *Aphr.* 75 ff.).

69–74. Aphrodite is fawned upon by normally ferocious beasts as she makes her way across Ida. Pleased at the sight of them, she casts desire into their breasts and they couple in the shady valleys of the mountain. Her control over animals in this passage has led some to believe that Aphrodite is represented here as πότνια θηρῶν, identified with the Asiatic Magna Mater/Cybele (cf. Rose 1924, *Gesch.* i. 522–3, Lenz 1975, 124, Càssola 1975, 547, etc.); a view which has also encountered significant opposition (AHS 351, Podbielski 1971, 39–41, VE 35, VB 8–9, etc.).

Those who support such a reading have certainly overstated the case. Aphrodite is not actually called πότνια θηρῶν here (although Lenz and Càssola speak almost as if she were); the traditional formula at v. 68 μητέρα θηρῶν is used of Ida, just the place one might expect to meet such animals in epic (cf. on *Aphr.* 70–1). In fact, the scene is perfectly explicable in terms of epic conventions: as Poseidon makes his way across the ocean *Il.* 13. 21 ff., dolphins follow after him and the sea rejoices; at *Od.* 10. 210–19 the animals which Circe has bewitched fawn (σαῖνον v. 219) around Odysseus' men, as the animals here fawn (σαίνοντες v. 70) after the goddess; dogs crowd around Odysseus when he arrives in disguise at the hut of Eumaeus at 14. 29 ff. and the same dogs fawn (περίσσαινον v. 4) around Telemachus when he arrives at 16. 4–6; the dogs also react to Athena's arrival at the hut in disguise at 16. 157–63. Outside this hymn, Aphrodite's power does not extend to the animal world in early epic (cf. West 1966*a*, 225), her control over nature being limited to an effect on vegetation in Homer and Hesiod (grass grows under foot as she moves at *Th.* 194, and grass and flowers spring up at *Il.* 14. 347 while Zeus and Hera make love); but it is a trait found in later literature (see on *Aphr.* 2–6 for examples; note also the reaction of the animals to Aphrodite's giving birth at Nonn. *D.* 41. 185 ff.).

Nonetheless, Aphrodite's control over animals may ultimately owe something to conceptions of the love-goddess in the Near East. Scholars have focused upon the possible links between Aphrodite and the Magna Mater in the Troad (see Farnell ii. 641), but this is not the only possible eastern source for the πότνια θηρῶν motif. Ištar has control over animal reproduction in the *Descent of Ištar to the Nether*

World; when she leaves the earth 'The bull would not mount the cow, | [the ass would not impregnate the jenny]' (*BTM 501*; cf. Penglase 1994, 173–4). She elsewhere has the title 'mistress of animals' (*bēlet nammašti*; see West 1997, 56). Also connected to animals is Ištar's Ugaritic counterpart Astarte (*ʿAθ*tartu), a possible eastern precursor of the Paphian Aphrodite (see Budin, 2003, 237 ff.). In glyptic of the Late Cypriote Bronze Age (LC II, 1450–1200 BC) there seems to be some interchangeability between representations of a nude goddess and a πότνια θηρῶν; the two types may represent the same divinity, possibly an early conception of Aphrodite; see Budin (2003), 146–54.

Podbielski, followed by VE 35, argues that this episode has internal justification; it is explained by the poet elaborating upon the motif already presented at vv. 3–4 ἐδαμάσσατο ... θηρία πάντα, and foreshadowing the power which she will have over Anchises. Indeed, the passage is internally coherent and dramatically effective; it shows off Aphrodite's power just as she arrives at Anchises' hut.

69 βῆ δ' ἰθὺς σταθμοῖο: for similar phrasing see *Od.* 1. 119 βῆ δ' ἰθὺς προθύροιο, 17. 325 βῆ δ' ἰθὺς μεγάροιο; also *Il.* 5. 849 βῆ δ' ἰθὺς Διομήδεος, 8. 322 βῆ δ' ἰθὺς Τεύκρου.

δι' οὔρεος: note *Herm.* 231 ὀδμὴ δ' ἱμερόεσσα δι' οὔρεος ἠγαθέοιο. Elsewhere only later at Q.S. 10. 458, Nonn. *D.* 1. 365, etc.

οἱ δὲ μετ' αὐτήν: the animals are introduced and left behind by the narrator in similar language; οἱ δὲ μετ' αὐτήν (5⏑⏑6×) and following necessary enjambment (cf. *Sc.* 248 ff. αἳ δὲ μετ' αὐτούς | ...) is balanced by v. 73 οἱ δ' ἅμα πάντες (5⏑⏑6×) and necessary enjambment.

70–1 λύκοι ...: mountains are the domain of beasts in Homer; boars, lions, wolves etc. (cf. *Il.* 11. 474 ff., 12. 146 ff., 16. 156 ff., etc.). Ida itself receives the title of μητέρα θηρῶν (used only of Ida; *Il.* 8. 47, 14. 283, 15. 15) and is thus just the place one might expect to encounter such a troupe of beasts. The formula may have originated in a reality known to shepherds and hunters in the Troad; villagers around the modern-day Kaz Dağ (identified with Ida) 'report hares, jackals, boar, badgers, deer, wild cats ... partridge, bears ... and leopards' on the mountain (Cook 1973, 306). As for lions, Woronoff (1989) suggests that a type of lion might even have inhabited the

Troad, but their presence in Homer more probably comes from knowledge of them further east (see Richter 1968, 37–8 and Buchholz et al. 1973, 8 ff.).

The grouping of wolves, lions, bears, and leopards is found later at Nonn. *D.* 41. 185 ff., when beasts react to the birth of Aphrodite's daughter Beroe. Most similar in early poetry is *Herm.* 223–4 οὔτε λύκων πολιῶν οὔτ' ἄρκτων οὔτε λεόντων | οὔτέ τι κενταύρου, or *Hy.* 14. 4 εὖαδεν ἠδὲ λύκων κλαγγὴ χαροπῶν τε λεόντων. Otherwise together: lions, wolves, and boars (*Od.* 10. 212, 433); bears, boars, and lions (*Od.* 11. 611); leopards and wolves (*Il.* 13. 103); or lions, leopards, and boars (*Il.* 17. 20–1). Compare the group of animals in the *Epic of Gilgamesh*, during the lament of Gilgamesh for Enkidu: 'May bear, hyena, panther, leopard, deer, jackal, | Lion, wild bull, gazelle, ibex, the beasts and creatures of the steppe, weep for you' (Foster, 60 = Tablet VIII. 16 ff.).

70 σαίνοντες: this is a gesture normally expected from domesticated dogs in Homer. At *Od.* 10. 210–19 wolves and lions bewitched by Circe fawn around Odysseus and his men as dogs fawn around their master coming from the table (v. 215 περισσαίνοντες, v. 217 σαίνωσ', v. 219 σαῖνον). Cf. above on 69–74. The verb is used of wild beasts divinely enchanted by Rhea at A.R. 1. 1144–5 θῆρες ...| οὐρῇσιν σαίνοντες ἐπήλυθον. At Q.S. 5. 95 it describes dolphins, animals known for being tame.

πολιοί τε λύκοι: for the grey wolf cf. the disguise of Dolon at *Il.* 10. 334 ῥινὸν πολιοῖο λύκοιο and *Herm.* 223 λύκων πολιῶν; later at Theoc. *Id.* 11. 24 and A.R. 2. 124. πολιοί wolves and χαροποί lions appear together at *PMG* 935. 17–18 (= *IG* iv/1². 131), a hymn to the Mother of the Gods. The adjective πολιός is used of the grey hair of old age below at v. 228.

χαροποί τε λέοντες: the adjective should be translated as 'Kampfesfreude blickend' (Bechtel 1914, 332; most recently West 2003, 'fierce-eyed'), or 'greedy-eyed' (Latacz 1966, 38–43, followed by VE 35–6); the former based upon an etymology from χάρμη, the latter from the IE *gher- 'desire'. Maxwell-Stuart (1981) suggests that Polemon of Laodicea's use of χαροπός in his *Physiognomy* = 'amber', thus 'tawny-eyed' of lions, but this is based upon a faulty emendation of the Arabic translation of the word, which is certainly 'dark blue' (see Elsner 2007, 220 n. 55). See the adjective elsewhere of lions at *Od.* 11.

611, *Herm.* 569, *Hy.* 14. 4, *Th.* 321. *Sc.* 177; later Theoc. *Id.* 25. 142, [Opp.] *C.* 1. 310 etc.

71 ἄρκτοι: the asyndeton is not inappropriate to a list (see VE 36, who points to the list of Nereids at *Th.* 243–6; also *Il.* 18. 39–40). In any case, asyndeton occurs elsewhere in *Aphr.* at vv. 12, 153, 173 and 273 (cf. Janko 1982, 270 n. 70) and there is no reason to suspect it here; Kamerbeek (1967), 391 tentatively suggests reading κἄρκτοι.

παρδάλιες: a minority of MSS, all in the *p* group, contain πορδάλιες. πορδ- is a variant in the Homeric MSS as well (*Il.* 13. 103 etc.; cf. West 1998, *Praefatio*, p. xxxiv), where, however, παρδ- is the sole reading at *Il.* 3. 17, 10. 29; given the Homeric tradition it seems best to follow the majority reading. The variant form might be of Aeolic origin, given that ο for α before or after liquids is most common in Lesbian (see Buck 1955, 20; also Boeotian). Shipp (1972), 18, 146 thinks it is an Atticism, based upon some evidence for its use by later Attic authors (cf. LSJ s.v and Strabo 13. 2. 6), but the spelling seems to have been variable in classical literature, and ΠΑΡΔΑΛΙΣ is the form known on an Attic black-figure vase (see Henderson 1987, 188 on Ar. *Lys.* 1014); cf. Ael. Dion. π 18 (Erbse 1950, 135) πάρδαλιν Ἀττικοί, πόρδαλιν Ἴωνες, not that there is any reason to think παρδ- strictly Attic either. In fact, the evidence seems too slight to attach either form to any particular dialect (cf. also Janko 1982, 170).

θοαί: the adjective never describes animals in Homer and Hesiod, but ships (*Il.* 2. 619 etc.), chariots (*Il.* 11. 533 etc.), warriors in battle (2. 758 etc.), etc. (cf. *LfgrE* s.v.). See its use of horses at Pi. *P.* 4. 17 etc. θοαὶ πορδάλιες are found elsewhere only at [Opp.] *C.* 1. 433, 3. 130. The adjective is used later of horses and deer in the bucolic setting of Theoc. *Id.* 2. 49 and 30. 18, and of dogs at A.R. 3. 1373.

προκάδων: this form, as if derived from προκάς, appears only here; πρόξ is the only known nominative. The morphology is not surprising however; a double form exists for the similar δόρξ (cf. AS 206 and Zumbach 1955, 5). D'Orville ap. Allen 1897, 257 rather wildly conjectures ἄρκτοι, παρδάλιες θωοί τε πρόκων ἀκόρητοι, which in any case deepens the asyndeton at the beginning of the line.

72 ἤϊσαν: all MSS have ἤεσ(σ)αν, corrected to the Homeric ἤϊσαν by Ilgen (1796, 485); so in this *sedes* at *Il.* 10. 197, 13. 305, 17. 495, *Od.* 20. 7, 24. 13.

ἡ δ' ὁρόωσα μετὰ φρεσὶ τέρπετο θυμόν: for similar expressions of divine pleasure at sight see *Il.* 20. 23 ἔνθ' ὁρόων φρένα τέρψομαι, *Od.* 5. 74 θηήσαιτο ἰδὼν καὶ τέρφθειη φρεσὶν ᾗσιν, *Apoll.* 204 οἱ δ' ἐπιτέρπονται θυμὸν μέγαν εἰσορόωντες and 341–2 ἡ δὲ ἰδοῦσα | τέρπετο ὃν κατὰ θυμόν. Cf. as well the language at *Il.* 23. 600, where Menelaus' θυμός warms in reconciliation μετὰ φρεσί.

Aphrodite has a similar reaction to animals later at Nonn. *D.* 41. 204–6 γαληναίῳ δὲ προσώπῳ | ἠθάδα πέμπε γέλωτα φιλομμειδὴς Ἀφροδίτη | τερπομένων ὁρόωσα λεχώια παίγνια θηρῶν.

73 ἐν στήθεσσι βάλ' ἵμερον: desire is once again cast, as at vv. 45 and 53, but this time it is Aphrodite (not Zeus) who does the throwing. This repetition at the height of her display of power helps to recall the irony of the situation; this phrasing will also recur later at v. 143 when she finally seduces Anchises (on the repetition cf. Porter 1949, 258). For similar language see strength cast in the breast at *Il.* 5. 513 ἐν στήθεσσι μένος βάλε; also a spear at 5. 317 and an arrow at *Od.* 20. 62.

οἱ δ' ἅμα πάντες: 'all at the same moment' (N. Richardson 1993, 214 on ἅμα on *Il.* 23. 362). See the phrase at line-end at *Od.* 8. 121, *Little Iliad* fr. 32. 7 (Bernabé); cf. also at line-beginning *Il.* 23. 362 and *Od.* 10. 130.

74 σύνδυο: the word is not found in early hexameter; elsewhere in poetry at Pi. *P.* 3. 81 and later in the comic poet Machon fr. 8. 63 (for examples in prose see the note there of Gow 1965, 75). This is not necessarily a later form, however; Homer has σύντρεις at *Od.* 9. 429 and note σύν τε δύ' ἐρχομένω at *Il.* 10. 224 (cf. Heitsch 1965, 26, Janko 1982, 156).

κοιμήσαντο κατὰ σκιόεντας ἐναύλους: see the very similar *Od.* 10. 479 οἱ μὲν κοιμήσαντο κατὰ μέγαρα σκιόεντα (note also 23. 299 αὐτοὶ δ' εὐνάζοντο κατὰ μέγαρα σκιόεντα). The epithet σκιόεις is nowhere else used of ἔναυλος. In this respect the end of the line most resembles *Th.* 129 χαρίεντας ἐναύλους, where ἔναυλος is first used with the meaning of 'haunt' (elsewhere in the *Hymns* at 14. 5 and 26. 8). In Homer ἔναυλος always means 'stream', where, however, it is possibly a separate word derived from αὐλός; ἔναυλος with the meaning 'haunt' might instead be derived from αὐλή (see Heitsch 1965, 21, *LfgrE* s.v.).

75 ff. Leaving the impassioned animals in her wake, Aphrodite finally arrives at her intended destination. The bucolic life of Anchises, of which a brief glimpse was given above at vv. 53–7, now comes into full view. She finds the hero alone, as he wanders to and fro beside his hut playing the cithara. This rustic atmosphere will colour the entire affair: Aphrodite and Anchises even later go to bed upon the skins of animals, which Anchises is said to have killed himself (vv. 159–60). The setting is far from the luxurious Trojan palaces known in the *Iliad*. But this quiet, idealistically simple life is nonetheless appropriate to the noble character of Anchises and his son Aeneas. Open-air sexual encounters with nymphs and goddesses result in the birth of several prominent Trojans in the *Iliad* (Aesepus and Pedasus of Boucolion and a nymph, at 6. 21–8 etc. Anchises is of course himself known as a herdsman at 5. 313).

Griffin (1992), 201–4 points out that this pastoral feature of semi-divine progeny seems to be particular to the Trojans in Homer. On the Greek side such business is an indoor activity: Hermes sleeps with the Greek Polymele εἰς ὑπερῷ᾽ ἀναβάς (*Il*. 16. 184), while the *Catalogue of Women* frequently records semi-divine births ἐνὶ μεγάροισιν ([Hes.] frr. 5. 1, 17a. 14 etc.); even the coupling of the Achaean Peleus and the nymph Thetis is not described in Homer as having taken place outside. This observation is part of a wider argument in which he convincingly demonstrates eastern features in bucolic scenes in early Greek poetry, and identifies Homer and *Aphr*. as precursors for later bucolic poetry. Such an affair suits the eastern Trojan, but not the western Greek.

75 αὐτὴ δ᾽ ἐς κλισίας ... ἀφίκανε: for similar language see *Il*. 11. 618 οἱ δ᾽ ὅτε δὴ κλισίην Νηληϊάδεω ἀφίκοντο, and the imagined arrival of Priam at the hut of Achilles at 24. 431 ὄφρα κεν ἐς κλισίην Πηληϊάδεω ἀφίκωμαι.

κλισίας εὐποιήτους: Anchises' hut and its μέλαθρον at v. 173 are both qualified as 'well-built'. The adjective εὐποίητος, which is used also in *Aphr*. of Anchises' bed (v. 161), does not appear elsewhere of a hut, but see κλισίην ἐΰτυκτον at *Il*. 10. 566, 13. 240, *Od*. 4. 123; note also *Od*. 8. 458 (Nausicaa) στῆ ῥα παρὰ σταθμὸν τέγεος πύκα ποιητοῖο. It is used of cowhide shields at *Il*. 16. 636, weapons at *Od*. 3. 434, clothes at 13. 369, coverings at 20. 150, chariots at *Apoll*. 265 etc. (see *LfgrE* s.v.). Note later Q.S. 6. 187 ἐς τέγος εὐποίητον.

Anchises' dwelling is part of the more inclusive term σταθμός, used at vv. 69 and 76: see Knox (1971), 30 on huts and farm buildings in Homer; 'a pastoral establishment consists of a κλισίη (or sometimes, perhaps several κλισίαι, as in *H. Ven.* 75), a yard or αὐλή adjoining it in which animals are kept loose or in pens, and (at least sometimes) a fenced pasture too.'

76–9 λελειμμέν-ον/ος οἶ-ον/ος ἀπ' ἄλλων: v. 79 is largely a repetition of 76. This led Hermann tentatively to suggest a double recension here, and the removal of either 76–7 or 78–80 (1806, pp. xci f.: 'difficilius est de hoc loco iudicare'). Both sets of lines, however, perform an integral function. In the first instance, the finding of Anchises alone at v. 76 is typical of an arrival scene (see on *Aphr.* 64–91). The second set of lines then indicates the further information of why he is alone: because the other shepherds are off in the hills. The poet will in fact return to this theme in vv. 168–9, framing the seduction in a ring-composition which provides a certain bucolic reality to the episode; it opens by telling that the other shepherds are off in the hills, and is completed by a reminder of their return (cf. Podbielski 1971, 41). As Càssola 547–8 suggests, the poet is emphasizing the point of Anchises' solitude through the repetition (cf. also VE 36 and Turkeltaub 2003*a*, 57; the latter identifies 'dramatic isolation' as a characteristic of epiphany scenes).

76 τὸν δ' εὗρε: a form of the deictic pronoun + δ' εὗρ- at line-beginning is formulaic (*Il.* 3. 125, 6. 321, 7. 382 etc.).

σταθμοῖσι: Hermann (1806) proposed inserting ἐν (σταθμοῖσι) here to avoid the local dative. There is no reason to suspect the syntax, however. A locatival dative occurs again at *Aphr.* 173 and is attested both in Homer and elsewhere in the *Hymns* (*Od.* 6. 162, *Dem.* 99 etc.; see Monro 1891, 139–40, AHS 358).

λελειμμένον οἶον ἀπ' ἄλλων: Polyphemus is compared to a mountain-peak which stands out alone from all others in similar phrasing at *Od.* 9. 192 ὑψηλῶν ὀρέων, ὅ τε φαίνεται οἶον ἀπ' ἄλλων. Anchises' separation from the other shepherds not only facilitates the privacy necessary for his intimate encounter with Aphrodite, but also indicates his privileged position. Similarly, Zeus sits apart from the other gods at *Il.* 1. 498–9 'to emphasise his independence and superiority, as well as to make it easy for Thetis to approach him' (Kirk 1985, 106). In Homer, οἶος often designates someone who is isolated because of a distinctive quality which others do not have, or who is distinguishing himself in battle (see Biraud 1990, 92–3). See later A.R. 1. 60–1 οἷος ἀπ' ἄλλων | ἤλασ' ἀριστεύων etc.

77 Ἀγχίσην ἥρωα: cf. *Th.* 1009 Ἀγχίσῃ ἥρωι μιγεῖσ' ἐρατῇ φιλότητι. As in Homer, the term ἥρως is used as a secular, honorific title (see West 1978, 370–3); the religious sense, cult-hero, known in later Greek, most probably developed alongside the secular one in the Dark Ages, even though the former does not appear in epic, with the exception perhaps of Hes. *Op.* 172 (cf. Currie 2005, 64).

θεῶν ἄπο κάλλος ἔχοντα: of Nausicaa at *Od.* 8. 457 θεῶν ἄπο κάλλος ἔχουσα, and of her companions at *Od.* 6. 18 Χαρίτων ἄπο κάλλος ἔχουσαι (= [Hes.] fr. 215. 1); also possibly [Hes.] fr. 171. 4 θεῶν ἄπ]ο κάλλος ἔ[χουσαν. Homeric heroes, who have an intermediate status between gods and men (see Dietrich 1965, 24–8), are often likened to the divine as Anchises is here (cf. ἀντίθεος Τελαμωνιάδης of Ajax at *Il.* 9. 623). Anchises' beauty has already been compared to the gods above at v. 55 and is a motif in the poem (see Introd., pp. 9–10).

78–9 οἱ δ' ἅμα . . . | πάντες: 'the others . . . all of them'. There is emphasis placed upon πάντες here by its enjambment, which stresses the point of Anchises' solitude (cf. on *Aphr.* 76–9). This phrasing is reminiscent of vv. 73–4 οἱ δ' ἅμα πάντες | σύνδυο, of the lusty animals. Note a similar enjambment of πάντες at *Il.* 15. 636–8.

78 οἱ δ' ἅμα βουσὶν ἕποντο: there is similar phrasing in the *Catalogue of Ships* at *Il.* 2. 637 τῷ δ' ἅμα νῆες ἕποντο. For a cowherd following after cattle see *Il.* 18. 524–5 βοῦς | . . . δύω δ' ἅμ' ἕποντο νομῆες, 577 νομῆες ἅμ' ἐστιχόωντο βόεσσιν, *Herm.* 209 ὅς τις ὁ παῖς ἅμα βουσὶν ἐϋκαίρῃσιν ὀπήδει and *Op.* 406 ἥτις καὶ βουσὶν ἕποιτο. At *Op.* 441 τοῖς [βουσίν] δ' ἅμα . . . ἕποιτο means 'to plough'.

VE's absurd suggestion (36) that the imperfect ἕποντο has pluperfect force here is well refuted by VB 9; 'the herdsmen "were following the cows" precisely *during* the time of the encounter'.

νομούς . . . ποιήεντας: this adjective meaning 'grassy' is used nowhere else with νομός. As below at *Aphr.* 99, it is used of πίσεα at *Il.* 20. 9 and *Od.* 6. 124, and of ἄγκεα at *Od.* 4. 337, 17. 128, and *Dem.* 381. It also describes named places at *Il.* 2. 503, 9. 150, 9. 292, *Od.* 16. 396, *Apoll.* 243, *Herm.* 190, *Sc.* 381. Note, however, E. *Cyc.* 61 ποιηροὺς λιποῦσα νομούς.

80 πωλεῖτ' ἔνθα καὶ ἔνθα: Anchises wanders to and fro while playing his lyre. Cf. φοίτων ἔνθα καὶ ἔνθα at *Il.* 2. 779 of the Myrmidons and φοιτᾷ δ' ἔνθα καὶ ἔνθα at *Hy.* 19. 8 of Pan. VB 9 claims that this implies Anchises' impatience and boredom with his simple life. Other instances, however, of wandering ἔνθα καὶ ἔνθα do not convey this idea by default: in *Il.* 2 it is unclear whether the Myrmidons are bored with their idleness from battle or are enjoying it (so Kirk 1985, 242; 'presumably they are doing both at different times'); but even if the former is the case there, Pan is hardly bored with his wandering in *Hy.* 19. As regards the verb πωλέομαι: it describes the solitary Cyclops at *Od.* 9. 189 (who may well be bored), but also the wandering bard (Homer) at *Apoll.* 170 etc. Achilles takes to his lyre out of boredom at *Il.* 9. 186, but his situation in the middle of war cannot be compared with that of Anchises; shepherds are known to delight in making music (see *Il.* 18. 525–6 νομῆες | τερπόμενοι σύριγξι). A love-goddess is of course just the thing to spice up Anchises' quiet life, but there is no implication of 'restless impatience' on his part. For a complete list of ἔνθα καὶ ἔνθα in Homer see Bolling (1950); note also *Apoll.* 361, *Herm.* 279, *Hy.* 7. 39.

διαπρύσιον κιθαρίζων: on the meaning of διαπρύσιον, often of shouting, see on *Aphr.* 19. It is used uniquely here of the lyre; the instrument is known to be loud in Homer (cf. *Il.* 9. 186 φόρμιγγι λιγείῃ, *Od.* 8. 67 φόρμιγγα λίγειαν). Compare *Herm.* 425 τάχα δὲ λιγέως κιθαρίζων and later *Orph. Arg.* 408 διωλύγιον κιθαρίζων. As an adjective it later describes the sound of a trumpet at Crinagoras *AP* 6. 350. 1 κελάδημα διαπρύσιον σάλπιγγος. Note the phonetically similar *Od.* 2. 213 οἵ κέ μοι ἔνθα καὶ ἔνθα διαπρήσσωσι κέλευθον.

κιθαρίζων: one more naturally expects a shepherd to have a pan-pipe (so *Il.* 18. 526, Theoc. *Id.* 1. 3, 14 etc.). Griffin (1992), 199 comments: 'that he plays on the heroic lyre, like Achilles, and not on the humbler pipes, is presumably a curtsey to his status as a Homeric hero'. However, 'heroic' is perhaps the wrong word for the κίθαρις, an accoutrement of the heroic-antitype Paris mentioned in Hector's rebuke of his brother (whom the normally heroic Achilles perhaps resembles in his withdrawal from battle in *Il.* 9) for not fighting at *Il.* 3. 54 οὐκ ἄν τοι χραίσμῃ κίθαρις τά τε δῶρ' Ἀφροδίτης [ὅτ' ἐν κονίῃσι μιγείῃς]; one might rather say 'noble', or alternatively, as its placement next to τά τε δῶρ' Ἀφροδίτης at *Il.* 3. 54 may suggest, the lyre is an appropriate instrument for a Trojan hero who is about to have an affair with the goddess of love.

81–90. Aphrodite appears before Anchises, but in the disguise of a young maiden so as not to frighten him. Presumably there is little chance that he would have agreed to sleep with her if she had appeared in her full divine stature. At the same time, of course, she is no ordinary maiden: not only does she appear out of the blue on the slopes of a quiet mountain, but she comes dressed in the most glamorous fashion, wearing a fine robe and jewellery. On Anchises' reaction, see on *Aphr.* 83–90, 92–106.

The description of her clothing and jewellery is on a grand scale. These lines expand upon the brief mention of her dressing immediately after her bath (vv. 64–5). Nor is this the last we see of her clothing; she is later described undressing before going to bed with Anchises, and putting her clothes on afterwards (see on *Aphr.* 162–5, 168–83), and it is fair to say that her adornment is a recurring motif in the poem. As Sowa (1984), 77–9, West (1997), 203–5, and Penglase (1994), 165 ff. point out, this emphasis on her clothing may owe something to eastern conceptions of the love-goddess. The love-goddess Inanna covers herself in jewels from head to vulva to foot before encountering the mortal herdsman Dumuzi in a Sumerian text (*ETCSL* 4. 08. 20 = *ANET* 638). And most striking for its symbolism of clothing is the descent of Ištar into the Nether World (*BTM* 500–1): as the goddess descends through the seven gates of the Nether World a piece of clothing is removed at each gate (including a crown, earrings, beads around her neck, pins on her breast, a girdle of birth stones, clasps around her hands and feet, and a robe) until she arrives in the underworld naked. When later Ereshkigal has her sprinkled with the water of life and she returns through the gates to earth, she receives her items of clothing one by one in reverse order. The removal of Ištar's clothing symbolizes her death and weakness, while the subsequent rehabilitation symbolizes her life and strength. It is perhaps going too far to suggest as Sowa does that Aphrodite's later removal of her clothes before sleeping with Anchises is a symbol of her 'death', but it is possibly a symbol of her weakness (cf. on *Aphr.* 162–5). Conversely, like Ištar, her elaborate ornamentation here represents her strength and power as she embarks upon her sexual conquest.

In Greek poetry also, the description is the stuff of seduction scenes (cf. Janko 1992 173). An even more elaborate list of Hera's clothing precedes her seduction of Zeus in *Il.* 14. 173–87, making up part of her bath. It is remarkable, however, that in *Aphr.* the full description is delayed until the encounter instead of being included in the bath scene. On the narratological level, the delay until this point allows the audience to join more actively in Anchises' reaction of amazement at seeing the goddess (see Smith 1981*a*, 44, de Jong 1989, 14–15). In this respect, the description owes more to the appearance of the goddess in physical disguise than to seduction. In the *Odyssey*, Athena appears several times in disguise, as Mentor (3. 12 ff., 222 ff., 22. 205 ff.), a shepherd (13. 221 ff.), and a mortal woman (13. 288 ff., 16. 154 ff., 20. 30 ff.). In the case of *Od.* 13, she appears close to Odysseus, her form as a male shepherd is announced, a short description of her clothes follows (a cloak, sandals and staff), and Odysseus addresses her. *Aphr.* follows this same pattern. Also similar is the visit of Demeter to Eleusis in *Dem.* When she first appears next to a well she takes the disguise of an old woman (101 ff.). There is no immediate description of her clothing, but when she later arrives at the palace of Celeus, a short description of her attire (182–3) precedes her appearance before Metaneira (on the similar reaction of Metaneira and Anchises see on *Aphr.* 83–90). This combination of length and timing has a powerful effect; the audience meets the full glamour of the goddess at the same time as Anchises, a coincidence which makes his amorous reaction all the more tangible (cf. Podbielski 1971, 43: 'il y a liaison complète entre l'aspect de la déesse et l'évolution de la situation').

It is also worth mentioning that clothes play an appropriate part in deception. Odysseus' famous transformation into a beggar by Athena (*Od.* 13. 429 ff.; cf. also his transformation at 16. 457) includes a description of the dirty rags he dons, and his clothes are central to deception/recognition throughout the latter half of the *Odyssey* (see Block 1985).

81 στῆ δ' αὐτοῦ προπάροιθε: so Zeus attracted to Hera at *Il.* 14. 297 στῆ δ' αὐτῆς προπάροιθε. Aphrodite is the one making the approach this time, but she has a strong feeling of attraction in common with Zeus. See also Zeus' arrival (as a bull full of desire) before Europa at Mosch. *Eur.* 93 στῆ δὲ ποδῶν προπάροιθεν ἀμύμονος Εὐρωπείης (with the note of Campbell 1991, 90–1). The formulaic στῆ δ(έ) is a common way of introducing speech. Someone stands close and makes an address (see Kirk 1990, 76 and cf. Arend 1933, 28). In this case the pattern is subverted; not only does speech not follow immediately (as at *Il*. 14. 297), but after the description of clothes it is Anchises who speaks first (on which see on *Aphr*. 91–106).

Διὸς θυγάτηρ Ἀφροδίτη: this formula, metrically equivalent to φιλομμειδὴς Ἀφροδίτη, occurs twice more later in the hymn at vv. 107 and 191; the use of φιλομμειδὴς Ἀφροδίτης is instead concentrated at the beginning of the poem (four before v. 65, with only one after this point at v. 155). Janko (1981*b*, 254–5) argues that the two equivalent formulae are interchanged at random, without consideration of a difference in meaning. It has already been suggested above, however, that φιλομμειδής shows a connection to the smiles of erotic trickery, at least explicitly at *Aphr*. 49 (see on *Aphr*. 17). Boedeker (1974), 36–7 instead proposes that the choice of Διὸς θυγάτηρ here underlines both Aphrodite's subjugation by Zeus and the irony of her immortal nature as she takes the disguise of a young maiden. At least an understood difference in tone between the two formulae better explains their distribution in *Aphr*. than Janko's suggestion that in the beginning 'the composer temporarily forgot about the existence of the doublet [Διὸς θυγάτηρ]'. The encomium of her sexual power in the first part of the poem would seem to facilitate φιλομμειδής. Also, at v. 155 her ruse has worked and she is about to do what she does best; but she has little reason to smile at v. 191.

The formula is used eight times in the *Iliad* (3. 374, 5. 131, etc.), once in the *Odyssey* (8. 308), and at *Apoll*. 195. It then appears only once more much later at Nonn. *D*. 31. 210.

82 παρθένῳ ἀδμήτῃ ... εἶδος ὁμοίη: there is nothing more opposite to Aphrodite's true nature than this disguise. ἄδμητος is used only of animals in early epic (see Heitsch 1965, 28), although cf. at line-end παρθένος ἀδμής (*Od*. 6. 109, 6. 228, *Dem*. 145 and [Hes.] fr. 59. 4; for later examples see Campbell 1994, 12 on A.R. 3. 4–5). Note also at line-beginning the metrically equivalent παρθένος αἰδοίη (*Il*. 2. 514; acc. *Hys*. 27. 2 and 28. 3); and the thematically similar 'like ... ' παρθένῳ αἰδοίῃ ἴκελον (*Th*. 572 | *Op*. 71). This pairing occurs only once more later at *Orph*. *Hy*. 55. 25 παρθένοι ἄδμηται. The line

is comparable to *Dem.* 145–6 παρθένος ἀδμής | ... εἶδος ἀρίστη (cf. Janko 1982, 164, N. Richardson 1974, 42), although given line-final παρθένος ἀδμής in Homer the parallel is not particularly suggestive of direct imitation.

μέγεθος καὶ εἶδος ὁμοίη: more usual is εἶδός τε μέγεθός τε at line-beginning, used just a few lines below at *Aphr.* 85 (cf. *Il.* 2. 58, *Od.* 6. 152, 11. 337, 18. 249, 24. 374 and 24. 253). In this order and place in the line, the pair is elsewhere only at *Dem.* 275 μέγεθος καὶ εἶδος ἄμειψε (Demeter resumes her true form). Note at line-end φυὴν καὶ εἶδος ὁμοίη at *Od.* 6. 16 of Nausicaa.

83–90 μή μιν ταρβήσειεν ἐν ὀφθαλμοῖσι νοήσας. | Ἀγχίσης δ' ὁρόων ἐφράζετο θάμβαινέν τε ...: Aphrodite's disguise may stop Anchises from reacting with fear at the sight of her, but he is nonetheless amazed. This is perhaps not surprising given the sudden appearance of his visitor. Amazement is a common motif at the arrival of an unexpected guest; cf. (of Achilles) *Il.* 9. 193 ταφὼν δ' ἀνόρουσεν, 24. 483–4 θάμβησεν ... | θάμβησαν when Priam shows up unexpectedly, etc. (see further N. Richardson 1993, 324). Amazement is also, however, a characteristic reaction to epiphany (for this and other features of epiphany see N. Richardson 1974, 208, who provides comprehensive lists of examples, and cf. on *Aphr.* 168–83), and other elements of this scene suggest that partial epiphany is in fact what is happening here (cf. Smith 1981*a*, 44 ff., Sowa 1984, 241 ff.; Turkeltaub 2003*a*, 57–60 calls this 'Hint of Divinity'): (i) an emphasis on radiance characterizes the description of Aphrodite's clothes, εἵματα σιγαλόεντα, πέπλον ... φαεινότερον πυρὸς αὐγῆς, κάλυκάς τε φαεινάς, ὡς δὲ σελήνη | ... ἐλάμπετο: now, radiance can be a quality of beautiful mortal girls (cf. Alcm. fr. *Parth.* 1. 39–43, where the maiden Agido is said to emit a φῶς which is compared to the sun), but it is also a common motif of epiphany and this young girl's emphatic shine seems to be beyond that of the ordinary mortal. Hera has a similar shine about her before setting out to seduce Zeus (*Il.* 14. 183 ff.; ἀπελάμπετο πολλή, λευκὸν δ' ἦν ἠέλιος ὥς, ποσσί ... λιπαροῖσιν; on her shine cf. Bremer 1975, 6–8). (ii) more subtly (for the moment, she does not hit the rafters like Demeter in her partial epiphany at *Dem.* 188–9; see on *Aphr.* 173–4), Anchises is amazed at the εἶδός τε μέγεθός τε of the girl; supernatural stature is a third common feature of epiphany. If Anchises' first words to his visitor indeed suggest that he thinks she is a goddess, her divine flare has given him good reason to think so (cf. on *Aphr.* 91–106).

83 ταρβήσειεν ... ἐν ὀφθαλμοῖσι νοήσας: for ταρβέω of fearing a god see Telemachus' fear (ταρβήσας) of Odysseus μὴ θεὸς εἴη at *Od.* 16. 179. Elsewhere, Poseidon tells Achilles μήτέ τι τάρβει when he appears at *Il.* 21. 288 (cf. also 24. 171 and *Od.* 7. 50–1). For similar language of fear at sight note *Il.* 6. 469–70; Astyanax fears (ταρβήσας) Hector upon seeing (νοήσας) his helmet. Cf. ἐν ὀφθαλμοῖσι νοήσας in v. 179.

84 ὁρόων ἐφράζετο: 'gazed and took stock of her' (West 2003); Anchises considers her marvellous appearance. For this reaction at an unexpected guest, see the surprised Dolion and sons upon encountering Odysseus at *Od.* 24. 391–2 οἳ δ' ὡς οὖν Ὀδυσῆα ἴδον φράσσαντό τε θυμῷ | ἔσταν ἐνὶ μεγάροισι τεθηπότες. For general consideration of something wondrous see *Apoll.* 415 φράσσασθαι μέγα θαῦμα (cf. *Sc.* 218), and the verb can simply mean 'to perceive', as at *Il.* 10. 339. For the phrasing cf. also *Il.* 16. 646 of Zeus watching battle ὅρα καὶ φράζετο θυμῷ.

θάμβαινέν: the *p* MSS have the rare θάμβαινέν (the others θαύμαινέν), which appears only once more as a variant, in one MS of Pi. *O.* 3. 32 δένδρεα θάμβαινε; the other MSS there have θαύμαινε, θαύμαζε, or θάμαινε (cf. AHS 358). θαυμαίνω is itself a rare term, but is known to early epic; once in Homer at *Od.* 8. 108 (ἀέθλια θαυμανέοντες), at *Herm.* 407 (θαυμαίνω ... κράτος), and later Anacr. *PMG* 501. 11. VE prefers θαμβαίνω (printed also by Hermann 1806, Càssola 1975) as the 'stronger' term in reaction to a god, citing Achilles' response to Athena at *Il.* 1. 199 θάμβησεν (Helen reacts in the same way to Aphrodite at 3. 398). As VB 9 points out, however, this is not a full epiphany (even if it is a partial one; see above on 83–90), and one might not expect the same reaction. In any case, amazement at the divine is catered for with θαυμαίνω as well; at *Herm.* 407 Apollo wonders at Hermes' strength as an infant; cf. also the thematically similar *Hy.* 6. 18 εἶδος θαυμάζοντες [the gods] ἰοστεφάνου Κυθερείης (on the sense of wonder present in θαυμάζω and component terms see Mette 1961). In short, the context provides no reason to prefer θάμβαινεν, but equally none to exclude it. But as *lectio difficilior* θάμβαινέν does seem preferable. The known form θαύμαινεν could easily have been introduced in place of the rarer form. It is impossible to be certain, but it is at least more difficult to see how θάμβαινέν should come to replace the known form.

85 εἶδός τε μέγεθός τε: see on *Aphr*. 82.

τε καί: so all MSS. Flach (see Càssola's app. crit.) deletes τε (which is impossible), while Fick prefers τ' ἰδέ (presumably following *Aphr*. 164), both unnecessarily in order to preserve the digamma in εἵματα. Digamma in εἵματα is neglected also later at *Aphr*. 232, and elsewhere in early epic at *Il*. 24. 162, *Od*. 7. 259, *Op*. 556. The neglect here is perhaps a signal of modification by permutation of P$_2$ and T$_2$ formulae (ὅθι εἵματα σιγαλόεντα *Il*. 22. 154 and ἰδέ εἵματα σιγαλόεντα *Aphr*. 164 beside καὶ ῥήγεα σιγαλόεντα *Od*. 6. 38 [*καὶ Ϝείματα σιγαλόεντα]; cf. καὶ ἡνία σιγαλόεντα *Il*. 5. 226 etc.); see Hoekstra (1965), 61–2 and on the notation P$_2$ and T$_2$ above on 29 δῶκε καλὸν γέρας ἀντὶ γάμοιο.

εἵματα σιγαλόεντα: at line-end as here also at *Aphr*. 164, and in Homer at *Il*. 22. 154, where of washed clothes; the noun–epithet combination otherwise occurs only once more in early epic at *Od*. 6. 26 εἵματα ... σιγαλόεντα, again of washed clothes. The adjective σιγαλόεις is used elsewhere in Homer of different types of clothing (ῥῆγος *Od*. 6. 38 etc. and χιτών *Od*. 15. 60), as well as reins (*Il*. 5. 226 etc.), a throne (*Od*. 5. 86), and a chamber (*Od*. 16. 449). Szemerényi (1969), 243–5, with a summary of early literature (cf. *Dictionnaire* s.v.), derived the word from Hittite and Luwian šeḫeli- 'clean', ultimately Sumerian sikil 'pure', and perhaps to Greek through Ugaritic sihala- (Eastern h rendered by Greek γ). It is later connected with the shine of oil (Hermipp. *PCG* fr. 63. 20 ἀμύγδαλα σιγαλόεντα); LSJ s.v. also link σιγαλόω 'to smooth, polish' to the adjective, but this cannot be certain. But whatever its exact etymology, the Homeric contexts in which it is used clearly imply a meaning of 'glittering' or 'shining' (so ancient lexicographers and scholiasts, e.g. Hsch. s.v.: λαμπρά, ποικίλα, καὶ τὰ ὅμοια; cf. Handschur 1970, 84–5). The shine of cloth in Homer may reflect the practice of treating clothes with oil, known in Mycenaean times (see Shelmerdine 1998; cf. on *Aphr*. 63 ἑανῷ). When openly a goddess in *Aphr*. (64 and 171) Aphrodite's clothes are described as καλά, but both times when she is in mortal disguise (here and 164) they are σιγαλόεντα.

This rare noun–epithet combination is elsewhere found only later in the poetry of Gregory of Nazianzus; at line-end as here at *Carm*.

I 2. 1. 613 (*PG* 37. 569) and *Carm.* II. 2. 1. 241 (*PG* 37. 1468); cf. also *Carm.* II. 2. 6. 6–7 (*PG* 37. 1542. 11–1543. 1).

86 πέπλον: the πέπλος is the most frequently named item of female apparel in Homer. It has traditionally been identified with the Doric robe, a folded blanket held at the shoulders by two pins (after Studniczka 1886, 97 ff.). This assumption has more recently been challenged by Marinatos (1967), 42 ff. (followed by Pekridou-Gorecki 1989, 77–80), who suggests the term means 'Schleier' (veil or shawl) rather than 'robe' at all, the latter indicated only by ἑανός. The matter of exactly what a peplos was thought to consist of in Homer, and how it might have been pinned, remains unclear (that πέπλοι are even chariot covers at *Il.* 5. 194 suggests that the term was flexible), but that the peplos was not a dress at all is highly improbable (cf. Snodgrass 1969, 391–2). The two terms ἑανός and πέπλος seem to have been equated on some level in Homer (see, among other ancients, Hsch. ἑανός· πᾶν λαμπρὸν ἱμάτιον, ὃ καὶ πέπλον λέγει Ὅμηρος; cf. Lorimer 1950, 403–4, Janko 1992, 177). It is thus not so difficult, especially given the contextual similarity of seduction, to compare Aphrodite's πέπλος with Hera's elaborate ἑανός at *Il.* 14. 178–9; embroidered (ἐνὶ δαίδαλα πολλά), and pinned (κατὰ στῆθος περονᾶτο), hers is a grand affair (see Lorimer 1950, 378–80). There is no suggestion here that Aphrodite's peplos is decorated, nor any indication of how it hung (although see on *Aphr.* 163 πόρπας), but it must at least be a dress, and a fancy one at that. In art Aphrodite wears a Doric peplos, hung from both shoulders, in a few figures from the first half of the fifth century BC (*LIMC* ii Aphrodite, nos. 111 ff.), but she is generally well known in robes of various shapes and sizes (ibid., *passim*).

φαεινότερον πυρὸς αὐγῆς: also of the θώραξ of Achilles at *Il.* 18. 610. Aphrodite's robe is said to be shining at *Il.* 5. 315 πέπλοιο φαεινοῦ. The comparison to the light of fire here may imply that the garment was considered to be red (Marinatos 1967, 11; see more generally on coloured clothing Losfeld 1991, 262–7). It is also a sign of its great beauty; see *Il.* 6. 294–5/*Od.* 15. 107–8 (πέπλος) ὃς κάλλιστος ἔην ποικίλμασιν ἠδὲ μέγιστος, | ἀστὴρ δ' ὣς ἀπέλαμπεν.

87 ἐπιγναμπτάς: Kamerbeek (1967), 391 suspects this unique compound (only here) and prefers to read ἐπὶ γναμπτάς; 'là-dessus', i.e. upon the robe. If, however, one accepts ἕλικας and κάλυκας as 'bracelets' and 'earrings' (see next n.), they cannot be attached to the peplos. Heitsch's proposal (1965), 24 of reading ἔπι adverbially 'as well' is a more plausible route for separation (cf. *Il.* 18. 529, *Od.* 5. 443). But there seems to be no strong reason to reject the compound. The fact that At, D, and most MSS of the *p* group contain ἐπὶ γναμπτάς gives no particular justification for the separation (cf. Càssola 548); a knowledge of γναμπτάς θ' ἕλικας *Il.* 18. 401 (= *Aphr.* 163) could have led to the division. The neologism seems natural enough. A verb ἐπιγνάμπτω (to bend) occurs more than once in Homer (*Il.* 21. 178; metaphorically 2. 14 etc.). Furthermore, a compound εὔγναμπτος is known at *Od.* 18. 294 (adopted here by Baumeister 1860, 258) of golden hooks of brooches which the suitors give to Penelope to woo her; the list there of clothes and jewellery, including a peplos and necklace, is similar to *Aphr.* Cf. also the rare ἐπικαμπύλος *Op.* 427 (also *Herm.* 90) of bent timber, which has the parallel verb ἐπικάμπτω (see West 1978, 266, who rejects attempts at separation of that adjective).

ἕλικας κάλυκάς τε: the meaning of these two words is uncertain. Outside *Aphr.* both are mentioned as pieces of jewellery in early epic only at *Il.* 18. 401 (= *Aphr.* 163). They are paired once later (in an erotic context) at Nonn. *D.* 43. 401 ὅρμον ἄγων κάλυκάς τε φέρων ἕλικας τε τιταίνων (the works of Hephaestus as at *Il.* 18. 401).

The consensus of modern scholarly opinion is that κάλυκες are earrings in the shape of flower-buds (see AHS 359, Renehan 1982, 83 etc.), and this indeed seems most probable. That it indicates a piece of jewellery in the shape of a flower is clear; at *Dem.* 247 ῥοδέας κάλυκας are 'rose-buds' plain and simple (cf. *Cypr.* fr. 4. 5; see N. Richardson 1974, 291–2). Not only does Aphrodite certainly have flower-shaped earrings when she dresses at *Hy.* 6. 8–9 ἐν δὲ τρητοῖσι λοβοῖσι | ἄνθεμ' ὀρειχάλκου χρυσοῖό τε τιμήεντος (cf. Bielefeld 1968, 6), but earrings seem to be a common feature of such toilettes; Hera has a pair at *Il.* 14. 182–3 (also Penelope at *Od.* 18. 297–8), and earrings may have been in the mind of the poet. In art, Aphrodite is frequently portrayed wearing earrings, both in sculpture and in vase-painting. An early-fourth-century bust of the goddess even displays a large flower-shaped pair (*LIMC* ii, Aphrodite, no. 1049). Otherwise, several Cyprian statues of Aphrodite have crowns inlaid with rosettes (see V. Karageorghis 1998, 203–9 and *LIMC* ii,

Aphrodite, nos. 107–10). J. Karageorghis (1984), 363–5 has compared this epic description with figurines found at Paphos (possible representations of the goddess and her attendants) which are portrayed with ear-caps in the shape of a flower, among other jewellery.

More difficult is ἕλικας. They are spirals of some sort, connected with the verb ἑλίσσω 'to twist' (see *Dictionnaire* s.v. ἕλιξ; cf. *Sc.* 295, where they are tendrils of the vine). As with κάλυκας, ancient guesswork abounds; they could be hairbands, earrings, finger-rings, or bracelets (Homeric scholia, Eustathius, etc.). Most probable is that they are bracelets or armbands of some sort (so Müller 1887, 410, followed by AHS 359). Helbig (1884), 191–4 thinks that they might be brooches, but their differentiation from πόρπας at *Il.* 18. 401 (= *Aphr.* 163; see ad loc.), which are pins or brooches of some sort, suggests that they are something different; if one accepts κάλυκας as earrings, these cannot be earrings as well (cf. Càssola 548). Images of Aphrodite in art may indicate that bracelets are more likely than golden spirals or bands for the hair (preferred by M. W. Edwards 1991, 194). Aphrodite wears spiralled bracelets and armbands in both sculpture (*LIMC* ii, Aphrodite, nos. 54, 65 etc.), and vase-painting (*LIMC* ii, Aphrodite, no. 1434 etc.).

In both these cases it is interesting also to compare the jewellery which Ištar wears in *Descent to the Nether World* (*BTM* 500–1). It corresponds very well: Ištar loses to the gatekeeper a crown (ἐϋστέφανος, *Aphr.* 6), earrings (κάλυκας?, *Aphr.* 87), beads around her neck (ὅρμοι, *Aphr.* 88), pins on her breast (στήθεσσιν ἀμφ' *Aphr.* 90, πόρπας 163), a girdle of birth stones (ζώνην, *Aphr.* 164), and clasps round her hands and feet (ἕλικας?, *Aphr.* 87). The clasps around her hands and feet (Akkad. *semerū*; 'bracelets' or 'anklets' is the certain meaning; see *CAD* v. 219 ff.) and the absence of hair decoration other than a crown perhaps speaks in favour of ἕλικας as 'bracelets'. On the eastern nature of these themes (introduced to Greece at least partially through Cyprus?) cf. N. Richardson (1991) and see J. Karageorghis (1977), 58–60 on the frequent representation of women and goddesses with elaborate jewellery in the East.

88–9 ὅρμοι ... καλοὶ χρύσειοι παμποίκιλοι: the description of Aphrodite's necklaces is similar to that of the necklace which Eurymachus gives to Penelope at *Od.* 18. 295–6 ὅρμον δ' Εὐρυμάχῳ πολυδαίδαλον αὐτίκ' ἔνεικε | χρύσεον, ἠλέκτροισιν ἐερμένον, ἠέλιον ὣς (cf. also 15. 460). For the pile-up of adjectives here see the description of Aphrodite's diadem at *Hy*. 6. 7–8 στεφάνην ... | καλὴν χρυσείην, and Heracles' armour at *Sc*. 124–5 θώρηκα ... | καλὸν χρύσειον πολυδαίδαλον.

Aphrodite wears golden necklaces at *Hy*. 6. 11, and Pandora is adorned with golden necklaces by Peitho and the Charites in order to make her beautiful at *Op*. 74. Statues of Aphrodite from Cyprus have conspicuously large necklaces (see *LIMC* ii, Aphrodite, nos. 98–110), and the goddess frequently wears necklaces in vase painting (see *LIMC* ii, Aphrodite, nos. 212, 214, 806, 830, 932, etc.).

88 ἀμφ' ἁπαλῇ δειρῇ: Aphrodite's neck is soft also at *Hy*. 6. 10 δειρῇ δ' ἀμφ' ἁπαλῇ, as well as her breasts below in v. 90 (for which cf. [Hes.] fr. 75. 10). Although the necks of warriors can also be soft (i.e. *Il*. 13. 202), this is a feature of female beauty: at *Il*. 19. 285 the attractive Briseis, who is said to be ἰκέλη χρυσῇ Ἀφροδίτῃ, has ἁπαλὴν δειρήν. Later in Theoc. *Id*. 11. 20, the beautiful sea-nymph Galateia is described as ἁπαλωτέρα ἀρνός etc. If restored correctly, see also the phrasing at Sappho fr. 94. 16 πλέκ[ταις ἀμφ' ἁ]πάλαι δέραι.

περικαλλέες: the adjective, which describes a wide array of beautiful things in Homer (see *LfgrE* s.v.), is not used elsewhere of ὅρμοι. It does, however, describe the neck of Aphrodite at *Il*. 3. 396 περικαλλέα δειρήν, around which these necklaces are here specified as sitting (ἀμφ' ἁπαλῇ δειρῇ).

89 ὡς δὲ σελήνη: the comparison of jewellery to a heavenly body is not out of place here. Hera's κρήδεμνον is said to be white like the sun (ἠέλιον ὥς) in her dressing-scene at *Il*. 14. 185 and such a simile was 'perhaps traditional in toilette-scenes' (Janko 1992, 178). The golden ὅρμος given to Penelope at *Od*. 18. 295–6 is compared to the sun in the same way (cf. on *Aphr*. 88–9), as are the clothes of Odysseus at 19. 234. The likening of her attire to the moon is perhaps less expected, but again not unknown. The robe Penelope weaves to deceive the suitors is likened to the 'moon or the sun' at *Od*. 24. 148 (cf. also of Menelaus' house at 4. 45), and in *Hy*. 32. 8, the radiant Selene herself wears εἵματα τηλαυγέα. See also *Dem*. 278–9 τῆλε δὲ φέγγος ἀπὸ χροὸς ἀθανάτοιο | λάμπε θεᾶς; φέγγος 'not in Homer or Hesiod ... in classical Attic prose it seems to be used normally of moonlight' (N. Richardson 1974, 253). VE 39 points also to a possible simile of a woman standing out amongst the Lydian women like the moon amongst the stars at Sappho fr. 96. 7 ff. ὣς ποτ' ἀελίω | δύντος ἀ βροδοδάκτυλος σελάννα | πάντα περρέχοισ' ἄστρα (σελάννα is a conjecture by Schubart, rejected by *PLF*, which reads †μήνα, but adopted by Voigt).

It is in Near Eastern literature, however, that the most striking parallel is found. In a Sumerian sacred-marriage text, the love-goddess Inanna bathes and anoints herself, dresses in fine clothing and jewellery, and appears to her mortal lover Dumuzi 'like a moon-beam' (*ETCSL* 4. 08. 29 = *ANET* 639. Cf. West 1997, 204–5 and Penglase 1994, 174). Much later (12th c. AD) in Greek literature, one might wonder whether Theodoros Prodromos was thinking of this passage at *Carmina Historica* 6. 42–3 ὡς δὲ σελήνη | χρυσείοισι πέπλοισι φαείνεται (a simile for the shine of a city).

90 ἐλάμπετο: it is uncertain how to understand this singular verb after the plural ὅρμοι. The most plausible, and favoured, reading is that it acts impersonally (see Gemoll 1886, 266, VE 39, VB 10). Although rare, an impersonal use of shining is known at *Il.* 22. 319 ὡς αἰχμῆς ἀπέλαμπ' εὐήκεος (N. Richardson 1993, 138 compares φαίνετο at 22. 324; see also *Od.* 9. 143 προὐφαίνετ' ἰδέσθαι, although this may refer to the god who leads the ship there). One might also consider that adaptation of an already established simile, such as the metrically equivalent and similar ἀμφὶ δὲ χαλκὸς ἐλάμπετο εἴκελος αὐγῇ | ἢ πυρὸς αἰθομένου ἢ ἠελίου ἀνιόντος at *Il.* 22. 134–5, may have influenced the poet to use the singular here.

Other suggestions are no more convincing: AHS 359 propose that this is a case of attraction to the number of σελήνη, but this has no parallel in early epic. Baumeister (1860), 258 thinks that Aphrodite is the subject, but this would be a rather abrupt switch, and as AHS point out, it would be awkward to say that she herself shines στήθεσιν ἀμφ' ἁπαλοῖσιν. Càssola 548–9 believes that the verb is singular because the subject is 'things', which can be treated syntactically as neuter (a *schema Pindaricum*; see GG ii. 607–8). But this occurs only twice in epic at *Th.* 321 and 825, on both occasions where ἦν is followed by a plural subject; not only is ἦν no parallel for ἐλάμπετο (ἦν was originally plural and remained so in several dialects; see Buck 1955, 128), but N. Richardson (1974), 253 points out (apropos of a refutation of the singular κατενήνοθεν as a *schema Pindaricum* at *Dem.* 279) that it is very unusual for the subject to precede the verb in such cases. Nor can one move the lines around at whim as some have thought acceptable (see the discussion at AS 207).

θαῦμα ἰδέσθαι: a common formula, *Il.* 5. 725, 10. 439 etc.

91 ἔρος εἷλεν: the same formula has Anchises seized by love now and later at v. 144. Peppmüller (1889), 16 here conjectures τάφος 'astonishment' for δ' ἔρος, on the grounds that ἔρος does not fit the context; why is Anchises said to be seized by love at this point, if he does nothing about it until after Aphrodite's tale? Lenz (1975), 37 n. 1 also thinks that ἔρος is an inaccuracy on the part of the poet here; if Anchises is seized by love now, what is the point of Aphrodite's long speech to convince him to sleep with her? A simple answer is that, given the stunning beauty which has just been described, it is entirely natural that Anchises should feel love of some sort, which returns more strongly at v. 144 'after all difficulties have been removed' (VE 39; cf. Allen 1898, 24). However, a more exact and convincing explanation of the use of ἔρος here has been offered by VB 10–11. He notes an important difference between the two uses of the formula ἔρος εἷλεν in the hymn; here Anchises is seized only by ἔρος, whereas at v. 144 he is seized by ἔρος and also struck with ἵμερος (in the previous line γλυκὺν ἵμερον ἔμβαλε θυμῷ). It is only after being struck with ἵμερος that Anchises takes action. VB goes on to draw a distinction between ἵμερος and ἔρος as the marked and the unmarked term respectively: ἔρος indicates a more general 'disposition' to love, while the stronger term ἵμερος indicates a desire which is to be fulfilled immediately; his distinction seems broadly applicable to the use of the two terms in the hymn and elsewhere in early epic (cf. de Jong, *LfgrE* s.v. ἵμερος). In other words, Anchises is attracted to Aphrodite, but he is not yet overcome by an immediate desire to sleep with her, suspicious as he is of her divinity (see on *Aphr.* 92–106).

ἔπος δέ μιν ἀντίον ηὔδα: this formula occurs elsewhere only at *Il.* 5. 170 ἔπος τέ μιν ἀντίον ηὔδα (Kirk 1990, 76 apparently missed *Aphr.* in commenting there that the 'present formulation is unique in having plain ηὔδα rather than προσηύδα or προσέειπε, followed by a double accusative'). Podbielski (1971), 46 thinks it remarkable that Anchises is the first to speak, but this is the norm for a host in epic (see Smith 1981a, 46), while Aphrodite, although a goddess who might speak first, is trying to pass herself off as a mortal (see de Jong 1989, 15).

92–106. Anchises' speech confirms that he has a strong suspicion this beautiful intruder is a goddess (on Aphrodite's partially divine appearance and Anchises' reaction see on *Aphr.* 81–90 and 83–90). He does not, however, know which goddess, and so offers a lengthy list of possibilities, including Artemis, Leto, Aphrodite herself, Themis, Athena, the Charites, and the nymphs. Allen (1898), 25 and Bickerman (1976), 231 argue that this is just a flattering address to a beautiful woman, comparing Odysseus' first words to Nausicaa at *Od.* 6. 149 ff.; but these two speeches differ in several significant respects. First, Odysseus is cautious by asking whether Nausicaa is a god or a mortal (*Od.* 6. 149 θεός νύ τις ἢ βροτός ἐσσι etc.), whereas Anchises asks more bluntly which goddess Aphrodite is, with no mention of possible mortality (cf. VE 40 and Podbielski 1971, 45). Second, Anchises' claim is on a much larger scale; he lists a multitude of goddesses, while Odysseus is content to liken Nausicaa to Artemis alone (*Od.* 6. 151). Third, Anchises' pledge to build an altar and the requests he makes thereafter (vv. 100 ff.) are appropriate only for a divinity, whereas the requests which Odysseus makes to Nausicaa accord with her mortality (cf. de Jong 1989, 16). It therefore seems best to follow Smith (1981a), 46–9 in supposing that Anchises genuinely suspects that his visitor is a goddess. Cf. also *Apoll.* 464 ff., where the Cretans compare Apollo to a god, but ask questions reasonable for a mortal (Apollo is on this occasion then frank with them that he is a god), and *Od.* 13. 221 ff., where Odysseus beseeches Athena in disguise 'as to a god' (ὥς τε θεῷ), but clearly believes she is a mortal man. On the other hand see *Od.* 16. 181–5, where Telemachus likens Odysseus to a god after his sudden change of appearance (a good reason to think he is a god), and offers to propitiate him with sacrifices and gifts.

Anchises' speech is in fact perfectly structured as a mini-hymn appropriate for a god: he begins by addressing the stranger with χαῖρε, a typical hymnic invocation (on which see on *Aphr.* 92 and cf. Podbielski 1971, 43); in his list of possible goddesses he uses relative expansion three times to elaborate upon the Charites and the nymphs (αἵ τε vv. 95, 97, 98), a common device in hymns (cf. on *Aphr.* 1–6); he then concludes with a prayer in which he asks for long life, strong offspring etc. in return for worship, a frequent closing feature in hymns (see Furley i. 60 and cf. Smith 1981a, 46–9). The prayer is not dissimilar to Nestor's prayer to Athena at *Od.* 3. 380–4, where he addresses the goddess as ἄνασσα, asks for glory for himself, his children, and his wife, and promises to make sacrifices to her (cf. on *Aphr.* 100 σοὶ δ' ἐγώ). On the structural level, note also that the speech can be divided neatly into two equal halves: the first half (7 lines; see below on 97–9 on the deletion of v. 98) consists of the initial address and lists and expands upon possible goddesses, while the second half (7 lines) is devoted to the prayer.

His belief that this visitor is a goddess is also, as de Jong (1989), 16–17 puts it, a 'masterful stroke of storytelling'. In love, but still in control of himself, Anchises has the sense to react piously to this visitor whom he suspects is a goddess (for the pious reaction here cf. Reinhardt 1956, 9, VE 40), and Aphrodite is thereby forced, to the delight of the audience, to convince him of her mortality with a long and elaborate tale (vv. 107–42). De Jong (1989), 16 suggests that this address does not present Anchises as a pious young shepherd at all, arguing instead that he is portrayed in this speech as 'a self-confident and ambitious prince' requesting favours from the goddess. In support of this she also remarks that his second speech in the hymn (vv. 149–54), in which he passionately addresses his visitor before sleeping with her, 'shows him to be not exactly god-fearing'. But I see good reason to think that Anchises is here presented as pious. (i) While it is certainly true that Anchises is not seized at v. 91 by desire (ἵμερος), which would lead one to expect immediate action, he is at least attracted to her (ἔρος εἷλεν); it is still surprising then, if he is not displaying piety towards the divine, that he does not make any reference to his attraction or to Aphrodite's beauty in his speech (Odysseus, for example, makes explicit reference to Nausicaa's beauty). (ii) A request for favours, which does not necessarily imply overt self-confidence (Hector, in the terror of war, makes similarly grand requests at *Il.* 6. 475–81), does not preclude piety; rather, it is the prerogative of the pious to make requests. (iii) If Anchises is bold in his second speech (vv. 149–54), it must be remembered that this is made after Aphrodite's tale of explanation, when Anchises has been sufficiently swayed to lay aside his convictions and take action (see on *Aphr.* 143–54).

92 χαῖρε ἄνασσ': a hymnic formula; cf. *Hy.* 32. 17 χαῖρε ἄνασσα, θεά, *Hy.* 15. 9, 31. 17 χαῖρε ἄναξ. Janko (1982), 160 claims that observance of digamma in the formula is unparalleled in Homer, but digamma is never certainly neglected in the three occurences of the feminine ἄνασσα in Homer (*Od*. 3. 380, 6. 149, 175), and is frequently observed in the masculine forms; the formula (which does not appear in Homer) is probably old, but observance of digamma is no sure sign of archaism (see on *Aphr*. 10).

Mortals can also be greeted with χαίρω, a common use which extends to modern Greek; see Achilles to his guests χαίρετον (*Il*. 9. 197), or Telemachus to Mentor (Athena) χαῖρε (*Od*. 1. 123), whom he believes to be entirely mortal. But ἄνασσα is a term reserved for goddesses (cf. Hainsworth, *OC* i. 303; the only exception is Odysseus' compliment to Nausicaa at *Od*. 6. 149, but there not with χαῖρε; rather γουνοῦμαί σε, ἄνασσα).

ἥτις ... τάδε δώματα ἱκάνεις: AHS 359 compare the superficial structure of *Dem*. 119–20 αἵ τινές ἐστε γυναικῶν θηλυτεράων | χαίρετε. Cf. also *Od*. 20. 295/21. 313 (ἀτέμβειν) ξείνους Τηλεμάχου, ὅς κεν τάδε δώμαθ' ἵκηται.

μακάρων: here and at v. 195 μακάρων is on its own without θεῶν stated, an absolute use of the epithet found only once in Homer (*Od*. 10. 299, also in the gen. plural). It is far more common in Hesiod (6×: *Th*. 33, *Op*. 136, 171, 549, 718, 730; cf. West 1966*a*, 166) and the *Hymns* (cf. *Dem*. 303 and see Janko 1982, 156 for more examples).

93–9. This list of possible identities is striking, because of its length and the divinities it includes. The closest parallel is *Hy*. 7. 17 ff.: when the helmsman of the pirate ship recognizes that their prisoner is probably a god (Dionysus), he falls to similar guessing (τίνα τόνδε θεόν ... | ... | ἢ γὰρ Ζεὺς ὅδε γ' ἐστίν, ἢ ἀργυρότοξος Ἀπόλλων, | ἠὲ Ποσειδάων); but he stops at three famous gods. As to the content of the list in *Aphr*.: the five individual goddesses named are all included in the long list of gods whom the Muses hymn at the beginning of the *Theogony* vv. 11–21 (West 1966*a*, 156 notes that Themis and Aphrodite appear side by side here and at *Th*. 16). Otherwise, certain of these are grouped only separately: Penelope's comparison to Artemis or Aphrodite at *Od*. 17. 37/19. 54 Ἀρτέμιδι ἰκέλη ἠὲ χρυσῇ Ἀφροδίτῃ is very similar to v. 93; Leto and Artemis are a natural pair as mother and daughter (cf. *Apoll*. 159 and *Th*. 918). The sense at *Th*. 11 ff. seems to be of an almost exhaustive list, abridged at v. 21 with ἄλλων τ' ἀθανάτων ἱερὸν γένος αἰὲν ἐόντων (as at *Il.* 18. 38 ff. a similarly long list of the Nereids begins with πᾶσαι ὅσαι ... Νηρηΐδες ἦσαν and is then abridged), and that might be the underlying point here too. This stranger could be any goddess, and Anchises covers a wide field to underline the statement ἤ τις μακάρων. This may partially explain the mention of the Charites and the nymphs here as well. At *Il.* 20. 7–9 it is said that none of the Rivers, except Ocean, or the nymphs (almost identical lines in *Aphr.*; see on *Aphr.* 97–9) failed to attend the important council of Zeus, in order to exemplify the inclusiveness of the meeting. Similarly, the placement of the Charites and nymphs here stresses the exhaustive guessing of the hero. The mention of Aphrodite may be a light touch of irony, but ultimately hers is just another name in the list (cf. de Jong 1989, 15; *contra* Podbielski 1971, 43–4, who understands a more direct suspicion of Aphrodite here).

It is also appropriate that the nymphs should be included here thematically. Trojan shepherds were known to have had affairs with nymphs (Boucolion and Abarbaree at *Il.* 6. 21–2, Enops and a nymph 14. 444–5, or Otruntes and a nymph 20. 384; cf. Griffin 1992, 201), and Anchises might have considered this possibility when a beautiful female appeared before him. The Charites too come to mind naturally here, known for their beauty in Homer (cf. *Od.* 6. 18). They sing together with the nymphs on Mount Ida at *Cypr.* fr. 5. 4–5.

93 χρυσῆ Ἀφροδίτη: all MSS have the contracted form of the adjective. Barnes (1711) corrected to χρυσέη, although in the MSS of Hesiod and (for the most part) Homer there is a distinction between contracted forms of χρύσεος in this formula, and uncontracted forms elsewhere, suggesting that the contraction should be kept in this case (see West 1966a, 383–4 on *Th.* 822; 1998, *Praefatio*, pp. xxxvi f.). For more on this epithet and Aphrodite's connection with gold see on *Aphr.* 1 πολυχρύσου.

94 Θέμις ἠϋγενής: this form of εὐγενής (in Homer only the abnormal form εὐηγενής; as below at v. 229) is found only here. The lengthened grade ἠϋ- may be ancient (see Janko 1992, 257), in which case, given its placement in Anchises' mini-hymn, one might see this as a relic of hymnic language (cf. the *hapax* ἠϋθέμεθλον at *Hy.* 30. 1).

95–6 Χαρίτων: here the Charites are said to be the consorts of all gods. They appeared above at v. 61 in their best-known role as the attendants of Aphrodite, but she is not their only associate. In Homer, Hephaestus marries Charis at *Il.* 18. 382 (named Aglaïe at *Th.* 945; he is married to Aphrodite at *Od.* 8. 266 ff.), and Hera promises one of the Charites to Hypnos at *Il.* 14. 267–8. The breadth of their group of companions expands after Homer, when they are often grouped together with the Muses (*Th.* 64, *Hy.* 27. 15 etc.; see further West 1966a, 177), as well as with Artemis (*Hy.* 27. 15) and the nymphs (*Cypr.* fr. 5. 4). Later they are connected with Dionysus (see Furley ii. 376), Hecate (see *OCD* s.v.), and other gods (see AHS 359–60). This statement, after hymnic relative expansion, may be intended simply to indicate the honoured position of the Charites; cf. *Hy.* 12. 4–5 ἣν πάντες μάκαρες κατὰ μακρὸν Ὄλυμπον | ἀζόμενοι τίουσιν or *Hy.* 29. 1–3 ἣ πάντων ἐν δώμασιν ὑψηλοῖσιν | ἀθανάτων τε θεῶν . . . | ἕδρην ἀΐδιον ἔλαχες (note also Hestia's honoured place at *Aphr.* 31 πᾶσιν δ' ἐν νηοῖσι θεῶν).

95 ἦ πού τις: 'I suppose'; the particle που, which conveys a 'feeling of uncertainty in the speaker' (Denniston 1954, 490–1), underlines the fact that Anchises is just hazarding guesses. See Andromache guessing possibilities as to how the Greeks thrice attacked the weak spots in the wall of Troy at *Il.* 6. 438 ἦ πού τίς σφιν ἔνισπε θεοπροπίων εὖ εἰδώς (cf. on *Aphr.* 93–9).

δεῦρ' ἤλυθες: cf. Penelope's question to the figure who visits her in a dream at *Od.* 4. 810 τίπτε, κασιγνήτη, δεῦρ' ἤλυθες;

96 πᾶσιν: note the enjambment here, placing emphasis on 'all'. Cf. the passages cited on 95–6.

ἑταιρίζουσι: 'to act as a companion to' (N. Richardson 1993, 308) or 'to associate with' (cf. Stagakis 1971). The verb is rare and occurs only twice in Homer (*Il.* 13. 456 ἑταρίσσαιτο (+ acc.), 24. 335 ἑταιρίσσαι). See later its use at Call. *Hy.* 3. 206, of Artemis' connection with Cyrene.

καὶ ἀθάνατοι καλέονται: cf. *Il.* 5. 342 καὶ ἀθάνατοι καλέονται, generically of the gods (the Charites are mentioned there just four lines above). VE 41 thinks that this formula has been used here to distinguish the immortal Charites from the nymphs who follow in the list; yet, even if the nymphs are classed as semi-mortal later in the poem (vv. 256–73), there is no reason to suspect such a distinction here. The nymphs are traditionally immortal in Homer (see *Gesch.*

i. 245–6) and this is after all a list of μάκαρες (cf. VB 11–12). The phrase is more probably just honorific.

97–9. Ruhnken (1749), 25–6 suspected the similarity of vv. 97 and 98 and deleted the latter (E and T omit v. 97; 'wohl nur durch Zufall', Gemoll 1886, 267). With it out of the way, vv. 97 and 99 neatly form a pair almost identical with *Il.* 20. 8–9, and Ruhnken's move was followed by several early editors (Ilgen 1796, Hermann 1806, etc.). Most modern editors, however, have kept the line (Gemoll 1886, AHS 1936, Càssola 1975) with the exception of West (2003). There is good reason for doubting its authenticity. Certainly, the repetition itself does not provide adequate grounds for dismissal. There is very similar repetition above at vv. 62–3 (see ad loc.), and on that occasion as well two verses which form a pair in Homer are divided by another verse (see on *Aphr.* 58–63; cf. AHS 360). In any case, the fact that vv. 97 and 99 form a pair in Homer is weak evidence for suspecting v. 98; vv. 98–9 are themselves similar to *Od.* 6. 123–4 νυμφάων, αἳ ἔχουσ' ὀρέων αἰπεινὰ κάρηνα | καὶ πηγὰς ποταμῶν καὶ πίσεα ποιήεντα (the description seems formulaic and there is no reason to suppose direct imitation of Homer here). On the other hand, unlike in the case of vv. 62–3, the second of these lines is redundant. It has been argued by some that the two lines refer to different groups of nymphs, v. 98 singling out those who live on Ida (see AHS 360, Càssola 549, VE 42), but this seems forced. There is no reason to think that the general statement 'nymphs who live in the fair groves' does not encompass those who live on Ida as well. The mountain is covered with trees suitable for a grove (cf. v. 285 καταειμένον ὕλῃ), and the nymphs later in the hymn (who are specified as living on τόδε ... ὄρος as here, v. 258) have an explicit connection with trees on the mountain (vv. 264–72). Mountain nymphs in Homer too are connected with trees (they plant elms around the tomb of Eetion at *Il.* 6. 419–20).

The structure of the passage also seems to favour the removal of v. 98. Without it, the guessing is introduced by a line which greets the visitor and poses the general question (ἤ τις μακάρων), after which three pairs of lines follow; two listing individual goddesses, two devoted to the Charites, and two devoted to the nymphs. The latter two pairs are then balanced by ἤ (πού) τις + relative expansion (αἵ τε), + one line of further description (note that the first pair is balanced internally by ἠέ after the caesura in both lines). The inclusion of v. 98 seems to upset this, a point perhaps all the more noteworthy given that the poet shows himself to be concerned with structural balance and symmetry above at *Aphr.* 58–63 (see ad loc.). Finally, although the Attic contraction νυμφῶν is not itself a certain criterion for rejecting the second line (the Ionic νυμφέ͡ων with synizesis, *Od.* 12. 319, *Th.* 130, is equally admissible; cf. Janko 1982, 156–7), it may, given the other reasons for suspecting the verse, be a further suggestion that v. 98 is a later variant (on other possible Atticisms in *Aphr.* see Introd., p. 45).

97 ἄλσεα καλά: the noun–epithet combination is rare; apart from the almost identical verse at *Il.* 20. 8 (cf. on *Aphr.* 97–9), it occurs in the plural only three more times in later literature, at Gr. Naz. *Carm.* II 1. 1. 77 (*PG* 37. 976), Nonn. *D.* 13. 237, 13. 288. Callimachus adapts it to the singular, again with reference to the nymphs, at *Hy.* 6. 25 (cf. Hopkinson 1984a, 101), as does Q.S. at 2. 588–9; see also of the grove of Eros at Marianus Scholiasticus *AP* 9. 668. 1.

98 καλὸν ὄρος τόδε: see τόδε . . . ὄρος later in the hymn at vv. 258 and 285.

99 πηγὰς ποταμῶν . . . πίσεα ποιήεντα: outside this formulaic verse (identical with *Il.* 20. 9 and *Od.* 6. 124) πηγὰς ποταμῶν occurs only once more at [Opp.] *C.* 3. 195; πίσεα ποιήεντα not at all. On the adjective ποιήεντα cf. on *Aphr.* 78.

100–2. Podbielski (1971), 44–5, Càssola 549, and VE 42 think that the first two lines of this prayer refer to the foundation of an actual cult on Ida, but there is nothing to suggest this in the text. Elsewhere in the *Hymns*, the foundation of a particular precinct of a god is accompanied by a geographical reference, or the name of the god to whom the altar is built: at *Dem.* 270 ff. Demeter requests that an altar be built above the Callichoron in Eleusis, at *Dem.* 296–7 Demeter is named as the recipient of the altar, at *Apoll.* 490–6 Apollo orders an altar to be built which will be called Delphinios. In contrast, Anchises neither names a location, nor in fact knows to which god he is promising to found this altar. Also, the foundation of an altar is not referred to anywhere else in the hymn (cf. Lenz 1975, 27), which overall shows no explicit interest in cult. Anchises seems merely to be proposing the appropriate propitiatory action, although any ancient audience of the hymn could of course have thought of a local cult of Aphrodite upon hearing this.

100 σοὶ δ' ἐγώ: this juxtaposition of pronouns adds rhetorical power to Anchises' promise; cf. the very similar σοὶ δ' αὖ ἐγώ in Nestor's prayer to Athena at *Od.* 3. 332 (on which cf. on *Aphr.* 92– 106; cf. also Diomedes to Athena at *Il.* 10. 292). It is used several times in Homer, before a speech which promises to be informative (cf. *Il.* 8. 286, *Od.* 24. 123; so too *Op.* 286, and before speech Thgn. 27, 1049, S. *Trach.* 468, Eur. *Hec.* 1232), or before a boast or a brave claim (in a boast before killing an opponent in battle at *Il.* 5. 652/11. 443, or the brave words of Dolon at 10. 324). It also begins Aphrodite's promise of return to Anchises later in the hymn at v. 276. Note also the emphatic statement of promise proposed by Hera to Zeus at *Il.* 4. 62–3 ὑποείξομεν ἀλλήλοισιν | σοὶ μὲν ἐγώ, σὺ δ' ἐμοί. The contrast of pronouns continues throughout the prayer, reversed at vv. 102 ff. when Anchises switches from promise to request, σὺ δέ ... | δός με ... | αὐτὰρ ἔμ' αὐτόν.

ἐν σκοπιῇ περιφαινομένῳ ἐνὶ χώρῳ: for the foundation of an altar in a lofty place see *Dem.* 272 and 297–8 ἤνωγ' ... | ποιῆσαι καὶ βωμὸν ἐπὶ προὔχοντι κολωνῷ (note the use of ποιέω; see on *Aphr.* 101). The nymphs have an elevated altar at *Od.* 17. 209–10 κατὰ δὲ ψυχρὸν ῥέεν ὕδωρ | ὑψόθεν ἐκ πέτρης· βωμὸς δ' ἐφύπερθε τέτυκτο, but this does not imply that Anchises is thinking in particular of them here, as VB 12 suggests, nor of Aphrodite (cf. above on 100–2). Apart from the examples of altars on high to Demeter cited above, Zeus has his sanctuary in Gargaron high up in the peaks of Ida (*Il.* 8. 47–8). Hector sacrificed to him there, or at other times upon the citadel of Troy, another elevated location (*Il.* 22. 171–2; cf. his prayer at *Il.* 6. 257). A high place is simply an honoured location (cf. the lofty places of the Old Testament, ἱερεῖς τῶν ὑψηλῶν 3 *Ki.* 12. 32 etc.), and a natural one for a shepherd on Ida to mention. Also, elevation is a general characteristic of altars in cult. From the eighth century BC, stepped monumental altars, which raised the priest performing sacrifice at an elevation above the worshippers, became the most popular type in Greece, especially before large temples; they were very expensive to build, and thus presumably a mark of honour (see Yavis 1949, 115 ff., 140 ff.).

As for the phrasing here, it is uniquely assembled: the σκοπιή is the high point where a look-out sat to see most clearly (cf. *Il.* 5. 771 ἥμενος ἐν σκοπιῇ) and περιφαινόμενος is used of a mountain at *Il.* 13.

179. The poet may have been thinking of the formula περισκέπτῳ ἐνὶ χώρῳ, found at *Od.* 1. 426, 10. 211, 10. 253, 14. 6; even if in its Homeric appearances it means 'protected on all sides', the ancients interpreted it as 'conspicuous'/'seen from all around' (see S. West, *OC* i. 125–6 and Hoekstra, *OC* ii. 193). Cf. also Odysseus' naked retreat to the forest, which is ἐν περιφαινομένῳ at *Od.* 5. 476.

101 βωμὸν ποιήσω: for the establishment of an altar with ποιέω see in particular *Dem.* 298 ποιῆσαι καὶ βωμὸν ἐπὶ προὔχοντι κολωνῷ (cf. n. prec.); also *Apoll.* 384, 490, 508. Later see A.R. 2. 522 βωμὸν ποίησε (to Zeus), followed in the next line by ἱερά τ' εὖ ἔρρεξεν, and 4. 1715–16 (to Apollo).

ῥέξω δέ τοι ἱερὰ καλά: ἔρδω + ἱερὰ καλά is formulaic language for making a sacrifice, but never quite as here; cf. *Il.* 11. 727, *Od.* 4. 473, 7. 191, 11. 130, etc. (see more examples at *LfgrE* s.v. ἔρδω). Note σοὶ δ' αὖ ἐγὼ ῥέξω βοῦν at *Il.* 10. 292/*Od.* 3. 382. For the structure of this phrase, see the metrically equivalent δώσω δέ τοι ἀγλαὰ δῶρα *Od.* 4. 589.

102 ὥρῃσιν πάσῃσι: for ὥρῃσιν used to mean 'in due season' cf. *Dem.* 265, which refers to a ritual mock-battle at Eleusis held in honour of Demophon (see N. Richardson 1974, 245–8 ad loc., with parallels; add *Hy.* 26. 12 ἐς ὥρας). The sense here is most probably similar, 'in every due season' (West 2003; *contra* VE 43 'at all seasons'). See, however, *Cypr.* fr. 4. 6–7 ὥδ' Ἀφροδίτη | ὥραις παντοίαις τεθυωμένα εἵματα ἕστο; Aphrodite wears perfumed clothes, which the Hours and Charites dip ἐν ἄνθεσιν εἰαρινοῖσιν (vv. 1–2). This could mean 'in every due season', i.e. every spring when there are spring flowers, but given that fragrance is a general characteristic of the goddess (cf. on *Aphr.* 58–9), it perhaps more probably means 'in all seasons', i.e. 'all year round'. In any case, the context there is very different from *Aphr.* Note also Ar. *Nu.* 308–10 εὐστέφανοί τε θεῶν | θυσίαι θαλίαι τε | παντοδαπαῖσιν ὥραις; the point is that there are festivals and sacrifices in Athens all year round, but the reference is to many gods, and thus to many different seasons of worship.

Janko (1982), 155 points out that nu mobile makes position both here and at *Dem.* 265, a feature which may point to modification; if so, however, a prototype formula has not survived (cf. Hoekstra 1965, 85).

εὔφρονα θυμὸν ἔχουσα: Kamerbeek (1967), 387–8 (cf. Janko 1982,

157) points out that εὔφρων means 'gracious' or 'kindly', 'comme évidemment ici', nowhere else in early epic; otherwise first in Pi. *O.* 4. 12–13 θεὸς εὔφρων εἴη λοιπαῖς εὐχαῖς (see LSJ s.v. for more examples). In Homer the adjective means 'merry' or 'cheerful' (see Latacz 1966, 161–73), where the noun–epithet combination θυμὸς εὔφρων is found once at *Od.* 17. 531 (cf. εὔφρονι θυμῷ at *Hy.* 30. 14 and Panyassis fr. 12. 17). Very similar to *Aphr.*, but again with the sense 'merry', is Thgn. 765 εὔφρονα θυμὸν ἔχοντας (see also the comparable ὁμόφρονα/σαόφρονα θυμὸν ἔχ- at *Il.* 22. 263, *Herm.* 391, *Dem.* 434, *Hy.* 7. 49 and Thgn. 81, or ταλασίφρονα θυμὸν ἔχοντες Tyrt. fr. 5. 5). This may be a neologism based upon πρόφρονι θυμῷ/θυμῷ πρόφρονι 'wholeheartedly', used of willingness in Homer (Zeus at *Il.* 8. 39–40 etc.; see N. Richardson 1993, 290 on *Il.* 24. 139–40). For a list of the great number of -φρων adjectives applied to θυμός see Darcus (1977); cf. ἄφρονι θυμῷ below at v. 286.

103–6. In the first few lines of his prayer Anchises asks for a θαλερόν γόνον. This is a significant request here, as it introduces for the first time the theme of Anchises' lineage, in particular his fathering of Aeneas, which will be so prominent later in the hymn (see Introd., pp. 7–10); if this seems at first glance to be a standard request in a prayer, it should be remembered that an ancient audience would very probably have known the story of Aeneas' parentage and brought it to mind here.

The final lines of the prayer also seem to allude to a theme which appears prominently later in the poem. Anchises asks to live long (δηρὸν ἔτι ζώειν v. 105) and to reach the threshold of old age (γήραος οὐδὸν ἱκέσθαι v. 106), words which haunt the memory when Anchises later pleads for his life (vv. 188–90) and Aphrodite tells the tragic story of the eternally ageing Tithonus (on the motif of mortality in the poem see Introd., p. 11). For more on the foreshadowing here see on 191–9 on Aphrodite's 'response' to this prayer.

The first two lines of Anchises' prayer share language with Hector's prayer for his son Astyanax at *Il.* 6. 476–7 Ζεῦ, ἄλλοι τε θεοί, δότε δὴ καὶ τόνδε γενέσθαι | παῖδ' ἐμόν, ὡς καὶ ἐγώ περ, ἀριπρεπέα Τρώεσσιν.

103 δός με ... ἔμμεναι: for the acc. + infinitive construction with δός see the prayers of Priam to Zeus at *Il.* 24. 309 δός μ' ἐς Ἀχιλλῆος φίλον ἐλθεῖν and Odysseus to Athena at *Od.* 6. 327 δός μ' ἐς Φαίηκας φίλον ἐλθεῖν (possibly also Diomedes' prayer to Athena at *Il.* 5. 118 δός δέ [v.l. τόνδε] τέ μ' ἄνδρα ἐλεῖν).

ἀριπρεπέ'... ἄνδρα: as above cf. *Il.* 6. 477 παῖδ' ἐμόν... ἀριπρεπέα Τρώεσσιν. The adjective, generally of things which are conspicuous or stand out, is combined with ἀνήρ only once at *Il.* 9. 441 ἄνδρες ἀριπρεπέες, but that is sufficient to make Hermann's αἰεί (1806) unnecessary (cf. AS 208). Cf. also of the εἶδος of the Phaeacian prince Laodamas at *Od.* 8. 176 and kings at 390 (for more uses see *LfgrE* s.v.).

104 ποίει... θαλερὸν γόνον: the function of ποίει here has caused some difficulty. VE 43–4 thinks that it means 'to cause' or 'bring about', with εἶναι understood and θαλερόν as predicate: 'cause my offspring [to be] strong'. VB 12–13 follows a similar reading, but takes the adjective as attributive 'cause that there will be flourishing offspring for me'. The actual sense seems to be 'make my offspring healthy' (so West 2003), with no infinitive understood and θαλερόν predicate. Similarly in Homer, the gods can make gifts rich (δῶρα, τά μοι θεοὶ Οὐρανίωνες | ὄλβια ποιήσειαν *Od.* 13. 41–2) or people mad (μάργην σε θεοὶ θέσαν, οἵ τε δύνανται | ἄφρονα ποιῆσαι καὶ ἐπίφρονά περ μάλ' ἐόντα *Od.* 23. 11–12). It is not particularly problematic that after this clause the prayer continues with acc. + infinitive constructions, in which ποιέω needs to play no part. At *Il.* 7. 179–80 Nestor launches into a short prayer to Zeus with only an infinitive (Ζεῦ πάτερ, ἢ' Αἴαντα λαχεῖν ...), where an imperative such as δός is apparently understood (cf. *Il.* 2. 412–13, 3. 285; see Goodwin 1900, 330); δός, already stated at the beginning of the prayer, can reasonably be understood to govern αὐτὰρ ἐμ' αὐτόν... as well (cf. AS 208). Gemoll (1886), 267 unnecessarily conjectured ἔα for ἔϋ in the next line.

εἰσοπίσω: Heitsch (1965), 40 n. 2 notes that this first appears elsewhere in Solon fr. 27. 10 καὶ παίδων ζητεῖν εἰσοπίσω γενεήν; the context is strikingly similar. Also alike is Tyrt. fr. 12. 30 καὶ παίδων παῖδες καὶ γένος ἐξοπίσω. Analogous to ἐξοπίσω (which is in the same place in the verse several times in Homer, *Il.* 11. 461, 13. 436 etc.), the formation of εἰσοπίσω is entirely natural, perhaps from an earlier separation such as γένοιτό τοι ἐς περ ὀπίσσω | ὄλβος (*Od.* 18. 122–3, 20. 199–200; again see Heitsch 1965, 24). The word remains rare, later at S. *Ph.* 1104, then [Opp]. *C.* 4. 362 and four times in Quintus (1. 243, 5. 55, 6. 584, 13. 424).

θαλερὸν γόνον: the adjective θαλερός 'healthy/full of strength' (cf. LfgrE s.v.: 'kraftstrotzend, im Vollbesitz der Vitalität') is joined with γόνος only here, but θαλερὸν γάμον (cf. Od. 6. 66, 20. 74 and Hy. 19. 35) is unnecessarily conjectured by Köchly (1881), 221. If not of γόνον, it is used in Homer of fertility and lineage, of wives (Il. 3. 53, Th. 921 etc.) and husbands (Il. 6. 430, 8. 156 etc.); from the same root, children can of course be called θάλος (Il. 22. 87 etc.). For a full discussion of the use of the adjective in early epic see Lowenstam (1979).

αὐτὰρ ἔμ᾽ αὐτόν: cf. in the same position in the line Il. 1. 133 αὐτὰρ ἔμ᾽ αὔτως; also, although at line-beginning, note 20. 240 αὐτὰρ ἔμ᾽ Ἀγχίσης, of Aeneas being fathered by Anchises.

105 δηρὸν ἔϋ ζώειν καὶ ὁρᾶν φάος ἠελίοιο: 'to live and see the light', ζώειν/ζώει και ὁρᾶν/ὁρᾷ φάος ἠελίοιο is an old and well-established formula (Il. 18. 61, 18. 442, 24. 558, Od. 4. 540, 4. 833, 10. 498, 14. 44, 20. 207); see West (1988), 154 for the same idea in Rigvedic poetry. For δηρόν at line-beginning, cf. Il. 5. 120 δηρὸν ἔτ᾽ ὄψεσθαι λαμπρὸν φάος ἠελίοιο. Note later v. 256, where to be born is 'see the light of the sun' (only here and Apoll. 71).

ἔϋ ζώειν: cf. ἔϋ ζώ- at Od. 17. 423, 19. 79 and Apoll. 530. On the accentuation ἔϋ for ἐΰ see West (1998), Praefatio, pp. xx f. The MSS transmit εὐζώειν, an unparalleled verb in early Greek, corrected by Barnes (1711).

106 ὄλβιον: on the material connotations of this word, yet with religious overtones as well, see N. Richardson (1974), 314 on Dem. 480.

γήραος οὐδὸν ἱκέσθαι: for arrival at the 'threshold' of old age cf. Od. 23. 212 ἥβης ταρπῆναι καὶ γήραος οὐδὸν ἱκέσθαι and Od. 15. 246 ἵκετο γήραος οὐδόν; see also ἐπὶ γήραος οὐδῷ at Il. 22. 60, 24. 487, Od. 15. 348, Op. 331. The meaning of the phrase γήραος οὐδός is not entirely clear but probably 'the threshold consisting of old age', with old age understood as a transitional stage between life and death (see Kakridis 1971, 512–13); thus effectively 'old age' (cf. Wyatt 1969, 227–8). This is consistent with the fact that all three cases of ἱκέσθαι + acc. must mean 'to arrive at old age', i.e. the beginning (cf. Heubeck, OC iii. 336 on Od. 23. 212), while, with the exception of the ambiguous Od. 15. 348 (did Odysseus leave his father 'in old age' or 'on the threshold of old age'?), all instances of ἐπί + dat. clearly mean that one is already in, lit. upon, old age. The regular distinction elsewhere may suggest that at *Od*. 15. 348 too the sense is that Odysseus left his father when he was already old (cf. Falkner 1989, 33–4).

107–42. Aphrodite responds to Anchises. Her physical disguise, while certainly enchanting, has not convinced the hero of her mortality, and she is now forced to win him over with mendacious words. The speech is well organized and unfolds in three main phases: (i) vv. 108–16, direct rebuttal of Anchises' claims that she is a goddess and insistence upon her 'true' identity; (ii) vv. 117–30, explanation of how she came to arrive on the mountain; (iii) vv. 131–42, supplication of Anchises, with the request that he take her as his lawful wife (for the tripartite division cf. Podbielski 1971, 46). Her story is made more credible by an abundance of specific details (common also in other lies in epic; see examples below) and the content has been well calculated to persuade Anchises: she is a young maiden of nobility, in particular the daughter of a famous Phrygian king, and therefore the perfect match for a Trojan hero; she speaks the Trojan language because she was reared by a Trojan nurse; she was brought to the mountain by Hermes with the express purpose of being his wife, which gives divine sanction to the match, and explains both how she knows Anchises' name and how she appeared before him so suddenly; and she assures him that her parents will reward him generously for taking her as his wife. All in all a story difficult for a Trojan prince not to want to believe (on the persuasive content of the speech cf. de Jong 1989, 20, Smith 1981*a*, 49–54). The tailor-made quality of this lie (combining a broad range of epic material; see below *passim*) is spoken for by its distinctiveness from the tall tales told elsewhere in early poetry.

Perhaps the closest parallel is found in *Dem*. 118 ff., where Demeter, disguised as an old woman, tells a fictitious story to the daughters of Celeus in order to conceal her identity. It has a similar tripartite structure: Demeter begins by giving her identity (v. 122), explains in some detail (place-names etc.) how she arrived at Eleusis (vv. 123–34; beginning with νῦν as in *Aphr*. 117), and finally beseeches the girls to pity her and grant her work in their household (vv. 135–44). But, despite such skeletal similarities, there are significant differences. Demeter's tale is cast in a more traditional mould. Having been asked where she is from, Demeter gives a remarkable but plausible story of having been kidnapped in Crete by pirates and brought across the sea. The fictitious origin in Crete is a typical element in Odysseus' lies in the *Odyssey* (for this and more similarities see N. Richardson 1974, 188, on *Dem.* 120–5). In comparison, the content of Aphrodite's tale is far more original and exotic, and unlike Demeter's story it moves beyond what is plausible for a mortal, introducing an element of divine involvement. She does not claim to arrive by human hands but to have been whisked to the mountain by Hermes, and this fantastic quality is emphasized by the vivid description of her journey over four whole lines of the speech (v. 122–5). Unlike Demeter, Aphrodite has already been taken for a god and she must come up with something more original than pirates to satisfy Anchises!

From the point of view of Aphrodite's amorous intention, one can also compare the lies of Hera to win over Zeus in *Il.* 14. 300 ff. Sexuality and deception go together (cf. vv. 7 and 38, ἀπατάω), and it is a common element of epic seduction scenes that one must overcome the objections of the person one is seducing (see Sowa 1984, 83–7; cf. *Il.* 3. 441–6, *Od.* 23. 166 ff.). Like Aphrodite, Hera must explain her arrival on the mountain to Zeus, and she concocts a fantastic tale suitable for a goddess. She wants to head off to the ends of the earth in order to reconcile the feuding Ocean and Tethys, but she has come first to see Zeus lest he should be angry with her for leaving without a word; accordingly, her horses and chariot, which Zeus remarks she did not bring with her, are waiting at the foot of the mountain to take her away. The tale is certainly inventive and, as in *Aphr.*, the details are well suited to the situation: the mention of a feuding couple who keep away from love-making (*Il.* 14. 305–6) is the perfect thing to incite the already attracted Zeus to sleep with his wife (cf. Janko 1992, 200). However, in many respects, Hera's lie is again very different from the one in *Aphr.* Unlike Aphrodite, she is not trying to hide her identity, but only her intention. She is a god addressing a god, and the need for disguise and false identity in Aphrodite's speech seems far closer to the tales of Odysseus than to this one (cf. *Od.* 13. 256 ff., 14. 192 ff., 16. 61 ff., 19. 165 ff.; cf. also the story of Hermes to Priam at *Il.* 24. 389 ff.). Also, Hera's victim is far more compliant than Anchises; Zeus cannot wait to get into bed, and Hera daringly refuses his first assent to her secret wish out of a mock sense of decency (*Il.* 14. 329 ff.). Once again, it is the differences which stand out more than the similarities. For more discussion of these epic parallels see Luther (1935), 158–60, Reinhardt (1956), 10–12, Podbielski (1971) 46–53, Lenz (1975), 38–40, 126.

107–8. On the almost *verbatim* repetition of these lines later in the hymn see on *Aphr.* 191–9.

107 τὸν δ' ἠμείβετ' ἔπειτα: = *Il.* 5. 375/14. 193 (τὴν ...). The speech-introduction τὸν/τὴν δ' ἠμείβετ' ἔπειτα is formulaic and very common in Homer (47× *Il.*, 24× *Od.*), but never in Hesiod or the *Hymns* apart from the two occurrences in *Aphr.* (also at v. 191). Nor does it appear anywhere in later poetry.

Διὸς θυγάτηρ Ἀφροδίτη: see on *Aphr.* 81.

108 Ἀγχίση κύδιστε: see the metrically equivalent Ἀτρείδη κύδιστε *Il.* 1. 122, 2. 434. etc. On κύδιστος, only of Zeus and Agamemnon in Homer, see on *Aphr.* 42 on κυδίστην of Hera.

χαμαιγενέων ἀνθρώπων: the formula appears first in Hesiod; cf. *Th.* 879, *Dem.* 352, and later *Orac. Sib.* 1. 308; see also the separated noun–epithet combination at Thgn. 870 (v.l.) and Pi. *P.* 4. 98. It is a doublet of the more common καταθνητῶν ἀνθρώπων, used five times in *Aphr.* (cf. on *Aphr.* 3). N. Richardson (1974), 186 on *Dem.* 113 notes that in its other uses in early poetry χαμαιγενέων ἀνθρώπων 'is used of men in relation to the superior (and destructive) powers of the gods', though that particular connotation would make its use here rather odd in the mouth of Aphrodite in mortal disguise; especially as when she retakes her divine form later in the hymn καταθνητῶν ἀνθρώπων is substituted into the otherwise identical v. 192. That is, of course, unless the poet intends an ironic allusion to her divinity! The suggestion of Smith (1981*a*), 126 n. 79 that the later substitution of καταθνητῶν underlines his mortality at that point in the poem, while χαμαιγενέων rather 'connotes lowliness and ties with the earth', is attractive. Janko (1982), 25 instead thinks the two phrases are equivalent in meaning and suggests that this could be a 'clash of two "regional" formulae', χαμαιγενέων adopted here because of 'Hesiodic' influence.

109–10 οὔ τίς τοι θεός ... | ἀλλὰ καταθνητή τε: the particle ἀλλά in the second line contrasts with Aphrodite's first statement 'I am not a goddess ... but a mortal woman' (adversative ἀλλά is frequent after negative statements; see Denniston 1954, 1 and cf. *Il.* 1. 125 etc.). The interceding 'why do you liken me to the immortals' should therefore be understood in parenthesis (cf. VE 45, VB 13). Also on the structural level, note the balance in these lines, each with two halves clearly divided at the weak caesura (οὔ τίς τοι..., τι... | ἀλλὰ...γυνὴ δέ). There is alliteration as well with repetition of τ- and θ-. Smith (1981a), 50 points out that this once again directly contrasts the idea of mortal and immortal in the poem (see Introd., p. 11).

These lines are extremely similar to *Od.* 16. 187–8 οὔ τίς τοι θεός εἰμι· τί μ' ἀθανάτοισιν ἐΐσκεις; | ἀλλὰ πατὴρ τεός εἰμι, where Odysseus assures Telemachus that he is not a god. If the poet was thinking of that passage, there is a certain irony in the echo; Odysseus is for once telling the truth with these words, whereas in the mouth of Aphrodite they are full of deceit. Whether, however, there is direct imitation here is uncertain; the lines could be a formulaic response to being likened to a god (cf. Introd., p. 33).

110–11. On the later repetition of these lines in Anchises' response to Aphrodite see below on 143–54.

110 τε ... δέ: this sequence of particles, transmitted by all MSS, 'is often unnecessarily emended by editors' (Denniston 1954, 513; listed, however, under his irregular corresponsions); so Gemoll (1886), 269 proposed γε for τε, while almost a century before him Ilgen (1796) had played with the other half of the line by substituting τε for δέ (τε is a variant for δέ later at the almost identical v. 145). AHS and Humbert follow Gemoll, but as Denniston has since shown, the correspondence is common enough to be acceptable (in Homer *Il.* 23. 277; retained by VE, Càssola, and West 2003).

γυνὴ δέ με γείνατο μήτηρ: most similar is the exact opposite claim at *Il.* 21. 109 (= 1. 280 σε pro με) θεὰ δέ με γείνατο μήτηρ; but there is no particular reason to suppose direct imitation. The expression is formulaic; γείνατο μήτηρ is relatively common at line-end in Homer, where it is used of mortal mothers too (see *Il.* 3. 238, 5. 896, 6. 24, 13. 777, 19. 293, *Od.* 6. 25).

111 Ὀτρεύς ... ὀνομάκλυτος: despite being ὀνομάκλυτος, Otreus is mentioned only once outside *Aphr.* At *Il.* 3. 181–90 Priam briefly recalls having fought alongside the king of the Phrygians against the Amazons. The name is well chosen, distant enough not to raise suspicion, but at the same time a name which Anchises, a member of Priam's family, is sure to have heard. Also, an eastern princess is a good match for a Trojan hero (cf. on *Aphr.* 107–42). There is certainly no reason to follow Ferri (1960), 299–300 in understanding in the name a reference to the Etruscans, with whom he implausibly tries to connect this hymn (against Ferri's position see Lenz 1975, 125 n. 1, VE 46). The name is perhaps originally derived from Ὀτροία, a place on the Ascanian Lake known in later Bithynia (see von Kamptz 1982, 299), but whatever its origins, it is here most probably just a literary reminiscence.

ὀνομάκλυτος: this epithet is rare; outside *Aphr.* twice in early epic at *Il.* 22. 51 and *Herm.* 59 (although cf. ὄνομα κλυτόν, *Od.* 9. 364 and 19. 183), and then Pi. *Paian* 6. 123 (fr. 52f), Semon. fr. 7. 87 (κὠνομάκλυτον), Ibyc. fr. 306. 1, Simias fr. 1. 13 (*CA*) and Nonn. *D.* 3. 261. It may have a long history in the tradition, however; West (1988), 155 notes a correspondence to Rigvedic *nāma śrúityaṃ*. See also Tocharian A *ñom-klyu* and Tocharian B *ñem-kälywe* (Watkins 1995, 65).

All MSS here divide the adjective to ὄνομα κλυτός, although M reads ὀνομακλυτός at v. 146 (presumably here as well, but there is a lacuna in M at this point; cf. *Herm.* 59). M should be followed given the tradition at *Il.* 22. 51; a few MSS divide the word there as well, but the majority do not. The formation is paralleled by τοξόκλυτος B. *Epin.* 11. 39. The proper accentuation for the compound is proparoxytone, ὀνομάκλυτος (see West 1998, *Praefatio*, p. xxviii on δουρικλυτός).

εἴ που ἀκούεις: this would certainly be 'rhetorical doubt' in the mouth of Aphrodite (cf. Càssola 549), but then she is playing an innocent young maiden here, for whom a bit of uncertainty is not inappropriate. The phrase is all part of the act, yet touched with irony for the audience who know who the speaker really is (cf. VB 13). Cf. Eumaeus recounting his own history at *Od.* 15. 403 νῆσός τις Συρίη κικλήσκεται, εἴ που ἀκούεις and Penelope asking Telemachus for news of Odysseus at 17. 106 εἴ που ἄκουσας. On the particle που see on *Aphr.* 95.

112 ὃς πάσης Φρυγίης ... ἀνάσσει: for the phraseology cf. *Il.* 12. 242 ὃς πᾶσι ... ἀνάσσει and 13. 217 [Θοάς] ὃς πάσῃ Πλευρῶνι ... | Αἰτωλοῖσιν ἄνασσε; also [Hes.] fr. 23a. 32–3 [Ἔχεμος] ὃς πάσης Τεγέης ... | ἀφνειὸς ἤνασσε. In Homer, Phrygia is said to be by the Sangarios river, east of Troy (cf. *Il.* 3. 185–7, 16. 719).

εὐτειχήτοιο: this form is found only here; Homer has εὐτείχεος (*Il.* 1. 129 etc.) and εὐτειχής (*Il.* 16. 57). Hoekstra (1969), 12–13 follows Zumbach (1955), 26 in regarding the form as post-Homeric, as derived from τειχέω, which first appears at Hdt. 1. 99. 1 (cf. Heitsch 1965, 24–5). It is, however, formed to fit metre easily enough by association with adjectives such as ἐϋδμήτοιο [πόληος] (*Il.* 21. 516 etc.), or even εὐποιήτοιο (*Aphr.* 173 etc.) and does not need to be very late (see Janko 1982, 29). Phrygia is ἀμπελόεσσαν at *Il.* 3. 184, and nowhere else εὐτείχητος. VE 46 claims that its use here of a region rather than a city is 'awkward'; a bold claim for a *hapax*, which of a region must be taken to mean something approximating 'with well-walled cities'; cf. O'Sullivan, *LfgrE* s.v.: 'well-fortressed, i.e. well-furnished with fortifications.'

113–16. Aphrodite's explanation of her bilingualism is framed by repetition, which helps to highlight this striking detail: 113 γλῶσσαν δ' ὑμετέρην τε καὶ ἡμετέρην σάφα οἶδα ~ 116 ὡς δή τοι γλῶσσάν γε καὶ ὑμετέρην εὖ οἶδα (noted by Heitsch 1965, 37). The existence of languages other than that spoken by Achaeans is alluded to in Homer, apropos of the Trojans' allies (*Il.* 2. 803–4, 2. 867, 4. 437–8) and the Cretans (*Od.* 19. 175), but this is the first explicit reference in Greek literature to bilingualism. Mention of interaction with foreign languages and dialects becomes more common in later authors: so Solon (fr. 36. 11–12), Aeschylus (*Ch.* 563–4 etc.), and the other tragedians etc. (see further Werner 1983); note in later epic A.R. 4. 730–2, where Medea speaks Colchian with Circe (in indirect speech). This is not, however, any indication of a late date. The more unequivocal comments of Aphrodite are not a far step from the Homeric knowledge cited above, even if in Homer the Trojans themselves speak the same language as the Achaeans. Moreover, it is significant for the understanding of this passage that the detail of language already has a place in a lie in Homer; the reference to the many languages in Crete at *Od.* 19. 175 forms part of Odysseus' lie to Penelope about his Cretan origins. The mention of language here may be more elaborate, but just as in Odysseus' story, it is an element of the lie intended to persuade.

AHS 360 suggest that this knowledge of different tongues points to an Asiatic or Aeolic origin. This is a distinct possibility. Recent Phrygian inscriptions found at Daskylion near the Hellespont speak in favour of a long tradition of Greek and Phrygian interaction in the area (see Brixhe 2002, 1–2). Combined with other factors, there is a good case for *Aphr.* having been composed in northern Asia Minor (see Introd., pp. 49–50).

113 ὑμετέρην τε καὶ ἡμετέρην: none of the MSS has τε, but its insertion by Wolf (1807) is attractive. It avoids hiatus after καί, which is rare before words which did not originally begin with digamma (see West 1982, 15), and could easily have dropped out in the transmission.

σάφα οἶδα: the formula σάφα οἶδ- is at line-end elsewhere in early poetry only at *Od.* 17. 307, found more commonly in Homer at ‿‿3‿/‿‿5‿ (*Il.* 20. 201 etc.). Similarly, εὖ οἶδ- at v. 116 is elsewhere at line-end only at *Herm.* 467, in Homer at —3‿/—5‿ (*Il.* 7. 237 etc.; once εὖ οἶδ᾽ 4— *Od.* 23. 175). In this position, these may be later modifications from the seemingly more established line-ending σάφα εἰδώς (*Il.* 15. 632 etc. and at *Aphr.* 167) and εὖ εἰδώς (*Il.* 2. 718 etc.). Later, the phrase σάφα οἶδ- is at line-end several times in Gr. Naz. (*Carm.* I 2. 2. 363, *PG* 37. 607 etc.). The meaning is 'to know clearly' (see on *Aphr.* 167).

114–15 μεγάρῳ με τροφὸς τρέφεν ... | ... ἀτίταλλε: this is appropriate language for a nurse; so Eurycleia rearing Odysseus εὖ τρέφεν ἠδ᾽ ἀτίταλλε (*Od.* 19. 354). The verb ἀτιτάλλω, which is often joined with τρέφω, is almost always, when of humans, used of someone rearing a child who is not his own (see Moussy 1972, 161–5; the only exception in Homer is *Od.* 11. 250); see Phylas' adoption of Eudorus εὖ τρέφεν ἠδ᾽ ἀτίταλλε *Il.* 16. 191, Hera reared away from her parents by Ocean and Tethys οἵ μ᾽ ἐν σφοῖσι δόμοισιν εὖ τρέφον ἠδ᾽ ἀτίταλλον *Il.* 14. 202/303 or [Hes.] fr. 165. 6 κούρην δ᾽ ἐν μεγάροισιν εὖ τρέφεν ἠδ᾽ ἀτίταλλε (cf. also *Il.* 24. 60 and *Th.* 480). For a nurse rearing a child in a μέγαρον see Eurymedusa ἣ τρέφε Ναυσικάαν λευκώλενον ἐν μεγάροισιν *Od.* 7. 12, Eumaeus' nurse παῖδα ... ἐνὶ μεγάροις ἀτιτάλλω, or Demeter acting as nurse to Demophon ἔτρεφεν ἐν μεγάροις (*Dem.* 235; cf. also 164–5). As in the case of Nausicaa, this is the type of upbringing one would expect a young princess to have (cf. later A.R. 3. 528 where Medea is said to be reared in the μέγαρον of Aietes).

114 Τρῳάς: only *M* transmits the correct reading, while the other MSS have the obviously wrong Τρωός; the error may be due to association with τροφός. This nom. sing. is rare and attested elsewhere in poetry only at Ps.-Arist. fr. 640, no. 38.2 (Rose) and Ps.-Eur.

ap. Apsin., *Ars.* i. 394. 14 (Spengel), although see the graphically equivalent accusative plural Τρῳάς at *Il.* 5. 461 etc. (modifying a noun as here cf. acc.. plur. *Il.* 9. 139 and gen. sing. *Od.* 13. 263).

ἣ δὲ διάπρο: cf. *Il.* 5. 66, 7. 260, 20. 276 and *Meropis* fr. 4. 1 (Bernabé), of arrows and spears going 'right through' armour. This is the only temporal use of διάπρο (= διαμπερές 'throughout'); Heitsch (1975), 29 and Janko (1982), 157 follow Suhle (1878), 18 in saying that this meaning is known later in the Hellenistic period, but none states the example, which is not forthcoming; this seems to be its only occurrence. The meaning is not attested in Hsch. and other ancient lexica, and modern scholars are silent on the matter; LSJ s.v. διά says nothing, while Renehan (1982), 53 cites this instance in his supplementary note on adverbial διάπρο, but does not comment on the temporal use.

The MSS have διὰ πρό or διαπρό. Such adverbs and prepositions seem to have been treated together as compounds from an early stage; on this and the accentuation see West (1998), *Praefatio*, pp. xviii f.

115 σμικρὴν παῖδ': for a child qualified as small cf. Sappho fr. 49. 2 σμίκρα μοι πάϊς and Alcaeus fr. 75. 7–8 πάϊς | . . . σμῖκρ[ο]ς. See also Tyrt. fr. 10. 6 παισί τε σὺν μικροῖς and Thgn. 254 μικρὸν παῖδα.

φίλης παρὰ μητρὸς ἑλοῦσα: for the phrasing see *Od.* 15. 127 φίλῃ παρὰ μητρί and *Th.* 914 ἥρπασεν ἧς παρὰ μητρός; cf. also *Th.* 932 παρὰ μητρὶ φίλῃ.

116 γε: the MSS all transmit the nonsensical τε, for which Hermann's (1806) γε has been adopted universally by editors. Only VB 13–14 argues that γε 'lends unsuitable stress to γλῶσσαν'. There is certainly emphasis conveyed by γε, 'I know *even* your language' (for 'even' cf. Denniston 1954, 116), but it is unclear why this should be unsuitable. Aphrodite is summing up a point about language which she has spent the previous three lines making, and the particle focusing γλῶσσαν is very apt. If τε καί was originally in *Aphr.* 113 (see ad loc.), its proximity may have led to the error; Ruijgh (1971), 844 even explains the variant τε for γε at *Od.* 22. 167 by recollection of the similar yet distant 18. 83, although the corruption is in any case an easy one.

117–29. The story of Aphrodite's abduction by Hermes is a central part of her tale. The introduction of a divinity into the equation provides an explanation for her sudden arrival in front of Anchises and her knowledge of his name, while intimating that the match is 'made in heaven' (cf. on *Aphr.* 107–42). It also gives Aphrodite the direct motive she needs to request marriage from Anchises. The episode can be divided into three parts according to content: (i) vv. 117–20: explanation of the circumstances of the abduction; (ii) vv. 121–5: vivid description of the journey itself; (iii) vv. 126–30: report of the information imparted by Hermes and her arrival.

The depiction of a young girl playing with her companions (sometimes in a chorus) is a typical prelude to divine rape: the involvement of Hermes is similar to *Il.* 16. 179 ff., where the god falls in love with Polymele after seeing her in a chorus of Artemis, and then sneaks into her chamber to rape her (on this cf. on *Aphr.* 118); also, at *Dem.* 2 ff. Persephone plays with her companions before being abducted by Hades. Later too, Europa is abducted by Zeus while she is playing with her companions at Mosch. *Eur.* 28 ff. (cf. [Hes.] fr. 140), and see Boreas and Oreithyia at A.R. 1. 213 ff. On these motifs cf. N. Richardson (1974), 140–2. It is striking here then that Hermes does not whisk this stunning beauty away for himself, but for the benefit of Anchises (cf. Reinhardt 1956, 11); he is supposedly acting in his role of messenger, as in the affair of Zeus and Ganymedes later in the hymn (vv. 212–13), but it is Zeus who does the actual abducting on that occasion (vv. 202–3). Gods steal away young maidens in epic to rape them, not to give them to someone else; closest to this is E. *Hel.* 44–6, where Helen claims that Hermes abducted her at the behest of Zeus in order to keep her pure for Menelaus, sending a replica of her to Troy instead. The image created by the supposed altruistic abduction is a rather awkward mix between divine rape and the divinely encouraged romance of Nausicaa and Odysseus in *Od.* 6. There, after receiving instructions from Athena in a dream (vv. 25 ff.), Nausicaa sets out with her companions. She plays ball with them and leads them in song 'just like Artemis' (vv. 99 ff.) before her famous romantic encounter with Odysseus. Abduction is of course not an issue on that occasion, in what is a more innocent meeting of two mortals. The mixture between these two types of encounters here adds sharp irony to Aphrodite's deceitful words, for while she is kindling romance in the mind of Anchises, her story contains undertones of divine rape.

117 ἀνήρπαξε: the typical word for abduction, ἁρπάζω occurs several times in the poem, both in its plain form and in the compound ἀναρπάζω (see v. 121 ἥρπαξε, v. 203 ἥρπασεν, v. 208 ἀνήρπασε, v. 218 ἥρπασεν). VE 48 and VB 14 think that the compound ἀνα- implies an abduction through the air, but there is no such connotation in the form; cf. the abduction of Eumaeus' nurse by pirates at *Od.* 15. 427 ἀλλά μ' ἀνήρπαξαν Τάφιοι ληϊστορες ἄνδρες (across the sea). The lack of difference in the essential meaning is also indicated by the alternation between the compound and the simple form here to describe the same abduction (vv. 117, 121), as again later in the Ganymedes episode (vv. 203, 208). The compound may convey a slight nuance of emphasis 'snatched me *up*', but any difference in sense is surely secondary to its role as a metrical convenience.

χρυσόρραπις Ἀργειφόντης: the name–epithet combination (also at v. 121) is relatively rare; twice in early epic at *Od.* 10. 331 and *Dem.* 335 (acc.), and then once later at *Orph. A.* 137.

For the epithet χρυσόρραπις 'of the golden wand' (cf. *Od.* 5. 87, 10. 277 etc.) see the gift which Apollo gives Hermes at *Herm.* 529–30 ῥάβδον | χρυσείην τριπέτηλον, known as his κηρύκειον (caduceus) at *Il.* 24. 343 and *Od.* 24. 2. His wand has magic powers, as well as being a herald's sceptre and a shepherd's staff (see N. Richardson 1974, 265; 1993, 308–9). Ἀργειφόντης was understood by several ancient sources as 'slayer of Argos', in reference to Hermes' slaying of Argos in the myth of Io; as a popular etymology alongside ἀνδρειφόντης 'man-killer' (*Il.* 2. 651 etc.) this may well be how Homer and the poet of *Aphr.* understood it, although its actual origins are obscure. See the discussion of S. West, *OC* i. 79, who lists the many modern suggestions: most notably 'dog-slayer' (defended by West 1978, 368–9 and others), but also 'shining in splendour', 'shining at Argos', 'killer at Argos' (to her bibliography add Davis 1953, who proposes 'snake-slayer', from ἀργῆς 'snake' and Athanassakis 1989, 39 who also defends 'dog-slayer'); she may well be right in following Chantraine (1935a), 79 that this is 'une vieille épithète préhellénique devenue inintelligible de bonne heure'; at least the ancients were no less divided as to its meaning (see the most recent discussion by Lightfoot 1999, 197–8 on Parth. fr. 38).

118. This line is almost identical with *Il.* 16. 183 ἐν χορῷ Ἀρτέμιδος χρυσηλακάτου κελαδεινῆς, where Hermes espies Polymele in dance before raping her (cf. on *Aphr.* 117–29). The similarity of these two lines, combined with the presence of Hermes in both episodes, makes a possible case for imitation of the Homeric passage, although one cannot rule out the possibility that the language was established in a traditional account of Hermes' rape of Polymele. The contracted genitive χοροῦ (not in Homer, where once χοροῖο *Il.* 3. 394, or Hesiod) is another possible case of post-Homeric innovation by declension. On Artemis' connection with the choruses of young girls cf. on *Aphr.* 19.

119–23. Note the repetition of πολλ- at the beginning of these lines; v. 119 πολλαί, v. 122 πολλά, v. 123 πολλήν (the alliteration on π- at line-beginning is also effected by παίζομεν in v. 120, which almost creates two doublets separated by ἔνθεν in v. 121, πολλαί/παίζομεν><πολλά/πολλήν). These combine with another expression of size in the passage, ὅμιλος ἀπείριτος v. 120, to lend an emphatic sense of grandeur to the scene, and perhaps even a 'naïve excitement' in the mouth of Aphrodite (Smith 1981a, 52).

119–20. Similarities of diction between these lines and the episode of dancing depicted on Achilles' shield at *Il.* 18. 590–606 (ἀλφεσίβοιαι ~ 18. 593; v. 120 ~ 18. 603) suggest traditional language for dance.

119 νύμφαι: here 'young women' and not the goddesses whom Anchises earlier evoked in his prayer. Cf. VE 48 and see *LfgrE* s.v. for examples of the meaning.

ἀλφεσίβοιαι: only here and at *Il.* 18. 593, both times of παρθένοι who are dancing. The first part of the adjective is derived from the root of ἀλφάνω 'to earn', thus 'cattle-earning' (cf. M. W. Edwards 1991, 229 and *LfgrE* s.v.: 'Rinder erbringend'). It refers to the marriage-gifts (ἔδνα) of cattle which a father received from a suitor (on this practice in Homer see Finley 1955, 177–87, Snodgrass 1974, 115–22 and Hoces de la Guardia y Bermejo 1990, 209–18). Love, dance, and marriage go together: in a later dialogue περὶ ὀρχήσεως, Lucian has Lycinus say that dance came into being in most ancient times, appearing together with Eros (*Salt.* 7 Ἔρωτι συναναφανεῖσαν, cf. on *Aphr.* 117–29 on the connection between the chorus and rape). Female dance was often connected with rites of initiation, where the participants were at the age of puberty preparing for marriage (see Calame 1977, i. 63 *et passim*); T. S. Eliot accordingly writes in his *Four Quartets* (*East Coker,* Stanza I) 'And see them dancing around the bonfire | The association of man and woman | In daunsinge, signifying matrimonie' (this line has as its source *The Boke Named the Gouernour* Bk 1, Ch.21, written in 1531 by Eliot's ancestor Sir Thomas Elyot of East Coker).

The adjective is later applied by Aeschylus to water (*Supp.* 855 ἀλφεσίβοιον ὕδωρ), which 'yields cattle' in the sense of nourishing them. See also the proper name Ἀλφεσίβοια (Theoc. *Id.* 3. 45 etc.), the daughter of Bias and Pero; she is so named after the history of her mother, whose father would only accept the suitor who recovered his own mother's herds from Phylacus (see further Gow ii. 73–4).

120 ἀμφὶ δ' ὅμιλος ἀπείριτος ἐστεφάνωτο: for the phraseology cf. *Il.* 15. 153 ἀμφὶ δέ μιν θυόεν νέφος ἐστεφάνωτο, *Od.* 10. 195 νῆσος τὴν πέρι πόντος ἀπείριτος ἐστεφάνωται, *Sc.* 204 περὶ δ' ὄλβος ἀπείριτος ἐστεφάνωτο (all noted by Heitsch 1965, 36 n. 1). For the idea of a crowd surrounding dancers, see *Il.* 18. 603 πολλὸς δ' ἱμερόεντα χορὸν περιίσταθ' ὅμιλος (cf. as well *Il.* 24. 712 ἀμφίσταθ' ὅμιλος and *Od.* 8. 109 πουλὺς ὅμιλος). On the circular structure of a lyric chorus see Calame (1977), i. 77–84. The adjective ἀπείριτος appears only the once in Homer, but twice more in Hesiod, *Th.* 109 (πόντος) and 878 (γαῖαν). Its use here with ἐστεφαν- seems traditional (see West 1966*a*, 397).

ἐστεφάνωτο: E reads the plural ἐστεφάνωντο, which VE 49 is surely incorrect in adopting as the *lectio difficilior*, by *constructio ad sententiam*; his parallel of ὣς φάσαν ἡ πληθύς (*Il.* 2. 278) is not convincing for ὅμιλος, which is treated as singular in Homer (*Il.* 18. 603 etc.). The plural probably sneaked in after the preceding plural nouns (νύμφαι καὶ παρθένοι).

121. The poet returns to the focal point of abduction through repetition of v. 117 (νῦν δέ μ' ἀνήρπαξε . . . | ἔνθεν μ' ἥρπαξε . . .), as a means of transition to the description of the journey.

122–5. Hermes travels across the cultivated land of humans, and the wild earth where the beasts roam. Such description of a divine journey is paralleled in Homer: the narrative of Poseidon's journey across the sea at *Il.* 13. 27–31 is no less elaborate, including the mention of sea creatures which accompany him on his route (Aphrodite mentions animals here too, which, apart from adding detail, serves to recall the truth of her actual journey across Ida at vv. 69–74; cf. Smith 1981*a*, 52); Hera travels along the snowy peaks of the Thracian mountains and then across the sea at *Il.* 14. 225–30; and Hermes himself swoops down from heaven before travelling across the sea like a bird at *Od.* 5. 49–54. The details are certainly new (the seemingly standard route across the sea in such fabulously long journeys would clearly not have been appropriate for a trip from Phrygia to Troy), but there is no reason to assume that the level of detail here is a departure from epic style towards the picturesque description of lyric poetry (so VE 49), even if one might associate the decorated quality of such epic passages with Romantic lyric (cf. Kirk 1962, 172–3).

Scholars have assumed that this is a journey high up through the air (N. Richardson 1974, 278, VE 49, VB 14–15), comparing in particular *Dem.* 380–3, where Hermes and Persephone travel high above the mountain-peaks. Now, in *Aphr.* Hermes is clearly covering a lot of distance (πολλά ... πολλήν ...) and must therefore be 'flying' along at an incredible speed; but exactly how high he is from the ground is far from evident. In *Dem.* it is said that Persephone and Hermes are above the ἄκριες of the mountains, cutting through the ἠέρα: compare the first part of Hera's journey at *Il.* 14. 225–30, specifically said to be across mountains (ὄρεα ... | ἀκροτάτας κορυφάς), or the description of the flight of Zeus' eagle at B. *Epin.* 5. 16–30, which travels through the αἰθέρα and above κορυφαί; cf. Ibyc. PMGF S223a ii. 7 βαθ[ὺν ἀ]έρα τάμνων, probably part of an account of the abduction of Ganymedes in a love–poem to Gorgias (Ibyc. fr. 289a; see Barron 1984, 16–17, Bowra 1961, 259). On the similarities of these lyric passages to *Dem.* see N. Richardson (1974), 279–81. Later see the journey of Eros at A.R. 3. 159–63 οὐρέων ... κορυφαί; on Eros' 'panoramic' view there see Campbell (1983,) 21–2. In contrast, things in *Aphr.* remain remarkably grounded; Hermes simply travels ἐπὶ ἔργα, and there are no explicit indications of height (mountain-peaks, aither). The impression is thus far more similar to *Il.* 13. 27–31, where Poseidon drives his chariot ἐπὶ κύματα; there the god is not high up in the air but skimming along the surface of the ocean, presumably at a distance above the water just great enough for the axles of his chariot not to get wet (vv. 29–30 τοί τ' ἐπέτοντο | ῥίμφα μάλ', οὐδ' ὑπένερθε διαίνετο χάλκεος ἄξων; Janko 1992, 45 on 13. 27–31, thinks that this does not indicate actual flight, but just speed, in which case the horses are moving so fast that they do not touch the water). So too Hermes skims ἐπὶ κῦμα after descending from the heavens at *Od.* 5. 50–1 (cf. Hainsworth, *OC* i. 259); perhaps also Hera (ἐπὶ πόντον ἐβήσετο, *Il.* 14. 229) after a jaunt in the mountains. Later at Mosch. *Eur.* 113 ff., Zeus even takes Europa on this style of journey after he abducts her; in the form of a bull he travels ἐπ' εὐρέα κύματα (v. 114), managing to do so with dry hooves (χηλαῖς ἀβρέκτοισιν; for an analysis of that episode see Campbell 1991, 102 ff.). The switch from skimming over the sea to skimming over the land is not great, and if this is what the poet had in mind here, it has the advantage of making Aphrodite's statement οὐδὲ ποσὶ ψαύειν δόκεον φυσίζοον αἴης at v. 125 far more explicable (cf. ad loc.).

122 πολλὰ δ' ἐπ' ἤγαγεν: cf. the metrically equivalent *Il.* 23. 705 πολλὰ δ' ἐπίστατο ἔργα. The MSS read the compound ἐπήγαγεν, which makes no sense here, corrected by Barnes (1711).

ἔργα: on the repetition of this word in the hymn see on *Aphr.* 1. The meaning here 'cultivated farm land' is common; see *LfgrE* s.v.

123 πολλήν: it is not surprising to find nouns for land or sea omitted (see a list at AHS 361; of land, *Il.* 14. 308, *Od.* 20. 98, *Dem.* 43, *Apoll.* 529). Nonetheless, the sudden switch to the fem. sing. here with γαῖαν understood is rather inelegant after ἔργα in the previous line.

ἄκληρον: uniquely here of land 'unallotted'/'unowned'. The adjective appears only once in Homer at *Od.* 11. 490, of a poor man (i.e. 'with no allotment'), and then not until A. *Eu.* 352, again of poverty. At E. *Tr.* 32 it is used of the Trojan women who have not been allotted to a new Greek master. Cf. also πολυκλήρων ἀνθρώπων at *Od.* 14. 211.

ἄκτιτον: although it appears only here in Greek literature, the adjective is ancient, known in Mycenaean *a-ki-ti-to* with the same meaning 'uncultivated'. See Ruijgh (1967), 364–5 and Pavese (1974), 76 who derive it from the athematic stem *κτει-, meaning 'to cultivate or to build'. Cf. ἐϋκτίμενος, which in Homer means both 'well-built' (*Il.* 2. 570) and 'well-cultivated' (*Od.* 9. 130, 24. 226, 336)—Ruijgh points out that the latter must have been the original sense—and see also ἐΰκτιτον Αἰπύ (*Il.* 2. 592).

124 ὠμοφάγοι: 'carnivorous', the adjective adds a rather exotic flavour. It is at this position in the line at *Il.* 11. 479 of mountain jackals and 16. 157 of wolves, and elsewhere of lions (15. 592, 5. 782,

7. 256); but never in the *Od.* or Hesiod. Although in this case it is with the generic θήρ, one naturally thinks of the lions and leopards 'insatiable for deer' which Aphrodite encountered above at vv. 70–1. See Thgn. 542, where it is used of the Centaurs, and Ibyc. *PMGF* 321. 4, where it is used of fish; it grimly describes the 'delight' of Bacchic ritual at E. *Ba.* 139. Theoc. later uses it of a lion in the mountains at *Id.* 13. 62.

κατὰ σκιόεντας ἐναύλους: repeated from v. 74, κατὰ σκιόεντας ἐναύλους strengthens the allusion to Aphrodite's actual approach to Anchises, when she caused all sorts of wild animals to sleep together in the shady haunts of the mountain.

φοιτῶσι: used of frequent or habitual action; see *Hy.* 26. 8 δὴ τότε φοιτίζεσκε καθ' ὑλήεντας ἐναύλους where it is used of Dionysus roaming in valleys (cf. of birds at *Od.* 2. 182 or the nymphs at *Hy.* 19. 20; later of foxes at Theoc. *Id.* 5. 113). There may also be some sexual implication; it describes the sexual intercourse of Zeus and Hera at *Il.* 14. 296 εἰς εὐνὴν φοιτῶντε (for later examples of this meaning see LSJ s.v.).

125 οὐδὲ ποσὶ ψαύειν δόκεον: M alone reads the future infinitive ψαύσειν, the other MSS the present tense. The future, which would mean 'I thought I should never touch the ground [again]' (preferred by AHS and Càssola), makes for a rather odd expression (although VE 50 thinks that it fits as a description of a long journey, πολλά . . . | πολλή; cf. above on 119–23). VB 14–15 recognizes the awkwardness of such a statement, but still prefers the future, instead with the sense 'I did not think that I should touch the earth with my feet there [in the wilderness described at vv. 123–4]'; but this is rather forced; the expression refers to land generally, not to a specific region over which she passed. The most natural sense is provided by the present tense 'I thought that my feet were not touching the ground' (adopted by Humbert and West 2003). Not touching the earth with one's feet during a journey is paralleled by *Il.* 14. 227–8 σεύατ' ἐφ' ἱπποπόλων Θρηκῶν ὄρεα νιφόεντα | ἀκροτάτας κορυφάς, <u>οὐδὲ χθόνα μάρπτε ποδοῖιν</u>, where Hera's feet do not touch the ground as she travels over the mountains. In *Aphr.* of course it is an impression rather than a statement of fact, implying that this was a journey across the earth rather than through the air; 'I was travelling over the earth, but I did not think that I was touching the ground with my feet' (cf. Erichthonius' mares, *Il.* 20. 226–9, which move so nimbly across the tops of flowers that the plants remain unharmed). This has formed the main objection to the present tense for those who insist that this must be a journey high up through the air (so AHS 361, VB 14), but a sort of skimming along the earth in fact seems to be what is envisaged here (see on *Aphr.* 122–5). The impression is what one might expect from a mortal companion on such a journey, and Aphrodite is making a clever play at mortal bewilderment.

δόκεον: all MSS transmit the contracted form ἐδόκουν. The meaning of δοκέω here 'to think' (frequent in later Greek), although less common than 'to seem' in early poetry, is paralleled at *Il.* 7. 192, *Od.* 18. 382, and *Herm.* 208 (cf. *LfgrE* s.v., Kirk 1990, 259). Accordingly, the sense cannot be considered Attic as Zumbach (1955), 61 claimed (cf. Janko 1982, 171, who points out that the meaning 'to think' is well-attested also in the Ionic Greek of Herodotus). The contracted form ἐδόκουν certainly is Attic (ε + ο = ου is Attic only; see Buck 1955, 40), but it could easily be due to later scribal interference (cf. the similar case υἷας v. 51 and see Introd., p. 45). Given the absence of any sign in *Aphr.* of Attic influence, it seems reasonable to follow West (2003) in adopting La Roche's δόκεον (cited ibid.); the form is not in Homer but cf. in later epic A.R. 4. 666. Also possible would be ἐδόκεον, the Ionic form used commonly by Herodotus.

φυσιζόου αἴης: see the nom. φυσίζοος αἶα at *Il.* 3. 243 and *Od.* 11. 301 (once later in Mesomedes *AP* 14. 78. 4), and cf. at line-beginning γῆ φυσίζοος *Il.* 21. 63. Given its short vowel, the second half of the adjective -ζόος is most probably derived originally from ζειά 'wheat' ('wheat-producing') rather than ζωή ('life-producing')—ζωή and its cognates have a long vowel; see *Dictionnaire* and Frisk s.v. ζειαί, Kirk (1985), 300–1 and cf. the comparable ζείδωρος ἄρουρα, *Il.* 2. 548 etc.—although see Floyd (1989), 339–40 who argues for a derivation from ζω-. The latter was at least a popular etymology amongst the ancients (by the time of A. *Supp.* 584 it had so much lost any sense of 'wheat-producing' that it is used of Zeus, and cf. Hsch. s.v.: ἡ τὰ πρὸς τὸ ζῆν φύουσα) and, regardless of true etymology, this may well be how Homer and the poet of *Aphr.* understood the word. Floyd (ibid. 337–42) is justified in thinking that the epithet is used to contrast life and death in Homer (i.e. the 'life-producing' earth holds the 'dead'

Dioscuri at *Il.* 3. 243; cf. N. Richardson 1993, 58), although his claims for such a contrast in *Aphr.* (because Hermes is also the guide of the dead and Anchises later says that he is willing to go to Hades after he has slept with Aphrodite) are unconvincing. All MSS except L have φυσιζώον, a variant reading also at *Il.* 21. 63; it is a form in later Greek, which could easily have been substituted by a scribe.

126–7 παραὶ λέχεσιν καλέεσθαι | κουριδίην ἄλοχον: Hoekstra (1969), 41 calls the expression παραὶ λέχεσιν καλέεσθαι (possibly also at [Hes.] fr. 22. 9) 'very queer', suggesting modification by transposition of line-end παραὶ λεχέεσσι κλιθῆναι *Od.* 1. 366/18. 213, 'or something like it'; this is made probable by nu mobile making position in λέχεσιν (the form is not in Homer, who has λέχεσσι/ λεχέεσσι; cf. on *Aphr.* 54 ὄρεσιν, 67 νέφεσιν and see Janko 1982, 155). Also, παραὶ λέχεσιν does not fit naturally into the sentence in *Aphr.* At *Od.* 1. 366 the suitors desire 'to lie beside [Penelope] in bed', with παραί an adverb and λεχέεσσι a local dative (cf. S. West, *OC* i. 121 ad loc.). The same must be true in *Aphr.*, rendering the passage 'and he claimed that I should be called the young wife of Anchises, next to him in bed' (see Kamerbeek 1967, 391–2); it is grammatically possible, but this is not smooth Greek (cf. Càssola 550, 'stilisticamente infelice'). In a Homericizing mood, van Herwerden (1878), 198 conjectured Ἀγχίσῃ . . . κλινέεσθαι. Janni (1967), 13–15 suggests that the poet of *Aphr.* misunderstood παραί as a preposition when adapting the earlier phrase, which can only mean 'next to' and not 'in bed' as would be required; but there is no particular reason to assume such a misunderstanding. For the genesis of this phrase, AHS 361 point also to *Od.* 7. 313 ἐμὸς γαμβρὸς καλέεσθαι; cf. later on 148 ἐμὴ δ' ἄλοχος κεκλήσεαι.

126 φάσκε . . . καλέεσθαι: for the verb φάσκω + fut. infin. cf. *Od.* 10. 331 φάσκεν ἐλεύσεσθαι, where Circe recalls Hermes' prophecy about the coming of Odysseus.

127 κουριδίην ἄλοχον: 'young bride'; the formula occurs several times in Homer (*Il.* 1. 114, 7. 392, etc.), always of a mortal wife. Only in *Hy.* 6. 17 is it used of a goddess, Aphrodite herself whom the gods would all like to take as a wife after seeing her beauty! Kirk (1985), 65 notes that it often has 'an affectionate and pathetic ring', which would be appropriate to the emotional plea made here. Primarily though it implies the proper legal status of 'wedded wife', for which

Aphrodite will soon ask in detail (on the sense of 'wedded wife' cf. *LfgrE* s.v. κουρίδιος; also of husbands, *Il.* 5. 414 etc.).

ἀγλαὰ τέκνα τεκεῖσθαι: Hermes makes a standard claim of activity for a future wife; see τέκνα τεκέσθαι at *Od.* 22. 324 (Odysseus speaking of Leodes' desire for Penelope to be his wife) and *Dem.* 136 (Demeter wishing the daughters of Celeus children in their future marriages); cf. also [Hes.] fr. 31. 4 ἵν' ἀγλαὰ τέκνα τ[εκ. The audience of course know exactly what child will come of the union.

The *hapax* future form τεκεῖσθαι, otherwise τέξεσθαι (*Il.* 19. 99 and *Apoll.* 101), is remarkable, but not a monstrosity worth deleting in favour of τεκέσθαι (as Kamerbeek 1967, 388). Zumbach (1955), 31 notes the linguistic parallel ἔπεσον ~ πεσέεσθαι (cf. Càssola 127, Janko 1982, 272, who parallel *Il.* 2. 366 μαχέονται ~ 20. 26 μαχεῖται for the contraction). Its formation here from τέκνα τεκέσθαι was probably influenced by the appropriateness of the future infinitive in the recollection of a prophecy, especially after καλέεσθαι in v. 126 (see ad loc. for *Od.* 10. 331). Hoekstra (1969), 15 points to similar 'formulaic conjugation' in Homer, such as *Od.* 18. 146 δηρὸν ἀπέσσεσθαι ~ 19. 302 δηρὸν ἀπεσσεῖται, thus making it very doubtful that this artificial form can be considered evidence for a later stage of composition (as Hoekstra himself seems inclined to think).

128–9 αὐτὰρ ἐπεὶ δὴ δεῖξε ... | ... ἀπέβη: cf. *Od.* 5. 241–2 αὐτὰρ ἐπεὶ δὴ δεῖξ' ὅθι δένδρεα μακρὰ πεφύκει, | ἡ μὲν ἔβη πρὸς δῶμα Καλυψώ.

δεῖξε καὶ ἔφρασεν: 'after he showed [the way] and pointed out [my future with you]'; the sense seems to be similar to *Od.* 12. 25–6 αὐτὰρ ἐγὼ δείξω ὁδὸν ἠδὲ ἕκαστα | σημανέω, where Circe tells Odysseus about his future journey (cf. VE 51 'place ... and what has been told'). VB 15 suggests that δείκνυμι refers to the way (ὁδός) and φράζω to the place where Anchises is (χῶρος; cf. *Il.* 23. 138, *Od.* 11. 22 and 14. 3), but there is nothing in the preceding lines to lead one to this distinction. Rather, Aphrodite has said that Hermes carried her to Ida and prophesied her future. Others have taken both verbs to refer pleonastically to the prophecy (cf. Humbert 1936 'après m'avoir indiqué sa pensée', and *LfgrE* s.v. δείκνυμι: 'Bezug wahrscheinlich auf vorgehende Rede: mein künftiges Schicksal erklärt hatte'; of δείκνυμι alone, or both verbs together?), but then this ignores the journey. Given what precedes, δεῖξε seems to refer most naturally to the journey (ὁδόν) and ἔφρασεν to the prophecy. It is not surprising to find φράζω, originally 'to show', connected with speech (cf. *Od.* 1. 272–3 αὔριον εἰς ἀγορήν καλέσας ἥρωας Ἀχαιούς | μῦθον πέφραδε πᾶσι). Fournier (1946), 51 thinks that this passage represents a stage in the development from 'to show' towards 'to say' in δείκνυμι, unjustifiably if it refers primarily to the journey (in any case it seems to have developed towards this sense quite early; cf. *Od.* 12. 25 and *Op.* 502 with West 1978 ad loc.).

For δείκνυμι and φράζω used one after the other to show two different things cf. *Dem.* 474–6 δ[εῖξε . . . | . . . δρησμοσύνην θ' ἱερῶν καὶ ἐπέφραδεν ὄργια πᾶσι.

ἔφρασεν ἤτοι: Hoekstra (1969), 23 suggests that nu mobile obviating hiatus here may show innovation.

ἤτοι ὅ γ'. . . αὐτάρ: 'he left . . . . while I . . .'; on ἤτοι as a preparative particle in epic, a slightly stronger equivalent of μέν, see Ruijgh (1981). VB 15 lists examples of similar corresponsion with αὐτάρ in Homer. Cf. below on 202 ἤτοι μέν. On the accentuation of ἤτοι see Denniston (1954), 553.

129 ἀθανάτων μετὰ φῦλ' ἀπέβη: the expression θεῶν φῦλ-ον/α is almost always used of going to join the gods; see West (1966*a*), 224, N. Richardson (1974), 160. Most similar to this line is *Op.* 199 ἀθανάτων μετὰ φῦλον. Also see Hermes rushing off at *Od.* 5. 148 ὣς ἄρα φωνήσας ἀπέβη κρατὺς Ἀργειφόντης.

κρατὺς Ἀργειφόντης: κρατύς 'strong/mighty' appears to be an ancient relic, found only as an epithet of Hermes (elsewhere at *Il.* 16. 181, 24. 345, *Od.* 5. 49, 5. 148, *Dem.* 346, 377, *Herm.* 294, 414); cf. Breuil (1989), 40–1. For Ἀργειφόντης see on *Aphr.* 117.

130 αὐτὰρ ἐγώ . . . κρατερὴ δέ μοι ἔπλετ' ἀνάγκη: cf. *Od.* 10. 273 αὐτὰρ ἐγὼν εἶμι· κρατερὴ δέ μοι ἔπλετ' ἀνάγκη, of Odysseus' necessity to go to Circe's house; also *Il.* 6. 458 κρατερὴ δ' ἐπικείσετ' ἀνάγκη, of Andromache as an imagined captive, of which Kirk (1990), 222 ad loc. thinks *Od.* 10. 273 δέ μοι ἔπλετ' 'is an awkward adjustment' (for 'strong necessity' note as well *Th.* 517, and see West 1966*a*, 311 ad loc. for more parallels). On ἀνάγκη as a binding force see N. Richardson (1974), 227–8 with bibliography.

The unwillingness of Persephone to be abducted by Hades is a recurring motif in *Dem.*; 19, 30, 72, 344, 413, 432 (cf. Moschus' playful reversal of this motif at *Eur.* 14, where Europa is pulled in her dream οὐκ ἀέκουσαν; on which see Campbell 1991, 24–5). Now, Aphrodite does not actually use the term 'unwilling' here, but this nonetheless seems to be part of what she is playing at with her claim of ἀνάγκη. The two ideas are explicitly linked on other occasions: when Demeter tells Helios that her daughter was abducted unwillingly at *Dem.* 72, the phrase she uses is ἀέκουσαν ἀνάγκῃ; she employs the same phrase of her abduction by pirates at v. 124; Penelope completes her web for the suitors οὐκ ἐθέλουσ᾽ ὑπ᾽ ἀνάγκης, *Od.* 2. 110/19. 156/24. 146; and again see Andromache at *Il.* 6. 458 πόλλ᾽ ἀεκαζομένη ... ἀνάγκῃ (note later Musae. 226 ἀλλήλων ἀέκοντες ἐνοσφίσθησαν ἀνάκγῃ). In the case of a young maiden, compulsion in the face of abduction is just the thing to appeal to Anchises' sense of propriety. It serves as well to raise the level of pathos in her situation as suppliant; again, Demeter appeals to 'necessity' as a suppliant before the daughters of Celeus (*Dem.* 124), and Odysseus raises the point of his 'neccessity' as a beggar at *Od.* 15. 310–11.

Moreover, the term probes below the surface of Aphrodite's disguise, acting as a delicate bridge between fiction and reality. By presenting herself as a captive of Hermes, the messenger of Zeus, Aphrodite implies quite directly that her compulsion as a young maiden is brought about by Zeus, whose name she invokes in the next line, ἀλλά σε πρὸς Ζηνὸς γουνάζομαι (Zeus is behind Persephone's abduction in *Dem.* as well; on his involvement there see N. Richardson 1974, 138). This is ironic for the audience which knows that, as a goddess, her desire for Anchises has in fact been brought about by the will of Zeus (see vv. 45 and 53; cf. Lenz 1975, 39). And the irony may go deeper. De Jong (1989), 21 suggests that Aphrodite herself is not aware that Zeus is behind the affair. This is not clear either way at this point, but if she is not, her claim of ἀνάγκη and the mention of Zeus' name in the following line underline her own misunderstanding in this mendacious affair.

Across these various levels of narrative, the mention of ἀνάγκη seems also to reflect the ambiguity of Aphrodite's sexual desire here. H. Parry (1986), 257 ff. goes too far in connecting this mention of ἀνάγκη, and the later statement that the union is brought about θεῶν ἰότητι καὶ αἴσῃ (v. 166), generically with 'the pivot between the male's pre-coital and post-coital experience of *eros*': first of all the experience is not just male—the ἀνάγκη at least is Aphrodite's; cf. de

Jong 1989, 21 n. 26—and then not all love-affairs are as regretful as this one. Similarly forced psychological interpretations of the poem also abound in Bergren 1989; see below on 167 οὐ σάφα εἰδώς. Nonetheless ἀνάγκη seems to inform the sexual encounter at hand. Even if Aphrodite does not know that Zeus is the instigator of her desire, she must have some idea that this affair with a mortal can lead to no good, but just as Anchises ignores his suspicions of her divinity in a frenzy of passion (cf. on *Aphr.* 143–54), she can do nothing but submit to the necessity of her desire. After the consummation of their love, both awaken to the harsh and sombre reality of what they have done (see on *Aphr.* 168–90).

131 ἀλλά σε πρὸς Ζηνὸς γουνάζομαι: the grasping or touching of knees is a common element of supplication (see Gould 1973, 75–7 = 2001, 24–6). It is uncertain, however, whether Aphrodite actually grasps Anchises' knees here. Rather, this could be a case of what Gould (ibid. 77 = 26–7 *et passim*) calls 'figurative' supplication, 'the verbal forms of the act of supplication without the physical contact.' The obvious parallel to this situation is Odysseus' supplication of Nausicaa at *Od.* 6. 149 ff.; after debating whether to grasp her knees or stay at a distance, he opts for the latter, nonetheless beginning his speech γουνοῦμαί σε ἄνασσα. Odysseus refrains from contact partially out of decorum—a dirty, nude man would make a rather shocking sight at a young maiden's knees (cf. Pedrick 1982, 138)—and there is also the awkwardness of physical contact between two young lovers to consider there. In this situation, Aphrodite might not be so awkward about her desire, and grasping Anchises' knees would allow her to touch the object of her desire. On the other hand, one wonders how low she will stoop; this is the reverse of *Od.* 13. 324 νῦν δέ σε πρὸς πατρὸς γουνάζομαι, where Odysseus, a mortal, supplicates Athena, a goddess.

Aphrodite is switching the tables of supplication at this point, after Anchises has supplicated her in his prayer at vv. 100–6. Things will switch over again after they have slept together, when this line will be repeated almost *verbatim* by Anchises at v. 187 (see on *Aphr.* 184–90). For the phrasing of this line cf. also Pi. *Paian* 9. 7 ἀλλά σε πρὸς Διός (fr. 52k).

γουνάζομαι ... ἠδὲ τοκήων: to supplicate in the name of absent family members is a common device of persuasion. Note in particular Nestor's exhortatory supplication to the Greeks to keep fighting at *Il.* 15. 660–6, invoking their children, wives, property, and parents (vv. 663–5 παίδων ἠδ' ἀλόχων καὶ κτήσιος ἠδὲ τοκήων ... | ... | τῶν ὕπερ ἐνθάδ' ἐγὼ γουνάζομαι). Also see *Il.* 22. 338, 24. 466–7, 485–92, *Od.* 11. 66 ff. (cf. N. Richardson 1993, 141).

131–2 τοκήων | ἐσθλῶν· οὐ μὲν γάρ κε κακοὶ τοιόνδε τέκοιεν: for the rhetoric of coming from good parents see *Od.* 4. 63–4 ἀλλ' ἀνδρῶν γένος ἐστὲ διοτρεφέων βασιλήων | σκηπτούχων, ἐπεὶ οὔ κε κακοὶ τοιούσδε τέκοιεν and *Dem.* 213–14 χαῖρε γύναι, ἐπεὶ οὔ σε κακῶν ἄπ' ἔολπα τοκήων | ἔμμεναι ἀλλ' ἀγαθῶν. On both occasions royalty is intended. Emphasis is placed on ἐσθλῶν by its enjambment; cf. *Od.* 8. 585, 20. 86.

132 οὐ μὲν γάρ κε: this is the reading of M; the other MSS read the unmetrical οὐ γάρ τε, apart from V οὐ γάρ τοί. There seems to be no reason to doubt the metrical reading of M; the same run is at *Il.* 9. 545 (also cf. later Theoc. *Id.* 25. 183 οὐ μὲν γάρ κε τοσόνδε) and κε seems to be supported by *Od.* 4. 64 ἐπεὶ οὔ κε κακοὶ τοιούσδε τέκοιεν (cf. AHS 361 who point to the confusion of κε and τε at *Il.* 15. 224). On οὐ μέν adverbially 'assurément', see Ruijgh (1971), 741 ff., Denniston (1950), 362. Stephanus (1566) preferred to emend the reading of V to οὐ γάρ τοι γε (cf. *Op.* 726).

133 ἀδμήτην μ' ἀγαγών: 'leading me a virgin...'; ἀδμήτην must here be governed by ἄγω, not δεῖξον as VE 52 thinks; see VB 12— 'word-order seems to tell against this; and "present me as a virgin" is an unlikely meaning'—who also makes short work of Reinhardt's suggestion (1956, 8) that this is a request to remain a virgin, the whole point being that Aphrodite wants desperately to sleep with him! For active ἄγω of taking a woman as booty see *Il.* 23. 512 δῶκε δ' ἄγειν ἑτάροισιν ὑπερθύμοισι γυναῖκα; of bringing home a wife for oneself or a family member, the middle is usual (cf. *Od.* 4. 10, 14. 211 etc.; see *LfgrE* s.v. III. 2 for more examples). Although of a bull, cf. similar language at *Il.* 10. 293/*Od.* 3. 383 ἀδμήτην, ἥν οὔ πω ὑπὸ ζυγὸν ἤγαγεν ἀνήρ and see later of a captive virgin being led down from a tree at Nonn. *D.* 47. 236 παρθενικὴν ἀδμῆτα κατήγαγον. On ἀδμήτην see on *Aphr.* 82.

ἀπειρήτην φιλότητος: the adjective ἀπείρητος 'inexperienced' is found only twice in Homer *Il.* 12. 304 and *Od.* 2. 170 (once with a passive sense, *Il.* 17. 41 'untried'), but never of sexual experience. See later Manetho, *Apotel.* 1. 125–6 γυναῖκας | ... ἀπειρήτους φιλότητος and cf. Nonn. *D.* 15. 171–2 Ἄρτεμις ἄλλη | ἀλλοτρίη φιλότητος, ἀπειρήτη Κυθερείης. Cf. Pi. *O.* 11. 18 ἀπείρατον καλῶν.

134 πατρί τε σῷ: cf. *Il.* 3. 50, 8. 283, later Q.S. 3. 486 and the anonymous *App. Anth.* 1. 298. 9 (Cougny); note also line-beginning πατρί τ' ἐμῷ, *Od.* 3. 209, 18. 140 (later A.R. 1. 907), which appears below at v. 138 (there at 2∪∪3).

μητέρι κεδν' εἰδυίῃ: see on *Aphr.* 44.

135 σοῖς τε κασιγνήτοις: possible modification by transposition of line-end κασιγνήτοισί τε σοῖσι *Il.* 5. 474, the innovation signalled by the short dative plural; see Janko (1982), 155 who compares also οἷο κασιγνήτοιο *Il.* 3. 333 and οὕς τε κασιγνήτους *Hy.* 7. 31. Cf. as well πατρί τ' ἐμῷ πίσυνος καὶ ἐμοῖσι κασιγνήτοισι *Od.* 18. 140 and at line-beginning πάρ τε κασιγνήτῳ *Od.* 3. 39. Càssola 551 comments that this is the only mention of Anchises' brothers; whether they exist or not, the inclusion of all possible family members adds to the emotional power of her plea.

τοι ὁμόθεν γεγάασιν: 'born of the same blood'; cf. the similar *Op.* 108 ὡς ὁμόθεν γεγάασι θεοί. This sense is not Homeric, where ὁμόθεν appears only once with the meaning 'from the same place' *Od.* 5. 477 [δοιοὺς θάμνους] ἐξ ὁμόθεν πεφυῶτας. West (1978), 178, however, compares *Il.* 4. 58 (Hera to Zeus) καὶ γὰρ ἐγὼ θεός εἰμι, γένος δέ μοι ἔνθεν ὅθεν σοι, and cf. also *Od.* 4. 723 ὁμοῦ τράφεν ἠδ' ἐγένοντο; these parallels suggest how the sense 'of the same blood' is a natural extension of 'from the same place/origin' and so could well have been traditional. Accordingly, it is doubtful whether there is a direct connection with *Op.* 108 (Janko 1982, 165 points out simply that there is nothing to establish priority). For ὁμόθεν with this meaning in later Greek see S. *El.* 156, E. *Or.* 456, *IA.* 501, Xen. *Cyr.* 8. 7. 14 (ἀπὸ τοῦ ὁμόθεν γενομένου) etc.; A.R. 1. 90–1 uses the term (perhaps playfully) of two brothers who do not come to join Jason from the same place. Note also phrasing similar to this line later at A.R. 3. 731 οἳ δή μοι ἀδελφειοὶ γεγάασιν and Q.S. 13. 554 αἳ δή οἱ ἀδελφειαὶ γεγάασιν.

136–136a εἴ τοι ἀεικελίη γυνὴ ἔσσομαι ἠὲ καὶ οὐκί: M and Θ have this line after 136, while the *p* MSS have conflated the two into the nonsensical οὔ σφιν ἀεικελίη γυνὴ ἔσσομαι ἠὲ καὶ οὐκί. Three things are clear here: (i) both lines have a long history in the tradition; (ii) the lines make no sense one after the other: Aphrodite is hardly saying 'I shall not be an unsuitable daughter-in-law to them [your family], but a suitable one, whether or not I am a good wife to you'; (iii) 'they do not seem corruptions either one of the other or of a common original' (AHS 361). One line needs to go, and most modern editors have chosen to solve the problem by deleting 136a (Gemoll 1886, AHS, Càssola, West 2003, etc.). This seems the best course of action on the grounds that 136 makes far better sense here. VE 53 comments that 136a is inappropriate 'because at 141 Aphrodite commands Anchises to prepare the marriage, not reckoning with a possible disapproval'. The clause ἦε καὶ οὐκί can be used as a rhetorical device in Homer (so Thersites at *Il.* 2. 238, or Odysseus exhorting the troops with imperatives at 2. 299–300 τλῆτε φίλοι, καὶ μείνατ' ἐπὶ χρόνον, ὄφρα δαῶμεν | ἢ ἐτεὸν Κάλχας μαντεύεται ἦε καὶ οὐκί; it is implied that he is a true prophet); but such rhetoric seems feeble, overdone modesty in this situation when compared with the powerful and straightforward statement of v. 136 (so Gemoll 1886, 269: 'wieder wird übrigens hier das Schickliche betont'). The same objection can be raised against Shackle's combination (1915, 163) of the two lines to form εἴ σφιν ἀεικελίη νυὸς ἔσσομαι ἢ εἰκυῖα. AHS 361 cite Flach's preference for 136a because ἀλλ' εἰκυῖα neglects digamma; this is certainly no reason to favour the line.

It remains, however, to explain how 136a entered the text. Càssola 551 suggests that the variant was born from a feeling that the rare νυός, properly 'daughter-in-law', could not follow after brothers as well (on the frequency and sense of this word see n. below), an elaborate argument which fails to explain why the rest of 136a was added as well; if νυός was the problem, why did the interpolator not just substitute γυνή for νυός (as Humbert does)? VB 15–16 offers the solution of transposing 136a to follow 138, thus reading [πέμψαι δ' ἄγγελον] εἰπεῖν πατρί τ' ἐμῷ καὶ μητέρι κηδομένῃ περ | εἴ τοι ἀεικελίη γυνὴ ἔσσομαι ἦε καὶ οὐκί; but this gives an odd sense, and once again the question of approval seems out of place. Moreover, it is not easy to explain how such a transposition took place over two lines here. If, as he suggests, the similarity of the lines had caused confusion, one might expect further corruption (i.e. vv. 137–8 missing, or 136a repeated twice). And it is not true that 'transposition of lines is a less radical device than deletion', at least not for an editor of early epic; Homer is full of possible interpolations and this poem significantly has two other strong cases (see on *Aphr.* 97–8 and 274–7 which could be an interpolation). Verse 136a is best taken as a marginal variant that has entered the text.

Some comment must finally be made on VB's argument that his transposition solves the 'problem' of absolute εἰπεῖν in 138; what exactly is the messenger supposed to tell? He admits that absolute εἰπεῖν is known in Homer (citing *Il.* 17. 692; for several more examples see *LfgrE* s.v. I. 5d), but suggests that there the meaning is clear from the context, whereas it is not here. However, the request to be led and shown to the family, and the straightforward claim to be a good νυός at 136, are more than enough to make it evident that their marriage is what the messenger is to announce; and that is why her parents will respond with gifts.

136 οὔ σφιν ἀεικελίη νυὸς ἔσσομαι: comparable to *Dem.* 83–4 οὔ τοι ἀεικὴς | γαμβρός (cf. also v. 363). Given the other similarities between these two poems, the enjambment in *Dem.* may suggest that it has been adapted from the line in *Aphr.*, but one should perhaps be more cautious than to say that this 'is certainly a case of formulaic modification over line-end from *Aphr.* 136' (Janko 1982, 227); for more on the relationship between the two poems see Introd., pp. 38–40. For parallels for such an expression in later Greek (οὐ μεμπτός) and Latin literature see N. Richardson (1974), 175 on *Dem.* 83 ff.

νυός: 'daughter-in-law' at *Il.* 22. 65, 24. 166 and *Od.* 3. 451; it here seems to encompass 'sister-in-law' as well, as apparently at *Il.* 3. 49 it more broadly means 'member of the household' (cf. Kirk 1985 ad loc.). Apart from these cases, this word does not surface again until Theoc. *Id.* 15. 77, 18. 15, where it appears to be used simply as 'wife' (see Gow ii. 285–6), and it remains rare; cf. A.R. 4. 815, fr. 12. 15 *CA* (the Λέσβου κτίσις, *FGrH* 479F1), Posidipp. *Ep.* 114. 20, [Mosch.] *Meg.* 61, Q.S. 10. 383. M's νηός is just a simple error (cf. A.R. 2. 1126 νηὸς ἀεικελίης).

137 πέμψαι δ' ἄγγελον ὦκα: messengers are traditionally swift; cf. *Od.* 24. 413–14 ὅσσα δ' ἄρ' ἄγγελος ὦκα κατὰ πτόλιν ᾤχετο πάντῃ | μνηστήρων στυγερὸν θάνατον καὶ κῆρ' ἐνέπουσα, or Iris at *Il.* 23. 198–9. But here it is not just the messenger who should be quick; Anchises should be quick in dispatching him. The request for speed adds a sense of pathetic urgency to her demand, reinforcing the image of her worrying mother in the next line.

Φρύγας αἰολοπώλους: cf. *Il.* 3. 185 Φρύγας ἀνέρας αἰολοπώλους. Apart from these two occurrences, the epithet is found only at Theoc. *Id.* 22. 34, of Castor (known elsewhere as ἱππόδαμος), and possibly in a fragment of Cercidas (fr. 6a. 1 Lomiento = fr. 8. 1 *CA*). See also Achilles' horse at *Il.* 19. 404 πόδας αἰόλος ἵππος. The adjective most probably means 'of the swift horses' (cf. Kirk 1985, 291); αἰόλος almost certainly had an original meaning of 'rapid, lively', developing later the sense of 'shining' found in αἰολοθώρηξ, αἰολομίτρης, or κορυθαιόλος (see *Dictionnaire* s.v.). M. W. Edwards (1991), 283 ad loc., however, may be right that at *Il.* 19. 404 there is 'a connotation of shining hoofs as well as speed', citing the name of Achilles' horse Ποδάργης 'White-foot' (19. 400). Might this ambiguity extend to the epithet as well (the always swift-footed Iris is also χρυσόπτερος, with golden wings on her heels, at *Il.* 11. 185 and *Dem.* 314; cf. Θέτις ἀργυρόπεζα *Il.* 9. 410)? One thinks of the connection of light and speed in the English phrase 'quick as lightning'. The Phrygians were clearly well-known for their horses, called ἱππόμαχοι at *Il.* 10. 431.

138 εἰπεῖν: see on *Aphr.* 136–136a.

μητέρι κηδομένη περ: cf. in particular *Il.* 1. 586 τέτλαθι, μῆτερ ἐμή, καὶ ἀνάσχεο κηδομένη περ; the formula κηδομένη περ occurs also at *Il.* 5. 382, 24. 104 and *Od.* 18. 178. VE 53 points out that while the particle περ is often used concessively after a participle (cf. Denniston 1954, 485), it can here only be understood as intensifying the reference to her grieving mother, as apparently it intensifies Zeus' mention of Thetis' suffering at *Il.* 24. 104.

139. This line is almost identical with *Od.* 13. 136/16. 231 χαλκόν τε χρυσόν τε ἅλις ἐσθῆτά θ' ὑφαντήν. Also, in particular for πέμψουσιν in the next line, cf. 5. 37–8 πέμψουσιν δ' ἐν νηΐ φίλην ἐς πατρίδα γαῖαν | χαλκόν τε χρυσόν τε ἅλις ἐσθῆτά τε δόντες (very similar as well is 23. 340–1). The Homeric formula is modified later at *Herm.* 180–1 χρυσόν ἅλις τ' αἴθωνα σίδηρον | καὶ πολλὴν ἐσθῆτα (cf. Janko 1982, 134).

οἱ δέ κέ τοι χρυσόν τε: there is considerable corruption at the beginning of this line. M reads οἱ δέ κε χρυσόν τε, while the other MSS have οἱ δέ τε χρυσόν κεν (AQ οὐδέ τε!); both are unmetrical. Most editors have followed Matthiae's insertion (1805) of τοι into

M, which seems to be by far the best solution. The run οἱ δέ κέ τοι + fut. indic. πέμψουσιν is fully justified by *Il*. 14. 267–8 ἀλλ' ἴθ', ἐγὼ δέ κέ τοι Χαρίτων μίαν ὁπλοτεράων | δώσω ὀπυιέμεναι καὶ σὴν κεκλῆσθαι ἄκοιτιν (even the context of marriage is similar; for more examples of κε(ν) + fut. indic. in Homer cf. GG ii 369, although Schwyzer, GG ii 351, understands πέμψουσιν here to be a subjunctive), and χρυσόν τε ... perhaps gains some support from *Od*. 13. 136 etc. (cited in prec. n.). VE 53 takes the opposite position, that M has 'restored' a Homeric phrase, and follows Gemoll (1886), 269 in starting from the reading of the other MSS (οἳ δ' ἤτοι χρυσόν κεν | οἳ δή τοι χρυσόν κεν). Both, however, ignore the fact that κεν after χρυσόν is far less likely than τε, which supplies the common corresponsion τε ... τε in the line (for examples of which see Denniston 1950, 503 ff.); indeed, κε(ν) + fut. indic. is 'chiefly found after δέ' (Monro 1891, 297). VB 18 is troubled by the use of κε(ν) at any point here, calling it 'virtually otiose' in comparison to *Il*. 14. 267–8, and cautiously proposes οἱ δὲ τότε χρυσόν τε (also οἱ δ' αὖ τοι and οἱ δ' αὖτε). It is difficult, though, to see the objection. As at *Il*. 14. 267–8 Hera will (would) give Sleep one of the Graces, *should* he agree to help her, Aphrodite's imaginary parents will (would) send many gifts, *should* Anchises dispatch a messenger announcing marriage (cf. Goodwin 1900, 277–8 on *Il*. 1. 174–5 ἄλλοι | οἵ κέ με τιμήσουσι 'the future with ἄν [κε] seems to be an intermediary form between the simple future, *will honor*, and the optative with ἄν [κε], *would honor*'); in any case, the fact that κε(ν) appears in all MSS suggests that it was at least somewhere in the original line.

140 πέμψουσιν: this recalls πέμψαι at line-beginning in 137; the effect is a verbal strengthening of the idea that if Anchises sends a messenger with good news, her parents will send something in return. At line-beginning with nu mobile making position as here see *Od*. 5. 37 πέμψουσιν δ' ἐν νηΐ (on nu mobile cf. Hoekstra 1965, 81).

σὺ δὲ πολλὰ καὶ ἀγλαὰ δέχθαι ἄποινα: the end of the line is identical with *Il*. 1. 23/377, of the ransom of Chryseïs; see also *Il*. 6. 46/11. 131 σὺ δ' ἄξια δέξαι ἄποινα and 24. 555 σὺ δὲ δέξαι ἄποινα. There has been much controversy over the use of ἄποινα in this line. It properly means 'ransom/compensation' in Homer, while here the relationship with dowry seems undeniable; marriage is the point in question, and the gifts which Anchises will supposedly receive from the maiden's parents can be little but dowry. These, however, are normally called μείλια (*Il.* 9. 147/289) or ἕεδνα (*Od.* 1. 277/2. 196); on this custom, known alongside the practice of the suitor paying a bride-price in Homer (see on *Aphr.* 119 ἀλφεσίβοιαι), see N. Richardson (1993), 111 with bibliography. Some have attempted to construe this as 'ransom/compensation', with unconvincing results: Càssola 551–2, followed by Smith (1981*a*), 119 n. 56, suggests that as a stranger devoid of legal rights, Aphrodite appeals with ransom not to be made a slave, while Rüter (*LfgrE* s.v. ; followed by VE 54) offers the fanciful proposal that as an abducted young maiden she asks first to be made a free woman through the exchange of ransom before she will marry Anchises. But this is a unique situation where the normal rules of abduction cannot be thought to apply; she has been snatched away by a god and brought to a mountain to meet her destined lover (cf. VB 17–18, who, however, also rejects 'dowry', proposing that the exchange of ἄποινα 'compensation' makes the marriage a 'binding transaction'). Gemoll (1886), 269 cites Suhle as taking ἄποινα in a positive sense of 'reward' as at Pi. *P.* 2. 14 ἄποιν᾽ ἀρετᾶς.

Heitsch (1965), 29–30 and Hoekstra (1969), 48 n. 20, accept that a dowry must be intended, but label it a 'misuse' of the word. That ἄποινα is simply a 'misuse', born of ignorance or metrical constraint, is difficult to justify when the metrically equivalent ἕεδνα could easily have been substituted for ἄποινα, and the poet uses ἄποινα in its usual sense later at v. 210. One should rather ask why the word has been employed in a unique way. Keaney (1981) has done much to shed light on this question by highlighting the use of ἄποινα in the context of supplication; as the Homeric parallels cited above show, ἀγλαὰ δέχθαι ἄποινα is part of the vocabulary of supplication in Homer, and Aphrodite is here presenting herself as a suppliant. Its unusual application to dowry (in this entirely unusual situation!) underlines Aphrodite's position of suppliant in a way that ἕεδνα would not have done; the ambiguity of the term enhances the rhetoric of her persuasion, also by stressing the material advantages of her marriage.

141 ταῦτα δὲ ποιήσας: 'and having done these things'; cf. *Od.* 17. 148 ταῦτα τελευτήσας νεόμην.

δαίνυ γάμον ἱμερόεντα: δαίνυμι + γάμον = 'to give a marriage-feast' (cf. *LfgrE* s.v.). For the active verb see *Il.* 19. 299 and *Od.* 4. 3; also the middle 'to take part in a feast', *Il.* 24. 63 (the wedding of Peleus and Thetis), *Od.* 4. 15, etc. (cf. Archil. fr. 197 Ζεῦ πάτερ, γάμον μὲν οὐκ ἐδαισάμην). It is perhaps odd that Anchises should be asked to give the marriage-feast, which seems properly to have been the responsibility of the parents; so at *Od.* 4. 3 Menelaus gives the marriage-feast for his son and daughter (in classical times the feast was the responsibility of the bride's father; cf. E. *IA* 720 of Agamemnon—hypothetically—giving a feast for Iphigenia, and see Redfield 1982, 188). Several scholars (see Leaf ii ad loc.) have suggested that the subject of the infinitive δαίσειν γάμον at *Il.* 19. 299 is Achilles, of his own wedding to Briseis; but this rests on an awkward switch from Patroclus as the subject of the preceding infinitive θήσειν, which is only possible if one adopts the δ' of the inferior MSS for the more established τ' (see M. W. Edwards 1991, 270; West 2000 reads τ'); why, however, Patroclus should be responsible for this is unclear. Both these passages might be understood more clearly if one admits also the sense 'to enjoy/celebrate a wedding feast' in the active form; the same meaning seems to be required at Pi. *N.* 1. 71–2 γάμον | δαίσαντα, where the subject of the verb is Heracles 'celebrating' (cf. Braswell 1992, 82 ad loc.) his wedding-feast πὰρ Δὶ Κρονίδᾳ (Zeus is presumably putting on the event). Alternatively, the situation in *Aphr.* is unusual (her parents are far away and her supposed husband is a shepherd on a mountain) and Aphrodite may well be asking Anchises to put on the event even if it would not be the norm for the bridegroom to do so (nor would the situation between Achilles and Briseis have been typical).

The versification is more like the gloomy *Od.* 3. 309 ἤτοι ὁ τὸν κτείνας δαίνυ τάφον Ἀργείοισι 'gave a funeral feast' (cf. also simply 'to give a feast' δαίνυ δαῖτα *Il.* 9. 70). A γάμος is never ἱμερόεις in Homer, although cf. *Il.* 5. 429 ἀλλὰ σὺ γ' ἱμερόεντα μετέρχεο ἔργα γάμοιο. The noun–epithet combination occurs elsewhere first at [Hes.] frr. 37. 6, 211. 6; cf. also Phoc. fr. 14. 8 (*TP*) and Thgn. 1293; later Q.S. 4. 131, Gr. Naz. *Carm.* II 2. 3. 188 (*PG* 37. 1493) and Nonn. *D.* 16. 291.

142 τίμιον ...: Janko (1982), 161 compares Apoll. 482–3 ἀλλ' ἐνθάδε πίονα νηὸν | ἕξετ' ἐμὸν πᾶσιν μάλα τίμιον ἀνθρώποισι and [Hes.] fr. 240. 7 τίμιον ἀνθρώποις. Cf. also *Od.* 10. 38–9 ὅδε πᾶσι φίλος καὶ τίμιός ἐστιν | ἀνθρώποισ' and *Th.* 203–4 τιμὴν ἔχει ἠδὲ λέλογχε |

μοῖραν ἐν ἀνθρώποισι καὶ ἀθανάτοισι θεοῖσιν. A τίμιος γάμος is unique in early poetry; cf. later *Orac. Sib.* 8. 27, and of a Christian marriage *Heb.* 13. 4. This final comment about a wedding honoured amongst both men and gods is, at face value, tantamount to saying 'honoured amongst everybody' (cf. on *Aphr.* 35); but it also ends Aphrodite's speech on a supreme note of irony. In reality, their union may be honoured amongst men, but it will be a mark of shame for Aphrodite amongst the gods (cf. Smith 1981a, 54).

143–54. At the close of her speech Aphrodite casts ἵμερος into the heart of Anchises; in other words, the tall tale has had the intended effect and Anchises is overcome with an immediate desire to sleep with her (on the force of ἵμερος see on *Aphr.* 91). However, before proceeding to the act itself he expresses his strong desire for her in words, which appears to be a typical element for males in seduction scenes (cf. Paris to Helen *Il.* 3. 438–46 and Zeus to Hera at 14. 312–28). Podbielski (1971), 54 and Keaney (1981), 264 think that by expressing his will to sleep with Aphrodite immediately he is rejecting her request for marriage. On the contrary, sexual intercourse represents the entrance into marriage (as perhaps for Helen and Paris; see Erdmann 1934, 199), and regardless of his taking this step before the feast he has been asked to throw, and before informing the parents, it signals his acceptance of the offer. After all, his own words express that he will sleep with her on the assumption that all she has said to make her an appropriate wife is true, and it is unlikely that Aphrodite should have made an offer which would not lead to the immediate fulfilment of her own desire.

That he agrees to sleep with her, however, does not mean that he fully believes what he has heard. Rather, as Smith (1981a), 55–7 and de Jong (1989), 17 have suggested, his response seems to betray uncertainty. Some caution, however, is required in reaching this conclusion. Smith (1981a), 55, 120 n. 58 begins by noting that the speech opens without a vocative address formula, calling this abrupt and unusual; but εἰ quite frequently begins responses in Homer (4× *Il.*, 12× *Od.*; *Il.* 10. 242, 11. 138 etc.) where there is regularly no hint of uncertainty, and one might not necessarily expect a vocative after ἔπος τ᾽ ἔφατ᾽ ἔκ τ᾽ ὀνόμαζεν (see on *Aphr.* 144). Nor does the construction εἰ + indic. found here necessarily betray uncertainty; often in Homer it expresses 'mere *supposition* . . . where there need be no implication either for or against the truth of the supposition made' (Monro 1891, 293–4; cf. the two examples given under speeches beginning with εἰ).

More suggestive is the phrase ὡς ἀγορεύεις (v. 146; substituted for εἴ που ἀκούεις in the otherwise identical v. 111), in which de Jong, loc. cit. rightly sees an implication of scepticism on the ground that 'instead of acknowledging that he has heard of Otreus, as Aphrodite invited him to do, he stresses that it is she who claims to be his daughter.' While the phrase again may not *a priori* imply mistrust (cf. *Il.* 24. 373, *Od.* 4. 157 etc.), it is frequently associated with scepticism; in particular with respect to this passage, it is combined with εἰ in several speeches in Homer where mistrust is almost a certainty: when Penelope begins her speech to Eurycleia at *Od.* 23. 35–8 with εἰ, she is questioning the truth of what the nurse has just told her about Odysseus' return; εἰ δ' ἄγε δή μοι, μαῖα φίλη, νημερτὲς ἐνίσπες | εἰ ἐτεὸν δὴ οἶκον ἱκάνεται, ὡς ἀγορεύεις. Also similar is *Od.* 19. 215–19; Penelope directly challenges the truth of the false tale which Odysseus (in disguise) has told to her, beginning with the words νῦν μὲν δή σευ ξεῖνε ὀΐω πειρήσεσθαι | εἰ ἐτεὸν δὴ κεῖθι σὺν ἀντιθέοις ἑτάροισι | ξείνισας ἐν μεγάροισιν ἐμὸν πόσιν, ὡς ἀγορεύεις (see ὡς ἀγορεύεις when questioning truth also at *Il.* 9. 41, 17. 180, *Od.* 23. 62). She is emotionally moved (to tears) by what he has said, and would clearly like to believe that he has once hosted Odysseus, but she is openly cautious after so many years of vain hoping. Anchises has also heard a tale which he would like to believe, and his ὡς ἀγορεύεις perhaps suggests some of the same hopeful scepticism which Penelope shows. Cf. as well Zeus' response to the trickery of Hera at *Il.* 15. 49–55: he begins his response with εἰ before exclaiming ἀλλ' εἰ δή ῥ' ἐτεόν γε καὶ ἀτρεκέως ἀγορεύεις (v. 53).

Also noteworthy is the fact that Anchises traces meticulously over each claim which Aphrodite has made; the first two lines of his reply (vv. 145–6) repeat almost *verbatim* her own words (vv. 110–11). This summary makes even the audience step back and reconsider the magnitude of the assertions which have just been heard, and if it does not show a certain incredulity on Anchises' part, it at least puts any blame for what he is about to do on Aphrodite (cf. van der Ben 1981, 76 and see on *Aphr.* 185–6). Finally, Smith (1981*a*), 57 suggests that Anchises' boast at the end of his speech, saying he would face Apollo and accept death in order to sleep with Aphrodite (vv. 149–54), also reveals that he still entertains the possibility of divine punishment; a suggestion which he reinforces by pointing to the tantalizing vocative address γύναι εἰκυῖα θεῇσιν (v. 153). If these elements are merely high rhetoric, they are at least full of irony.

If, however, he is unsure that things are on the level, why does he so vehemently pursue the risky *copula carnalis*? De Jong, loc. cit. cuts to the heart of the matter: 'Anchises remains rationally sceptical about the alleged human nature of the woman facing him, yet emotionally lets himself be swayed by her words.' Indeed, the triumph of emotion over his rational musings is plain to see in the development of his speech, itself a crescendo of passion: Anchises starts calmly enough by listing her supposed mortality, origin, and mode of arrival, but once he repeats to himself the claim that she might be his wife at v. 148, things start to heat up (on the rising passion of vv. 149–54 see ad loc.).

143. This line is an exact copy of *Il.* 3. 139, where, however, the sense is very different from that here: Iris casts ἵμερος 'longing' into the heart of Helen for her homeland and family. The casting of desire into the heart of Aphrodite by Zeus at vv. 45 and 53 set the narrative in motion; the same action by the goddess now moves the plot into its final stage of completion, recalling at this crucial moment the ultimate source of the affair (cf. Podbielski 1971, 53–4).

144 ἔπος τ' ἔφατ ἔκ τ' ὀνόμαζεν: whereas before at v. 91 when Anchises was seized by love the formula introducing his speech was ἔπος δέ μιν ἀντίον ηὔδα, his reply is now introduced by ἔπος τ' ἔφατ' ἔκ τ' ὀνόμαζεν; the latter is common in Homer (17× *Il.*, 26× *Od.*; not outside Homer other than in *Aphr.*) and may be a simple variation of formulae with little distinction in sense; alternatively, however, it is worth considering that the alliteration of hard sounds π, τ, κ in the formula is more expressive of the emotion which Anchises' speech will contain on this occasion; cf. Calhoun (1935), 23–5, who notes that the formula suggests 'emotion . . . earnest, affectionate, or cordial address', and Couch (1937), 140, who reaches the similar conclusion that 'the words that follow are usually of marked emphasis, though they may express a wide variety of emotions'. Some will not agree (see M. W. Edwards 1970, 2), but such a nuance at least seems to fit the use of this formula in *Aphr.*; cf. below on 176. The literal force of ὀνομάζω has long ago disappeared. Actually to name an addressee after this formula is rare, and six times no vocative follows ἔπος τ᾽ ἔφατ᾽ ἔκ τ᾽ ὀνόμαζεν as here; see Heubeck (OC iii. 271).

145–6. On the repetition of vv. 110–11 see on *Aphr.* 143–54, and on 110–11 for more detailed comments on individual constituents.

147–8 ἀθανάτου δὲ ἕκητι διακτόρου ... | Ἑρμέω: cf. line-beginning *Od.* 15. 319 Ἑρμείαο ἕκητι διακτόρου. Hoekstra (1969), 42 labels this 'an extreme case of separation', pointing to the use of the metathesized genitive Ἑρμέω and the contracted genitive singular ἀθανάτου, neither of which is found in Homer (Ἑρμέω first at *Herm.* 413, cf. later Theoc. *Id.* 25. 4). The latter is in fact transmitted only by M (ἀθανάτου δ᾽ ἕκατι, corr. Hermann 1806), while the other MSS read the lengthened genitive with a neglect of digamma in ἕκητι (ἀθανάτοιο δ᾽ ἕκητι, printed by Gemoll 1886 and Càssola). It is impossible to decide definitively between the two (the poet elsewhere both uses contracted genitives singular and neglects digamma; see Introd., pp. 26–8), but M's reading seems to be the more likely. In four appearances of ἕκητι in Homer and Hesiod (*Od.* 15. 319, 19. 86, 20. 42 and *Op.* 4) digamma is never neglected (not until *Hy.* 26. 5, which is probably a later creation than *Aphr.*), while the contracted ἀθανάτου is confirmed by metre at *Th.* 191. M retains digamma against the other MSS also at *Apoll.* 341.

147 διάκτορος: a frequent epithet of Hermes in epic (*Il.* 2. 103, 21. 497 etc.); cf. v. 213. As with so many epithets, its etymology is obscure: the most convincing argument comes from Janko (1978), who derives it from the (now rare) διάκτωρ 'guide/conductor' (see Hsch. διάκτορσι· ἡγεμόσι, βασιλεῦσι), as χρυσάορος from χρυσάωρ; alternatively, Chantraine, *Dictionnaire*, s.v. suggests it is connected to διάκονος, used of the god at [A.] *PV* 941–2, and Bechtel (1914), s.v. prefers a development from κτέρας, given Hermes' position as 'giver of good things' (*Od.* 8. 335 etc.; cf. his assumed name Πολύκτωρ at *Il.* 24. 397, which von Kamptz 1982, 69, also connects to κτέρας). See further the discussions of S. West (*OC* i. 85 on *Od.* 1. 84) and Hoekstra (*OC* ii. 253). Later ancient authors understood the epithet as 'messenger'; Hsch. glosses the word ἀπὸ τοῦ διάγειν τὰς ἀγγελίας, and Call. fr. 519 (also Ant. Sid. *AP* 7. 161. 1, Nonn. *D.* 31. 107 etc.) uses it in that sense (see Rengakos 1992, 26); and this may be how it was understood earlier too (cf. West 1978, 160). However, a meaning 'guide/conductor' often seems best suited to the context; N. Richardson (1993), 308 notes its appropriateness at *Il.* 24. 339 where Hermes leads Priam to Achilles' tent, and cf. *Herm.* 392 Ἑρμῆν δὲ διάκτορον ἡγεμονεύειν. This meaning is also most fitting here, although 'messenger' is better suited below at v. 213.

148 ἐμὴ δ' ἄλοχος κεκλήσεαι ἤματα πάντα: cf. *Il.* 3. 138 φίλη κεκλήσε' ἄκοιτις and 14. 268 σὴν κεκλῆσθαι ἄκοιτιν; similarly, *Il.* 4. 61/18. 366, *Th.* 410, *Dem.* 79, [Hes.] fr. 26. 24, 105. 3. Cf. also on 126–7, where Hermes claims that she will be his wife. For the phrasing note *Herm.* 292 ἀρχὸς φιλητέων κεκλήσεαι ἤματα πάντα.

ἤματα πάντα: see on *Aphr.* 28 πάντ' ἤματα.

149–54. Anchises moves from one bold statement to the next: neither god nor man will hold him back from sleeping with her, not even if Apollo himself should shoot arrows at him; for he is willing in that case to die after having gone to bed with her! These hyperbolic expressions of passion bring the exchange of speech between Aphrodite and Anchises to a climactic close (cf. Smith 1981a, 57, 'aptly marked'), making the transition to action natural, if not inevitable. Kamerbeek (1967), 392 must be right to place a comma after νῦν in v. 151, the boast against Apollo being an elaboration upon the statement that nothing will hold Anchises back. However, he then places a full stop at the end of v. 152, where West's colon (2003) seems preferable: both ἔπειτα and the asyndeton (cf. VE 56) in v. 153 indicate that the claim to be willing to die is directly related to the mention of Apollo's arrows; 'I should want, in that case [that Apollo fires arrows at me], to die having slept with you' (cf. West 2003 'I should choose in that case'; *contra* VB 18 n. 27, who takes ἔπειτα in a temporal sense, connected to σῆς εὐνῆς ἐπιβάς).

His expressed willingness to die in order to fulfil his erotic desire is unique in early literature, although several people claim to be willing to die to achieve a goal in Homer (see van der Ben 1981, 19, who provides a list; *Il.* 15. 115–18, 17. 415–22 etc.); one might compare the *femme fatale* par excellence Helen, for whom Paris was willing to lead a nation to war. Podbielski (1971), 57 likens these lines to Zeus' words to Hera during their affair at *Il.* 14. 342–5 (Ἥρη, μήτε θεὸν τό γε δείδιθι μήτέ τιν' ἀνδρῶν | ὄψεσθαι), but both the content and the tone are very different. The desire for death in the face of unrequited or missing love is known from Homer onward (Penelope at *Od.* 18.

201–5, [Stesich.] *PMGF* 277 (Καλύκη), Sapph. fr. 94 etc.; see Bickermann 1976, 245–7, who provides a useful list of the motif in Greek and Latin literature, but mistakenly thinks that this is Anchises' point here; see *contra* his position VB 18); but Anchises is far from unrequited! His fatal attraction does not find voice again until much later, in the mouth of 'every man' (τις) for the beautiful Hero in Musaeus 79 αὐτίκα τεθναίην λεχέων ἐπιβήμενος Ἡροῦς (noted by AHS 362); for which these lines may have been a model (see Kost 1971, 266 ad loc., who compares also Nonn. *D*. 4. 147 ff., where the disguised Aphrodite speaks to Harmonia as if she were in love with Cadmus in order to win the girl's heart for the man; καὶ ἡμετέρου διὰ κόλπου | τεθναίην ὅτε μοῦνον ἀφειδέα χεῖρα χαλάσσας | ἀμφοτέρων θλίψειεν [Cadmus] ἐλεύθερον ἄντυγα μαζῶν etc.). See also *Od*. 8. 334–42 where Hermes says that he would endure three times the chains which bound Ares and Aphrodite and the mockery of the gods in order to sleep with Aphrodite.

149. On the antithesis of gods and mortals see on *Aphr*. 35. Cf. *Il*. 1. 547–8 οὔ τις ἔπειτα | οὔτε θεῶν πρότερος τόν γ' εἴσεται οὔτ' ἀνθρώπων and *Od*. 7. 246–7 οὐδέ τις αὐτῇ | μίσγεται οὔτε θεῶν οὔτε θνητῶν ἀνθρώπων.

150 ἐνθάδε με σχήσει: 'nobody will hold me [back] here now before . . .'. AHS 362 and others compare *Il*. 17. 502–4 οὐ γὰρ ἐγώ γε | Ἕκτορα Πριαμίδην μένεος σχήσεσθαι ὀΐω | πρίν . . . βήμεναι ἵππω; with coupling in mind, cf. also Circe holding Odysseus against his will at *Od*. 10. 339–40 αὐτὸν δ' ἐνθάδ' ἔχουσα δολοφρονέουσα κελεύεις | ἐς θάλαμόν τ' ἰέναι καὶ σῆς ἐπιβήμεναι εὐνῆς. VE 56 suggests taking ἐνθάδε temporally, reinforced by αὐτίκα νῦν in the next line; the sense may be something like the emphatic 'here and now', known in Homer (for a list of examples see *LfgrE* s.v. 2; cf. in particular *Il*. 21. 92 νῦν δὲ δὴ ἐνθάδ' ἐμοὶ κακὸν ἔσσεαι). ἐνθάδε is later used temporally in S. *OT* 488, *OC* 992.

σῇ φιλότητι μιγῆναι: cf. *Hy*. 19. 33–34 θάλε γὰρ πόθος ὑγρὸς ἐπελθὼν | νύμφῃ ἐϋπλοκάμῳ Δρύοπος φιλότητι μιγῆναι. Heitsch (1965), 21–2 notes that the possessive adjective takes on the function of a genitive, the latter often found in the phrase 'to mingle in love' in Hesiod and the *Hymns* (Διὸς φιλότητι μιγεῖσα *Th*. 920, *Herm*. 4, *Hy*. 7. 57, 18. 4 etc.; in particular *Th*. 980 μιχθεῖσ' ἐν φιλότητι πολυχρύσου Ἀφροδίτης). In Homer the phrase is used only with the dative of the person with whom one is involved, as later at v. 287 ἐν φιλότητι μιγῆναι ἐϋστεφάνῳ Κυθερείῃ (cf. Il. 6. 165 etc.; also in Hesiod, Th. 125 etc.). See later App. Anth. 6. 19. 2 (Cougny), an oracle of Pythian Apollo, Φλεγυηὶς ἔτικτεν ἐμῇ φιλότητι μιγεῖσα. On the frequency of μείγνυμι of sexual intercourse see above on 39 συνέμειξε.

151 αὐτίκα νῦν: 'immediately, now!'; the immediacy of his desire is stressed even further by the enjambment. See the combination enjambed at Od. 5. 205 of Odysseus' ardent desire to return home, or 18. 203 of Penelope's strong wish for death to end the terrible suffering of longing for her husband.

οὐδ' εἴ κεν ... | ... προΐῃ: the p MSS have the optative προῖοι (M et Θ προίη, corr. Gemoll 1886, 269–70). The optative could be acceptable after εἴ κεν if the clause were a conditional protasis attached to βουλοίμην κεν vv. 153–4 (in any case 'a comparatively rare form'; Monro 1891, 285). It seems, however, to be connected to the previous sentence (see on Aphr. 149–54 and cf. VE 57). The p group elsewhere has the optative against the other MSS; see v. 269 opt. παρεστήκοι vs. MΘ indic. παρεστήκει (cf. also v. 38, pΘ opt. ἐθέλοι vs. M subj. ἐθέλῃ). The optative could have suggested itself to a scribe who took the clause with βουλοίμην; cf. Il. 23. 591 ff. ἵππον δέ τοι αὐτός | δώσω, τὴν ἀρόμην. εἰ καί νύ κεν οἴκοθεν ἄλλο | μέζον ἐπαιτήσειας, ἄφαρ κέ τοι αὐτίκα δοῦναι | βουλοίμην ...; cf. also Il. 9. 444–5 οὐκ ἐθέλοιμι | λείπεσθ', οὐδ' εἴ κέν μοι ὑποσταίη θεὸς αὐτός.

For the phrasing here with the subjunctive note Od. 21. 364–5 εἴ κεν Ἀπόλλων | ἡμῖν ἰλήκῃσι καὶ ἀθάνατοι θεοὶ ἄλλοι.

ἑκηβόλος αὐτὸς Ἀπόλλων: emphatic, 'far-shooting Apollo himself' (cf. VE 57, contra Humbert 'le grand Apollon'). For αὐτός + Apollo compare Il. 2. 827 Πάνδαρος, ᾧ καὶ τόξον Ἀπόλλων αὐτὸς ἔδωκεν and 17. 322–3 ἀλλ' αὐτὸς Ἀπόλλων | Αἰνείαν ὤτρυνε. See N. Richardson (1974), 275 on Dem. 371–2 where αὐτός is used of Hades: 'this use, of Apollo, might suggest that it was applied to a god to emphasize his dignity, i.e. "Himself"'; in later literature he points to αὐτός + Apollo at [Mosch]. Meg. 13 and αὐτός + Zeus at Mosch. Eur. 155. Cf. its use also of Poseidon at Il. 12. 27, where the bT scholia comment τὸ τοιοῦτον ἐπὶ δεσπότου καὶ βασιλέως τίθεται. N. Richardson also compares the use of the definite article with ἄναξ, ἥρως, and γέρων; see Monro (1891), 230 and note αὐτός of Anchises 'himself' below at v. 160. The doublet is paralleled by Herm. 234 ἑκατηβόλος αὐτὸς Ἀπόλλων. There, 'the usage has simply become stereotyped' (Janko 1982, 140, following AHS 316), with little trace of the emphatic sense of αὐτός in *Aphr.* (Radermacher 1931, 122 suggests unconvincingly that there is some emphasis in *Herm.* because Apollo came in person when he could have sent a messenger); this may be one hint (among others: Janko 1982, 133–50 *passim*) that *Herm.* is later than *Aphr.* The two passages have nothing to suggest any direct relationship.

The epithet ἐκηβόλος is commonly attached to Apollo (*Il.* 1. 14 etc.; 11× Homer, Hesiod and the *Hymns*). On its meaning, properly from *ἑκαβόλος 'he who shoots at will' (ἑκών) but by popular etymology understood by bards as 'far-shooting' through association with ἑκάς, see Janko (1992), 251 on *Il.* 15. 231–2.

152 τόξου ἄπ' ἀργυρέου: the contracted genitive ἀργυρέου, not in Homer, suggests modification of line-ending (ἀπ') ἀργυρέοιο βιοῖο (*Il.* 1. 49, 24. 605), although whether this is post-Homeric is called into question by line-beginning τόξου ἄπο κρατεροῦ *Il.* 8. 279 (see Hoekstra 1969, 44 and Janko 1982, 155). Apollo is often called ἀργυρότοξος (*Il.* 1. 37 etc.).

βέλεα στονόεντα: 'groan-causing arrows'; in this metrical position cf. *Il.* 17. 374, *Od.* 24. 180 (preceded by ἐφίει) and *Th.* 684; see also *Il.* 8. 159, 15. 590 and cf. Artemis' στονόεντα βέλη at *Hy.* 27. 6. On all these occasions the arrows are explicitly bringing death (in Hesiod of the gods during the Titanomachy, and in *Hy.* 27 of Artemis on the hunt). Later Q.S. makes use of the noun–epithet combination several times (10. 223, 11. 370 etc.).

153–4 βουλοίμην κεν ἔπειτα: with κεν/ἄν, 'the optative does not express *wish*, or even direct *willingness* on the part of the speaker, but only *willingness to admit* a consequence' (Monro 1891, 273). He does not want to die but will if he has to; 'I should be willing in that case'. Another possible translation of βουλοίμην is 'would rather, *malim*' (cf. van der Ben 1981, 18), and see West (2003) 'I should choose'. For βουλοίμην κε(ν) at line-beginning + infin. see *Od.* 11. 489 and 16. 106 (τεθνάμεν) and cf. on *Aphr.* 151 οὐδ' εἴ κεν. On the function of ἔπειτα see on *Aphr.* 149–54. The asyndeton adds emphasis (cf. Longin. 19. 2), which is expressive of Anchises' passionate language.

γύναι εἰκυῖα θεῇσι: cf. *Il.* 11. 638 and 19. 286 γυνὴ εἰκυῖα θεῇσιν. On the irony of this comparison here see on *Aphr.* 143–54.

154 σῆς εὐνῆς ἐπιβάς: similar phrasing is found throughout the Circe episode in *Od.* 10: εὐνῆς ἡμετέρης ἐπιβήομεν (334), σῆς ἐπιβήμεναι εὐνῆς (340), τεῆς ἐπιβήμεναι εὐνῆς (342), ἐπέβην περικαλλέος εὐνῆς (347) and ἐπιβὰς περικαλλέος εὐνῆς (480). Cf. also Agamemnon's oath not to sleep with Briseis, μή ποτε τῆς εὐνῆς ἐπιβήμεναι ἠδὲ μιγῆναι (*Il.* 9. 133/275/19. 176), and ἀλόχου ἐπιβήμεναι εὐνῆς (*Sc.* 40). VE 58 insists upon the fact that it is properly Anchises' bed which they will mount, not Aphrodite's, but the sense here is surely more metaphorical than literal, to mount 'her' bed being to have intercourse with her.

δῦναι δόμον Ἄϊδος εἴσω: a rather round-about way to say 'to die'; it is more vivid, adding emphasis to Anchises' boast. The phrase is formular: as here at *Il.* 3. 322 and 7. 131 (cf. also 11. 263 ἔδυν . . .), while all told δόμον Ἄϊδος εἴσω is at line-end 5× *Il.* and 4× *Od.* Outside Homer, however, it is not common: cf. Thgn. 917, and then only later *Orac. Sib.* 8. 199 etc. Note the combination with the verb δύω twice more later at Cometas, *AP* 15. 42. 1, Leontius Scholasticus, *AP* 16. 365. 1. In a bitter reversal of the motif of a maiden's desire for death because of unrequited love (cf. on *Aphr.* 149–54), Theocritus has the witch Simaetha threaten that not she, but her beloved Delphis, will knock on the gate of Hades if her love is not returned (*Id.* 2. 160 τὰν Ἀΐδαο πύλαν, ναὶ Μοίρας, ἀράξει).

155–67. Anchises takes Aphrodite by the hand and leads her to bed, while she continues to play the innocent young virgin, casting her eyes down towards the ground in mock shame; she might almost need to turn her head away to conceal a sly smile (φιλομμειδής) at her success. The male leading the female to bed is a common element of seduction: after expressing his desire, Paris heads to bed with Helen in tow at *Il.* 3. 447 ἦ ῥα, καὶ ἄρχε λέχοσδε κιών· ἅμα δ' εἵπετ' ἄκοιτις, Zeus takes Hera into his arms after his speech at *Il.* 14. 346 ἦ ῥα, καὶ ἀγκὰς ἔμαρπτε Κρόνου πάϊς ἣν παράκοιτιν, and Ares takes Aphrodite's hand even before speaking to her at *Od.* 8. 291 ἔν τ' ἄρα οἱ φῦ χειρί (also a typical element of arrival, Arend 1933, 29).

In such episodes the act itself can then be passed over in a simple statement of its completion worthy of the strictest Victorian censorship (so *Il.* 3. 448 τὼ μὲν ἄρ' ἐν τρητοῖσι κατηύνασθεν λεχέεσσιν is all one hears of Paris and Helen in bed, before the scene switches abruptly to Menelaus wandering in search of his vanished foe;

cf. Ares and Aphrodite *Od.* 8. 297 and Odysseus and Circe *Od.* 10. 347 etc.: Odysseus passes swiftly to what the servants were doing), or there can be further elaboration (grass and flowers grow under Zeus and Hera at *Il.* 14. 347 ff., in which they lie surrounded by a golden cloud, while at *Od.* 23. 205 ff. the amorous encounter of Odysseus and Penelope is touchingly extended by an alternation between love-making and conversation). The scene in *Aphr.* falls into the latter category, as it really only could, being the culmination of a long seduction which occupies over 100 lines of the poem; a one- or two-line summary simply would not have done (cf. Podbielski 1971, 54). Similarly, the elaboration in *Il.* 14 comes after a long seduction by Hera, and the extended encounter of Odysseus and Penelope in *Od.* 23 reflects their lengthy struggle for reunion.

The details of the elaboration in *Aphr.* are unique to a seduction scene: a four-line (vv. 157–60) description of the bed-covering precedes the announcement of their arrival onto it (v. 161), after which a four-line (vv. 162–5) description of the removal of Aphrodite's clothes precedes the announcement of the completion of the act (vv. 166–7). For the description of the bed one can compare broadly *Il.* 14. 367 ff., where the flowers and the golden cloud described are the *locus* of action for Zeus and Hera (cf. *ETCSL* 4. 08. 20 = *ANET* 638, where Inanna's bed is covered with plants), but the details are of course very different. Otherwise, note Penelope's brief command to Eurycleia to make the bed for her and Odysseus at *Od.* 23. 177–80 with fleece and blankets, or *Il.* 9. 658–61 where beds are prepared for Achilles and Patroclus in which they will sleep with captured women; although the former is a test and removed from the actual love-making while the latter is a scene of hospitality (for Phoenix) rather than seduction (cf. on *Aphr.* 158–60). Nor is there any real parallel for the undressing. The removal of a girdle (v. 164) is found in Poseidon's romance with Tyro at *Od.* 11. 235–52, where the god covers them in a wave and then at v. 245 loosens her girdle (λῦσε δὲ παρθενίην ζώνην, κατὰ δ' ὕπνον ἔχευεν, although the line may be a later interpolation; it is condemned by Aristarchus, but defended by van der Valk 1949, 260–1; in any case see more examples below on 164), but the scale of the undressing in *Aphr.* has no counterpart in Greek literature (see on *Aphr.* 162–5).

This all makes for a very evocative scene. Podbielski (1971), 56 does his best to reassure the modern reader that 'le tableau n'a aucun caractère pornographique'; perhaps not pornographic (there is not the lewd detail of Archilochus' seduction-epode, fr. 196a. 42 ff.), but the description nonetheless gives the scene a strong eroticism (cf. Sowa 1984, 89–90). The representation of the well-laid bed and the tantalizing removal of clothing (piece by piece) rouse the imagination to fill in the more explicit detail, such that, reflecting the position of Aphrodite at this point in the poem, the sexually explicit is shrouded in a seductive innocence.

155 ὡς εἰπὼν λάβε χεῖρα: the combination λαμβάνω + χεῖρα is used in Homer for shaking hands on an agreement (*Il.* 6. 233) and for consolation and greeting (*Il.* 21. 286, 24. 671–2, *Od.* 24. 398); for a possibly romantic greeting see Penelope's thoughts of what action to take when she first confronts Odysseus at *Od.* 23. 87 (either stand aloof . . . ἢ παρστᾶσα κύσειε κάρη καὶ χεῖρε λαβοῦσα; cf. their farewell also at 18. 258). For grasping the hand with sexual intentions see the preceding note.

φιλομμειδὴς Ἀφροδίτης: see on *Aphr.* 17, 155–67.

156 ἕρπε: 'move' or 'go'; the specialized sense 'to crawl' or 'to creep' which the verb has elsewhere (cf. Sk. *sarpati*, Lat. *serpere*) is not present in Homer. On this see Létoublon (1985), 110–13, who points out also that the four examples of the verb in Homer (*Il.* 17. 447, *Od.* 12. 395, 17. 158, 18. 131) and one in *Dem.* 365 all refer to general movement without a particular direction, while here the verb is used of motion *towards* the bed. She may be right that this suggests a more developed stage of the epic language; the one other occurrence of ἕρπω in the *Hymns* has Pan moving towards the centre of the dance at *Hy.* 19. 22 ἐς μέσον ἕρπων, but that poem is generally considered to be late (see AHS 402–3). For movement towards a bed with the verbs ἔρχομαι and κίω see *Il.* 3. 447 and *Od.* 23. 294. For this movement of Aphrodite, see later Theoc. *Id.* 1. 105–6 οὐ λέγεται τὰν Κύπριν ὁ βουκόλος; ἕρπε ποτ' Ἴδαν, | ἕρπε ποτ' Ἀγχίσαν.

μεταστρεφθεῖσα: VE 58 suggests that Aphrodite turns herself about to go off to bed, *contra* Humbert (1936), who translates 'détournait la tête'. Turning herself around to go to bed would be a curious detail given that there is little indication in which direction the bed is, or how they were standing when talking. It is true that the verb, common in Homer in both the active and the passive (see in particular the metrically equivalent στῆ δὲ μεταστρεφθείς Il. 11. 595/15. 591/17. 141, and τῷ δὲ μεταστρεφθέντι Il. 8. 258/11. 447), does not elsewhere mean to turn just the head, but this seems to be the most natural sense here; in complement to κατ' ὄμματα καλὰ βαλοῦσα, Aphrodite would then be turning her face away in (mock) maidenly shame (cf. n. seq.). One might, however, imagine her turning more of her body than just her head.

See later Mosch. Eur. 111 ἡ δὲ μεταστρεφθεῖσα φίλας καλέεσκεν ἑταίρας, a possible reminiscence of this line. There the young maiden Europa is turning around (presumably most of her body) to call out to her companions whilst she is being carried off on the back of Zeus (as a bull) to be raped.

κατ' ὄμματα καλὰ βαλοῦσα: Demeter does the same at Dem. 194 after entering the house of Celeus (in disguise), where the action is apparently an indication of her sorrow. The phrase does not occur elsewhere and is another indication of the direct connection between Aphr. and Dem. (see Introd., pp. 38–40). But this case offers no indication of priority; Heitsch (1965), 39 argues that the phrase is better suited to Aphrodite's show of modesty and is therefore prior to Dem., but as a sign of sorrow it seems 'perfectly appropriate' (N. Richardson 1974, 218, cf. Janko 1982, 164).

For the gesture cf. Il. 3. 217 ὑπαὶ δὲ ἴδεσκε κατὰ χθονὸς ὄμματα πήξας, where Odysseus is said by Antenor to have fixed his eyes upon the ground (in feigned modesty?) when addressing the Trojans. Also, Il. 3. 427 ὄσσε πάλιν κλίνασα, where Helen averts her eyes from Paris. Later, lovers casting their eyes downward becomes a standard motif of love poetry: in Greek Theoc. Id. 2. 112 (Delphis in assumed modesty; see Gow ii. 55 ad loc.), Call. fr. 80. 11, A.R. 1. 790–1, 3. 1008–9, 1022–4, Irenaeus Referendarius, AP 5. 253, Musae. 160, Colluth. 305, etc., and see in Latin Verg. A. 11. 480 oculos deiecta decoros (Lavinia) which may be an imitation of Aphr. (cf. N. Richardson, loc. cit.; for many more examples of the motif in Latin poetry see Watson 1983, 261, 262 n. 49). More generally on the gesture, whether of maidenly shame, sorrow, or contemplation, see Muecke (1984), Campbell (1994), 34–5, West (1997), 200.

157 λέχος εὔστρωτον: 'well-spread bed'. Not in Homer or Hesiod, the rare adjective occurs also at Dem. 285 κὰδ δ' ἄρ' ἀπ' εὐστρώτων λεχέων θόρον; elsewhere at Alc. fr. 283. 8 εὔστρωτον λέχος and then twice later at Nonn. *D.* 18. 164 and 45. 345 ἐϋστρώτων ἐπὶ λέκτρων (Somolinos 1998, 56 n. 100 points also to a late inscription (5th c. AD) *IEphesos* 1304 = *IGChr.* 99, where the adjective is used of streets, ἀγυιαί). The rareness of the term points once again to a direct connection between *Dem.* and *Aphr.*; Janko (1982), 164, 227 follows Heitsch (1965), 38 and Podbielski (1971), 91 n. 16 in claiming that *Aphr.* is earlier because ἐστρωμένον in the next line glosses the neologism, while in *Dem.* the word is used absolutely, but this on its own is not convincing evidence (see N. Richardson 1974, 255). Also of interest is the parallel in Alcaeus, another connection between *Aphr.* and Lesbian poetry (see Introd., pp. 45–7). There is no reason to assume a direct connection between the two poems, but this might suggest that the adjective εὔστρωτος has a tradition in Aeolic poetry. If so, this would favour its having been borrowed by *Dem.* from *Aphr.*, which shows other signs of Aeolic origin (cf. above on 31–2 τιμάοχος and see Introd., pp. 44–5). The adjective is paralleled in Hesiod by *Th.* 798 στρωτοῖς ἐν λεχέεσσι and cf. later Mosch. *Eur.* 16 στρωτῶν λεχέων, a possible imitation of *Dem.* (see N. Richardson, loc. cit.). For the compound, Somolinos (1998), 57 compares Alcmaeonis 2. 1–2 Davies νέκυς δὲ χαμαιστρώτου ἔπι τείνας | εὐρείης στιβάδος.

ἐς λέχος . . . ὅθι: for the structure cf. *Il.* 23. 206 Αἰθιόπων ἐς γαῖαν, ὅθι etc. and in particular *Od.* 8. 277 βῆ ῥ' ἴμεν ἐς θάλαμον, ὅθι οἱ φίλα δέμνια κεῖτο of Hephaestus setting his trap for Aphrodite and Ares.

ὅθι περ πάρος ἔσκεν: cf. *Od.* 4. 627/17. 169 ὅθι περ πάρος, ὕβριν ἔχοντες. For πάρος + iterative ἔσκεν see *Il.* 11. 669 = *Aphr.* 238 of power formerly in now old limbs. The sense here, however, is similar to *Il.* 1. 609–11 Ζεὺς δὲ πρὸς ὃν λέχος ἤϊ' Ὀλύμπιος ἀστεροπητής | ἔνθα πάρος κοιμᾶθ' ὅτε μιν γλυκὺς ὕπνος ἱκάνοι. | ἔνθα καθηῦδ' ἀναβάς, a fact which has relevance for the present moment, 'up until this point' (cf. VE 58); see West (2003) 'where the lord kept it spread with soft blankets'.

ἄνακτι | . . . ἐστρωμένον: the dative ἄνακτι is best understood as a 'dative of agent'; see Monro (1891), 136: 'the "Dat. of the Agent" with Passive Verbs seems to be a special application of the true Dat.; cf. *Il.* 13. 168 ὅ οἱ κλισίηφι λέλειπτο *which for him was (= which he had) left in the tent,* [Ἀνδρομάχη] ἔχεθ' Ἕκτορι [*Il.* 6. 398] *was had as wife by Hector.* So Τρωσὶν δαμναμένους [*Il.* 13. 16/353], Πηλείωνι δαμείς

[*Il.* 20. 294/22. 40] etc., because the victory is gained by the victor' (*contra* VE 59 'a possessive dative').

158–60. The coverings of Anchises' bed include blankets and the more exotic skins of bears and lions. A detailed description of the bed is not typical in seduction scenes (see above on 155–67), but it is formulaic in scenes of hospitality in Homer. See in particular the extensive preparation of beds by Achilles' attendants at *Il.* 24. 643–8, where ῥήγεα, τάπητες, and χλαῖναι are all piled on to make a comfortable resting-place, and the almost identical preparation for guests at *Od.* 4. 294–305 and 7. 335–47; also less elaborately *Il.* 9. 658–68, *Od.* 10. 352–3, etc. (see further Arend 1933, 99–105 and schema 12). Blankets (χλαῖναι) are standard fare, while the addition of animal skins is just the rustic touch which one might expect of a shepherd living in the mountains; at *Od.* 14. 50–1 Eumaeus covers his couch with the skin of a shaggy wild goat on which he sleeps, ἐστόρεσεν δ' ἐπὶ δέρμα ἰονθάδος ἀγρίου αἰγός | αὐτοῦ ἐνεύναιον, μέγα καὶ δασύ.

Apart from adding a rustic flavour, the introduction of the animals has further significance. Anchises' skins are not those of mere wild goats, but of bears and roaring lions, which 'he himself killed in the high mountains' (v. 160 τοὺς αὐτὸς κατέπεφνεν ἐν οὔρεσιν ὑψηλοῖσιν). This last phrase in particular sets the animal skins as a symbol of Anchises' power, just as Heracles' lion skin is a symbol of his strength; see Smith (1981*a*), 59 'the appearance of the skins on Anchises' bed has an oddly balancing effect . . . this helps to prevent our seeing him as a hopelessly weaker and inappropriate partner in the love-making which is to follow' (cf. Podbielski 1971, 55). Furthermore, the bears and lions recall the same beasts which Aphrodite lulled into sexual submission earlier in the poem while crossing Ida to confront Anchises (see on *Aphr.* 69–74 and 70–1). By doing so the animal skins become more than just an abstract symbol of Anchises' power, and underline Aphrodite's own loss of power in the face of Anchises' momentary strength; she is now conquered on top of the very beasts she earlier controlled. This symbolic loss of strength which recalls an earlier display of power is paralleled in the second half of this scene by the description of clothes, which previously symbolized Aphrodite's sexual power when setting out to seduce Anchises (see on *Aphr.* 162–5).

158 χλαίνῃσιν μαλακῇς: χλαῖναι are in Homer never μαλακαί; although cf. χλαῖναι οὖλαι (*Od.* 4. 50 etc.). For the soft blanket as an erotic instrument see, if the reconstruction is correct, Archil. fr. 196a. 42–5 παρθένον δ' ἐν ἄνθ]εσιν | τηλ]εθάεσσι λαβὼν | ἔκλινα, μαλθακῇ δ[έ μιν | χλαίν]ῃ καλύψας, αὐχέν' ἀγκάλης ἔχων. This combination appears first in Hes. *Op.* 537 χλαῖνάν τε μαλακήν, 1—2⏑⏑3 as here; cf. later Ar. *Ves.* 738 χλαῖναν μαλακήν, σισύραν.

βαρυφθόγγων: lions do not roar in Homer, where they move silently as stealthy creatures; this is the first reference to their roar in Greek literature (see Lonsdale 1990, 44–5). This is also the first occurrence of the adjective βαρύφθογγος, although Heitsch (1965), 24 points to *Od.* 9. 257 φθόγγον ... βαρύν of the fearful voice of Polyphemus. It appears elsewhere first at Pi. *I.* 6. 34 of a bowstring (βαρυφθόγγοιο νευρᾶς), and of a lion at B. *Epin.* 9. 9 and Nic. *Ther.* 171, the latter in the gen. plur. as here εἰς ἐνοπὴν ταύρων τε βαρυφθόγγων τε λεόντων; it is connected with lions also later at Nonn. *D.* 2. 610–11 πῇ χάσματα κεῖνα λεόντων | καὶ χθόνιον μύκημα βαρυφθόγγων σέο λαιμῶν.

160 τοὺς αὐτὸς κατέπεφνεν ἐν οὔρεσιν ὑψηλοῖσιν: this line is very similar to *Od.* 11. 574 τοὺς αὐτὸς κατέπεφνεν ἐν οἰοπόλοισιν ὄρεσσι, describing the great hunter Orion whom Odysseus sees in Hades (cf. Podbielski 1971, 55). For the killing of a beast 'oneself' for a trophy Reinhardt (1956), 12 also compares Pandarus' killing of a wild goat for his bow at *Il.* 4. 105–9. On the dignity conveyed by αὐτός 'himself' see on *Aphr.* 151 ἑκηβόλος αὐτὸς Ἀπόλλων.

The formula ἐν οὔρεσιν ὑψηλοῖσιν recurs at *Aphr.* 266, but not elsewhere except at *Orac. Sib.* 3. 682. See however the metrically equivalent *Il.* 24. 614 ἐν οὔρεσιν οἰοπόλοισιν, and the gen. ὑψηλῶν ὀρέων at *Il.* 12. 282, *Od.* 9. 113 etc.; also later Q.S. 10. 348 ἐν ὑψηλοῖσιν ὄρεσσι.

161 οἱ δ' ἐπεὶ οὖν: very common in Homer *Il.* 1. 57, 3. 340 etc. (7× *Il.*, 5× *Od.*); note in particular *Il.* 24. 329 οἱ δ' ἐπεὶ οὖν πόλιος κατέβαν. On the frequency of the combination ἐπεὶ οὖν see Denniston (1954), 417: 'In 33 places there is a reference to something already described or foreshadowed'.

λεχέων εὐποιήτων ἐπέβησαν: the λέχος is not otherwise εὐποίητος; Gerstinger supplements the word at Pamprepius fr. 4. 50 (*GDK*; see app. crit. ad loc.) εἰς λέχος εὐ[ποίητον ἐπήλυθε Δ]ηιαν[εί]ρης, but it is impossible to know if this is correct. For more on the adjective see on *Aphr.* 75. For the mounting of a λέχος see *Sc.* 16 πρὶν λεχέων ἐπιβῆναι; later Isyllus 50 λεχέων δ' ἱμεροέντων ἐπέβας (*CA*) and Paulus Silentiarius, *AP* 5. 275. 3 τολμήσας δ' ἐπέβην λεχέων. Cf. on *Aphr.* 154 for the verb used of mounting an εὐνή.

162–5. The removal of Aphrodite's clothing and jewellery echoes its description when she appeared before Anchises at vv. 81–90, with the addition of two items, πόρπαι and a ζώνη (for detailed discussion of the other items mentioned here see on *Aphr.* 81 ff. *passim*). The addition of the πόρπαι is formulaic, while the removal of the ζώνη is an important symbol of sexual submission. The detailed removal of the rest of the clothing, however, finds no parallel in Greek literature. Once again this feature has an eastern ring to it. Very similar is the *Descent of Ištar into the Nether World* (*BTM* 500–1), where the goddess has all her clothing and jewellery (including a girdle) removed piece by piece as she passes through the seven gates of the Nether World. Also, parallel to Aphrodite's redressing after this sexual encounter (vv. 171–2), Ištar regains her clothing as she re-ascends to the earth (see a more detailed description on 81–90 and 87 ἕλικας κάλυκάς τε). In these eastern texts the clothing of the love-goddess is a symbol of her strength; its removal represents her death and its retrieval her rebirth. Here too Aphrodite's attire perhaps symbolizes her strength, and its removal her weakness (see Sowa 1984, 79 and on 81–90). The main point here, however, must be that Aphrodite is taking off her clothes in order to have intercourse.

162 κόσμον μέν οἱ πρῶτον ἀπὸ χροὸς εἷλε φαεινόν: nowhere else is κόσμος called φαεινός, until Nonn. *D.* 5. 83 ἕκτην Ζηνὸς ἄγαλμα φαεινοτέρῳ κάμε κόσμῳ. But this line has similarities with *Il.* 14. 169–71 of Hera's toilette before seducing Zeus, ἔνθ' ἥ γ' εἰσελθοῦσα θύρας ἐπέθηκε φαεινάς | ἀμβροσίῃ μὲν πρῶτον ἀπὸ χροὸς ἱμερόεντος | λύματα πάντα κάθηρεν. On the brightness of Aphrodite's jewellery, see on *Aphr.* 83–90.

μέν οἱ πρῶτον: this is picked up by δέ ... οἱ in v. 164, providing an ordered structure to the undressing; first Anchises takes off her jewellery, then he loosens her girdle and takes off her clothes. This meticulous removal of her attire piece by piece enhances the eroticism of the passage.

163. This line is an exact replica of *Il.* 18. 401. In a departure from his usual care, Hoekstra (1969), 41 claims that 'there is no Homeric parallel at all' for this line, suggesting that the neglect of digamma in ἕλικας (not neglected in its two other occurrences at *Aphr.* 87 and *Sc.* 295) is a sign of modification. This may be the case, but *Il.* 18. 401 rules out any claim that it is post-Homeric. For more on this line cf. on *Aphr.* 87.

πόρπας: only here and at *Il.* 18. 401 in early epic. The word means a 'pin' or 'brooch', used in some way for holding a garment together (so later ancients; Hsch. σχιστός· χιτών τις ποιὸς γυναικεῖος, κατὰ τὸ στῆθος πόρπῃ συνεχόμενος etc.). It is probably related to περόνη 'pin' through a derivation from πείρω 'to pierce' (*Dictionnaire* s.v. πείρω). Pollux, *Onomast.* 7. 54 differentiates πόρπη from περόνη as a pin on the breast rather than on the shoulder, but Hsch. treats them as synonyms (περόναι explained by πόρπαι); in any case, it is difficult to be certain what the earlier meaning was from later testimony (it is also unclear exactly what type of pin is implied by Hera's golden ἐνεταί at *Il.* 14. 180; cf. Bielefeld 1968, 6–8, Janko 1992, 176–7). The choice between 'pin' and 'brooch' is a delicate matter of date; the brooch seems for the most part to have replaced the metal pin and fibula before 600 BC and could easily be intended here, but following *Il.* 18. 401 'pin' is probably still the best translation (see Lorimer 1950, 401–4, 512 n. 3; so also West 2003). This was not mentioned in the earlier description of her clothing (see on *Aphr.* 86 πέπλον).

164 λῦσε δέ οἱ ζώνην: the loosening of the woman's girdle by the man is a typical prelude to sexual activity (cf. on *Aphr.* 155–67). See Poseidon and Tyro at *Od.* 11. 245 λῦσε δὲ παρθενίην ζώνην and Peleus and Thetis at Alc. fr. 42. 9–10 ἔλ]υσε δ' —— | ζῶμα παρθένω; later, Mosch. *Eur.* 164 [Ζεὺς] λῦσε δέ οἱ μίτρην, Nonn. *D.* 1. 347 [Ζεὺς] μίτρην πρῶτον ἔλυσε. For the middle form of λύω, properly used of a woman removing her own girdle (although the active is used of the wearer at Pi. *I.* 8. 45, A.R. 1. 288; see McLennan 1977, 52–3), cf. [Hes.] fr. 1. 4 μίτρας τ' ἀλλύσαντο, and the anonymous *AP* 7. 324 ἃδ' ἐγὼ ἁ περίβωτος ὑπὸ πλακὶ τῇδε τέθαμμαι | μούνῳ ἐνὶ ζώναν ἀνέρι λυσαμένα. Otherwise, the middle form of λύω + ζώνην/μίτρην is used also of childbirth (Call. *Hy.* 1. 21, 4. 209 etc.; cf. Pi. *O.* 6. 39); and see below v. 255 ὑπὸ ζώνῃ of pregnancy.

The ζώνη in Homer is properly a belt worn by women (twice

the term apparently refers to the 'waist', of Ares *Il.* 2. 479 and Agamemnon 11. 234, although in the latter case it is possibly synonymous with ζωστήρ; see Hainsworth 1993, 250 ad loc.), but specifics as to how it was worn are unknown (see Marinatos 1967, 12; Losfeld 1991, 222–6); apart from the example of Tyro above, both Calypso and Circe wear one (*Od.* 5. 231 and 10. 544), and Hera puts on an elaborate one before setting out to seduce Zeus at *Il.* 14. 181 (on which see Janko 1992, 177 ad loc.). Other than on this occasion, however, Aphrodite is not described wearing a ζώνη, which cannot be identified with her famous κεστὸς ἱμάς loosened from her breast to give to Hera at *Il.* 14. 214 ᾗ καὶ ἀπὸ στήθεσφιν ἐλύσατο κεστὸν ἱμάντα (on this as a 'saltire' or 'breast-strap' see Bonner 1949, Brenk 1977, Janko 1992, 184–5 ad loc.). As above, its inclusion here is entirely within the realm of Greek epic, but one can perhaps also compare Ištar's girdle of birth stones in Akkadian poetry (Foster 501; see on *Aphr.* 162–5). Aphrodite is represented with a girdle in art (see *LIMC* ii, Aphrodite 85, 87, etc.); J. Karageorghis (1984), 364–5 reports bronze-age figurines of the fertility-goddess found in Cyprus with an embroidered girdle.

εἵματα σιγαλόεντα: see on *Aphr.* 85.

165 ἔκδυε: for the compound of taking clothes off someone else see *Od.* 14. 341 ἐκ μέν με χλαῖνάν τε χιτῶνά τε εἵματ' ἔδυσαν; elsewhere, the active form ἐκδύνω has a middle sense, as when Telemachus takes off his cloak at *Od.* 1. 437 ἕζετο δ' ἐν λέκτρῳ, μαλακὸν δ' ἔκδυνε χιτῶνα. The middle is used of taking off armour at *Il.* 3. 114. The enjambment places emphasis on the verb, and thereby on the removal of Aphrodite's clothing.

κατέθηκεν ἐπὶ θρόνου ἀργυροήλου: for the phrasing see in particular *Od.* 20. 95–7 χλαῖναν μὲν συνελὼν καὶ κώεα, τοῖσιν ἐνεῦδεν, | ἐς μέγαρον κατέθηκεν ἐπὶ θρόνου, ἐκ δὲ βοείην | θῆκε θύραζε φέρων; while ἐπὶ θρόνου ἀργυροήλου is four times at this place in the line in Homer (*Il.* 18. 389, *Od.* 7. 162, 10. 314, 366). Note as well for placing clothes on a throne χλαίνας μὲν κατέθεντο κατὰ κλισμούς τε θρόνους τε *Od.* 17. 86/179/20. 249 (cf. also *Od.* 10. 352 and 20. 150).

The adjective ἀργυρόηλος 'silver-studded' is combined in Homer with θρόνος as here (5× gen. -ου 1× acc. *Od.* 8. 65), twice with φάσγανον (*Il.* 14. 405, 23. 807), and most commonly with ξίφος (11×, *Il.* 2. 45 etc.); it is not otherwise found outside Homer. V. Karageorghis

(1976) compares a throne found in a tomb in Salamis, Cyprus, dated to 700 BC; the throne is wooden, covered with sheets of silver and decorated with silver rivets (on silver used in furniture in Homer see Laser 1968, 42–3). The silver-studded sword is a Mycenaean item, and the components of the formula are known in Linear B tablets (see Kirk 1985, 118), but this formulation with θρόνος is probably a later innovation given the contracted gen. sing. in all but one instance (cf. Janko 1992, 213–14). The throne has many other decorative epithets (one example of each given): δαιδάλεος (*Od.* 17. 32), φαεινός (*Il.* 11. 645), περικαλλής (*Od.* 22. 438), ξεστός (*Od.* 16. 408), εὐποίητος (*Od.* 20. 150), and σιγαλόεις (*Od.* 5. 86).

166–7 Ἀγχίσης . . .: the enjambment of the name here emphasizes that it is Anchises performing all these actions. This leads the audience out of the dreamy description of the love-making back to the cold hard fact which the next two lines will recall: he, a mortal, is sleeping with a goddess! As Smith (1981*a*), 60–1 points out, these two verses put 'a kind of narrative seal on what precedes them', announcing the completion of the long-awaited sexual encounter and opening the way for a new phase in the narrative (cf. also Podbielski 1971, 56).

166 θεῶν ἰότητι καὶ αἴσῃ: Anchises sleeps with Aphrodite 'by the will of the gods and by destiny'. The phrase 'by the will of the gods' (θεῶν ἰότητι) appears seven times in Homer (*Il.* 19. 9, *Od.* 7. 214 etc.) and αἶσα is frequently invoked as a force which directs the lives of men and gods alike; but αἶσα is never combined with the phrase as here. That is not to say of course that the will of the gods and fate are two separate things, as they most often overlap, at least ultimately; only occasionally does Zeus have to forgo his own desire in deference to fate (see his acceptance of the death of his son Sarpedon, *Il.* 16. 431–61). Cf. phrases such as Διὸς αἴσῃ *Il.* 9. 608, ὑπὲρ Διὸς αἶσαν 17. 321, Διὸς αἶσα *Od.* 9. 52, etc. (also δαίμονος αἶσα *Od.* 11. 61, *Dem.* 300). On the undefined borders between the gods and fate, and fate and free will, see a good summary by Janko (1992), 4–7 with further bibliography (also VE 59). Ultimately, the insistence here upon the role of fate and the will of the gods is surely intended to recall and underline the central role which Zeus has played in bringing about this union (see on *Aphr.* 45–52, 53–199).

167 ἀθανάτῃ . . . θεᾷ βροτός: the immediate juxtaposition of θεᾷ and βροτός sums up the union taking place (see Podbielski 1971, 56, VE 60, VB 19). Compare in particular *Il.* 2. 821 θεὰ βροτῷ εὐνηθεῖσα of Aphrodite and Anchises; as well, 16. 176 γυνὴ θεῷ εὐνηθεῖσα, *Od.* 5. 129 θεοί, βροτὸν ἄνδρα παρεῖναι (the gods jealous of Calypso having a mortal man as a consort), and [Hes.] fr. 30. 33 φιλότητι θεὸς βροτῶι. Without an erotic context, cf. gods and mortals juxtaposed also at *Il.* 24. 67, *Od.* 1. 32 and 4. 397. Also often in the *Rigveda*, e.g. 3. 9. 1 *devám mártāsaḥ* (= θεὸν βροτοί) or 8. 48. 12 *ámartiyo mártiyām* (= ἀθάνατος θνητούς). In Latin, see Naevius' epitaph (Gell. 1. 24. 2) *immortales mortales si foret fas flere | flerent diuae Camenae Naeuium poetam.*

ἀθανάτῃ παρέλεκτο θεᾷ: note [Hes.] fr. 343. 16 ἔνθα θεὰ παρέλεκτο Θέμις; for the verb form also [Hegesinus], *Atthis* 1 (*Dubia et Spuria* fr. 3 Davies) Ἄσκρῃ δ' αὖ παρέλεκτο Ποσειδάων ἐνοσίχθων and Nonn. D. 13. 350 Ἁρμονίῃ παρέλεκτο ῥοδώπιδι Κάδμος ἀλήτης. The verb frequently describes sexual union: *Il.* 2. 515 (Ares and Astyoche), 6. 198 (Zeus and Laodameia), 14. 237 (Zeus and Hera), 16. 184 (Hermes and Polymele), 24. 676 (Achilles and Briseis), etc.

οὐ σάφα εἰδώς: 'not knowing for sure'; for a robust defence of this meaning see Smith (1981a), 122–3 n. 67, *contra* Bickerman's *nesciens* 'not knowing [at all]' (1976, 247 n. 73): among other examples he compares *Il.* 5. 183 σάφα δ' οὐκ οἶδ' εἰ θεός ἐστιν, where Pandarus seems genuinely uncertain of whether Diomedes is a god or not. Cf. also the herdsman at *Il.* 15. 632–3 οὔ πω σάφα εἰδὼς | θηρὶ μαχέσσασθαι, unsure of what to do when a lion attacks his cattle; and *Od.* 1. 202, where Athena, disguised as Mentes, says that she will prophesy to Telemachus οὔτε τι μάντις ἐὼν οὔτ' οἰωνῶν σάφα εἰδώς. On Anchises' scepticism, and then cautious acceptance of his visitor's claims, see on *Aphr.* 92–106, 143–54.

VB 19 debates whether this is a general statement about the unwitting nature of mortals, parallel to Ζεὺς δ' ἄφθιτα μήδεα εἰδώς v. 43, or a specific qualification of παρέλεκτο θεᾷ; the latter is surely what is intended (his reference to *Il.* 18. 363 ὅς περ θνητός τ' ἐστὶ καὶ οὐ τόσα μήδεα οἶδε is no parallel for οὐ σάφα εἰδώς), although Anchises' position is certainly in contrast to Zeus' supreme knowledge. After the comparison of mortal and immortal earlier in the line, the phrase serves to underline Aphrodite's successful deception of her mortal lover. Bergren's suggestion (1989, 25) that this can be understood to mean that 'from the perspective of Anchises—of any man whom Aphrodite and ἔρος deceive—the inside of the woman, her truth, remains impenetrable even to intercourse' is entirely unjustified.

168–83. At the time when herdsmen drive their flocks back from the fields, the love-making comes to a close. Aphrodite puts Anchises to sleep, dresses, assumes her true divine form, and then wakes him. When he sees the goddess in her full glory he is terrified and pathetically reduced to hiding behind his blanket.

Aphrodite's dressing introduces for the final time in the poem the recurring motif of her clothing (see on *Aphr.* 81–90). As a symbol of her power, her dressing is an appropriate element of the epiphany, and the natural counterpart to the removal of her clothes before sleeping with Anchises (see on *Aphr.* 162–5). One will also recall here Aphrodite's retreat to her sanctuary in Paphos after her sordid affair with Ares (*Od.* 8. 362–6), where she bathes and dresses. In both instances she has good reason to be ashamed and her preparation after intercourse marks a return in the direction of respectability. The mention of the dressing also brings a neat structural close to the seduction, which began at v. 64 with Aphrodite dressing and setting out to confront Anchises on Ida. The ring-composition is even effected verbally, with v. 172 almost an exact replica of v. 64, save for the substitution of δῖα θεάων for εἵματα καλά (here in the previous line). While the similarity recalls what has come before, the important difference highlights her emerging divinity; whereas earlier her clothing represented her disguise, it now forms part of the revelation of her true identity. A third integral function of the reference to the clothing here is to recall its detailed description above in vv. 83–90. On that occasion Anchises reacted to Aphrodite's luminous appearance with awe (θάμβαινεν v. 84), the whole scene giving the impression of a partial-epiphany (see above ad loc.). Its recollection imports the vividness of that description to the full epiphany here without the need for further repetition; this time there will be no doubt that Aphrodite is a goddess.

The epiphany contains three standard elements: (i) supernatural stature (vv. 173–4); (ii) divine radiance (v. 174); (iii) the human reaction of awe and terror (vv. 181–3)—on these see N. Richardson (1974), 208–9, 252; with a comprehensive list of parallels—and cf. above on 83–90. If divine fragrance, another common feature of epiphany, is not explicitly mentioned here (a fact noted by VE 60), the fact that her κάλλος is ἄμβροτον (vv. 174–5) perhaps recalls the emphasis on scent in Aphrodite's earlier toilette (see on *Aphr.* 58–9). On top of this traditional base, however, the epiphany is not quite the norm. First, it is worth pointing out a general difference between epiphanies in Homer and the *Hymns*. As Lenz (1975), 131–4, comparing in particular the epiphany of Aphrodite to Helen in *Il.* 3. 386 ff., and Sowa (1984), 241 note, those in *Aphr.* and the other *Hymns* (see *Dem.* 188 ff., 275 ff., *Apoll.* 440–7, and Dionysus at *Hy.* 7. 32 ff.) pay more attention to the god involved than in Homer, where the mortal is the 'Hauptperson' (*contra* Podbielski 1971, 62–3 'le récit insiste notamment moins sur la démonstration de la majesté de la divinité que sur la réaction d'Anchise terrifié'; that the gods receive more attention is of course not to say that the reaction of mortals is ignored); this difference reflects one of the major distinctions between the two genres, epic focusing primarily upon the lives of men and the *Hymns* upon the gods. In *Aphr.* this attention is focused upon the goddess. Aphrodite sends Anchises to sleep as soon as they finish making love, meaning that her epiphany, although it takes place right in front of the hero, is in effect enacted in the first instance for the audience alone. This creates a separation between the goddess and her lover (cf. Smith 1981*a*, 63 on her sending Anchises to sleep being 'a gentle step in the role of overt control which she now assumes'), singling her out for individual attention while engendering a suspense in anticipation of his reaction upon awakening. One can perhaps compare the transformation of Odysseus at *Od.* 16. 154 ff., where Athena makes him young and beautiful in secret away from the hut and Telemachus then reacts upon his return; but Odysseus is not a god, nor is sleep involved. It seems rather that the theme of epiphany has here been combined with a common motif of seduction and intercourse; sleep of one or both partners after intercourse is frequent in epic: so Paris and Helen (*Il.* 3. 448), Zeus and Hera (*Il.* 14. 352–3), Ares and Aphrodite (*Od.* 8. 295), Poseidon and Tyro (*Od.* 11. 245), and Odysseus and Penelope (*Od.* 23. 342–3).

Along with the transformation of the goddess comes a transformation of the tone of the poem. Up until this point the prevailing mood has been one of playful irony and deception, appropriate to the flirtatious exchange between two lovers. Everything must now be seen in a new light as Aphrodite and Anchises both awaken (whether literally or metaphorically) to the reality of what has been accomplished (on Parry's suggestion of post-coital clarity see on *Aphr.* 130 ἀνάγκη). A similar switch in tone occurs after the deceptive seduction of Zeus at *Il.* 14. 292 ff. In the lead-up to sexual intercourse there, Zeus' listing of his numerous amours in an apparent attempt to convince Hera of his strong attraction is highly comical in its tastelessness (312 ff.), yet sleep brings this atmosphere to an abrupt close; Sleep runs to the Achaean ships to tell Poseidon that the coast is clear, returning the audience to the harsh and brutal world of human war (354 ff.), and Zeus himself will see things with a different eye when he wakes up at 15. 4 ff. Podbielski (1971), 62–3 insists that in comparison to the solemn epiphanies in *Dem.* and *Apoll.*, Aphrodite's epiphany is a humorous event, but it is difficult to see the humour in what follows: the extreme fear and pleading of Anchises, the horrific tale of Tithonus, the deep regret of Aphrodite for having slept with a mortal, and her strong warnings to Anchises.

168 ἦμος . . . (τῆμος): the new phase in the poem is marked by a general indication of time; the love-making has finished at dusk, when herdsmen lead their cattle back from pasture. This is the only occurrence of ἦμος in the *Hymns*, which 38 times in Homer is used to locate an event in the narrative within the framework of a proverbial event (see Radin 1988, who gives a full survey of Homeric usage). Here the reference is slightly more than proverbial, recalling Anchises' fellow herdsmen, who were said to be away in the fields when Aphrodite arrived (a quaint bucolic touch; see on *Aphr.* 76–9 and cf. VE 60), but it nonetheless functions mainly as a generalization. Smith (1981a), 62–3 goes too far in supposing that the recollection of the real herdsmen gives the impression of a narrated event and thus a temporal discontinuity. Not only do the Homeric associations of ἦμος speak against a specific reference, but any suggestion of the imminent return of Anchises' companions would be sorely out of place; at least the two long tales about Ganymedes and Tithonus which Aphrodite tells do not suggest that she is in any rush to get out of the way before they return, which she would surely want to do given her later warning to Anchises.

For the ἦμος … τῆμος construction see *Il.* 7. 433–4, 11. 86–90 etc. The measurement of time by the proverbial action of herdsmen is paralleled by ἦμος δ' ἠέλιος μετενίσετο βουλυτόνδε (*Il.* 16. 779, *Od.* 9. 58). Radin (1988), 302–5 also compares this passage with two ἦμος clauses which refer to the mealtime of man in the middle of a battle (*Il.* 11. 86–90, *Od.* 12. 439–40; the only two in Homer which do not refer to a natural phenomenon such as the setting of the sun), noting that in all three instances 'the evocation of ordinary life intensifies the extra-ordinariness, the uniqueness, of [the] moment in the narrative' (cf. Podbielski 1971, 60: the time of day marked by the return of the herdsmen 'souligne l'heure non usuelle pour le sommeil.').

ἂψ εἰς αὖλιν: the term αὖλις is used only twice in Homer, of the shelter of humans at *Il.* 9. 232 and birds *Od.* 22. 470. Elsewhere of a cattle-fold in early poetry see *Herm.* 71–2 ἔνθα θεῶν μακάρων βόες ἄμβροτοι αὖλιν ἔχεσκον | βοσκόμεναι λειμῶνας ἀκηρασίους ἐρατεινούς (later Call. *Hy.* 6. 106, Theoc. *Id.* 16. 92 and 25. 18). For the phrasing cf. *Il.* 10. 211 ἂψ εἰς ἡμέας ἔλθοι and 15. 550 ἂψ εἰς Ἴλιον ἦλθε.

ἀποκλίνουσι: the meaning is to 'turn back' (+ ἂψ). This particular sense does not appear anywhere else. In its one appearance in Homer the verb means 'to turn aside [a dream]' *Od.* 19. 556. AHS 362 compare *Herm.* 76 ἴχνι' ἀποστρέψας, where Hermes magically turns the hooves of the cattle backwards as he drives them away in theft, but the sense there is really quite different.

169 βοῦς τε καὶ ἴφια μῆλα: the neglect of digamma in ἴφια (never neglected in Homer) suggests modification by transposition of line-end βόας καὶ ἴφια μῆλα *Il.* 5. 556 etc. (including nom. 4× *Il.*, 6× *Od.*; also [Hes.] fr. 204. 50); see Janko (1982), 153. Cf. ἴφια μῆλα in the same metrical position as here at *Il.* 9. 466/23. 166 πολλὰ δὲ ἴφια μῆλα καὶ εἰλίποδας ἕλικας βοῦς. Given the neglect of digamma elsewhere in the poem (see Introd., pp. 29–31 for examples), there is certainly no good reason to delete τε in order to restore it here (see Hoekstra 1965, 62).

νομῶν ἐξ ἀνθεμοέντων: 'flowery pastures'; the adjective is not elsewhere used with νομός until Nonn. *D.* 5. 266, 47. 180. See, however, of meadows (λειμῶνας) *Il.* 2. 467 and *Od.* 12. 159, ground in general (γαῖα) *Th.* 878 and notably at *Herm.* 96 (πεδί᾽ ἀνθεμόεντα) of mountain plains over which Hermes is driving cattle.

170–1 γλυκὺν ὕπνον … | νήδυμον: sleep is both γλυκύς (*Il.* 2. 71

etc.) and νήδυμος (Il. 2. 2 etc.) in Homer, but the two epithets are never combined as here. Heitsch (1965), 30 argues from this that in Aphr. νήδυμον has lost its individual meaning, combined with γλυκύν to lend 'episch-archaisches Kolorit' (followed by Hoekstra 1969, 48 n. 36). His own parallel, however, of Od. 13. 79–80 καὶ τῷ νήδυμος ὕπνος ἐπὶ βλεφάροισιν ἔπιπτε | νήγρετος ἥδιστος hinders the assumption both that this combination is post-Homeric and that νήδυμος is a meaningless gloss (cf. Janko 1982, 157, VE 61). In the Homeric passage there is emphasis on the sweetness of sleep for Odysseus, a hero who has suffered much (cf. also 13. 90–3; after all his toils he then slept ἀτρέμας). Here the emphasis on Anchises' sweet sleep will heighten the sense of his rude awakening in a few lines.

On νήδυμος, probably originally from ἥδυμος (so Herm. 241, 449 and a variant in Homer) by misdivision of nu mobile in the previous word as at Il. 2. 2 ἔχε-ν ἥδυμον ὕπνον, see Leumann (1950), 44–5, with further discussion and bibliography given by Càssola 552, VE 61–2, S. West, OC i. 242; less convincing is Wyatt's belief (1969, 71–2) that νήδυμος is the original form, later becoming ἥδυμος by analogy with ἡδύς. For νήδυμος enjambed as here see Il. 14. 253, 23. 62–3.

170 ἐπὶ γλυκὺν ὕπνον ἔχευεν: = Od. 2. 395; cf. also 18. 188 κατὰ γλυκὺν ὕπνον ἔχευεν. Of sleep related to intercourse, see Hera's plan to send Zeus to sleep at Il. 14. 164–5 τῷ δ᾽ ὕπνον ἀπήμονά τε λιαρόν τε | χεύῃ ἐπὶ βλεφάροισιν; see also Poseidon and Tyro at Od. 11. 245 κατὰ δ᾽ ὕπνον ἔχευεν (for sleep and χέω cf. Il. 2. 19, Od. 7. 286, 12. 338, 13. 70). On sleep 'poured', envisaged as a liquid in ancient thought, see Onians (1951), 31–2, West (1997), 234–5.

171–2. On the repeated point of Aphrodite's dressing and the similarity of v. 172 to v. 64 see on Aphr. 168–83.

171 αὐτὴ δέ: 'but she . . .'; the mortal and goddess have been close, both physically and in the verse (see on Aphr. 167 θεᾷ βροτός), but now their separation is signalled by the demonstrative and adversative δέ (on the separation effected by Anchises' sleep see on Aphr. 168–83).

χροΐ: for the locatival dative VE 62 compares Od. 14. 506 (= 23. 115) κακὰ χροΐ εἵματ᾽ ἔχοντα; see also Cypr. fr. 4. 1 εἵματα μὲν χροΐ ἕστο.

173–5. These lines are very similar to Dem. 188–9, where Demeter makes a partial epiphany upon arrival at the palace of Celeus: ἡ δ᾽ ἄρ᾽

ἐπ' οὐδὸν ἔβη ποσὶ καί ῥα μελάθρου | κῦρε κάρη, πλῆσεν δὲ θύρας σέλαος θείοιο. In particular, the identical phrase μελάθρου | κῦρε κάρη has prompted scholars to suppose a direct relationship between the two passages. This seems all the more probable given the two parallels with *Dem.* just a few lines above (see on *Aphr.* 156, 157). If so, the case for priority is as usual a delicate one. Outlined by N. Richardson (1974), 209–10, the linguistic criteria are the following:

(i) In *Aphr.* μέλαθρον has its proper meaning 'roof-beam' or 'rafter' (see scholia T on *Od.* 8. 279 μέλαθρον δὲ κυρίως τὸ μέσον τῆς στέγης; cf. in Homer *Il.* 2. 414 etc., later Sapph. fr. 111. 1 etc.); Aphrodite is presumably inside the hut while she is dressing and her head naturally reaches the rafters. In *Dem.* on the other hand, Demeter stands upon the threshold of the room, filling the doorway with light; μέλαθρον should therefore logically mean 'lintel' (although see Beck, *LfgrE* s.v., who argues against that meaning on the ground that the οὐδός extends within the door), a sense not attested elsewhere except for a late gloss in Hsch.: μέλαθρα· οἰκίαι, ὑπέρθυρα. This mild stretch in meaning may suggest that the use in *Dem.* is secondary.

(ii) Heitsch (1965), 39 condemns *Dem.* as secondary because of a 'hard' switch of subject: he holds that in *Aphr.* κάρη is the subject of κῦρε, that it is therefore also the subject in *Dem.*, and that the latter thus awkwardly switches from the goddess as subject, to her head, and then once again back to her (πλῆσεν). In fact, in both cases it is also possible for κάρη to be an acc. of respect. As N. Richardson, loc. cit. points out, the asyndeton in *Aphr.* makes it easier for κάρη to be the subject, separate from that (the goddess) in the previous clause, but in *Dem.* it is more natural for Demeter to be the subject in all three connected clauses (with κάρη acc. of respect); of course, there is nothing in particular stopping κάρη from being an acc. of respect in *Aphr.* also. Yet even if both cases are nom., in *Dem.* κάρη could govern πλῆσεν as a common part of the body from which divine light radiates (see N. Richardson 1974, 210 on *Dem.* 189 and cf. *Aphr.* 174), therefore largely negating Heitsch's claim of difficulty. In any event this is hardly reliable evidence for establishing priority.

(iii) The asyndeton in *Aphr.* has caused some controversy. Ruhnken (1782), 33 proposed εὐποιήτου δέ, while AS 212 preferred to assume a lost crasis κεὐποιήτοιο (Allen changed his mind in 1936;

they also note a most intrusive emendation ἀτὰρ ἐυτύκτοιο by Brunck); neither is required. Asyndeton occurs several times in *Aphr.* (see above on 71 ἄρκτοι), frequently enough to allow this as a stylistic feature of the poet, even if it is not elsewhere in the middle of the line as here. On more subjective ground, Smith (1981*a*), 63–4 defends the asyndeton as reflecting 'a striking disjunction on the factual level in the events he is describing'; in other words, appropriate to the shock and awe of the epiphany (cf. Humbert 1936, 157 n. 2). As regards the poem's relationship with *Dem.*, the asyndeton is certainly not evidence that *Aphr.* is later (for asyndeton in the middle of the line in Homer, see in speech at *Il.* 22. 393; cf. *Grammaire*, ii. 351).

(iv) Similar to the question of asyndeton is that of the locatival dative ἔστη ἄρα κλισίῃ. N. Richardson (1974), 210 comments that this is odd 'as one expects a preposition, and ἄρα comes very late in the sentence'; Stephanus had proposed πάρ for ἄρα. Again, however, the locatival dative is a frequent stylistic feature in *Aphr.* which does not cause great surprise here (note the proximate χροΐ in v. 171). As for the position of ἄρα in the sentence, it is indeed unusually late (VE 62 attempts to argue *contra* N. Richardson that 'ἄρα often comes late in the sentence' by referring to Denniston 1954, 41–2, but all the examples given there are later and none are in hexameter verse); this, and the enjambment of the phrase, which might elsewhere have stood on its own at line-beginning (with ἄρα in its normal place, second in the clause), may suggest adaptation of an earlier model. But as this particular phrase is not paralleled in *Dem.* it can have no bearing on the relationship between the two poems.

In summary the only linguistic criterion worth considering for the issue of priority is the first, a suggestion perhaps that *Dem.* is secondary (cf. Janko 1982, 164). Otherwise, a general impression that *Aphr.* is the lender may be supported by the fact that several parallels are clustered in close proximity in *Aphr.* (vv. 156, 157, 173–4), which are then somewhat more spread out in *Dem.* (vv. 188–9, 194, and *285), although one might not want to put too much weight on this. Reinhardt (1956), 13, Heitsch (1965), 39, and Lenz (1975), 56 all argue for this on the grounds that the epiphany is more appropriate here than in *Dem.*, but such arguments seem rather too subjective (cf. again Janko, loc. cit.). See further Introd., pp. 38–40.

εὐποιήτοιο: on this adjective, uniquely here with μέλαθρον, see on Aphr. 75 κλισίας εὐποιήτους and 161 λεχέων εὐποιήτων. Cf. Od. 11. 278 ὑψηλοῖο μελάθρου.

μελάθρου | κῦρε κάρῃ: a version of this motif is found at Il. 4. 443 [Ἔρις] οὐρανῷ ἐστήριξε κάρη καὶ ἐπὶ χθονὶ βαίνει. On the similarity with Dem. 188–9 see on Aphr. 173–4. Callimachus later seems to have Dem. (and Aphr.?) in mind at Hy. 6. 57–8 Δαμάτηρ ... γείνατο δ' αὖ θεύς | ... κεφαλὰ δέ οἱ ἅψατ' Ὀλύμπω—see Hopkinson (1984a) ad loc., who lists several later Greek and Latin parallels for divine heads reaching great heights (among them note Nonn. D. 29. 320–1 and Q.S. 8. 349–50—after Il. 4. 443: Tryph. 562–3, Verg. A. 4. 177, 10. 767, etc.). N. Richardson (1974), 210 asks whether Claudian had the Hymns in mind at Cons. Stil. 2. 277 summae tangunt laquearia cristae (the epiphany of Roma); at least the touching of a roof with the head in an epiphany does not seem to exist elsewhere.

Bulloch (1977), 116–21 suggests that Callimachus also had the Hymns in mind at Hy. 6. 37 μέγα δένδρεον αἰθέρι κῦρον, a tree in the sacred grove of Demeter (conflating for the first time the epic construction κυρέω + dat., 'to meet with', always with this case in Homer and Hesiod, with the sense of κυρέω + gen. 'to reach/hit'; for later examples with the gen. see N. Richardson 1974, 209 and LSJ s.v.); the context makes it an attractive possibility, but as for a conscious echo it is not an open and shut case (see the reservations of Hopkinson 1984a ad loc.).

κῦρε: only M preserves the κ of κῦρε; the other MSS have βύρε ET, ηὗρε LΠp, ἦρε AtD; on the common confusion of κ, η and β in the early period of minuscule see AHS 362.

174–5 κάλλος ... | ἄμβροτον, οἷον ...: cf. the very similar Od. 18. 192–4 κάλλεϊ μέν οἱ πρῶτα προσώπατα καλὰ κάθηρεν | ἀμβροσίῳ, οἵῳ περ ἐϋστέφανος Κυθέρεια | χρίεται, where Athena enhances Penelope's beauty. For similar enjambment of ἄμβροτος see vv. 62–3.

174 κάλλος δὲ παρειάων ἀπέλαμπεν: for divine radiance emanating from the head or face cf. N. Richardson (1974), 210 with other parallels; Il. 5. 7, 18. 205 ff. etc. (on Aphrodite's radiance in Aphr. and its importance in epiphanies see on Aphr. 83–90). Generally on beauty as a physical emanation from a girl, often from the eyes, see West (1966a), 409. Note in particular the bright cheeks of Helios at Hy. 31. 11–13 παρὰ κροτάφων τε παρειαὶ | λαμπραὶ ἀπὸ κρατὸς χαρίεν κατέχουσι πρόσωπον | τηλαυγές. Also, see later the moving description of Neoptolemus at Q.S. 7. 361–4 ἀμφὶ δ' ἄρ' αὐτῷ | ὄμματα μαρμαίρουσιν ἴσον πυρί, τοῦ δὲ παρειαὶ | κάλλος ὁμοῦ κρυόεντι φόβῳ καταειμέναι αἰεὶ | φαίνοντ' ἐσσυμένου, τρομέουσι δὲ καὶ θεοὶ αὐτοί. Otherwise, beauty does not appear to shine specifically from the cheeks as it does here, although cheeks were praised for their beauty early on; as attested by the common epithet καλλιπάρῃος Il. 1. 143, 184 etc. Note the verb ἀπέλαμπεν in the same position as here at Il. 19. 381 ἡ δ' ἀστὴρ ὣς ἀπέλαμπεν.

175 οἷόν τ'. . . : 'such as is the beauty of Aphrodite', greater even than her astounding beauty when disguised as a mortal girl! Note the use of adverbial τε here for the indication of an attribute (see on Aphr. 3).

ἰοστεφάνου: yet another unique reading of M, where the other MSS have ἐϋστεφάνου (cf. vv. 6 and 287). The choice between the two is extremely difficult. It is very tempting to follow Ruhnken (1782), 57, Càssola, and VE 63 in reading the rarer ἰοστεφάνου, as *lectio difficilior*. It is not known in Homer, but is common enough later: Hy. 6. 18, Solon fr. 19. 4, several times in the *Theognidea* (250, 1304, 1332, 1382, amongst which ἐϋστέφανος sits once at 1339), Simon. fr. 22. 6, Pi. fr. 76 (*Dith.*), B. *Epin.* 3. 2 etc.; the poet of *Aphr.* could well have known it. The substitution of ἐϋστεφάνου here is at least easier to explain, since the word is known in Homer and used twice more in this poem; it is a variant in *p* for ἰοστεφάνου at Hy. 6. 18. On the other hand, this case bears similarities to *M*'s individual, and probably wrong, κῆπον above at v. 66, there a garden and here a flower-garlanded Aphrodite (see ad loc.); could a similar motivation have inspired both instances? But if so, why only here and not in the other two occurrences of ἐϋστέφανος in the poem? It seems impossible to know for certain.

176 ἐξ ὕπνου τ' ἀνέγειρεν: Janko (1982), 155 lists this as a case of modification by insertion of τ' into ἐξ ὕπνου ἀνέγειρεν (Il. 10. 138; at line-end Od. 23. 22). However, it is hardly a reliable sign of post-Homeric composition as he suggests, given that τ' does not alter the phrase in any substantial way; cf. at line-end ἐξ ὕπνου μ' ἀνεγείρεις Od. 23. 16.

ἐξ ὕπνου τ' ἀνέγειρεν . . .: VE 64 is right to reject claims of asyndeton here, as if τε . . . τε . . . τε connected the three verbs in the line but not the preceding sentence (so Càssola 553 following Hermann 1806; 'si apre una nuova scena'; others have substituted δέ for the first τε; Ilgen 1796, Gemoll 1886, 270). He compares, however, the dissimilar *Il.* 1. 459–60. More relevant are parallels involving the formular unit ἔπος τ' ἔφατ' ἔκ τ' ὀνόμαζεν; cf. *Il.* 1. 360–1 καί ῥα πάροιθ' αὐτοῖο καθέζετο δάκρυ χέοντος | χειρί τέ μιν κατέρεξεν ἔπος τ' ἔφατ' ἔκ τ' ὀνόμαζεν, 5. 371–2 ἣ δ' ἀγκὰς ἐλάζετο θυγατέρα ἥν | χειρί τέ μιν κατέρεξεν ἔπος τ' ἔφατ' ἔκ τ' ὀνόμαζεν etc. In many such cases the first τε is better understood as connecting the previous phrase; here West (2003) might be followed in treating this as following on from v. 172–3 ἑσσαμένη δ'... | ἔστη ἄρα κλισίῃ, with the intervening description of the epiphany, introduced by asyndeton (see on *Aphr.* 173–4), a kind of parenthesis.

ἔπος τ' ἔφατ' ἔκ τ' ὀνόμαζεν: one might assume that Aphrodite speaks out with renewed force (ὄρσεο) and confidence now, having regained her divine form; on the choice (?) of the formula see on *Aphr.* 144.

177 ὄρσεο Δαρδανίδη: Apollo rouses Hippocoon with the verb at *Il.* 10. 518 (ὦρσεν; cf. in the middle form of waking 11. 2 etc.). For ὄρσεο followed by the patronymic, see *Il.* 3. 250 ὄρσεο Λαομεδοντιάδη. The patronymic Δαρδανίδης is used similarly with other imperatives: *Il.* 24. 171 θάρσει Δαρδανίδη Πρίαμε, 24. 354 φράζεο Δαρδανίδη. Its use here introduces from the very moment of Anchises waking a concern with his genealogy which will take a prominent role in the latter half of the poem (see Introd., pp. 7–10).

τί νυ νήγρετον ὕπνον ἰαύεις: this question is filled with mockery; Aphrodite knows full well why Anchises is sleeping (she sent him to sleep!). One might recall her earlier rhetorical question to the hero τί μ' ἀθανάτῃσιν ἐΐσκεις; (v. 109). For τί νυ beginning a question see *Il.* 1. 414, 16. 859, etc. AHS 362 point to the similarity between this line and *Herm.* 289 ἀλλ' ἄγε, μὴ πυματόν τε καὶ ὕστατον ὕπνον ἰαύσῃς; however the sense is quite different, Apollo ordering Hermes to act if he does not want to be put to 'sleep'. See more similarly the later Leontius Scholasticus, *AP* 16. 375. 1 ἔγρεο, Κωνσταντῖνε. τί χάλκεον ὕπνον ἰαύεις; Also, for ὕπνον ἰαυ- see later Theoc. *Id.* 3. 49 ἄτροπον ὕπνον ἰαύων, Call. *Aetia* fr. 75. 2 προνύμφιον ὕπνον ἰαῦσαι, Opp. *H.* 2. 111 βαθὺν ὕπνον ἰαύειν, Q.S. 13. 27 πανύστατον ὕπνον ἴαυον (after *Herm.* 289?), Nonn. *D.* 16. 98 γλυκὺν ὕπνον ἰαύεις, etc.

νήγρετον ὕπνον: 'deep sleep'. The adjective is rare; cf. *Od.* 13. 79–80 καὶ τῷ νήδυμος ὕπνος ἐπὶ βλεφάροισιν ἔπιπτε | νήγρετος ἥδιστος, θανάτῳ ἄγχιστα ἐοικώς and once as an adverb of sleep at 13. 74 νήγρετον εὕδοι. Otherwise not until later: [Mosch.] *Bion* 104, Tryph. 378 and the anonymous *AP* 7. 338. 6 (cf. also 7. 305. 3 νήγρετον ὕπνωσας), where νήγρετον ὕπνον does not just resemble death as in Homer, but is death. Of sleep as here, Gow ii. 74 compares ἄτροπον ὕπνον ἰαύων at Theoc. *Id.* 3. 49, of the eternal sleep of Endymion.

178–9 καὶ φράσαι εἴ ...: following on from ὄρσεο Δαρδανίδη, 'wake up, son of Dardanus, ... and', the interceding rhetorical question should be treated in parenthesis (cf. VE 64 and West 2003). This structure is extremely similar to vv. 109–10, Aphrodite's first words to Anchises (see ad loc.). Contrast *Od.* 22. 157–9 ἀλλ' ἴθι, δῖ' Εὔμαιε, θύρην ἐπίθες θαλάμοιο | καὶ φράσαι ἤ τις ἄρ' ἐστὶ γυναικῶν, ἢ τάδε ῥέζει | ἢ υἱὸς Δολίοιο Μελανθεύς, τόν περ ὀΐω.

ὁμοίη ἐγὼν ἰνδάλλομαι εἶναι: cf. *Od.* 3. 246 ὥς τέ μοι ἀθάνατος ἰνδάλλεται εἰσοράασθαι, where Telemachus pays the compliment to Nestor that he looks like a god; in a more literal sense this is of course the point of Aphrodite's question here. The verb ἰνδάλλομαι 'to seem/appear' is used three more times in Homer, *Il.* 17. 213, 23. 460, *Od.* 19. 224 (the last case in the same metrical position as here). With ὅμοιος cf. later Ar. *Ves.* 188–9 ὥστ' ἔμοιγ' ἰνδάλλεται | ὁμοιότατος κλητῆρος εἶναι πωλίῳ, and Opp. *H.* 2. 233 πέτρῃσιν ὁμοίϊοι ἰνδάλλονται.

179 οἵην δή με τὸ πρῶτον ... νόησας: cf. *Od.* 1. 257 τοῖος ἐὼν οἷόν μιν ἐγὼ τὰ πρῶτ' ἐνόησα. On the combination οἷος δή, often conveying disparagement, irony, or contempt, see Denniston (1950), 220–1; he lists this passage, however, as an exception with no irony present, a position against which VE 65 justifiably protests. Aphrodite's questions at this point, to which she well knows the answers, seem filled with provocation and mockery; see on *Aphr.* 177 τί νυ νήγρετον ὕπνον ἰαύεις; and cf. Smith (1981*a*), 124–5 n. 74.

τὸ πρῶτον: in no case of τὸ πρῶτον/τὰ πρῶτα in Homer is τό/τά scanned short as here (cf. v. 185). Some have suggested emendations to the text to remove the irregularity; Hermann (1806) proposed omitting τό (see AS 212). There is no reason to doubt the transmission, but this may be a sign of later modification; see Kamerbeek

(1967), 389, Janko (1982), 157, who, however, note *Od.* 3. 320 ὅν τινὰ πρῶτον; cf. also *Od.* 17. 275 ἠὲ σὺ πρῶτος.

ἐν ὀφθαλμοῖσι νοήσας: repeated from v. 83 (νόησας for νοήσας) where Anchises first perceived the goddess in disguise; the verbal similarity helps to contrast the two very different appearances. Cf. the formula at *Il.* 24. 294 and 24. 312.

180 ὣς φάθ'· ὁ δ' ἐξ ὕπνοιο μάλ' ἐμμαπέως ὑπάκουσεν: Anchises is startled awake; cf. *Il.* 10. 162 (Diomedes) ὣς φάθ'· ὁ δ' ἐξ ὕπνοιο μάλα κραιπνῶς ἀνόρουσε and *Od.* 14. 485 (Odysseus) ὁ δ' ἄρ' ἐμμαπέως ὑπάκουσε. The adverb ἐμμαπέως is otherwise rare (elsewhere at *Il.* 5. 836, *Sc.* 442, Ion *IEG* 28).

181–2. There are certain similarities between Anchises' recognition of Aphrodite and Helen's realization that she is speaking to the goddess at *Il.* 3. 396–8 καί ῥ' ὡς οὖν ἐνόησε θεᾶς περικαλλέα δειρὴν | στήθεά θ' ἱμερόεντα καὶ ὄμματα μαρμαίροντα | θάμβησέν τ' ἄρ' ἔπειτα, ἔπος τ' ἔφατ' ἔκ τ' ὀνόμαζεν; in both cases their attention is focused upon the neck and the eyes (cf. Aeneas' recognition of Venus at Verg. *A.* 1. 402 ff.). These are also points of focus when describing beautiful young women; see Briseis mourning Patroclus at *Il.* 19. 284–5 χερσὶ δ' ἄμυσσεν | στήθεά τ' ἠδ' ἁπαλὴν δειρὴν ἰδὲ καλὰ πρόσωπα.

ὣς δὲ ἴδεν δειρήν: Hoekstra (1969), 41 notes that nu mobile makes position here in ἴδεν, where it does not in Homer; cf. *Il.* 5. 846 ὣς δὲ ἴδε(ν). This, however, requires dismissing *Il.* 4. 151 ὡς δὲ ἴδεν νεῦρον and 17. 198 ἴδεν νεφεληγερέτα Ζεύς on the assumption that the lengthening in these cases goes back to the doubling of nasals (see Hoekstra 1965, 73, 80–1; cf. *Il.* 1. 396 ἐνὶ [μ]μεγάροισιν). Perhaps so, but this is shaky ground for claiming a post-Homeric modification.

ὄμματα κάλ' Ἀφροδίτης: for the phraseology cf. *Il.* 23. 66 ὄμματα κάλ' ἐϊκυῖα, *Od.* 1. 208 ὄμματα καλὰ ἔοικας. Aphrodite had cast her beautiful eyes down towards the ground earlier at v. 156 ὄμματα καλὰ βαλοῦσα.

182 ταρβησέν τε καὶ ὄσσε . . . ἔτραπεν ἄλλῃ: Anchises now reacts exactly as Aphrodite wanted to prevent him from doing earlier by taking the disguise of a young girl; v. 83 μή μιν ταρβήσειεν (see ad loc., and on fear as a standard reaction to epiphany on 168–83). For the casting of the eyes away in fear of a god, see *Od.* 16. 179 ταρβήσας δ' ἑτέρωσε βάλ' ὄμματα, μὴ θεὸς εἴη, where Telemachus suspects that Odysseus might be a god after his sudden transformation. The phraseology here, however, is more similar to turning the eyes away for other reasons: cf. τρέπεν ὄσσε φαεινώ *Il.* 13. 3/7, Zeus turning his eyes away from the human battle, and 21. 415, Athena turning her eyes away from Ares after defeating him. Compare also Helen averting her eyes from Paris at *Il.* 3. 427 ὄσσε πάλιν κλίνασα (cf. Aphrodite above on v. 83 ὄμματα καλὰ βαλοῦσα): 'Helen evidently cannot bear to look at her lover' (Kirk 1985, 327); for different reasons, neither can Anchises! In a completely different context, ἔτραπεν ἄλλη occurs at line-end as here at *Il.* 5. 187, of a god turning aside Pandarus' arrow.

παρακλιδόν: 'aside'; the adv. occurs only twice in Homer, where it is used of deviating from speaking the truth, *Od.* 4. 348, 17. 139 [οὐκ ἂν ἐγώ γε] ἄλλα πάρεξ εἴποιμι παρακλιδὸν οὐδ' ἀπατήσω. Used of the direction of eyes, see later Nonn. *D.* 29. 151–2 εἶπε καὶ ἐπτοίητο παρακλιδὸν ὄμματι λοξῷ | ὠτειλὴν χαρίεντος ὀπιπεύων Ὑμεναίου, and of the lusty Poseidon surveying Beroe 42. 451–2 οἷά τε γυμνωθέντα παρακλιδὸν ἄκρα δοκεύων | στήθεα μαρμαίροντα; also note similar phrasing of Hera turning a spear aside at 28. 68 ἀλλὰ δόρυ προμάχοιο παρακλιδὸν ἔτραπεν Ἥρη.

183 ἂψ δ' αὖτις: 'back again'; the combination is reasonably common in Homer (Zeus stirs up strength 'once again' amongst the Trojans at *Il.* 8. 335, and four times of sitting 'back down again' in the place from where one stood in the *Od.* 18. 157 etc.).

χλαίνης ἐκαλύψατο καλὰ πρόσωπα: having been awakened from a sweet sleep to find himself faced with a goddess, the best Anchises can do is to hide pathetically behind his blankets. This use of his blankets is all the more pathetic when one recalls that they were a symbol of his strength and grandeur as he took Aphrodite to bed (see on *Aphr.* 158–60). See similar language of Odysseus covering his face in shame at shedding tears after hearing Demodocus sing of the Trojan war; *Od.* 8. 84–5 πορφύρεον μέγα φᾶρος ἑλὼν χερσὶ στιβαρῇσι | κὰκ κεφαλῆς εἴρυσσε, κάλυψε δὲ καλὰ πρόσωπα. See later Oenone at Q.S. 10. 466 καλυψαμένη πέρι φάρεϊ καλὰ πρόσωπα; stricken with grief at the loss of her lover Paris, and remorse for not having helped him, she covers her face and leaps on the pyre with him.

The MSS all have χλαίνῃ τ' ἐκαλύψατο (Θ τε καλύψατο). The τε, however, can make little sense after ἂψ δ' αὖτις. The problem was first recognized by VB 19, who conjectured either χλαίνης ἐκαλύψατο or χλαίνῃσι καλύψατο; while both are plausible, the former seems preferable as a less radical change. West (2003) subsequently conjectured χλαίνῃ ἐκαλύψατο; certainly possible as well, it nonetheless has the disadvantage of introducing hiatus, while the plural proposed by VB has the added advantage that Anchises was said to have blankets in the plural above at v. 158 (although he might reasonably just hide behind one of them now).

184–90. Anchises speaks out in prayer (λισσόμενος). He has already prayed to the goddess in a more elaborate fashion above at vv. 100–6 (see on *Aphr.* 92–106), the main themes of which this shorter, desperate plea now echoes: his request not to be left ἀμενηνός amongst men corresponds to his desire to live long and prosperously as a leading man amongst the Trojans (vv. 103, 104–6), and although his earlier petition for a strong offspring (θαλερὸν γόνον v. 104) is not directly paralleled here, a concern with reproduction does seem to be implied in the terms ἀμενηνός and βιοθάλμιος (for these correspondences cf. Smith 1981*a*, 65–6 and on the latter two terms see on *Aphr.* 188–90). The roles of supplication are now put back in their proper order, after having been reversed earlier by Aphrodite; one is reminded of this reversal by Anchises' repetition of Aphrodite's words to him at v. 131 ἀλλά σε πρὸς Ζηνὸς γουνάζομαι (= v. 187). His pleading tone is certainly at odds with his confident claim above that he would be willing to die to sleep with his visitor.

184. This line is formular, identical with *Od.* 22. 311, 22. 343, 22. 366; possibly also *Il.* 21. 73 (variant for καί μιν φωνήσας; see N. Richardson 1993, 59). As for the common speech introduction ἔπεα πτερόεντα προσηύδα (55× *Il.*, 52× *Od.*), Vivante (1975), 6 offers an appealing argument that it conveys 'spontaneity of expression', noting that 'recognition ... produces winged words, not so much because of the emotions involved as because of the shock' (cf. Achilles' reaction to Athena at *Il.* 1. 199–201); some will see no such implication in the formula (so M. W. Edwards 1970, 2; see above on 144 ἔπος τ' ἔφατ' ἔκ τ' ὀνόμαζεν).

185–6 αὐτίκα σ' ὡς τὰ πρῶτα ... | ἔγνων ὡς θεὸς ἦσθα, σὺ δ' οὐ νημερτὲς ἔειπες: Anchises confirms his initial suspicion that Aphrodite was a goddess (see on *Aphr.* 92–106), and puts all the blame upon her for having lied to him. He implied that he would do as much above by meticulously retracing her words when accepting her false identity (see on *Aphr.* 143–54), and he now falls back on this crutch to save his skin. He can hardly relieve himself of all responsibility though, and his words here have something of the helplessness of the schoolboy caught at mischief: 'she did it, not me'! With the clarity of hindsight he is now regretting his actions.

θεά: Anchises addresses her straightforwardly as a goddess now that he is certain, whereas above at v. 92, when he only supposed she was a goddess, the term used was ἄνασσα (on its implications see ad loc.).

186 ἔγνων ὡς θεὸς ἦσθα, σὺ δ'...: cf. Apollo's remark to Achilles at *Il.* 22. 9–10 οὐδέ νύ πώ με | ἔγνως ὡς θεός εἰμι, σὺ δ' ἀσπερχὲς μενεαίνεις. For γιγνώσκω of recognizing a god see also *Il.* 5. 815 (Diomedes to Athena) γιγνώσκω σε θεά, *Od.* 1. 420 (Telemachus, not in speech) φρεσὶ δ' ἀθανάτην θεὸν ἔγνω and 13. 299–300 (Athena to Odysseus) οὐδὲ σύ γ' ἔγνως | Παλλάδ' Ἀθηναίην. Later see the goatherd at Theoc. *Id.* 3. 15 coming to know Eros, νῦν ἔγνων τὸν Ἔρωτα.

σὺ δ' οὐ νημερτὲς ἔειπες: cf. Antenor to Helen at *Il.* 3. 204 ὦ γύναι, ἦ μάλα τοῦτο ἔπος νημερτὲς ἔειπες; also at line-end νημερτέα εἴπῃ *Od.* 3. 19, νημερτέα εἶπεν 5. 300, νημερτέα εἴπω 11. 96. See also *Od.* 2. 251 σὺ δ' οὐ κατὰ μοῖραν ἔειπες and for συ δ' cf. *Il.* 22. 10 cited in the previous note.

187. On the repetition from v. 131 see on *Aphr.* 184–90.

188–90. Anchises begs Aphrodite not to leave him living amongst men ἀμενηνόν, for he knows that οὐ βιοθάλμιος ἀνὴρ γίγνεται ὅς τε θεαῖς εὐνάζεται ἀθανάτῃσιν. Rose (1924; cf. *Gesch.* i. 22–3, Ferri 1960, 301, etc.) suggests that behind these words lies an indication of the Anatolian origin of the hymn, interpreting the two terms ἀμενηνός and βιοθάλμιος as referring to Anchises' fear of losing his virility after sleeping with Aphrodite/Magna Mater; parallel to Attis and other eunuch lovers of eastern fertility goddesses. Others (AHS 363–4, VE 66, VB 19–21, etc.) disagree, arguing that the two terms refer generally to physical strength rather than sexual potency, and that in any case the idea that sleeping with a goddess is dangerous is paralleled in Homer; Gemoll (1886), 270 compares Hermes' advice to Odysseus about sleeping with Circe at *Od.* 10. 301 μή σ' ἀπογυμνωθέντα κακὸν καὶ ἀνήνορα θήῃ (= 341 ὄφρα με [Odysseus] γυμν-...). As often, the truth seems to lie somewhere between the two positions.

First, it is not unreasonable to see in both ἀμενηνός and βιοθάλμιος some reference to sexual potency and reproductive power. The latter is a *hapax* (cf. Pi. *O*. 7. 11 ζωθάλμιος), with a fairly transparent derivation from βίος and θάλλω 'strong, full of vitality' (cf. *LfgrE* s.v.). However, behind a more general meaning may also lurk an implication of reproductive power, through recollection of Anchises' earlier request for a θαλερὸν γόνον at v. 104; see Smith (1981*a*), 66, who also points out that Aeneas is referred to as a θάλος below at v. 278, and Tsomis (2004), 26–9. With regard to ἀμενηνός, both VE and VB reject the possibility of a sexual implication on the ground that there are no parallels; but this is not true. Admittedly much later, the word refers specifically to a man unable to take part in sexual activity at *Orph. L*. 469–71 (Euphorbus, son of Abarbaree) ἤδη καί τινα φῶτα χόλῳ χρυσέης Ἀφροδίτης | ἔργα πρὸς ἱμερόεντα γάμων ἀμενηνὸν ἐόντα | μεμνῆσθαι φιλότητος ἀκεσσάμενος προΐαλλεν. In early poetry too, although less explicitly, the term seems to be linked at times with reproduction: at *Dem*. 352–4 it is used as a general epithet of mortal men, but significantly in connection with Demeter having hidden the reproductive seed (σπέρμα) under the ground, φθεῖσαι φῦλ' ἀμενηνὰ χαμαιγενέων ἀνθρώπων | σπέρμ' ὑπὸ γῆς κρύπτουσα, καταφθινύουσα δὲ τιμὰς | ἀθανάτων; also, the positive term μένος, from which ἀμενηνός is almost certainly derived, is clearly connected with ejaculation at Archil. fr. 196a. 52]ὸν ἀφῆκα μένος (it is impossible to know what preceded: Merkelbach suggests λευκ]όν and West θερμ]όν; for the former see the later erotic epigram of Dioscorides *AP* 5. 55. 7 ἀπεσπείσθη λευκὸν μένος, and for the latter—outside the erotic sphere—Parm. fr. 11. 5 DK ἄστρων θερμὸν μένος).

Yet, accepting that this is one implication of the word does not necessitate the belief that it is the only, or even primary, one here: at *Il*. 5. 887 ἤ κε ζὼς ἀμενηνὸς ἔα χαλκοῖο τυπῇσι (a line very similar to this one, although very possibly a later interpolation; see Kirk 1990, 152 ad loc.) the word is used of an injured, debilitated Ares, while its most frequent use in Homer is of the dead (νεκύων ἀμενηνὰ κάρηνα *Od*. 10. 521, 536, 11. 29 and 49; once more of dreams at *Od*. 19. 562 and cf. the verb ἀμενήνωσεν at *Il*. 13. 562 of Poseidon taking away the μένος of a spear). Giacomelli (1980), 13–19 makes an important connection between ἀμενηνός and the debilitating effects of old age and mortality: among other later examples, she points to Pi. *O*. 8.

70–1, where μένος is the adversary of old age (γήραος ἀντίπαλον; cf. [Mosch.] *Meg.* 113 ff. γέρων ... ἀμενηνός), and Ar. *Av.* 685–9, where the φῦλ' ἀμενηνά of mortal men are compared to the immortal birds (τοῖς ἀθανάτοις ἡμῖν, τοῖς αἰὲν ἐοῦσιν). This latter example is particularly striking when one recalls *Dem.* 352–4 cited above; there, along with the implication of the loss of fertility, is the juxtaposition of the effect of Demeter's action upon mortal men (φῦλ' ἀμενηνὰ χαμαιγενέων ἀνθρώπων) and the effect upon immortals (ἀθανάτων). A link between the term and the general effects of mortality seems to be present in *Aphr.* as well. Later, in an explicit comparison of mortality and immortality, Aphrodite tells the tale of the eternally ageing Tithonus (vv. 218–38). His ageing brings about the loss of strength (κῖκυς) in his arms and a physical fragility (vv. 237–8), included in which is his loss of virility and sexual attractiveness as Eos stays away from his bed (v. 228–30); Anchises clearly fears a more exaggerated feebleness (a punishment of some sort) for having slept with a love-goddess than that generally accorded to mankind at *Dem.* 352, but a similar range of debilitations to those which Tithonus suffers might nonetheless be understood in the term ἀμενηνός.

To return then to the question of whether Anchises' comments here are an indication of immediate Asiatic influence on the hymn, the term ἀμενηνός offers no particular suggestion of this. Generally, there would seem to be sufficient precedent in Greek thought for a male hero to fear sleeping with a goddess. If, as AHS 363 point out, Gemoll's Homeric parallel of Odysseus' fear of sleeping with Circe (cited above) is partially negated by the fact that Circe is a malevolent witch from whom one might naturally expect harm, the universal danger of mortal men sleeping with goddesses is expressed elsewhere. At *Od.* 5. 118 ff. Calypso expands upon how the gods jealously harm men who have had divine lovers (cf. Podbielski 1971, 63–4). Giacomelli (1980), 16–17, followed by Clay 1989, 182–3, rejects this as a parallel because it refers to punishment through revenge, whereas she sees Anchises' comments as referring strictly to a fear of 'the physical effects of the act of love itself.' He may fear a bit of both, but Aphrodite's reply οὐ γάρ τοί τι δέος παθέειν κακὸν ἐξ ἐμέθεν γε | οὐδ' ἄλλων μακάρων at least suggests that he fears direct punishment from either Aphrodite or the other gods (cf. de Jong 1989, 18 n. 17). The comparison with the Calypso passage is strengthened by a verbal parallel; Calypso says [θεοὶ ζηλήμονες] οἵ τε θεαῖς ἀγάασθε παρ' ἀνδράσιν εὐνάζεσθαι, comparable to ὅς τε θεαῖς εὐνάζεται (on possible imitation see Introd., p. 32).

On the other hand, this concern expressed by Anchises is entirely in line with Near Eastern parallels. The fate of lovers of eastern fertility-goddesses is not confined to castration or impotency; in the *Epic of Gilgamesh* (Foster 46; Tablet VI 32 ff.) Gilgamesh angers Ištar by refusing to sleep with her because of dangerous precedent, listing the many lovers who have come to harm because of affairs with her: she whipped and drove the stallion she loved, turned a shepherd into a wolf, Ishullanu into a mole, etc. (cf. West 1997, 411–12). Such Near Eastern myths must be the origin of the parallel figure of Adonis in Greek (his name is a West Semitic word meaning 'lord'), and could ultimately be behind the tradition of Anchises' divine punishment for boasting of his affair with Aphrodite (cf. Penglase 1994, 171–2). Even the danger of Odysseus sleeping with Circe at *Od.* 10. 301/341 probably has an oriental origin like Circe herself (see Germain 1954, 262 ff., West 1997, 404–10). The motif appears to have made its way into the Greek tradition already by the time of Homer.

ζῶντ' ἀμενηνὸν ἐν ἀνθρώποισιν ἐάσῃς | ναίειν, ἀλλ' ἐλέαιρ': 'do not leave me to dwell amongst mankind as a living invalid' (West 2003). VB 21 proposes that behind Anchises' plea to the goddess for pity is a request for immortality: assuming that no good comes to men who have slept with goddesses, Anchises asks specifically 'not to be left to dwell amongst men enfeebled', i.e. to be made immortal. He understands this to introduce what follows in the narrative, thus explaining why Aphrodite tells two stories about mortal lovers who are taken to dwell amongst the gods; she uses the disastrous fate of Tithonus to demonstrate why she cannot take Anchises to live amongst the gods (he points to her statement at vv. 239–40 οὐκ ἂν ἐγώ γε σὲ τοῖον ἐν ἀθανάτοισιν ἑλοίμην | ἀθάνατόν τ' εἶναι καὶ ζώειν ἤματα πάντα).

This theory is certainly ingenious in its explanation for the development of the narrative, but there are substantial difficulties in accepting it. First and foremost, the meaning 'take me to dwell amongst the gods' can only be extracted laboriously from the text; if this is what was intended by the poet, he has left the sense remarkably obscure. VB takes issue with translators for having reduced ἐν ἀνθρώποισιν . . . | ναίειν 'to little more than a periphrastic equivalent of εἶναι'; it certainly is not that, but it does seem to be a periphrastic equivalent of 'to dwell', as suggested by *Od.* 17. 419–20/19. 75–6 καὶ γάρ ἐγώ ποτε οἶκον <u>ἐν ἀνθρώποισιν ἔναιον</u> | ὄλβιος ἀφνειόν; the point here is that Odysseus once lived as a wealthy man, with little significance attached to ἐν ἀνθρώποισιν; it amounts to a formular use and this is the most natural way to read it in *Aphr.* as well. On more subjective grounds, it would, as de Jong (1989), 22 n. 28 points out, be rather 'odd that Anchises, who fears to be punished by the gods, should ask to be transported to the gods' (on his fear see n. prec.).

Neither is there any support for VB's belief (20) that ζῶντα is 'hypothetical', thus 'do not, should I live, leave me to dwell enfeebled amongst men'. This interpretation is based upon a hypothetical substitution of κε ἔθανον for κε δηρὸν πήματ' ἔπασχον at *Il.* 5. 885–7 ἀλλά μ' ὑπήνεικαν ταχέες πόδες· ἦ τέ κε δηρὸν | αὐτοῦ πήματ' ἔπασχον ἐν αἰνῇσιν νεκάδεσσιν | ἤ κε ζώς ἀμενηνὸς ἔα χαλκοῖο τυπῇσι: he comments, 'if, however, we substitute this ... the lines make good sense—in the mouth of a mortal', and then applies this supposed contrast between life and death to *Aphr.*; but Ares is not a mortal and ἔθανον is not in the text (κε δηρὸν πήματ' ἔπασχον ἐν αἰνῇσιν νεκάδεσσιν is not just a euphemism for ἔθανον; Ares is hardly saying that he would have died amongst the dead 'for a long time'). Rather, ζῶντα, like ζώς in the *Il.*, is most naturally understood as an emphatic complement to ἀμενηνόν; among other translations, see Crudden (2001) 'don't let me dwell amongst humans in strengthless existence', or even Smith (1981a), 74 '[to live] among men a <u>creature</u> enfeebled'. In fact, ζώς/ζῶντα ἀμενην-ός/όν can perhaps best be taken as a set phrase: 'living invalid' (contrasting with the apparently more traditional νεκύων ἀμενηνὰ κάρηνα, 4× *Od.* 10. 521 etc.; again, *Il.* 5. 887 may well be a later interpolation; see n. prec.).

ἀλλ' ἐλέαιρ': cf. *Od.* 5. 450 ἀλλ' ἐλέαιρε ἄναξ, 6. 175 ἀλλὰ ἄνασσ' ἐλέαιρε.

ἐπεὶ οὐ ... | γίγνεται, ὅς ... : for the structure of these lines see *Od.* 8. 585–6 ἐπεὶ οὐ μέν τι κασιγνήτοιο χερείων | γίγνεται, ὅς κεν ἑταῖρος ἐών πεπνυμένα εἰδῇ.

βιοθάλμιος: on this *hapax* see on *Aphr.* 188–90.

θεαῖς: the dative -αις (once again in *Aphr.* at v. 249 αἶς) is attested in Homer at *Il.* 12. 284 ἀκταῖς (all MSS; although West 2003 prefers Rzach's conjecture ἀκτῆς), *Od.* 5. 119 θεαῖς (v.l. θεάς; on the thematic link between these two passages see on *Aphr.* 188–90) and 22. 471 πάσαις; then more frequently in Hesiod and the *Hymns*; see West (1966a), 176–7 on *Th.* 61, N. Richardson (1974), 53–4, 163. Wackernagel (1916), 53 considered the form an Atticism, but this cannot be true; as N. Richardson, loc. cit. and Janko (1982), 171 point out, the archaic Attic forms were -ησι, -ᾱσι (cf. Buck 1955, 86), and the established presence of the form in the textual tradition tells against later interpolation (cf. Hainsworth, *OC* i. 265–6).

191–290. Aphrodite's final speech to Anchises takes up approximately a third of the entire poem. With the central action of the narrative now complete, her address acts as a sort of epilogue (cf. Podbielski 1971, 64; what Clay 1989, 180 calls the 'aftermath'), exploring the consequences of their love-affair and instructing Anchises as to the future. The speech can be divided into five main sections: (i) vv. 191–9, Aphrodite reassures Anchises that he will not suffer harm from her or the other gods and announces that she will give birth to his son Aeneas; (ii) vv. 200–40, she recounts the two stories of Zeus and Ganymedes and of Eos and Tithonus, and explains that she cannot take Anchises to live with her amongst the gods; (iii) vv. 241–255, she underlines Anchises' future as a mortal (old age will soon envelop him), juxtaposing this with her own future of shame amongst the gods as a result of their union; (iv) vv. 256–73, she elaborates upon the rearing of Aeneas by nymphs; (v) vv. 274–90, she instructs Anchises that he must take Aeneas to Troy once he has reached adolescence, then finally reveals her name and gives him a warning not to speak of their union to others for fear of punishment by Zeus.

The speech is broadly comparable with Poseidon's much shorter oration at *Od.* 11. 248–52, which concludes his love-affair with Tyro (cf. [Hes.] fr. 31): after sleeping with her, he tells her that (i) v. 248 she should take heart (χαῖρε γύναι φιλότητι ~ *Aphr.* 193), (ii) v. 249 she will give birth to his children (~ *Aphr.* 196), (iii) v. 250 she will rear them herself (~ *Aphr.* 256 ff. nymphs will rear Aeneas), (iv) v. 251 she should return home and not tell of the affair (ἴσχεο μηδ' ὀνομήνῃς ~ *Aphr.* 290 ἴσχεο μηδ' ὀνόμαινε), and finally (v) v. 252 he is Poseidon (~ *Aphr.* 287). He then disappears under the sea, while Aphrodite rushes off into the sky (*Aphr.* 291). Also, later in Mosch. *Eur.* 154–61 Zeus' address to Europa follows a similar pattern (although this time just before he sleeps with her; cf. the comparison of Campbell 1991, 122–3 ad loc.): he tells her (i) v. 154 not to be afraid (θάρσει παρθενική· μὴ δείδιθι πόντιον οἶδμα ~ Aphr. 193 θάρσει, μηδέ τι σῇσι μετὰ φρεσὶ δείδιθι λίην), (ii) vv. 160–1 she will bear his children, who will be kings amongst men (~ Aphr. 196 σοί δ' ἔσται φίλος υἱὸς ὃς ἐν Τρώεσσιν ἀνάξει), (iii) vv. 158–9, Crete, which reared Zeus, will now rear her offspring (Κρήτη δέ σε δέξεται ἤδη | ἥ μ' ἔθρεψε καὶ αὐτόν ~ Aphr. 256 ff. rearing by nymphs), (iv) this speech contains no warning, and (v) v. 155 he is Zeus (~ Aphr. 287).

There is no parallel, however, for the length and level of detail of Aphrodite's closing remarks. The two parallels adduced above have in common that they bring a swift close to the episode, or in the latter case the poem, and one might have expected something similar here; the goddess has just made her epiphany, most common in epic at the arrival and departure of a deity (see N. Richardson 1974, 208); cf. *Hy.* 7. 55–7, where Dionysus' post-epiphany address to the helmsman, inciting courage (θάρσει) and revealing his name, brings the poem to a swift close. Indeed, had a version of *Aphr.* been transmitted in which vv. 200–55 were omitted, an audience which knew no other would have had little reason to think something was amiss. As it stands, far from bringing a close to the poem, Aphrodite's address extends the boundaries of the narrative. She goes beyond the imparting of necessary information and confesses 'much more to Anchises than she really has to' (Smith 1981*a*, 67).

This is not to say that anything in vv. 200–55 is inappropriate for the development of the poem. There can be little doubt as to the unity of the final third of the hymn and its coherence with what has preceded. The stories of Ganymedes and Tithonus (vv. 200–40) are certainly appropriate to the theme at hand, while the expression of her grief at Anchises' mortality and her shame amongst the gods (vv. 241–55), naturally mentioned as a consequence of the union, exposes the success of Zeus' revenge, which began the whole affair at v. 45 (Zeus is also significantly a character in the Ganymedes story). Moreover, this entire final third of the poem is united by two central themes: (i) the contrast of mortality and immortality (the two stories about divine-mortal affairs, the description of the semi-divine nymphs etc.), a significant *leitmotiv* of the poem (cf. Podbielski 1971, 65, Smith 1981*a*, 67), and (ii) the ancestors and descendants of

Anchises (Ganymedes, Tithonus, and the regal future of Aeneas), a concern foreshadowed earlier in the hymn and now treated in depth; on both of these themes see Introd., pp. 7–10.

191–9. Aphrodite bids Anchises to take courage and promises that no harm will come to him from either herself or the other gods. She then reveals that she will give birth to his son Aeneas, who will rule amongst the Trojans, and that he will have a long line of descendants (v. 197 παῖδες παίδεσσι διαμπερὲς ἐκγεγάονται). The calming of his fears with the pledge that he will not be harmed responds directly to his preceding reaction (hiding behind his blankets) and prayer in vv. 184–90. The promise of a beloved son who will be a king of the Trojans, and a long line of descendants, also responds to his prayer, most directly to his request for a θαλερὸν γόνον in his first prayer at 103–6, which is perhaps also alluded to in his second prayer (see on *Aphr.* 184–90). There are more reasons too to recall his first prayer at this moment: vv. 191–2, the introduction and first line of her reply, are almost identical with vv. 107–8 (only καταθνητῶν substituted for χαμαιγενέων; on this see on *Aphr.* 108), which themselves followed directly after his previous prayer, while the announcement that Aeneas will rule ἐν Τρώεσσιν perhaps echoes Anchises' own request earlier to be an honoured man μετὰ Τρώεσσιν (v. 103).

193. This line is almost identical with *Od.* 4. 825 θάρσει, μηδέ τι πάγχυ μετὰ φρεσὶ δείδιθι λίην; cf. also the similar structure of *Il.* 4. 184 θάρσει, μηδέ τί πω δειδίσσεο λαὸν Ἀχαιῶν and 18. 463 (*Od.* 13. 362 etc.) θάρσει· μή τοι ταῦτα μετὰ φρεσὶ σῇσι μελόντων. Later, see Zeus' words to Europa at Mosch. *Eur.* 154, cited on 191–290.

194 οὐ γάρ τοί τι δέος παθέειν: the neglect of digamma in δέος is not known in Homer (cf. *LfgrE* s.v.) and may be due to a modification by inversion of οὐδέ τί τοι παθέειν δέος *Od.* 5. 347 (see Janko 1982, 154); the neglect in δέος is otherwise first at [Hes.] fr. 239. 3. The Homeric parallel may help to explain MS M's inversion of τοί τι (τί τοι), facilitated also by the identical pronunciation of ι and οι for a Byzantine scribe.

κακὸν ἐξ ἐμέθεν γε: cf. *Il.* 1. 525 τοῦτο γὰρ ἐξ ἐμέθεν γε (1∪∪2∪∪3∪).

195 μακάρων: on its own without θεῶν, see on *Aphr.* 92.

ἐπεὶ ἦ: the MSS give ἐπειή or ἐπείη. On the correction see *HT*

267–8; the MSS of the *Iliad* often have ἐπεὶ ἦ (*Il.* 1. 156 etc.; cf. AHS 211 on *Apoll.* 72).

φίλος ἐσσὶ θεοῖσι: cf. *Il.* 20. 347 where his son Aeneas is said to be φίλος ἀθανάτοισι θεοῖσιν (the same compliment is paid to Aeolus at *Od.* 10. 2 and Peleus at [Hes.] fr. 211. 3); for the structure here see in particular *Il.* 24. 749 φίλος ἦσθα θεοῖσιν (Hector) and *Od.* 24. 92 μάλα γὰρ φίλος ἦσθα θεοῖσιν (Achilles).

196–7. These lines are very similar to Poseidon's prophecy at *Il.* 20. 307–8 νῦν δὲ δὴ Αἰνείαο βίη Τρώεσσιν ἀνάξει | καὶ παίδων παῖδες, τοί κεν μετόπισθε γένωνται. The poet may well have been drawing directly upon that passage given the specific nature of the content (see Introd., p. 32). The two prophecies have often been taken to indicate the existence of a family of Aineiadai, for whom the Iliadic passage and *Aphr.* were written. Despite recent criticism of the stance, this seems very probable; Anchises' genealogy and the birth and fate of his son Aeneas feature prominently in the poem (see Introd., pp. 3–10).

196 φίλος υἱός: note the acc. in the same metrical position at vv. 208 (of Ganymedes) and 282 (again Aeneas); the noun–epithet combination is very common in Homer in this position (*Il.* 3. 307 etc.).

197 ἐκγεγάονται: this unique form is most convincingly understood as a future, modelled on the perfect (note γεγάασιν used above on v. 135); so Chantraine (1935*b*), who proposes that the σ was omitted by analogy with future forms such as ἐλάω or καμοῦμαι. Hoekstra (1969), 39 prefers to follow previous suggestions that the form is a reduplicated *praesens propheticum* (see in support Càssola 553); but he unconvincingly (46 n. 8) rejects Zumbach's observations (1955), 31–2 that the context seems to require a future and the surrounding verbs in the prophecy are future (ἔσται, ἀνάξει, ἔσσεται). See in support of the future form also Janko (1982), 157, who parallels ἐρχατόωντο (*Od.* 14. 15)/ἔρχαται (*Il.* 16. 481/*Od.* 10. 283), rightly dismissing the claims of Pavese (1974), 152 that the thematic ending is Aeolic.

Baumeister (1860), 265, followed most recently by West (2003), suggests rejecting the form altogether and conjectures ἐκγεγάοντες. This is possible, and would make the line closer to *Il.* 20. 308 καὶ παίδων παῖδες, τοί κεν μετόπισθε γένωνται; his descendants will rule forevermore, rather than just continue as a race. To explain the change in meaning brought about by ἐκγεγάονται, Hoekstra (1969), 39–40, followed by VE 42, proposes that the author of *Il.* 20 was writing to a family of Aineiadai in the height of power, while *Aphr.* was written for members of the family after they had been reduced to oligarchs (i.e. part of a nobility but no longer called kings); it would therefore not have been appropriate to speak of them ruling (on the Aineiadai see Introd., pp. 3–10). This theory is merely hypothesis (as Hoekstra himself recognizes), and the change could be attributed to nothing more than poetic licence; VB 22 notes that the difference is only one of emphasis, stressing the longevity of the race rather than the rule. I see no reason to prefer the sense given by the participle and retain the unique form ἐκγεγάονται. The participle ἐκγεγάοντες would itself be a *hapax* and one might have expected a perfect participle ἐκγεγα-ῶτες/-ότες, proposed by Ilgen (1796, 491; cf. the form at A.R. 1. 952); although Baumeister parallels κεκλήγοντες *Il.* 16. 430 etc.

198–9. Aeneas' name is introduced for the first time, and an etymology is given for it based upon the present narrative; he will be called Aeneas because of the αἰνὸν ἄχος which he has caused Aphrodite. It is an obvious popular etymology for the name, seemingly exploited also at *Il.* 13. 481–2 δείδια δ' αἰνῶς | Αἰνείαν (cf. Janko 1992, 108–9), and known later in *EM* alongside one from αἶνος. Puns on names are well known in Homer; see AHS 365. This one bears particular similarity to Patroclus' wordplay on Ἀχιλλεύς, ἄχος, and Ἀχαιοί at *Il.* 16. 22 (see Smith 1981a, 126 n. 82); cf. *Od.* 1. 62/19. 407–9 Ὀδυσσεύς and ὀδύσσομαι (with the note of S. West, *OC* i). For the directness of this etymology see [Hes.] fr. 235 Ἰλέα, τόν ῥ' ἐφίλησεν ἄναξ Διὸς υἱὸς Ἀπόλλων | καί οἱ τοῦτ' ὀνόμηνʼ ὄνομʼ ἔμμεναι, οὕνεκα νύμφην | εὑρόμενος ἵλεων μίχθη ἐρατῇ φιλότητι etc. (cf. VE 72). Etymological puns on names are common later in tragedy, particularly in Aeschylus and Euripides (see Dodds 1960, 116 on E. *Ba.* 367, where there is a pun on Pentheus and πένθος); see the list of examples given by Elmsley (1822), 68 on E. *Ba.* 508. There is another possible pun on Anchises' name in ἀγχίθεοι below in v. 200.

198 τῷ δὲ καὶ Αἰνείας ὄνομʼ ἔσσεται: cf. *Od.* 19. 409 τῷ δʼ Ὀδυσεὺς ὄνομʼ ἔστω. On the particle combination δὲ καί, used 'to supplement the adversative or disjunctive sense with the idea of addition', see

Denniston (1950), 305–6: it here lays greater emphasis on the introduction of the name; compare *Il.* 16. 148 τῷ δὲ καὶ Αὐτομέδων etc.

αἰνόν . . . | ἄχος: the relatively frequent pairing αἰνὸν ἄχος (*Il.* 4. 169 etc.) is split within the line in Homer (*Il.* 22. 43, *Od.* 16. 87), but as Janko (1982), 35 points out, never across two lines as here; another possible sign of later modification; cf. the similar case of separation and enjambment across two lines at vv. 147–8. The enjambment gives added weight to αἰνόν at the end of the line.

199 ἔσχεν ἄχος: grief does not have hold (ἔχειν) of someone in Homer; although see ἄχος εἷλε *Il.* 13. 581 or ἄχος ἔλλαβε 14. 475 etc. (cf. *LfgrE* s.v. ἄχος). With ἔχειν see Alcm. fr. 116, *Meropis* fr. 2. 4 Bernabé; note also *Sc.* 457 ἄχος εἷλεν and later A.R. 3. 464 (significantly, perhaps, in the erotic context of Medea loving Jason; cf. Campbell 1994, 377).

ἕνεκα: this fits most naturally into the sentence as a conjunction 'because'; so, 'his name will be Aeneas because (οὕνεκα) I was seized by a terrible sorrow, because (ἕνεκα) I fell into the bed of a mortal man'. The rareness of this meaning has troubled commentators; in Homer and Hesiod it is always a preposition attached to a gen. (as at *Aphr.* 248 εἵνεκα σεῖο). Suhle (1878), 17 and Freed–Bentman (1954), 158 took this as evidence that *Aphr.* was late, even Hellenistic; ἕνεκα is known as a conjunction in Hellenistic poetry at A.R. 4. 1523, Call. *Aetia* fr. 1. 3. Others have proposed emendations on the basis that this is not appropriate to early poetry: Kamerbeek (1967), 388 offers the plausible solution of placing a colon after ἄχος, thus attaching ἕνεκα to βροτοῦ 'because I was seized by a terrible sorrow; because of a man I fell into bed'; but this has the disadvantage that βροτοῦ is most naturally governed by εὐνῇ, 'I fell into the bed of a man'; simply 'I fell into bed' is rather clumsy (cf. σῆς εὐνῆς above at v. 154). VB 22–3 offers ἔσχ' ἄχος, οὗ ἕνεκα βροτοῦ etc.; but while this may keep βροτοῦ with εὐνῇ, it relies upon the premise that Aphrodite's ἄχος is the reason for which her affair with a mortal was brought about (despite his comparison with *Il.* 18. 88, her ἄχος is most naturally the result of sleeping with a mortal man; cf. Clay 1989, 184–5), and requires a rather violent change to the transmitted text. Others: Hermann (1806) proposed ἔσχ' ἄχος οὕνεκ' ἄρα, Gemoll (1886), 271 ὅτε τε following the similar *Il.* 18. 85 ἤματι τῷ ὅτε σε βροτοῦ ἀνέρος ἔμβαλον εὐνῇ and Suhle, loc. cit. ὅτι ῥα.

There is no particular reason to exclude the possibility that ἕνεκα/ εἵνεκα as a conjunction, although rare, was in use relatively early: Pindar has a mid-way use at *I.* 8. 32 (εἵνεκα = 'that'), while it may well have meant 'because' at [Hes.] fr. 180. 10; also, even though great faith cannot be placed in a conjecture, Pfeiffer (Pf. i. on Call. *Aetia* 1. 3) has proposed emending *Apoll.* 308 (M ἤνεκ' ἄρα, Ψ εὖτ' ἄρα) to εἴνεκ' ἄρα, a use which would lend considerable support to this instance in *Aphr.* (cf. Janko 1982, 158). As above, the conjunction is defended in *Aphr.* by its providing the most natural sense, and it is best kept without attaching much significance to it for purposes of dating, although it may reasonably be said to be post-Homeric; cf. Hoekstra (1969), 47 n. 14 who, however, unnecessarily supposes that the poet mistakenly thought ἕνεκα = οὕνεκα to be epic (Heitsch 1965, 30–1 suggests that a 'mißbräuchliche Wortverwendung' was influenced by the proximity of οὕνεκα).

200–38. Aphrodite now expands upon the close proximity of Anchises' lineage to the gods, recounting the stories of Ganymedes' abduction by Zeus and Tithonus' affair with Eos. This digression is entirely in keeping with the style of this poet, who above in vv. 7–33 included a digression about three goddesses who were exceptions to Aphrodite's universal dominion, and will later in vv. 257–73 again have Aphrodite enter into a digression, about the life of the tree-nymphs who will rear Aeneas.

The connection, however, of these two stories to the main narrative of the poem is unquestionable: as two examples of relationships between gods and mortals, they follow naturally upon the affair which Aphrodite has just concluded. The expansion upon two members of Anchises' family is also another example of the marked concern for Aeneas' lineage shown in the poem, which perhaps supports the hypothesis that the poet was composing with a group of Aineiadai in mind (see further Introd., pp. 3–10); the two lines introducing the section (vv. 200–1 ἀγχίθεοι δὲ μάλιστα καταθνητῶν ἀνθρώπων | αἰεὶ ἀφ' ὑμετέρης γενεῆς εἶδός τε φυήν τε) suggest that this is a central point to draw from the two stories. As well, both tales reflect upon the juxtaposition of mortality and immortality, another major theme in the poem (see further on this theme Introd., p. 11).

These two stories do not, however, form an equal pair. The affair of Tithonus and Eos has horrific consequences, whereas the other has a seemingly happy ending; Ganymedes lives with Zeus ageless and immortal amongst the gods, while his father rejoices in Zeus' present of immortal horses and the news of his son's elevated position (vv. 210–17). Smith (1981a), 71–7 argues that the first story has a negative cast as well, with the eternally subordinate position of Ganymedes to Zeus implied, and an ironically unequal exchange of horses for a son, but this is far from clear; nothing negative is said about Ganymedes' position, and Tros, although initially grieved at the loss of his son, is ultimately presented as happy: Tros' joy at hearing of his son's immortality and at receiving the divine horses is emphatically contrasted with his former grief across the final two lines of the story (vv. 216–17 οὐκέτ' ἔπειτα γόασκε, γεγήθει δὲ φρένας ἔνδον, | γηθόσυνος δ' ἵπποισιν ἀελλοπόδεσσιν ὀχεῖτο). Both stories do not need to carry a negative message to make sense as a pair. As Clay (1989), 187–91, van der Ben (1981), 87, and VB 25 have insightfully pointed out, 'it is essential not to overlook the emphasis laid on Zeus: Zeus made Ganymedes ἀθάνατος καὶ ἀγήρως, the implication being "quod licet Iovi non licet Veneri."' Eos made a serious oversight in forgetting to ask Zeus to make Tithonus ageless, for Zeus is the only one capable of granting such a request. Aphrodite might not forget, but she is neither able nor willing to ask Zeus for such a favour because of her situation: he might, given their history, simply refuse to grant the request, and she could in any case hardly put the question to him out of shame, the result of her union which Aphrodite dwells upon in the lines immediately following these two stories (cf. below on 239–55).

A scholiast on A.R. reports that Ibycus included an account of how Eos carried off Tithonus when he told of the abduction of Ganymedes (Ibyc. *PMGF* 289a; see Bowra 1961, 259). The two are also mentioned together later at Nonn. *D.* 15. 279–82 (cf. below on 203 ὃν διὰ κάλλος). Goddesses who fall in love with mortal men act similarly to *erastai*, and later vase paintings depicting Eos and Tithonus can assimilate Tithonus to Ganymedes or other anonymous *eromenoi*; see Dover (1989), 172.

200–1. The δέ in v. 200 seems to carry explanatory force, as in v. 6 (cf. VE 73 and above on 2–6); these two lines explain why Aphrodite has fallen into bed with Anchises (because of his immortal beauty) and act as an introduction for the stories of Ganymedes and Tithonus (see further below on μάλιστα).

200 ἀγχίθεοι: the subject of the sentence, the word here must mean 'godlike', as signalled by the accusatives of respect εἶδός τε φυήν τε at the end of v. 201 (cf. VE 73). It is only used twice in Homer of the Phaeacians (*Od.* 5. 35, 19. 279), where it means 'close to the gods', referring either to the special relationship they have with the divine or to their descent from Poseidon (cf. Hainsworth, *OC* ii. 258). Hsch. s.v. is aware of all three possible meanings (ἀγχίθεοι· οἱ Φαίακες. καθότι τρίτοι εἰσὶν ἀπὸ Ποσειδῶνος οἱ βασιλεῖς. ἢ ὅτι θεοὶ συνδιέτριβον αὐτοῖς. ἢ ὅτι εὐδαίμονες καὶ ἰσόθεοι).

Here, the adjective is surely also intended as an etymological pun on the name Ἀγχίσης, who by nature of his affair with Aphrodite is quite literally close to a god (see VB 24); the poet has made a similar pun on Aeneas' name just two lines earlier (see on *Aphr.* 198–9).

The word does not appear again until Lucian *Syr. D.* 31 (οὐ μέντοι πάντες οἱ ἱρέες, ἀλλὰ οἳ μάλιστα ἀγχίθεοί τέ εἰσιν καὶ οἷσι πᾶσα ἐς τὸ ἱρὸν μέλεται θεραπηίη), where it refers to the special connection certain priests have with the divine. It later occurs frequently in Nonnus' *Paraphrasis* (1. 147 etc.).

μάλιστα: Nordheider (*LfgrE* s.v.) and Humbert (1936) take this adverb with the adjective ἀγχίθεοι, 'most godlike' (cf. *Od.* 19. 160 etc.). VB 23 prefers to take it with the partitive genitive ἀνθρώπων (cf. *Il.* 2. 21 etc.), on the grounds that 'the context requires that Aphrodite's remark should refer to Anchises' family surpassing all others in the bringing forth of ἀγχίθεοι, rather than about degrees of ἀγχίθεος-ness'; cf. West (2003) 'Of all humankind, those close to the gods in appearance and stature always come especially from your family.'

Either meaning is possible, and the context could as easily favour the former over the latter; ἀγχίθεοι refers to the godlike beauty of Anchises (see n. prec.), beauty which also tempted Zeus and Eos and in part offers an explanation for Aphrodite's behaviour (cf. on *Aphr.* 200–201).

201 αἰεὶ ἀφ' ὑμετέρης γενεῆς: VB 24 suggested reading εἰσίν for αἰεί, but there is no compelling reason to doubt the unanimous MS tradition. Barnes (1711) had proposed αἰέν to avoid correption. Cf. ἡμετέρην γενεήν in the same metrical position at *Od.* 16. 117.

εἶδός τε φυήν τε: this phrasing does not occur elsewhere. For the pairing of the two words in early poetry see *Il.* 2. 58/*Od.* 6. 152 beginning εἶδός τε μέγεθός τε φυήν, *Il.* 22. 370 φυὴν καὶ εἶδος ἀγητόν, *Od.* 6. 16 φυὴν καὶ εἶδος ὁμοίη, *Th.* 259 φυὴν ἐρατὴ καὶ εἶδος ἄμωμος, [Hes.] fr. 229. 16 φυὴν καὶ εἶδος; cf. above on 82 μέγεθός τε εἶδός τε.

202–17. The story of Ganymedes' abduction by Zeus is recounted at *Il.* 20. 232–5:

> Ἶλός τ' Ἀσσάρακός τε καὶ ἀντίθεος Γανυμήδης,
> ὃς δὴ κάλλιστος γένετο θνητῶν ἀνθρώπων·
> τὸν καὶ ἀνηρέψαντο θεοὶ Διὶ οἰνοχοεύειν
> κάλλεος εἵνεκα οἷο, ἵν' ἀθανάτοισι μετείη.

The episode is also alluded to at *Il.* 5. 265–7, where Aeneas' horses are said to be descended from those which Zeus gave to Tros in return for his beautiful son. Some linguistic similarity between *Il.* 20. 235 κάλλεος εἵνεκα οἷο, ἵν' ἀθανάτοισι μετείη and *Aphr.* 203 ἥρπασεν ὃν διὰ κάλλος, ἵν' ἀθανάτοισιν μετείη could suggest *imitatio* of the passage in *Il.* 20, especially given the likelihood of imitation of *Il.* 20. 307–8 above at vv. 197–8 (see Introd., p. 32), but even if the poet knew the Homeric version it seems probable that he had another model in mind here. The account of the abduction in *Aphr.* is far more detailed than in the *Iliad* and it differs in an important respect; whereas in *Il.* 20 it is the gods who take Ganymedes up to heaven, it is Zeus himself who seizes the boy on this occasion, as often in early Greek art (see *LIMC* iv, Ganymedes, nos. 7–56). The role which Hermes plays in the exchange between Zeus and Tros in *Aphr.* and the initial grief of Tros at the loss of his son are not known elsewhere, but these are not necessarily innovations of the poet as VE 76 suggests. Hermes is involved in the abduction of Ganymedes in art and later literature, as is Zeus' other personal messenger Iris (see further Sichtermann, *LIMC* iv/1. 154–69; in literature see Lucian *DDeor.* 20. 6 and Mart. 9. 25. 8), and his role as messenger to Tros could easily have been part of other early versions of the abduction. Tros' grief, which functions well here as a foil to his eventual joy at the reception of the horses, is also natural enough in such a story.

There is no direct statement in *Il.* 20 that Ganymedes has been taken to be the beloved of Zeus, but the emphasis placed there on his beauty and the fact that wine-pouring, along with paederasty, was an important initiation ritual for young boys, seems to imply this; see Bremmer (1980), 285 ff. and M. W. Edwards (1991), 319–20. The erotic implications of the abduction are even stronger in *Aphr*. The context of the story alone suggests this reading; Aphrodite has just slept with a mortal, and the subsequent story of Eos and Tithonus has the same theme (cf. VE 73–4; *contra* VB 24). Paederasty is perhaps also implied in the verb ἁρπάζω, used of Zeus seizing Ganymedes (vv. 203; cf. also v. 208 ἀνήρπασε θέσπις ἄελλα and v. 218 of Eos abducting Tithonus); ἁρπαγή seems to be a technical term used for a man who captures a young lover (see Bremmer 1980, 285): the verb is later used by Theognis 1347 in his account of Ganymedes' abduction, where the homoerotic element is made clear; cf. also the scholiast's report of the version told by Ibycus in his encomium to Gorgias (Ibyc. *PMGF* 289a). Rape is implied in the use of the simple verb and its compound ἀναρπάζω earlier in the poem also at vv. 117 and 121, when Aphrodite in mortal disguise claims that Hermes snatched her away from dancing with her young companions (on the implication of rape there see on *Aphr*. 117–29). On the absence of overt homosexuality in the Homeric epics, see Dover (1989), 194, 196 ff.

202 ἤτοι μέν: this combination of preparative particles is picked up in v. 218 by ὣς δ' αὖ, which provides a structural link between the Ganymedes and Tithonus episodes; VB 24–5 notes that balance is also provided by the occurrence of ἥρπασεν in both lines. The combination ἤτοι μέν is an emphatic equivalent of preparative μέν or ἤτοι alone; see Ruijgh (1981), 276–9.

ξανθὸν Γανυμήδεα: the adjective is used in early epic of horses, rivers, and hair, and as an epithet of heroes and gods; see *LfgrE* s.v. for a full list of occurrences. The exact colour which the word denotes is uncertain, but it is some shade of 'light-brown' or 'blond'; see Edgeworth (1983), 32–3, Handschur (1970), 144–7, Kober (1932), 55–8. Ganymedes is not elsewhere called ξανθός, but the epithet is here appropriate to his godlike beauty; Demeter's ξανθαὶ κόμαι at *Dem*. 279 are described as part of the transformation from her disguise of an old mortal woman to her true divine beauty (cf. J. G.-J. Abbenes, *LfgrE* s.v.). Plato (*R*. 474 D–E) later has Socrates tell Glaucon that lovers are apt to call the 'fair' (λευκούς) youths they are enamoured with the 'children of the gods' (θεῶν παῖδας); cf. Irwin (1974), 135.

203 ἥρπασεν ὃν διὰ κάλλος ἵν' ἀθανάτοισι μετείη: cf. the very similar *Il.* 20. 234/*Od.* 15. 251 κάλλεος εἵνεκα οἷο ἵν' ἀθανάτοισι μετείη, the former of Zeus' abduction of Ganymedes, the latter of Eos' abduction of Cleitus. On the verb ἁρπάζω see above on 202–17.

ἥρπασεν ὅν: Dp transmit ἥρπασ' ἑόν, x ἥρπασ' ἐνόν, presumably misarticulations of ἥρπασε ὅν and ἥρπασεν ὅν (M reads ἥρπασ' αἰνόν). Matthiae (1805) prints ἥρπασε ὅν (followed by Càssola), preserving digamma in ὅν. However, neglect of digamma in this possessive pronoun is not uncommon in Homer (see *Grammaire*, i. 147, Monro 1891, 370, Leaf i. 494 ad *Il.* 11. 403), and evidence of a Naxian dedication (*CEG* 403) suggests that poets were using nu mobile to obviate digamma-hiatus as early as the mid-seventh century (see West 2001*a*, 163). There is therefore no certainty that nu mobile is a later addition here, and I prefer to follow Hermann (1806) in printing ἥρπασεν ὅν. Cf. above on *Aphr.* 6 πᾶσιν δ' ἔργα.

ὃν διὰ κάλλος: when the possessive ἑός, ὅς does not refer to the subject of the sentence it is often emphatic; see Monro (1891), 220 and GG ii. 204. Cf. *Od.* 11. 281–2 τήν ποτε Νηλεὺς | γῆμεν ἑὸν διὰ κάλλος, where Neleus marries Chloris because of her beauty. Similar language is used of Ganymedes' abduction later at Nonn. *D.* 15. 281–2 ὃν διὰ κάλλος | φειδομένοις ὀνύχεσσιν ἐκούφισεν ὑψιπέτης Ζεύς (there mentioned together with Eos' rape of Tithonus).

204–6 ἐπιοινοχοεύοι | ... τετιμένος | ... ἀφύσσων: M once again departs from the other MSS with three unique readings ἐπιοινοχοεύειν | ... τετιμένον | ... ἀφύσσειν (on the other unique variants in M see Introd., pp. 54–5). The infinitive construction ἥρπασεν [Γανυμήδεα] ... ἐπιοινοχοεύειν is possible, but would be extremely awkward after ἵνα and the optative μετείη (cf. AHS 365). Both VE 74–5 and VB 25 adopt the infinitive on the grounds that ἔπι οἰνοχοεύειν are two separate words, with ἔπ' standing for either ἔπεστι 'he is present amongst the gods' or ἔπεστί οἱ 'it is his share'. VE compares *Od.* 2. 58–9 οὐ γὰρ ἔπ' ἀνήρ | οἷος Ὀδυσσεὺς ἔσκεν, ἀρὴν ἀπὸ οἴκου ἀμῦναι, but such ellipsis seems strained here; θεοῖς ἔπεστι would repeat the sense of ἀθανάτοισι μετείη and there is no strong reason to divide the compound (see below). The infinitive may have been suggested to the scribe by familiarity with *Il.* 20. 234 τὸν

[Γανυμήδεα] καὶ ἀνηρείψαντο θεοὶ Διὶ οἰνοχοεύειν (cf. Baumeister 1860, 257); the infinitive occurs at line-end also at *Il.* 2. 127.

After the optative, the nominatives τετιμένος and ἀφύσσων describe Ganymedes as the subject of the sentence. M's τετιμένον could be supported by the conflation τετιμένονος in *x* (cf. AHS 365), but this is a simple error which might be explained separately as assimilation to the neuter θαῦμα at the beginning of the line (cf. VE 75). In M, both the accusative τετιμένον and the infinitive ἀφύσσειν conform to the infinitive construction. For pouring and drawing wine together, see the description of Hephaestus at *Il.* 1. 597–8 αὐτὰρ ὃ τοῖς ἄλλοισι θεοῖς ἐνδέξια πᾶσιν | οἰνοχόει γλυκὺ νέκταρ ἀπὸ κρητῆρος ἀφύσσων.

204 καί τε: see above on 3.

ἐπιοινοχοεύοι: *x* and *Γ* separate this compound, but there is no compelling reason to follow them here, as do VE 74–5 and VB 25 on the grounds that ἐπι- cannot mean 'to pour out for'. A similar compound is found at Thgn. 971 πίνοντ' ἐπιοίνιον ἆθλον, and there seems to be little difference in meaning between οἰνοχοεύοι and the compound, which is probably a poetic variation; cf. ἐπιβουκόλος (*Od.* 3. 422 etc.) for βουκόλος, ἐπιβώτορι (*Od.* 13. 222) for βώτορι, and ἐπίουρος (*Od.* 13. 405/15. 39) for οὖρος (see Hoekstra, *OC* ii 178). The compound could have been suggested by a line such as *Od.* 1. 143 κῆρυξ δ' αὐτοῖσιν θάμ' ἐπῴχετο οἰνοχοεύων (cf. Heitsch 1965, 24). The form ἐποίνιος is later used several times by Nonnus (*D.* 11. 301 etc.).

205. Most similar is *Dem.* 397 ναιετάοις πάντεσσι τετιμ[ένη ἀθανάτοι]σιν (on the reading there see N. Richardson 1974, 283; on the close relationship between *Aphr.* and *Dem.* see Introd., pp. 38–40); cf. *Il.* 24. 533 φοιτᾷ δ' οὔτε θεοῖσι τετιμένος οὔτε βροτοῖσι, *Th.* 415 ἀθανάτοις τε θεοῖσι τετιμένη, 449 πᾶσι μετ' ἀθανάτοισι τετίμηται and *Apoll.* 479/522 πολλοῖσι τετιμέν-ον (-οι) ἀνθρώποισιν. Janko (1981*a*), 161 also points to *Certamen* 220 Allen (§13 West 2003, 340) Ἡσίοδος Μούσῃσι τετιμένος ἀθανάτῃσιν.

θαῦμα ἰδεῖν: elsewhere only at Hes. *Sc.* 318 and [Hes.] fr. 145. 16. More common is θαῦμα ἰδέσθαι, above at v. 90 (see ad loc.).

206 χρυσέου ἐκ κρητῆρος ἀφύσσων: cf. *Il.* 23. 219–20 χρυσέου ἐκ κρητῆρος . . . | οἶνον ἀφυσσάμενος, of Achilles drawing wine from his golden bowl to pour out on the ground for Patroclus. Note also *Il.* 1. 598 ἀπὸ κρητῆρος ἀφύσσων, 3. 295 οἶνον δ' ἐκ κρητῆρος ἀφυσσάμενοι and *Od.* 9. 9 μέθυ δ' ἐκ κρητῆρος ἀφύσσων.

νέκταρ ἐρυθρόν: this combination recurs at *Il.* 19. 38, *Od.* 5. 93. The adjective ἐρυθρόν is used also of wine at *Od.* 5. 165 etc. Nectar is usually the drink of the gods, although it is not certain exactly what the substance was imagined to be composed of. It is used as an unguent at *Il.* 19. 38, where Thetis drips nectar and ambrosia into Patroclus' nose to keep his corpse firm. On both nectar and ambrosia, the food of the gods, see further Hainsworth, *OC* i. 264 and *OCD* s.v. ambrosia. The etymology of νέκταρ is uncertain. It has often been derived from *ṇ privative and κταρ < κτέρες (νεκροί) 'immortal', but it could come from the Semitic root *qṭr* 'burning incense' (see S. Levin 1971, Càssola 555); Griffith (1994) suggests a derivation from the Egyptian *nṯry* 'divine'.

207 Τρῶα: Tros is the father of Ganymedes and the great-grandfather of Tithonus and Anchises. The genealogy is given at *Il.* 20. 215 ff.; cf. M. W. Edwards (1991), 316.

Τρῶα δὲ πένθος ἄλαστον ἔχε φρένας: cf. *Th.* 467 Ῥέην δ' ἔχε πένθος ἄλαστον and *Od.* 24. 423 παιδὸς γάρ οἱ ἄλαστον ἐνὶ φρεσὶ πένθος ἔκειτο. See also *Il.* 24. 105 [Θέτις] πένθος ἄλαστον ἔχουσα μετὰ φρεσίν, where πένθος is the object possessed (cf. *Od.* 7. 218, 10. 376 etc.). On the double-accusative construction with φρένας see above on 7.

ἄλαστον: this adjective is most often used of πένθος or ἄχος. The etymology is uncertain, but the word could derive from λαθεῖν + *ṇ privative 'not forgotten' (see *Dictionnaire* s.v. ἀλάστωρ, Frisk s.v., VE 75). In any case, it seems to have come to mean something like 'insufferable' (cf. LSJ s.v.) or 'severe/terrible' (cf. *LfgrE* s.v.: 'heftig'). It is used also as a verbal insult against Hector at *Il.* 22. 261, where it appears to mean 'accursed' (see N. Richardson 1993, 133).

οὐδέ τι εἴδη: this phrase is formulaic; cf. οὐδέ τι εἴδη *Il.* 13. 674 and οὐδέ τι οἶδ- *Il.* 11. 657, *Od.* 3. 184, etc. The digamma is respected here, as at *Il.* 1. 70, whereas it is neglected at *Od.* 23. 29. On the spelling εἴδη for ᾔδει transmitted by the MSS see West (1998), *Praefatio*, p. xxxiii, *Grammaire*, i. 438.

208 φίλον υἱόν: see above on 196.

θέσπις ἀέλλα: Ganymedes is taken up by a 'divine wind'. Later versions of the myth have Ganymedes abducted by an eagle (cf. Apollod. 3. 12. 2, Verg. *A.* 5. 252 ff., Ov. *Met.* 10. 155 ff., etc.), but in early art he is most often depicted being abducted by Zeus, or his messengers Hermes and Iris (see *LIMC* iv, Ganymedes, nos. 7–56). As Zeus is above said to have seized Ganymedes (ἀνήρπασε here echoes ἥρπασεν v. 202), the idea could be that Zeus appeared as a 'divine wind' to seize the boy (cf. VB 25–6). Alternatively, to be whisked away by storm-winds (ἄελλαι, θύελλαι, ἅρπυιαι) seems to be equivalent to a mortal saying that someone has 'disappeared into thin air' (see Russo, *OC* iii. 112): at *Od.* 4. 727–8 Penelope explains Telemachus' sudden disappearance without her knowledge with the phrase νῦν αὖ παῖδ᾽ ἀγαπητὸν ἀνηρείψαντο θύελλαι; cf. *Il.* 6. 345–8 (Helen wishes she had been whisked away at birth), *Od.* 1. 241–2 (Telemachus describes Odysseus' disappearance), 20. 61 ff. (Penelope's wish and fate of the daughters of Pandareus). The main point here is that Tros has no idea where his son has gone.

209 τὸν δὴ ἔπειτα: see on *Aphr.* 56.

γοάσκε: here and at v. 216, this contracted form of γοάασκε occurs only in this poem. However, even γοάασκε occurs only once in early poetry at *Od.* 8. 92 ἂψ Ὀδυσσεὺς κατὰ κρᾶτα καλυψάμενος γοάασκε (cf. later A.R. 1. 264 etc.), and there is insufficient evidence to suppose that the contraction is a case of modification of a formula (see Hoekstra 1968, 44).

διαμπερὲς ἤματα πάντα: on ἤματα πάντα see above on 28; whereas on the other four occasions it is used in *Aphr.* (28, 148, 221, 240) the phrase applies to a future state of affairs and means 'always/for ever', it here refers to a finite time and must have the sense 'all the time/ every day', for Zeus soon stops Tros' sorrow with the gift of the horses. See *Od.* 4. 209, where διαμπερὲς ἤματα πάντα refers to all the days of Nestor's long life; for the formula cf. *Apoll.* 485.

210 Ζεὺς ἐλέησε: it is a common motif that Zeus takes pity on mortals; see *Il.* 15. 12, 16. 431, 17. 441, 19. 340 (cf. Janko 1994, 375).

δίδου οἱ υἷος ἄποινα: on ἄποινα see above on 140. For ransom given in return for Ganymedes, cf. *Il.* 5. 266 δῶχ᾽ υἷος ποινὴν Γανυμήδεος and *Little Iliad* fr. 6. 1 Davies ἄμπελον ἣν Κρονίδης ἔπορεν οὗ παιδὸς ἄποινα. See also for the phraseology *Il.* 2. 230 υἷος ἄποινα.

211 ἵππους ἀρσίποδας: this appears to be a modification of the formula ἵπποι ἀερσίποδες (*Il.* 3. 327 and 23. 475; cf. *Il.* 18. 532); see Hoekstra (1969), 39, Heitsch (1965), 31. The contracted form of the adjective is found only here and much later in an anonymous epigram, *AP* 7. 717. 3 (of hares). The adjective, derived from ἀείρω, means 'which lift their feet/high-stepping', with the implication of speed (see *LfgrE* s.v.); cf. West (2003) 'prancing horses'. Horses are commonly ὠκυπόδες in Homer (*Il*. 5. 732 etc.).

The story of Zeus' gift of horses to Tros in return for his son is recounted by Diomedes at *Il*. 5. 265; the swiftness of their descendants is lauded by Aeneas at 5. 222–3. Another tradition makes Laomedon the father of Ganymedes, who receives a golden vine for his son; see *Little Iliad* fr. 6 Davies.

τοί τ' ἀθανάτους φορέουσι: cf. *Il*. 10. 322–3 ἧ μὲν τοὺς ἵππους τε καὶ ἅρματα ποικίλα χαλκῷ | δωσέμεν, οἳ φορέουσιν ἀμύμονα Πηλείωνα.

212 εἶπέν τε ἕκαστα: the nu mobile of εἶπε(ν) makes position here, but never in Homer. This could be the result of modification by conjugation of εἴπω τε ἕκαστα (*Od*. 3. 361); see Hoekstra (1969), 39. Wolf (1807) proposed reading δέ for the τε of the MSS. However, τε is possible as a simple connective of two words, clauses, and sentences in verse (a use much rarer in prose); see Ruijgh (1971), 175 ff. and Denniston (1954), 497.

213 Ζηνὸς ἐφημοσύνῃσι: the word ἐφημοσύνη is rare in early poetry (*Il*. 17. 697, *Od*. 12. 226, 16. 340), where it otherwise appears only in the singular; the conjugation could have been suggested by *Op*. 245 Ζηνὸς φραδμοσύνῃσιν, *Th*. 626 Γαίης φραδμοσύνῃσιν. The plural becomes common in Hellenistic poetry and later; cf. A.R. 1. 3, 4. 818 etc. Colluthus might have had *Aphr*. in mind at 19 Ζηνὸς ἐφημοσύνῃσιν ἐῳνοχόει Γανυμήδης.

διάκτορος Ἀργειφόντης: see on *Aphr*. 147.

214 [εἶπεν] ὡς ἔοι: this and the similar *Od*. 24. 237–6 ἕκαστα | εἰπεῖν, ὡς ἔλθοι καὶ ἵκοιτ' ἐς πατρίδα γαῖαν are the earliest cases of *oratio obliqua* with the optative. It has been proposed that in *Od*. 24. 237–6 the ὡς-clause can be understood as an indirect question ('tell how . . .'; see GG ii. 232, *Grammaire*, ii. 224, Cooper iii. 2420), a construction with the optative known elsewhere in Homer, but this is questionable. It seems best to take both cases as examples of *oratio obliqua* + opt., a contruction well developed in Herodotus: see Monro (1891), 281, VB 26, Heubeck, *OC* iii. 388, with further bibliography.

ἀθάνατος καὶ ἀγήρως ἶσα θεοῖσιν: on the common formula ἀθάνατος καὶ ἀγήρως (-αος) ἤματα πάντα (*Il*. 8. 539 etc.), see Janko (1981c), West (1966a), 246 on *Th*. 277. The MS D has the uncontracted form ἀγήραος, but it is best to follow the majority reading; the contracted form is guaranteed by the metre on several occasions in Homer (see N. Richardson 1974, 240 on *Dem.* 242). M and *a* (in the margin) have ἶσα θεοῖσιν, while the others transmit ἤματα πάντα; the former should be favoured as *lectio difficilior*, for which the common formula could easily have been substituted.

215. This line bears similarities to *Od.* 5. 150 [πότνια νύμφη] ἤϊ᾽, ἐπεὶ δὴ Ζηνὸς ἐπέκλυεν ἀγγελιάων (cf. Heitsch 1965, 23), where Hermes tells Calypso that she must send Odysseus away. Tros leaves behind his sorrow only after having heard that his son will be immortal and ageless, not by the gift of the horses themselves. He takes pleasure in the latter only after he is secure in the fate of his son.

αὐτὰρ ἐπεὶ δή: this formula is common at line-beginning (*Il.* 4. 124, 6. 178, etc.). Cf. above on 128–9.

216–17. There is alliteration of γ- across these two lines: γόασκε, γεγήθει, γηθόσυνος. The immediate juxtaposition of γόασκε/γεγήθει at the feminine caesura in v. 216 helps to convey Tros' rather sudden switch from sorrow to joy, and this joy is then emphasized by the enjambment of γηθόσυνος in v. 217. The beginning of v. 216 οὐκέτ᾽ ἔπειτα γόασκε also echoes 209 above, bringing a structural end to the description of Tros' sorrow.

216 γεγήθει δὲ φρένας ἔνδον: VE 77 compares *Il.* 11. 683 γεγήθει δὲ φρένα Νηλεύς and *Od.* 11. 337 ἰδὲ φρένας ἔνδον ἐΐσας (= *Od.* 18. 249). Cf. γεγήθει φρένα also *Il.* 8. 559, *Od.* 6. 106 and *Dem.* 232.

217 γηθόσυνος: this adjective and the noun γηθοσύνη are commonly found in the first position of the line in early epic; cf. *Il.* 7. 122, 13. 29 etc. It is also very common in later verse; see Campbell (1991), 104 on Mosch. *Eur.* 117.

ἵπποισιν ἀελλοπόδεσσιν: the adjective ἀελλόπος 'storm-footed' is used in Homer only of Iris (*Il.* 8. 409, 24. 77, 24. 159), who is also called ποδήνεμος. It is elsewhere used of horses at Simon. *PMG* 515, Pi. *N.* 1. 6, fr. 221. 1, and later at A.R. 1. 1158, Q.S. 4. 536 etc. Another tradition (*Il.* 20. 221–9) has the wind-god Boreas sleep with twelve mares of Erichthonius, son of Dardanos, to produce a divine breed of horses which might naturally be called 'storm-footed'. Similarly, Achilles' divine horses are sired by the West Wind (*Il.* 16. 148–51);

see further Janko (1992), 336–7. On the swiftness of these horses, cf. above on 211 ἵππους ἀρσίποδας.

218–38. Tithonus is known to be the husband of Eos in Homer and Hesiod (*Il.* 11. 1–2, *Od.* 5. 1–2 and *Th.* 984), but the story of his deathless ageing is not found elsewhere until Mimn. fr. 4 *IEG* and Sappho fr. 58 (as in West 2005). The latter has several thematic similarities to the narrative in *Aphr.*: v. 227 ναῖε παρ' Ὠκεανοῖο ῥοῆς ἐπὶ πείρασι γαίης ~ fr. 58. 10 βᾶμεν' εἰς ἔσχατα γᾶς φέροισα[ν, v. 228 πρῶται πολιαὶ κατέχυντο ἔθειραι ~ fr. 58. 4 ἐγ]ένοντο τρίχες ἐκ μελαίναν, 12 πόλιον γῆρας, v. 233 κατὰ γῆρας ἔπειγεν ~ fr. 58. 3–4 ποτ' [ἔ]οντα χρόα γῆρας ἤδη and v. 234 οὐδέ τι κινῆσαι μελέων δύνατ' (~ *Od.* 8. 298) ~ fr. 58. 5 βάρυς δέ μ' ὁ [θ]ῦμος πεπόηται, γόνα δ' οὐ φέροισι. There is, however, no good reason to suppose direct borrowing; the language is not particularly close and the thematic similarities would be well explained by a common model (see further Introd., pp. 45–7).

It has been suggested that the story of Tithonus' deathless ageing is the invention of this poet, because the motif fits the narrative so well (see Podbielski 1971, 70, VB 26–7; cf. Smith 1981*a*, 84). This is possible, but the poet could equally well have adapted an earlier account because of the appropriateness of the motif. The version of the story in *Aphr.* is at odds with the genealogy of the Dardanians found at *Il.* 20. 237, where Tithonus is the son of Laomedon and of the same generation as Anchises: here he must be of a previous generation. However, alternative genealogies of this family were circulating—at *Little Iliad* fr. 6 Davies, Laomedon is said to be the father of Ganymedes—as might the story of Tithonus' deathless ageing (cf. Lenz 140–1). In later versions of the myth, Tithonus is the one who forgets to ask for agelessness when requesting immortality and Eos turns him into a cicada (see below on 237). Eos is well known for taking mortal lovers; apart from Tithonus, she abducts Orion, Cephalus, Cleitus, and even Ganymedes; see further Hainsworth, *OC* i. 266 on *Od.* 5. 121.

After the story is introduced in vv. 218–19, the narrative progresses in four distinct parts: (i) vv. 220–4 Eos' request of Zeus, (ii) vv. 225–7 Tithonus' youth, (iii) vv. 228–32 Tithonus' approach to old age, and (iv) vv. 233–8 Tithonus' extreme old age (cf. Smith 1981*a*, 77–82). This story provides a counterexample to the happy outcome to Zeus' abduction of Ganymedes (see above on 200–40), but also works alongside it as an exploration of mortality and immortality; on this theme in the Tithonus episode cf. in particular Segal (1974, 1986) and King (1989), and see Introd., p. 11.

218 ὥς δ' αὖ: on δέ picking up μέν at 202 see above ad loc. This phraseology occurs elsewhere only at *Od.* 5. 129, as part of Calypso's account of love-affairs between goddesses and mortal men.

χρυσόθρονος ἥρπασεν Ἠώς: cf. the rape of Cleitus at *Od.* 15. 250–1 ἀλλ' ἤτοι Κλεῖτον χρυσόθρονος ἥρπασεν Ἠώς. See also the formular χρυσόθρονος ἤλυθεν Ἠώς (*Od.* 10. 541, 12. 142, 15. 56, 20. 91). The epithet χρυσόθρονος is used in early epic of Eos, Artemis, and Hera, and was most probably understood at an early stage to mean 'golden-throned'. It might, however, have an original derivation from θρόνον 'flower' (cf. *Il.* 22. 441 θρόνα ποικίλ' and compare Aphrodite's epithet πο]ικιλόθρο[ν' at Sappho fr. 1. 1); see Hainsworth, *OC* i. 266–7 on *Od.* 5. 123, Càssola 556, and VE 78. 'Golden-flowered' would be more appropriate of Eos, and 'golden-throned' of Hera.

219. This line recalls the point made at vv. 200–1 above, that those of Anchises' race are the most ἀγχίθεοι of mortal men, acting structurally as a second point of departure. For the formulaic ἐπιείκελος ἀθανάτοισιν cf. *Il.* 4. 394, 11. 60, etc.

220 βῆ δ' ἴμεν αἰτήσουσα: cf. *Od.* 17. 365 βῆ δ' ἴμεν αἰτήσων, of Odysseus begging from the suitors. The future participle αἰτήσουσα occurs in the same metrical position also at *Od.* 20. 74, of Aphrodite going to Olympus to ask for the accomplishment of marriages for the daughters of Pandareus. βῆ δ' ἴμεν, equivalent to βῆ, is formulaic; cf. *Il.* 10. 32 etc.

κελαινεφέα Κρονίωνα: 'dark-clouded son of Kronos'; a common formula in the dative (*Il.* 1. 397 etc.), but only once more in the accusative at *Il.* 11. 78.

221 ἀθάνατόν τ' εἶναι καὶ ζώειν ἤματα πάντα: perhaps a variation upon the common formula ἀθάνατος καὶ ἀγήρως (-αος) ἤματα πάντα (see above on 214); Tithonus will of course not be ἀγήρως. For the versification cf. in particular *Od.* 7. 94 ἀθανάτους ὄντας καὶ ἀγήρως ἤματα πάντα and *Dem.* 260 ἀθάνατόν κέν τοι καὶ ἀγήραον ἤματα πάντα. On ἤματα πάντα see above on *Aphr.* 28.

222 Ζεὺς ἐπένευσε: Zeus nods forward to give his assent (= κατανεύω, *Il.* 1. 524 etc.); for the gesture cf. *Il.* 15. 75, *Dem.* 169,

466. Nodding the head backwards (ἀνανεύω, Il. 6. 311 etc.) indicates refusal, as still in modern Greece.

ἐκρήηνεν ἐέλδωρ: for this formular phrase see Il. 1. 41 and 1. 504. Cf. ἐπικρήηνον/κρήηνατ' ἐέλδωρ Il. 1. 455, 8. 242, etc.

223 νηπίη, οὐδ' ἐνόησε: for the phraseology cf. Il. 20. 264 νήπιος, οὐδ' ἐνόησε κατὰ φρένα καὶ κατὰ θυμόν, 22. 445 νηπίη, οὐδ' ἐνόησεν, as well as Th. 488 σχέτλιος, οὐδ' ἐνόησε μετὰ φρεσί; cf. West (1966a), 301, who lists more parallels. The adjective νήπιος is often used of children, but also of adults whose lack of foresight leads to horrendous consequences; see the comprehensive study of the word by Edmunds (1990); on its use for adults, esp. 60 ff.

πότνια Ἠώς: only here and below at v. 230, although cf. Sappho fr. 157 πότνια Αὔως. The noun–epithet pair is formed by analogy with πότνια Ἥρη (Il. 8. 198), πότνια Δηώ (Dem. 47) etc. Cf. Janko (1982), 275–6 n. 16, who also compares Dem. 51 φαινόλις Ἠώς (cf. Sapph. 104. 1). On πότνια cf. above on 24.

224 ἥβην αἰτῆσαι: the enjambment places emphasis on ἥβην at the beginning of the line; Eos has made a grave mistake in not asking for youth as well. For the versification, cf. the enjambed ἥβην ἵξεσθαι at Il. 24. 728.

ξῦσαί τ' ἄπο: for the scraping-off of old age cf. Il. 9. 446 γῆρας ἀποξύσας and Nostoi fr. 6. 2 γῆρας ἀποξύσασα; see also later Greg. Nanz. Carm. I. 2. 2. 483 (PG 37. 616) γῆρας ἀποξύσειε, Cometas AP 15. 37. 3 γῆρας ἀποξύσας. Griffin (1995), 128 relates it to the idea of old age as a skin that can be shed, as that of a snake (cf. Theodoros Prodromos, Carmina Historica 24. 18 ἀπόξυσαι τὸ γῆρας ὥσπερ ὄφις).

γῆρας ὀλοιόν: 'destructive old age'; cf. Hes. Th. 604 ὀλοὸν δ' ἐπὶ γῆρας ἵκηται and see Il. 24. 487 ὀλοῷ ἐπὶ γήραος οὐδῷ. The lengthened form of the adjective ὀλοιός for ὀλοός occurs elsewhere only twice in the feminine ὀλοιή (-ῇσι); Il. 1. 342 and 22. 5. This unique masculine form could suggest post-Homeric modification by lengthening—see Janko (1982), 158—but it is impossible to be certain.

225 τὸν δ' ἤτοι εἵως μέν: repetition of this structure punctuates the Tithonus narrative; see v. 230 τοῦ δ' ἤτοι εὐνῆς μέν and v. 237 τοῦ δ' ἤτοι φωνὴ ῥέει (cf. Smith 1981a, 78, Heitsch 1965, 37). ἤτοι μέν is here corresponsive with αὐτάρ (v. 228); at v. 230 with αὐτὸν δ' αὖτ' (v. 231), where it contrasts Eos' avoidance of Tithonus' bed and her nursing of him (cf. VE 81); on ἤτοι μέν cf. above on 202. ἤτοι in v. 237 is corresponsive with οὐδέ of the same line, contrasting the flowing voice and loss of strength.

εἵως: on the form ἕως/εἵως, often transmitted by the MSS as here and corrected by editors to ἧος, see West (1966c).

ἔχεν πολυήρατος ἥβη: cf. the noun–epithet combination at Od. 15. 366, [Hes.] fr. 30. 31, 205. 2 and 229. 8 (v.l.). Youth (ἥβη) is said to have hold of someone only here and below at v. 274, where it seizes Aeneas, ἕλῃ πολύρατος ἥβη. However, this is a natural corollary to old age seizing someone (cf. Il. 18. 515, Od. 11. 497). One can elsewhere possess the 'flower of youth' (ἄνθος ἥβης); cf. Il. 13. 484, Th. 988, Simon. IEG 20. 5, etc.

226–7 Ἠοῖ τερπόμενος ... | ναίει: cf. Hy. 15. 8 [Ἡρακλῆς] ναίει τερπόμενος καὶ ἔχει καλλίσφυρον Ἥβην; also Thgn. 566 Ἥβηι τερπόμενος παίζω.

ἠριγενείη: 'early born', a common epithet of Eos (Il. 1. 477 etc.), but not elsewhere in early poetry in the dative. Cf. in particular Od. 23. 347 αὐτίκ᾽ ἀπ᾽ Ὠκεανοῦ χρυσόθρονον ἠριγένειαν, the only other instance where χρυσόθρονος and the adjective appear together. On χρυσόθρονος see above on 218.

227 ναῖε πὰρ᾽ Ὠκεανοῖο ῥοῆς: the uncontracted o-stem genitive -οῖο could be an archaism, from which Od. 24. 11 Ὠκεανοῦ τε ῥοάς/Th. 841 Ὠκεανοῦ τε ῥοαί are modified by separation, although the short dative ῥοῆς might itself be modification of line-end ποταμοῖο ῥοῆισιν (Il. 16. 669, 16. 679, Od. 6. 216); see Janko (1982), 160–1. For the phraseology, cf. Il. 13. 176, 15. 551 ναῖε δὲ πὰρ Πριάμῳ. Eos makes her home at the ends of the earth with Ocean (cf. Il. 19. 1–2, Od. 12. 1–6).

ἐπὶ πείρασι γαίης: cf. Od. 9. 284 ἐπὶ πείρασι γαίης and Th. 622 ἐν πείρασι γαίης; also πείρατα γαίης (Il. 14. 200 etc.). The πείρατα γαίης are frequently associated with Ocean, although they are sometimes situated in the underworld; see West (1966a), 258–9.

228 πολιαί ... ἔθειραι: the grey/white hair of old age is described as πολιός in Homer (cf. Il. 22. 77 πολιὰς τρίχας, of Priam), and elsewhere as λευκός; see Irwin (1974), 194 for a full list of parallels. Heads and chins are also πολιός (Il. 22. 74, 24. 516, of Priam; cf. Anacr. PMG 395. 1–2 πολιοὶ μὲν ἡμὶν ἤδη | κρόταφοι κάρη τε λευκόν), while Laertes and Dolius are themselves described as πολιός at Od.

24. 499. Old age itself is grey at Sapph. fr. 58. 12 πόλιον γῆρας. Used with ἔθειραι, cf. later *Anacreontea* 51. 2 τὰν πολιὰν ἔθειραν and Strato, *AP* 12. 240. 1 ἤδη πολιαὶ μὲν ἐπὶ κροτάφοισιν ἔθειραι.

ἔθειραι: in Homer used only of horse hair, on the living creature or in the crest of helmets (*Il.* 8. 42, 16. 795, etc.); cf. LSJ s.v. See, however, ἐθειράδες (v.l. for γενειάδες) of Odysseus' beard at *Od.* 16. 176. The word describes Dionysus' hair at *Hy.* 7. 4, P. *I.* 5. 9, etc.

228–9 κατέχυντο | ... ἐκ κεφαλῆς: 'spread down from his head'; Tithonus grows his first grey hairs. The language recalls descriptions of hair being pulled out (cf. *Il.* 10. 15 πολλὰς ἐκ κεφαλῆς προθελύμνους εἵλκετο χαίτας, 22. 77–8 τρίχας εἵλκετο χερσίν | τίλλων ἐκ κεφαλῆς; Agamemnon and Priam) or falling out (*Od.* 13. 399, 431 ξανθὰς δ' ἐκ κεφαλῆς ὀλέσω/ὄλεσεν τρίχας; Odysseus' transformation into a beggar), but that cannot be meant here. There is no reason to follow VE 80 in reading 'were poured over' (κεφαλῇ supplied; cf. *Od.* 6. 235 κατέχευε χάριν κεφαλῇ τε καὶ ὤμοις, of Athena); as VB 27 points out, ἐκ does not necessarily imply separation.

For the verb χέω of hair, cf. later Theoc. *Id.* 20. 23 χαῖται δ' οἷα σέλινα περὶ κροτάφοισι κέχυντο and Call. *Hy.* 6. 5 καταχεύατο χαίταν.

229. Note the balanced alliteration of this line; κ-/λ- sounds in the first half, γ-/ν- sounds in the second half.

εὐηγενέος: twice in Homer of people (*Il.* 11. 427 and the vulgate at 23. 81; v.l. εὐηφενέων, see N. Richardson 1993, 174), but not of a body part as here. Heitsch (1965), 31 suggests that the poet misunderstood the word to mean 'well-bearded' ἠϋγένειος, but there is no good reason to suppose this; cf. Janko (1982), 158–9 and VE 80, who point out that the poet may have intended some humorous play between words here. The adjective is later used of the neck and face at E. *Hel.* 136, *Med.* 1072.

M alone transmits εὐηγενέος. The other MSS have the more regular form εὐγενέος, here *contra metrum*.

230 τοῦ δ' ἤτοι εὐνῆς μέν: see above on 225.

ἀπείχετο: of keeping away from a bed or sexual activity, cf. *Il.* 14. 206–7/305–6 ἀλλήλων ἀπέχονται | εὐνῆς καὶ φιλότητος.

231 ἀτίταλλεν ἐνὶ μεγάροισιν: on the verb ἀτιτάλλω, usually used of nursing small children, see above on 114–15. Eos could be envisaged as treating Tithonus like a child, although the verb can later have a sense of 'to pamper' that would be appropriate here;

cf. Theoc. *Id.* 15. 111 Ἀρσινόα πάντεσσι καλοῖς ἀτιτάλλει Ἄδωνιν and Gow ii. 294 ad loc.

232 σίτῳ τ' ἀμβροσίῃ: the combination of mortal and immortal food is representative of Tithonus' intermediary status between mortal and divine (see VE 81). Odysseus in contrast receives mortal food from Calypso (*Od.* 5. 195–9). For the versification of this line, cf. *Th.* 640 νέκταρ τ' ἀμβροσίην τε, τά περ θεοὶ αὐτοὶ ἔδουσι.

εἵματα καλὰ διδοῦσα: equivalent to εἵματα σιγαλόεντα above at v. 85 (on which see ad loc.); cf. Hoekstra (1969), 48 n. 27. Cf. εἵματα καλά at line-end in vv. 64 and 171. For the gift of clothes from a goddess to a mortal lover, cf. *Od.* 7. 255–60 and 264–5 (Calypso to Odysseus).

233 ἀλλ' ὅτε δὴ πάμπαν: ἀλλ' ὅτε δή is very common in Homer (*Il.* 1. 493 etc.). Cf. *Il.* 13. 111 ἀλλ' εἰ δὴ καὶ πάμπαν.

στυγερὸν κατὰ γῆρας ἔπειγεν: cf. *Il.* 23. 623 χαλεπὸν κατὰ γῆρας ἐπείγει (v.l. for vulgate ἔπεισιν); cf. old age as a companion at *Il.* 1. 29 ἔπεισιν and 8. 103 γῆρας ὀπάζει. For the combination στυγερὸν γῆρας see *Il.* 19. 336 γήραϊ τε στυγερῷ, στυγερόν μ' ἐπὶ γῆρας ἱκέσθαι, and later at A.R. 1. 684, 4. 872, Posidipp. *Ep.* 118. 5 AB, and Gr. Naz. *Carm.* II 1. 1. 107 (*PG* 37. 978). Cf. γῆρας ὀλοιόν above at v. 224.

234. This line is almost identical with *Od.* 8. 298 οὐδέ τι κινῆσαι μελέων ἦν οὐδ' ἀναεῖραι, which describes Aphrodite and Ares trapped under the chains of Hephaestus. The phrasing is otherwise unparalleled; this could be a case of direct imitation of the episode of Aphrodite's affair with Ares (see further Introd., p. 34).

235. This line is formulaic and found frequently in early epic; cf. *Il.* 2. 5, 10. 17, etc. AHS 367 compare in particular *Od.* 9. 424 and 11. 230, where there is explanatory asyndeton in the next line as here; cf. VB 27.

236 ἐν θαλάμῳ κατέθηκε: for the phraseology, cf. the description of Odysseus taking the armour out of the main hall at *Od.* 24. 166 [τεύχεα] ἐς θάλαμον κατέθηκε; note also 21. 45 ἐν δὲ σταθμοὺς ἄρσε, θύρας δ' ἐπέθηκε φαεινάς.

θύρας δ' ἐπέθηκε: cf. on *Aphr.* 60, where Aphrodite puts to the doors of her temple.

237 τὸν δ' ἤτοι: see above on 225.

φωνὴ ῥεῖ ἄσπετος: cf. *Il.* 18. 402–3 περὶ δὲ ῥόος Ὠκεανοῖο | ἀφρῷ μορμύρων ῥέεν ἄσπετος, which may have served as a model for this line (cf. also Thgn. 1017 ῥέει ἄσπετος ἱδρώς). There the adjective ἄσπετος, originally 'unspeakable/unutterable', signifies the 'strong/immense' flow of Ocean, but that sense is awkwardly used of Tithonus' voice. VE 82 favours it, comparing the old men of Troy who have stopped from war but continue to speak like cicadas (*Il*. 3. 150–2), but Tithonus is no normal old man and it is difficult to see how a powerful voice would accord with a body as diminished as his (cf. VB 28; although it is used of loud noises at *Od*. 14. 412, *Apoll*. 360). The most probable meaning here is 'endless/ceaseless' (cf. *LfgrE* s.v.), for which there is support in a similar expression of the voice of the Muses at *Th*. 39 τῶν δ' ἀκάματος ῥέει αὐδή (cf. AHS 368). Maxwell-Stuart (1977), 160 proposes 'inarticulate', but the parallels he provides do not support the sense (e.g. *Il*. 16. 157, 17. 332).

Kakridis (1930) argues that Tithonus' metamorphosis into a cicada is alluded to here and Dornseiff (1931) that the poet of *Aphr*. invented the story, but there is no reason to understand any allusion to the metamorphosis here. The story of Tithonus' transformation into a cicada is known first in scholia of a Hellenistic date (cf. schol. *Il*. 11. 1, schol. Lyc. A. 18 etc.): it is referred to in a fragment of Hellanicus (*FGrH* 4 F 140), but this might not be from Hellanicus (see Smith 1981a, 129–30 n. 96).

ῥέει: Wolf (1807) proposed ῥέει for the MSS ῥεῖ, which resolves the hiatus, otherwise infrequent in the hymn (see Introd., p. 24). For a flowing voice, see Nestor's at *Il*. 1. 249 and the Muses' at *Hy*. 25. 5, *Th*. 39, 97. Words flow at *Th*. 84. Smith (1981a), 81 points out that the present tense here 'reaches forward to us in the present time of the poem's performance'.

237–8. The language of these lines is formulaic. Cf. *Il*. 11. 668–9, *Od*. 11. 394, 21. 283.

238 γναμπτοῖσι μέλεσσιν: the adjective γναμπτός is often used of limbs in contexts where there is a contrast of youth and old age (of Nestor *Il*. 11. 669 etc.), and could refer to the 'bent' limbs of old age; this seems to be the sense at *Il*. 24. 359, of Priam's aged limbs. However, an original meaning was probably 'supple/curved', referring generically to the joints or the muscles; as perhaps at *Od*. 11. 394, where the phrase refers to the limbs which the soul of Agamemnon once possessed in life. This sense could also be understood here, with reference to the former state of Tithonus' limbs in youth. It is impossible to be certain, although the evocation of his formerly youthful limbs would perhaps provide a more poignant contrast to his complete inability to move them in v. 234. See further *LfgrE* s.v., Hainsworth (1993), 296, N. Richardson (1993), 311, Maxwell-Stuart (1977), 160–1, VE 83.

239–55. Aphrodite returns to the situation at hand, the consequences of her shameful affair with a mortal man. The juxtaposition of mortality and immortality, a theme throughout the poem (see Introd., p. 11), is now treated explicitly and with gravity (cf. Podbielski 1971, 72–2). The terrible description of Anchises' impending old age (vv. 244–6) highlights the mortal condition of humanity, contrasted with the comparably trivial shame that Aphrodite will suffer amongst her peers (vv. 247–5).

Aphrodite uses the *exemplum* of Tithonus to explain that she would not choose for Anchises to be immortal like him. She would have been pleased if he could have remained for ever young and been her husband, but it is not possible. This is not false logic (Smith 1981*a*, 87–9), for although Aphrodite, unlike Eos, is aware that a request for both immortality and agelessness must go to Zeus, she is unable to petition him out of her sense of shame (cf. above on 200–38); if Anchises were to live amongst the gods as her immortal husband he would serve as a constant reminder of her shame. This is true even though it remains unclear whether Aphrodite yet knows that Zeus actually instigated her affair (see de Jong 1989, 19–23). The claim that she cannot have Anchises as her immortal husband does not imply that Anchises has asked to be made immortal above (cf. on *Aphr.* 188–9). Aphrodite is musing on the difficulty of her own situation in these lines, before she moves to the business of her child.

The eventual old age of Anchises as the lover of Aphrodite is the subject of a later epigram of Agathias Scholasticus, *AP* 6. 76.

239 οὐκ ἂν ἐγώ γε σὲ τοῖον: the asyndeton immediately after the story of Tithonus serves to set the present situation against the preceding tale and add emphasis; 'I would not choose for *you* to be like Tithonus'; σέ should be accented accordingly. τοῖον 'such' = 'like Tithonus'. For the language of this line compare *Il.* 9. 517 οὐκ ἂν ἐγώ γέ σε μῆνιν ἀπορρίψαντα κελοίμην.

ἐν ἀθανάτοισιν ἑλοίμην: Janko (1981a), 161 compares *Dem.* 328 ἐθέλοιτο μετ' ἀθανάτοισιν ἑλέσθαι (for which, however, Hermann conjectured ἕλοιτο μετ' ἀθανάτοισι θεοῖσιν—as at *Dem.* 444—to avoid the otherwise unknown middle form of ἐθέλω; see N. Richardson 1974, 264).

240. This line is identical with 221 (see ad loc.). The repetition helps to effect comparison between the situations of Tithonus and Anchises.

241–6. The sequence of optatives in these lines expresses an unfulfilled condition; on the use of the optative after ἄν see above on 153–4 (cf. VB 30). N. Richardson points out that the structure of these lines is similar to Sarpedon's words to Glaucus about the thematically comparable inevitability of death at *Il.* 12. 322–8; where εἰ + opt . . . κεν (=ἄν) + opt . . . νῦν δέ.

241 ἀλλ' εἰ μέν: cf. *Il.* 1. 135 and 22. 49.

τοιοῦτος ἐών: 'as you are now'. M reads the unmetrical τοῖος where all other MSS have τοιοῦτος. The conjecture of Hermann (1806) τοιόσδε ἐών is unnecessary. Cf. later Theoc. *Id.* 11. 34 ἀλλ' οὗτος τοιοῦτος ἐὼν βοτὰ χίλια βόσκω. τοῖος ἐών is common in Homer (*Il.* 17. 170, 18. 105, etc.).

εἶδός τε δέμας τε: for this formular phrase cf. *Od.* 8. 116, 11. 469 etc.

242 ζώοις: the enjambment of this word highlights the focus on mortality; cf. ζώει (-ειν) at line-beginning at *Il.* 18. 91, 24. 526, *Od.* 17. 391, 22. 222 and *Th.* 606 with West (1966a), 334 ad loc.

πόσις κεκλημένος εἴης: cf. the hope of Nausicaa concerning Odysseus at *Od.* 6. 244–5 αἲ γὰρ ἐμοὶ τοιόσδε πόσις κεκλημένος εἴη; also *Il.* 2. 260 πατὴρ κεκλημένος εἴην.

243–4. The repetition of ἀμφικαλύπτω at the end of these two lines serves to contrast the two fates of Anchises and Aphrodite; he will be enfolded by old age, while she will be enfolded by grief (cf. above on 239–55).

243 ἄχος πυκινὰς φρένας ἀμφικαλύπτοι: this seems to be a mixture of language normally used of love and the idea that death 'enfolds'; see the seduction of Zeus at *Il.* 14. 294 ἔρος πυκινὰς φρένας ἀμφεκάλυψεν and Helen *Il.* 3. 442 ἔρως φρένας ἀμφεκάλυψεν, and for death enfolding *Il.* 5. 68, 16. 350 etc. The echo of phrasing appropriate to love could be thought to add irony to the statement in the mouth of Aphrodite, for it is love which has brought this ἄχος upon her.

Cf. also Od. 8. 541 ἄχος φρένας ἀμφιβέβηκεν and ἄχος πύκασε φρένας (Il. 8. 124, 8. 316 and 17. 83). Later see Q.S. 4. 471 Τρῶας δ' ἄχος ἀμφεκάλυψεν.

πυκινὰς φρένας: cf. above on 38.

244 νῦν δέ σε μέν: cf. Il. 22. 508, Od. 11. 66 and 13. 324. σε will be picked up below in v. 247 αὐτὰρ ἐμοί (cf. VE 85, VB 30).

τάχα: D and b (ss. τάχα) transmit κατά for τάχα. There is no reason to doubt the vulgate, which is more expressive of the short span of mortal life than κατά (cf. VE 84); Anchises will age soon as compared with divine immortality. κατά may have been introduced by familiarity with the language of v. 233 στυγερὸν κατὰ γῆρας ἔπειγεν. Cf. later Q.S. 3. 614 ἀνέρι ὃν τάχα γῆρας ἀμείλιχον ἀμφιμέμαρφε.

γῆρας ... ἀμφικαλύψει: on ἀμφικαλύπτω used of death enfolding someone, see above on 243. For old age covering all around, cf. later Q.S. 12. 276 ἀλλά σε γῆρας ἀμείλιχον ἀμφιμέμαρφε (compared by Campbell 1991, 93; cf. n. prec.) and A.R. 1. 263–4 σὺν δέ σφι πατὴρ ὀλοῷ ὑπὸ γήραι | ἐντυπὰς ἐν λεχέεσσι καλυψάμενος γοάασκεν.

ὁμοίιον: cf. Il. 4. 315 ἀλλά σε γῆρας τείρει ὁμοίιον; cf. the combination of noun and adjective also in later literature at Q.S. 13. 197, Gr. Naz. AP 8. 50. 1. ὁμοίιος, of uncertain meaning, is also used of strife (Il. 4. 444), death (Od. 3. 236), and war (Il. 9. 440 etc.) in Homer. Hesiod uses it as an equivalent to ὁμοῖος at Op. 182 (see West 1978, 199 ad loc.), but this could be due simply to the aural similarity of the two words rather than to any deeper connection. It has often been translated as 'distressing', as it was connected with κακός in antiquity (cf. LSJ ad loc.), but this cannot be trusted. Better is the proposal of Athanassakis (1976), who derives the word from ὁμός and the root of Ϝίς, Ϝίεμαι. This gives a meaning 'forcing to the same place' or 'levelling' that fits its application to the destructive forces of death, old age, war, and strife, which affect all equally. Catenacci (1996) maintains that it derives from ὅμοιος/ὁμοῖος through lengthening, and proposes a similar meaning 'equal (for all)'. See further Dictionnaire s.v., Russo, OC iii. 65–6.

245 νηλειές: this lengthened form of νηλεής is found also at Hes. Th. 770, but not in Homer; it is more common in later literature (A.R. 1. 1214 etc.). This could once again be a case of post-Homeric modification by lengthening (Janko 1982, 159), although it is impossible to be certain (see Hoekstra 1969, 45); cf. above on 224 γῆρας ὀλοιόν.

νηλεής 'pitiless' is not used elsewhere of old age, but it is applied to a broad range of nouns: bronze, the heart, sleep, the day, etc.; see LfgrE s.v. for a full list of occurrences.

ἔπειτα: this is awkward after τάχα; it must mean either 'at some point' or, as VB 30 suggests, refer to the time after the passage of youth (here unexpressed) when old age takes hold of men. It could have been introduced here through the appropriation of a general statement about death and old age into this specific situation (cf. VE 85), or it could have suggested itself as corresponding to the ἔπειτα of Aphrodite's imagined situation in v. 243.

παρίσταται ἀνθρώποισιν: cf. the fated day attending the suitors at Od. 16. 280 δὴ γάρ σφι παρίσταται αἴσιμον ἦμαρ. See later Q.S. 6. 427 παρίσταται οὐλομένη Κήρ. Cf. below on 269.

246. For this line cf. σμερδαλέ'/ἀργαλέ' εὐρώεντα, τά τε στυγέουσι θεοί περ (Il. 20. 65, Th. 739, 810), where the gods shudder at the house of Hades and the extremities of the earth. Death is is said to be hateful to the gods at Th. 766.

οὐλόμενον καματηρόν: these complete a string of adjectives which characterize old age as a powerful and destructive force; ὁμοίιον, νηλειές, οὐλόμενον, and καματηρόν. Podbielski (1971), 72 compares the build-up of adjectives to descriptions of old age found in lyric poetry (e.g. Mimn. frr. 1, 5 IEG), but it is not unepic. Old age is a destructive force in Homer too (see Byl 1976).

For οὐλόμενος (common at line-beginning in Homer; Il. 1. 2 etc.) of old age, cf. Th. 225, Thgn. 272, 527, 768, 1012, 1021, Pi. P. 10. 41 and later at the anonymous AP 9. 118. 1 and App. Anth. 2. 681. 3. καματηρός, attested only here in surviving epic, is derived from the o-stem κάματος, modelled upon ἀνιηρός through misdivision (cf. πονηρός); see Hoekstra (1969), 19 n. 39, Janko (1982), 159. It appears later in prose (Hdt. 4. 135 etc.) and in poetry at Ar. Lys. 542 and A.R. 2. 87.

247–55. Aphrodite now turns to the consequences of the union for herself. Zeus' revenge has been successful and she will no longer be able to boast about her activities to the gods. On the interpretation of these lines, which are taken by some to imply that Aphrodite renounces altogether mixing gods and mortals in love, see Introd., pp. 10–18.

247 αὐτὰρ ἐμοί: see above on 244 νῦν δέ σε μέν. For adversative αὐτάρ and the pronoun cf. *Il.* 1. 118 etc.

μέγ' ὄνειδος: first and foremost in the mind of Aphrodite is the great shame she will suffer amongst the gods because of her affair with a mortal. As she goes on to explain in vv. 252–5, she will no longer be able to boast about her activities, because the gods now have something with which to mock her in return. Cf. Thgn. 508 μέγ' ὄνειδος ἔχω. For the structure of the line cf. *Il.* 4. 38 σοὶ καὶ ἐμοὶ μέγ' ἔρισμα μετ' ἀμφοτέροισι γένηται.

248. For this line cf. *Il.* 16. 499 ἔσσομαι ἤματα πάντα διαμπερές. On ἤματα πάντα see above on 28 and 209. εἴνεκα σεῖο appears at line-end at *Il.* 6. 525 and *Od.* 6. 156.

249 ἐμοὺς ὀάρους καὶ μήτιας: for the ὄαροι 'intimate whispers' of Aphrodite see *Th.* 205 [Ἀφροδίτη ἔχει] παρθενίους τ' ὀάρους μειδήματά τ' ἐξαπάτας τε and note *Hy.* 23. 3 πυκινοὺς ὀάρους ὀαρίζει (Zeus to Themis). Cf. also the personified ὀαριστύς at *Il.* 14. 216, and the verb ὀαρίζω of the speech of young girls at *Il.* 22. 128. VE 86 argues that these ὄαροι are the conversations of the gods with mortal women rather than Aphrodite's conversations with other gods. The most natural sense is that they are in fact the intimate whispers of the goddess herself, which go alongside her tricky plans. However, one does not need to draw a fine distinction between the two ideas. Just as ὀαριστύς can be personified at *Il.* 14. 216, Aphrodite is here depicted as performing the activity of which she is representative. On the term in later literature, see Bulloch (1985), 174 on Call. *Hy.* 5. 66. The accusative plural form μήτιας occurs only here.

250. For the language of this line, see above on 39 and 50.

251. τάρβεσκον: the delay and enjambment of the main verb in these lines places strong emphasis upon the fact of the gods' fear. This iterative form of ταρβέω occurs only here (cf. below on δάμνασκε νόημα).

πάντας ... δάμνασκε: πάντας here most naturally refers to all the gods rather than all living creatures; see VB 32 *contra* Podbielski (1971), 74. On the repetition of πάντας in this passage, here and above in v. 249, see Introd., pp. 15–16.

δάμνασκε νόημα: for the mind of a god taming someone, cf. *Il.* 16. 103 δάμνα μιν Ζηνός τε νόος καὶ Τρῶες ἀγανοί. This iterative form of δάμνημι occurs only here (cf. above on τάρβεσκον).

252 νῦν δὲ δὴ οὐκέτι μοι: Aphrodite returns to the present reality with νῦν δέ, just as she did above at v. 244 νῦν δέ σε μὲν τάχα when discussing the fate of Anchises.

στόμα τλήσεται ἐξονομῆναι: the MSS all transmit the incomprehensible στοναχήσεται. Several acceptable conjectures have been offered: στόμα χείσεται (Martin 1605), στόμα τλήσεται (Matthiae 1800), στόματ' ἔσσεται (Clarke 1740), στόμ' ἀχήσεται (Buttmann 1846), and στόμα χ' ἥσεται (Ludwich 1908). Most modern editors read either Martin's στόμα χείσεται (cf. AHS and West 2003) or Matthiae's στόμα τλήσεται (cf. Càssola). The former has the advantage of being close to the transmitted στοναχήσεται, and the future form of χανδάνω is found in the same metrical *sedes* at *Od.* 18. 17. However, there are problems with the sense of χανδάνω, which elsewhere in epic means 'to contain/hold' (see Kamerbeek 1967, 392–3, Smith 1979, 34–5). Others seem to have taken χείσεται to be an otherwise unattested future form of χάσκω 'to open wide' (see West 2003; cf. Càssola 557 on χήσεται). ἀχήσεται is also possible, but the verb is not well attested in early epic (see N. Richardson 1974, 309–10) and the required sense of shouting loudly is awkward in this phrase; cf. Càssola 557. Ludwich's ἥσεται would be an otherwise unattested future form of ἥδομαι (ἥσομαι is elsewhere attested as the future middle of ἵημι; see LSJ ad loc.); Shackle (1915), 164 compares the aorist ἥσατο at *Od.* 9. 353, but ἥδομαι is in any case not elsewhere construed with the infinitive and would be clumsy here.

The best sense is offered by στόμα τλήσεται 'my mouth will not dare to mention this', itself not a far departure from the transmitted text. As Smith, loc. cit. points out, τλάω is used several times in the *Odyssey* of a speech act (5. 178, 11. 438, etc.), and there is no reason to doubt that the α of στόμα can be short before τλ-. Mute + liquid combinations at the beginning of a word often do not lengthen the final vowel of the preceding word, as in *Aphr.* at 114, 131, 179, 187 (πρ-); see further *Grammaire*, i. 108–9, and for τλ- not lengthening the proceeding vowel within a word cf. *Il.* 3. 414.

VE 86–7 objects to the use of στόμα altogether because it is not elsewhere an organ of speech until Pi. *N.* 10. 19, but this is not a far step from the tongue and mouth as organs of singing at *Il.* 2. 489–90 and speech διὰ στόμα at 14. 91. His own conjecture στοναχή 'σεται, to mean 'that will no longer be a reason for sighing among the immortals to mention', is extremely strained. Nor is there anything to recommend VB's radical departure (32–3) from the transmitted στοναχήσεται; he reads γάμον ἔσσεται (after *Od.* 6. 66) and changes τοῦτο μετ' in the next line to τοῦτον ἐν.

253 τοῦτο: this is best taken to refer inclusively to her description of mixing gods and mortal women in vv. 249–51, the central point being that she will no longer be able to boast about these activities amongst the gods (see further Introd., pp. 16–18). οὐκέτι speaks against its referring specifically to her affair with Anchises.

ἐπεί μάλα πολλὸν ἀάσθην: Aphrodite was temporarily blinded by her infatuation with Anchises, and only now does she fully comprehend the result of sleeping with a mortal man. VB 33 points out that the result of ἄτη is 'disaster' or 'distress', which Aphrodite is certainly feeling now. For the language cf. *Il.* 19. 112–13 Ζεὺς δ' οὔ τι δολοφροσύνην ἐνόησεν | ἀλλ' ὄμοσε μέγαν ὅρκον, ἔπειτα δὲ πολλὸν ἀάσθην, and later A.R. 4. 412 ἐπεὶ τὸ πρῶτον ἀάσθη.

254 σχέτλιον οὐκ ὀνομαστόν: 'terribly, unspeakably'; these two neuter singulars should be taken adverbially with ἀάσθην. All MSS transmit ὀνοτατόν, for which ὀνομαστόν (Martin 1605) is the best conjecture, adopted by most editors; for οὐκ ὀνομαστήν (-οί, -ά) see *Od.* 19. 260, 19. 597, 23. 19, *Th.* 148, [Hes.] fr. 33a. 18, and cf. VE 87, Smith (1979), 36–7. Clarke (1740) proposed ὀνοταστόν 'to be blamed' (from the rare verb ὀνοτάζω), which appears elsewhere only as a variant at [Hes.] fr. 33. a. 18 and gives a less satisfactory sense alongside σχέτλιον.

ἀπεπλάγχθην δὲ νόοιο: Aphrodite leads the mind of Zeus astray (cf. v. 36 above), but has now herself wandered from her senses. Cf. *Od.* 20. 346 παρέπλαγξεν δὲ νόημα, where Athena leads astray the mind of the suitors. The passive is elsewhere used of a spear going astray (*Il.* 22. 291) or Odysseus' wanderings (*Od.* 8. 573). A similar idea is contained in ἐν κάλλει γυναικὸς πολλοὶ ἐπλανήθησαν Sir. 9. 8.

255 παῖδα δ' ὑπὸ ζώνῃ ἐθέμην: M reads the accusative ζώνην, which is paralleled by A. *Ch.* 992 τέκνων ἤνεγχ' ὑπὸ ζώνην βάρος. However, the dative is the unanimous reading below at v. 282 ὑπὸ ζώνῃ θέτο μήτηρ and should be kept here as well.

βροτῷ εὐνηθεῖσα: cf. *Il.* 2. 820–1 Αἰνείας τὸν ὑπ' Ἀγχίσῃ τέκε δῖ' Ἀφροδίτη | Ἴδης ἐν κνημοῖσι θεὰ βροτῷ εὐνηθεῖσα; note also 16. 176 γυνὴ θεῷ εὐνηθεῖσα and and *Th.* 380 θεὰ θεῷ εὐνηθεῖσα.

256–90. The final section of Aphrodite's speech focuses on the fate of Aeneas. She explains that their son will be reared by mountain nymphs (vv. 256–73) and that when he reaches adolescence he will be brought to Anchises (vv. 274–80), who should immediately take him to Troy. She then closes (vv. 281–90) by warning Anchises not to reveal to anyone that Aphrodite is the mother of his son; he is threatened with punishment by Zeus if he transgresses.

The focus upon the future of Aeneas in the final section of the poem once again underlines the importance given to his lineage (see Introd., pp. 7–10). There is a long digression on the nature of the nymphs who will rear their son (vv. 258–73; see ad loc.), but the poet returns to focus on Aeneas through repetition of the language of v. 256 τὸν μὲν ἐπὴν δὴ πρῶτον in v. 274, and then again in v. 278 (such repetition seems to be a stylistic feature of this poet; cf. above on 225 τὸν δ' ἤτοι εἵως μέν). Verses 254–5 have made it clear that Aeneas is a source of shame for Aphrodite, but he will nonetheless be well looked after by the goddess and become a great man amongst the Trojans.

256–7. It is common for nymphs to rear gods and mortals in their role as *Kourotrophoi*; see *Th.* 346–8, West (1966*a*), 263–4 ad loc., Jeanmaire (1975), 283–96. Cf. the nymphs rearing Dionysus at *Hy.* 26. 3–4.

256 τὸν μὲν ἐπὴν δὴ πρῶτον: see above on 256–90.

τὸν . . . ἴδῃ φάος ἠελίοιο: the phrase 'to see the light of the sun' = 'to live' is well established (see above on 105), but it is used of birth only once more at *Apoll.* 71; the neglect of digamma in ἴδῃ in both these instances is indicative of modification of a traditional formula (see Janko 1982, 153), which indeed is not elsewhere found with the aorist. Heitsch (1965), 31 believes that this is also a reversal of the usual subject, with the φάος ἠελίοιο said to look upon Aeneas, but this awkward switch is easily avoided by placing a comma after τὸν μέν, 'As for him, when he first sees the light of the sun, the nymphs will nurse him'; cf. *Od.* 16. 78–9 ἀλλ' ἤτοι τὸν ξεῖνον, ἐπεὶ τεὸν ἵκετο δῶμα, | ἕσσω μιν χλαῖνάν τε χιτῶνά τε εἵματα καλά (cf. Cassola, 558).

257 ὀρεσκῷοι: this adjective is used elsewhere of Centaurs (*Il*. 1. 268, [Hes.] fr. 209. 5), goats (*Od*. 9. 155; where the nymphs are said to rouse the goats), a tortoise (*Herm*. 42), a hare (*Hy*. 19. 43), and beasts generally (Alcm. *PMGF* 89. 4), but not nymphs. But cf. νύμφαι ὀρεστιάδες (*Il*. 6. 420, *Hy*. 19. 19) and [Hes.] fr. 10a. 17, 123. 1 οὔρειαι νύμφαι. Nymphs are common inhabitants of mountains; cf. v. 118 above and see Kirk (1990), 215. On the etymology of the word, the second element from the root κει- (κεῖμαι), see Heubeck (*OC* ii. 23).

βαθύκολποι: 'deep-bosomed'; in Homer this epithet is used only of Trojan women (*Il*. 18. 339, 18. 122, 24. 215), although it is a variant with Μοῦσαι at *Il*. 2. 484 (cf. Pi. *P*. 1. 12). It is elsewhere in early epic used of nymphs only at *Dem*. 5 κούρῃσι σὺν Ὠκεανοῦ βαθυκόλποις, a possible case of imitation; Janko (1982), 165, 226–7 notes that the short dative plural in *Dem*. suggests later modification (on the relationship of *Aphr*. and *Dem*. see Introd., pp. 38–40). The adjective is naturally applied to nymphs as *kourotrophoi*; cf. *Hy*. 26. 3–4 [Διόνυσον] ὃν τρέφον ἠΰκομοι νύμφαι παρὰ πατρὸς ἄνακτος | δεξάμεναι κόλποισι and N. Richardson (1974), 140. See its use later of Thetis at Theoc. *Id*. 17. 55 and a nymph at Nonn. *D*. 42. 99.

258–72. Aphrodite now enters upon a lengthy digression about the life of the nymphs who will rear Aeneas. This section has often been considered an interlude with little relevance to the progression of the narrative—see Baumeister (1860), 252, Gemoll (1886), 274, van Groningen (1958), 106—but recent scholars have understood better its integral value. On the thematic level, this excursus about semi-divine nymphs, who live a long life in the bloom of youth, continues the exploration of mortality and immortality in the poem; the immortal Aphrodite sleeps with the mortal Anchises, Ganymedes was immortal and unageing, Tithonus immortal and ageing, the nymphs mortal and unageing; see Podbielski (1971), 75–7, Segal (1974), Smith (1981*a*), 92–5, VB 34–5, Clay (1989), 193–6, and cf. Introd., p. 11. Such a digression is also very much in the style of this poet (cf. above on 7–33 and 200–239), and Aphrodite's concern with the nymphs echoes Anchises' expansion upon them in vv. 95–9, where he suggested that the disguised Aphrodite might actually be a nymph. Nymphs are erotic beings who have affairs with mortals (cf. above on 93–9), and this will soon once again become relevant to the progression of the narrative. Before her departure

Aphrodite will order Anchises to claim, should anyone ask, that a nymph is the mother of his child (vv. 281–85) and this expansion gives him all the information he will need to tell that story convincingly.

The nymphs are often said to be immortal, ἀθάναται (*Il.* 18. 86, *Od.* 24. 47) or θεαί (*Il.* 24. 615–16, *Od.* 12. 131–3, *Hy.* 26. 7, *Th.* 129–30, [Hes.] fr. 123). They are mortal and long-lived also at [Hes.] fr. 304. On the connection of these mortal nymphs to trees, see below on 264–72.

258–61. On the relationship of these lines to the proem of the *Theogony* (2 αἵ θ' Ἑλικῶνος ἔχουσιν ὄρος μέγα τε ζάθεόν τε and 7–8 χοροὺς ἐνεποιήσαντο | καλούς ... ἐπερρώσαντο δὲ ποσσίν) see Introd., pp. 35–6.

258 ὄρος μέγα τε ζάθεόν τε: this phrase appears elsewhere only at *Th.* 2 and here violates economy alongside the Homeric ὄρος καταειμένον ὕλῃ used below at v. 285 (see Introd., pp. 35–6). ζαθεός 'holy/ numinous' (cf. *LfgrE* s.v., West 1966*a*, 152) is combined with ὄρος also *Apoll.* 223.

259 αἵ ῥα: the particle ῥα, which expresses 'a lively feeling of interest' (Denniston 1954, 33), frequently follows a relative in Homer (cf. *Il.* 12. 454 etc.), where it focuses attention upon the expansion. VE 88 compares *Od.* 17. 292 Ἄργος ... ὅν ῥά ποτ', for the introduction of a digression (there about Odysseus' dog).

οὔτε θνητοῖς οὔτ' ἀθανάτοισιν ἕπονται: the sense of the verb here seems to be 'count amongst' rather than 'follow' (cf. AHS 339), similar to the positive expression above in vv. 95–6 αἵ [Χάριτες] τε θεοῖσιν | πᾶσιν ἑταιρίζουσι καὶ ἀθάνατοι καλέονται, where the fact that the Graces accompany the gods is linked to their being called immortal. This meaning of ἕπομαι is not elsewhere attested in early epic. Heitsch (1965), 22 and Podbielski (1971), 87 argue that this sense is developing also at *Th.* 268 αἵ [Ἅρπυιαι] ῥ' ἀνέμων πνοιῇσι καὶ οἰωνοῖς ἅμ' ἕπονται, but there the Harpies actually follow along with the winds and the birds; cf. Janko (1982), 159, VE 88–9. Cf. Thgn. 327–8 ἁμαρτωλαὶ γὰρ ἐν ἀνθρώποισιν ἕπονται | θνητοῖς, Κύρνε. θεοὶ δ' οὐκ ἐθέλουσι φέρειν.

260 δηρὸν μὲν ζώουσι: on the mortal nature of the nymphs, see above on 258–72. For the language here cf. above v. 105 δηρὸν ἐὺ ζώειν, and see later A.R. 3. 729 μηδέ με δηρὸν ἔτι ζώουσαν ἴδοιο.

μέν: this is perhaps best understood to correspond to ἀλλά in v. 269, where the death of the nymphs is contrasted with their long life; cf. VE 89. VB 35 suggests instead that it corresponds to δέ in v. 264. This is possible, but there is no strong contrast of life and death there as in v. 269. For μέν followed by ἀλλά, a mostly poetic construction, see Denniston (1954), 5–7.

ἄμβροτον εἶδαρ ἔδουσι: ambrosia is the food of the gods (see above on v. 206 νέκταρ ἐρυθρόν). For ambrosial εἶδαρ, cf. Il. 5. 369 and 13. 35 (the food of Achilles' horses) and Apoll. 127 (the food of Apollo). εἶδαρ ἔδουσι occurs at line-end at Od. 9. 84 (where ἄνθινον εἶδαρ is equivalent to ἄμβροτον εἶδαρ), 11. 123 and 23. 270.

261 καί τε ... ἐρρώσαντο: the aorist is 'omnitemporal', describing a general characteristic of the nymphs; see Faulkner (2006) and cf. above on 3 for the particle combination καί τε.

κᾰλὸν χορόν: digamma is neglected in κᾰλὸν also above in v. 29; see ad loc.

καλὸν χορόν ἐρρώσαντο: perhaps modelled upon Th. 7–8 χορούς ἐνεποιήσαντο | καλούς ... ἐπερρώσαντο δὲ ποσσίν (see further Introd., p. 35). However, see also Il. 24. 616 νυμφάων, αἵτ' ἀμφ' Ἀχελώϊον ἐρρώσαντο and Od. 12. 138 ἔνθα δ' ἔσαν νυμφέων καλοὶ χοροὶ ἠδὲ θόωκοι (cf. Hoekstra 1965, 43).

262 τῆσι δέ: note the repetition in v. 264. Cf. Od. 6. 101, Dem. 212.

Σιληνοί: the Silens are first named here in Greek literature. They are later equated with the Satyrs, hybrid characters (part human part horse) who are continuously aroused and in pursuit of nymphs or maenads (cf. OCD s.v. satyrs and silens); an individual figure named Silenus is the father or leader of the Satyrs in Pindar (fr. 156–7) and Attic satyr-plays (e.g. E. Cyc.). The Silens are first labelled in art on the Attic François vase (c.570 BC; see LIMC viii, Silenoi no. 22), where they are depicted together with Dionysus, Hephaestus, and nymphs. Horse-human figures appear as early as the seventh century (see LIMC viii, Silenoi no. 29c) and are later frequently shown in pursuit of nymphs; see Hedreen (1994) and cf. LIMC viii, Silenoi, passim.

The form Σιληνοί with long ι (MDb) is found in the earliest inscriptions (see Simon, LIMC viii/2. 1108) and should perhaps be favoured here over Σειληνοί.

τε καὶ εὔσκοπος Ἀργειφόντης: Hermann (1806) omitted τε to conform to the Homeric form ἐΰσκοπος, but there is no reason to assume this; the trisyllabic form is paralleled at *Apoll.* 36 Ἴμβρός τ' εὐκτιμένη (cf. Janko 1982, 159). For the formula εὔσκοπος Ἀργειφόντης cf. *Il.* 24. 24, 24. 209, *Od.* 1. 138, 7. 137, *Herm.* 73. The meaning of εὔσκοπος is 'keen-sighted' or 'watchful' (cf. N. Richardson 1993, 278 on *Il.* 24. 24). On Ἀργειφόντης see above on 117.

Hermes is frequently associated with the nymphs in mythology: he fathers Pan with the nymph Dryops (*Hy.* 19. 32 ff.), and Autolycus with Philonis ([Hes.] fr. 64). At *Od.* 14. 435–6 a sacrifice is made to both Hermes and the nymphs; cf. Hoekstra, *OC* iii. 223–4, and for Hermes' connection with the nymphs in art see *LIMC* v, Hermes, nos. 347–57.

263 μίσγοντ' ἐν φιλότητι: cf. above on 150.

μυχῷ σπείων: cf. *Od.* 5. 226 μυχῷ σπείους γλαφυροῖο. For μυχός of the depth of a cave, cf. its combination also with ἄντρον (*Od.* 9. 236, 13. 363, 24. 6).

ἐροέντων: this adjective is not found in Homer, and is nowhere else used of a cave; cf., however, *Od.* 13. 103–4 ἄντρον ἐπήρατον ἠεροειδής | ἱρὸν νυμφάων αἳ νηιάδες καλέονται. In Hesiod ἐροέις is used of nymphs (*Th.* 245, 251, 357), and it is elsewhere applied to both objects and people; the daughters of Metaneira (*Dem.* 109), flowers (*Dem.* 425), a tortoise (*Herm.* 31), and the mouths of the Muses (*Hy.* 32. 20).

264–72. This is the most explicit identification of the life of nymphs with trees in early literature, although the idea seems to be implied elsewhere in Hesiod and the *Hymns*; at *Th.* 187 nymphs are called Μελίαι 'tree-nymphs' (see West 1966a, 221 ad loc.), while at *Dem.* 22–3 ἀγλαόκαρποι Ἐλαῖαι 'fruit-bearing olive trees' are grouped together with gods and mortals in not hearing the cries of Persephone (cf. Humbert 1936, 146). The relationship may even be foreshadowed at *Il.* 6. 419–20, where mountain-nymphs are said to plant trees around the tomb of Eetion (cf. VE 90). Cf. later Pi. fr. 165 ἰσοδένδρου τέκμαρ αἰῶνος θεόφραστον λαχοῖσα. Tree-nymphs are later referred to as Hamadryads (see in poetry A.R. 2. 477 etc.).

Callimachus, who authored a work περὶ νυμφῶν, might have been thinking of this passage when in his fourth hymn to Delos (82–5) he asks the Muses whether it is really true that the lives of nymphs are linked to trees (cf. Call. *Hy.* 6. 37–8). See also Prop. 2. 32. 33 ff., where what is possibly a reference to the affair between Aphrodite and

Anchises (see Butler–Barber 1933, 252, L. Richardson 1977, 306) includes mention of both the Silens and the Hamadryads.

264 ἐλάται ἠὲ δρύες: fir and oak trees are frequently paired; cf. *Op.* 509, E. *Ph.* 1515–16, *Ba.* 109–10, 684–5, A.R. 3. 968, Lucillius *AP* 11. 246. 3–4, Anon. *AP* 12. 130. 3. See also *Il.* 11. 494 (where δρῦς ... πεύκας). Note the pairing also in Milton, *Paradise Lost* 6. 575 'Oak or Firr | With branches lopt in Wood or Mountain fell'd'.

ὑψικάρηνοι: once more in early poetry at *Il.* 12. 132 δρύες οὔρεσιν ὑψικάρηνοι. Oak trees are more commonly called ὑψίκομοι (*Il.* 14. 398, 23. 118 etc.). The adjective next appears in Call. fr. 309. 2 Pf. (possibly part of the *Hecale*; see Hollis 1990, 305) of a mountain glen and then becomes common in later literature of trees and mountains, especially in Nonnus (*D.* 18. 237 etc.).

265 ἐπὶ χθονὶ βωτιανείρῃ: 'man-nourishing earth'; once in Homer at *Il.* 1. 155 of Phthia and of the earth as here at *Apoll.* 363 and [Hes.] fr. 165. 16 χθονὶ βωτιανείρῃ. This is a variation on the more common formula ἐπὶ χθονὶ πουλυβοτείρῃ (*Il.* 3. 89, 195 etc.); cf. *Od.* 19. 408 ἀνὰ χθόνα πουλυβώτειραν (v.l. βωτιάνειραν). The adjective is rare in Greek literature; cf. Alcm. *PMGF* 77, Maxim. Astrol. περὶ καταρχῶν 10. 510, Procl. *Hy.* 7. 23, Colluth. 221.

266 καλαὶ τηλεθάουσαι: cf. the participle 'flourishing' of trees at *Il.* 17. 53–5 ἔρνος... ἐλαίης | ... | καλὸν τηλεθάον, *Od.* 7. 114–16 δένδρεα μακρὰ πεφύκασι τηλεθόωντα | ... | ... ἐλαῖαι τηλεθόωντα (= 11. 590) and 13. 196 πέτραι τ' ἠλίβατοι καὶ δένδρεα τηλεθάοντα; of a forest at *Il.* 6. 147–8 and *Od.* 5. 63. The verb is elsewhere in Homer used of children (*Il.* 22. 423) and hair (23. 142).

The punctuation of this line is disputed. AHS place a full stop at the end of 266, VE 91 after καλαὶ τηλεθάουσαι, while West (2003) punctuates at the end of 265. The latter seems most natural, with the asyndeton at the beginning of v. 266 introducing the description of the trees. Asyndeton is a stylistic feature of this author (see above on 71 ἄρκτοι).

ἐν οὔρεσιν ὑψηλοῖσιν: see above on 160.

267 ἠλίβατοι: in Homer only of rocks (*Il.* 15. 273 etc.), but cf. *Sc.* 421–2 ὡς ὅτε τις δρῦς ἤριπεν ἢ ὅτε πέτρα (v.l. πεύκη) | ἠλίβατος, and note the association of πέτραι ἠλίβατοι and δένδρεα τηλεθάοντα at *Il.* 13. 196. The sense of ἠλίβατος here seems to be 'high' (cf.

290   Commentary

Th. 786–7 and *LfgrE* s.v.), complementing the position of the trees ἐν οὔρεσιν ὑψηλοῖσιν, but the etymology of the word is obscure; it could derive from *ἠλιτό-βατος (ἀλιταίνω) 'inaccessible'; see *Dictionnaire* s.v., Càssola 558–9.

τεμένεα: the MSS all transmit the contracted Attic form τεμένη, which is paralleled by *Od.* 11. 185. However, in the latter case the scholia report that Aristarchus read τεμένεα, which should perhaps be restored as the older form in both instances. There is no other sure Atticism in *Aphr.* and the form could have been introduced in an Attic phase of transmission (see Introd., p. 45). The plural is used in later poetry at E. *Supp.* 1211, *HF* 1329, and is common in prose.

τεμένεα δέ ἑ κικλήσκουσιν: cf. *Od.* 4. 355 Φάρον δέ ἑ κικλήσκουσιν. ἑ is usually singular and Hoekstra (1969), 41 suggests that its use as a plural here was introduced by an ungrammatical modification of traditional language. However, there is some reason to think that this is a rare but legitimate use. ἑ might follow a plural at *Il.* 2. 196–7, if one adopts Zenodotus' βασιλήων for βασιλῆος, and οἱ refers collectively to δώματα at *Od.* 17. 266. Moreover, the adjective ἑός/ὅς is used of the plural in Homer; see Monro (1891), 222. The pronoun derives from an Indo-European reflexive *swe (see Frisk, 431), originally used of all persons and numbers, and its use as a plural here could be an archaism; see Pavese (1974), 68, Càssola 559, Janko (1982), 159–60.

268 τὰς δ' οὔ τι βροτοί κείρουσι σιδήρῳ: mortals who cut sacred trees suffer dire consequences; cf. Erysichthon (Call. *Hy.* 6) and Paraibius' father (A.R. 2. 476–89). For a tree or forest being cut with iron see *Il.* 4. 482 ff., *Op.* 420–1, and cf. *Herm.* 109 ὄζον ἑλὼν ἐπέλεψε σιδήρῳ. For the beginning of the line τὰς δ' οὔ τι cf. *Il.* 1. 511, 4. 401, etc.

269 ἀλλ' ὅτε κεν μοῖρα παρεστήκῃ θανάτοιο: cf. *Il.* 16. 853 (= 24. 132) ἄγχι παρέστηκεν θάνατος καὶ μοῖρα κραταιή. For the verb παρίστημι of old age or death, cf. above on 245; see also [Hes.] fr. 25. 24 τέλος θανάτοιο παρέστη, Mimn. fr. 2. 5 Κῆρες δὲ παρεστήκασι μέλαιναι and Tyrt. fr. 7. 2 εὖτέ τιν' οὐλομένη μοῖρα κίχοι θανάτου.

270 ἀζάνεται: this form does not occur elsewhere, although cf. the compound καταζήνασκε at *Od.* 11. 587. Heitsch (1965), 23 compares the description of a felled tree at *Il.* 4. 487 ἡ μέν τ' ἀζομένη κεῖται ποταμοῖο παρ' ὄχθας.

Lines 268—274-7

δένδρεα καλά: this noun–epithet combination does not occur in Homer, but cf. δένδρεα μακρά *Il.* 9. 541. Later at Call. *Hy.* 6. 41, Demeter responds to Erysichthon's *hubris* by asking τίς μοι καλὰ δένδρεα κόπτει.

271 φλοιός: 'bark'; cf. *Il.* 1. 237, where it is said to have been stripped off from the sceptre of the speaker. Otherwise, the word is rare in poetry; cf. Emp. fr. 81 DK, Theoc. *Id.* 18. 47, Call. *Aet.* fr. 73. 1, Nic. *Ther.* 676, 842, fr. 70. 9. It is common in prose.

ἀμφιπεριφθυνύθει: this is a *hapax* in Greek literature; cf. *Il.* 8. 348 ἀμφιπεριστρώφα, *Od.* 8. 175 ἀμφιπεριστρέφεται and later *Orph. L.* 521 φύλλα περιφθινύθουσιν. The compound could be separated to ἀμφὶ περιφθυνύθει, but should be printed together; see above on 114 ἡ δὲ διάπρο, Hainsworth, *OC* i. 357, Heitsch (1965), 24.

πίπτουσι δ' ἀπ' ὄζοι: for the language cf. *Hy.* 7. 13 λύγοι δ' ἀπὸ τηλόσ' ἔπιπτον (the bonds holding Dionysus).

272 δέ θ'... λείπει: the MSS transmit δέ χ' and the indicative λείπει, which cannot stand; Ludwich (1908), 270 compares *Il.* 14. 484 τῶ καί κέ τις εὔχεται ἀνήρ for the construction, but there either the variant τε should be read for κε (West 2000; see Ruijgh 1971, 773–4), or εὔχεται should be taken as a short–vowel subjunctive (see Janko 1992, 220). AHS conjecture the optative λείποι, but the indicative is preferable amid the general statements in the preceding lines and the best solution is Hermann's conjecture δέ θ' (1806), a combination which often signals a general statement (cf. Smith 1979, 37–9, Denniston 1954, 520 ff.). VE 93 proposes δέ γ' on the grounds that θ' for χ' 'is not likely from a palaeographic point of view', but such corruption of a single letter is in fact very easy (cf. VB 35).

ψυχὴ λείπει φάος ἠελίοιο: the soul itself does not elsewhere leave the light of the sun, but the soul can leave one behind, and one can leave the light of the sun. Cf. *Il.* 5. 696 τὸν δὲ λίπε ψυχή, 16. 453 τόν γε λίπῃ ψυχή, *Od.* 14. 426 τὸν δ' ἔλιπε ψυχή, 18. 91 ψυχὴ λίποι alongside *Il.* 18. 11 λείψειν φάος ἠελίοιο, *Od.* 11. 93 λιπὼν φάος ἠελίοιο, *Op.* 155 ἔλιπον φάος ἠελίοιο.

273. The relative construction αἵ ... recalls vv. 256–7, providing structural closure to the expansion upon the nymphs.

274–7. Verses 274–5, in which Aphrodite says that the nymphs will bring Aeneas to Anchises when ἥβη takes hold of him, are incompatible with 276–7, in which the goddess claims that she herself will bring her son to Anchises after five years. In epic ἥβη always refers to the prime of life at the beginning of manhood, just as above in vv. 223–7 the poet has used the term to refer to the youth of the lover Tithonus (cf. *LfgrE*); *contra* AHS 371, who retain both sets of lines by suggesting that ἥβη here refers to an earlier age. One pair of lines should be bracketed as an interpolation.

Verses 274–5 have been suspected because the nymphs are referred to as θεαί, when the preceding lines have expanded upon their mortality; see Smith (1979), 39–41, Càssola 560, Breuning (1929), 112–13. On the other hand, the language of v. 276 is extremely problematic (see below ad loc.). On balance, despite the inexactitude of θεαί, whose use could be due to adaptation of traditional language applied to the nymphs (cf. above on 258–72), it seems to me best to follow Hermann (1806) in preferring vv. 274–5. The role of the nymphs bringing Aeneas to Anchises follows naturally from their rearing him (cf. Jeanmaire 1975, 286), and is also more appropriate given Aphrodite's embarrassment about the affair; by handing Aeneas off to the nymphs she is able to wash her hands of the business. Nor should the repetition of τὸν μὲν ἐπὴν δὴ πρῶτον in v. 278 make one suspect this version (*contra* Smith 1979, 40); such repetition seems characteristic of this poet (cf. above on 256–90). Verses 276–7 may have been inserted to correct the inappropriate use of θεαί. VB 35–6 proposes a rearrangement of the lines (placing 275 after 277 and 274 after 279), but this seems far less probable than interpolation.

274 ἔλῃ ... ἥβη: see above on 225 ἔχεν πολυήρατος ἥβη.

275 τοι: only M reads τοι, where the other MSS transmit σοι. Enclitic σοι is possible in early epic (cf. *Il.* 1. 170, *Od.* 11. 381 and 22. 167), but τοι is usual (see *Enchiridium*, 253). It is also in this instance easier to explain how τοι was changed to σοι than the other way around; for a medieval scribe σοι was pronounced like -σι at the end of ἄξουσιν, and σοι at the beginning of the next line could also have influenced the change. VE 94 rejects M's reading on the weak grounds of his belief that M tends to restore Homeric forms (on M see Introd., pp. 54–5).

276 σοί δ' ἐγώ: cf. above on 100.

ὄφρα τ<οι> αὖ τὰ μετὰ φρεσὶ πάντα διέλθω: the line, as it is transmitted (ὄφρα ταῦτα μετὰ φρεσί), is unmetrical, making emendation necessary. Several editors insert κε after ὄφρα, proposed by Barnes (1711), cf. AHS and West (2003); along the same lines, VE 94 suggests ὄφρ' ἄν as being palaeographically easier. VB 36–7, who himself offers ὄφρ' ἐμά γ' αὖ τὰ μετὰ φρεσί, argues that in final clauses ὄφρα + subj. never takes κε or ἄν in Homer, but this does occur; see Cooper iii. 2430–1 and Monro (1891), 262. Nonetheless, the best solution is perhaps offered by Kamerbeek (1967), 363, who emends to ὄφρα τοι αὖ τὰ μετὰ φρεσὶ πάντα διέλθω 'go through with you again all the things I have in mind' (adopted by Càssola). This could easily have been corrupted to the transmitted text through familiarity with the formulaic ταῦτα μετὰ φρεσί (cf. Il. 14. 264, 18. 463, etc.) and provides superior sense with τοι; on its own ταῦτα μετὰ φρεσὶ διέλθω 'go over these things in my mind' is elliptical (although one might understand the force of σοι at the beginning of the line to apply to this clause as well), and cannot mean 'put in your [Anchises'] mind' as suggested by Heitsch (1965), 32, Hoekstra (1969), 41: in epic this is expressed by ἐνὶ φρεσὶ βάλλω/τίθημι, while μετὰ φρεσί is used of the mind of the subject (cf. Od. 10. 438 ἐγώ γε μετὰ φρεσὶ μερμήριξα). τὰ μετὰ φρεσί is not elegant composition, but the use of the pronoun followed by a preposition and the dative is paralleled by Il. 17. 375 τοὶ δ' ἐν μέσῳ ἄλγε' ἔπασχον (cf. VB 36–7).

But the language and sentiment of the line are in any case very strained. διέρχομαι is not elsewhere used with the sense 'go over/recount' until Pi. N. 4. 72, [A.] PV 872; although note πάντα διίξομαι, Il. 9. 61, 19. 186, Dem. 416; cf. Janko (1982), 160, Hoekstra (1969), 41. Also, the idea that Aphrodite should want to go through again what she is revealing in her present speech is awkward. These infelicities support the possibility that the line is a later interpolation (see above on 274–7).

277 ἐς πέμπτον ἔτος: 'in the fifth year'; cf. Od. 24. 309 αὐτὰρ Ὀδυσσῆϊ τόδε δὴ πέμπτον ἔτος ἐστιν.

αὖτις ἐλεύσομαι: cf. Il. 1. 425 δωδεκάτῃ δέ τοι αὖτις ἐλεύσεται Οὐλυμπόνδε.

278 τὸν μὲν ἐπὴν δὴ πρῶτον: repeated from v. 256; see on Aphr. 256–90. τόν is here governed by ὁρόων, while θάλος is the direct object of ἴδῃς in the ἐπήν clause; cf. VB 37.

θάλος: 'scion', used of sons and daughters as flourishing offspring;

cf. *Il.* 22. 87, *Od.* 6. 157, *Dem.* 66, 187 and see Chadwick (1996), 140–1.

279 γηθήσεις ὁρόων: cf. [Hes.] fr. 302. 21 γηθήσω δ' ὁρόων. Rejoicing at sight is a commonplace; cf. ἰδὼν γήθησεν, *Il.* 1. 330, 4. 255 etc.

μάλα γὰρ θεοείκελος ἔσται: cf. *Dem.* 159 δὴ γὰρ θεοείκελός ἐσσι, another possible case of direct borrowing (see Introd., pp. 38–40). The adjective θεοείκελος is used in Homer of Achilles (*Il.* 1. 131, 19. 155), Telemachus (*Od.* 3. 416), Deiphobos (4. 276) and Alcinous (8. 256). It is used of children at [Hes.] fr. 70. 32. On the recurring theme of the godlike nature of Anchises and Aeneas, see Introd., pp. 7–10.

280 μιν: the usual epic form, conjectured by Hermann (1806), should be adopted over the Doric form νιν transmitted by MSS Ψ. Otherwise the Doric form is transmitted at [Hes.] fr. 296. 3 as reported by Stephanus Byzantinus, *Cypria* fr. 7. 12 as reported by Athenaeus, and as a v.l. in one papyrus at *Il.* 18. 64; cf. Thgn. 364 (itself the only instance in Thgn., which should perhaps be emended to μιν; see van Groningen 1966, 145). The change could have been brought about during transmission through familiarity with the formulaic αὐτίκα νῦν, where νῦν and νιν were pronounced identically by Byzantine scribes; M actually transmits αὐτίκα νῦν. Familiarity with the form νιν in Callimachus (Call. *Hy.* 1. 4 etc.), whose *Hymns* were often transmitted together with the *Homeric Hymns*, could also have influenced the change; cf. Kamerbeek (1967), 388, Janko (1982), 171. The Doric form is common in lyric and tragedy.

Ἴλιον ἠνεμόεσσαν: the noun–epithet combination is formulaic; cf. *Il.* 3. 305, 8. 499 etc. The site of Troy in northern Turkey is very windy, making the application of the epithet particularly appropriate (see Bowra 1960, 19), although its use is not unique to Troy in Homer (cf. Enispe in Arcadia *Il.* 2. 660 and the mountain Mimas *Od.* 3. 172).

281–90. Aphrodite closes her speech with a warning to Anchises not to tell other mortals of their union. If he transgresses, he should expect punishment from Zeus. Aphrodite's warning is motivated by her embarrassment about the affair (cf. vv. 239–55), but secrecy is a common motif in love-affairs between gods and mortals: Ares lies in secret with Astyoche at *Il.* 2. 512–15, as does Hermes with Polymele at 16. 179–85, and Poseidon gives a similar warning to Tyro at *Od.* 11. 248–52 (for more on the similarities between the speeches of

Aphrodite and Poseidon, see above on 191–290 and cf. below on 290 ἴσχεο μηδ' ὀνομήνῃς). A final warning is also a motif found at the end of other *Homeric Hymns*; Apollo warns the priests of Delphi to guard both their speech and their actions (*Apoll.* 540–4; cf. below on 289), and Demeter warns the Eleusinians not to reveal her mysteries (*Dem.* 478–9).

281–4 ἢν δέ τις εἴρηταί σε ... φάσθαι: cf. Odysseus' departing comment to Polyphemus at *Od.* 9. 502–3 Κύκλωψ, αἴ κέν τίς σε | καταθνητῶν ἀνθρώπων | ὀφθαλμοῦ εἴρηται ἀεικελίην ἀλαωτύν, | φάσθαι.

282 φίλον υἱόν: see above on 196.

ὑπὸ ζώνῃ θέτο: cf. v. 255.

283 μυθεῖσθαι μεμνημένος ὥς σε κελεύω: for the structure of the imperatival phrase cf. *Op.* 623 γῆν δ' ἐργάζεσθαι μεμνημένος ὥς σε κελεύω. The participle μεμνημένος is absolute; in a command cf. *Il.* 19. 153. The formulaic ὥς σύ/ ὥς σε/με κελεύ- is common in early epic; *Il.* 8. 35, 10. 516, etc.

284 φάσθαι τοι ... ἔκγονον εἶναι: the MSS read φασίν, adopted by AHS, Càssola, and others, who take v. 284–5 as direct speech; Anchises is to say to anyone who asks, 'they say that he is the off-spring of a nymph with eyes like buds.' It is, however, unclear why Anchises should be commanded to tell those who ask that 'others' have said his son is the offspring of a nymph; would he himself not know with whom he slept? Matthiae (1800), 347 offers better sense with his conjecture of the imperatival φάσθαι, based upon the parallel of *Od.* 9. 502–3 (quoted above on 281–4): 'speak as I tell you ... I say that he is the offspring of a nymph with eyes like buds.' This line is similar to *Il.* 20. 206 φασί σε μὲν Πηλῆος ἀμύμονος ἔκγονον εἶναι (Aeneas says that others claim Achilles is the son of Peleus and Thetis; cf. also 20. 105–6, *Od.* 11. 236), knowledge of which could have influenced the change to φασί during transmission. AHS 372 and VE 97 argue that two imperatives are not required here, but the second specifies exactly how Aphrodite commands him to speak; see further Smith (1979), 41–3.

καλυκώπιδος: the adjective is very rare and occurs elsewhere in early epic only at *Dem.* 8 καλυκώπιδι κούρῃ (Persephone) and 420 Ὠκυρόη καλυκῶπις, and is perhaps a post-Homeric formation; cf. Heitsch (1965), 25, Hoekstra (1969), 13. This is another example of rare language linking *Aphr.* and *Dem.* (see Introd., pp. 38–40). The word is later found only at B. fr. 20a. 17 and then *Orph. Hy.* 24. 1, 60. 6 and 79. 2. On its meaning 'with eyes like buds', see N. Richardson (1974), 144.

285 ὄρος καταειμένον ὕλῃ: this formula occurs at *Od.* 13. 351 and *Herm.* 228 (note also *Od.* 19. 431). In later literature see Q.S. 13. 488 ὄρος . . . καταειμένον ὕλης. Cf. above on 258.

286–8. Anchises' transgression and punishment are known in later accounts of the story (see above on 53–199). Similarities between Soph. *Laocoon* fr. 373 (D.H. 1. 48), in which Anchises has been wounded by a thunderbolt, and Proclus' paraphrase of the *Ilioupersis* (pp. 62–3 Davies), as well as depictions of Aeneas carrying a crippled Anchises in art from the sixth century BC onwards (see *LIMC* i, Aeneas, nos. 59–93), suggest that the punishment was known to the Epic Cycle (see Lenz 1975, 146–9). It is at least possible that the poet of *Aphr.* also knew the tradition; *contra* VB 37–40. The claim that Zeus will punish Anchises has a certain irony here given that Zeus is the one who brought about the love-affair in the first place.

286 ἐξείπῃς καὶ ἐπεύξεαι: Anchises is not to boast about his affair. The warning underlines how Aphrodite's opinion has changed on the matter; Zeus intended to end her own boasting by turning the tables on the goddess (see v. 48 ἐπευξαμένη εἴπῃ); cf. VB 40 n. 68.

ἄφρονι θυμῷ: the combination occurs once elsewhere in early epic at *Od.* 21. 105; in later literature *Orac. Sib.* 3. 687, 3. 722, Q.S. 3. 245, 5. 421, Gr. Nanz. *Carm.* II. 1. 1. 434 (*PG* 37. 1002), Procl. *Hy.* 7. 39 and Nonn. *Para.* 5. 57. ἄφρων is one of many -φρων adjectives applied to θυμός; cf. above on *Aphr.* 102 εὔφρονα θυμόν and see Darcus (1977), 179–81.

287 ἐν φιλότητι μιγῆναι: see above on *Aphr.* 150 σῇ φιλότητι μιγῆναι.

ἐϋστεφάνῳ Κυθερείῃ: see above on *Aphr.* 6.

288 Ζεύς σε χολωσάμενος: the participle χολωσαμεν- often sits in this metrical *sedes* (*Il.* 2. 599 etc.); of Zeus, cf. in particular *Op.* 53 τὸν δὲ χολωσάμενος προσέφη νεφεληγερέτα Ζεύς.

βαλέει ψολόεντι κεραυνῷ: the thunderbolt is a frequent weapon of Zeus; for the expression here cf. in particular *Od.* 23. 330–1 ἔβαλε ψολόεντι κεραυνῷ | Ζεὺς ὑψιβρεμέτης, and [Hes.] fr. 51. 1–2 πατὴρ ἀνδρῶν τε θεῶν τε | χώσατ' ἀπ' Οὐλύμπον δὲ βάλων ψολόεντι κεραυνῷ.

289 εἴρηταί τοι πάντα, σὺ δὲ φρεσὶ σῇσι νοήσας: almost identical is Apoll. 544 εἴρηταί τοι πάντα, σὺ δὲ φρεσὶ σῇσι φύλαξαι, part of the god's departing warning to the Delians (cf. above on 281–90).

290 ἴσχεο μηδ' ὀνόμαινε: cf. Od. 11. 251 ἴσχεο μηδ' ὀνομήνῃς, at line-end (also ἴσχεο μηδ' Il. 2. 247, Od. 22. 356, 411). When the aorist is used in prohibitions the subjunctive is normal, a fact which prompted Hermann (1806) to conjecture the present imperative ὀνόμαινε for the transmitted ὀνόμηνε. The construction μή + the aorist imperative is attested three times in Homer (Il. 4. 410, 18. 134 and Od. 24. 248) and could plausibly be retained here as the unanimous reading, with the rare construction the result of adaptation of traditional language (transposition of ἴσχεο μηδ' ὀνομήνῃς); see Smith (1979), 43–50. However, also problematic is the imperatival ending -ε, where in the weak aorist one would expect -ον (cf. κραίνω, κρῆνον, etc.). The present stem ὀνομαίνω is itself not found anywhere in early epic (where ὀνομάζω is used) and would be an unusual form, but it seems easier to accept this as formed by analogy with φαίνω, ὑφαίνω. etc. than both the abnormal imperative form and the rare construction with the aorist; cf. VB 40–1. VE 98–9 proposes reading the imperatival infinitive ὀνομῆναι by scanning θεῶν as one syllable through synizesis (elsewhere at Il. 1. 18, Od. 14. 251, Th. 44, Dem. 55, 259, 355; cf. N. Richardson 1974, 170), in which case one could also read the aorist ὀνομήνῃς, but this strains the metre by removing the caesura in the third foot where there is a natural break in sense (elsewhere in the hymn there is no caesura in the third foot only in vv. 4 and 271, where the long words διειπετέας and ἀμφιπεριφθινύθει push it to the fourth foot; cf. VB 40–1).

θεῶν δ' ἐποπίζεο μῆνιν: cf. Od. 5. 146 Διὸς δ' ἐποπίζεο μῆνιν, and notably later Thgn. 1297 θεῶν δ' ἐποπίζεο μῆνιν.

291 ὣς εἰποῦσ' ἤϊξε πρὸς οὐρανόν: the narrative ends abruptly on this note of warning and Aphrodite goes away into the heavens, as gods often do after interacting with mortals; cf. Il. 1. 221–2 (Athena), 24. 694 (Hermes), and the return of Demeter and Persephone to Olympus at the end of Dem. (483–4). For the language cf. Il. 23. 868 ἤϊξε πρὸς οὐρανόν, of an arrow rushing into the sky.

οὐρανὸν ἠνεμόεντα: the usual noun–epithet combination is οὐρανὸν ἀστερόεντα (Il. 4. 44, 5. 769 etc.), and ἠνεμόεις is not elsewhere applied to οὐρανός. The poet may have been influenced by

Ἴλιον ἠνεμόεσσαν above in v. 280 to make the substitution (cf. Janko 1982, 160), which perhaps adds more descriptive force to the swiftness of her departure (i.e. like the wind); cf. *Il.* 8. 549 κνίσην δ' ἐκ πεδίου ἄνεμοι φέρον οὐρανὸν εἴσω. There is no good reason to suspect scribal error and to follow Ruhnken in restoring ἀστερόεντα (Mahne 1832, 25).

292–3. The closing of the poem is typical for a *Hymn*, including an address of farewell to the goddess with χαῖρε and a formula of transition to another song. For χαίρω (25 times in the *Hymns*) cf. *Apoll.* 545, *Herm.* 579, *Hy.* 6. 19, 7. 58, 9. 7, 10. 4, etc. The formula stating the poet's intention to go on and sing another song (σεῦ δ' ἐγὼ ἀρξάμενος μεταβήσομαι ἄλλον ἐς ὕμνον, also *Hy.* 9. 9, 18. 11; cf. *Dem.* 495 etc. αὐτὰρ ἐγὼ καὶ σεῖο καὶ ἄλλης μνήσομ' ἀοιδῆς) evinces the tradition that the *Hymns* were in origin προοίμια or 'preludes' to longer epic recitations, as said of *Apoll.* by Th. 3. 104. This is demonstrated in the epic tradition; Demodocus begins his song with an invocation to a god at *Od.* 8. 499, and Pindar says at *N.* 2. 1–3 that the Homeridae began their songs Διὸς ἐκ προοιμίου (cf. Furley i. 41–3). It has been doubted that poems as long as *Dem., Apoll., Herm.*, and *Aphr.* could have preceded the recitation of longer epics (AHS, pp. xciii–xcv), but this perhaps underestimates the ability of an ancient audience to listen over a long span of time; see N. Richardson (1974), 3–4, cf. 324–5 on *Dem.* 495. However, one should not exclude the possibility that the longer *Hymns* also at times functioned independently; see Clay (1997), 494–8.

292 χαῖρε θεά . . . ἐϋκτιμένης μεδέουσα: cf. *Hy.* 10. 4–5 (to Aphrodite) χαῖρε θεὰ Σαλαμῖνος ἐϋκτιμένης μεδέουσα | εἰναλίης τε Κύπρου. The epithet ἐϋκτίμενος 'well-built/well-established' (cf. *LfgrE* s.v.) is often used of cities in Homer (cf. *Il.* 2. 570 etc.) but is here first applied to Cyprus; used of an island, cf. Anacr. *PMG* 358. 5–6 ἀπ' εὐκτίτου | Λέσβου.

293 σέο: all MSS transmit the contracted form σεῦ, which should be restored to the earlier uncontracted form σέο; see West (1998), pp. xxii f.

μεταβήσομαι ἄλλον ἐς ὕμνον: cf. *Od.* 8. 492 ἀλλ' ἄγε δὴ μετάβηθι καὶ ἵππου κόσμον ἄεισον, where Odysseus asks Demodocus to go on to another song.

Works Cited

Abbreviations of journal titles follow *L'Année philologique*.

ABRAMOWICZ, S. (1972), 'Répétitions et hantises verbales chez Homère', *Eos*, 60: 223–34.
ADKINS, A. W. H. (1969), '*ΕΥΧΟΜΑΙ, ΕΥΧΩΛΗ*, and *ΕΥΧΟΣ* in Homer', *CQ*² 19: 20–33.
ADRADOS, F. R. (1964), 'Sobre el aceite perfumado: Esquilo, Agamemnón 96, las tablillas Fr. y la ambrosia', *Kadmos*, 3: 122–48.
AITCHISON, J. M. (1963), 'Homeric ἄνθος', *Glotta*, 41: 271–8.
ALDUS (1504) = *Homeri opera omnia*, ed. Aldus Manutius (Venice).
ALEXANDER, J. A. (1963), *Potidaea: Its History and Remains* (Atlanta).
ALLEN, T. W. (1895), 'The Text of the Homeric Hymns: I', *JHS* 15: 136–83.
—— (1897), 'D'Orville's Notes on the Homeric Hymns', *Journal of Philology*, 25: 250–60.
—— (1898), 'The Text of the Homeric Hymns: Part V', *JHS* 18: 23–32.
ANDERSON, J. K. (1985), *Hunting in the Ancient World* (California).
AREND, W. (1933), *Die typischen Scenen bei Homer* (Berlin).
ATHANASSAKIS, A. (1976), 'The Etymology and Meaning of ὁμοίιος', *RhM*² 119: 4–7.
—— (1989), 'From the Phallic Cairn to Shepherd God', *Eranos*, 87: 33–49.
BAILEY, C. (1947), *Lucretius: De Rerum Natura*, 3 vols. (Oxford).
BAKKER, E. J. (1988), *Linguistics and Formulas in Homer: Scalarity and the Description of the Particle περ* (Amsterdam).
BALLABRIGA, A. (1996), 'Survie et descendance d'Énée: le mythe grec archaïque', *Kernos*, 9: 21–36.
BARCHIESI, A. (1999), 'Ovidian Transformations: Essays on Ovid's *Metamorphoses* and its Reception', *PCPhS Supp.* 23: 112–26.
BARNES, J. (1711), *Homeri Ilias et Odyssea: accedunt Batrachomyomachia, hymni et epigrammata* (Cambridge).
BARRETT, W. S. (1964), *Euripides: Hippolytos* (Oxford).
BARRON, J. P. (1984), 'Ibycus: Gorgias and Other Poems', *BICS*, 31: 13–24.
BAUMEISTER, A. (1860), *Hymni Homerici* (Leipzig).
BECHTEL, F. (1914), *Lexilogus zu Homer* (Halle).

BEN, N. van der (1980), 'De Homerische Aphrodite-hymne I: De Aeneas-passages in de *Ilias*', *Lampas*, 13: 40–77.
—— (1981), 'De Homerische Aphrodite-hymne 2: Een interpretatie van het gedicht', *Lampas*, 14: 67–107.
BERGREN, A. (1989), 'The Homeric Hymn to Aphrodite: Tradition and Rhetoric, Praise and Blame', *ClAnt* 8: 1–44.
BICKERMAN, E. J. (1976), 'Love Story in the Homeric Hymn to Aphrodite', *Athenaeum*, 54: 229–54.
BIELEFELD, E. (1968), *Schmuck* (Archaeologia Homerica, C; Göttingen)
BIRAUD, M. (1990), 'Conceptions dynamiques de la totalité et de la restriction dans la langue homérique: études sémantiques des couples de lexèmes οὖλος et πᾶς, οἶος et μοῦνος', in J. Granarolo and M. Biraud (eds.), *De la préhistoire à Virgile: Hommage à René Braun* (Nice), 83–94.
BLOCK, E. (1985), 'Clothing Makes the Man: A Pattern in the Odyssey', *APhA* 115: 1–11.
BOEDEKER, D. (1974), *Aphrodite's Entry into Greek Epic* (Leiden).
BOLLING, G. M. (1950), '*ΕΝΘΑ* in the Homeric Poems', *Language*, 26: 371–8.
BONNER, C. (1949), 'Kestos Himas and the Saltire of Aphrodite', *AJPh* 70: 1–6.
BORNMANN, F. (1968), *Callimachi Hymnus in Dianam* (Florence).
BOSSI, F. (1978), '[Hom.] Hymn. Ven.', *MCr* 13–14: 23–4.
BOWRA, C. M. (1926), 'Homeric Words in Arcadian Inscriptions', *CQ* 20: 168–76.
—— (1960) 'Homeric Epithets for Troy', *JHS* 80: 16–23.
—— (1961), *Greek Lyric Poetry* (Oxford).
BRASWELL, B. K. (1992), *A Commentary on Pindar Nemean One* (Fribourg).
BREMER, D. (1975), 'Die Epiphanie des Gottes in den homerischen Hymnen und Platons Gottesbegriff', *ZRGG* 27: 1–21.
BREMMER, J. N. (1980), 'An Enigmatic Indo-European Rite: Pederasty', *Arethusa*, 13: 279–98.
BRENK, F. E. (1977), 'Aphrodite's Girdle: No Way to Treat a Lady (*Iliad* 14. 214–23)', *CB* 54: 17–20.
BREUIL, J. (1989), '*ΚΡΑΤΟΣ* et sa famille chez Homère: étude sémantique', in Casevitz (1989), 17–53.
BREUNING, P. S. (1929), *De Hymnorum Homericorum memoria* (Diss. Utrecht).
BRIXHE, C. (2002), 'Interactions between Greek and Phrygian under the Roman Empire', in J. N. Adams, M. Janse, and S. Swain (eds.), *Bilingualism in Ancient Society* (Oxford), 246–66.
BROWN, J. P. (1965), 'Kothar, Kinyras and Kythereia', *JSS* 10: 197–219.
—— (1995) *Israel and Hellas*, i (Berlin).

BÖCHELER, F. (1869), *Hymnus Cereris Homericus* (Leipzig).
BUCHHOLZ, H.-G., JÖHRENS, G., and MAULL, I. (1973), *Jagd und Fischfang mit einem Abhang: Honiggewinnung* (Archaeologia Homerica, J; Göttingen).
BUCHNER, G., and RUSSO, C. F. (1955), 'La coppa di Nestore e un'inscrizione metrica da Pitecusa dell'VIII secolo av. Cr.', *RAL*[8] 10: 215–34.
BUCK, C. D. (1955), *The Greek Dialects* (Chicago).
BUDIN, S. (2003), *The Origin of Aphrodite* (Bethesda, MD).
BULLOCH, A. W. (1977), 'Callimachus' Erysichthon, Homer and Apollonius Rhodius', *AJPh* 98: 97–123.
—— (1985), *Callimachus: The Fifth Hymn* (Cambridge).
BURKERT, W. (1985), *Greek Religion: Archaic and Classical* (Cambridge, MA).
—— (1992), *The Orientalizing Revolution: Near Eastern Influence on Greek Culture in the Early Archaic Age* (Cambridge, MA).
—— (2001), *Kleine Schriften*, i: *Homerica*, ed. C. Riedweg (Göttingen).
—— (2002), 'Die Waffen und die Jungen: Homerisch OPLOTEROI', in Reichel–Rengakos (2002), 31–4.
BUTLER, H. E., and BARBER, E. A. (1933), *The Elegies of Propertius* (Oxford).
BUTTMANN, P. (1846), *Lexilogus; or, A Critical Examination of the Meaning and Etymology of Numerous Greek Words and Passages: Intended Principally for Homer and Hesiod*, tr. J. R. Fishlake, 3rd edn. (London).
BYL, S. (1976), 'Lamentations sur la vieillesse', *LEC* 44: 234–44.
CALAME, C. (1977), *Les Chœurs de jeunes filles en Grèce archaïque*, 2 vols. (Rome).
CALHOUN, G. M. (1935), 'The Art of Formula in Homer—ΕΠΕΑ ΠΤΕΡΟΕΝΤΑ', *CPh* 30: 215–27.
CAMPBELL, M. (1981), *Echoes and Imitations of Early Epic in Apollonius Rhodius* (Leiden).
—— (1991), *Moschus: Europa* (Hildesheim).
—— (1994), *A Commentary on Apollonius Rhodius: Argonautica III 1–471* (Leiden).
CAMPS, W. A (1967), *Propertius: Elegies Book II* (Cambridge).
CASABONA, J. (1966), *Recherches sur le vocabulaire des sacrifices en grec* (Publications des Annales de la Faculté des lettres, Aix-en-Provence, NS 56; [Gap]).
CASEVITZ, M. (1989) (ed.) *Études homériques: séminaire de recherche* (Travaux de la Maison de l'Orient, 17; Lyon).
CATENACCI, C. (1996), 'Aggiustamenti metrici nell'esametro', *QUCC* 81: 133–44.
CHADWICK, J. (1957), 'Potnia', *Minos*, 5: 117–29.
—— (1996), *Lexicographica Graeca* (Oxford).

—— and Ventris, M. (1973), *Documents in Mycenaean Greek*, 2nd edn. (Cambridge).

Chantraine, P. (1935a), 'L'Épithète homérique *Ἀργεϊφόντης*', in *Mélanges offerts à O. Navarre* (Toulouse), 69–79.

—— (1935b) 'Grec *ἐκγεγάονται* (Hymne homérique à Aphrodite, 197)', *BSL* 36: 131–2.

—— (1956), *Études sur le vocabulaire grecque* (Paris).

—— (1967), 'Exemples de la loi de Caland', *Beiträge zur Indogermanistik und Keltologie*, 13: 21–4.

Cianni, M. G. (1974), *ΦΑΟΣ e termini affini nella poesia greca* (Florence).

Clarke, S. (1740), *Homeri Odyssea, graece et latine, item Batrachomyomachia, hymni, et epigrammata*, 2 vols. (London).

Clay, J. (1989), *The Politics of Olympus: Form and Meaning in the Major Homeric Hymns* (Princeton).

—— (1997), 'The Homeric Hymns', in I. Morris and B. Powell (eds.), *A New Companion to Homer* (Leiden), 489–507.

Clinton, K. (1986), 'The Author of the Homeric Hymn to Demeter', *Opuscula Atheniensia*, 16: 43–9.

Cook, J. M. (1973), *The Troad: An Archaeological and Topographical Study* (Oxford).

Couch, H. N. (1937), 'A Prelude to Speech in Homer', *TAPhA* 68: 129–40.

Crudden, M. (2001), *The Homeric Hymns* (Oxford).

Currie, B. (2005), *Pindar and the Cult of Heroes* (Oxford).

Darcus, S. (1977), '-phrōn Epithets of thumos', *Glotta*, 55: 178–82.

Davies, A. M. (1964), '"Doric" Features in the Language of Hesiod', *Glotta*, 42: 138–65.

Davis, S. (1953), 'Argeiphontes in Homer—The Dragon-Slayer', *G&R* 22: 33–8.

Denniston, J. D. (1954), *The Greek Particles*, 2nd edn., rev. K. J. Dover (Oxford).

Deubner, L. (1941), *Ololyge und Verwandtes* (Abhandlungen der Preußischen Akademie der Wissenschaften, phil-hist. Kl. 1941/1 (Berlin).

Devlin, N. G. (1994), 'The Hymn in Greek Literature' (D.Phil. thesis, Oxford).

Dietrich, B. C. (1965), *Death, Fate and the Gods* (London).

Dodds, E. R. (1960), *Euripides: Bacchae* (Oxford).

Dornseiff, F. (1931), 'Der homerische Aphroditehymnos', *ARW* 29: 205–6.

Dover, K. J. (1989), *Greek Homosexuality*, 2nd edn. (Cambridge, MA).

Drees, L. (1968), *Olympia: Gods, Artists and Athletes* (London).

Due, O. S. (1965), 'The Meaning of the Homeric Formula *χρυσηλάκατος κελαδεινή*', *C&M* 26: 1–9.

DUNBAR, N. (1995), *Aristophanes: Birds* (Oxford).
EDGEWORTH, R. J. (1983), 'Terms for "Brown" in Ancient Greek', *Glotta*, 61: 31–40.
EDMUNDS, S. T. (1990), *Homeric Nēpios* (New York).
EDWARDS, G. P. (1971), *The Language of Hesiod in its Traditional Context* (Oxford).
EDWARDS, M. W. (1970), 'Homeric Speech Introductions', *HSCPh* 74: 1–36.
—— (1991), *The Iliad: A Commentary: Books 17–20* (Cambridge).
ELMSLEY, P. (1822), *Euripidis Bacchae* (Leipzig).
ELSNER, J. (2007), 'Physiognomics: Art and Text', in S. Swain (ed.), *Seeing the Face, Seeing the Soul: Polemon's Physiognomy from Classical Antiquity to Medieval Islam* (Oxford), 203–24.
ERBSE, H. (1950), *Untersuchungen zu den attizistischen Lexika* (Berlin).
ERDMANN, W. (1934), *Die Ehe im alten Griechenland* (Munich).
FAERBER, H. (1932), *Zur dichterischen Kunst in Apollonios Rhodios' Argonautica* (Diss. Berlin).
FALKNER, T. M. (1989), 'Ἐπὶ γήραος οὐδῷ: Homeric Heroism, Old Age and the End of the Odyssey', in Falkner–de Luce (1989), 21–67.
—— and LUCE, J. DE (eds.), *Old Age in Greek and Latin Literature* (New York).
FAULKNER, A. (2003), review of Reichel–Rengakos (2002), *BMCR* 2003.05.25.
—— (2006), 'Aphrodite's Aorists: Attributive Sections in the *Homeric Hymns*', *Glotta*, 81: 60–79.
FEHLING, D. (1969), *Die Wiederholungsfiguren und ihr Gebrauch bei den Griechen vor Gorgias* (Berlin).
FERRI, S. (1960), 'L'inno omerico a Afrodite e la tribù anatolica degli Otrusi', in Rostagni (1960), i. 293–307.
FINLEY, M. I. (1955), 'Marriage, Sale and Gift in the Homeric World', *RIDA* 3: 167–94.
FLOYD, E. D. (1989), 'Homer and the Life-Producing Earth', *CW* 82: 337–49.
FOURNIER, H. (1946), *Les Verbes 'dire' en grec ancien* (Paris).
FRAENKEL, E. (1942), 'An Epodic Poem of Hipponax', *CQ* 36: 54–6.
FRANGESKOU, V. (1995), 'The *Homeric Hymn to Aphrodite*: A New Interpretation', *SCI* 14: 1–16.
FRÄNKEL, H. (1955), *Wege und Formen frühgriechischen Denkens* (Munich).
—— (1962), *Dichtung und Philosophie des frühen Griechentums* (Munich).
FREED, G., and Bentman, R. (1954), 'The *Homeric Hymn to Aphrodite*', *CJ* 50: 153–9.
GELZER, T. (1994), 'Zum Codex Mosquensis und zur Sammlung der Homerischen Hymnen', *Hyperboreus*, 1: 113–36.

GEMOLL, A. (1886), *Die Homerischen Hymnen* (Leipzig).
GEORGIADES, T. (1958), *Musik und Rhythmus bei den Griechen* (Hamburg).
GERMAIN, G. (1954), *Genèse de l'Odyssée* (Paris).
GIACOMELLI, A. (1980), 'Aphrodite and After', *Phoenix*, 34: 1–19.
GOODWIN, W. W. (1900), *A Greek Grammar* (Boston).
GOULD, J. (1973), 'Hiketeia', *JHS* 93: 74–103; repr. *Myth, Ritual, Memory, and Exchange* (Oxford, 2001), 22–77.
GOW, A. S. F. (1965), *Machon: The Fragments* (Cambridge).
GRAF, F. (1985), *Nordionische Kulte: religionsgeschichtliche und epigraphische Untersuchungen zu den Kulten von Chios, Erythrai, Klazomenai und Phokaia* (Rome).
GRIFFIN, J. (1980), *Homer on Life and Death* (Oxford).
—— (1992), 'Theocritus, the *Iliad*, and the East', *AJPh* 113: 189–211.
—— (1995), *Homer: Iliad Book Nine* (Oxford).
GRIFFITH, R. D. (1994), 'Nektar and Nitron', *Glotta*, 72: 20–3.
—— (1997), 'Homeric ΔΙΙΠΕΤΕΟΣ ΠΟΤΑΜΟΙΟ and the Celestial Nile', *AJPh* 118: 353–59.
GRONINGEN, B. A. van (1958), *La Composition littéraire archaïque grecque* (Amsterdam).
—— (1966), *Theognis: Le premier livre, édité avec un commentaire* (Amsterdam).
GUTTMANN, A. (1869), *De Hymnorum Homericorum historia critica particulae quattuor* (Greifswald).
HAHN, E. A. (1953), *Subjunctive and Optative: Their Origin as Futures* (New York).
HAINSWORTH, J. B. (1968), *The Flexibility of the Homeric Formula* (Oxford).
—— (1993), *The Iliad: A Commentary: Books 9–12* (Cambridge).
HALL, E. (1996), *Aeschylus' Persians* (Warminster).
HANDSCHUR, E. (1970), *Die Farb- und Glanzwörter bei Homer und Hesiod, in den homerischen Hymnen und den Fragmenten des epischen Kyklos* (Diss. Wien).
HEITSCH, E. (1965), *Aphroditehymnos, Aeneas und Homer* (Göttingen).
HELBIG, W. (1884), *Das homerische Epos aus den Denkmälern erläutert* (Leipzig).
HENDERSON, J. (1987), *Aristophanes: Lysistrata* (Oxford).
HEDREEN, G. (1994), 'Silens, Nymphs and Maenads', *JHS* 114: 47–69.
HERMANN, G. (1806), *Homeri hymni et epigrammata* (Leipzig).
HERWERDEN, H. van (1878), 'Observationes Criticae', *RPh* 2: 195–203.
HOCES DE LA GUARDIA Y BERMEJO, A. L. (1990), '*ΕΔΝΑ* y *ΔΩΡΑ* en el matrimonio homérico', *Veleia*, 7: 209–23.

HOEKSTRA, A. (1965), *Homeric Modifications of Formulaic Prototypes* (Amsterdam).
—— (1969), *The Sub-Epic Stage of the Formulaic Tradition* (Amsterdam).
HOFFMANN, C. A. (1848), *Quaestiones Homericae: Vol. 2* (Clausthal).
HOLLIS, A. S. (1990), *Callimachus: Hecale* (Oxford).
HOOKER, J. (1979), 'Three Homeric Epithets—$αἰγίοχος$, $διπετής$, $κορυθαίολος$', *IF* 84: 113–19.
—— (1987), 'Homeric Society: A Shame Culture?', *G&R* 34: 121–5.
HOPKINSON, N. (1984a), *Callimachus: Hymn to Demeter* (Cambridge).
—— (1984b), 'Rhea in Callimachus' Hymn to Zeus', *JHS* 104: 176–7.
HUMBACH, H. (1967), '$διπετής$ und $διοπετής$', *ZVS* 81: 76–283.
HUMBERT, J. (1936), *Homère: Hymnes* (Paris).
—— (1954), *Syntaxe grecque*, 2nd edn. (Paris).
HUNTER, R. (1989), *Apollonius of Rhodes: Argonautica, Book III* (Cambridge).
—— (1999), *Theocritus: A Selection* (Cambridge).
HURST, A. (1976), 'L'huile d'Aphrodite', *Živa Antika*, 26: 23–5.
ILGEN, C. D. (1796), *Hymni Homerici cum reliquis carminibus minoribus* (Halle).
IRIGOIN, J. (1970), 'Les manuscrits grecs I: quelques catalogues récents', *REG* 83: 500–29.
IRWIN, E. (1974), *Colour Terms in Greek Poetry* (Toronto).
JAMES, M. R. (1888), 'Excavations in Cyprus', *JHS* 9: 147–271.
JANKO, R. (1978), 'A Note on the Etymologies of $διάκτορος$ and $χρυσάορος$', *Glotta*, 56: 192–5.
—— (1981a), 'Structure of the Homeric Hymns—A Study in Genre', *Hermes*, 109: 9–24.
—— (1981b), 'Equivalent Formulae in the Greek Epos', *Mnemosyne*[4], 34: 251–64.
—— (1981c), '$ΑΘΑΝΑΤΟΣ\ ΚΑΙ\ ΑΓΗΡΩΣ$: The Genealogy of a Formula', *Mnemosyne*[4], 34: 382–5.
—— (1982), *Homer, Hesiod and the Hymns: Diachronic Development in Epic Diction* (Cambridge).
—— (1991), review of Clay (1989), *CR*[2] 41: 12–13.
—— (1992), *The Iliad: A Commentary: Books 13–16* (Cambridge).
JANNI, P. (1967), 'Due note omeriche', *QUCC* 3: 7–30.
—— (1968), '$ΘΕΟΙ\ ΑΙΕΝ\ ΕΟΝΤΕΣ$', *SIFC* 40: 148–68.
JEANMAIRE, H. (1975), *Couroi et courètes* (New York).
JOHANSEN, H. F., and WHITTLE, E. W. (1980), *Aeschylus: The Suppliants*, 3 vols. (Copenhagen).
JONG, I. J. F. DE (1989), 'The Biter Bit: A Narratological Analysis of *H. Aphr.* 45–291', *WS* 102: 13–26.

—— (2001), *A Narratological Commentary on the Odyssey* (Cambridge).
Jouan, F. (1956), 'Thétis, Hestia et Athéna', *REG* 69: 290–302.
Kakridis, J. Th. (1930), 'Tithonos', *WS* 48: 25–38.
—— (1971), 'Neugriechische Scholien zu Homer', *Gymnasium*, 78: 505–24.
Kamerbeek, J. C. (1967), 'Remarques sur l'Hymne à Aphrodite', *Mnemosyne*[4], 20: 385–95.
Kamptz, H. von (1982), *Homerische Personennamen* (Göttingen).
Karageorghis, J. (1977), *La Grande Déesse de Chypre et son culte* (Lyon).
—— (1984), 'Appendix: Mythology and Cult', in G. Maier and V. Karageorghis, *Paphos: History and Archaeology* (Nicosia), 357–75.
Karageorghis, V. (1976), 'Θρόνος ἀργυρόηλος', *Kadmos*, 15: 176–7.
—— (1998), *Greek Gods and Heroes in Ancient Cyprus* (Athens).
—— (2002), *Ancient Art from Cyprus in the Collection of George and Nefeli Giabra Pierides* (Cyprus).
Keaney, J. J. (1981), 'Hymn. Ven. 140 and the Use of ἌΠΟΙΝΑ', *AJPh* 102: 261–4.
King, H. (1989), 'Tithonos and the Tettix', in Falkner–de Luce (1989), 68–9.
Kirk, G. S. (1962), *The Songs of Homer* (Cambridge).
—— (1966), 'Formular Language and Oral Quality', *YCS* 20: 153–74.
—— (1985), *The Iliad: A Commentary: Books 1–4* (Cambridge).
—— (1990), *The Iliad: A Commentary: Books 5–8* (Cambridge).
Kirster, E., and Kraiker, W. (1967), *Griechenlandkunde: Ein Führer zu klassischen Stätten* (Heidelberg).
Knox, M. O. (1971), 'Huts and Farm Buildings in Homer', *CQ*[2] 21: 27–31.
Kober, A. (1932), *The Use of Color Terms in the Greek Poets* (Diss. Columbia).
Köchly, H. (1881), *Gesammelte kleine philologische Schriften*, ed. G. Kinkel, i (Leipzig).
Kost, K. (1971), *Musaios: Hero und Leander* (Bonn).
Kraus, T. (1960), *Hekate* (Heidelberg).
Labat, R., Caquot, A., Sznycer, M., and Vieyra, M. (1970), *Les Religions du Proche-Orient asiatique* (Paris).
Laser, S. (1968), *Hausrat* (Archaeologia Homerica, P; Göttingen).
Latacz, J. (1966), *Zum Wortfeld 'Freude' in der Sprache Homers* (Heidelberg).
Lejeune, M. (1963), 'Hom. ἐδανός', *BSL* 58: 81–4.
Lenz, L. H. (1975), *Der homerische Aphroditehymnus und die Aristie des Aineias in der Ilias* (Bonn).
—— (1980), *Das Proöm des frühen griechischen Epos: Ein Beitrag zum poetischen Selbstverständnis* (Bonn).
Létoublon, F. (1985), *Il allait, pareil à la nuit: les verbes de mouvement en grec* (Paris).

LEUMANN, M. (1950), *Homerische Wörter* (Basel).
—— (1959), *Kleine Schriften* (Zürich).
LEVIN, S. (1971), 'The Etymology of νέκταρ: Exotic Scents in Early Greece', *SMEA* 13: 31–50.
LEVINE, D. B. (1982), 'Homeric Laughter and the Unsmiling Suitors', *CJ* 78/1: 97–104.
LIBERMAN, G. (1999), *Alcée: Fragments* (Paris).
LIGHTFOOT, J. L. (1999), *Parthenius of Nicaea* (Oxford).
LILJA, S. (1972), *The Treatment of Odours in the Poetry of Antiquity* (Commentationes Humanarum Litterarum, 49; Helsinki).
LIVREA, E. (1968), *Il ratto di Elena: Colluto* (Bologna).
—— (1973), *Apollonii Rhodii Argonauticon Liber IV* (Florence).
LOBEL, E., and PAGE, D. L. (1952), 'A New Fragment of Aeolic Verse', CQ^2 2: 1–3.
LONSDALE, S. H. (1990), *Creatures of Speech: Lion, Herding and Hunting Similes in the Iliad* (Stuttgart).
LORIMER, H. L. (1950), *Homer and the Monuments* (London).
LOSFELD, G. (1991), *Essai sur le costume grec* (Paris).
LOWENSTAM, S. (1979), 'The meaning of IE **dhal-*', *TAPhA* 109: 125–35.
LUDWICH, A. (1908), *Homerischer Hymnenbau* (Leipzig).
LUTHER, W. (1935), *'Wahrheit' und 'Lüge' im ältesten Griechentum* (Diss. Göttingen).
MAHNE, G. L. (1832), *Epistolae mutuae duumvirorum Davidis Ruhnkenii et Lud. Casp. Valckenaerii* (Vlissingen).
MARINATOS, S. (1967), *Kleidung, Haar- und Barttracht* (Archaeologia Homerica, AB; Göttingen).
MARTIN, B. (1755), *Variarum lectionum libri quatuor, editio altera* (Utrecht; 1st edn. Paris, 1605).
MARZULLO, B. (1958), *Studi di poesia eolica* (Florence).
MATTHIAE, A. (1800), *Animadversiones in hymnos Homericos* (Leipzig).
—— (1805), *Homeri Hymni et Batrachomyomachia* (Leipzig).
MAXWELL-STUART, P. G. (1977), 'Tithonus: A Medical Note', *LCM* 2: 159–62.
—— (1981), *Studies in Greek Colour Terminology*, ii: ΧΑΡΟΠΟΣ (Leiden).
MCLENNAN, G. R. (1977), *Callimachus: Hymn to Zeus: Introduction and Commentary* (Rome).
MEISSNER, T. (2006), *S-Stem Nouns and Adjectives in Greek and Proto-Indo-European* (Oxford).
METTE, H. J. (1961), '"Schauen" und "Staunen"', *Glotta*, 39: 49–71.
MINEUR, W. H. (1984), *Callimachus: Hymn to Delos, Introduction and Commentary* (Leiden).
MOMMSEN, A. (1878), *Delphika* (Leipzig).

MONRO, D. B. (1891), *A Grammar of the Homeric Dialect* (Oxford).
MORGAN, G. (1978), 'Aphrodite Cytherea', *TAPhA* 108: 115–20.
MOUSSY, C. (1972), 'Sur ἀταλός, ἀτάλλω, ἀτιτάλλω', in *Mélanges de linguistique et de philologie grecques offerts à P. Chantraine* (Paris), 157–68.
MUECKE, F. (1984), 'Turning Away and Looking Down: Some Gestures in the Aeneid', *BICS* 31: 105–12.
MUGLER, C. (1964), *Dictionnaire historique de la terminologie optique des grecs* (Paris).
MÖLLER, I. (1887), 'Privataltertümer', *Handbuch der klassischen Altertums-Wissenschaft*, iv (Nördlingen), 335–480.
NAGY, G. (1979), *The Best of the Achaeans* (Baltimore).
NORDEN, E. (1913), *Agnostos Theos* (Leipzig).
NOTOPOULOS, J. A. (1962), 'The Homeric Hymns as Oral Poetry: A Study of the Post-Homeric Oral Tradition', *AJPh* 83: 337–68.
OLSON, S. D. (1998), *Aristophanes: Peace* (Oxford).
ONIANS, R. B. (1951), *The Origins of European Thought* (Cambridge).
PAGE, D. (1955), *Sappho and Alcaeus* (Oxford).
—— (1960), 'Anacreon Fr. I', in Rostagni (1960), ii. 661–7.
PARKE, H. W., and Wormell, D. E. W. (1956), *The Delphic Oracle II: The Oracular Responses* (Oxford).
PARRY, A. (1971), *The Making of Homeric Verse: The Collected Papers of Milman Parry* (Oxford).
PARRY, H. (1986), 'The Homeric Hymn to Aphrodite: Erotic ANANKE', *Phoenix*, 40: 253–64.
PAVESE, C. (1972), *Tradizioni e generi poetici della Grecia arcaica* (Rome).
—— (1974), *Studi sulla tradizione epica rapsodica* (Rome).
PEDRICK, V. (1982), 'Supplication in the Iliad and the Odyssey', *TAPhA* 112: 125–40.
PEKRIDOU-GORECKI, A. (1989), *Mode im antiken Griechenland: Textile Fertigung und Kleidung* (Munich).
PELLIZER, E. (1978), 'Tecnica compositiva e struttura genealogica nell'inno omerico ad Afrodite', *QUCC* 27: 115–144.
PENGLASE, C. (1994), *Greek Myths and Mesopotamia: Parallels and Influence in the Homeric Hymns and Hesiod* (London).
PEPPMÖLLER, R. (1889), 'Zu den homerischen Hymnen', *Philologus*, 47: 13–24.
PIRENNE-DELFORGE, V. (1994), *L'Aphrodite grecque* (*Kernos*, Supp. 4; Athens).
PLANTINGA, M. (2004), 'A Parade of Learning: Callimachus' *Hymn to Artemis* (vv. 170–268)', in M. A. Harder, R. F. Regtuit, and G. C. Wakker (eds.), *Hellenistica Groningana: Callimachus II* (Leuven), 257–77.

PODBIELSKI, H. (1971), *La Structure de l'Hymne homérique à Aphrodite* (Wrocław).
PORTER, H. N. (1949), 'Repetition in the *Homeric Hymn to Aphrodite*', *AJPh* 70: 249–72.
—— (1951), 'The Early Greek Hexameter', *YCS* 12: 3–63.
POSTLETHWAITE, N. (1979), 'Formula and Formulaic: Some Evidence from the Homeric Hymns', *Phoenix*, 33: 1–18.
PRESTON, K. (1916), *Studies in the Diction of the Sermo Amatorius in Roman Comedy* (Menasha, WI), repr. in B. Lier (ed.), *Ad topica carminum amatoriorum symbolae* (New York, 1978).
PREZIOSI, P. G. (1966), 'The *Homeric Hymn to Aphrodite*: An Oral Analysis', *HSCP* 71: 171–204.
RACE, W. H. (1982), 'Aspects of Rhetoric and Form in Greek Hymns', *GRBS* 23: 5–14.
—— (1992), 'How Greek Poems Begin', *YCIS* 29: 13–38.
RADERMACHER, L. (1931), *Der homerische Hermeshymnus* (Wien).
RADIN, A. (1988), 'Sunrise, Sunset: ἦμος in Homeric Epic', *AJPh* 109: 293–307.
REDFIELD, J. (1982), 'Notes on the Greek Wedding', *Arethusa*, 15: 181–201.
REICHEL, M., and Rengakos, A. (2002), *EPEA PTEROENTA — Beiträge zur Homerforschung: Festschrift für Wolfgang Kullmann zum 75. Geburtstag* (Stuttgart).
REINHARDT, K. (1956), 'Zum homerischen *Aphroditehymnus*', in *Festschrift für Bruno Snell zum 60. Geburtstag* (Munich), 1–14.
RENEHAN, R. (1972), '*ΔΙΑΙΠΕΤΗΣ* in Alcman', *RhM*² 115: 93–6.
—— (1982), *Greek Lexicographical Notes* (Hypomnemata, 74; Göttingen).
RENGAKOS, A. (1992), 'Homerische Wörter bei Kallimachos', *ZPE* 94: 21–47.
RICHARDSON, L. (1977), *Propertius: Elegies I–IV* (Oklahoma).
RICHARDSON, N. (1974), *The Homeric Hymn to Demeter* (Oxford).
—— (1991), 'Homer and Cyprus', in V. Karageorghis (ed.), *The Civilizations of the Aegean and their Diffusion in Cyprus and the Eastern Mediterranean, 2000–600 B.C.* (Larnaca), 124–7.
—— (1993), *The Iliad: A Commentary: Books 21–24* (Cambridge).
RICHTER, W. (1968), *Die Landwirtschaft im homerischen Zeitalter* (Archaeologia Homerica, H; Göttingen).
RISCH, E. (1985), 'Homerische *ΕΝΝΕΠΕΩ*, lakonisch *ΕΦΕΝΕΠΟΝΤΙ* und die alte Erzählprosa', *ZPE* 60: 1–9.
ROSE, H. J. (1924), 'Anchises and Aphrodite', *CQ* 18: 11–16.
ROSTAGNI, A. (1960) (ed.), *Studi in onore di Luigi Castiglioni*, 2 vols. (Florence).

Ruhnken, D. (1749), *Epistola Critica I: in Homeridarum hymnos et Hesiodum* (Lugduni Batavorum).

—— (1782), *Homeri Hymnus in Cererem: accedunt duae epistolae criticae ex editione altera* (Lugduni Batavorum).

Ruijgh, C. J. (1958), 'Les datifs pluriels dans les dialectes grecs et la position du Mycénien', *Mnemosyne*[4], 11: 97–116.

—— (1967), *Études sur la grammaire et le vocabulaire du grec mycénien* (Amsterdam).

—— (1971), *Autour de 'τε épique'* (Amsterdam).

—— (1981), 'L'Emploi de *HTOI* chez Homère et Hésiode', *Mnemosyne*[4], 34: 272–87.

Salmon, J. B. (1984), *Wealthy Corinth* (Oxford).

Schamp, J. (1976), 'Sous le signe d'Arion', *Ant. Cl.* 45: 95–120.

Schmitt, R. (1967), *Dichtung und Dichtersprache in indogermanischer Zeit* (Wiesbaden).

Schulze, W. (1892), *Quaestiones epicae* (Gütersloh).

Schwyzer, E. (1923), *Dialectorum Graecarum exempla epigraphica potiora* (Leipzig).

Segal, C. (1974), 'The Homeric Hymn to Aphrodite: A Structuralist Approach', *CW* 67: 205–12.

—— (1986), 'Tithonus and the Homeric Hymn to Aphrodite: A Comment', *Arethusa*, 19: 37–46.

Shackle, R. J. (1915), 'Some Emendations of the Homeric Hymns', *CR* 29: 161–5.

Shelmerdine, C. W. (1985), *The Perfume Industry of Mycenean Pylos* (Göteborg).

—— (1998), 'Shining and Fragrant Cloth in Homeric Epic', in J. B. Carter and S. P. Morris (eds.), *The Ages of Homer: A Tribute to Emily Townsend* (Austin, TX), 99–107.

Shipp, G. P. (1972), *Studies in the Language of Homer* (Cambridge).

Simon, E. (1985), *Die Götter der Griechen* (Munich).

Smith, P. (1979), 'Notes on the Text of the Fifth *Homeric Hymn*', *HSCPh* 83: 29–50.

—— (1981a), *Nursling of Mortality: A Study of the Homeric Hymn to Aphrodite* (Frankfurt).

—— (1981b), 'Aineiadai as Patrons of Iliad XX and the Homeric Hymn to Aphrodite', *HSCPh* 85: 17–58.

Snodgrass, A. M. (1969), review of Marinatos (1967), *Gnomon*, 41: 389–94.

—— (1974), 'An Historical Homeric Society', *JHS* 94: 114–25.

Solmsen, F. (1960), 'Zur Theologie im großen Aphrodite-Hymnus', *Hermes*, 88: 1–13.

SOMOLINOS, H. (1998), *Léxico de los poetas lesbios* (Madrid).
SOWA, C. A. (1984), *Traditional Themes and the Homeric Hymns* (Chicago).
SPENCER, N. (1995), 'Early Lesbos between East and West', *BSA* 90: 269–306.
STAGAKIS, G. J. (1971), '*ETA(I)PIZ-*, in Homer, as Testimony for the Establishment of an Hetairos Relation', *Historia*, 20: 524–33.
STEPHANUS, H. (1566), *Poetae Graeci principes heroici carminis* (Geneva): *Aphr.* pp. 762–90.
STUDNICZKA, F. (1886), *Beiträge zur Geschichte der altgriechischen Tracht* (Vienna).
STUMPP, B. E. (1998), *Prostitution in der römischen Antike* (Berlin).
SUHLE, B. (1878), *De hymno Homerico quarto εἰς Ἀφροδίτην* (Stolp [Słupsk]).
SZEMERÉNYI, O. (1969), 'Etyma Graeca II (8–15)', in *Studia classica et orientalia Antonino Pagliaro oblata* (Rome), iii. 233–50.
—— (1977), review of P. Chantraine, *Dictionnaire étymologique de la langue grecque*, in *Gnomon*, 49: 1–10.
THEANDER, C. (1937), 'Zum neuesten Sapphofund', *Philologus*, 92: 465–9.
THESLEFF, H. (1965), *The Pythagorean Texts of the Hellenistic Period* (Acta Academiae Aboensis, 30/1; Åbo [Turku]).
TÖLLE, R. (1964), *Frühgriechische Reigentänze* (Waldsassen).
TREU, M. (1958), 'Homerische Flüsse fallen nicht von Himmel', *Glotta*, 37: 260–75.
—— (1968), *Sappho* (Munich).
TSOMIS, G. (2004), '$μένος$ in der frühgriechischen Dichtung und $ἀμενηνός$ im homerischen Aphrodite-Hymnos (5, 188)', *WS* 117: 15–29.
TURKELTAUB, D. W. (2003*a*), 'The God's Radiance Manifest: An Examination of the Narrative Pattern Underlying the Homeric Divine Epiphany Scenes' (Diss. Cornell).
—— (2003*b*), 'The Three Virgin Goddesses in the *Homeric Hymn to Aphrodite*', *Lexis*, 21: 101–16.
VALK, M. VAN DER (1949), *Textual Criticism of the Odyssey* (Leiden).
VERDENIUS, W. J. (1971), 'Hesiod, *Theogony* 507–616: Some Comments on a Commentary', *Mnemosyne*[4], 24: 1–10.
VIVANTE, P. (1975), 'On Homer's Winged Words', *CQ*[2] 25: 1–12.
WACKERNAGEL, J. (1916), *Sprachliche Untersuchungen zu Homer* (Göttingen).
WALCOT, P. (1991), 'The Homeric Hymn to Aphrodite: A Literary Appraisal', *G&R* 38: 137–55.
WATKINS, C. (1995), *How to Kill a Dragon: Aspects of Indo-European Poetics* (Oxford).
WATSON, L. C. (1983), 'Three Women in Martial', *CQ*[2] 33: 258–64.
WERNER, J. (1983), 'Nichtgriechische Sprachen im Bewußtsein der antiken Griechen', in *Festschrift für Robert Muth* (Innsbruck).

WEST, M. L. (1966a), *Hesiod: Theogony* (Oxford).
—— (1966b), 'Conjectures on 46 Greek Poets', *Philologus*, 110: 147–68.
—— (1966c), 'ἕως oder ἧος', *Glotta*, 44: 135–9.
—— (1967), 'The Contest of Homer and Hesiod', *CQ*² 17: 433–50.
—— (1970), 'The Eighth *Homeric Hymn* and Proclus', *CQ*² 20: 300–4.
—— (1978), *Hesiod: Works and Days* (Oxford).
—— (1982), *Greek Metre* (Oxford).
—— (1983), *The Orphic Poems* (Oxford).
—— (1985), *The Hesiodic Catalogue of Women* (Oxford).
—— (1988), 'The Rise of the Greek Epic', *JHS* 108: 151–72.
—— (1995), 'The Date of the *Iliad*', *MH* 52: 203–19.
—— (1997), *The East Face of Helicon* (Oxford).
—— (1998), *Homerus:Ilias, Volumen Prius, Rhapsodiae I–XII* (Stuttgart).
—— (2000), *Homerus: Ilias, Volumen Alterum, Rhapsodiae XIII–XXIV* (Stuttgart).
—— (2001a), *Studies in the Text and Transmission of the Iliad* (Munich).
—— (2001b), 'Some Homeric Words', *Glotta*, 77: 118–35.
—— (2001c), '*The Fragmentary Homeric Hymn to Dionysus*', *ZPE* 134: 1–11.
—— (2002), 'The View from Lesbos', in Reichel–Rengakos (2002), 207–19.
—— (2003), *Homeric Hymns, Homeric Apocrypha, Lives of Homer* (London).
—— (2005), 'The New Sappho', *ZPE* 151: 1–9.
WILAMOWITZ-MOELLENDORFF, U. von (1931–2), *Der Glaube der Hellenen*, 2 vols. (Berlin).
WILLETTS, R. F. (1962), *Cretan Cults and Festivals* (London).
WILLIAMS, F. (1978), *Callimachus: Hymn to Apollo* (Oxford).
WILSON, N. G. (1974), 'A Puzzle in Stemmatic Theory Solved', *RHT* 4: 139–42.
WOLF, F. A. (1807), *Homeri et Homeridarum opera et reliquiae* (Leipzig).
WORONOFF, M. (1989), 'Les lions de l'Ida', in Casevitz (1989), 103–6.
WYATT, W. F. (1969), *Metrical Lengthening in Homer* (Rome).
YAVIS, C. G. (1949), *Greek Altars: Origins and Typology* (St. Louis).
YEGÜL, F. (1992), *Baths and Bathing in Classical Antiquity* (New York).
ZUMBACH, O. (1955), *Neuerungen in der Sprache der homerischen Hymnen* (Diss. Zürich).

General Index

Abarbaree 176, 249
accentuation 79, 184, 189, 192, 203, 277
  recessive 75
accusative:
  double accusative construction 84, 120, 172, 266
  plural prevocalic 27
Achilles:
  age relative to Aeneas 9, 12
  horses 210, 269, 287
  lyre playing 160
  marriage to Briseis 213, 233
Adonis 251
aegis 106–7
Aeneas:
  birth and lineage 7–10, 134, 135–6, 182, 243, 255, 256, 259–60, 266, 270, 284
  name, etymological pun on 257
Aeolic dialect 38, 44–5, 75, 114–15, 117, 155, 226, 256
  distinct tradition 41–2
Agamemnon:
  marriage feast for daughter 213
  oath not to sleep with Briseis 112, 222
Aineiadai 3–18, 49–50, 256–7, 259
Alcmene 119
alliteration 121, 133, 141–2, 188, 195, 216, 269, 274
altars on high 180
Amaltheia 106–7
ambrosia 146, 266, 287
anaphora 116
Anchises:
  beauty 9–10, 139, 159, 261
  brothers 207
  lineage, *see* Aeneas
  name, etymological pun on 261
  punishment by Zeus 136, 296
  reaction to Aphrodite's appearance on Ida 162, 164–6, 172–4
  shepherd on Ida 157, 160

Andromache 113, 177, 203–4
  marriage to Hector, *see* Hector
animal skins, symbol of strength 227
Aphrodite:
  Ares, affair with, *see* Ares
  bathing and adornment 20–1, 32–3, 141, 144–8, 161–72, 229–31, 234
  birth of 92
  boasting 14–18, 131, 133, 280–3, 296
  conducted by Hermes, *see* Hermes
  development as a goddess 18–19
  disguise 11, 161–72
  ἐν κήποις 150
  fragrance 142–3, 146–8
  garlanded 81
  laughter 92–3, 133, 163
  power over animals 19–20, 74, 152–6, 227
  power over Zeus 13–18
  shame 214, 234, 253–4, 277, 281, 284
  universal power 14, 74–5, 118–19, 122–3
  'works' (ἔργα) of 72–3
Apollo:
  birth of 97
  far-shooter 220–1
  Hestia, pursuer of 101, 106, 107–10; *see also* Poseidon
  lyre player 95
  warning to priests of Delphi 295
Ares 136
  Aphrodite, affair with 17–18, 34, 136, 141, 219, 222–3, 226, 234–5, 275
  Astyoche, affair with 233, 294
  'works' (ἔργα) of 73
Artemis:
  chorus of 33, 95–6, 193
  cities and justice 35, 98–101
  huntress 91–5
  Leucophryene 98
  patron of childbirth 97
  virgin 84–5, 90–1, 103, 104, 110–12
  worship of 96, 98–101

assonance 121, 135, 141–2
Astarte 20, 153
Astyanax, *see* Hector
Astyoche, *see* Ares
asyndeton 155, 218, 221, 239–40, 242–3, 275, 277, 289
Athena:
  daughter of Zeus 85
  disguised 152, 162, 173, 233
  patron of crafts 37, 88
  virgin 83–5, 103
  war goddess 86–7
  worship of 87
Athens 87, 100, 150, 181
Attic dialect 45, 117, 134, 155, 179, 200, 253, 290
  phase of transmission 45
Attis 248

bathing, *see* Aphrodite; type scenes
beds, preparation of 223, 225–9
Beroe 154, 246
bilingualism 49, 190–1
Bishop Melito of Sardes 82
Boucolion 157, 176
Briseis 170, 245; *see also* Achilles; Agamemnon
bucolic setting 137, 156–8, 227

Calypso 22, 32, 231, 271
  Odysseus, affair with 12, 142, 233, 250–1, 269, 275
Cephalus 270
Charites 81, 83, 91, 141, 145, 150, 170, 176–7, 181, 286
cheeks, radiating beauty 241–2
chiasmus 88, 133, 144
Circe:
  control over animals 152
  Odysseus, affair with 12, 22, 219, 222–3, 248–51
  oriental origin 251
  prophecy 202
Cleitus, abducted by Eos 264, 270–1
clothing and jewellery 20–1, 161–71, 229–31; *see also* Aphrodite
  gift from a goddess 275
  perfumed with oil 147, 166
  removal of 223–4, 229
  symbolic of power 20–1, 161–2, 234

Colchian language 190
Corinth 109
Crete 100, 106, 186, 190, 254
cult worship, lack of direct connection to 3–4, 179–80
Cybele 20, 22, 100, 152, 248
Cyprus 18–19, 21, 49, 75, 82–3, 169–70, 231, 232, 298
Cythera 82–3

Danae 119
dance, connected to marriage 195–6; *see also* Artemis
dative:
  of agent 226–7
  locatival 158, 238, 240
  plural, long and short 27, 127, 135, 285
δέ, 'explanatory' 74–5, 260–1
Delphi 103, 108–9, 115; *see also* Apollo
Demeter:
  disguise and lies to the daughters of Celeus 162, 185–7, 204, 225, 263
  epiphany 164, 238–42, 254
  foundation of cult in Eleusis 179
  nursing Demophon 191
  refusal of Zeus' pleas in mourning for Persephone 112
  warning to Eleusinians 295
Demetrius of Scepsis 5. n. 10
Demodocus 95, 246, 298
  Lay of 17–18, 143
digamma, neglect of 26–7, 28–31, 41, 81, 86, 87, 166, 175, 191, 208, 217, 230, 237, 255, 264, 266, 284, 287
digression 259, 284, 285
Dike 102–3, 118
Diomedes 6, 86, 113, 133, 180, 183, 233, 268
Dionysus 199, 274, 287
  birth and rearing 14 n. 43, 284
  Tyrrhenian pirates 175, 235, 254
  worship of 126
disguise, *see* Aphrodite; Athena; Demeter; Odysseus
Dolon 73, 113, 120, 154, 180
dowry 195, 211–12
Dumuzi 19–21, 135, 144, 161, 171

General Index 315

Eliot, T.S., *Four Quartets*, 195–6
enjambment 24, 105, 117, 129, 144, 146, 153, 159, 177, 206, 220, 231, 232, 238, 240, 241, 258, 268, 272, 278, 281
Eos 92, 270–1, 273
   Cleitus, affair with, *see* Cleitus
   Tithonus, affair with, *see* Tithonus
Ephesus 100
epiphany 10, 164–6, 234–5, 238–42, 245–6, 254–6, 294–5
Erichthonius' mares 199–200, 269
Eros 74, 76, 92, 128, 151, 179, 195, 197, 248
Etruscans 189
Eumaeus 152, 189, 191, 194, 227
Europa, abduction of 119, 140, 162, 193, 198, 203–4, 225, 253–4, 255
Eurycleia 113, 191, 215, 223
eyes, averting of
   fear 245–6
   maidenly shame 224–5

formulae:
   measure of oral composition 23–4
   modification of 27–31, 79, 80, 86, 114–15, 121, 127, 129, 133, 135, 138, 139, 144, 166, 181, 195, 201, 207, 209, 210, 217, 237, 242, 244–5, 255, 258, 267–8, 272, 273, 284, 285, 290
fragrance, *see* Aphrodite

Ganymedes 9–10, 193, 197, 253–5, 259–60, 262–70, 270, 285
Gargaron, Zeus' sanctuary 180
genitive, contracted -ου 27–31, 33, 41, 121, 127, 195, 217, 221, 273
Gilgamesh 22, 154, 251
Girard of Old Patras 52 n. 159
girdle 161, 169, 223, 229–31
'gnomic' aorist 13–14, 75, 76–7, 86, 90, 115, 119, 122–3
   augment of 76–7
gods and mortals:
   juxtaposition of 5, 7, 11, 133, 219, 232–4, 249–50, 254–5, 259–60, 271, 277, 285
   permanent separation of 10–18

gold, of Aphrodite and eastern adornment 73–4; *see also* Aphrodite
Gortyn Law Code 27 n. 100

Hades 222, 280; *see also* Persephone; Zeus
hand-holding 224
head nod, of assent and refusal 271–2
Hecate 35, 99–100, 177
Hector 120, 148, 160, 174, 180, 256
   Astyanax 165, 182
   marriage to Andromache 89, 226
   mourned after death 113
Helen 130, 142, 216, 248, 267
   abducted by Hermes 193
   Paris, affair with 130, 136, 141, 165, 214, 218, 222–3, 225, 235, 245–6, 278
Hephaestus 17–18, 82, 88, 168, 177, 226, 265, 275
Hera:
   birth and family 33, 34–5, 101–2, 105, 124–9
   journey over the Thracian mountains 196–9
   seduction of Zeus 32–3, 77, 92, 123, 130, 136, 138, 140, 141, 144, 148–9, 151, 162, 164, 168, 170, 186–7, 214, 218, 222–3, 229, 231, 235–6, 238, 278
   worship of 126
Heracles 9, 170, 213, 227
Hermann's bridge 77
Hermes:
   Aphrodite, conductor of 33, 185–6, 192–203
   Argeiphontes 194
   conductor/messenger 217–18, 262, 269
   lie to Priam 186
   Tros, messenger to 262, 268, 269
   nymphs 288
   Persephone conductor of 197
   Polymele, abduction of 33, 96, 140, 157, 193, 194–5, 233, 294
   precociousness 165
Hero 219
ἥρως, meaning of 159

General Index

Hestia 34–5, 46, 101–18, 125, 129, 136, 177; *see also* Apollo; Poseidon; Zeus
hiatus 24–5, 28, 80, 190, 203, 276
Homeric Hymns, collection of 3
homoeomeson 93
horses, *see* Achilles; Erichthonius' mares; Phrygia; Tros
hymnic conventions 69–72, 174–5, 295, 298

Ida 97, 137–8, 151–4, 178
impotence 22, 248–51
Inanna 19–20, 135, 144–5, 161, 171
interpolation 178–9, 207–9, 291–3
Ioannes Eugenikos 53 n. 159
Iris 130, 209–10, 216, 262, 267, 269
Ištar 20–1, 148, 152–3, 161, 169–70, 229, 231, 251

Kaz Dağ 138, 153
Kothar 82
Kronos 33, 35, 101, 104–5, 124
Kuthar 82

Lais, prostitute 143
Laomedon 268, 270
laughter, *see* Aphrodite; Paris
Lemnian women 76
Lesbos 41, 45–7, 49 n. 152, 117, 126–7
Leto 91, 128, 175
lies 8, 185–6, 190, 204, 214–16, 247–8; *see also* Demeter; Odysseus
lions 153–4, 228
list, expressing 'all nature' 74
love at first sight 137, 140
  unrequited 218–19, 222
lyre 95, 160–1; *see also* Apollo; Paris

Magna Mater, *see* Cybele
Magnesia 98
manuscript M, unique readings of 54–5, 98, 122–3, 133, 134, 150–1, 189, 191–2, 199–200, 206, 210, 217, 241, 242, 264–5, 278, 283, 292
marriage 73, 195–6, 201–2, 214
  feast 212–13
  gifts, *see* dowry
Medea 76, 190, 258
metathesis 28–31, 120–1, 217
Miletus 100

Milton, *Paradise Lost* 146, 289
modern Greek 74, 175
moon, comparison to 21, 170–1
Muses 35, 70–2, 85, 175, 177, 276, 288

Naevius' epitaph 233
names:
  as first word in poem 70–1
  etymological wordplay on 257, 261
Nausicaa 90, 113, 159, 164, 191
  meeting with Odysseus 8 n. 19, 173–5, 193, 205, 278
Near Eastern, literature and themes 18–22, 82, 94, 135, 144–5, 148, 152–4, 161, 169–171, 223, 229, 231, 251
nectar 266
Nereids 91, 155, 176
Nestor 174, 180, 183, 206, 244, 267, 276
Nestor's cup 81
nu mobile 28–31, 41, 80, 81, 138, 139, 151, 181, 201, 203, 211, 238, 245, 264, 268
nurses 191
nymphs 35, 85, 151–2, 176, 177–8, 284–94
  Hamadryads 288–91
  mortality 285–6, 292

oaths 90, 100, 110–13
Ocean 176, 186, 191, 273, 276
Odysseus:
  Calypso, affair with, *see* Calypso
  Circe, affair with, *see* Circe
  disguise 152, 162, 173, 235, 274
  lies 33, 186, 188, 190, 215
  Nausicaa, affair with, *see* Nausicaa
  reunion with Penelope 136, 215, 223, 235
  sons of 12
Oenone, affair with Paris 136, 246
old age 184–5, 249–50, 272, 273–4, 275, 276–7, 279–80
Olympia 100, 103, 109
opus, erotic sense 73
oral poetry 23–5
oratio obliqua 268
Orion 228, 270
Otreus 188–9
Otruntes 176

General Index

paederasty 262–3
Pan 95, 160, 224, 288
Pandora 36–7, 149, 170
Paphos 19, 21, 33, 169, 234
Paris:
   judge of beauty contest 127
   Helen, affair with, *see* Helen
   laughter at Diomedes 133
   lyre playing 160
   Oenone, affair with, *see* Oenone
Patroclus 112, 213, 223, 245, 257, 265–6
Peleus, *see* Thetis
Penelope 170, 175, 177, 204, 204, 218, 220, 241
   Odysseus, reunion with, *see* Odysseus
perfect, 'intensive' 80
performance context of *Hymns* 298
Persephone 90, 104, 295, 297
   abducted by Hades 193, 203–4, 288
Phrygia 49, 189
   horses of 210
Polymele, *see* Hermes
Polyphemus 158, 160, 228, 295
Poseidon; *see also* Zeus
   Hestia, pursuer of 101, 107–10; *see also* Apollo
   journey across the sea 152, 196–8
   prophecy about Aeneas 4, 6, 32, 256
   Tyro, affair with 223, 230, 235, 238, 253, 294
Potidaea 109
πότνια θηρῶν 20, 94, 152–3
praesens propheticum 256
prayer 173–4, 179–85, 247, 255
Priam 157, 164, 182, 186, 188, 218, 273, 276
Priamel 69–70

ransom 211–12, 267; *see also* dowry
relative clause expansion 71, 138, 173, 177, 178, 286
repetition 72–3, 83, 121, 137, 141–2, 158, 178, 188, 190, 195, 196, 215, 234, 245, 247, 255, 272, 278, 284, 287, 292, 293
Rhea 33, 104, 125, 128, 154

Rigveda 233
ring composition 149, 151, 234

sacrifice, language of 181
schema Pindaricum 171
Semele 119, 128
Silens 287, 289
Simaetha, and Delphis 222
sleep
   and death 244
   and love 76, 235–6, 237–8
softness, feature of female beauty 170
supplication 113, 158, 205–6, 212, 247
synizesis 117, 137, 179, 297

Telemachus 152, 165, 173, 188, 231, 233, 235, 244–5, 248, 267, 294
Teos 100
Themis 118, 173, 175, 281
Thetis:
   Peleus, marriage to 77, 107, 112, 157, 213, 230, 295
   pursued by Zeus 107–8
   supplicating Zeus 113, 158
Thor 107
time, passage of 236–7
Tithonus:
   cicada 270, 276
   Eos, affair with 9–10, 46, 144, 253–5, 259–60, 270–7, 285
tone of *Aphr.* 3, 235–6
transposition of lines 208–9
Troad 41, 49–50, 152, 153–4
Tros 140, 260, 262–3, 266
   horses of 267–70
Troy, windy 294
type scenes:
   arrival 148–9, 163, 222
   bathing and adornment 141, 144–5; *see also* Aphrodite; clothing and jewellery
   hospitality 227
   seduction 136, 162, 186, 214, 222–4, 227; *see also* Hera
Tyro, *see* Poseidon

Virgin Mary 90

war, compared to love 86–7

Zeus:
- aegis bearing 107
- affairs with mortal women 119–20, 140
- βουλή of 106, 232
- division of world, shared with Poseidon and Hades 121
- Hestia, relation to 35, 90, 102, 104–5, 111–17
- immortality, dispenser of 260
- justice, dispenser of 99–100
- pity on mortals 267
- pursuit of Thetis 107
- rearing in Crete 106
- revenge on Aphrodite 7–18, 118, 125, 129–31, 136, 204, 254, 277, 280–1
- weather god 106–7, 120–1

Index Locorum

ACUSILAUS (FOWLER)
fr. 39: 136

AESCHINES
Ctesiph.
108: 114

AESCHYLUS
A.
140: 99
1207: 73

Ch.
463–4: 190
585: 80
992: 283

Eu.
352: 198

Pers.
1–53: 74

Supp.
584: 200
676: 99
855: 196

fr. (*TrGF*)
174 (*Ὅπλων κρίσις*): 118

[AESCHYLUS]
PV
650: 75
872: 293
922–5: 107
941–2: 217

AGATHIAS SCHOLASTICUS
AP 6. 76: 136, 277

ALCAEUS (VOIGT)
frr.
3. 1: 109

42. 9–10: 230
75. 7–8: 46, 192
129: 126
130b. 19–20: 97
283. 8: 46, 225

ALCMAEONIS (DAVIES)
fr.
2. 1–2: 226

ALCMAN (PMGF)
frr.
1. 39–43 (*Parth.*): 164
3. 66–7: 79
77: 289
89: 78
89. 3–5: 80
89. 4: 285
116: 44, 258

ANACREON (PMG)
frr.
348: 98
358. 5–6: 298
388. 10: 45, 49 n. 154, 89
395. 1–2: 273
501. 11: 165

ANACREONTA (WEST)
51. 2: 274

ANTHOLOGIA GRAECA
5. 55. 7: 249
5. 139. 4: 83
5. 194. 1: 83
5. 253: 225
5. 275. 3: 229
6. 76: 136, 277
6. 283: 74
6. 350. 1: 160
7. 17. 3: 267

7. 161. 1: 217
7. 218. 8–10: 143
7. 221: 73
7. 305–3: 244
7. 324: 230
7. 338. 6: 244
7. 648. 2: 113
8. 50. 1: 279
9. 118. 1: 280
9. 416: 73
9. 668. 1: 179
11. 246. 3–4: 289
11. 380. 1: 118
12. 130. 3: 289
12. 240. 1: 274
14. 78. 4: 200
15. 37. 3: 272
15. 42. 1: 222
16. 168: 136
16. 357: 136
16. 365. 1: 222
16. 375. 1: 52, 243

APP. ANTH. (COUGNY)
1. 264: 136
1. 264. 4: 137
1. 298. 9: 207
2. 681. 3: 280
3. 281. 18: 127
6. 19. 2: 220

ANTIPATER SIDONIUS
AP 7. 161. 1: 217
AP 7. 218. 8–10: 143

ANTONINUS LIBERALIS
Met.
21. 1. 5: 73

APOLLODORUS
3. 12. 2: 266
3. 141: 136

APOLLONIUS RHODIUS
1. 3: 268
1. 18–19: 88
1. 60–1: 159
1. 90–1: 207
1. 130: 120
1. 132: 120
1. 213–18: 193
1. 263–4: 279
1. 264: 267
1. 288: 230
1. 307: 143
1. 615: 75
1. 684: 275
1. 790–1: 225
1. 803: 51, 75
1. 850: 51, 76
1. 907: 207
1. 952: 257
1. 1144–5: 154
1. 1158: 269
1. 1214: 279
1. 1272: 96
2. 87: 280
2. 124: 154
2. 227: 79
2. 424: 75
2. 476–89: 290
2. 477: 288
2. 501–2: 86
2. 522: 181
2. 719: 128
2. 1126: 209
3. 4–5: 163
3. 108: 83
3. 152: 51, 84
3. 159–63: 74, 197
3. 185: 132
3. 292: 80
3. 388: 103
3. 464: 51, 258
3. 528: 191
3. 530: 80
3. 532: 91
3. 536: 84
3. 558–63: 86
3. 729: 286
3. 731: 207
3. 883: 139
3. 968: 289

3. 1008–9: 225
3. 1022–4: 225
3. 1105: 87
3. 1373: 155
4. 1–2: 72
4. 102: 120
4. 412: 283
4. 648: 43, 114
4. 666: 200
4. 730–2: 190
4. 794–5: 81
4. 800: 118
4. 815: 209
4. 818: 268
4. 872: 275
4. 1133: 116
4. 1165: 77
4. 1491: 43, 103
4. 1523: 44, 258
4. 1715–16: 181
4. 1715: 97

fr.
12. 15 (CA
  Λέσβου κτίσις): 209

ARATUS
20: 114
204: 114
869: 132

ARCHILOCHUS (IEG)
frr.
19. 1: 73
122. 7: 78
124b. 4: 120
196: 92
196a. 42–53: 224
196a. 42–5: 228
196a. 52: 249
197: 213

ARISTONOUS OF CORINTH (CA)
2. 2–3: 103

ARISTOPHANES
Ach.
883: 118

Av.
214–22: 97
685–9: 250
798: 78
1067: 150
1442: 78
1731–42: 126

Eq.
616: 97
1327: 97

Lys.
86: 118
542: 42, 280
1014: 155

Nu.
308–10: 181

Pax.
775: 71
1099: 84
1270: 106

Ran.
674: 71

Thesm.
891: 124

Ves.
188–9: 244
738: 226

ARISTOTLE
Rh.
1413a 1: 95

AULUS GELLIUS
1. 24. 2: 233

BACCHYLIDES
Dith.
17. 10: 75

Enc.
20B. 8: 75

Index Locorum

Epin.
3. 2: 242
5. 16–30: 197
5. 175: 75
6. 1: 122
9. 1: 91
9. 9: 42, 228
11. 39: 189
fr. 20a. 17: 296

BATRACHOMYOMACHIA
172: 133

CALLIMACHUS
Aetia (frr. Pf.)
1. 3: 258–9
1. 25–8: 99
73. 1: 291
75. 2: 243
80. 11: 225
86. 1: 72
110. 56: 75

Hec. (frr. Pf.)
234: 120
260. 51: 114
309. 2: 289

Hy. 1
4: 294
14–20: 128
21: 230

Hy. 2
34: 74
95: 110

Hy. 3
1: 71
2–3: 93
3: 96
6–28: 111
6: 90
13–15: 96
18: 99
26–7: 50, 113
33–5: 99
110–12: 94
122: 50, 98–9
181: 96

183: 86
187: 86
206: 177
225: 99–100
240–3: 96
266: 96

Hy. 4
209: 230
258: 50, 96, 97
308: 75
325: 105, 115

Hy. 5
15–22: 84
66: 281
139: 97

Hy. 6
5: 274
25: 179
37–8: 288
37: 50, 241
41: 291
57–8: 50, 241
106: 237

CATULLUS
64. 8–10: 88

CERCIDAS (LOMIENTO)
fr.
6a. 1 (8. 1 *CA*): 210

CERTAMEN (ALLEN)
220: 265

CHRISTUS PATIENS
336: 80

CLAUDIAN
Cons. Stil.
2. 277: 51, 241

COLLUTHUS
19: 268
221: 289
229: 80
279: 110
305: 225

COMETAS
AP 15. 37. 3: 272
AP 15. 42. 1: 222

CRINAGORAS
AP 6. 350. 1: 160

CYPRIA (DAVIES)
frr.
1: 12
2: 107
4–5: 20 n. 62, 33 n. 115, 150
4. 1: 238
4. 5: 168
4. 6–7: 181
4. 7: 147
5: 145
5. 1–2: 81
5. 1: 92
5. 2: 150
5. 4–5: 176
5. 4: 177
5. 5: 138
7. 4: 41, 131
7. 12: 41, 78, 79, 294

DIOGENES (*TrGF*)
fr.
45. 1. 8: 97

DIOSCORIDES
AP 5. 55. 7: 249

EMPEDOCLES (DK)
frr.
21. 15: 78
81: 291

EPIGONI (DAVIES)
fr.
1: 106

EUDOCIA
de Martyrio Sancti Cypriani
30: 52, 72

Homerocentones
1. 1–3: 52, 77

Index Locorum

EURIPIDES
Alc.
1136: 122

Ba.
109–10: 289
139: 199
367: 257
508: 257
684–5: 289

Cyc.
61: 44, 159

Hec.
645–6: 83
1181: 80
1232: 180

Hel.
44–6: 193
136: 274
1308: 96
1311: 49 n. 154, 89

HF
1329: 290

Hipp.
447–61: 74
1129: 94
1268–81: 74
1287: 80
1301–2: 90

Hyps.
133: 79

Ion
465–6: 84
1606: 122

IA
501: 207
720: 213

IT
963: 42, 118
977: 78

Med.
1072: 274

Or.
456: 207

Ph.
1515–16: 289

Phaeth. (DIGGLE)
228–31: 109

Supp.
1211: 290

Tr.
32: 198
979–81: 111–12

frr. (*TrGF*)
815. 2: 78

GREGORY NAZIANZUS
AP 8. 50. 1: 279
Carm.
I 2. 1. 613 (*PG* 37. 569): 167
I 2. 2. 363 (*PG* 37. 607): 191
I 2. 2. 483 (*PG* 37. 616): 272
II. 1. 1. 77 (*PG* 37. 976): 179
II 1. 1. 107 (*PG* 37. 978): 275
II 1. 1. 434 (*PG* 37. 1002): 296
II. 2. 1. 241 (*PG* 37. 1468): 167
II 2. 3. 188 (*PG* 37. 1493): 213
II. 2. 6. 6–7 (*PG* 37. 1542. 11–1543. 1): 167

[HEGESINUS] (DAVIES, *DUBIA ET SPURIA*)
Atthis
fr. 3. 1: 233

HELLANICUS (*FGrH*)
4 F 140: 27

HERMIPPUS (*PCG*)
fr.
63. 20: 166

HERODOTUS
1. 91. 9: 190
1. 105: 83
4. 114: 43, 124
4. 135: 280

HESIOD
Op.
1–8: 142
1–2: 71
4: 217
48: 105
53: 296
62: 127
63–4: 37, 88
63: 34, 37 n. 127
71: 163
72: 149
73: 109, 145
74: 170
99: 106
108: 34, 207
136: 175
146: 80
155: 291
167: 12
171: 175
172: 159
182: 279
199: 203
225–47: 35, 99
230: 91
238: 80
245: 268
256–7: 103
256: 37–8, 89, 102
259: 102
277: 78
286: 180
300: 81
331: 184
347: 121
373: 84

Index Locorum

377: 90
406: 159
416: 132
420–1: 290
427: 168
430: 88
441: 159
483: 121
484: 131
502: 203
509–10: 37–8
509: 289
519–20: 36–8, 89
521: 36, 73
522–3: 144
526: 34, 36, 38, 86
529–30: 194
531: 36, 38, 80
534: 38
537: 34, 228
549: 175
556: 166
618–94: 38
623: 295
661: 121
699: 37 n. 127
718: 175
726: 206
730: 175
734: 34, 105

Th.
1: 71
2–8: 35
7–8: 286, 287
11–21: 175
11: 109
13: 35, 85, 85
16: 119
18: 105
22: 71
25: 106
28: 122
33: 175
39: 276
44: 297
49: 122
52: 106
61: 253
64: 145, 177

84: 276
97: 276
107: 34, 80
109: 196
114: 72
120: 127
121–2: 74
121: 76
122: 92
125: 220
129–30: 286
129: 34, 156
130: 179
135: 128
137: 105
148: 283
153: 127
168: 105
187: 288
191: 217
192–3: 82
194: 103
195: 119
196: 81
198–9: 82
199: 75
200: 92
203–4: 213
205: 92, 281
225: 280
228: 87
243–6: 155
245: 34, 288
251: 288
254: 123
259: 262
268: 286
277: 268
291: 129
321: 155, 171
328: 128
346–8: 284
357: 288
374: 92
380: 284
384: 90
393: 104
395–6: 104
404–52: 35, 99
405: 140

410: 218
415: 39, 265
426–7: 104
449: 39, 265
452–3: 101
453–500: 35, 104
453: 128
454: 34, 104–5
457: 104
467: 266
473: 105
480: 191
488: 272
495: 105
514: 113
517: 203
523: 76
537: 123
545: 128
546: 105
550: 128–9
561: 128
562: 140
570–89: 37
572: 103, 163
573: 34, 149
582: 36, 79, 115
585: 34, 36, 114
588: 39
602–4: 36, 115
604: 272
606: 278
622: 273
626: 268
640: 275
684: 221
721–5: 142
732: 144
735: 106
739: 280
766: 280
770: 34, 279
786–7: 290
796: 91
798: 226
802: 91
810: 280
822: 119, 176
825: 171
841: 273

HESIOD – (*Contd.*)
Th. – (*Contd.*)
878: 237
879: 187
887: 129
888: 85
889: 123
899: 87
918: 175
920: 219
921: 184
926: 34, 87, 109
945: 177
962: 119
966: 106
980: 34, 73, 219
984: 270
988: 273
989: 92
1006–10: 12, 107
1008–10: 135
1008: 81
1009: 137, 159
1022: 106

[HESIOD]
Sc.
8: 73
16: 229
40: 222
47: 73
124–5: 170
177: 155
204: 196
218: 165
248: 153
280: 95
295: 230
318: 265
322: 113
381: 159
421–2: 289
421: 44
442: 245
457: 258

frr.
1. 4: 230
1. 6–7: 12 n. 36
1. 7: 41, 135

5. 1: 157
10a. 17: 285
17a. 14: 157
22. 9: 201
23a. 19: 91
23a. 32–3: 189
25. 24: 290
25. 31: 119
26. 24: 218
30. 31: 273
30. 33: 233
31: 253
31. 4: 8 n. 21, 202
33a. 18: 283
37. 6: 41, 213
43a. 1: 81
43a. 6: 77
43a. 52: 121
51. 1–2: 296
59. 4: 163
64: 288
70. 32: 294
70. 40: 77
75. 10: 170
105. 3: 218
123: 286
123. 1: 285
124. 2: 73
140: 193
141: 140
141. 26: 128
145. 16: 265
165. 6: 191
165. 16: 289
171. 4: 159
176. 1: 92
180. 10: 41, 44, 259
180. 13: 103
185. 17: 73
185. 23: 127
197. 7: 41
199. 4: 41
204. 50: 237
204. 102–3: 12
204. 112: 77
204. 128: 132
205. 2: 273
209. 5: 285
210–11: 107
211. 3: 256

211. 6: 41, 213
215. 1: 159
229. 8: 273
229. 16: 262
233. 2: 41, 83
234. 2: 128
235. 1–3: 257
235. 5: 110
239. 3: 255
240. 4: 77
240. 7: 213
253. 3: 73
296. 3: 294
302. 21: 294
303. 2: 121
320: 78
343. 15: 77,
343. 16: 233

HIPPONAX (IEG)
fr.
128. 1: 71

HOMER
Il.
1. 2: 280
1. 5: 106
1. 14: 221
1. 18: 297
1. 23: 44, 211
1. 29: 275
1. 37: 221
1. 39–41: 16 n. 48
1. 41: 272
1. 49: 221
1. 55: 90
1. 57: 228
1. 61: 77
1. 68: 115
1. 70: 266
1. 114: 201
1. 118: 281
1. 122: 128, 187
1. 125: 187
1. 129: 43, 189
1. 131: 294
1. 133: 184
1. 135: 278
1. 143: 242
1. 155: 91, 289

Index Locorum

1. 156: 256
1. 157: 97
1. 170: 292
1. 174–5: 211
1. 177–80: 87
1. 184: 142
1. 185: 115
1. 199–201: 247
1. 199: 165
1. 213: 132
1. 218: 122
1. 221–2: 297
1. 237: 291
1. 240: 134
1. 249: 276
1. 268: 285
1. 280: 33, 188
1. 290: 146
1. 330: 294
1. 339: 119
1. 342: 272
1. 360–1: 243
1. 362: 84
1. 377: 211
1. 388: 112
1. 396: 245
1. 397: 271
1. 414: 243
1. 418: 90
1. 425: 293
1. 436: 141
1. 437: 130
1. 449: 139
1. 455: 272
1. 459–60: 243
1. 477: 273
1. 489: 134
1. 493: 275
1. 498–9: 158
1. 501: 113
1. 504: 272
1. 511: 290
1. 520: 127
1. 524: 271
1. 525: 255
1. 547–9: 219
1. 586: 210
1. 597–8: 265
1. 598: 265
1. 603: 95

1. 609–11: 226
2. 2: 238
2. 5: 26, 275
2. 14: 168
2. 19: 238
2. 21: 261
2. 45: 231
2. 58: 164, 262
2. 71: 237
2. 82: 127
2. 103: 217
2. 118: 122
2. 127: 265
2. 196–7: 290
2. 205: 105
2. 219: 145
2. 230: 267
2. 238: 208
2. 247: 297
2. 260: 278
2. 270: 133
2. 278: 196
2. 285: 75
2. 299–300: 208
2. 338: 80
2. 348: 106
2. 366: 202
2. 412–13: 183
2. 412: 122, 128
2. 414: 239
2. 434: 187
2. 445: 78
2. 467: 237
2. 479: 231
2. 484: 72, 285
2. 489–90: 283
2. 491: 106
2. 503: 159
2. 512–15: 294
2. 514: 103, 113, 163
2. 515: 233
2. 547: 71
2. 548: 200
2. 554: 149
2. 570: 198, 298
2. 592: 198
2. 599: 296
2. 600: 126
2. 614: 80
2. 619: 155

2. 637: 159
2. 651: 194
2. 660: 294
2. 669: 75
2. 693: 134
2. 715: 127
2. 718: 191
2. 758: 155
2. 761: 72
2. 779: 160
2. 803–4: 49 n. 155, 190
2. 820–1: 132, 135, 284
2. 821: 233
2. 827: 220
2. 867: 49 n. 155, 190
3. 5: 150
3. 17: 155
3. 50: 207
3. 53: 184
3. 54: 160
3. 64: 73
3. 89: 289
3. 114: 231
3. 124: 127
3. 125: 158
3. 138: 218
3. 139: 75, 130, 216
3. 149: 26
3. 150–2: 276
3. 158: 127
3. 173: 87
3. 181–90: 188
3. 184: 190
3. 185–7: 189
3. 185: 210
3. 195: 289
3. 204: 248
3. 217: 225
3. 236: 84
3. 238: 188
3. 243: 200, 201
3. 250: 243
3. 285: 183
3. 295: 265
3. 301: 77
3. 305: 294
3. 307: 256
3. 322: 222
3. 327: 43, 267
3. 333: 207

HOMER – (*Contd.*)
Il. – (*Contd.*)
3. 340: 228
3. 374–447: 136
3. 374: 163
3. 386–98: 235
3. 394: 195
3. 396–8: 245
3. 396: 170
3. 398: 165
3. 414: 282
3. 415: 140
3. 424: 92
3. 426: 85
3. 427: 225, 246
3. 438–46: 214
3. 441–6: 186
3. 442: 141, 278
3. 446: 76, 130, 141
3. 447: 222, 224
3. 448: 222, 235
4. 10: 92
4. 38: 281
4. 44: 44, 297
4. 58: 105, 207
4. 59–61: 33, 125–6, 128
4. 59: 101, 104–5
4. 61: 218
4. 62–3: 180
4. 105–9: 228
4. 124: 269
4. 151: 245
4. 169: 258
4. 184: 255
4. 255: 294
4. 262–3: 122
4. 315: 279
4. 394: 271
4. 401: 290
4. 410: 297
4. 437–8: 49 n. 155, 190
4. 441: 127
4. 443: 241
4. 444: 75, 279
4. 465: 131
4. 473: 134
4. 482: 290
4. 487: 290
4. 515: 128
5. 7: 241

5. 29: 75
5. 51–2: 94
5. 61: 88
5. 66: 192
5. 68: 278
5. 118: 183
5. 120: 184
5. 127–8: 123
5. 131: 163
5. 170: 172
5. 183: 233
5. 187: 246
5. 194: 167
5. 215: 144
5. 222–3: 268
5. 226: 166
5. 248: 119
5. 265–7: 262
5. 265: 268
5. 266: 267
5. 312–13: 135
5. 312: 24 n. 79
5. 313: 139, 144, 157
5. 315: 167
5. 317: 156
5. 330: 75
5. 332: 118
5. 338–9: 145
5. 342: 177
5. 347–51: 86
5. 369: 287
5. 371–2: 142
5. 375: 24 n. 79, 92, 187
5. 381: 114
5. 382: 210
5. 414: 202
5. 423: 140
5. 427: 119
5. 428–30: 86
5. 429: 73, 213
5. 458: 75
5. 461: 43, 192
5. 464: 134
5. 474: 30, 207
5. 489: 153
5. 513: 156
5. 520: 130
5. 523: 29, 138
5. 555: 144
5. 556: 30, 237

5. 592: 109
5. 652: 180
5. 696: 291
5. 700: 150
5. 721: 117
5. 725: 172
5. 732: 268
5. 751: 79
5. 769: 297
5. 771: 180
5. 773: 85
5. 782: 198
5. 815: 248
5. 836: 245
5. 846: 245
5. 876: 29, 80
5. 883: 75
5. 885–7: 252
5. 887: 249
5. 896: 188
6. 21–8: 157
6. 21–2: 176
6. 24: 188
6. 46: 211
6. 119–236: 6
6. 123: 29, 77
6. 140: 133
6. 147–8: 289
6. 165: 220
6. 178: 269
6. 198: 233
6. 200: 133
6. 233: 224
6. 250: 129
6. 257: 180
6. 294–5: 167
6. 301: 97
6. 304: 85
6. 305: 109
6. 311: 272
6. 321: 158
6. 339: 113
6. 345–8: 267
6. 398: 226
6. 402–3: 5 n. 13
6. 418: 87
6. 419–20: 178, 288
6. 420: 285
6. 430: 184
6. 438: 177

Index Locorum

6. 458: 203–4	8. 299: 84	9. 588–9: 150
6. 459: 132	8. 305: 127	9. 608: 232
6. 469–70: 165	8. 316: 279	9. 623: 159
6. 475–81: 174	8. 322: 153	9. 658–68: 227
6. 475: 132	8. 325: 132	9. 658–61: 223
6. 476–7: 182	8. 335: 246	10. 15: 274
6. 477: 183	8. 348: 291	10. 17: 26, 275
6. 479: 132	8. 383: 117	10. 29: 155
6. 488: 119	8. 395: 79	10. 32: 271
6. 505: 150	8. 409: 269	10. 134: 145
6. 525: 281	8. 453: 88	10. 138: 242
7. 45: 75	8. 499: 294	10. 162: 245
7. 60: 113	8. 539: 268	10. 197: 155
7. 87: 132	8. 549: 298	10. 211: 237
7. 102: 127	8. 559: 269	10. 224: 156
7. 122: 269	9. 41: 215	10. 242: 214
7. 131: 222	9. 61: 293	10. 292: 180, 181
7. 179–80: 183	9. 70: 213	10. 293: 206
7. 180: 73	9. 132: 112	10. 315: 73
7. 207: 149	9. 133: 222	10. 322–3: 268
7. 208: 150	9. 139: 192	10. 324: 180
7. 237: 191	9. 147: 212	10. 334: 154
7. 256: 199	9. 150: 159	10. 339: 165
7. 260: 192	9. 159: 117	10. 368: 133
7. 382: 158	9. 183: 164	10. 391: 120
7. 392: 201	9. 184: 84	10. 403: 77, 131
7. 433–4: 237	9. 186: 160	10. 431: 210
7. 446–53: 110	9. 197: 175	10. 439: 172
8. 2: 121	9. 228: 80	10. 441–2: 131
8. 35: 295	9. 232: 237	10. 454–5: 113
8. 39–40: 182	9. 274: 112	10. 516: 295
8. 42: 274	9. 275: 222	10. 518: 243
8. 47–8: 180	9. 289: 212	10. 552–3: 85
8. 47: 26, 138, 151, 153	9. 292: 159	10. 566: 157
8. 48: 143, 144	9. 389: 71	11. 1–2: 270
8. 103: 275	9. 390: 37	11. 2: 243
8. 124: 279	9. 410: 210	11: 46: 73
8. 143: 121	9. 431: 112	11. 60: 271
8. 156: 184	9. 440: 279	11. 66: 113
8. 159: 221	9. 441: 183	11. 78: 271
8. 162: 116	9. 444–5: 220	11. 86–90: 237
8. 198: 272	9. 446: 272	11. 89: 141
8. 203: 207	9. 466: 237	11. 131: 211
8. 218: 90	9. 503: 85, 96	11. 138: 214
8. 227: 96	9. 510: 112	11. 183: 138
8. 242: 272	9. 517: 277	11. 185: 210
8. 258: 225	9. 538: 114	11. 218: 72
8. 279: 30, 221	9. 539: 76	11. 234: 231
8. 286: 180	9. 541: 291	11. 263: 222
8. 296: 94	9. 545: 206	11. 266: 145

HOMER – (*Contd.*)
Il. – (*Contd.*)
11. 378–9: 133
11. 403: 264
11. 427: 44, 274
11. 438: 41, 131
11. 443: 180
11. 447: 225
11. 461: 183
11. 474–81: 153
11. 479: 198
11. 494: 289
11. 533: 155
11. 550: 116
11. 595: 225
11. 618: 157
11. 638: 127, 221
11. 645: 232
11. 657: 266
11. 668–9: 276
11. 669: 26, 226, 276
11. 683: 269
11. 727: 181
11. 741: 80
11. 811: 141
12. 17: 108, 110
12. 27: 220
12. 34: 108, 110
12. 63: 112
12. 132: 289
12. 146–50: 153
12. 242: 189
12. 252: 29, 121
12. 282: 228
12. 284: 252
12. 304: 206
12. 311: 116
12. 322–8: 278
12. 439–40: 237
12. 454: 286
13. 3: 146
13. 16: 226
13. 21–31: 152
13. 21: 143
13. 27–31: 196–7
13. 29: 269
13. 35: 287
13. 103: 154, 155
13. 111: 275
13. 121: 90
13. 168: 226
13. 176: 273
13. 179: 180
13. 196: 289
13. 202: 170
13. 217: 189
13. 240: 157
13. 305: 155
13. 353: 226
13. 436: 183
13. 456: 177
13. 481–2: 257
13. 483: 94
13. 484: 273
13. 562: 249
13. 581: 44, 258
13. 665: 150
13. 674: 266
13. 716: 87
13. 777: 188
14. 76: 114
14. 91: 283
14. 153–351: 136
14. 157: 138
14. 158: 138
14. 160: 123
14. 161: 26
14. 163–5: 131
14. 164–5: 238
14. 166–86: 32–3
14. 168: 105
14. 169–71: 229
14. 169: 26, 141, 144
14. 172: 26, 141, 147–8
14. 173–87: 20, 162
14. 178–9: 167
14. 178: 147
14. 181: 231
14. 182–3: 168
14. 183–6: 164
14. 185: 170
14. 187: 149
14. 188: 119, 151
14. 193: 187
14. 194: 118
14. 198–9: 74, 77
14. 200: 273
14. 202: 191
14. 203: 128
14. 206–7: 274
14. 211: 92
14. 214–17: 33 n. 114
14. 214: 231
14. 216: 281
14. 222–3: 92
14. 225–30: 197–8
14. 227–8: 199
14. 227: 150
14. 234: 79
14. 237: 233
14. 243: 118
14. 253: 238
14. 264: 293
14. 267–8: 177
14. 267–8: 211
14. 268: 218
14. 281–93: 149
14. 282: 151
14. 283: 151, 153
14. 292–15. 13: 236
14. 294: 123, 140, 141, 278
14. 296: 199
14. 297: 51, 162
14. 300–40: 186–7
14. 303: 191
14. 305–6: 186, 274
14. 307: 138
14. 308: 198
14. 312–28: 214
14. 313–28: 119
14. 315–16: 77
14. 328: 76, 130, 141
14. 340: 29, 86
14. 342: 218
14. 346: 222
14. 347–9: 223
14. 347: 152
14. 352–3: 235
14. 361: 77
14. 398: 289
14. 405: 231
14. 427: 119
14. 444–5: 176
14. 475: 258
14. 484: 291
14: 508: 72
15. 12: 267
15. 37–8: 122
15. 49–55: 215

Index Locorum 329

15. 75: 271
15. 107: 127
15. 115–18: 218
15. 144: 75
15. 151: 151, 153
15. 153: 196
15. 175: 106
15. 184–99: 108
15. 189: 121
15. 224: 206
15. 231–2: 221
15. 273: 289
15. 412: 88
15. 461: 123
15. 550: 237
15. 551: 273
15. 590: 221
15. 591: 225
15. 592: 198
15. 632–3: 233
15. 632: 191
15. 636–8: 159
15. 660–6: 206
16. 22: 157
16. 57: 189
16. 103: 282
16. 112: 72
16. 148–51: 269
16. 148: 258
16. 156–63: 153
16. 157: 198, 276
16. 174: 78
16. 176: 233, 283
16. 179–85: 193, 294
16. 181–2: 140
16. 181: 203
16. 183: 26, 30, 33, 91, 96, 194
16. 184: 157, 233
16. 191: 191
16. 232: 121
16. 325: 141
16. 350: 278
16. 395: 79
16. 430: 257
16. 431: 267
16. 432: 29, 127
16. 453: 291
16. 481: 256
16. 499: 281
16. 636: 96, 157
16. 646: 165
16. 650–1: 131
16. 669: 273
16. 679: 273
16. 719: 189
16. 779: 237
16. 795: 274
16. 853: 290
16. 859: 243
17. 5: 129
17. 20–1: 154
17. 41: 206
17. 53–5: 289
17. 77: 131
17. 83: 279
17. 141: 225
17. 170: 278
17. 176: 29, 121
17. 180: 215
17. 198: 245
17. 213: 244
17. 263: 78
17. 321: 232
17. 322–3: 220
17. 323: 140
17. 332: 276
17. 374: 221
17. 375: 293
17. 415–82: 218
17. 441: 267
17. 447: 224
17. 495: 155
17. 502–4: 219
17. 593: 107
17. 647: 86
17. 659: 116
17. 692: 209
17. 697: 268
17. 748: 96
18. 4: 113
18. 11: 291
18. 38–51: 176
18. 39–40: 155
18. 61: 31, 184
18. 64: 294
18. 85: 132, 258
18. 86–7: 11 n. 29
18. 86: 286
18. 88: 258
18. 91: 278
18. 105: 278
18. 122: 285
18. 134: 297
18. 184: 128
18. 205: 241
18. 283: 91
18. 289: 73
18. 308: 131
18. 339: 285
18. 356: 29, 127
18. 363: 233
18. 366: 218
18. 382: 177
18. 389: 231
18. 401: 26, 168–9, 230
18. 402–3: 275
18. 432–3: 77
18. 434: 112
18. 442: 184
18. 463: 255, 293
18. 495: 96
18. 515: 273
18. 524–5: 159
18. 525–6: 160
18. 529: 168
18. 531: 150
18. 532: 267
18. 567: 37 n. 127
18. 569–72: 95
18. 577: 159
18. 590–606: 195
18. 593: 195
18. 603: 196
18. 610: 167
19. 1–2: 273
19. 9: 232
19. 38: 266
19. 86: 119
19. 99: 43, 81, 202
19. 112–13: 283
19. 113: 112
19. 153: 295
19. 155: 294
19. 175: 49 n. 155
19. 176: 222
19. 186: 293
19. 284–5: 245
19. 285: 170
19. 286: 127, 221

HOMER – (Contd.)
Il. – (Contd.)
19. 293: 188
19. 299: 212–13
19. 336: 275
19. 340: 267
19. 381: 242
19. 400: 210
19. 404: 210
20. 7–9: 176
20. 8–9: 178
20. 8: 26, 179
20. 9: 26, 159, 179
20. 23: 156
20. 40: 92
20. 65: 280
20. 96: 94
20. 102: 132
20. 105–7: 108
20. 105–6: 295
20. 105: 73, 85
20. 133: 120
20. 146: 147
20. 201: 191
20. 203–9: 108
20. 206: 295
20. 208–9: 135
20. 209: 119
20. 215–41: 266
20. 215: 105
20. 221–9: 269
20. 234: 264
20. 235: 33, 262
20. 236–9: 128
20. 237: 270
20. 240: 184
20. 264: 272
20. 266: 131
20. 276: 192
20. 293–308: 6
20. 294: 227
20. 305: 124
20. 307–8: 4, 32, 256–7, 262–3
20. 347: 256
20. 384: 176
21. 63: 200, 201
21. 73: 26, 247
21. 92: 219
21. 109: 33, 188
21. 178: 168
21. 268: 78
21. 286: 224
21. 288: 165
21. 326: 78
21. 415: 246
21. 448–9: 139
21. 448: 30
21. 460: 129
21. 470: 94, 109
21. 476: 127
21. 485: 94
21. 497: 217
21. 507: 147
21. 511: 81
21. 516: 190
21. 599: 132
22. 5: 43, 272
22. 9–10: 248
22. 40: 227
22. 43: 258
22. 49: 278
22. 51: 189
22. 60: 184
22. 65: 209
22. 74: 273
22. 77–8: 274
22. 77: 273
22. 87: 184, 294
22. 128: 113, 281
22. 134–5: 171
22. 154: 30, 166
22. 171–2: 180
22. 221: 113
22. 261: 266
22. 263: 182
22. 291: 283
22. 319: 171
22. 324: 171
22. 338: 206
22. 370: 262
22. 393: 240
22. 423: 289
22. 441: 271
22. 445: 272
22. 508: 279
23. 14: 76
23. 42: 112
23. 62–3: 238
23. 66: 245
23. 67: 149
23. 81: 44, 274
23. 108: 76
23. 118: 289
23. 138: 202
23. 142: 289
23. 144: 96
23. 148: 144
23. 166: 237
23. 175: 134
23. 181: 134
23. 186–7: 148
23. 198–9: 209
23. 206: 226
23. 208: 91
23. 219–20: 165
23. 277: 188
23. 362: 156
23. 460: 244
23. 475: 267
23. 501: 151
23. 512: 206
23. 591–4: 220
23. 600: 156
23. 623: 275
23. 705: 198
23. 807: 231
23. 868: 297
24. 24: 288
24. 60: 191
24. 63: 95, 213
24. 67: 233
24. 77: 269
24. 88: 128
24. 104: 210
24. 105: 266
24. 132: 290
24. 139–40: 182
24. 159: 269
24. 162: 166
24. 166: 209
24. 171: 165, 243
24. 209: 288
24. 215: 285
24. 259: 131
24. 282: 123
24. 294: 245
24. 309: 182
24. 312: 245
24. 329: 228

Index Locorum

24. 335: 177
24. 339: 218
24. 343: 194
24. 345: 203
24. 354: 243
24. 359: 276
24. 373: 215
24. 387: 134
24. 389–404: 186
24. 397: 217
24. 431: 157
24. 434: 120
24. 466–7: 206
24. 483–4: 164
24. 485–92: 206
24. 487: 184, 272
24. 497: 134
24. 516: 273
24. 526: 278
24. 529: 124
24. 533: 265
24. 555: 211
24. 558: 184
24. 605: 30, 221
24. 614: 228
24. 615–16: 286
24. 616: 31, 35, 287
24. 643–8: 227
24. 671–2: 224
24. 675: 123
24. 676: 233
24. 694: 297
24. 699: 87
24. 712: 113, 196
24. 728: 272
24. 730: 129
24. 749: 256

Od.
1. 1: 71
1. 14: 109
1. 32: 233
1. 39: 110
1. 62: 257
1. 71: 75
1. 84: 217
1. 119: 153
1. 123: 175
1. 138: 288
1. 143: 265

1. 156: 85
1. 202: 233
1. 208: 245
1. 241–8: 267
1. 257: 244
1. 263: 146
1. 272–3: 203
1. 277: 212
1. 365–6: 97
1. 366: 30, 201
1. 378: 146
1. 420: 248
1. 426: 181
1. 428: 129
1. 432: 129
1. 437: 231
2. 58–9: 264
2. 110: 204
2. 120: 81
2. 143: 146
2. 170: 206
2. 182: 199
2. 196: 212
2. 213: 160
2. 251: 248
2. 395: 76, 238
3. 12: 162
3. 19: 248
3. 39: 207
3. 42: 106
3. 49: 209
3. 114: 77
3. 159: 143
3. 171: 150
3. 172: 294
3. 184: 266
3. 209: 207
3. 222: 162
3. 224: 126
3. 236: 279
3. 246: 244
3. 259: 87
3. 282: 77
3. 296: 132
3. 304: 73
3. 309: 213
3. 320: 43, 245
3. 332: 180
3. 361: 30, 268
3. 380–4: 174

3. 380–1: 8 n.20
3. 380: 175
3. 382: 181
3. 383: 206
3. 394: 106
3. 416: 294
3. 422: 265
3. 434: 157
3. 451: 209
3. 465: 106
3. 468: 139
4. 3: 212–13
4. 10: 206
4. 15: 213
4. 45: 170
4. 50: 228
4. 63–4: 206
4. 64: 206
4. 121: 91, 142
4. 123: 157
4. 157: 215
4. 188: 144
4. 209: 267
4. 276: 294
4. 294–305: 227
4. 337: 159
4. 348: 51, 84, 246
4. 355: 31, 290
4. 397: 233
4. 473: 181
4. 477: 78
4. 540: 184
4. 581: 77
4. 589: 181
4. 627: 226
4. 723: 207
4. 727–8: 267
4. 729: 90
4. 810: 177
4. 825: 26, 255
4. 833: 184
5. 1–2: 270
5. 4: 122
5. 27: 79
5. 32: 119
5. 35: 261
5. 37–8: 210
5. 37: 211
5. 49–54: 197–8
5. 49: 203

HOMER – (Contd.)
Od. – (Contd.)
5. 51: 150
5. 56: 80
5. 63: 289
5. 64: 98
5. 67: 80
5. 74: 156
5. 86: 166, 232
5. 93: 266
5. 118–36: 11 n. 29, 22, 250–1
5. 119: 32, 252
5. 123: 90
5. 129: 233, 271
5. 146: 297
5. 148: 203
5. 149: 109
5. 150: 26, 269
5. 165: 266
5. 178: 282
5. 195–9: 275
5. 205: 220
5. 215: 109
5. 226: 288
5. 231: 231
5. 241–2: 202
5. 264: 142, 147
5. 300: 248
5. 340: 140
5. 347: 30
5. 366: 76
5. 385: 76
5. 427: 90
5. 443: 168
5. 450: 252
5. 476: 181
5. 477: 207
6. 16: 164, 262
6. 18: 159, 176
6. 19: 144
6. 25 ff.: 193
6. 25: 188
6. 26: 166
6. 33: 113
6. 38: 30, 166
6. 66: 44, 184, 283
6. 101: 287
6. 106: 269
6. 109: 90, 113, 163
6. 111: 30
6. 123–4: 178
6. 124: 159, 179
6. 149–85: 8 n. 19, 173, 205
6. 149: 175
6. 152: 164, 262
6. 156: 281
6. 157: 294
6. 162: 158
6. 175: 175, 252
6. 216: 273
6. 228: 163
6. 232–4: 88
6. 235: 274
6. 244–5: 278
6. 270: 98
6. 327: 182
7. 12: 191
7. 20: 37 n. 127
7. 50–1: 165
7. 57: 127
7. 94: 271
7. 109–11: 37
7. 114–16: 289
7. 137: 288
7. 162: 231
7. 180: 75
7. 191: 181
7. 201–2: 13 n. 39
7. 214: 232
7. 218: 266
7. 221: 126
7. 246–7: 219
7. 255–60: 275
7. 259: 166
7. 264–5: 275
7. 284: 78
7. 286: 238
7. 291: 127
7. 313: 201
8. 14: 139
8. 65: 231
8. 67: 160
8. 84–5: 246
8. 92: 267
8. 99: 96
8. 108: 165
8. 109: 196
8. 116: 127, 278
8. 121: 156
8. 175: 291
8. 176: 183
8. 212: 119
8. 248–55: 95
8. 256: 294
8. 266–366: 136, 177
8. 267: 81
8. 277: 226
8. 279: 239
8. 288: 81
8. 291: 222
8. 295: 235
8. 297: 223
8. 298: 18, 26, 34, 46, 270, 275
8. 308: 163
8. 334–42: 219
8. 335: 217
8. 321–27: 17–18
8. 362–5: 17, 32–3, 141, 234
8. 362: 92, 143
8. 363–6: 142
8. 363: 26, 143, 144
8. 364–5: 145
8. 364: 26
8. 365: 26, 145, 146
8. 390: 183
8. 448: 109
8. 457: 159
8. 458: 157
8. 461: 132
8. 492: 298
8. 493: 88
8. 499: 298
8. 541: 279
8. 573: 283
8. 585–6: 252
8. 585: 206
9. 9: 265
9. 52: 232
9. 58: 237
9. 84: 287
9. 113: 228
9. 130: 198
9. 135: 116
9. 143: 171
9. 155: 285
9. 189: 160

Index Locorum

9. 192: 158
9. 236: 288
9. 257: 228
9. 284: 273
9. 353: 282
9. 364: 189
9. 424: 275
9. 429: 156
9. 502–3: 295
9. 502: 77
9. 516: 76
9. 521: 26, 119
10. 2: 256
10. 11: 129
10. 38–9: 213
10. 56: 150
10. 130: 156
10. 171: 78
10. 180: 78
10. 195: 196
10. 210–19: 152, 154
10. 211: 181
10. 212: 154
10. 223: 87
10. 230: 144
10. 235: 124
10. 253: 181
10. 273: 203
10. 283: 256
10. 299: 175
10. 301: 22, 248, 251
10. 306: 131
10. 314: 231
10. 331: 194, 201, 202
10. 334–480: 222
10. 339–40: 219
10. 341: 251
10. 347: 223
10. 352–3: 227
10. 352: 231
10. 366: 231
10. 376: 266
10. 433: 154
10. 438: 293
10. 479: 156
10. 498: 184
10. 521: 249, 252
10. 536: 249
10. 541: 271
10. 544: 231

11. 22: 202
11. 29: 249
11. 39: 37 n. 127
11. 49: 249
11. 61: 232
11. 66–8: 206
11. 66: 279
11. 93: 291
11. 96: 248
11. 123: 287
11. 130: 181
11. 146: 90
11. 175: 115
11. 184: 29, 115
11. 185: 290
11. 186: 87
11. 230: 275
11. 235–52: 223
11. 236: 295
11. 244: 124
11. 245: 230, 235, 238
11. 248–52: 10 n. 24, 253, 294
11. 250: 191
11. 251: 297
11. 278: 241
11. 281–2: 264
11. 283: 106
11. 286: 96
11. 301: 200
11. 337: 164, 269
11. 381: 292
11. 386: 90
11. 394: 276
11. 438: 282
11. 469: 278
11. 489: 221
11. 490: 44, 198
11. 497: 273
11. 536: 146
11. 574: 228
11. 580: 128
11. 587: 290
11. 611: 154
11. 612: 87
11. 623: 132
12. 1–6: 273
12. 25–6: 202
12. 25: 203
12. 116: 80

12. 131–3: 286
12. 138: 287
12. 142: 271
12. 159: 237
12. 226: 268
12. 318: 31
12. 319: 179
12. 338: 238
12. 395: 224
13: 41–2: 183
13. 70: 238
13. 74: 244
13. 79–80: 238, 244
13. 83: 151
13. 90–3: 238
13. 103–4: 288
13. 136: 26, 210, 211
13. 196: 289
13. 221–7: 162, 173
13. 222: 265
13. 231: 173
13. 256–86: 186
13. 263: 192
13. 288: 162
13. 289: 87
13. 299–300: 248
13. 324: 205, 279
13. 351: 296
13. 362: 255
13. 363: 288
13. 369: 157
13. 391: 109
13. 399: 274
13. 405: 265
13. 429–38: 162
13. 431: 274
14. 3: 202
14. 6: 181
14. 15: 256
14. 29–36: 152
14. 44: 184
14. 50–1: 227
14. 154: 149
14. 159: 105
14. 192–359: 186
14. 205: 138
14. 211: 198, 206
14. 251: 297
14. 331: 112
14. 341: 231

HOMER – (Contd.)
Od. – (Contd.)
14. 395–400: 142
14. 412: 276
14. 423: 133
14. 426: 291
14. 435–6: 288
14. 436: 133
14. 485: 245
14. 488: 92
14. 506: 238
15. 39: 265
15. 56: 271
15. 60: 166
15. 107–8: 167
15. 185–6: 122
15. 234: 90
15. 246: 184
15. 248: 134
15. 250: 271
15. 251: 264
15. 310–11: 204
15. 319: 30, 217
15. 348: 184
15. 366: 273
15. 403: 189
15. 418: 87
15. 427: 194
15. 460: 170
16. 4–6: 152
16. 28: 86
16. 61–7: 186
16. 78–9: 284
16. 79: 149
16. 87: 258
16. 106: 221
16. 117: 261
16. 154–80: 162, 235
16. 157–63: 152
16. 158: 87
16. 176: 274
16. 179: 165, 245
16. 181–5: 173
16. 187–8: 33, 188
16. 187: 26
16. 231: 26, 210
16. 280: 280
16. 282: 90
16. 340: 268
16. 396: 159

16. 408: 232
16. 449: 166
16. 457: 162
17. 32: 232
17. 37: 175
17. 86: 231
17. 106: 189
17. 128: 159
17. 139: 51, 84, 246
17. 148: 212
17. 156: 105
17. 158: 224
17. 169: 226
17. 179: 231
17. 203: 149
17. 209–10: 180
17. 262: 96
17. 266: 290
17. 270: 145
17. 275: 245
17. 292: 286
17. 307: 191
17. 325: 153
17. 365: 271
17. 391: 278
17. 419–20: 252
17. 423: 184
17. 485: 76
17. 531: 182
17. 587: 77
18. 17: 282
18. 91: 291
18. 111: 133
18. 122–3: 183
18. 131: 224
18. 140: 207
18. 146: 202
18. 157: 246
18. 158: 90
18. 178: 210
18. 188: 238
18. 192–4: 146, 241
18. 193–4: 145
18. 193: 81
18. 201–5: 218
18. 202: 90
18. 203: 220
18. 213: 30, 201
18. 249: 164, 269
18. 258: 224

18. 294: 168
18. 295–6: 169, 170
18. 297–8: 168
18. 382: 200
19. 54: 175
19. 75–6: 252
19. 79: 184
19. 86: 217
19. 113: 134
19. 156: 204
19. 160: 261
19. 165–202: 186
19. 175: 190
19. 183: 189
19. 205: 29, 138
19. 215–19: 215
19. 224: 244
19. 234: 170
19. 260: 283
19. 279: 261
19. 285: 77
19. 302: 202
19. 304: 105
19. 329–34: 142
19. 346: 129
19. 353: 123
19. 354: 191
19. 407–9: 257
19. 408: 289
19. 431: 296
19. 473: 113
19. 545: 132
19. 547: 113
19. 556: 237
19. 562: 249
19. 597: 283
20. 7: 155
20. 30: 162
20. 42: 217
20. 57: 129
20. 61–90: 267
20. 61: 109
20. 62: 156
20. 71: 90
20. 72: 37
20. 73: 71
20. 74: 184, 271
20. 76: 77
20. 85–6: 13, 123
20. 86: 206

Index Locorum

20. 91: 271
20. 95–7: 231
20. 98: 198
20. 150: 157, 231, 232
20. 199–200: 183
20. 207: 184
20. 226–9: 200
20. 231: 105
20. 238: 133
20. 249: 231
20. 295: 175
20. 347: 133
20. 358: 133
20. 390: 133
21. 1: 90
21. 17: 147
21. 45: 144, 275
21. 100: 76
21. 105: 296
21. 203: 133
21. 221: 132
21. 313: 175
21. 364–5: 220
21. 376: 133
22. 157–9: 244
22. 167: 192, 292
22. 205: 162
22. 222: 278
22. 223: 129
21. 283: 276
22. 311: 26, 247
22. 324: 8 n. 21, 202
22. 343: 26, 247
22. 356: 297
22. 366: 26, 247
22. 411: 297
22. 438: 232
22. 444: 126
22. 470: 237
22. 471: 253
22. 500: 76
23. 11–12: 183
23. 16: 242
23. 19: 283
23. 22: 242
23. 29: 266
23. 35–8: 215
23. 62: 215
23. 87: 224
23. 115: 238

23. 126: 77
23. 144: 76
23. 153–372: 136
23. 163: 139
23. 166–72: 186
23. 175: 191
23. 177–80: 223
23. 182: 129
23. 205–87: 223
23. 212: 184
23. 232: 129
23. 270: 287
23. 294: 224
23. 299: 156
23. 330–1: 296
23. 340–1: 210
23. 342–3: 235
23. 347: 273
24. 2: 194
24. 6: 288
24. 11: 273
24. 13: 155
24. 47: 286
24. 92: 256
24. 123: 180
24. 146: 204
24. 148: 170
24. 166: 275
24. 180: 221
24. 226: 198
24. 237–6: 268
24. 248: 297
24, 253: 164
24. 291–2: 78
24. 309: 293
24. 336: 198
24. 374: 164
24. 391–2: 165
24. 398: 224
24. 413–14: 209
24. 423: 266
24. 499: 273

HOMERIC EPIGRAMS
4. 3: 41, 106
7. 1: 109

HOMERIC HYMNS
Dion.
2: 114

Dem.
2–21: 193
2: 71
5: 37 n. 125, 39–40, 285
8: 39, 295
11: 135
19: 203
22–3: 188
30: 203
43: 198
47: 272
49: 91
51: 272
55: 297
66: 294
72: 203–4
79: 218
83–4: 39, 209
97: 138
99: 158
101–4: 162
102: 73
109: 288
113: 187
118–44: 185–6
119–20: 175
124: 204
136: 8 n. 21, 202
145–6: 39, 164
145: 163
146: 127
159: 39, 294
164–5: 191
169: 271
182–3: 162
187: 294
188–90: 235
188–9: 39, 50, 164, 238–41
194: 39, 225
195: 129
202: 129
203: 109
205: 86
212: 287
213–14: 206
224: 81
231: 147
232: 269
235: 191

Index Locorum

HOMERIC HYMNS –
(Contd.)
Dem. – (Contd.)
242: 269
247: 168
259: 297
260: 271
265: 181
268–9: 39, 116
268: 45, 117
270–4: 179
272: 180
275–83: 235
275: 39, 164
278–9: 170
279: 145, 171, 263
285: 39, 46, 225
296–7: 179
297–8: 180
298: 181
300: 232
303: 175
314: 210
321: 128
328: 278
330: 112
331: 142
335: 194
344: 203
346: 203
352–4: 249–50
352: 77, 187
355: 39, 143, 297
365: 224
371–2: 220
374: 104
377: 203
380–3: 197
381: 159
385: 39, 143
397: 39, 265
401: 150
413: 203
416: 293
420: 39, 295
424: 84
425: 288
432: 203
434: 182
444: 278

474–6: 203
478–9: 295
480: 184
483–4: 297
486: 104
492: 109
495: 298

Apoll.
1:70
2: 71
21: 40, 79, 80
22: 87
34: 97
36: 288
49: 150
60: 116
62: 128
71: 40, 184, 284
72: 256
85: 122
87–8: 143, 144
101: 202
119: 97
127: 287
148: 129
159: 175
170: 160
182–206: 95
184: 147
194–6: 145
195: 163
204: 156
209: 110
223: 286
243: 159
265: 157
275: 84
308: 40–1, 44, 259
309: 140
311–13: 129
313: 40
316: 133
323: 85
325: 132
341–2: 156
341: 217
347: 117
360: 276
361: 160

363: 289
379: 123
384: 181
415: 165
440–70: 235
445: 97
461: 141
464–73: 173
479: 265
482–3: 213
485: 267
490–6: 179
490: 181
508: 181
522: 265
529: 198
530: 184
534: 90
540–4: 295
541: 77
544: 40, 297
545: 298

Herm.
1–19: 14 n. 43
3: 71
4: 219
5: 104
31: 288
42: 285
59: 189
71–2: 237
71: 40
73: 288
76: 237
81: 124
90: 168
95: 91
96: 237
105–41: 3
109: 290
144: 119
180–1: 210
190: 159
208: 200
209: 159
223–4: 154
228: 296
231: 153
234: 220

237: 147
241: 238
267: 80
274: 112
279: 160
289: 40, 243
292: 218
294: 203
322: 142
336: 40, 96
385: 132
391: 182
392: 218
407: 165
413: 217
414: 203
425: 160
449: 238
458: 127
505: 95
545: 51, 84
547: 120
548: 146
569: 155
570: 80
578: 77
579: 298

Hy. 6
1: 71, 103, 119
2: 82
5–13: 20 n. 62
6: 149
7–8: 170
8–9: 168
10: 170
11–12: 149
11: 170
14: 149
17: 201
18: 40, 82, 165, 242
19: 298

Hy. 7
4: 274
13: 291
17–21: 175
31: 207
32–7: 235
39: 160

49: 182
55–7: 254
56–7: 14 n. 43
57: 219
58: 298

Hy. 9
4: 94
7: 298
9: 298

Hy. 10
1: 71, 82
3: 92
4–5: 298

Hy. 11
2–3: 87

Hy. 12
1–4: 125–6
1: 128
4–5: 177
4: 128
3: 127

Hy. 14
4: 86, 154, 155
5: 156

Hy. 15
1–6: 14 n. 43
8: 273
9: 174

Hy. 18
4: 219
11: 298

Hy. 19
1: 70, 72
8: 160
12–13: 95
19: 285
20: 199
22: 40, 224
25–6: 150
30: 139
31–2: 142
31: 143

32–7: 288
33–4: 219
33: 131
35: 184
43: 285

Hy. 20
2–3: 88

Hy. 23
1: 122
3: 281

Hy. 24
1–2: 103
1: 105
5: 102

Hy. 25
5: 276

Hy. 26
3–4: 284, 285
5: 217
7: 286
8: 156, 199
12: 181

Hy. 27
1: 91
2–15: 93
2: 84, 103, 163
4: 97
5: 91, 94
6: 221
7–10: 91
15: 96, 176

Hy. 28
1–16: 14 n. 43
2: 84
3: 103, 163

Hy. 29
1–5: 112
1–3: 116, 177
1: 105
3–4: 104
3: 115, 118
6: 105

HOMERIC HYMNS –
  (*Contd.*)
Hy. 29 – (*Contd.*)
10: 103
11: 105

Hy. 30
1: 176
3: 80
6: 109
14: 182

Hy. 31
11–13: 241
17: 174

Hy. 32
8: 170
16: 127–8
17: 174
20: 288

Hy. 33
1: 70

HYGINUS
Fab.
94: 136

IBYCUS (*PMGF*)
frr.
S223a ii. 7: 197
289a: 197, 260, 263
306. 1: 189
321. 4: 199

ION (*IEG*)
fr.
28: 245

IRENAEUS
  REFERENDARIUS
AP 5. 253: 225

ISYLLUS (*CA*)
50: 229

LEONIDAS
AP 7. 648. 2: 113

LEONTIUS SCHOLASTICUS
AP 16. 357: 136
AP 16. 365. 1: 222
AP 16. 375. 1: 52, 243

LIBANIUS
Or.
5. 34: 99

Little Iliad (DAVIES)
frr.
6: 268, 270
6. 1: 267
2. 1 *Dubia*: 41, 72

(BERNABÉ)
32. 7: 156

LONGINUS
19. 2: 221

LONGUS
4. 17. 6: 136

LUCIAN
DDeor.
20. 6: 262

Salt.
7: 195

Syr. D.
31: 261

LUCILLIUS
AP 11. 246. 3–4: 289

LUCRETIUS
1. 19: 74

LYCURGUS
Orat. AL
77: 87

LYRICA ADESPOTA (PMG)
935. 17–18: 154
938e. 1: 71

MACEDONIUS
AP 11. 380. 1: 118

MACHON (Gow 1965)
fr.
8. 63: 156

MANETHO
Apotel.
1. 125–6: 207

MARCELLUS SIDETES
81: 90

MARIANUS
  SCHOLASTICUS
AP 9. 668. 1: 179

MARTIAL
9. 25. 8: 262

MAXIMUS ASTROL.
περὶ καταρχῶν
10. 510: 289

MELEAGER
AP 5. 139. 4: 83
AP 5. 194: 1: 83

MEROPIS (BERNABÉ)
frr.
2. 4: 258
4. 1: 192
6. 5: 149

MESOMEDES
AP 14. 78. 4: 200

MIMNERMUS (*IEG*)
frr.
1: 280
2. 5: 290
4: 270
4: 46
5: 280

MOSCHUS
Eur.
1: 51, 76
14: 203
16: 226
28–71: 193
71: 145

74–6: 140
76: 51, 75, 120
78: 51, 123
93: 51, 162
111: 51, 225
113–30: 198
117: 269
154–61: 253–4
155: 220
164: 230

[MOSCHUS]
Bion.
104: 244

Meg.
13: 220
61: 209
113–17: 250

MUSAEUS
79: 52, 219
141: 73
160: 52, 225
198: 92

NAUPACTIA (DAVIES)
fr.
7a 1–2: 130

NEW TESTAMENT
Heb.
13. 4: 214

NICANDER
Ther.
171: 228
676: 291
842: 291

fr.
70. 9: 291

NONNUS
D.
1. 365: 153
1. 347: 230
2. 276: 139
2. 610–11: 228
3. 261: 189

3. 308: 86
4. 147–9: 219
5. 83: 44, 229
5. 266: 237
5. 270: 143
9. 175: 128
11. 241: 128
11. 296: 52, 95
11. 301: 265
13. 237: 179
13. 288: 179
13. 350: 233
15. 171–2: 44, 207
15. 210–12: 136
15. 279–82: 260
15. 281–2: 264
16. 98: 243
16. 291: 213
18. 164: 226
18. 237: 289
28. 68: 246
29. 151–2: 44, 246
29. 320–1: 241
31. 10: 163
31. 107: 217
33. 36: 93
33. 316: 92
34. 274: 149
35. 148: 93
41. 185–211: 152, 154
41. 204–6: 156
42. 99: 285
42. 105: 93
42. 451–2: 246
42. 467: 83
43. 93: 149
43. 401: 168
45. 345: 226
47. 180: 237
47. 236: 206
48. 893: 43, 132

Paraphrasis
1. 147: 261
5. 57: 296

NOSTOI (DAVIES)
fr.
6. 2: 272

OPPIAN
H.
1. 687–8: 93
1. 704: 78
2. 21–3: 89
2. 111: 243
2. 233: 244
2. 665: 118

[OPPIAN]
C.
1. 310: 155
1. 433: 155
2. 31: 92
3. 48: 114
3. 130: 155
3. 195: 179
3. 461: 72
4. 362: 183
4. 391: 79

ORPHICA
A.
137: 194
408: 160
475: 127
477: 76
479: 92
868: 76
1007: 77

Hys.
1. 8–9: 122
10. 2: 118
17: 126
24. 1: 296
27. 13: 118
41. 2: 119
55. 25: 44, 163
60. 6: 296
79. 2: 296
84. 3: 115
84. 5–6: 116
85. 2: 80

L.
254: 114
469–71: 249
521: 291

340 Index Locorum

ORPHICA
frr. (BERNABÉ)
236: 107
269. 2–3: 89
702. 4: 118

OVID
Am.
1. 9. 1: 87

Ep.
16. 203–4: 136

Met.
5. 366: 74
5. 375–6: 84
10. 15561: 266

PAMPREPIUS (GDK)
fr.
4. 50: 228

PANYASSIS (DAVIES)
fr.
12. 17: 182

PARMENIDES (DK)
fr.
11. 5: 249

PAULUS SILENTARIUS
AP 5. 275. 3: 229

PAUSANIAS
1. 8. 4: 87
1. 28. 5: 87
2. 2. 8: 109
2. 24. 1: 43, 132
3. 23. 1: 83
5. 15. 4: 100
5. 15. 6: 87
5. 15. 9: 103
5. 26. 2: 109
7. 25. 1: 143
9. 4. 1: 87

PHILIP OF
    THESSALONICA
AP 9. 416: 73

PHILOSTRATUS
VA
1. 30: 111

PHOCYLIDES (TP)
fr.
14. 8: 213

PHORONIS (DAVIES)
fr.
3. 3: 149

PINDAR
I.
1. 48: 80
5. 9: 274
6. 34: 42, 228
8. 26–35: 107
8. 32: 259
8. 36: 43, 132
8. 45: 230

N.
1. 6: 269
1. 71–2: 213
2. 1–3: 298
3. 23: 78
4. 72: 44, 293
5. 23–4: 95
5. 36: 91
6. 36: 91
8. 1–2: 71
10. 19: 282
10. 84: 87
11. 1: 71
11. 41: 150

O.
3. 32: 42, 165
4. 12–13: 44, 182
5. 4: 71
6. 39: 230
6. 104: 91
7. 11: 42, 249
8. 70–1: 249
11. 18: 207

P.
1. 12: 285
2. 14: 212

3. 81: 42, 156
4. 17: 43, 155
4. 98: 187
5. 24: 150
8. 80: 83
10. 41: 280
11. 24: 92

Paians
6. 123 (fr. 52f): 189
9. 7 (fr. 52k): 205

frr.
76 (Dith.): 242
156–7: 287
165: 288
221. 1: 269

PLATO
Phdr.
260 A: 146

R.
406 D: 44
474 D: 263

PLINY
Nat.
36. 32: 100

PLUTARCH
Sept. Sap. Conv.
154 A: 41, 72

POLLUX
Onomast.
7. 54: 230

POSIDIPPUS (AB)
114: 20: 209
118. 5: 275
119. 2: 75
126. 2: 75
141. 1: 75

PROCLUS
Hys.
4. 13: 52, 80
7. 6: 132
7. 8: 52, 77

7. 23: 289
7. 39: 296

PROPERTIUS
2. 32. 33–40: 136, 288

QUINTUS SMYRNAEUS
1. 135: 77
1. 243: 183
1. 457: 86
1. 667: 81
2. 588–9: 179
3. 104: 78
3. 245: 296
3. 486: 207
3. 614: 279
4. 131: 213
4. 471: 279
4. 536: 269
5. 45: 77
5. 55: 183
5. 95: 154
5. 421: 296
6. 141: 106
6. 160: 116
6. 187: 157
6. 309: 140
6. 427: 280
6. 584: 183
7. 361–4: 242
8. 349–50: 241
8. 466–7: 52, 80
10. 223: 221
10. 318: 81
10. 348: 228
10. 383: 209
10. 458: 153
10. 466: 246
11. 370: 221
12. 276: 279
13. 27: 243
13. 197: 279
13. 402–3: 52, 74, 77
13. 424: 183
13. 488: 296
13. 554: 207
14. 482: 91

RUFINUS
10. 19. 2: 107

SAPPHO (VOIGT; FR. 58 WEST 2005)
frr.
1. 1: 271
1. 3: 92
1. 14: 92
17: 126
44. 13–17: 45–6, 89
44. 13: 42, 49 n. 154
44. 15: 90
44a. 1–11: 46, 50, 110–12
49. 2: 46
58: 46, 270
58. 12: 274
86. 6: 151
94: 219
94. 16: 170
96. 7–9: 171
102. 2: 92
111. 1: 239
140. 1: 82
157: 272

SEMONIDES (*IEG*)
fr.
7. 63–6: 144
7. 87: 189

SEPTUAGINT
3 *Ki*. 12. 32: 180

Sir. 9. 8: 283

SIBYLLINE ORACLES
1. 296: 81
1. 308: 187
3. 682: 228
3. 687: 296
3. 697: 78
3. 722: 296
8. 27: 44, 214
8. 199: 222

SIMIAS (*CA*)
fr.
1. 13: 189

SIMONIDES (*IEG*)
frr.
15. 1: 139

20. 5: 273
22. 6: 242
92. 1: 71

PMG
515: 269

SOLON
frr.
19. 4: 242
27. 10: 183
36. 11–12: 190
37. 8: 116

SOPHOCLES
Ant.
787–90: 119
1082: 78

El.
156: 207

OC
992: 219

OT
164: 83
488: 219

Ph.
955–6: 94
1104: 183

Trach.
468: 180

frr. (*TrGF*)
373 (*Laocoon*): 296
373. 2–3 (*Laocoon*): 136
941. 9–17: 74

STESICHORUS (*PMGF*)
frr.
S17. 8–9: 97
223. 3: 75
S88. 19: 123

[STESICHORUS] (*PMGF*)
fr.
277: 219

Index Locorum

STRABO
13. 1. 43: 138
13. 1. 52: 5 n. 10
13. 2. 6: 155
14. 1. 39: 98

STRATO
AP 12. 240. 1: 274

SYNCELLUS
Apocalypsis Henochi Graece
8. 1: 89

THEOCRITUS
Ep.
4. 4: 73

Id.
1. 3: 160
1. 14: 160
1. 105–6: 136, 224
2. 49: 155
2. 112: 225
2. 160: 222
3. 15: 248
3. 45: 196
3. 46: 83
3. 49: 243, 244
5. 113: 199
7. 8: 97
8. 59–60: 90, 120
11. 20: 170
11. 24: 154
11. 34: 278
13. 62: 199
15. 77: 209
15. 111: 275
16. 92: 237
17. 55: 285
17. 123: 143
18. 15: 209
18. 47: 291
20. 23: 274
20. 34: 136
22. 34: 210
24. 6: 113
25. 4: 217
25. 18: 237
25. 31: 139
25. 40: 127
25. 142: 155
25. 183: 206
30. 18: 155

THEODOROS PRODROMOS
Carmina Historica
6. 42–3: 52, 171
24. 18: 272

THEOGNIS
27: 180
81: 182
250: 242
254: 46, 192
272: 280
327–8: 286
364: 294
508: 281
527: 280
542: 199
566: 273
765: 182
768: 280
870: 187
897: 131
904: 128
917: 222
971: 265
1010: 113
1012: 280
1017: 276
1021: 280
1049: 180
1252: 43, 97
1277: 151
1293: 213
1297: 297
1304: 242
1332: 242
1339: 81, 242
1347: 263
1382: 242
1385–8: 123
1386: 82

THUCYDIDES
3. 104: 3, 298
7. 48: 118

TRYPHIODORUS
378: 144
562–3: 241

TYRTAEUS (*IEG*)
frr.
5. 5: 182
7. 2: 290
10. 6: 192
12. 30: 183

VERGIL
A.
1. 402–9: 245
2. 649: 136
4. 177: 241
5. 252–7: 266
10. 16: 74
10. 767: 241
11. 480: 225

XENOPHON
Cyr.
8. 7. 14: 207

HG
7. 4. 31: 103

INSCRIPTIONS
CEG
24: 115
403: 81, 264
454: 81

IG iv/1°. 131: 154
IGChr. 99 (=*IEphesos* 1304): 226
GVI
1330. 6: 115